P9-CSE-369

Exploring Your Role

Exploring

Your Role

A Practitioner's Introduction to Early Childhood Education

Mary Renck Jalongo, Ph.D.
Indiana University of Pennsylvania

Joan P. Isenberg, Ed.D.
George Mason University

MERRILL, AN IMPRINT OF PRENTICE HALL
Upper Saddle River, New Jersey • Columbus, Ohio

Library of Congress Cataloging-in-Publication Data

Jalongo, Mary Renck
Exploring your role : a practitioner's introduction to early
childhood education / Mary Renck Jalongo, Joan P. Isenberg.
    p. cm.
    Includes bibliographical references and index.
    ISBN 0-13-526915-6 (case)
    1. Early childhood education—United States. 2. Early childhood
teachers—United States. I. Isenberg, Joan P.
II. Title.
LB1139.25.J35   2000
372.21'0973—dc21   99-12749
                                              CIP

Cover photo: Photo Edit
Editor: Ann Castel Davis
Developmental Editor: Linda Scharp McElhiney
Production Editor: Sheryl Glicker Langner
Design Coordinator: Diane C. Lorenzo
Text Designer: John Reinhardt
Cover Designer: Rod Harris
Production Manager: Laura Messerly
Electronic Text Management: Karen L. Bretz
Editorial Assistant: Pat Grogg
Director of Marketing: Kevin Flanagan
Marketing Manager: Meghan Shepherd
Marketing Coordinator: Krista Groshong

This book was set in Palatino and Antique Olive by Carlisle Communications Inc. and was printed and bound by World Color. The cover was printed by World Color.

© 2000 by Prentice-Hall, Inc.
Pearson Education
Upper Saddle River, New Jersey 07458

All rights reserved. No part of this book may be reproduced, in any form or by any means, without permission in writing from the publisher.

Photo Credits: pp. xxiv, 34, 72, 118, 121, 132, 146, 170, 180, 194, 224, 282, 287, 293, 312, 316, 320, 323, 328, 332, 361, 387, 393 by Anthony Magnacca/Merrill; pp. xxv, xxvi, 2, 7, 20, 59, 68, 108, 129 135, 161, 164, 184, 188, 190, 197, 214, 253, 301, 358, 388 by Scott Cunningham/Merrill; pp. 38, 151 (right) by Silver Burdett & Ginn; pp. 46, 151 (left) courtesy of the Library of Congress; pp. 55, 280 (right) by James L. Shaffer; p. 75 (left) by First Photo; p. 75 (right) by Nancy Ritz; p. 99 by Jo Hall/Merrill; pp. 113, 245, 336, 351 (right) by PhotoDisc, Inc.; pp. 215, 348 by Michael Newman/Photo Edit; p. 229 by Laura Dwight/Photo Edit; p. 274 by Robin L. Sachs/Photo Edit; p. 280 (left) by Alan Oddie/Photo Edit; p. 308 by Mary Kate Denny/Photo Edit; p. 351 (top left) by Corbis Bettmann; pp. 351 (bottom left), 382 by Lawrence Migdale/PIX; p. 401 by Cindy Charles/Photo Edit.

Printed in the United States of America

10 9 8 7 6 5 4 3 2 1

ISBN: 0-13-526915-6

Prentice-Hall International (UK) Limited, *London*
Prentice-Hall of Australia Pty. Limited, *Sydney*
Prentice-Hall of Canada, Inc., *Toronto*
Prentice-Hall Hispanoamericana, S. A., *Mexico*
Prentice-Hall of India Private Limited, *New Delhi*
Prentice-Hall of Japan, Inc., *Tokyo*
Prentice-Hall (Singapore) Pte. Lt., *Singapore*
Editora Prentice-Hall do Brasil, Ltda., *Rio de Janeiro*

For Marianne Maxwell Latall, a cherished friend and valued colleague whose vision for all teachers, children, and families is an inspiration for all early childhood educators.

J. P. I.

To practitioners everywhere who devote their professional lives to the education and care of young children. It is through the concerted efforts of early childhood educators that the world learns to appreciate the importance of the early years and recognizes the enduring benefits of high-quality programs for all young children and their families.

M. R. J. AND J. P. I.

Preface

Why does anyone decide to make the care and education of young children their life's work? When we ask undergraduate students this question, their answers vary. Some simply say, "I love kids." Others are more specific and respond with statements such as the following.

> "I idolized my second-grade teacher, Ms. Cardill. When I was in second grade, I found out that I had a learning disability. Ms. Cardill helped me learn how to cope and inspired me to become a teacher in the process."
>
> "My mother and sisters are teachers; so is one of my uncles. I grew up with teaching and come from a teaching family. I guess you could say that I am carrying on the family tradition."
>
> "Because I am the oldest and my aunts and uncles lived nearby, my job when I was growing up was to babysit for my little brother, nieces, and nephews. There were always kids around the house, and I found that I really enjoyed their company."

By way of introduction, here is what we have to say about what precipitated our decisions to pursue careers in early childhood.

> Mary: "I've always wanted to be a teacher just like Miss Klingensmith, my kindergarten teacher. Throughout early childhood, my favorite play theme was school and I always played Miss Klingensmith. When I was in high school, my little sister was in first grade. After 6 months with a mean teacher who was a former Marine sergeant, my sister was crying and throwing up every morning before school started. At age 7, she developed a stomach ulcer. Her teacher was fired at the end of that year, but when I saw the damage that one bad teacher could do, I made the commitment to go into teaching and become a good teacher."

> Joan: "As the oldest of four siblings, I spent much of my childhood and adolescence with young children. When I was a teenager, my best friend and I planned and organized children's birthday parties. In the summers, I worked at a camp and was a swimming instructor for young children who were learning to swim for the first time. These experiences helped me to see many different ways to teach things that children really wanted to learn. These experiences also differed dramatically from the kind of in-school learning I remembered from my early childhood days, when I was expected to sit quietly, memorize information, and tolerate boredom.

My work at the camp and in my neighborhood allowed me to see children's delight in learning and led me to become an early childhood teacher."

Whether you are a beginner or a veteran in the field of early childhood, the underlying message is the same: We decide to teach young children because we feel it is one of the most delightful periods in life, because we are intrigued and charmed by the young child's newcomer's perspective on the world, and because we feel well suited to fulfill the early childhood educator's multiple roles. In short, we seek careers in early childhood education because we believe that we can exert a powerful and positive influence on the lives of the very young.

How does an educator of the very young move from dreams of teaching effectively to actually doing it? One thing is certain: In that journey from imagining ourselves as effective teachers and actually becoming outstanding teachers, good intentions are not enough. It is almost inconceivable that anyone would enter into teaching with the thought, "I plan to be a terrible teacher and make children's lives miserable," yet there are many examples of teachers who have drifted away from their original goals or completely lost their way. Generally speaking, they are the teachers who have neglected their own learning, who became jaded by the futile search for one method that works equally well with all children, who waited to be told what to do, or who failed to put children at the center of their practice. In his book *To Become a Teacher: Making a Difference in Children's Lives,* William Ayers (1995) raises and answers a simple yet profound question:

> What makes a good teacher? When I ask college students this question, they typically come up with a wide and interesting assortment of qualities: compassion, love of children, sense of humor, kindness, and intelligence. My own list includes passion, commitment, curiosity, a willingness to be vulnerable, and authenticity. When I ask kindergartners the same question, they too have ready answers: a good teacher is fair, funny, smart, nice. . . . Teaching at its best requires knowledge of students, knowledge of hopes, dreams, aspirations, skills, challenges, interests, preferences, intelligence, and values they bring with them to the classroom. Teaching at its best is first an act of inquiry, investigation, and research into the lives of children. (pp. 5–6)

Exploring Your Role: A Practitioner's Introduction to Early Childhood Education is designed to inaugurate your investigation into the lives of children, your research in the field of early childhood education, and your inquiry into the multiple roles that you will need to undertake as someone who cares deeply about the care and education of young children, ages birth through 8 years.

General Focus and Purpose

Traditionally, introductory textbooks in early childhood education have been organized in much the same way—a history of the field and a chapter on theory followed by one chapter on each major subject area: language arts, mathematics, science, the arts, and so forth. This text takes a more integrated and innovative approach. It is organized around the essential roles and responsibilities of an early childhood educator. Another fundamental difference between this book and traditional textbooks is that it is interactive. This means that readers are encouraged to respond to what they are reading while they are reading it. We rely upon case material and verbatim comments from students to make the content come alive. As you look through the book, you will notice sections called "Pause and Reflect About . . ." embedded within the chapters. This material will encourage you to relate what you have read to your own experiences and guide you to reflect more deeply upon the topics. For your convenience, we also have provided spaces where you can respond to the chapter material and note your ideas. Your instructor will determine the best way to use these responses within the context of your class, course, or program.

In *Guidelines for Preparation of Early Childhood Professionals*, the National Association for the Education of Young Children (NAEYC) (1995) characterizes early childhood education as "a diverse field encompassing a broad age-range of the life-span, birth through age eight, including children with special development and learning needs. Early childhood education occurs in diverse settings including public and private schools, centers, and home-based programs, and encompasses many roles in addition to the traditional role of 'teacher' " (p. 1). As a contemporary early childhood educator, you will need to fulfill at least 12 important roles that correspond to the content of this text. These roles, which the NAEYC (1995) has identified and which we have adapted, include the following:

1. The *reflective practitioner,* who carefully considers educational issues and is capable of ethical decision making (Chapter 1)
2. The *child advocate,* who is aware of the child-centered approaches that have dominated our field in the past and still dominate today (Chapter 2)
3. The *child development specialist* who uses professional knowledge about children's growth and development to address the needs of all children (Chapter 3)
4. The *facilitator of learning,* who understands both cognitive psychology and sociocultural theory in terms of their implications for practice (Chapter 4)
5. The *environment designer or arranger,* who knows how to create a safe, healthy, and developmentally appropriate physical environment for learning (Chapter 5)
6. The *curriculum developer,* who can plan lessons, thematic units, and programs that respect the diversity and uniquenesses of children, families, and communities (Chapter 6)
7. The *educational planner,* who understands different types and levels of collaborative planning and organization and can implement a meaningful curriculum that responds to children's needs and interests (Chapter 7)
8. The *evaluator,* who understands and applies principles of performance assessment when assessing children's progress and program effectiveness (Chapter 8)
9. The *mediator and role model,* who guides children's behavior and teaches them the skills of conflict resolution so necessary in our increasingly violent society (Chapter 9)
10. The *family resource person,* who builds trust and respect between, among, and with families and the larger community (Chapter 10)
11. The *emerging professional,* who seeks and self-monitors professional growth through research-based practice (Chapter 11)
12. The *manager of resources,* who knows how to locate and use physical and human resource materials to support children and their families (Compendium of Early Childhood Materials and Resources)

From this list alone, it is clear that working effectively with young children is a challenging and demanding vocation. Teaching young children is qualitatively different from the way it was 20, 10, or even 5 years ago. Our field has been profoundly affected by changes in American families, advances in cognitive psychology, perspectives on the preparation of teachers, political influences on early childhood education, and a new era of sensitivity to cultural diversity and young children with special needs. As you enter early childhood education, you will be engaged in the rigorous work of defining yourself professionally and flexibly adapting to a wide array of early childhood settings.

Audience for the Book

Exploring Your Role: A Practitioner's Introduction to Early Childhood Education is written for newcomers to the field of early childhood education. Typically, these students are enrolled in specialized programs at 2- or 4-year colleges or universities that prepare them to work with children ages birth through 8 years. This comprehensive introduction to the field is most appropriate as the primary textbook for the initial course. It will meet the needs of instructors who teach in baccalaureate (4- or 5-year programs) as well as the needs of instructors who teach in 2-year associate degree programs at community colleges.

Unique Features

This book is intended to be a departure in two senses of that word. First, it is a departure from the standard formula for an introductory textbook in early childhood. Secondly, it is a point of departure for novices who are beginning their exploration of the early childhood field and their roles within it. Notable features of the book are described in the following paragraphs.

Learning Outcomes

Every chapter begins with a list of outcomes for the student. This shift away from behavioral objectives to outcome statements is consistent with the very latest accreditation standards for teacher-education programs in America. Increasingly, teacher educators are being asked to provide more holistic and performance-based evidence that their early childhood programs make significant contributions to students' growth as professionals.

Meet the Teachers

Next, our readers will "Meet the Teachers" through case material that describes one infant and toddler caregiver, one preschool teacher, and one kindergarten or primary-grade teacher. In this way, we provide a balance of all of the three different age groups every early childhood teacher needs to know: infants and toddlers (ages birth through 2 years), preschoolers (ages 3 through 5 years), and children in the primary grades (ages 6 through 8 years). Unlike some introductory textbooks that focus almost exclusively on 3- to 5-year-olds, our emphasis is on the education and care of young children, ages birth through 8 years.

Body of the Chapters

As the Table of Contents details, the body of each chapter will follow a clear organizational pattern. Every chapter defines the professional role, provides a rationale for its importance, and addresses the classroom practices that support that role. The body of the chapter then moves to the most influential paradigms that have resulted from theory and research. (For example, Montessori is discussed in the chapter on early childhood programs, Vygotsky is discussed in the chapter on learning, and Howard Gardner's theory of multiple intelligences is included on the chapter on integrating the curriculum.) Finally, each chapter leads you to practical applications of what you have learned.

Ask the Expert

Each chapter includes one or two examples of the text feature we call "Ask the Expert." These profiles of leaders in the field of early childhood education are directly related to each chapter's content. In the chapter on curriculum development, for example, we profile Sue Bredekamp and her thoughts on developmentally appropriate practice. Given the complexity of early childhood education today, incorporating this collaborative approach within the text was one of the best ways we could imagine to ensure that all key topics were addressed in sufficient depth by leading experts. The conversations with prominent early childhood teacher educators will familiarize you with contemporary leaders in the field as you see their photographs and read what they have to say. In this way, *Exploring Your Role* provides the most up-to-date and authoritative information available on special topics of critical importance to early childhood practitioners. Information about the career paths and experiential backgrounds of each leader in the "Ask the Expert" features is included in the Instructor's Resource Manual.

One Child, Three Perspectives

Another distinctive characteristic of this textbook is the emphasis on the application of content. One text feature that makes our book exceptionally timely is what we call "One Child, Three Perspectives." This component of each chapter highlights a real child whom we have known and presents several different points of view on how best to meet that child's needs. Included among the perspectives are the views of parents, classroom teachers, social workers, school administrators, child guidance experts, health care professionals, and others who are committed to helping the child. This approach is in keeping with the new National Association for the Education of Young Children Standards that call for the preparation of early childhood professionals who have developed the skills of collaboration necessary to work with teams consisting of parents, families, colleagues, and professionals from many different fields who are committed to the education and care—the educare—of young children.

One of the complaints of trained professionals in virtually every field is that nobody ever told them how challenging it would be to work in the real world of the profession for which they were prepared. In *Exploring Your Role,* we attempt to rectify that error. Rather than restricting our accounts of young children to charming anecdotes, we present a wide array of more realistic situations that early childhood educators are likely to encounter. For instance, the case of a drug-exposed child and the case of a newly immigrated child with limited English proficiency are included. "One Child, Three Perspectives" develops your ability to consider different points of view, such as a parent's, psychologist's, and administrator's perspectives on how to support a child's growth and learning, and will equip you to work more skillfully with other professionals. This text feature also emphasizes the theory-research-practice connection. Each example shows how theory and research inform daily practice and provide a useful framework for problem solving.

Featuring Families

Families figure prominently in any successful early childhood program. Therefore, we not only have devoted an entire chapter to this topic, but we also have included a recommended strategy for working successfully with families in every chapter. "Featuring Families" illustrates specific ways that skillful practitioners we know convey information on a variety of topics to the significant adults in each child's life. These text features were collaboratively designed with the help of Ruth K. Steinbrunner.

In-class Workshop

The 11 chapters each conclude with a component that offers an additional opportunity to work with the information that you are learning in class. We call it an "In-class Workshop." These activities can be used with the total group or with small groups to give you a chance to apply the knowledge of the basic principles you have acquired from reading the chapter. In the professional development chapter, for example, we lead you in beginning to develop a teaching portfolio. All of these "In-class Workshop" activities have been extensively field-tested with students in our classes over the years and have been well received in presentations at professional conferences.

Instructor's Resource Manual, Student Study Guide, and Film

The exceptionally comprehensive Instructor's Resource Manual is another way in which our textbook supports instructors and distinguishes itself from other texts on the market. We include samples of classroom dialogue between teachers and children for students to analyze. We also include sample syllabi, an introductory activity for each chapter, objective test and essay test items, suggested in-class projects, and classroom observation forms that can be used during field experiences in early childhood settings or with a videotaped lesson supplied by the instructor. The Instructor's Resource Manual was developed by Ruth K. Steinbrunner, a doctoral candidate at George Mason University, and Natalie K. Conrad, M.A., teacher in the Penn-Cambria School District. We also provide a Student Study Guide, also developed by Ruth Steinbrunner, and an accompanying video, developed by Linda Scharp McElhiney.

A Final Word

In writing *Exploring Your Role: A Practitioner's Introduction to Early Childhood Education*, we drew upon our many years of teaching toddlers, preschoolers, and children in the primary grades, our supervision of student teachers, and our work with practitioners in child care, nursery schools, Head Start, and public schools so that we could offer a useful, contemporary, and comprehensive perspective on the field.

Welcome, then, to an exploration of your roles as an early childhood educator. You are joining the ranks of a profession with a long and distinguished history of dedication to the care and education of children. You are becoming a member of a field characterized by compassion, commitment, enthusiasm, and joy in the growth, development, and learning of young children.

Acknowledgments

Nearly 10 years ago, Joan and I were in Atlanta attending an NAEYC conference and standing in line, waiting to be seated for dinner. We saw Dave Faherty, then Merrill's Senior Editor, walk in with Joanne Hendrick, an early childhood educator and Merrill author whose books we both greatly admired. At the time, I dreamed aloud that that might be us some day as we approached the end of our careers. I imagined us celebrating with our editor after the successful publication of our book with Merrill. Little did we know that we would have two wonderful editors, Ann Davis and Linda McElhiney, to celebrate with. We thank them for their faith in us as thinkers, their unflagging support of us as authors, and their willingness to try a very different type of introductory textbook in early childhood education. We thank them also for their creativity and expert knowledge of the publishing field. Now that the book is published, we even thank them for the long conference calls on the telephone that crossed the line between nudging and pushing! It enabled us to write an introductory text sooner than we ever expected.

We also want to express our gratitude to the reviewers of this book, Jeri A. Carroll, Wichita State University; Elizabeth A. Eddowes, University of Alabama (Retired); Richard Fiene, Pennsylvania State University; Peg A. Ketron-Marose, United States Air Force; Patricia K. Lowry, Jacksonville State University; and Colleen K. Randel, The University of Texas at Tyler, for their thoughtful criticisms and many contributions that refined and polished our first draft of *Exploring Your Role*. Finally, we want to thank our graduate assistants, Ruth Steinbrunner and Natalie K. Conrad, who helped with the ancillary materials and suffered through the early drafts of the manuscript. Also, thanks are in order for Dr. Nancy L. Briggs, a former doctoral student who supplied the table about the history of childhood and families for Chapter 10. And, of course, we want to thank our families for helping out in myriad ways and tolerating our passion to try to make a contribution to the early childhood field.

Discover Companion Websites: A Virtual Learning Environment

Technology is a constantly growing and changing aspect of our field that is creating a need for content and resources. To address this emerging need, we have developed an online learning environment for students and professors alike—Companion Websites—to support our textbooks.

In creating a Companion Website, our goal is to build on and enhance what the textbook already offers. For this reason, the content for each user-friendly website is organized by chapter and provides the professor and student with a variety of meaningful resources. Common features of a Companion Website include:

For the Professor—

Every Companion Website integrates **Syllabus Manager**™, an online syllabus creation and management utility.

- **Syllabus Manager**™ provides you, the instructor, with an easy, step-by-step process to create and revise syllabi, with direct links into Companion Website and other online content without having to learn HTML.
- Students may logon to your syllabus during any study session. All they need to know is the web address for the Companion Website and the password you've assigned to your syllabus.
- After you have created a syllabus using **Syllabus Manager**™, students may enter the syllabus for their course section from any point in the Companion Website.
- Class dates are highlighted in white and assigned due dates appear in blue. Clicking on a date, the student is shown the list of activates for the assignment. The activities for each assignment are linked directly to actual content, saving time for students.
- Adding assignments consists of clicking on the desired due date, then filling in the details of the assignment—name of the assignment, instructions, and whether or not it is a one-time or repeating assignment.

- In addition, links to other activities can be created easily. If the activity is online a URL can be entered in the space provided, and it will be linked automatically in the final syllabus.
- Your completed syllabus is hosted on our servers, allowing convenient updates from any computer on the Internet. Changes you make to your syllabus are immediately available to your students at their next log in.

For the Student—

- **Chapter Objectives**—outline key concepts from the text
- **Interactive Self-quizzes**—complete with hints and automatic grading that provide immediate feedback for students

After students submit their answers for the interactive self-quizzes, the Companion Website **Results Reporter** computes a percentage grade, provides a graphic representation of how many questions were answered correctly and incorrectly, and gives a question by question analysis of the quiz. Students are given the option to send their quiz to up to four email addresses (professor, teaching assistant, study partner, etc.).

- **Message Board**—serves as a virtual bulletin board to post—or respond to—questions or comments to/from a national audience
- **Net Searches**—offer links to key terms from each chapter to related Internet content
- **Web Destinations**—links to www sites that relate to chapter content

To take advantage of these resources, please visit the *Exploring Your Role: A Practitioner's Introduction to Early Childhood Education* Companion Website at www. prenhall. com/jalongo

Contents

Introduction for the Student

For many years, teachers have made statements about the numerous roles they are expected to assume in children's care and education. Teachers may be overheard to say, "You get to be the nurse when it's time to take out the first-aid kit and treat a child's scraped knee on the playground," or "Sometimes you're like a social worker when you need to work with organizations and find services to solve a particular problem that a child and family face," or "I feel like the parent when a child is afraid and tearful and it's up to me to reassure and comfort. Sometimes my students even forget and call me Mom!" or "You feel like a counselor when a parent or colleague confides in you and asks for advice on a matter of great importance to him or her."

Recent developments in early childhood education have, if anything, expanded roles for early childhood practitioners in homes, centers, and schools, because educational programs serving very young children have become increasingly complex, diverse, and comprehensive. The same teacher who treats a minor playground injury now bears responsibility for adapting the physical environment of the classroom to accommodate one child in a wheelchair and for changing the feeding tube of another child. The teacher who saw a social-worker dimension to the role is now part of an instructional support team that includes a social worker, psychologist, health care professional, and parent, all of whom are responsible for arriving at educational plans and decisions to benefit the child. The educational professional who functioned in some ways like a parent now sits and chats with children as they eat the free breakfasts, snacks, and lunches provided by the program, while the teacher who saw a counseling dimension to her role now participates in a comprehensive family support program that provides a wide array of health, social, and psychological services on an as needed basis to all families served by the program.

We wrote this book not only out of the belief that teachers been right all along about the many different roles they are expected to fulfill, but also out of our conviction that early childhood teacher education needs to change in order to prepare college and university students for the realities of early childhood settings. Beginning professionals—and early childhood practitioners are no exception—typically approach their careers with a large measure of idealism. They frequently have a romanticized view of what their lives will be like. It is not uncommon for beginning teachers to imagine a large, sun-filled room with a small group of clean, healthy, bright, neatly dressed children who are eager to learn and devoted to their teacher. Over and over again, we hear our students make comments such as, "Observing in these child care settings has been a real eye-opener. I see how hard caregivers have to work and how much their working conditions need to improve," or "I

guess I've lived a sheltered life. I had no idea that children in my kindergarten class would arrive at school tired, cold, or hungry. Blaming the parents doesn't solve the child's problem. You have to take positive action," or "I think of myself as pretty personable, but when parents picked up their children after school at the synagogue doors, I just couldn't think of anything to say to them. I felt like an outsider. I felt like they probably didn't want to talk to me because they can see that I am young and don't have any kids yet," or "Student teaching in second grade was a shock. First of all, I never worked so hard in my life. There just wasn't enough time in the day to do everything I was expected to do. Second, I was surprised by the differences in children's abilities. In my math class, there is one child who can barely add by counting and another who can do long division in his head!" As these candid remarks from our students suggest, it is critically important for beginning early childhood practitioners to get a realistic perspective on the realities of child care and education from the very start. Otherwise, they feel disillusioned and defeated and leave the profession to which they were committed and for which they were trained, as many beginning teachers and caregivers do.

Teachers are not overstating the case when they talk about the many different roles they are expected to fill. Rather than disputing this notion, we and other teacher educators embrace it as an accurate portrayal of the lives of teachers (Carter & Curtis, 1994). Within each skilled teacher, there is the diagnostician who assesses children's strengths and plans successful learning experiences; the curriculum designer who draws upon theories and pedagogical knowledge to plan learning that the community considers important; the organizer of instruction who uses long-range and short-range planning to make the best possible use of resources; the manager of learning who creates a learning

environment and offers learning experiences that are relevant and interesting to the children; the counselor or advisor who interacts with children, provides guidance, and lends emotional support; the child advocate who champions children's causes in the larger community; and the decision maker who strives to be honest, fair, and ethical (Saracho, 1988).

As you begin your study of the early childhood field, it is essential that you acknowledge how perpetually challenging it is to teach well and to make the transition from novice to expert. The research on this process points to several important features that characterize the thinking of skilled professionals (Pressley, 1995), implications that we apply in this text to early childhood teaching:

- Newcomers to teaching tend to rely on others to gain a sense of their progress and achievement, while master teachers have more self-direction and have learned to monitor their own progress and practice the skills of self-evaluation. This is why we begin every chapter with a true account of an infant-toddler caregiver, a preschool teacher, and a teacher in the primary grades and then invite you to compare and contrast the three teachers' perspectives, and connect them with your own experiences. This need for teachers to become more self-directed with experience is also one of the reasons that you will be invited periodically in each chapter to "Pause and Reflect About" various issues. These activities are designed to help you become a more reflective practitioner.

- New teachers possess general knowledge about a variety of topics, while master teachers have developed highly specialized knowledge and skills that enable them to excel in the early childhood field; thus, we have provided learning outcomes at the start of each chapter so that you can preview the content that we include in the text. Our goal is not to merely cover content, but to engage you in really thinking about the issues; we therefore have included the best insights and advice from leading experts in the field in the "Ask the Expert" features, which are included in each chapter. Another aspect of the chapters that you will find helpful is the "In-Class Workshop," which allows you to delve into a topic in greater depth in ways that promote your professional development. Practical experiences with topics such as understanding inclusion, ways to arrange your classroom environment, and writing your teaching philosophy statement are all designed to develop your knowledge and skill.

- As new teachers begin to study the specialized content in their field, they know bits and pieces but sometimes find things difficult to synthesize, and they often feel overwhelmed or confused by problems. It is not until teachers have acquired a storehouse of cases, episodes, or accounts of classroom experiences that they begin to see the big picture, analyze problems at a deeper level, and approach solutions efficiently with few errors. In "One Child, Three Perspectives," you will be introduced to the problem of a child we have known and asked to *react* to the situation, *research* it further, and finally, *reflect* upon the proposed solutions. These situations will enable you to add to your repertoire of cases so that you can approach problems in a more thoughtful way. Because families figure so prominently in every high-quality early childhood program, each chapter also includes sample material that will enable you to synthesize what you are learning about working with families.

Instead of approaching your early teaching experiences with the sense that "Nobody told me it would be like this," we want you to be able to say, "Yes, I remember reading about a situation like this and discussing it in my intro class." We hope that this book and the learning experiences associated with it provide an introduction to the field that is accurate, appropriate, and empowering. We wish you success with your studies and hope that our book makes a contribution to your professional growth and commitment to care for and educate all of the young children in the settings where you work.

Exploring Your Role as a Reflective Practitioner

As teachers, we need to know a few things about ourselves as learners before we set out to plan for the learning of others. Maybe the primary question to ask here is, what led you to teaching in the first place? The reasons are familiar . . . I teach because I love teaching. I teach because I love kids. I've always wanted to be a teacher. Nothing is better than being a teacher . . . Teaching is hard work. Choose teaching because you want to teach. Teach because you believe that the human spirit is capable of learning at any age and you strongly desire to be part of the dynamic interactions that characterize positive learning—total engagement of the mind, body, and spirit in an inquiry about those things that are known as well as those that seem distant and impossible.

Susan Carothers, 1995, p. 27

Learning Outcomes

✔ Understand the characteristics and roles of effective practitioners in the field of early childhood education

✔ Consider the many different types of programs that comprise the field of early childhood education

✔ Appreciate and value the contributions of early education to children, families, and society at large

✔ Define reflective practice and apply the strategies of the reflective practitioner to case material

✔ Identify and use print and nonprint resources in the field of early childhood education

Meet the Teachers

Darlene has been a toddler caregiver for 7 years. She arrives at a Saturday workshop wearing a sweatshirt that shows a cartoon face shouting the word, "Mine!" If you spent the day with Darlene's toddler group, you would see that she spends most of her time on the floor interacting with the six toddlers for whom she is responsible. Darlene explains her perspective this way: "Toddlers need, first and foremost, to learn social skills. At this age, disputes over toys are common, and a frustrated toddler tends to respond physically—hitting, crying, or biting—because the words aren't there yet. I see my primary roles as caring deeply about them, teaching them to get along with one another, and meeting their basic needs (such as eating, resting, and toileting). I know that parents trust me to do what is right for their little ones, and I take that trust very seriously."

Ms. Thomas and her aide, Mrs. Grant, teach in a special public school prekindergarten program for children of low-income families. Family members drop off some children at the classroom, while other children arrive on the school bus. After coats and hats have been put away, the children's day begins with a complete breakfast served in the school cafeteria. As they eat, the children engage in informal conversations with their teachers and peers. After cleanup, the children return to the classroom and gather on the carpet for a planning session. They review the day's events and choose the centers that they will visit. Each day, one child is responsible for drawing a picture depicting an important classroom event and dictating a sentence about the picture. The picture and caption become part of a journal that chronicles the school year. After the children have finished their work at the centers, they meet in small groups to review and evaluate their accomplishments. Some of their comments are, "I made a farm with a fence out of blocks," "We put together a big dinosaur puzzle," and "Kerri and Lakisha and me played house."

 Ms. Ritchie is an experienced elementary school teacher who decided to change the way she started her school day after studying a new technique in her graduate class. For many years she had organized her classroom so that all of her first graders would begin completing the same worksheet the moment they arrived at school. After learning about the importance of providing time for children to make the transition from home to school each day, Ms. Ritchie changed her morning schedule. Instead of requiring every child to immediately begin working on a paper-and-pencil task, she offered many choices of activities for children: writing, science, building, puzzles, or drama. Within a few weeks of instituting this change, Ms. Ritchie began to see her first graders in a different way because she had more opportunity to talk with them, observe and assess their work, and help them to become independent learners. When Ms. Ritchie reported to her college class about the effects of the change, she said, "In all my years of teaching, this has been my easiest. Now I see the children beginning their long day happily. They are sharing and practicing different skills." For Ms. Ritchie, changing her schedule enabled her to work more closely with individual children (Isenberg, 1995, p. 121).

Each of these teachers is inviting children into the learning process as well as acting upon certain beliefs about early childhood education. Think about these teachers in relation to the five core attributes of outstanding early childhood practitioners outlined in Figure 1.1. Then respond to the following questions.

FIGURE 1.1	In a statement from the National Board for Professional Teaching Standards, the following five criteria were used to define the exemplary early childhood practitioner:
Five core attributes of exemplary early childhood practitioners	1. Has a commitment to students and their learning, including a willingness to adjust their teaching to meet differing needs and abilities
	2. Is knowledgeable about the subjects they teach and how to present this content to young children effectively
	3. Is able to create an ordered and productive learning environment in which student learning is thoughtfully managed and monitored
	4. Considers human development, subject matter, and young children's needs in thinking about professional practices
	5. Works in collaboration with families and professionals to create a productive and caring school and community
	SOURCE: Adapted from *Early Childhood/Generalist: Standards for National Board Certification*, National Board for Teacher Certification, 1995, Washington, DC.

COMPARE:	What are some commonalities that these three teachers share, even though they are working with children of various ages?
CONTRAST:	How do these teachers think about teaching? How would you characterize the outlook of each one?
CONNECT:	What aspect of these teachers' experiences made the greatest impression on you and how will you incorporate this into your teaching?

A Definition of Teaching

When you hear the word *teaching*, what is the first image that comes to mind? If you are like most people, you picture an adult standing in front of a group of students and presenting academic content. Teaching is far more complex than these first impressions suggest, however. Surely you have been in someone's class and felt as though you learned almost nothing. Does this qualify as teaching? According to several of the great contemporary thinkers in education, it does not. Elliott Eisner (1994) defines teaching as a "set of acts performed by people we call teachers as they attempt to foster learning" (p. 180). He refers to the notion of the great educational philosopher John Dewey that the word *teaching* is comparable to the word *selling* in that a transaction is implied: "That is, one could not teach unless someone learned, just as one could not sell unless someone bought . . . Thus, if a teacher attempts to teach but does not succeed in helping the student learn, then he or she may be said to have lectured, conducted a discussion, demonstrated, explained but *not* to have taught. To teach, in this sense, is known by its effects" (p. 179).

Suppose, for example, that an early childhood major decides to teach a lesson on colors to first graders. Even though this beginning teacher may prepare carefully and have excellent presentation skills, all of the children in the class already know the basic colors, so the opportunities to learn are extremely limited. If, however, the beginning teacher selects a more challenging concept, for example, how primary colors such as red and yellow are mixed to produce secondary colors and then gives the children an opportunity to discover this through direct experimentation with paints, that teacher is far more likely to teach in the true sense of the word.

Your Role as a Reflective Practitioner

Early childhood teachers perform several important functions, including caretaking, providing emotional support and guidance, instructing, and facilitating (Katz, 1972). How do they achieve these goals? Many experts believe that early childhood education students grow into effective teachers through the practice of reflection (see Ask the Expert: Elaine Surbeck on Keeping a Journal, later in this chapter). Cruickshank (1987) notes, "Literally, to reflect is to think. However, reflection is more than merely bringing something to mind. Once one brings something to mind, one must consider it . . . Rather than behaving purely according to impulse, tradition, and authority, teachers can be reflective—they can deliberate on their actions with open-mindedness, wholeheartedness, and intellectual responsibility" (pp. 3, 8). Prominent educator John Dewey (1933) described reflective thinking as "the active, persistent, and careful consideration of any belief or supposed form of knowledge in light of the grounds that support it" (p. 9). Teacher reflection starts with awareness of students' reactions, of teacher's feelings and thoughts, and of the consequences of teaching decisions (Glatthorn, 1996).

> Teaching demands thoughtfulness. There is simply no way to become an outstanding teacher through adherence to routine, formula, habit, convention, or standardized ways of speaking and acting. Thoughtfulness requires wide-awakeness—a willingness to look at the conditions of our lives, to consider alternatives and different possibilities, to challenge received wisdom and the taken for granted, and to link our conduct with our consciousness . . . [it also] requires strength and courage—the strength to think in a time of thoughtlessness, the courage to care in a culture of carelessness. (Ayers, 1995, p. 60)

In teaching, there are literally hundreds of daily decisions to be made. Anyone who aspires to become a good teacher will need to arrive at those decisions based on something more compelling than "We've always done it this way," or "I'm just following orders." To exert a powerful, positive influence on the field of early childhood education, teachers need content mastery as well as greater power over their professional lives.

Think for a moment about yourself at age 13. Remember how important it was to have certain clothes, musical tastes, hairstyles, or manners of speech? During that time in our lives, most of us go along with the crowd to a greater extent than at other times. Most teenagers try to be like other teenagers to win peer acceptance. It is not until later that they recognize the value of or even understand the expression "Be yourself."

> Inside each person there is a wonderful capacity to reflect on the information that the various sense organs register, and to direct and control these experiences. We take this ability so much for granted that we seldom wonder about what it is. . . . If we ever think about it, we give it such names as awareness, consciousness, self, or soul. Without it, we could only obey instructions programmed in the nervous system by our genes. But having a self-reflective con-

sciousness allows us to write our own programs for action, and make decisions for which no genetic instructions existed before. . . . Like air, it is always there; like the body, it has its limits. It is something that can get hurt, but it can also soar; it grows, and its powers slowly expand. Although every human brain is able to generate self-reflective consciousness, not everyone seems to use it equally. (Csikszentmihalyi, 1993, pp. 22–23)

Reflective practice is differentiated from routine practice by the number, richness, and flexibility of the scripts teachers bring to the classroom setting (Schon, 1983). By a *script* we mean an imaginary dialogue between a teacher and learners that is based on professional reading, pedagogical expertise, knowledge of child development, and familiarity with a particular child or group of children. Those scripts enable expert teachers to draw upon their reservoir of direct experience, and bring it to bear upon the current situation. Although a master teacher's response to a situation may appear to be intuitive or automatic, the teacher's skillful responses are rooted in reflective practice and the ability to adapt flexibly to a wide array of circumstances (Bruer, 1993; Carter & Doyle, 1989). From the earliest days of teaching, one of the defining characteristics of good teachers is reflective practice (McIntyre & O'Hair, 1996; Schubert & Ayers, 1992). These professionals, both the experienced and the novices, continually engage in a process of self-examination, all the while keeping the learners' needs uppermost in their minds. Teachers who fail to do this will discover that "chance and necessity are the sole rulers of those who are incapable of reflection" (Csikszentmihalyi, 1993, p. 17).

While teaching may look easy to outsiders, a teacher must make hundreds of decisions each day.

Common Issues and Concerns About Teachers' Journals

Elaine Surbeck

1. What is a teacher's journal? Who will read it?

I think it is natural that students are a bit uncertain about writing down their thinking, because often, their notion of a journal is similar to that of a diary. It is important to make the distinction that although a journal does contain personal contemplation and rumination, the focus of the journal is on professional development and their thinking about the process of becoming a teacher. In the context of teacher preparation, it is not intended to be a vehicle for revealing intimate details of personal existence. Unless the journal is specified as interactive among agreed-upon readers and participants, the information and thinking students share in dialogue journals with the professor is confidential. Students should be encouraged to write those things that they are comfortable revealing about themselves as developing prospective teachers. In many cases, the entries that students make grow in length and depth as they begin to trust me and to value their learning as they recognize the power of reflective thinking.

2. Why keep a teacher's journal?

While I have written rationales and voiced my beliefs, I think the best testimony comes directly from students themselves. With their permission, I am quoting two undergraduate students about what *they* found valuable in keeping a reflective dialogue journal.

Student 1: "I found keeping a journal this semester to be a very useful and insightful experience. When I look back to my beginning entries, it is easy to see how far I have come in my thinking. Before this semester, I don't think I could have expressed my philosophy about teaching as clearly as I feel I now can. Writing in my journal has helped me to bring my thoughts together. Drawing upon classroom experiences, lectures, notes, and readings to think about in my entries helped me make my own meaning from what I was learning. As I wrote, I felt I was constructing knowledge instead of just memorizing. . . . Journal writing is not an act of memorization; it is an act of thinking."

Student 2: "Journals . . . I am glad we were required to keep them—I wasn't at the time, of course, but now I am very glad. I learned so much more in this class than in any other class I have ever taken. The journal helped me to grow. I had to think, reflect, and think again, and that was good. I know more about who I am and what I want than ever before. What's more, I believe in what I am preparing to become. I know I will be the best teacher I can, and I know I will keep learning and learning and learning."

3. What is the process of reflection?

A common problem that is encountered in asking students to write in journals is how to help them take their reflections further and deepen their thinking about content. Through naturalistic research, my colleagues and I discovered that many students organized their journal entries using a particular sequence that started with *reactions* to something about teaching or the course, then they might continue on to *elaborate* more about the topic, and finally, some students progressed to the level of *contemplation*. Not all students do so, so the question becomes one of whether it is possible to encourage reflective thinking in all students. As one way to investigate this possibility, I now ask students to use this same framework to assess their own entries and challenge them to strive to reach the contemplative part of the sequence. (For more information about this framework, see E. Han, E. Surbeck and J. Moyer, Assessing reflective responses in journals [March, 1991]. *Educational Leadership, 48*[6].) Although additional research needs to be conducted to examine whether using the framework for self-assessment of journal entries increases students' ability to be reflective, we have some informal evidence that knowledge of the sequence and levels in the framework does encourage students to inquire further into their thinking. I believe that journal writing is one way to develop in our undergraduate students the disposition to be reflective and to assist them in creating their individual teaching theories, processes critical to becoming a child-sensitive teacher.

Elaine Surbeck is an associate professor of Early Childhood Education at Arizona State University in Tempe, Arizona.

Clearly, becoming a reflective practitioner is a desirable goal. You will know that you are moving toward reflective practice when you display the following characteristics, based on Dewey's definition (Eby & Kujawa, 1998):

Characteristics of the Reflective Teacher/Thinker

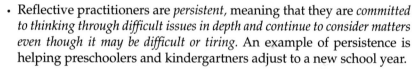

- Reflective practitioners are *active*, meaning that they *search energetically for information and solutions to problems that arise in the classroom.* An example of taking action is learning more about the medical condition of a child through collaboration with colleagues and professionals from other fields.

- Reflective practitioners are *persistent*, meaning that they are *committed to thinking through difficult issues in depth and continue to consider matters even though it may be difficult or tiring.* An example of persistence is helping preschoolers and kindergartners adjust to a new school year.

- Reflective practitioners are *careful*, meaning that they have *concern for self and others, respect students as human beings, and try to create a positive, nurturing classroom.* An example of behavior that demonstrates care is the practice of involving children in establishing and monitoring school rules.

- Reflective practitioners are *skeptical*. They *realize that there are few absolutes and maintain a healthy skepticism about educational theories and practices.* An example of skepticism is asking thoughtful questions about new assessment practices before implementing them in the classroom.

- Reflective practitioners are *rational*. They *demand evidence and apply criteria in formulating judgments rather than blindly following trends or acting on impulse.* An excellent example of rational behavior as it applies to teaching is referring to professional journal articles to gather additional information on a topic before arriving at an opinion.

- Reflective practitioners are *proactive*, meaning that they are *able to translate reflective thinking into positive action.* An example of being proactive is communicating the reasons underlying changes in classroom practices to parents so that their questions and concerns are addressed before problems arise. Figure 1.2 summarizes what outstanding teachers have in common. Note how each of these features depends upon reflective practice.

FIGURE 1.2

Characteristics of
outstanding early
childhood educators

Good teachers . . .
are able to view themselves as learners
are willing and able to grow
are keen observers
know the community in which they teach
possess a strong content background in child growth and development
have something they care to teach
understand how young children learn
need lots of energy
ask questions that motivate children
are able to take risks
understand that organization and order are important
are skilled at group management
possess a willingness to explore
are flexible
are filled with a sense of wonder
love teaching

SOURCE: Adapted from "Defining competence as readiness to learn" (pp. 29–36) by J. F. Kramer. In S. G. Goffin & D. E. Day (Eds.), *New perspectives in early childhood teacher education: Bringing practitioners into the debate*, 1994, New York: Teachers College Press.

What Is the Field of Early Childhood Education?

As you begin your professional career in the care and education of the very young, it is helpful to remember that "early childhood education is not an exercise or a schedule or a machine. It is young children exploring their world with sensory thoroughness, experimenting with people and places and materials, encouraged by a teacher who respects and uses their ideas and ways of learning to help them discover what has meaning for them in our society" (Law, Moffit, Moore, Overfield, & Starks, 1966, p. 12). Contemporary professional early childhood education includes several different broad categories of programs designed to support these goals (see Figure 1.3).

The field of early childhood education is diverse and frequently fragmented. Early childhood programs are characterized by diversity in the physical settings in which programs are offered, the types of programs, the funding sources used to support the programs, the population of children and families served, the roles of the early childhood professionals involved, and the certification or license required of early childhood professionals. Table 1.1 is an overview of the field of early childhood education in the United States. Programs may be public, meaning that they are funded by taxes and monitored by some government agency, or programs may be private, meaning that they are supported by other sources of revenue.

Characteristics of Effective Early Childhood Educators

For anyone who considers entering the field of early childhood education, the basic question is, "Do I have what it takes to become a good teacher or caregiver for the very young?" Other significant questions include the following:

- Why do I want to work with young children?
- What do I believe about how young children learn?

FIGURE 1.3

Categories of early
childhood programs

Family Day Care

Setting: The family child-care provider's home

Children/Families Served: The appeal of these programs is that young children are cared for in a very homelike and familylike setting. Children from 6 weeks to kindergarten-entry age may be enrolled in family day care. The number of children served is smaller than in group care, and the children are often of different ages, as they would be in a family.

Group Infant, Toddler, and Preschool Care

Setting: Rooms designed for very young children that may be located in child-care facilities, at parents' place of work, and so forth.

Children/Families Served: These programs typically offer extended hours that accommodate the needs of working parents or families. The adult-to-child ratios are governed by state regulations.

Preschool or Nursery School Programs

Settings: Programs for preschoolers may be housed in many different locations: at community centers, in churches or synagogues, in buildings provided by commercial chains such as Kindercare, at the YMCA, in private homes or special facilities built near private residences, and so forth.

Children/Families Served: Preschool is generally defined as the 3- to 5-year-old age group. Preschool programs may be half days, full days, alternating days (e.g., Tuesdays and Thursdays or Mondays, Wednesdays, and Fridays), combined with other programs (e.g., child care before and after regular preschool program hours), or some combination of these options.

Before- and After-School Child Care for School-Aged Children

Setting: Usually, these programs are in child-care centers or community centers, or they use the classroom space of public schools before and after regular school hours.

Children/Families Served: Children in these programs are already in school. The purpose of the programs is to provide supervised care and education—educare—for children whose parents and families are working during hours before and after the typical school day begins and ends.

Drop-In Child Care

Setting: Usually, these programs are in child-care centers, community centers, shopping malls, airports, or other public places convenient to the community.

Children/Families Served: The purpose of these child-care arrangements is to provide temporary care for young children. Rather than attending on a regular basis, children participate in the center on an as-needed basis. They may require 24-hour care if a parent needs to leave town for a family emergency, or just a few hours of care if a single parent needs to run errands and shop, for instance.

FIGURE 1.3

(continued)

Public School Prekindergarten, Kindergarten, and Elementary School

Setting: These programs are supported by tax dollars and are typically housed in public school buildings or in spaces rented by the public schools for that purpose.

Children/Families Served: Prekindergarten programs are typically for 3- and 4-year-old children; kindergarten is generally for 5- and 6-year-olds; and the primary grades in elementary school, grades 1 through 3, serve children from approximately age 6 or 7 up to and including age 8 or 9.

Private Prekindergarten, Kindergarten, and Elementary School

Setting: These programs are often housed in churches, synagogues, or other facilities secured or built for that purpose.

Children/Families Served: Families that can afford private school tuition are the ones that enroll their children in private schools.

- How do I think about concepts such as equality, freedom, individuality, and honesty as they relate to teaching and learning?
- What personal qualities and abilities do I possess that will make me successful in working with young children?
- What kind of early childhood teacher do I want to become?
- How will I demonstrate my commitment to young children through my work?

As Clark (1996) points out, "almost invariably, children's thoughts and stories about good teachers concern four fundamental human needs: (1) to be known, (2) to be encouraged, (3) to be respected, and (4) to be led" (p. 15). Over the years, we have worked with thousands of individuals who wanted to specialize in the care and education of young children. Based upon that experience and various sources (Ayers, 1989; Carter & Curtis, 1994), we have identified essential characteristics of outstanding early childhood educators. To become the best early childhood practitioner possible, you will need to achieve twelve important goals:

1. Make a firm commitment to the care and education of young children.
2. Take delight in, be curious about, and learn to understand children's development.
3. Maintain a fundamentally positive outlook on children, families, and teaching.
4. Understand the powerful influence that you exert over children's lives.
5. Concentrate on your goal of becoming the best teacher you can be.
6. Be willing to take the risks and make the mistakes that are part of the learning process.
7. Adapt flexibly to continuous change and expect perpetual challenge.
8. Acquire a specialized body of knowledge and skills.
9. Learn to use material and human resources.
10. Work to build a sense of community; seek collaboration and peer support.
11. Use problem-solving strategies to make ethical decisions.
12. Pursue professional growth as an educator of the very young.

The next section elaborates on each of these goals.

Table 1.1
Overview of The Field of Early Childhood Education

	Homes	Centers, schools, churches, synagogues	Homes, synagogues, churches, centers, schools	Centers on work sites	Hospitals	Public schools	Colleges and universities
				Settings			
Types	Family child care	Private child care and preschool programs	Special programs for students at-risk	Corporate-sponsored child care	Educational support programs for children with long-term and chronic illnesses	Pre-K, kindergarten, and 1st, 2nd, or 3rd grade	Professional preparation, teacher licensure, and in-service teacher professional development
Funding Source	Local, county, or state taxes; United Way; tuition on a sliding scale; or some combination thereof	Generally funded exclusively through tuition paid by parents and/or donations	Funded by the federal government	Funded by the employer as an employee benefit	Funded by various sources, including donations, United Way, and/or taxes; programs are often subcontracted to child-care companies	Funded by federal, state, and local taxes based on property values	Public institutions funded by federal and state taxes and private institutions funded by donations; both funded also by tuition and fees
Eligibility	Usually based on parent's proximity to home, ability to pay tuition, and eligibility criteria of specific programs	Generally based on parent's ability to pay tuition and fees	Reserved for low-income parents and children	Determined by the parent's employment status with the business or organization	Determined by the child's mental or emotional illness	All children of a specified age residing in a certain area are eligible to begin kindergarten	Adults are admitted to academic programs based upon ability to meet the entrance requirements

(continued)

Table 1.1
Continued

	Homes	Centers, schools, churches, synagogues	Homes, synagogues, churches, centers, schools	Centers on work sites	Hospitals	Public schools	Colleges and universities
Roles	Child caregiver, family child-care provider	Child-care providers	Teachers and aides	Child-care providers	Child-care providers	Public school teachers	Early childhood teacher educators
Specific Examples	County child-care programs American nanny program Home-based intervention programs	Montessori School Kindercare Child care on college campuses	Head Start Title I programs Reading Recovery	Xerox Corporation child care	Medical Center Child Life program	Multiage K, 1, and 2 full-day kindergarten	Child Development Associate programs (2 year); early childhood teacher certification programs (4 year); graduate programs
Certification or License Required*	High school diploma, state license or Child Development Associate (CDA)	High school diploma; state license, CDA, associate degree, or teaching certificate	High school diploma or equivalent; CDA, associate degree (2 year), or baccalaureate (4 year)	High school diploma, state license, CDA, possibly an associate degree or teaching certificate	State license, CDA	Early childhood teaching certificate, 4-year baccalaureate degree from an accredited institution	Prior experience with young children, at least a master's degree; usually a doctorate (Ed.D. or Ph.D.)

Settings

*Requirements vary considerably from state to state (see McCarthy, 1988).

Imagine that you had to trust someone else to help you care for and educate your sibling, your own child, or another child you love. What concerns would you have? What characteristics would you look for in the person responsible for your young child's care and education? Such questions are a good place to begin when thinking about the characteristics of effective early childhood educators. When you have determined your concerns and standards, compare them with the core attributes in Figure 1.1. Then look at the following Featuring Families to see a parent's checklist for evaluating early childhood programs. How did your ideas compare?

FEATURING FAMILIES

A CHECKLIST TO GUIDE PARENTS IN SELECTING AN EARLY CHILDHOOD PROGRAM

Parents choose a program for their children for a variety of reasons. According to the research (Fuller, Holloway, & Bozzi, 1997), the major considerations are as follows:

- Convenience and affordability
- Supportive relationships with teachers and providers
- Caregivers and teachers with positive affect (e.g., warm, sensitive, caring)
- Cognitive stimulation that will lead to children's success in school

The following checklist describes features of high-quality early childhood settings that parents should consider when they are seeking an early childhood program for their children.

THE TEACHER

_____ is warm, friendly, and supportive

_____ treats each child as a special person

_____ has training and experience working with children

_____ respects and accepts different races, cultures, religions, and ethnic groups

_____ listens to children intently

_____ interacts with children in positive ways, nonverbally and verbally

THE SCHOOL, CENTER, OR FAMILY CHILD-CARE SETTING

_____ is pleasant, comfortable, and clean

_____ has disease-prevention policies and first-aid procedures in place

_____ has space for both active and quiet play

_____ has appropriate light, heat, and ventilation

_____ is regulated and approved by a state and/or federal agency

_____ provides a safe outdoor play area

_____ is supplied with appropriate learning materials and equipment, indoors and out

THE FAMILY SUPPORT SYSTEM

_____ encourages family participation in the program

_____ provides information to families about the program and the child's progress on a regular basis

_____ offers scheduled opportunities for conferencing as well as informal opportunities for parents, families, and teachers to interact

_____ uses community resources to support families and children

THE PROGRAM

_____ gives every child a sense of belonging

_____ guides children in dealing with powerful emotions

_____ encourages self-help skills and builds independence

_____ prevents behavior problems and resolves conflicts in ways that respect children

Time is planned for

_____ active and quiet play

_____ indoor and outdoor activities

_____ trips, excursions, and special events

_____ artistic and musical expression

_____ creative expression and the arts

_____ language and literacy development activities

And opportunities to

_____ learn to get along, to share, and to respect differences

_____ learn about own and others' cultural and ethnic backgrounds

_____ speak English as well as to speak each family's native language

_____ develop each child's unique talents

_____ establish healthy self-esteem

_____ develop good health habits

Toys and equipment you should see include

For infants:

_____ cribs, mobiles, soft toys, and blankets

_____ rocking chairs, lullaby tapes, and soft lighting

_____ safe places to crawl and explore

For 1- and 2-year-olds:

_____ cloth, cardboard, and plastic books

_____ items to sort by shape and color, and large hollow blocks

_____ baby dolls, beds, bottles, and other related materials

_____ toys with which to practice filling and emptying, and pushing and pulling

_____ low climbing equipment with padding underneath

_____ simple equipment for practicing motor skills (e.g., rocking boat, large wooden wheeled toys)

For preschoolers:

_____ clay, paint, books, puzzles, games, and blocks

_____ tapes or CDs and simple musical instruments

_____ computers and software

_____ dress-up clothes, small toys (e.g., miniature farm or house setup), house area (with toy refrigerator, stove, etc.)

_____ tricycles, wagons, and climbing equipment

_____ sensory materials such as water and sand

Professional Goals of Early Childhood Educators

What is it that early childhood educators are expected to do in order to become outstanding teachers?

Make a Firm Commitment to the Care and Education of Young Children

Caring about children, enjoying their company, respecting them as individuals, and treating them equitably form the cornerstone of early childhood practice. In early childhood education, we speak of educating the "whole child"—the physical, social, emotional, cognitive, and aesthetic aspects (Hendrick, 1998). As a group, early childhood educators do not consider covering material to be their primary responsibility in the way that some teachers at other levels do. Rather, they see children first. For example, if you ask a high school biology teacher what she teaches, she is likely to say, "biology," while an early childhood practitioner is more apt to respond with the particular age of children taught (e.g., infants; toddlers; preschoolers; first, second, or third graders; a mixed-age group). The National Association for the Education of Young Children's *Code of Ethical Conduct and Commitment* (1998) provides guidelines about the type of commitment that is expected from early childhood educators (see the Compendium of Early Childhood Materials and Resources at the end of this book for the complete code). Those who work with young children have an obligation to do the following:

- Appreciate childhood as a unique and valuable stage in the human life cycle
- Base their work with children on knowledge of child development
- Appreciate and support the close ties between the child and family
- Recognize that children are best understood in the context of family, culture, and society
- Respect the dignity, worth, and uniqueness of each individual (child, family member, and colleague)
- Help children and adults achieve their full potential in the context of relationships that are based on trust, respect, and positive regard

Individuals who act upon these commitments are referred to as child advocates; therefore, their efforts on behalf of children and families are called child advocacy (Fennimore, 1989). When educators of young children act upon their care, concern, and commitment to the very young, their behavior speaks louder than words ever could.

Take Delight in, Be Curious About, and Learn to Understand Children's Development

Here is an example of a preservice teacher experiencing delight and curiosity in understanding a child:

> A group of children in my neighborhood were gathered for Scotty's third birthday party. The parents had made a videotape of the birthday boy at various ages. One of the things that he did when he was about 11 months old was to lie down on his stomach and slide quickly down five padded, carpeted stairs. One child begged to see the film run backwards, and the father obliged while the children laughed and squealed at the funny situations, such as a bite of birthday cake going backwards from a person's mouth and back onto the fork. When the film segment that showed Scotty shooting down the steps was run backwards, it looked like he was being propelled *up* the stairs. About half an hour later, a one-year-old who had watched the film was observed stretched out on the same stairs that were in the video. Suddenly I realized that he was trying to launch himself up the stairs, just as he had seen in the video run backwards! When I said this to my neighbors, they saw it too. This is an example of my being curious about why children do what they do. I was pleased that I was able to see more than the average person and make sense out of a child's behavior when no other adult at the party had seen it.

As this example illustrates, early childhood educators are intrigued by children's behavior and work harder than most to try to interpret it. Effective early childhood educators learn to be "kid watchers" (Goodman, 1978) who take the time to notice children's behavior and glean important information from those observations.

As you work with young children, you will want to maintain a focus on meeting children's needs and supporting their learning. Of course, you cannot achieve this goal unless you know young children well. That is why one of the key concepts in early childhood education is developmentally appropriate practice (Bredekamp & Copple, 1996). Developmentally appropriate practice has two key components: age appropriateness, what children of that age are capable of doing, generally speaking, and individual appropriateness, what is suitable for that particular child at that time and in that situation, including the child's culture and ethnicity.

Developmentally appropriate practice means that learning experiences are compatible "with the active, exploring mode that is natural to the child; encourage fantasy and playfulness; lay the groundwork for a vigorous style of intellectual curiosity and learning, personally motivated rather than externally dominated; and connect language concepts and the beginning process of reading and writing to meaningful experience and communication" (Minuchin, 1987, p. 250).

Maintain a Fundamentally Positive Outlook on Children, Families, and Teaching

No one goes into teaching with the thought, "I will become a mediocre, marginal, or destructive teacher who does whatever is minimally required or as little as possible," yet it is clear that such teachers exist. One indicator of whether a person will become one of these teachers is the current behavior of that person. Think about your own behavior and that of your classmates. Do some people drag themselves in, collapse into a chair at the back of the room, and complain when the work is demanding? If so, chances are that if these people manage to get into teaching, they will quickly deteriorate into poor teachers. Are you and your classmates willing to do more than what is required? How many of you would go to hear a guest speaker even though there is no extra credit involved? Students who will not do more than the minimum or what is rewarded now are unlikely to become teachers who will do more than the minimum later on. As you work with faculty and supervisors, they are continuously evaluating these traits because they will be asked to write recommendations of your performance. Those recommendations will be based not only on your current level of performance, but also on your teachers' and supervisors' predictions about how you will fare in an early childhood setting. Anyone who is lukewarm at the very beginning of a career can hardly be expected to become enthusiastic in later years.

Understand the Powerful Influence that You Exert over Children's Lives

Although educators often report feeling powerless to alter many of the circumstances that affect the students in their classes, caregivers and teachers do determine the quality of life within their centers and classrooms. In this sense, teachers are very powerful influences on children's lives. The belief that you can exert a powerful, positive influence on children's lives is referred to as teacher efficacy. Here is how Eleanore Zurbruegg, an award-winning teacher from Ridgeway Elementary School in Memphis, Tennessee, describes her views of a teacher's power over children and explains her efficacy beliefs: "What a teacher does and says can stay with a child forever. I try to build confidence, awaken curiosity, excite young minds, shape attitudes, encourage discoveries, and invite learning" (Boyer, 1995, p. 43).

A teacher's power emanates from several roles and responsibilities. Teachers have the power to establish and control the social environment of the classroom, exert an emotional influence over children's self-appraisals, exercise power over the content of a child's mind, negotiate meaning in classroom dialogue and interactions, and present a model of an educated adult who has certain habits of mind and work (Raywid, 1995).

"Kid watching" requires careful observation and interpretation of children's behavior.

PAUSE AND REFLECT ABOUT FIRST TEACHERS

Think about your first teachers. How did they influence your ideas about your talents and capabilities? How did they affect your sense of belonging to the group? What were the most important lessons that you learned from them? Did any of these teachers from your early years in school inspire you to become a teacher and play school? How will you use your power as a teacher to exert a powerful, positive influence on the lives of children and families?

When teachers do not exercise their power in positive ways, their classrooms become chaotic, and children feel confused or insecure. Imagine visiting a room for toddlers where there are two teachers and one aide who sit on a table and chat with one another and do not interact with the children unless a child begins to scream or cry. Because these three early childhood practitioners fail to exercise their power to guide the group and facilitate learning, the right of the toddlers to be nurtured and protected has been denied. Likewise, a teacher who shakes a child or pulls on a child's arm to gain the child's at-

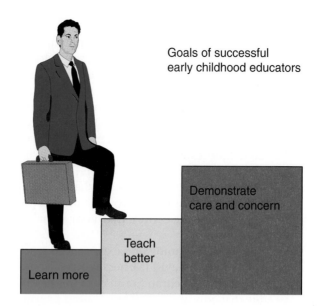

Goals of successful early childhood educators

Demonstrate care and concern

Teach better

Learn more

tention is abusing power. Ideally, the early childhood educator uses power to advocate for the needs of young children as well as to guide children in learning how to assert their independence in socially appropriate ways.

Concentrate on Your Goal of Becoming the Best Teacher You Can Be

Maria Montessori, one of the great pioneers in early childhood education, believed that the ability of the learner to focus and sustain concentration was one of the most important outcomes of an education. This outcome is just as important for adults as it is for young children. Are you genuinely interested in education and motivated to become the best teacher you can be? Achieving this goal requires sustained concentration throughout your program, even when the content of a particular course or the style of an instructor is not what you prefer. You will know that you are concentrating fully on your goal when you become so involved in learning activities that you lose track of time. Another indicator of this concentration on your goal is the tendency to seek feedback from others rather than fearing recommendations for improvement or resenting the extra effort it takes to become an even better teacher. Yet you could probably stand outside the classroom door of a typical education course on the day when major projects are returned to the students and overhear some students complaining bitterly because they were asked to revise their work. Although they are, in effect, saying, "How dare the instructor ask more of me!" the truth is that asking more of teachers is commonplace. Try chatting with any educator who has a wonderful reputation and you will undoubtedly be amazed by all of the duties, both required and volunteer, which this person has undertaken and the clear focus with which those duties are approached. If you immediately establish a sense of purpose, you will make the most of your education. The worst in our field are satisfied to be uninformed, less skilled, and disaffected. The best in our field are constantly striving to learn more, teach better, and demonstrate their care and concern for young children.

Be Willing to Take the Risks and Make the Mistakes that Are Part of the Learning Process

Psychologists usually define learning as a change in behavior. If your behavior remains the same, then you have not learned. The difficulty with changing behavior is that we feel unsure of ourselves, uncertain about whether we are acting appropriately.

A good example is writing a lesson plan for the first time. Students typically say such things as, "I never wrote a lesson plan before," "I'm so confused," or "I have no idea what to do." In other words, these students are being asked to change their behavior and they are afraid of taking a risk. Yet real learning is, by definition, risky—no risk of mistake, no learning. When you are confronted with new challenges and unfamiliar tasks such as lesson planning, it is helpful to take stock of what you *do* know based upon your experiences as a student. You probably know quite a few things about planning activities that are simply common sense, such as the need to teach something significant (a concept), the need to specify your goals (the objective), the need to capture children's attention at the beginning of the lesson (an introduction or motivation), the need to identify what materials are necessary to teach the lesson (materials), the need to think through your lesson in a logical sequence (the procedure), and the need to make certain that your information is current and accurate (resources or references).

For both beginning and experienced teachers, research indicates that the most effective teachers are avid learners who welcome the changes associated with new learning (Borko, 1989; Cochran-Smith & Lytle, 1990). Actually, there are several types of knowledge that educators at all levels need to acquire. They include the following:

- **content knowledge**—knowing the concepts, terminology, and principles related to the subject matter
- **general pedagogical knowledge**—knowing basic methods of teaching that pertain to all subject areas
- **curriculum knowledge**—understanding the big picture, the overall plan for learning and how what you are teaching contributes to those goals
- **pedagogical content knowledge**—knowing the specific instructional techniques that work best in different subject areas such as reading, science, mathematics, and so forth
- **knowledge of learners and their characteristics**—understanding children's growth, development, and needs
- **knowledge of educational contexts**—knowing how to adjust teaching to suit different contexts, such as addressing 300 children in an auditorium, communicating with one child in an assessment situation, or working with one small group while the remainder of the class works independently
- **knowledge of educational ends, purposes, and values**—knowing to delve beneath the surface and strive to understand what motives, goals, and ideals underlie actions (Shulman, 1986).

Adapt Flexibly to Continuous Change and Expect Perpetual Challenge

"Teaching is a complex, situation-specific, and dilemma-ridden behavior" (Sparks-Langer & Colton, 1991, p. 37). If you want a large measure of control, predictability, and guaranteed results, it is preferable to work with objects rather than human beings. As everyone knows, we human beings are highly individual. What encourages one person undermines the confidence of another. Often, the impact that you have on student learning is not immediately seen or easy to measure. Your effectiveness as an early childhood educator is judged not merely by your actions, but also by the influence of those actions on students and their families. Those who make a commitment to the field of teaching are entering a helping profession, a career dedicated to helping other people realize their optimal potential.

When you teach, you will be constantly adapting and adjusting your instructional strategies, the examples that you give, and the ways that you interact with students. For example, "Doctors do not walk into surgery with an instructional manual. Attorneys do not defend clients using prescribed dialogues that are guaranteed for all cases. These professionals interpret cases individually, and then apply the most appropriate interventions. Each patient is unique, each client an individual" (Glasgow, 1994, p. 132). In most cases, the work of the early childhood professional is accomplished in group rather than individual settings. You may have a child in your class who is disruptive, but that child will be just one of many others, each one of whom has different needs, interests, and abilities. Responding to these complex, multiple demands requires a large measure of flexibility. You can sit down with a group of children to read a story and within a few moments' time have multiple messages such as these running through your brain:

TEACHER'S THOUGHTS	QUESTIONS POSED TO STUDENTS
Using real objects to introduce the story has captured their attention. . . . Elisa seems very quiet today.	"Look at the cover of this book. Any ideas what it might be about?"
Taylor and Jason are lying down. Should I say something or ignore it? . . . It's raining outside. I hope that doesn't mean indoor recess. . . . Jaime leaves early for a doctor's appointment. . . .	"I want to see everyone sitting up. That way you can all see the pictures."
Maria really seems to be into the story today. . . . When we have our student teaching seminar, I want to be sure to share my idea for introducing the book. . . . Someone is outside my door—I hope it's not my supervisor because now Tyler and Jason are wrestling on the floor.	

Acquire a Specialized Body of Knowledge and Skills

It is a common misconception that those who work with young children have to know less than teachers in the upper grades because the information their students are capable of mastering is less sophisticated. Some people actually believe that a kindergarten or first-grade teacher is paid less, or should be. Yet those who teach young children need to be extremely resourceful and versatile in finding ways to make concepts understandable to young children. How do you get across the big ideas such as what a family is or how to be a friend? How can you teach a concept such as color or shape to preschoolers in ways that actively involve them? The answers to these questions are based on pedagogical knowledge. (Pedagogy is the science and art of teaching.) Rather than taking a single subject and delving into it in considerable depth, early childhood educators are laying the foundation for later learning. Although that foundation may not appear to be the most impressive part of each person's educational structure, later learning cannot be built without it.

An essential part of your knowledge and skills will be responding to the needs of diverse groups of learners. As a result of several pieces of federal legislation that were enacted into law, such as Public Law 94–142, the great majority of early childhood programs today include children with a much wider range of abilities and talents. Included are children with physical differences (e.g., those with hearing or vision impairments and those in wheelchairs), children with attentional difficulties (e.g., those who have attention deficit disorder or hyperactivity disorder), children with differing levels and profiles of achievement in various areas (e.g., those who are musically gifted or bilingual), children with different social and emotional needs (e.g., those who are aggressive or autistic), and children with a variety of hereditary syndromes (e.g., Down syndrome), birth defects (e.g., spina bifida), or diseases (e.g., multiple sclerosis). This nationwide effort to educate these young children with special needs alongside their peers to the fullest extent possible is referred to as inclusion. One of your roles as a teacher will be to work with other teams of professionals to decide what type of program would be best for each child, and clearly, that will require very sophisticated knowledge and skills. Some of the program placement options in inclusive early childhood settings, ranging from most to least inclusive, follow:

- Regular class—Young children with special needs are integrated fully into the class with their peers.
- Transition class—Young children with special needs are educated with peers in the regular classroom, but special education services are provided.
- Resource room—Young children are educated with their peers for most of the day, but they are pulled out for a portion of the day to work with a specialist.
- Separate class—Young children with similar disabilities are grouped together and placed in a special class for an intensive special education curriculum.
- Residential facility—This option is reserved for severe cases or cases in which the home is unable to provide needed care and the school is unable to provide an appropriate education.

Learn to Use Material and Human Resources

Students often express the concern that they will not be able to think of enough good ideas to enable them to teach well. The good news is that there are many excellent early childhood educators who are willing to share their experiences and ideas. Therefore, you can borrow and build upon their contributions rather than "reinventing the wheel." In fact, there is a vast amount of information that focuses exclusively on the care and education of young children of which newcomers to the field are frequently unaware. That information is contained in professional books, journals, magazines, nonprint media, and Web sites on the Internet. The Compendium of Early Childhood Materials and Resources at the end of this book highlights some of the most useful resources for early childhood educators. As you read more and discuss these ideas with practicing professionals, you will soon see that there is no lack of ideas in the early childhood field. More often than not, your task is one of carefully selecting from among many different options.

Work to Build a Sense of Community; Seek Collaboration and Peer Support

Have you ever felt a strong sense of affiliation with a group as people you could count on and with whom you truly belonged? If so, you were part of a community. Communities provide opportunities to reveal ourselves fully; know others well; and reach out, connect, and help (Sapon-Shevin, 1995).

As an early childhood educator, one of your primary goals is to create a sense of community in your center or classroom (Krall & Jalongo, 1998). A school community is characterized by a clear and vital mission and a shared sense of purpose (Boyer, 1995). This means that all stakeholders—children, parents, family members, teachers, administrators, support staff, and the community at large—understand what is happening in school and why. Another important dimension of a learning community is classroom climate, or the feeling or tone of a classroom. A classroom community that supports learning is

- *communicative,* meaning that all members strive to make themselves understood as well as understand others
- *just,* meaning that everyone expects and receives fair treatment
- *disciplined,* meaning that expectations for and limits on behavior are made clear
- *caring,* meaning that every person in the room is treated with love and respect
- *celebratory,* meaning that achievements and milestones are honored and savored (Boyer, 1995).

Whenever a sense of community is built, we feel responsible for ourselves yet committed to one another.

PAUSE AND REFLECT ABOUT BUILDING COMMUNITY

Think back to your very first college class. How did you respond to a new environment with unfamiliar people? How might those feelings help you to understand the child who cries on the first day of school? What is it that causes you to feel enthusiastic about a college course? What is it that causes you to dread attending a class? How might these feelings enable you to better understand the young child's perspective on a high-quality early childhood setting?

Use Problem-solving Strategies to Make Ethical Decisions

Suppose that a child in your class is being seriously neglected, arriving at school tired, hungry, unwashed, and dressed in clothes that will not protect her against the weather. Some teachers would complain bitterly about the family and call the local social services agency. Some would try to arrange a meeting at school with the family. Others would make a visit to the home. Still others would intervene directly and see to it that the child was fed, clothed, and bathed. At one time or another, most teachers have tried several of these strategies. Unlike situations in some other occupations, no one told the teacher precisely what to do or when to act. Rather, these teachers relied upon their general care and concern for children and families, the input of colleagues and other professionals, and their familiarity with the particular child's situation. When a teacher is solving a complex (yet common) problem such as helping a neglected child, breaking it down into smaller steps and proceeding confidently toward a solution seldom occurs. More often than not, teachers have to feel their way through many possible courses of action and proceed cautiously, guided by their "ethic of caring" (Noddings, 1984). A teacher who is acting in an ethical and principled fashion begins with questions such as the following:

- Who benefits from the decision?
- Whose interests are being served? With what effects?
- What is the significance of these effects on children's lives?
- To what extent do teacher decisions have a limiting or distorting effect on the opportunities open to children? (Tennyson & Strom, 1988)

William Ayers (1995) explains why this ethical dimension is so critical to becoming a successful teacher:

> Teaching is intellectual and ethical work. It requires the full attention—wide awake, inquiring, critical—of thoughtful and caring people if it is to be done well. Although there is always more to learn and more to know as a teacher, the heart of teaching is a passionate regard for students. With it, mistakes and obstacles will be met and overcome; without it, no amount of technical skill will ever fully compensate. The work of teaching involves struggling to see each student in as full and dynamic a way as possible, to create environments that nurture and challenge the wide range of students who are actually there in classrooms, and to construct bridges with each learner from the known to the not yet known. (p. 60)

Ethical teachers think logically and carefully about situations, use moral principles to guide behavior (e.g., equity, freedom, respect), and identify and empathize with the welfare of others beyond duty or common decency (Tennyson & Strom, 1988). Figure 1.4 summarizes the ethical responsibilities of early childhood educators.

Pursue Professional Growth as an Educator of the Very Young

Many psychologists contend that human beings naturally are growth seeking. Harvard psychologist Mihalyi Csikszentmihalyi (1993) explains it this way: "Boredom directs us to seek new challenges, while anxiety urges us to develop new skills; the net result is that, in order to avoid negative feelings, a person is forced to grow in complexity" (p. 191).

FIGURE 1.4

Ethical responsibilities of early childhood professionals

Section I: Ethical Responsibilities to Children

Childhood is a unique and valuable stage in the life cycle. Our paramount responsibility is to provide safe, healthy, nurturing, and responsive settings for children. We are committed to supporting children's development by cherishing individual differences, by helping them learn to live and work cooperatively, and by promoting their self-esteem.

Section II: Ethical Responsibilities to Families

Families are of primary importance in children's development. (The term *family* may include others, besides parents, who are responsibly involved with the child.) Because the family and the early childhood educator have a common interest in the child's welfare, we acknowledge a primary responsibility to bring about collaboration between the home and school in ways that enhance the child's development.

Section III Ethical Responsibilities to Colleagues

In a caring, cooperative work place human dignity is respected, professional satisfaction is promoted, and positive relationships are modeled. Our primary responsibility in this arena is to establish and maintain settings and relationships that support productive work and meet professional needs.

SOURCE: National Association for the Education of Young Children (NAEYC) *Code of Ethical Conduct* (1989). Washington, DC.

My Own Career Development

Lilian Katz

My interest in child development and the field of early childhood education grew out of my 5 years as a mother who participated with my three children in a cooperative nursery school in the San Francisco Bay Area. Their teachers, responsible for teaching not only them, but also their parents, were very impressive to me. They were knowledgeable and skillful in their work, and they encouraged me to read the literature on early development and education.

After my youngest child entered kindergarten, I enrolled in a class for preschool teachers at the local community college. The instructor was interesting and inspiring. Her name was Dr. Mary Lane (Professor Emerita from San Francisco State University), and she strongly encouraged me to complete my bachelor's degree, which I did in 1964. Dr. Lane also urged me to accept a position as a preschool teacher in a nearby parent cooperative nursery school. After teaching 3-year-olds for 2 years, I was able to get a scholarship to study child development at Stanford University with Professor Pauline Sears. Because Stanford had no master's program, I had to register for a Ph.D.—a completely unanticipated change in the direction of my life as the mother of three young children!

As I was completing my doctoral work, I was offered the position I now hold at the University of Illinois, Urbana–Champaign. The University housed what was then the National Laboratory of Early Childhood Education (a cluster of some dozen research centers around the country focusing on preschool education) and the ERIC Clearinghouse on Early Childhood Education, a national dissemination network. In 1970, I was appointed director of the Clearinghouse and continue in that role today, having participated in its development into the technological age.

In the nearly 30 years since my career began, I have engaged in a mix of teaching, lecturing, writing, and service to various groups, including 8 years on NAEYC's board, 4 as vice president and 2 as president (1992–1994).

What is a Key Issue in Teacher Development?

In several papers, I have discussed the "feed-forward" problem associated with teacher development. By feed forward, I mean that professional training experiences frequently give students answers to questions they have not yet asked. While that experience remains constant, the meaning attributed to it changes with subsequent experience, in retrospect. So that, for example, a student might say of an undergraduate course at the time of participation that it was not interesting, not practical enough, or too much work; but 5 years later, as a practitioner, the student might say retrospectively, "I hated it then, but now I'm so glad I had it." Or, vice versa, a student might say of a current experience, "This is fun," but later on say that it was a waste of time considering what he or she is now facing.

If this formulation of the feed-forward problem is accurate, then teacher education cannot be designed on the basis of how the student experiences it at the time. Rather, it must be designed on the basis of our very best understanding of the long-term developmental processes through which the professional must pass in the journey from novice undergraduate to in-service practitioner.

Lilian Katz is a professor of early childhood education at the University of Illinois, Urbana–Champaign and Director of the ERIC Clearinghouse on Elementary and Early Childhood Education.

This, of course, is what outstanding teachers do as they mature professionally—they become more complex and seek professional growth throughout their lives as educators.

You are embarking on a lifelong project—becoming a caring and competent teacher of the very young. Many students have the mistaken impression that if they put their 2 or 4 years into a program, they are finished with the project of becoming a teacher. Nothing could be further from the truth. Initial teacher preparation is just that, a beginning in the transition from novice to expert. Think about something that you do exceptionally well, then think about where you started and all the stages in between. Can you expect that any less effort would be expended in becoming a teacher than in learning to swim or cook or play a musical instrument, for instance? Yet over and over again, beginning teachers secure their first jobs and lament that they were not adequately prepared for the realities of teaching (Ryan, 1986), as if they expected to be a finished product churned out on an assembly line.

The truth is that most colleges and universities are all about possibilities—about what education could and should be rather than about what is or the status quo. In other words, there is a discrepancy between centers and schools as they routinely exist and centers and schools at their very best. If your college and university instructors are doing their jobs, they are preparing you to be the best possible early childhood educator, not a mediocre one. They are hoping that you will be strong enough to resist routine and expedience. They are trusting you to become a change agent, a person who will continually strive to improve centers, schools, and other educational contexts by making them more responsive to young learners.

Wondering about who you are as a beginning teacher opens the door for wondering who you will eventually become and how you will get there (Abbs, 1974). Gordon and Williams-Browne (1995) suggest that teachers ask themselves, "Do I see myself as a learner? Where does my learning take place? How? What happens to me when something is hard or when I make a mistake? Do I learn from other teachers? Do I learn from children?" (p. 148).

Both at this initial stage and throughout your career, you will want to remember the reasons why the early childhood years are so important.

The Importance of Education in the Early Years

The expression "First impressions are lasting ones" certainly applies to education. If you talk with teachers, they will tell you that at parent-teacher conference time, it is the kindergartners' parents and family members who attend in the greatest numbers. Evidently, families feel that getting children off to a good start is important. They want their children's first impressions of education to be positive ones. If you talk with adults, most of them can remember their first teacher even if it is difficult to recall the names of other teachers in their lives. Once again, those initial impressions about school are enduring ones. There are other reasons why early experiences matter.

Early educational experiences define the young child's overall perceptions of educational experiences. As an early childhood educator, you don't simply teach or care for young children, you define the quality of children's lives within an educational setting. The young child has no way of knowing whether a teacher is bad or mean, because the child has little or no basis for comparison. Teaching young children is an awesome responsibility, because your actions form the child's concept of care or education. You will play a formative role in children's lives.

Early experience affects later experience. What a person has learned so far exerts a tremendous influence on what he or she can learn in the future. A person's background knowledge is referred to as schema, and the theory that describes its importance is schema theory. Early childhood is undeniably an important time for forming the foundation of background knowledge. In fact, many experts argue that it is the most critical time for learning (Elkind, 1987).

Early education affects self-concept as a learner. Because children are embedded in their own point of view and have difficulty adopting a different perspective, they are likely to blame themselves for a dissatisfying school experience rather than attribute the problem to someone else. For example, in a study of young children's listening behaviors in which teachers gave deliberately ambiguous directions, the children attributed their lack of understanding to poor listening (McDevitt, 1990). This knowledge makes it particularly important for early childhood practitioners to be sensitive to children and skillful in working with them.

Early childhood is a period of rapid growth; it is a prime time for development. Gabriela Mistral, a poet from Chile, beautifully explains why enriched early childhood experiences are so essential: "Many things we need can wait. The child cannot. Now is the time his bones are being formed, his blood is being made, his mind is being developed. To him we cannot say tomorrow, his name is today" (quoted in Boyer, 1995, p. 12). The best teachers of young children go beyond fulfilling routine duties. They acquire skills in self-assessment that enable them to contrast the real ("How I am") with the ideal ("How I would like to be") (Burke, 1997).

PAUSE AND REFLECT ABOUT: THE BEST AGE FOR KINDERGARTEN

Parents and teachers often face the realities of developmental stage versus chronological age as they make decisions about children. For example, are all five-year olds ready to attend kindergarten? Considering Piaget's theories of cognitive development, it is not surprising that there is nothing magic that occurs on children's fifth birthdays that transforms them from preschoolers to kindergartners. Theory, observation, and experience demonstrate that each child develops physically, emotionally, and intellectually at her own rate.

For many years, age five was considered the "normal" time for a child to attend kindergarten, just as age seven was considered optimal for "reading readiness." Most schools require "kindergarten readiness" tests which measure small and large muscle coordination, hearing, vision, and facility with speech and language. We know that early childhood experiences define children's future perception of school and themselves as learners. We also know that each child does not progress through all areas of development at the same rate, for example, a child may be able to catch a ball (large muscle coordination), but not be able to use scissors (small muscle coordination). At another level, some children may have an extensive receptive vocabulary (understand what they hear), but have problems with speech production (may make them difficult to understand). For these reasons, the decision about whether a child is "ready" for kindergarten may be more critical and complex than it would seem to be on the surface.

This PrimeTime Parent Challenge video clip presents a discussion with two families who chose to delay their sons' entrance to kindergarten. These parents thought they were making a responsible and healthy decision for their children, but a research report says that there may be more consequences to this decision than we think. Now watch the video clip and think about the implication that delaying kindergarten could have on a child's future.

1. List at least six factors from the most important to least important that you would consider when determining a child's readiness for kindergarten. Compare and discuss your list with your classmates.

2. How do you interpret Dr. Byrd's research findings? Do you think his conclusions are appropriate? What other information would be useful to help you evaluate the significance of his research?

3. What types of productive activities would be beneficial to a child whose parents decide to delay kindergarten?

Conclusion

Perhaps the best way to conclude this chapter is to return to what has surely brought you to teaching in the first place: the children. Reflect for a moment on your personality and characteristics. If you were asked to identify what you like best about yourself, what would it be? If you had to identify five personal characteristics and qualities that will enable you to succeed as an early childhood educator, which ones would you choose? Why? This is how you can begin to explore your role as a practitioner. If you invest your heart and mind in becoming an effective early childhood practitioner, you will discover new ways to deepen insight about yourself as a professional, think systematically about your teaching practice, expand your repertoire of skills and techniques, and work with other professionals to improve your school or center (Kochendorfer, 1994).

One Child, Three Perspectives: **An Instructional Support Team Designs an Educational Plan for Michael**

The Instructional Support program was designed to reduce the number of students being placed in special education. It consists of a team approach to intervening when a child is experiencing serious difficulty in the classroom and has been identified as a possible candidate for special education. Members of the Instructional Support team (IST) include the principal, the guidance counselor, the Instructional Support teacher, the classroom teacher of the child, and the parent or parents. A teacher accesses these services by requesting assistance from the team. The process continues with the Instructional Support teacher collecting information, including observations of the child in class; an interview with the child, teacher, and parent(s); and other information as necessary. Then the IST meets to share information, set a reasonable goal, brainstorm about interventions to attain the goal, delegate responsibility for implementing the suggestions, and establish a timetable. The plan is put into action for 30 days, then the team meets to review the case. Several decisions are possible: (1) the child is making progress or has met the goal, (2) the interventions should continue and be monitored for another 30 days, or (3) the child should be referred for further evaluation and possible special education placement.

Ms. Mong has been the IST teacher for 2 years. In October, a second-grade teacher submitted a referral on five students in her second-grade class. Ms. Mong began with classroom observations. Michael was paired with a partner who had a higher reading level. When Ms. Mong interviewed Michael and asked him to read a passage from the new reading series, he said, "I can't read this book. Someone always reads it to me." Ms. Mong decided to check on Michael's progress during first grade. His teachers reported that his progress was slow but satisfactory. The first-grade teachers used a variety of children's books in addition to the reading series. They did not use workbooks or worksheets. They also mentioned that Michael's second-grade teacher, Ms. Orr, had been to see them to complain that "This kid can't read."

When she went to confer with Ms. Orr, the IST teacher suggested that it might be helpful to give Michael some reading choices. Ms. Orr refused, saying that this would single Michael out from his peers and be too confusing. She further pointed out that she was using a second-grade-level reading series, and said that therefore, a child assigned to her class ought to be able to read them. When the IST teacher invited her to bring some ideas to the team meeting, Ms. Orr said, "Why do I have to go through Instructional Support anyway? I just want him in remedial reading." When the IST meeting convened, Michael's father said angrily, "We never heard about any of these problems before. Why is this happening now? It's not *my* job to teach him to read, it's yours." Ms. Orr replied, "And that's exactly what I'm trying to do, but how can I give him the individual help he needs when there are 28 other children in the class? Now you see why I am for special placement." The IST teacher said, "Remember that our goal is to give Michael support and enable him to stay with his peers." "What should we do, then?" Michael's mother asked. "We only want what is best for Michael."

REACT:	With whom do you identify most strongly in this case and why?
RESEARCH:	What particular assessment challenges are represented by Michael's situation?
REFLECT:	What are the underlying issues?

Exploring Values Through Vignettes

It is common to speak about values, yet values are difficult to define. Hildebrand and Hearron (1998) have identified 10 characteristics of values:

Values . . .

may be defined as concepts of what is desirable.

are learned throughout life from example, study, and instruction.

can be consciously held and applied or subconscious.

can be brought to the level of awareness.

guide actions and decisions of individuals.

are both personal and professional (acquired through education, training, experience).

have been enshrined in the Constitution, laws, and regulations.

are rarely identical for two individuals.

are reflected in early childhood programs.

are the basis for regulations and standards in early childhood programs.

can be changed through conscious effort of individuals.

Individual Response

In an entry from her student teaching journal, Jane Mize describes how she overcame her initial disillusionment and made major changes in her teaching. As you read the excerpt, what can you infer about her values system? What kind of professional is she striving to become?

I had a lot of information I needed to "teach" to the children. I envisioned them, eyes glued, listening to me intently. In reality, I kept having to stop during the lesson to refocus the children or attend to behavioral problems, sometimes losing my calm demeanor. After one particular lesson that had not gone well, I just stopped and sent the children back to their seats early. I realized that I was getting more and more frustrated. At first, I thought it was the children. The more I thought about it and analyzed my teaching methods, the more I realized that I had to make some changes in my approach.

Within the next several days I had my "pet invention lesson" (where the children were to create imaginary pets out of cloth and other materials). I kept my focus on the children's literature that I selected to go along with the lesson and tried to concentrate on giving clear instructions to the children about the accompanying activities. Then off the children went, and for the rest of the morning I helped with the materials, observed children eagerly learning, and listened to them tell me excitedly about what they had made. This lesson was the beginning of the change in my approach to teaching. I realized that I had been keeping the children in their seats too long and doing most of the talking instead of engaging them in good dialogue, not only with me, but also with each other. Also, I realized that in my old approach I was getting responses from the same children while others were sitting there squirming or tuning me out. I was not using the time I had with the children to the best advantage.

I decided to try and revise my approach. We still came together as a group, but not as often and not as long. I tried doing more in small groups or pairs, having the children share information with each other. I hoped that this would encourage some of the more reticent children to become involved and gain confidence with their ideas. When we did come together as a group, I read good literature. I also attempted to improve my divergent questions and tried to encourage more children to participate. (Jalongo & Isenberg, 1995, pp. 192–193)

Discussion Questions

Now that you have collected your impressions of Jane Mize's experience, work in small groups and discuss the following questions, which are designed to encourage reflection on an episode of teaching (Cruickshank, 1987).

What happened?

What did the student teacher do? Why?

What would you have done in this situation?

Did learning take place?

What got in the way of learning?

What might the student teacher have learned?

What other ways might the experience have been organized?

Writing a Teaching Vignette

A vignette is a short description of an incident or episode about teaching and learning. A good teaching vignette includes the following elements.

Setting: Describe the who, what, when, and where involved in the situation. Include only those things that are essential to understanding the story.

Beginning: Start with something that will get the reader into your teaching vignette immediately. A good vignette does not necessarily arrange things chronologically. It starts with the most interesting part.

Reaction: A good teaching vignette is not like a book report; it does more than summarize. It also honestly and clearly describes your thoughts, feelings, and reflections as a teacher or as a learner.

Attempt: A vignette helps the reader to understand how you, as a teacher or learner, responded to the situation and why you responded as you did.

Outcome: A vignette makes the results of the actions for the teacher and the learner clear.

Ending: Every story needs to build to a satisfying conclusion. A vignette should give the reader a sense of completion, a sense that the incident has been "wrapped up."

You should choose a situation to write about that has powerful emotions associated with it, because these are the kinds of experiences that exert the greatest influence on behavior. Following are some ideas to get you started.

- Role Models and Mentors: Write a vignette about an educator who had a positive influence on your decision to become a teacher. What, exactly, did that person do for you? Why did it matter so much?

- Echoes of Childhood: Write about a particular incident from your childhood that has enabled you to develop greater empathy for students. How will you use that experience, good or bad, to be a more caring teacher?

- Best and Worst Learning Experiences: Write about a particular situation in which you felt very successful or unsuccessful as a learner. Why did this occur? What did you do about it?

Exploring Your Child Advocacy Role From a Historical Perspective

Where should teachers look for authority in reflecting on their work? Do we look only to ourselves and our past experience as reference points in understanding the teaching and learning process? Do we rely solely on the theoretical premises of scholars and the research paradigms of educational researchers, many of whom have never taught children, or taught little? Or do we look both in and out relying on our own instincts and our intuitive understandings of children, as well as on the body of knowledge that has come before us?

Karen Gallas, 1994, p. 8.

Learning Outcomes

✔ Gain a historical perspective on the field of early childhood education

✔ Identify the ways that teachers can function as child advocates

✔ Explore traditional and contemporary roles and responsibilities of early childhood educators in providing quality programs

✔ Describe the major models for programs serving young children, ages birth through 8 years

✔ Articulate a philosophy of teaching that reflects an understanding of the history of the field of early childhood education

Meet the Teachers

Marissa is an early childhood educator who is at an important stage in her professional life. She has been a parent volunteer in a county-sponsored child-care program for the past 3 years while she has earned her Child Development Associate (CDA) credential. Today is the day of her interview for a position as a family child-care provider. As she scans the faces of the interviewers seated at the conference table, she worries that she will have difficulty putting her ideas into words. When she is asked about her approaches to working with toddlers, she replies, "I believe that learning is natural and that a warm, homelike setting is the ideal way to offer care and education to toddlers. Although learning in the early years is playful, this is also a time of life when the brain is developing and a firm foundation for real learning is built."

Stephanie has taught kindergarten for 7 years in a parochial school, and she is meeting with a college faculty member who coordinates the master's program. Stephanie knows that the professor will expect her to give some reasons why she is interested in the graduate early childhood program. When the discussion comes around to her philosophy, Stephanie says, "After reading about the Project Approach, I have become very interested in curricula based on children's interests. I want to learn more about offering children interesting choices and encouraging children to explore a topic in greater depth."

Brian is a private nursery-school teacher in Miami, Florida. When parents visit the school, Brian knows that he must make the program philosophy clear so that families can make informed decisions about whether or not his program is right for their children. In

35

explaining his program to parents, Brian says, "Children need real-world experiences and meaningful learning activities, not mindless paper shuffling. The early childhood years are formative, so children need a balanced, whole-child approach that includes experiences to support their development physically, socially, intellectually, emotionally, and artistically."

REACT:	What are some commonalities among these three teachers' philosophical perspectives? What are some influences that might have shaped these teachers' ideas about early childhood education?
RESEARCH:	In what ways were the teachers' philosophies distinctive?
REFLECT:	Do you think that these ideas originated with these teachers? In what ways were their views alike or different from your own? Look ahead at the information about the early leaders in early childhood education in Figure 2.2. Did you encounter any philosophies that surprised you? Which of these notable individuals had views most consistent with your own? You might find it difficult to believe, but the views of each of the contemporary teachers just described can be traced to ideas about children, learning, instruction, curricula, and evaluation that have been in existence for decades or even centuries.

Your Role as a Child Advocate

Throughout history, there have been individuals who used their intelligence, influence, powers of persuasion, and monetary resources in the service of children and families. Child advocacy is the willingness to take a stand on behalf of children and families that goes beyond common decency or expectations. In 1997, the world mourned the loss of two prominent child advocates, Mother Teresa and Princess Diana. Mother Teresa used her unselfish commitment to humanitarian goals and the Catholic nuns who joined her order to help children around the world. In a very different way, England's Princess Diana used her access to power, wealth, and influence to raise money for various charities, particularly her goal of disarming land mines and bombs so that horrible injuries to children worldwide could be averted. To consider the contributions of well-known people such as Mother Teresa and Princess Diana can be rather daunting to a person who is just entering the early childhood field. You may ask yourself, "But what can *I*, as just one person, ever do that would qualify as being an advocate for young children?" Actually, as Goffin and Lombardi (1988) point out, there are many different types of child advocacy activities. Child advocacy might consist of speaking up when a child at the store counter is ignored by the clerk in favor of adults with larger purchases and saying, for example, "Excuse me, but I think this child was in line ahead of us." It might involve putting a child and family in contact with needed services, such as getting glasses through the local Lions Club for a visually impaired child from a low-income family. It might involve taking political action, such as participating in a Week of the Young Child gathering at the local, state, or national level. At other times, legal action, such as reporting a suspected case of child abuse, might be the most appropriate way to defend a young child.

As a first step in any child advocacy activity, you must *believe that just one person truly can make a difference*. After college student Jamie Barron Jones studied child advocacy, she found herself at a flea market where a vendor was selling a game that had been pulled off the market by the Product Safety Commission—large darts with weighted metal tips that were to be pitched like horseshoes outside in a yard. The darts had been responsible for the deaths or serious injuries of several children. Rather than remaining silent, Jamie deliberately made a scene and challenged the man at the booth about his unscrupulous business practices. She announced to all of the people there that these toys were dangerous. When the seller dismissed her concerns by saying that people were allowed to buy whatever they liked, she reported him to the police. Her reasoning was that even if she only prevented the man from selling a few sets of these banned toys, she might have protected a child from serious harm.

As Jamie's situation illustrates, another critical feature of child advocacy *is taking a stand and knowing to whom to turn for support*. Sources of support might be close to home, as in asking one of your family members to volunteer time to read to the children in your class. You might reach out to the community, inviting people, such as a florist, to speak about their jobs, to teach children a skill such as making tortillas, or to provide free services such as dental care to needy children. At other times, the special services, political influence, or financial resources represented by individuals or groups may be the resource that you need. A collaboration with the local librarian, a letter to your senator, or a donation from a local business can supply needed human and material resources. Mrs. Morrison, an infant-and-toddler caregiver, used local resources to create a playground for the young children in her center. She managed to get money for materials from local businesses, to convince parents to help assemble the play equipment at a Saturday picnic, and to publicize the event through the local media. Likewise, Mr. Shaughnessy helped to organize a community-wide effort to help families whose trailer homes had been destroyed in a tornado. By working with United Way, churches, the fire department, school personnel, and school students, he was able to collect many useful household items that enabled these families to rebuild their homes.

The third key element in child advocacy is *putting the child's agenda first*. When children are in desperate circumstances as a result of neglect, it is sometimes tempting to blame the victims rather than taking action. Ms. Ditka, an intern teacher, was surprised to learn from the school nurse that Autumn, an 8-year-old in her class, had head lice and fleas. Although it is common for head lice to appear at school and possible for anyone to get them, Autumn's situation was extreme. When an outbreak of head lice occurred in her classroom, many of the parents were angry with the teachers for not

The role of child advocate sometimes requires discovering and marshalling community resources.

noticing it sooner, and some blamed the school for unsanitary conditions. Soon, everyone was blaming Autumn and her family and treating them like outcasts. Ms. Ditka had to overcome her own fears about getting lice and fleas. She did this by getting accurate medical information about how to halt the transmission of these insects from one child to another and by working with the custodians to kill the insects that had infested her classroom. When Health Department officials went to Autumn's house to fumigate, they were met on the porch by her grandfather, his shotgun, and his hunting dogs. While the issue was being resolved with the help of the local authorities, Autumn was kept out of school for over a week. When she returned, Ms. Ditka had to confront her uneasiness about physical contact with Autumn. She also found it necessary to intercede on Autumn's behalf with the class because so many of the children had been cautioned to "stay away from that dirty girl." Mrs. Ditka knew that her response when Autumn walked into the room would speak volumes, so when Autumn stood hesitantly in the doorway, she welcomed her warmly and gave her a hug. What prevented Ms. Ditka from resenting Autumn, as many of her coworkers did, was simply her remembering that Autumn had no choices in or control over her physical environment. Without Ms. Ditka's advocacy, Autumn's second-grade year would have been a story of alienation from peers and damaged self-esteem. But because a caring teacher stood up for Autumn, calmed others, and controlled her own fears, Autumn was able to succeed academically and socially. She succeeded because her teacher approached the situation from the perspective of a child advocate rather than rushing to judge Autumn and her family. Figure 2.1 summarizes some of the different avenues that child advocacy can take.

FIGURE 2.1

Child advocacy
strategies

Speak Out on Issues of Concern to Children and Families

Lend your voice to public discussions of positive action on behalf of children. Write a letter to a legislator, create your own Web page about an issue of concern, write a letter to your local newspaper's editor, research a topic and share the information with others, work with professionals and parents to make a presentation at a conference, choose an assignment for a college course that will develop child advocacy skills, attend a meeting to find out more about what you can do, volunteer time to community service projects, offer to be a guest speaker for high school students who are considering the early childhood field, participate in a political protest against an injustice, advocate quality, compensation, and affordability (QCA) in a national system of child care

Share Knowledge and Experience

Draw upon and expand your knowledge base and experience so that you can become an information resource for others. Speak with families on issues of concern, create an information board for parents, plan cooperatively with fellow teachers, educate administrators about early childhood, join a chat group on the Internet, collect and disseminate information (newspaper articles, magazines written for parents, brochures from various organizations, items on the Internet from highly respected organizations), speak with your neighbors and community members about the challenges that today's children and families confront

Empower Parents and Families

Collaborate with colleagues, professionals from other fields, and families to find sources of support and to coordinate services. Develop good working relationships with child advocates from other fields so that you can make referrals; defend families' rights to services and show them how to cut through red tape; communicate in many ways (e.g., home visits, E-mail correspondence, notes home, telephone calls, informal conferences); share children's work in a variety of ways (e.g., on videotape; in photographs; in a class journal; in books that children author, illustrate, and take home); extend personal invitations to engage parents in school governance activities and shared decision making; donate time, materials, clothing, and household goods to charities

Stand Up for Yourself and Those in Your Profession

Educate others about the challenges the early childhood profession faces and affiliate with professional organizations that represent our needs and concerns. Get involved in a worthy-wage campaign for child care, conduct a survey and publish the results in a newsletter, join a professional association and bring along a friend, work toward accreditation and licensure for yourself and/or your program, participate in political lobbies designed to improve the working conditions for early childhood educators, read widely about a topic of concern and gather authoritative evidence to support your arguments

SOURCE: Adapted from *Speaking Out: Early Childhood Advocacy* by S. G. Goffin & J. Lombardi, 1988, Washington, DC: National Association for the Education of Young Children.

Historical Influences on Contemporary Programs

The field of early childhood owes much to the early leaders—philosophers, scholars, educators, theorists, religious leaders, physicians, and scientists—who have made significant contributions to contemporary thinking about young children. As you read their profiles in Figure 2.2, consider how the philosophy statements of the three early childhood practitioners from Meet the Teachers reflect these traditions.

FIGURE 2.2

Early leaders of early childhood education

Plato (427–347 B.C.) and Aristotle (394–322 B.C.)
Country: Ancient Greece
Occupation: Philosophers

Both believed that a child's education should begin well before age 6, and both discussed individual differences in children's learning and personalities.

Martin Luther (1483–1546)
Country: Germany
Occupation: Religious Leader

First to advocate universal education and teaching all children to read so that they could read the Scriptures in their native language (rather than Latin). Believed that the family was the most important educational institution. Is considered the father of religion-affiliated education.

John Comenius (1592–1671)
Country: Now the Czech Republic
Occupation: Educator and Bishop

Wrote the first known picture book, *Orbis Pictus* (*World of Pictures*) in 1658. Advocated that the child learn at the mother's knee until age 6. Believed that firsthand experiences were important to children's learning and that play was the natural learning medium of young children. Argued that the very young were more flexible in their thinking and that the early years were a crucial time for shaping character.

John Locke (1632–1714)
Country: England
Occupation: Medical Doctor, Philosopher, and Political Theorist

In his influential book, *Some Thoughts Concerning Education*, he took issue with the prevailing views of his contemporaries, who believed that heredity was the major influence on children's futures and that harsh discipline was necessary to keep children under control. He argued, rather, that the child's mind was comparable to a *tabula rasa*, or blank slate, upon which experience would draw the mind's contents. His belief that the child was impressionable and malleable had a profound influence on the promise of education to improve children's lives.

Jean-Jacques Rousseau (1712–1788)
Country: France
Occupation: Philosopher and Writer

Considered to be the originator of our modern concept of childhood development. Wrote a novel about a fictitious child named *Emile* in 1760. This book captured the imagination of many adults by enabling them to look at things from a child's point of view; this was a revolutionary way of thinking at the time. Believed that children are naturally good and innocent but that they are corrupted by society. Argued for greater freedom for children and believed that their education should be based upon their interests and adjusted to their innate timetables for learning, which he called unfolding. Also wrote *How Gertrude Teaches Her Children,* a book intended to model a natural style of educating the very young.

Johann Heinrich Pestalozzi (1746–1827)
Country: Italy
Occupation: Educator

Advocated teaching children with love, respect, patience, and understanding. Believed that the senses could be sharpened or cultivated by practice. Emphasized the importance of play and sensory experiences. Further developed Froebel's concept of the "object lesson," in which the child moves from concrete objects to ideas to words via careful observation and teacher-guided discussion, which often takes place outdoors. Designed schools based on Rousseau's idea of naturalism and argued for attention to three elements of the individual: the head, the heart, and the hand.

Robert Owen (1771–1858)
Country: Scotland
Occupation: Religious Leader, Educator

Fought against child labor and created the first factory day-nursery for children 18 months to 10 years to care for children while their parents worked in his mill. The program emphasized dance, song, and outdoor play. Disagreed with harsh punishment and fear as ways to train children.

Friedrich Froebel (1787–1852)
Country: Germany
Occupation: Educator

Considered to be the father of kindergarten (literally, "a garden of children"). Concluded that the early years were the most critical. Designed carefully sequenced materials and detailed instructions for their use. The program included gifts—toys such as balls, blocks, and cubes—and occupations—tasks that taught skills useful in later life such as weaving, folding paper, stringing beads, perforating paper, and modeling with clay. Children were brought closer to God through song, dance, plays, and games.

Horace Mann (1796–1859)
Country: United States
Occupation: Teacher, Lawyer, Senator,
Secretary of Massachusetts Board of Education

Initiated the Common School movement, the basis for public education. Argued that free education should be universal regardless of economic status, that religious training and schools should be distinct (separation of church and state), and that classrooms should be staffed by well-trained male and female teachers. Advocated the preparation of female teachers for work with younger children, an idea unheard of in his day. Started the first teacher-training school, an institution that prepared teachers by focusing on educational theories and giving them experiences with children that were closely supervised. Opposed the harsh punishment characteristic of the era and advocated a bond of mutual trust, respect, and rapport between teachers and children.

FIGURE 2.2

(continued)

Maria Montessori (1870–1952)
Country: Italy
Occupation: Medical Doctor, Program Developer

A medical doctor who was not permitted to practice because of the scandal associated with a woman studying anatomy. Was given a post working with slum children in Rome to try to resolve the problem of unsupervised, neglected children. Believed that children enjoy order and structure and should be taught practical, sensory, and formal skills, such as reading, writing, mathematics, and motor coordination. Her school, the Casi dei Bambini (Children's House) opened in 1908 and attracted attention because it taught academic skills, manners, and cleanliness to children younger than age 5. Promoted the idea of a prepared environment in which the teacher was a directress, and designed highly detailed instructions on how to teach. Believed that the major outcome of a quality education was the ability to focus and concentrate. Invented self-correcting materials, child-sized furniture, and a self-help skills curriculum. The focus of the program was unique in that it was child centered rather than group centered and children were encouraged to expand their interests.

John Dewey (1859–1952)
Country: United States
Occupation: Teacher, Scholar

Established the Dewey Laboratory School at the University of Chicago as a way of studying curricula (Tanner, 1997). Considered to be the father of progressive education. Dewey's primary concern was the preparation of citizens for a democratic society, as described in his major work, *Democracy and Education* (1916). Believed that curricula should be child-centered and include topics of study that would enable children to understand social purposes and community life. Topics of study began with the family and led out to the community. His emphasis was on active learning in which children used open-ended materials to understand problems, questions, relationships, and connections.

There are many compelling reasons for studying the historical foundations of early childhood education (Feeney, Christensen, & Moravcik, 1996). The study of history and an overview of the leaders in early childhood education will enable you to gain insight into the following questions: How have current policies and educational innovations evolved from past thought and practice? What are some of the enduring achievements and continuing controversies in the field of early childhood education?

What were the origins of many of the teaching methods and instructional materials in common use today? Figure 2.3 illustrates some of the teaching materials invented by leaders in the field of early childhood education that are standard equipment in most classrooms.

When we hear accounts of neglect or abuse of young children on the news, we cannot help wondering what this world is coming to. But before a culture can determine whether it has made progress, it must first review where it has been. In other words, you need a historical perspective on attitudes toward and treatment of children.

Actually, exploitation and abuse of young children has been in existence throughout history; at times, the maltreatment of children was commonplace and generally accepted as a prerogative of adults. Although contemporaries may argue that the treatment of children today is worse than ever before, the truth is that the further one goes back in history, the greater the likelihood that young children—particularly young

FIGURE 2.3

Where did they come from? A historical view of the originators of early childhood materials

1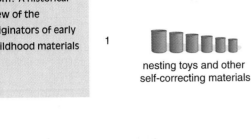
nesting toys and other self-correcting materials

2
wooden unit blocks

3
modeling clay

4
picture books for children

5
child-sized furniture

6
giant hollow blocks for building

7
school store and post office

8
sewing, weaving, and lacing cards

9
lacing frames to practice lacing and tying shoes

10
joint-and-stick construction toys, such as Tinkertoys

Answers: 1. nesting toys and self-correcting materials, Maria Montessori; 2. wooden unit blocks, Carolyn Pratt; 3. modeling clay, Friedrich Froebel; 4. picture books for children, John Amos Comenius; 5. child-sized furniture, Maria Montessori; 6. giant hollow blocks, Patty Smith Hill; 7. school store and post office, Carolyn Pratt; 8. sewing, weaving, and lacing cards (and follow-the-dots), Frederick Froebel; 9. lacing frames, Maria Montessori; 10. joint-and-stick construction toys, Frederick Froebel (who used toothpicks and peas).

FIGURE 2.4

Prevailing views of
children in different
historical eras

Antiquity	Little evidence of strong parental attachment; occasional infanticide was socially acceptable
Middle Ages	Poverty and high infant mortality rates contributed to indifference and abandonment
Renaissance	Ambivalent attitude toward children
18th Century	Children were valued for their potential as laborers; industrialization led to use of children as workers in factories, farms, mills, and mines
19th Century	Child labor and exploitation continued; significant medical and educational advances enabled a much higher percentage of children to survive to adulthood
20th Century	Concern with the rights and plights of children; however, instances of abuse, neglect, starvation, exploitation, and unnecessary mortality continue

SOURCE: Adapted from *Of children* by G. LeFrancois, 1998, Belmont, CA: Wadsworth.

children living in poverty—were mistreated and exploited by adults. By today's standards for the treatment of children (Cryan, 1995), the majority of children in previous eras would have been categorized as abused. This is not to say that adults who cared about children did not exist previously, only that prevailing views of children were far from positive in previous eras. Figure 2.4 is an overview of the dominant perspectives on children in different historical eras of Western culture.

Why were so many children treated with indifference or hostility in the past? Historians believe that there were several reasons, including (1) an infant mortality rate so high that few children lived to age 5 because of disease and poor living conditions; (2) the view of pregnancy as an often undesirable state and the absence of reliable methods of birth control; (3) the abject poverty in which large numbers of families existed as a result of the virtual absence of a middle class; and (4) perhaps most important, the fact that many adults lacked the ability to identify and empathize with children or to regard the early years of life as a qualitatively different and valuable time period in human beings' lives (DeMause, 1974; Postman, 1982; Tuchman, 1978).

PAUSE AND REFLECT ABOUT EARLY LEADERS AND PREVAILING VIEWS OF CHILDHOOD

After reviewing the material in Figures 2.2 and 2.3, consider these questions:

- What connections do you see between the ideas of the three teachers in Meet the Teachers and these early leaders in early childhood education? How are teaching philosophies built?

- Which of these notable individuals whose commitment to the very young has made an indelible impression on your field made the greatest impression on you? Why?

- Did you encounter any ideas that surprised you? Any that are consistent with your beliefs?

Of course, it can be demonstrated that deplorable examples of the treatment of young children continue to exist. Consider the following true incidents involving children that have recently been reported in the newspaper:

Two young children are left to fend for themselves while their parents go on a vacation.

Preschool girls with teased hair and heavy make-up compete in a beauty contest.

A mother is recorded on videotape attempting to sell her preschool daughter to the child's babysitter.

The nanny is convicted of shaking a crying infant and causing its death.

Each of these contemporary situations will be discussed in light of historical practices (Aries, 1962; Bloch & Price, 1994; Cleverly & Phillips, 1986; Osborn, 1980).

As to the first case, in which children were left home alone, child abandonment and neglect has been a recurrent practice throughout history. In different cultures and at various times, children were seen as a drain on limited resources. In ancient times, infants were left to die from exposure to the elements as a way of controlling family size and overpopulation. In the Greek city states, most children with physical defects were destroyed, and because grain allocations were limited to one female child per family (boys were more valued for their potential as warriors), firstborn girls were often the only ones saved. In Rome, "potting" children was common: Babies were abandoned by the roadside in clay pots or in the river in baskets and adorned with ornaments to invite others to take the children in if they wished. In other words, the Bible story of Moses as an infant floating down the Nile in a basket typified practices of the era. Even in the 20th century, children with disabilities were viewed by many people around the world as embarrassments or liabilities, and parents were pressured to institutionalize them. An excellent film that accurately portrays this attitude is *My Left Foot*.

In 318 A.D., during Roman Emperor Constantine's reign, killing a child became a crime. Emperor Augustus offered stipends to families who would raise foundlings. It was not until 400 A.D. that the first orphanages were established. Although laws against infanticide existed at that time, the practice of killing infants remained common. During the Dark Ages, most people were peasants who spent their short lives (life expectancy was about 30 years) working for landowners and the aristocracy. Disease, near starvation, and generally poor living conditions resulted in a high infant mortality rate. Children were frequently viewed as just another mouth to feed rather than a privilege or a treasure. During the Middle Ages, a distinction was made between willful disposal of children and other causes of death. One way of disposing of children was to smother them and claim that it was an accident. Even if a parent was convicted of willfully disposing of a child, the punishment for infanticide was only a year of penance. By the 1700s, opiates, starvation, dunking babies in cold water, and leaving them on doorsteps or at the hospital were ways to get rid of unwanted children. In 19th-century France, hospitals actually were equipped with turntables so that mothers could abandon their infants without being identified. This was more apt to occur when the child was disfigured in some way, and, with the high incidence of venereal disease, infants were frequently born blind until medical advances were made in the late 1800s. The novel *The Hunchback of Notre Dame* is representative of the way that children with disabilities were treated. Even during the Industrial Revolution, there were "nurses" who would take infants for the purpose of disposing of them and adults who bought children and turned them into slaves or criminals, as depicted in the Charles Dickens novel *Oliver Twist*.

As to the second news story, about a children's beauty pageant in which preschoolers are treated like Barbie dolls, the view of children as miniature adults has long been with us. If you examine pre-18th-century Western artwork, you will notice three things. First, children are seldom depicted (other than in a few pieces of sculpture), presumably because they were not considered worthwhile subjects. Second, when children were depicted, they usually were members of wealthy, titled families and were dressed exactly like the adults they were expected to become. Finally, you will notice that typical childish facial features (e.g., turned-up nose), body configuration (e.g., large head in proportion to the body), and interests (e.g., play) are rarely portrayed. Mainly, children were valued for their potential as adults. Throughout history, the point at which children were expected to think more logically has been age 6 or 7—the "age of reason." It was assumed that this ability to reason equipped them to take on adult roles, such as caring for other children, hunting, gardening, tending animals, performing household chores, and, in industrial societies, working in factory settings (Sameroff & McDonough, 1994). Anthropological studies of 50 cultures suggest that even now, most cultures begin assigning more responsibilities to children and initiate formal education for children between ages 5 and 7 (Rogoff, 1993). Two films, *The Last Emperor* and *Little Man Tate*, offer a valuable perspective on children being treated as adults, in the first case, a Chinese child of royal birth, and in the second, a child genius in mid-20th-century America.

As to the recent news account of the child being offered for sale, the treatment of children as property or as a commodity has long been in existence. Throughout his-

What does *childhood* mean to you?

tory, children have been exploited for their potential as workers in factories and on farms. In 1535, during English King Henry VIII's reign, a law was enacted to apprentice children so that they could begin working as early as possible. Beginning in 1618 and for many years thereafter, children as young as 10 years of age were shipped from London to work as indentured servants in colonial America. In 1619, the first African children landed in America and became slaves. In many states, African children were not viewed as human beings but as the property of slave owners, as depicted in the *Roots* television series. Because slaves were valuable property, some consideration was given to the care of the very young. But by age 5 or 6, most slave children were working, and by age 12, they were expected to perform one fourth of an adult's workload on a daily basis. The first factory to employ children opened in England in 1719, and it was not until The Factory Act was passed in 1833 that children under age 9 were prohibited from working in mines. After the American West was settled, "orphan trains" brought city children without families to work on farms. It was not until 1842 that the working day for children under age 12 was limited to 10 hours in Connecticut. Laws controlling the use of children as workers first were proposed in 1906, but 32 years passed before the first enforceable work law for the protection of minor children was passed in 1938. To this day, the notion that young children ought to be pushed to work very hard continues, although the definition of work differs. Most often, extreme pressure comes in the form of pushing children to achieve in sports, in the performing arts, in academic pursuits, or, in some cases, to achieve fame and fortune as a star in the media.

As to the recent case of the nanny who was convicted of murdering an infant, the view of the child as innately bad or needing harsh discipline has also been revisited throughout history. In the 1600s, children in America were expected to obey their parents without question and to address them as "honored sir" or "esteemed parent." Children were expected to be seen and not heard, and the prevailing opinion about child rearing was "Spare the rod and spoil the child." One of the first illustrated textbooks, *The New England Primer,* included the following verse to teach the letter *F:* "The Idle Fool is whipt at school." In colonial America, parents were advised to dress up as ghosts and enter a disobedient child's room at night to frighten the child into obedience. Children's natural playfulness and toddlers' willfulness were seen as the work of the devil, which had to be beaten out of them. Long after harsh discipline was generally frowned upon for most children in America, children who were from different cultures—such as Native Americans kidnapped from their families and forced by government law to attend boarding schools—were likely to be subjected to extreme methods of punishment in order to force them to fit into mainstream society. The film *The Dollmaker,* about an Appalachian woman and her family who moved to Detroit in the late 1940s, exposes the indifference and cruelty visited upon American children who were not part of the mainstream culture.

As the preceding historical overview suggests, conditions for children have improved, but there is still much work to be done. Fortunately, enlightened views on children's early years have existed alongside the more repressive views throughout history, and these ideas form the foundation for your role as a contemporary early childhood educator. Figure 2.5, based on survey data, lists some of the most prominent early childhood educators living today (Neugebauer, 1995). These individuals, combined with the early childhood experts whom we interviewed for the Ask the Expert feature that occurs throughout this book, form a veritable "who's who" of those who have exerted a profound influence on the early childhood education field.

FIGURE 2.5

Contemporary
leaders in early
childhood education

Scholars/ Researchers	Prominent Authors	Child Advocates	Practitioners	Experts from Other Fields
Urie Bronfenbrenner	Bettye Caldwell	James Hymes	Vivian Paley	T. Berry Brazleton
Constance Kamii	Alice Sterling Honig	Marian Wright Edelman	Docia Zavitkovsky	Howard Gardner
Bernard Spodek	Sue Bredekamp	Bertha Campbell	Loris Malaguzzi	Daniel Goleman
David Weikart	Barbara Bowman	Edward Zigler		Stanley Greenspan
Larry Schweinhart	Lilian Katz			

SOURCE: Adapted from The Movers and Shapers of Early Childhood Education by R. Neugebauer, November/December, 1995, *Child Care Information Exchange* (pp. 9–13).

Time-honored Precepts of Early Childhood Education

The leaders in early childhood education whom you read about at the beginning of this chapter are individuals whose lives and work have shaped current thinking. Throughout history, various facets of the child have been emphasized, such as physical development, religious training and character development, social and emotional growth, and intellectual growth (Osborn, 1980). Although different cultures and individuals have always differed in their responses to young children, some points of view have prevailed in Western thought. The field of early childhood education is part of a rich tradition of care, concern, and education for the very young. Teachers, researchers, and theorists in the field and in related fields have paved the way for your career by advocating for young children's needs, developing programs, and inventing the materials that are still in wide use. Some of the guiding principles of early childhood programs and their origins are discussed in the remainder of this section.

Young Children Need Special Nurturing

A recurring theme in early childhood has been the view that young children require special forms of care, protection, education, and sympathetic understanding from adults. Smith (1996) typifies this view: "If we are to make the best use of every country's most precious resource, its children, we must better define what we mean by quality and, through whatever means possible, deliver the resources necessary to foster and nurture children's development" (p. 330). How did kindergartens, nursery schools, and parent involvement in early childhood get their starts in the United States? Interestingly, the early efforts to provide care and education for the young were led by "dauntless women" who went against the general thinking of their day (Wortham, 1992; Snyder, 1972; Wyman, 1995).

The history of the kindergarten movement in the United States, prompted by Froebel's work in Germany, documents the growth of the commitment to the care and education of the very young. In 1855, inspired by the German kindergarten movement, Mrs. Carl Schurz opened the first kindergarten in Wisconsin for German immigrant children. Elizabeth Peabody established the first kindergarten for English-speaking children in 1860, and Susan Blow of St. Louis opened the first publicly supported kindergarten in 1873.

Nursery schools in the United States have a similar history. Carolyn Pratt founded the City and Country School in New York (now the Bank Street School). Her curriculum included field trips and child-run enterprises, such as a school store and post office. In 1922, Abigail Adams Eliot founded the Ruggles Street Nursery School in Boston, whose program was based on the work of the McMillan sisters in England. An early effort to involve parents meaningfully in programs for young children was the Parent Cooperative Nursery (a program in which parents volunteered to work in the classroom) which was established by wives of faculty members at The University of Chicago in 1915.

Professional organizations have long been a significant support system for educators acting upon their commitment to nurture the young. Patty Smith Hill (1868–1946), a professor at Teachers College, Columbia University, was the founder of two major professional organizations that play a vital role in professional development today. She worked with the International Kindergarten Union, now the Association for Childhood Education International (ACEI), and in 1929, she called a meeting of the National Association for Nursery Education, which changed its name to the National Association for the Education of Young Children in 1964 and includes nearly 100,000 members today.

Young Children Are the Future of Society

"I touch the future, I teach." Perhaps you have heard these words of the first American teacher to become an astronaut, Krista McAuliffe. Actually, this view of children as the future of society has an extensive history. Beginning in ancient times, philosophers noted the influence of early experience on later experience. Socrates (470–399 B.C.) spoke of the education of children under age 6, and Aristotle believed in educating the young and recognized individual differences. Much later, German religious leader Martin Luther (1483–1546) argued that girls as well as boys should be taught and advocated a wide range of courses in school, including music. In Czechoslovakia (now the Czech Republic), educator John Comenius (1592–1670) designed the first illustrated children's textbook, *Orbis Pictus* (*World of Pictures*) (1658), and one of the first books for parents, *School of Infancy* (1628), in which he advocated the "school of the mother's knee," whereby mothers would informally teach their children the basic foundations of all knowledge by age 6.

Young Children Are Worthy of Study

Recently published child development textbooks offer several reasons for studying children, including the following: studying children enables us to investigate development from its very beginnings and thus explain behavior; studying children offers practical guidance in child rearing, programs, and so forth; and studying children offers a means of predicting adult behavior. Again, there are long-standing traditions that emphasize the importance of child study, but they occurred much later than most people imagine. A survey of major research journals found only 35 empirical studies of children in the 9-year period from 1890 to 1899, and even in the time period from 1950 to 1958, only 362 studies of children were published (Cleverly & Phillips, 1986). One of the first published attempts at child study was written by physiologist William Preyer in 1881. His book *The Mind of the Child* was a 3-year diary about his son's behavior, which he studied from the normative perspective of when and in what order the child would display certain adult characteristics (Cleverley & Phillips, 1986). Evolutionist Charles Darwin and novelist Louisa May

Alcott, among other famous people, published biographies that described detailed observations of their infant children. In 1911, Arnold Gesell established the Child Development Clinic at Yale University, where he studied infants and identified general and predictable markers of development. Based on these studies, Gesell concluded that development must be controlled by an inner timetable of growth, or maturation. Jean Piaget (1926), who had completed advanced study in biology and was engaged in a study of epistemology (the study of knowledge), worked as a graduate student administering intelligence tests to young children. He became fascinated by the reasoning behind children's answers that he had to consider incorrect. Piaget studied his own children's intellectual development intensively and published *Language and Thought of the Child,* in which he set forth a proposal that was surprising for his day. Unlike his contemporaries, he did not argue that nature (heredity) was the most important influence on children's development, nor did he argue that nurture (environment) was the most important influence. Rather, he described a dynamic interaction between the child's heredity and environment and proposed a theory of cognitive (knowledge) development and stages of reasoning that children go through. Piaget also emphasized a concept called constructivism, or the belief that children actively build their own understandings about the world rather than merely soaking up information and experiences. This too was a departure from the thinking of the day.

Young Children's Potential Should Be Optimized

Another idea that is fundamental to early childhood education is the concept that every child is a unique individual who deserves to have her or his potential optimized. Some popular contemporary slogans include "Put children first," "Leave no child behind," and "Provide a level playing field" so that children can excel. Thoughtful discussions of young children's individuality first appeared in ancient times, when Aristotle wrote about differences in children and the importance of developing their talents.

There have been adults throughout history, then, who have advocated for children's basic needs and recommended educational programs for them, even when these adults were at odds with their contemporaries. Your role in providing quality care and education for the very young is consistent with the finest contributions of these leaders. Figure 2.6 summarizes the principles underlying quality programs. The following Ask the Expert feature, based on Amy Driscoll's book of case studies, also provides information about exemplary early childhood programs.

PAUSE AND REFLECT ABOUT YOUR PERSONAL HISTORY

Interview a partner using the questions provided. After the interview, be prepared to introduce your partner to the class. As the interviewer reporting to the class, you will do the following:

1. *Introduce your partner.* On the chalkboard, write your partner's first and last name large enough so that everyone can read it.

2. *Briefly summarize the interview responses your partner gave to each of the questions.* Choose the most interesting things that your partner said during the interview.

3. *Make a concluding statement.* While you are listening to your partner, try to "listen between the lines" and infer the values, beliefs, talents, strengths, and

attitudes that your partner might bring to teaching. Try to capture that in a sentence or two that characterizes your partner in a positive, memorable way for the class. When you are finished, switch roles.

Interview Questions

1. What is your first and last name?
2. When did you first say, "I want to work with young children"?
3. How did you get interested in becoming an early childhood educator? What influenced you the most?
4. If you were forced to choose a career other than teaching, what would it be? Why?

FIGURE 2.6

Programmatic
precepts

"Early childhood teaching is simply and completely about children and their well-being" (Glasgow, 1994, pp. 131–132).

Programmatic Precept 1: Learning is fundamentally social. Children's development and learning begin with social interaction. Close human relationships and mutual understandings facilitate learning. Therefore, adult-child intersubjectivity is important to the learning process, and teachers must get to know every child.

Programmatic Precept 2: Cultural contexts and environmental influences are powerful determinants of learning. Warm, secure, and responsive environments promote learning and development while cold, restrictive, and unsafe environments retard learning because they do not nurture children's physical and emotional well-being. Therefore, an early childhood perspective acknowledges the importance of providing children with opportunities to interact, understand, and cooperate in groups.

Programmatic Precept 3: Learning drives development rather than being driven by it. Early childhood teachers should set goals, implement them, and guide children's development rather than stand by and wait for development to occur spontaneously. Optimizing children's learning and development is the prime directive of early childhood education, irrespective of the setting.

Programmatic Precept 4: Children are not passive recipients of information; rather, they play an active role in the construction of their own understandings within the cultural context. Therefore, every society needs to carefully consider what is worthwhile for children to learn, the skills that they need to develop, and the dispositions they should have.

Programmatic Precept 5: Although patterns of development can be identified, each child is an individual with unique characteristics that have to be respected. Therefore, early childhood professionals are expected to plan flexible programs that accommodate individual growth.

SOURCE: Adapted from A Problem of Theory for Early Childhood Professionals by K. Glasgow, 1994, *Childhood Education, 70*(3) (pp. 131–132); and Quality Programs That Care and Educate by A. B. Smith, 1996, *Childhood Education, 72*(6), (pp. 330–336).

ASK the Expert — Amy Driscoll on Exemplary Early Childhood Programs

Common Issues and Concerns About Early Childhood Programs

Amy Driscoll

1. What's the best early childhood program you've seen?

It's impossible to respond to that question without one or two of my own. My response questions are "Best program for whom? Or for what community? Or for what purpose?" What became clear in my visits to exemplary programs for *Cases in Early Childhood Education* was the importance of the fit between the program and children, families, and the community. Programs must reflect the cultural values of the children and families they serve, so they must look different from place to place. Consequently, it is impossible to assess the quality of a program without looking at the context in which it serves children and families. While all good programs appear to be based on developmentally appropriate practices (DAP) and curricula, there is a huge variation in the way DAP is translated into these programs. That variation is connected to the diversity of children and families—their lifestyles and values, needs and strengths, and the environments in which they live. For that reason, I clearly avoid the idea of program models, because **model** suggests a framework that can be transported and duplicated in other places. I don't think that models are appropriate when we talk about programs for young children. Their individuality and that of their families must be cherished and strengthened, and to do that, a program must be developed with that individuality as a foundation.

The other aspect of fit is one that connects educators with specific beliefs about children and learning with an environment and curriculum that supports those beliefs. In my visits, I encountered early childhood professionals who placed a high priority on finding programs in which they could teach in ways that matched their philosophies. A number of those professionals had searched for and tried out various programs before finding the places where they could really be true to their beliefs. Once they found these places, these professionals were able to do their very best work for children.

2. What did the programs have in common to make them unique and outstanding?

I too was curious to answer that question as I began my visits. After much reflection, I have to say that the answer is people. In each case, it was an individual or a group of individuals who were committed to an idea or an ideal. For example, Bebe Fearnside in Gainesville, Florida, decided to abandon traditional approaches to serving children and families in order to meet their needs in a comprehensive program. In her words, she "colored outside the lines," interpreted policies and formed collaborations in ways that better served children. Like many other early childhood educators, she looked beyond what was happening and broadened her view of what was possible. The lesson we can learn from thinkers and professionals like her is that we have to push the boundaries of resources, of tradition, and even of policy and regulations to achieve the best programs for children.

3. What should parents look for in early childhood programs?

My answer is to go beyond what can be observed. You must begin, of course, with what you can see and hear, but after extensive observations, it is important to reflect and to inquire. The most outstanding programs I observed were those in which individuals reflected carefully about decisions and could articulate clear rationales. To learn about those reflections, I had to raise questions. Most educators are willing to talk about their ideas, so it is not a difficult process. What I learned from the conversations about decisions was that rationales were consistently based on children's needs, goals for children, or children's development. When Angela Pino, a teacher of 2-year-olds at City Country School in New York, was asked about why the staff went around cleaning up after children instead of leaving it all for cleanup time or insisting that children clean up before going to another activity, she could clearly describe the thinking behind their procedure: "We feel that teaching children of this age to clean up after themselves during play interferes with spontaneous play and creative activity. After we finish play, we all stop to pick up and ready the area for tomorrow. Then we're fostering the idea of group responsibility." When asked about the procedure of opening children's lunch boxes, and unscrewing tops from thermos bottles and other containers, Angela explained: "Children stay here for lunch for social reasons. For 2- and 3-year-olds, it could take the whole lunch period to get everything opened and arranged. Our goal during this period is not independence or fine motor skills; it's social development. The other aspect is that it's done for management reasons. It frees up the teachers to stay sitting at the tables to interact socially with the children."

Whether we agree with Angela's rationales or not, the important quality of her program is the reflection that goes into her decision making. She doesn't rely on tradition—the way it's always been done; she thinks through many of the daily management details with attention to what children need and to goals for them. Such reflection and decision making truly characterize the professional educator and quality programs.

Amy Driscoll is Director of Teaching, Learning, and Assessment, California State University, Monterey Bay

How Programs Begin and Change

There are several sources for and influences on early childhood programs. Each influence is described in its historical as well as contemporary context in the following paragraphs. *Influences on Early Childhood Programs*

Societal Trends

Societal trends, such as economic conditions, national and world events, political policies, and technological advances, influence early childhood programs. Despite the fact that today, the United States is one of the few developed countries without federally funded child care and nursery schools for all young children, such programs have existed in the past in the United States. After the Great Depression of the 1930s, the Works Progress Administration (WPA) established nursery schools to help address the social issues of unemployment and poverty. Later, during World War II, child-care centers were funded because men were at war and women were needed to work in munitions factories to support the war effort. The Lanham Act of 1942 authorized federal support for child-care centers, which were often located near women's places of employment. Today, parents, educators, and other child advocates are still lobbying for prekindergartens for 3- and 4-year-olds in public schools (Jalongo, Bauer, Conrad, & Cardy, 1998), and the United States remains without a national system of child care for infants, toddlers, or preschoolers, or before- and after-school care for children in the primary grades.

Educational Theories

Educational theories, research, and philosophies such as the ones you encountered in this chapter's Meet the Teachers are another influence on programs. Throughout the first half of the 20th century, many parents were encouraged to institutionalize children with special needs or to keep them at home. When children with disabilities were sent to school, it was often to sit in the back of the room or to perform some menial task in the building. Even after special education became widely available in public schools, these students were removed from the company of their peers and relegated to a remote area of the school, such as the furnace room or a storage area. When Public Law 94–142 was funded in 1977 with 1.1 billion dollars to support educational programs for children with disabilities, it called for mainstreaming, meaning that these children were to be taught in the least restrictive environment, in other words, in the company of their peers. Today, strategies for supporting the development of children with special needs have been clinically researched and carefully articulated (Greenspan & Wieder, 1998); young children with special needs are included in most early childhood settings; and most teachers study various handicaps and medical conditions as part of their preparation programs. Inclusion, the practice of adapting early childhood environments and curricula so that children with disabilities can be educated with their peers and experience success, is a major achievement of contemporary early childhood education (Clawson & Chick, in press).

Knowledge of Child Development

Knowledge of learners and child development, such as developmentally appropriate practice, observational research on young children, and educators' practical experiences, also influences programs. It has taken time for infants and children to be considered worthy of careful study. It was not until the early 20th century that child development emerged as a field of study. As recently as the 1970s, many people who had not studied child development continued to believe that babies were totally lacking in intellectual abilities. Some people actually thought that babies' senses, such as vision and hearing, were not operative during the early months! Today, brain research has persuaded educators and the general public that infants are much more competent than was previously imagined and that early experience exerts a profound influence on the mature human brain's capabilities (Grunwald, 1996/97; Jensen, 1998; Sylwester, 1995). As a field, early childhood education owes much to research on children's growth and development.

Curriculum Standards

Curriculum standards, such as the national curriculum, local policies, and school traditions, also affect early childhood programs. In the 1970s, many different projects and programs were funded by the federal government in an effort to determine which methods worked best. After Urie Bronfenbrenner (1974) published long-term studies evaluating these projects and it became clear that partnership with parents was a consistent feature of successful programs, more early childhood programs invested time and effort in these practices and continue to do so today (Roberts, Rule, & Innocenti, 1998).

Young children with special needs are included in most early childhood settings.

Community Expectations

Community expectations, such as national public opinion, regional issues, and local controversies, are another influence on programs. During the 1960s, *Life* magazine published pictures of FBI agents chasing Amish children through the fields to force them to attend the public school in accordance with the compulsory attendance laws. Today, it is considered perfectly acceptable for a wide array of schools and schooling methods with differing philosophies to exist, including home schooling, private programs, church-affiliated programs, programs that teach cultural perspectives different from the mainstream, university-affiliated preschools, and so forth (Driscoll, 1995). The history of education includes numerous examples of community pressures that shaped educational practices. For example, after *Sputnik* was launched in 1957 and the

United States feared that it would lose the space race to the Russians, there was tremendous pressure on public schools to increase students' achievement in science and mathematics.

Evaluation Criteria

Evaluation criteria, such as accreditation standards, large-scale testing programs, and the individual progress of children in the curriculum, affect early childhood programs. Head Start, a federally funded program for low-income families and their children, provided education, health care, nutrition, parent involvement and education, and career opportunities for adults commencing in the mid-1960s. Yet when it was evaluated in the 1970s based on increases in children's intelligence test scores alone, and these other important contributions were not considered, its funding declined. More recently, nationally recognized statistician Harold Howe calculated that every dollar invested in Head Start had saved approximately $7 in later support services, and the program's funding was increased.

Human Resources

Human resources, such as competent teachers and administrative support, as well as characteristics of the school as a learning organization, also affect programs. Recurring criticism of child care has been directed at its inadequate training for teachers and high turnover rates in centers. The difficulty with child care in the United States, of course, is that the salaries are low, the benefits are often nonexistent, the hours are long, and the expectations for professionalism from parents and the community are high. One major initiative that has attempted to address the professional status of child-care workers is the establishment in 1972 of the Child Development Associate (CDA) credential, which is based not only on coursework, but also on practical experience. In addition, the 2-year community college programs are assuming major responsibility for preparing America's child-care professionals. Through organizations such as the National Association for the Education of Young Children, the Day Care Workers of America, and the National Association of Early Childhood Teacher Educators, these community college programs are working to elevate the status of the profession and to improve working conditions for staff members.

Financial and Material Resources

Financial and material resources, such as funding, special grants, equipment, and curriculum materials, also have an influence on programs. During the 1800s and early 1900s, the majority of teachers were women without means; their families could not support them financially or find them suitable husbands. These women volunteered to teach in less populated areas in order to survive (at that time, states such as Michigan and Ohio were considered to be "out West"). Few towns had school buildings, much less equipment and materials, and it was common practice for teachers to move from home to home and rely upon the hospitality of families. Each year, the town decided whether it could afford the teacher's services, a site for the school, and so forth based on the success of farming and industry and on charitable contributions. Accounts of the "dame schools" for young children in the 1800s and historical accounts of teachers' lives based on their letters and diaries (Wyman, 1995) make interesting reading on this phenomenon in the field of early childhood. Eventually, property taxes were used to establish a funding base for schools and to provide free public education. This system is now under scrutiny as a result of Jonathan Kozol's (1991) exposé of inequities in school funding formulas; his book is appropriately titled *Savage Inequalities*. *Education Week* (Education Week and Pew Charitable Trust, 1998) reports that the average per pupil expenditure (the average amount spent to educate a child for 1 year of public school) in urban schools in the United States is $4,544. Yet some schools spend as little as $2,884 per pupil, while others—for example, nonurban school districts in the state of New York—spend as much as $7, 246 to educate each child for 1 year. When Kozol's book became a bestseller, it created a public outcry because it demonstrated how a system of school support based on property values consistently favors those residing in wealthy areas and puts those residing in low-income areas at a disadvantage.

Pedagogy

Pedagogy, or the agreed-upon set of standards for effective instructional practice, also has an impact on early childhood programs. It includes such things as integrated curricula, cooperative learning, and ways of presenting material to children. When the British infant schools that emphasized children's play and child-initiated activities were heralded as a major step forward during the 1970s, many American public schools attempted to transplant the ideas, most with limited success. Evidently, American educators found it difficult to abandon the assembly-line approach to education that dominated at the time. More recently, after the preschools in Reggio Emilia, Italy, were proclaimed the best in the world, it became popular for educators from around the globe to visit these schools and to attempt to emulate the practices of these schools in their own countries (Hendrick, 1996). It remains to be seen how successful these American endeavors to imitate the exemplary programs in Italy will be at a time when there is a public outcry for higher standards, accountability for public education, and increases in test scores.

Early Childhood Programs for the 21st Century

Throughout history, early childhood educators have been striving to develop high-quality programs for young children. Some of these programs have existed for centuries, such as the kindergarten concept that was begun by Friedrich Froebel in the 1800s. Other programs are 20th-century creations, such as the federally funded program for low-income families and their children, Head Start. We have adapted the following list of questions to stimulate reflection about the distinguishing features of the wide array of programs offered for the very young (Kammerman & Kahn, 1994; Isenberg & Jalongo, 1997).

Need for a Program. What is the apparent demand for early childhood education? For example, what percentage of mothers with young children at various ages are employed out of the home in this nation?

Types of Programs. What different kinds of programs for young children are offered? A system of family child care? Center-based care? Public school? On what hours, schedules, and calendars do these programs typically operate? How well do these programs meet the needs of families?

Children Served by a Program. Who is served by the program? All children? Children who are economically privileged? Children at risk? Children who have been identified as gifted and talented? What is the program's basic view of the child?

Funding for a Program. How is the program funded? With federal funds? Other public sources? Parents? Some combination of these?

Families in a Program. What forms of family support are available? Family leaves? After-school care? Health care? Social services? How are the roles of parents and families defined in the program?

Professionals in a Program. How are the staff members trained? What qualifications are necessary to work in the program? What is the status and income level of the profession? What benefits are offered? What is the turnover rate?

Goals of a Program. What is the program's primary focus? What purposes does it serve? What type of curriculum does it have, custodial or educational? How is the program's quality monitored?

Cultural Context of a Program. What uniquenesses does this early childhood program have? How has the culture and the society in which the program operates influenced standard practices?

Despite differences in specific characteristics, excellent early childhood programs share several important attributes (Carbo, 1995; Erwin, 1996); these are described in the following paragraphs.

Articulated Philosophy and Goals

In any excellent program, everyone clearly knows about the goals of the program, their specific roles, and the early childhood principles and practices that will support the program's purpose. A curricular philosophy is not a written statement of lofty ideals without much connection to classroom practices. Rather, the program's philosophy should be apparent in the daily experiences of children, families, and educators. A clearly articulated curricular philosophy is translated into goals and is evident to those who observe the program in action. Above all, the emphasis of a good early childhood program is on being of service to children and families. Respect for different family structures, cultural backgrounds, and community affiliations is essential in order to reach and teach every child.

Appropriate Structure and Organization

A good program is well organized so that it can make the most of team members' strengths and available resources. The program has leadership, yet it is characterized by a cooperative and democratic spirit. It has structure yet sufficient flexibility to adapt to individual needs, choices, and preferences of children, families, and educators. Evaluation is a major part of appropriate structure and organization. To monitor the program's progress, a high-quality curriculum includes an ongoing system of evaluation that guides improvement, acknowledges effort, and celebrates successes.

Emphasis on Concept Development

High-quality curricula emphasize concept development, depth of learning, and interpretation of meaning rather than the memorization of isolated bits of information. Good teaching involves more than telling children information. Perhaps the best indicator that meaningful concepts are being developed is the quality of children's work.

What does the similarity of these children's responses tell you about the value of the assignment?

If children's responses all look alike, there is little chance that real thinking is taking place, because the lesson was simply an exercise in following directions. Every early childhood curriculum should challenge young children's intellects by raising questions that intrigue young minds and encouraging the very young to explore answers in their own ways.

Attention to All Five Domains

Leaders in the field of early childhood education often speak of the whole child, which refers to supporting the young child's development and learning in five inter-related domains. In a high-quality curriculum, there are many activities that support every child's cognitive growth (the intellectual strategies used in learning), literacy learning (the ability to communicate through words), affective development (the emotional and social dimensions of development), psychomotor abilities (the mastery of physical motor skills), and aesthetic development (the ability to appreciate and respond via the arts).

Increased Opportunity for Social Interaction

An excellent early childhood program develops the group process skills of young children. Rather than working in solitude and silence on routine tasks, small groups of children are given interesting challenges and invited to use their problem-solving skills and seek guidance from the teacher as necessary. A good example might be a group of children who are asked to create a simple map of their indoor or outdoor play area.

Respect for Individual Differences

In an excellent early childhood program, children's interests, backgrounds, and learning styles are acknowledged, respected, and used as the basis for adapting the curriculum to meet their learning needs. Because the fundamental goal in an open society is for all children to experience success in school rather than to label and sort children, effective instructional practice means that teachers use diversified teaching strategies to optimize each child's potential. Too many early childhood curricula borrow their teaching strategies from the ones used with limited success with older children, yet it is obvious that early childhood is a unique phase of development that requires a different approach to instruction.

Recognition and Inclusion of the Contributions of Many Ethnic Groups

Yet another indicator of a high-quality curriculum is a multicultural perspective that appreciates the different people from every nation in our increasingly global society. Where cultures are concerned, the whole is truly more than the sum of its parts, because the contributions of each group interact with one another and are recombined to create something new. A high-quality early childhood curriculum does not emphasize the majority culture and disregard or ignore other groups that constitute the community at large.

Interdisciplinary Approaches to Subject-matter Teaching

In a high-quality curriculum, teachers help children to see the interrelationships between and among concepts and experiences. When early childhood programs have rigid schedules that provide a few minutes for each subject, children do not have sufficient time and opportunity to pursue ideas in depth, and the content becomes fragmented. Therefore, it is important to use the curriculum to demonstrate to children that ideas are connected and that what is learned in one context can be applied to similar situations or modified to fit a different situation. An evaluation of 390 child-care preschool classrooms using the 37-item Early Childhood Environment Rating Scale (Harms & Clifford, 1997) indicated that the features of early childhood programs that are ranked highest include scheduled time for gross motor activities, furnishings for routine care, supervision of creative activities, and fine-motor activities; those ranked lowest include a personal area for adults, meals and snacks, personal grooming, and displays of children's work (Cryer & Phillipsen, 1997).

PAUSE AND REFLECT ABOUT EXEMPLARY PROGRAMS

Work in small groups to identify the characteristics of your "dream program" in early childhood. Consider how teachers would behave, what the physical facility would look like, how the children would be taught, what equipment and materials would be provided, and how families would be supported. After brainstorming your list, compare and contrast it with the checklist in the Featuring Families section of Chapter 1. Reread Ask the Expert: Amy Driscoll on Exemplary Early Childhood Programs from earlier in this chapter and Ask the Expert: Jim Hoot on Early Childhood Programs Around the World, which follows. How have these experts enriched and enlarged your understanding of program quality? What evidence do you see of historical influences on contemporary programs?

ASK the Expert James L. Hoot on Early Childhood Programs Around the World

Common Issues and Concerns About Early Childhood Programs Outside the United States

James L. Hoot

1. Why should prospective teachers in the United States be interested in early education in other countries?

During my first 8 years of schooling, I attended a parochial school. Students at this school had many things in common. They were all residents of a suburban Midwestern community. They were all of Anglo-Saxon ancestry. They all spoke the same language, shared many of the same values, and were all American. As we begin the 21st century, America's classrooms are changing dramatically.

Demographic projections consistently support the view that within the next decade, those of Anglo-Saxon ancestry will be minorities in many of our nation's schools. Further, while minorities of earlier decades were composed primarily of blacks and Hispanics, today's growing minorities include children of Vietnamese, Hmong, Cantonese, Cambodian, Korean, Arabic, Eastern European, and other ancestries. Along with this diversity of students is a concomitant diversity of languages and values.

2. Why should we study what early childhood educators in other countries are doing?

Compared to other countries, America has truly been blessed. Our abundance in terms of wealth, however, often creates misleading notions that we are the best in everything we do. One has only to look at the Olympics and other international competitions to see the fallacy of this viewpoint. As it relates to children, this fallacy was recently well expressed by an American teacher attending a conference presentation on the topic "Excellence in Teaching Young Children—a World Perspective." After teachers from Australia, Finland, and Hungary made short presentations regarding child care in their respective countries, I overheard a stunned American teacher sheepishly whisper to her colleague, "My God! We're a third-world country when it comes to child care."

Clearly, the foundations of our field were laid by thinkers from abroad such as Pestalozzi, Froebel, Piaget, Vygotsky, and Montessori. Likewise, programs of today are enriched by the work of other international colleagues (e.g., Malaguzzi's work with Reggio Emilia). Considering international ideas provides us with an opportunity to assess what we have done and what we might do in the future to improve our own programs. While it would be a mistake to flit from one new international (or national) model to another for the sake of change, thoughtful consideration of the world of ideas for improving the lives of children can move us toward a better educational system for all children.

Learning about other approaches to early education can also provide dividends in advocating for all children of the world. Recently, a state politician was speaking to a group about what his administration was doing to improve child care. In a question-and-answer period following the session, this politician's self-accolades were quickly humbled by an educator who had just returned from Finland. The lady asked why people with as little as 12 hours of training and no formal postsecondary education were allowed to be preschool teachers. "Teachers in Finland," she continued, "must have 3 years of postsecondary education in early education to qualify." Both the politician and many other participants were quite surprised by such an inequity. Another teacher, who had just returned from a visit to Hungary, expressed amazement that preschoolers there nap in separate rooms on youth-sized beds complete with full bedding, in contrast to the cots and floors where children in the United States commonly take their naps. The remaining questions centered upon other inequities and what can only be interpreted as our national lack of commitment to very young children.

While some of the best early childhood programs I have seen are not in the United States, we have, nevertheless, made major contributions to the field. The relatively recent construct of developmentally appropriate practice by the National Association for the Education of Young Children and the resulting publication of its operational definition, for example, has advanced increased international discourse regarding acceptable practices for educating children. Use of this document by colleagues in other countries might assist their lawmakers in moving toward higher-quality programming for their children.

3. How can we learn more about what is going on in other countries?

There are a number of ways in which beginning professionals can learn about early education in other countries. One of the best ways is to travel. In Europe, preservice teachers frequently study in other countries as part of their teacher education programs through such programs as Erasmus, which is funded by the European Community. Over the past couple of years, many American universities have joined this early childhood teacher-exchange network. In addition, increasing numbers of universities (e.g., State University of New York at Buffalo) now have independent, year-long international student exchange programs for preschool teachers. If such travel or time commitment is not possible, preservice professionals can also join international early childhood education professional organizations, such as the World Organization of Early Childhood Education (OMEP) and the Association for Childhood Education International (ACEI). In addition to hosting a major professional conference outside of the United States every third year and producing numerous publications relating to international issues, the ACEI also has a home page on the Internet (http://www.udel.edu/bateman/acei/). This home page includes information about the organization, a system for setting up an international pen-pal program for your classroom, and a way of contacting international teaching colleagues.

Nations of the world are becoming increasingly interdependent. By working together with international colleagues, we are more likely to improve the quality of education for our world's children.

James Hoot is Director of the Early Childhood Research Center, State University of New York, Buffalo

Conclusion

Based not only upon the historical foundations of the early childhood field, but also upon current best practices, we know that high-quality programs for young children have enduring consequences. Early childhood programs, according to Schweinhart (1994), contribute to children's development when they *empower young children* by encouraging them to initiate their own learning activities; *empower parents* by involving them as partners with teachers in supporting their children's development, and *empower*

FIGURE 2.7	**Bank Street**
Internet sources for information about contemporary program models	www.edc.org/cct/mlf/bankst.html

Bank Street
www.edc.org/cct/mlf/bankst.html
www.cc.columia.edu/cu/cerc/wildones/bnkst.html

High/Scope
www.ed.gov/pubs/eptw/eptwII/eptwIId.html
www.sccoe.k12.ca.us/child/highscop.htp

Head Start
www.ci.chi.il.usworksmart/humanservices/childrenservices/headstart.html
www.cardmall.com/nbhs
www.infomagic.com~nacog/na01006.htm

Montessori
The Center for Contemporary Montessori Programs
www.stkate.edu/~mdorer/
The Montessori World Wide Web Site
www.montessori.co.uk/index.htm
www.montessori.org

Reggio Emilia
ericps.ed.uiuc.edu/eece/reggio.html
www.naeyc.org/naeyc/resource/affjul.htm

General Information: Educational Theory Home Page
www.ed.uiuc.edu/coe/eps/educational-theory/et-welcome.html

teachers by providing them with training and supervision that offer hands-on workshops, observation and feedback, and follow-up sessions. Figure 2.7 highlights and provides Internet addresses for some of the contemporary programs that are widely known, respected, and in use throughout the United States.

You can best fulfill your role as a child advocate when you work to provide early childhood programs that are "comprehensive, individualized, community based, generalizable, and age appropriate" (Erwin, 1996, p. 213). As Santrock (1997) reminds us, "the well-being of children is one of our nation's most important concerns. We all cherish the future of our children for they are the future of society. Children who do not reach their full potential, who are destined to make fewer contributions to society than society needs, who do not take their place as productive adults diminish that society's future" (Santrock, 1997, p. 549). Viewing children as the "living messages" that we send to a time we will not see (Postman, 1982) underscores the importance of understanding the traditions in the field and striving to become a child advocate.

One Child, Three Perspectives: Giselle's After-school Care

Giselle is an 8-year-old who lives in an upper-middle-class suburban neighborhood with her father, mother, and 4-year-old brother. Every day after school, she goes out into the yard with her brother and calls out to the retired woman who lives next door, "Anna, is it okay if we jump the fence?" Then the two young children climb over the fence that separates the two yards and spend the next hour or two on the patio with their neighbors. About this, Giselle says matter-of-factly, "My mom said that after-school care costs too much and that we can just play or watch TV until she gets home from work. This house cost a *lot* of money." The neighbor who unofficially watches Giselle and her brother says, "They are a nice family but I worry about those young children being by themselves. Giselle is really mature for her age, but she wouldn't know what to do in an emergency. My husband and I just try to arrange to be home every weekday afternoon. It's only for about an hour, and then their mom is home from her shift at the hospital." When Anna's daughter, who is a college student in education, visits her parents, she says, "I know you and Dad like children and all, but have you considered the legal implications? You don't really have any agreement with this neighbor about responsibility for care. If something happens to those children, they could sue you for trying to do them a favor." Giselle's mother says, "I don't know what I would do if we couldn't rely on Anna. It doesn't help me much to have my children in after-school care because I have to leave work on my break to take them there, take a chance on being late getting back to work, and then go through rush-hour traffic to pick them up after my shift. I think that after-school programs should be right in the school building and supported by the community like they were when we lived in Los Angeles. We were totally unprepared for the lack of services here."

REACT:	What is your initial response to Giselle's situation? What would you like to say to each of the adults in this scenario?
RESEARCH:	Go to the library and read a recent article about after-school programs, policies, curricula, or philosophies. Is your reading consistent with your reaction or not?
REFLECT:	Discuss what you and your classmates found in your readings. How has this information altered or enriched your initial reaction to the situation?

Developing a Personal or Program Philosophy Statement

When we hear the word *philosophy,* most of us tend to think of something that is very abstract, lofty, and divorced from everyday experience. Actually, nothing could be further from the truth, at least in the case of becoming an early childhood educator. Although a philosophy may be difficult to put into words, it is there nevertheless. A teaching philosophy drives decision making, and it is evident in the learning environments that we create. Remember that research suggests that classroom practice is "substantially influenced and even determined by teachers' underlying thinking" (Clark & Peterson, 1986, p. 255).

If someone asked you to explain your philosophy of teaching, what would you say? How would you begin to formulate a succinct statement that captures the essence of what you believe about teaching and learning? Whether you can articulate it or not, you have a rationale for your pedagogy, your methods of teaching children (Athey, 1990).

A teaching philosophy is a statement of beliefs that guides actions. Your personal or professional philosophy statement must communicate your beliefs about how children learn and grow, explain your view of the teacher's role, and emphasize what you believe to be most important for children to know, do, understand, and appreciate.

Begin a working draft of your teaching philosophy. In it, consider the following points.

- *What do you see as being your role?* Discuss your beliefs about to whom and for what you are responsible. Include children, families, the community, and colleagues.

- *What do you believe about how young children learn?* Write a series of statements that begin with the phrase "I believe that children learn best when . . ." Remember to consider how you will meet special needs and celebrate diversity.

- *What do you hope young children will become?* Write a series of statements that begin with the phrase "As a result of my influence, the children in my class would become . . ." Consider how you will guide children's behavior.

Read the following philosophy statement, written by an experienced teacher, before you begin to prepare a draft of your own statement.

Philosophy Statement of Maureen C. Busche

Children are our future. How we treat and educate young children will affect our future. I believe that positive early childhood experiences affect children's achievements and attitudes throughout their school careers and lives. By focusing on strengths—what a child can do—development in all areas can be achieved in a positive, natural, and meaningful way. With this positive influence, children will gain academic, social, and emotional success.

I consider the best learning environment to be one in which children are actively involved. Children need to create their own knowledge and express themselves creatively in order for meaningful learning experiences to take place. When children are actively engaged in their learning, they begin to take ownership of their education.

All children have special gifts and talents. These talents should be recognized and developed throughout a child's schooling through partnerships with families and strong community ties. By teachers' identifying the diversity in children and allowing them to develop areas of strength and interest, children will begin to value and feel good about their special gifts while developing an appreciation for and acceptance of differences in others.

Now, compose your personal philosophy statement, reread it, and revise it until it is well organized and flows well. Then meet with a small group and use the following checklist to assess the philosophy statements each person produced.

_____ Defines the teacher's role

_____ Presents a view of the child as a learner and celebration of diversity

_____ Explains the teacher's perspective on how all children learn

_____ Identifies a curricular orientation and a multicultural perspective

_____ Characterizes the teacher's approach to child guidance

_____ Addresses collaboration with families and the community

FEATURING  *FAMILIES*

A PROGRAM PHILOSOPHY STATEMENT

In addition to preparing a teaching philosophy statement, you may also be asked to write or revise a program philosophy statement. A program philosophy clarifies what is emphasized in the program, prioritizes long-range goals for students, and puts the entire program into perspective. The following is an excerpt from the Five Oaks School's program brochure and parent handbook that explains the program philosophy. Read it as you would if you were in the process of choosing a program for your sibling or child. How does this statement orient you to the goals and philosophy of the program? How does it communicate respect for your role? What questions do you still have about the program after reading it?

Five Oaks is a nondenominational early childhood program that is licensed by the state Board of Education and Department of Social Services to serve children from age 3 to 8 years. We have preschool groups and a primary school for grade kindergarten through third that conform to all state requirements.

Your child has learned a great deal during the first three years of life. When you compare the helpless infant you nurtured with the behavior of your talking, playful, active, competent three-year-old, what your child has learned in skills and knowledge is readily apparent. The early years from birth through eight lay the foundation for the learning that will continue throughout your child's entire life. Probably even more important than the knowledge and skills your child acquires are attitudes about school, learning, personal abilities, and work with others. The goal of Five Oaks is to promote learning, a venture that begins at home and continues through school. At Five Oaks, your child will learn to feel confident, capable, and accepted by the group.

Young children are naturally curious about their world and are motivated by that curiosity to make sense of their environments. Children learn from active interaction with their surroundings, with each other, and with caring adults. At Five Oaks, we nurture that curiosity and the development of skill and mastery of the whole child. The setting and the program are designed to be challenging, rewarding, and stimulating in all areas of the child's development—physical, social, emotional, and intellectual. We use a project approach to instruction and children often work in multi-age groups. Normally, one teacher will stay with a group of children throughout the preschool years and then will assist with the transition to the primary school. Each child will have the same lead teacher while attending the primary school.

You, as your child's first teacher, are an important member of the school community. Five Oaks looks to you for support and partnership that will further your child's development and learning.

3

Exploring Your Role as a Child Development Specialist

A society that stresses freedom and individuality makes knowledge of human development imperative for its educators. Early childhood teacher educators should help students think less about becoming "teachers of children" and more about becoming "students of children."

—Betty L. Hutchison, 1994, p. 146.

Learning Outcomes

✔ Understand the developmental characteristics of children from birth through age 8

✔ Apply knowledge of child development in early childhood settings

✔ Describe the leading theories influencing early childhood education

✔ Appreciate the importance of meeting young children's needs, interests, and abilities

Meet the Teachers

Ms. Mitchell has been providing care for infants and toddlers in her home for more than 15 years. She knows that infants and toddlers need varied sensory stimulation to help their brains make the necessary connections needed for learning, and she shares this information with the children's families. She also knows that very young children who do not have a stimulating environment develop smaller brains. So, in her home, you might see children's physical needs being met by being rocked or cuddled, playing pat-a-cake with an adult, or pushing and pulling toys by themselves. You would also notice bright objects or mirrors on the walls, colorful toys, and large pictures in books that are used to stimulate the infants' visual development. While feeding, diapering, or toileting these very young children, Ms. Mitchell talks to them in a soft, sing-song way to "bathe the children in language from the earliest days and to encourage them to explore and experiment with sounds."

Ms. Davis teaches in a county preschool program for children who are hearing impaired. The main goal of her program is to help the children learn to communicate. Ms. Davis makes weekly home visits to interact individually with each child and model appropriate ways for parents to work with their children who are hearing impaired. If you visit Ms. Davis's class, you will notice 3-year-old Morgan, a child with Down syndrome who is hearing impaired and does not yet walk or talk. During her weekly visits to Morgan's home, Ms. Davis uses pictures, picture books, props, gestures, and first-hand experiences to help Morgan communicate with others about her world. During Ms. Davis's visits, Morgan's mother discusses her own needs as well as Morgan's. Ms. Davis listens to Morgan's mother and offers suggestions about ways to improve Morgan's language development and senses other than hearing, but she tries to keep the conversation focused on the best ways to meet Morgan's developmental needs. Ms. Davis says,

"I am here to help Morgan grow and develop, but I also realize I must consider her mother's needs and education as well. This presents a real challenge for me."

Mr. Guthrie teaches third grade in a school where children speak 17 languages. Based on ideas from a book he recently read, *Positive Discipline* (1996) by Jane Nelsen, Mr. Guthrie uses class meetings as a means for meeting both individual and group needs. He notes that getting children to learn how to use a class meeting effectively takes a lot of time and reading at first. Thus, he usually spends the whole month of September teaching children how to give and receive compliments. He then uses the entire month of October to help children identify and solve real, problematic classroom situations. This year, for example, during reading workshop time, children often argued about who could use the couch in Mr. Guthrie's classroom. Once the children identified the problem and placed it in the problem box for discussion, Mr. Guthrie put it on the agenda for the next class meeting. After suggesting several possible solutions, the third graders finally decided to add a different colored set of cards to the book check-out pocket chart and rotate them daily to give everybody a turn using the couch. Mr. Guthrie says, "If you let yourself listen to children, they come up with great suggestions that are appropriate for solving problems."

These three teachers know what children are like. Now that you have met them, use the following questions to consider their understanding about child development and compare, contrast, and connect them to your own thinking at this time.

COMPARE:	What are some similarities in the ways these three teachers support children's growth and development?

CONTRAST:	What differences do you notice about the ways these teachers facilitate children's growth and development?

CONNECT:	What impressed you most about how these teachers meet the growth and developmental needs of the children in their care? How could you incorporate some of their ideas in your own teaching?

A Definition of Growth and Development

Consider the remarkable changes that have occurred in your body in your developmental journey from a newborn infant to a mature adult. Your growth and development depended on important biological and environmental factors. As you come to understand the process of normal development, it is easier to see how virtually any condition, biological or environmental, can contribute to or impair healthy growth and development.

When we refer to *growth*, we mean the increases in children's overall physical size or a specific aspect of size, such as height, weight, or strength. In contrast, *development* refers to the complex and dynamic cognitive, language, physical, motor, social, emotional, and moral changes that occur over time. Development is a life-long process (Hildebrand, 1997; Katz, 1996). Consider, for example, physical/motor development. You began your life not even able to hold your head up. As your muscle development matured, you were able to eventually roll over, sit, crawl, stand, walk, run, and engage in even more-complex physical skills. These changes over time are what make each person unique.

PAUSE AND REFLECT ABOUT GROWTH AND DEVELOPMENT

Make a list of the biological and environmental factors (e.g., good nutrition, physical health) that you needed to grow and develop into a healthy adult. Now think about what your own development would have been like if one or more of these factors had been lacking in your life. What observations can you make about the necessary resources and supports that facilitate healthy growth and development? Identify some current conditions that affect children's development.

Attributes of Young Children

All children, including those from diverse backgrounds and those with special needs, grow and develop in similar ways. They follow a predictable pattern of development, which is related to their age and influenced by their family and cultural backgrounds, individual temperament, and biological makeup. Although children of certain ages behave in similar ways and have particular characteristics and needs, variations in development are always evident. Knowledge of what young children are like is the first step toward making good decisions to support their healthy growth and development. Essentially, there are three primary attributes of what young children are like. These include: (a) predictable patterns of development, (b) essential needs, and (c) age-related characteristics.

Patterns of Development

Children all over the world grow and develop in the same way, yet each child has a unique pattern of development. The following five research-based principles of growth and development will help you better understand these patterns and provide guidelines for your work with children in all early childhood settings (Berk, 1996; Bredekamp & Copple, 1997; Erikson, 1963; Piaget, 1952; Santrock, 1995; Vygotsky, 1978).

1. *Development in each domain—physical, motor, social, emotional, and cognitive— influences and is influenced by development in other domains.* When children master any physical skill, such as climbing on a jungle gym, riding a bicycle, or kicking a soccer ball, their

self-confidence also usually increases. On the other hand, if children are unable to reach, grasp, crawl, or walk, they are limited in how they explore their world, which influences their cognitive development. The interrelatedness of each domain is an important principle of growth and development.

2. *Development occurs in an orderly and predictable sequence.* Growth occurs from the top of the body to the bottom (cephalocaudal) and from the center of the body outwards (proximodistal). Cephalocaudal development works its way down from the head, to the neck, trunk, and so forth. This is why an infant's head is proportionately so much larger than the rest of its body: The greatest growth in size, weight, and other features first occurs at the top of the body. Proximodistal development begins with the large trunk and arm muscles and works its way out to the smaller muscles in children's hands and fingers. This is why preschool children need lots of opportunities for large-muscle activities such as jumping, climbing, and running before they are expected to do activities that require control of the small muscles in their hands and fingers, such as writing and coloring in small spaces.

3. *Development proceeds at different rates within each individual and within each developmental area.* There is a wide range of individual variation in the timing of growth

While these children are the same chronological age, they show variation in the normal range of development.

and developmental changes that are influenced by biological and other factors such as sociocultural environment, family, temperament, learning style, and experience (Bredekamp & Copple, 1997). Children first sit up, roll over, take a step, lose a tooth, and learn to read at different rates. Only when children considerably deviate from the average ages for these developmental milestones is there cause to consider their development exceptional, either delayed or advanced.

4. *Development is greatly affected by the kinds of experiences children have.* Experiences are cumulative; therefore, they can either positively or negatively affect children's developing knowledge, skills, and abilities. Experiences that occur regularly have more powerful, lasting effects than those that occur rarely. For example, children who hear a great deal of spoken language in the home and use books early and consistently are likely to develop an understanding of the different functions of language, which is a clear advantage for later reading and writing. Conversely, young children who do not hear spoken language or have experiences with books are often at a disadvantage for later literacy development.

5. *Development results from the interaction of each child's biological, physical, and cultural environments.* No single theory adequately describes and explains the complex course of children's growth and development. Today, it is widely accepted that three major influences—biological, environmental, and cultural—are so intertwined that their combination makes each person unique. Biological influences originate in the genes, which determine such characteristics as height, weight, metabolism, and brain development; environmental influences include experiences, language, nutrition, and health care; and cultural influences come from family, peers, community, and the media. If, for example, your genetic makeup predisposes you to healthy growth and development but you have inadequate nutrition and medical care in your early years, your growth and development will be adversely affected (Bredekamp & Copple, 1997; Santrock, 1995).

Essential Needs

Just as there are universal principles of development, there are universal basic needs that affect children's well-being. Even though each child has a unique personality, family situation, and cultural background, all children have the same basic physical, social, emotional, and cognitive needs that contribute to their long-term health, well-being, and ability to thrive (Erikson, 1963; Garbarino, 1995; Maslow, 1954; Weissbourd, 1996).

Minimal physical needs include food, clothing, shelter, and medical care. Basic social and emotional needs include a consistent and predicable relationship with an attentive, caring adult, strong peer acceptance, and freedom from abuse and discrimination. Minimal cognitive needs include the "ability to communicate thoughts and feelings, to process information in a meaningful way, to engage in constructive problem solving, and to experience success both at school and in the community" (Isenberg, 1997, p. 30). How well early childhood practitioners meet the following essential needs of children strongly influences what children will be like.

Need for Security. Children need to feel safe and valued. Their world must be predictable and include at least one adult upon whom they can depend. Feelings of security influence children's ability to take risks, explore, and establish a positive sense of self (Bredekamp & Copple, 1997).

Need for Love. Children of all ages need love and affection from the significant adults in their lives in order to thrive and feel supported.

Need for Understanding and Acceptance. All children need adults in their lives who unconditionally understand and accept them as unique individuals throughout life.

Need for Competency, Responsibility, and Independence. From the earliest years, children gradually need to learn to become competent and responsible for themselves and their own actions. Infants have a need to feed themselves, toddlers have a need to dress themselves, and school-age children have a need to use the tools of reading and writing that will help them be competent students.

Need for Success. Closely related to children's need for competency is their need for success. Being successful in much of what they undertake helps children develop self-esteem, confidence, and motivation to learn.

Need for Guidance. All children need reasonable limits, suitable to their level of understanding and development, which allow them to maintain their dignity and self-respect.

Need for Respect. For children to show respect for others, they must be treated with respect by the adults who care for them.

Age-related Characteristics

All children develop in a universal sequence whose steps are often referred to as periods of development. Approximate age ranges that depict typical behaviors and abilities of children characterize each of these periods. As children develop, they and the adults in their lives face new and different demands and challenges. Knowing in advance what children are like during these periods will help you use the most suitable methods to help them learn and grow. The following sections describe four periods of development and key age-related characteristics of each period.

What Are Infants Like?

Infancy, the first 12 months of life, is a time of total dependency on adults; it also is the time of the most rapid changes in growth and development. By their first birthdays, infants, who were fully dependent upon adults to meet all of their needs as newborns, often can walk and feed themselves. Their well-being very much depends upon the nature of their early care and experiences. Infants vary in the rates at which they develop.

Physical/Motor Development. Physical development in infants is rapid and dramatic. Some of the more important milestones in infants' physical development are (a) increases in height and weight, (b) growth of the brain, bones, and muscles, and (c) a maturing central nervous system. During the first year, infants learn to sit up and move from place to place, hold and use objects, and increase their coordination. By 4 to 5 months of age, for example, an infant's birth weight will have doubled, and by 12 months, it will have tripled.

Social/Emotional Development. Healthy social and emotional growth and development begin at birth. During infancy, children need to learn that they can trust and depend on those who care for them. Trust is encouraged by consistency in the love, physical care, daily routines, and other experiences adults provide. Infants also must develop good feelings about themselves. They accomplish this by forming close attachments to loving, understanding adults who care for them and consistently meet their needs. By 6 months of age, infants need to have established one or more emotional ties to another human being–a process referred to as attachment. Developing trust and forming early attachments are essential for children's mental health. These early attachments have an enduring effect on later social and emotional development and behavior.

Cognitive Development. Infants grow and develop through sensory experiences with their surroundings. Their cognitive development begins with reflexes (e.g., eye blinking, grasping), moves to simple motor movements centered around their own bodies and then to repeated actions, and eventually shows the beginnings of goal-directed behavior that makes things happen (Piaget, 1952). In just a few short months, infants' rapid cognitive development enables them to move from accidentally making things happen (e.g., making sounds by dropping a rattle) to purposefully making things happen by thinking about their experiences and actions (e.g., deliberately dropping a rattle to hear the sounds it makes).

Language Development. Learning to speak and to understand what others say begin in the earliest days of infancy, when infants' parents or adult caretakers talk and respond to them. Babies listen to the words of the adults who care for them, begin to experiment with sounds, and try to repeat words they hear by cooing and babbling. Between 6 and 9 months of age, infants begin to name objects and imitate what they hear. Table 3.1 summarizes the major age-related characteristics of infants.

Physical development is dramatic and rapid during the first year of life.

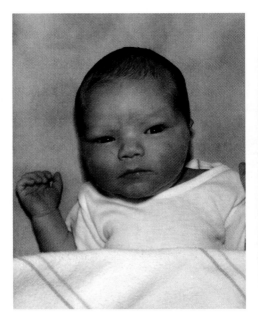

EXPLORING YOUR ROLE AS A CHILD DEVELOPMENT SPECIALIST

PAUSE AND REFLECT ABOUT: INVESTING IN INFANTS' BRAINS

As you have just read, infants have an enormous amount of "work" to accomplish in the areas of physical/motor, social/emotional, cognitive, and language development. What does all of this development work have in common? The brain. Did you know that the brain experiences the most development in the first three years of life? Research on brain functions tells us that each infant's brain contains about 100 billion neurons—quite an accomplishment for two cells "working" together for nine months or less!

So, how does what researchers have discovered about the brain affect your work with infants and young children? Over 30 states have used "brain research" to justify some level of funding for programs to support infant growth and development. As you'll see in the **video clip,** some governments believe that the investment they make now to build babies' brains will have a big payoff in the future. For example, Vermont has a program of early intervention with infants and their families. By providing resources and teaching parents about the importance of brain stimulation in infants, the Vermont government hopes to improve children's ability to learn as well as improve their chances of becoming productive members of society. As you watch the video clip, consider Table 3.1 which presents the Age-Related Characteristics of Infants.

1. After watching the video, list three ways early experiences affect an infant's brain.

2. Taking Dr. Greenspan's findings into consideration, what activity recommendations would you make to the parents of an infant that would make a difference in their child's development? What would you recommend to a toddler's parents?

3. How would you share and explain to parents the information Dr. Greenspan presents regarding brain development in light of the information in Table 3.1 (Age-Related Characteristics of Infants)?

Table 3.1
Age-related Characteristics of Infants

Age	Physical/Motor	Social/Emotional	Cognitive	Language
1–3 months	• hold head up • hold rattle briefly • glance from one object to another • reach toward object	• begin to smile • use smiles and gurgles to get responses • prefer people to objects	• look at colorful objects and faces • practice sucking, looking, grasping, and crying • accidentally discover what their bodies can do (e.g., sucking thumb)	• are calmed by familiar voices • cry when uncomfortable • listen to voices and sounds • coo and babble • show startle response to sharp noises

Table 3.1
(Continued)

Age	Physical/Motor	Social/Emotional	Cognitive	Language
3–6 months	• sit with support • double birth weight • visually follow ball • put objects in mouth • turn from stomach to back and then back to stomach • transfer object from hand to hand • grasp objects with thumb and four fingers	• begin to laugh and enjoy play • coo and smile at objects as well as people • cry in response to unpleasantness • anticipate and show interest in being picked up • show emotions: anger, surprise, sadness, fear	• try to make interesting sights and sounds last by repeating them (i.e., kicking to make a mobile move) • grasp reachable objects • recognize differences between self and objects • respond to own name • imitate interesting behavior	• have different cries for hunger, pain, and attention • babble with two syllables (e.g., ga-ga, goo-goo) • laugh • show interest in sounds • distinguish between friendly and angry sounds • imitate sounds • repeat vowels
6–9 months	• sit alone • crawl • pull string to obtain object • use pincer grasp • stand with help and by holding onto furniture • need help to sit down again • show hand preference	• are interested in social games (e.g., peek-a-boo) • sometimes react to strangers by screaming or crying • approach new situations and people with caution • consistently show emotions • shout to get attention • display shame and shyness	• intentionally try to make things happens (e.g., banging to make noise) • begin to recognize that objects can be used to cause things to happen (e.g., banging pot lids together to make noise)	• begin to understand first words • begin to say *mama* or *da da* and one or two other words • look at familiar objects when they are named • listen to own voice • respond to requests such as "Give me your rattle."
9–12 months	• pick up raisin with thumb and forefinger • push car along • pull up to stand beside furniture • take some steps • hold object with thumb and two fingers • triple birth weight	• may show possessiveness of adult by clinging or pushing others away • clearly communicate feelings and emotions • act socially toward other children by offering or taking away a toy • show affection by hugs • obey simple commands	• anticipate events (e.g., when mother gets the car keys, she is leaving) • look at object, reach for it, grasp it, and put it in mouth • search for hidden objects (e.g., look for a toy when they see it being hidden)	• babble to people • understand commonly used words and turn toward person saying them • understand 12 words (receptive vocabulary) • understand instructions (e.g., wave bye-bye) • speak first word between 10 and 15 months

What Are Toddlers Like?

The period of development from ages 1–3 can be somewhat challenging for toddlers and the adults caring for them. Toddlers are highly inquisitive and very active. They are determined to be independent and to make things happen. In addition, they tend to have frequent changes in mood. Because toddlers are into everything, they need constant supervision for their own safety. Toddlerhood is a time when children begin to become more competent and independent.

Physical/Motor Development. The average toddler is 32–36 inches tall and weighs 23–30 pounds. Even though physical growth slows during this period, toddlers' large muscles develop rapidly. Improved motor control, coordination, and balance keep toddlers constantly on the move, running, climbing, and jumping. As toddlers' small muscles develop, they become more skillful in using their hands; they can hold a cup with one hand, string beads, and stack objects. While they are not skilled at dressing, they are quite skilled at undressing, particularly undoing their shoes and taking off their socks. Toddlers use the new control they have over their bodies to express their feelings. They jump and chuckle when they are happy and kick and scream when they are unhappy. Because their rate of growth has slowed, they need less food. Thus, many toddlers become fussy eaters and prefer to play with their food rather than eat it. They also begin to use the toilet alone, and they continue to need periods of rest and quiet during the day.

Social/Emotional Development. Toddlers seek independence from adults and show interest in children their own ages. They demand to do things for themselves and typically respond to offers of help with a resounding "No!" or "Me do it!" These responses make them appear to be stubborn, willful, and defiant. In reality, however, they are simply trying to figure out who they are and to accomplish the important task of becoming more competent and independent. Toddlers also are meeting new expectations from parents and caregivers. When they were infants, the adults in their lives promptly and patiently responded to their needs and adjusted their own schedules to accommodate them. Now, these same adults often ask toddlers to wait and say "no" to them. Suddenly, toddlers' needs are not being met as promptly as they were during infancy, and conflicts arise. They often respond by crying or having temper tantrums.

Cognitive Development. Toddlers can recall and anticipate certain events they have experienced. For example, they not only ask for juice but also can remember where the juice is kept. This skill marks the beginning of memory. Toddlers also engage in imaginative play during which they act out their own ideas about objects and events without much regard for reality. What they think about their world depends upon the experiences they have had. These early concepts about their world are the basis upon which later concepts are formed.

Language Development. Most toddlers understand about 300 words. From ages 2 to 3, they learn new words and grammatical forms at an astounding rate. They enjoy language for its rhythm and like to hear the same stories over and over again, more for the rhythm than the content. They also enjoy looking at books and magazines and naming familiar objects they see in pictures. Toddlers' first words name familiar people (e.g., *da da, mama*), animals (e.g., *kitty, doggie*), and objects (e.g., *car, ball, cookie, nose*); they also include social interaction terms (e.g., *hi, bye-bye, up*). Toddlers' speaking vocabularies include single words that stand for a whole thought and average 200–275 words by age 2 (Santrock, 1995). Table 3.2 summarizes age-related characteristics of toddlers.

Table 3.2
Age-related Characteristics of Toddlers

Age	Physical/Motor	Social/Emotional	Cognitive	Language
12–18 months	**Gross Motor** • stand alone • walk without support • climb onto chair • push and pull toys • roll ball using both hands • squat to pick up objects • move in place to music **Fine Motor** • scribble on paper • pick up small objects with thumb and forefinger • feed self with fingers or spoon • pour, stack, and build • take off shoes and socks	• are deeply attached to adult who provides regular care • explore surroundings • can give and receive toys • enjoy chasing, hiding, and other games • play beside, but not with, other children	• try new ways to do things • imitate behavior of others • use trial-and-error method to learn	• say 2 words at 12 months, 4–5 words at 15 months, and 15–20 words by 18 months • use gestures, tone, and context • understand simple directions • repeat syllables • wave bye-bye • use words to make needs known at 12 months
18–24 months	**Gross Motor** • walk, run, and slide • throw and catch • balance self • bend to pick up objects • walk backward • imitate familiar adult behavior • move to music **Fine Motor** • use cup and spoon awkwardly • turn 2–3 pages of book • place large pegs in pegboard • hold crayon in fist • squeeze toys	• anticipate expressions of love and return them • recognize self in mirror • show intense likes and dislikes • are easily distracted and entertained by others • alternate between dependence on and independence from adults • understand ownership of own possessions • show contempt and guilt	• picture ideas, objects, and events in mind • think about and solves simple problems • imitate behavior seen days or even weeks earlier • are beginning to understand consequences of behavior	• understand simple questions • point to parts of body • have 20-word vocabulary at 18 months and a 272-word vocabulary by 24 months • use simple sentences and phrases by 24 months • begin to take turns in conversation

Table 3.2
(Continued)

Age	Physical/Motor	Social/Emotional	Cognitive	Language
24–36 months	**Gross Motor** • walk on toes • kick large ball • imitate animal movements • walk up and down stairs one at a time with alternating feet • ride tricycle • hang by hands from a support • jump in place **Fine Motor** • build towers • string 3–4 beads • manage spoon and fork easily • snip with scissors • hold crayon with thumb and forefinger • use one hand consistently • control grasp and release	• watch other children • make a choice between two alternatives • play house using simple role play • participate in small-group activities for 5–10 minutes • know gender identity • insist on doing things independently • take turns with one reminder • play independently for 15 minutes • express a range of emotions through actions, words, or facial expressions	• respond to simple directions • select and look at picture books, and identify several objects within one picture • touch and count 1–3 objects • match four colors • attempt to play with unfamiliar toys	• understand prepositions and pronouns • say "no" • use words to ask for things • make sounds for *p, m, n, w,* and *h* at the beginning of words • use question words (e.g., *why, when*) • use past tense and plurals • speak in 2–5–word sentences • understand negatives • enjoy simple storybooks for 10–15 minutes

What Are Preschoolers and Kindergartners Like?

The preschool–kindergarten period of development extends from 3 to 6 years. During this time, children show improved motor skills and make great strides in language development. Preschool children also become more self-sufficient in caring for themselves and begin to show less attachment to their parents. They engage in more-complex play activities, are very curious, and want to explore the world outside their familiar surroundings.

Physical/Motor Development. Physical development during the preschool years is steady. During this time, children's height increases each year by about 2 to 3 inches and their weight by about 4 to 6 pounds. Their body proportions change from chunky and chubby to lean and tall, and their muscles, bones, and brains continue to develop (Puckett & Black, 1996). By age 5, children's brains have reached about 90% of their adult weight, and myelination, the process that facilitates the transfer of messages, makes children's increased motor abilities possible. Preschoolers and kindergartners are usually very active and have lots of energy. Gross motor (i.e., large muscle) skills are rapidly expanding, and children show increased facility with their arms, hands, and legs. They enjoy practicing their newly learned hopping, throwing, catching, and jumping skills. Fine motor (i.e., small muscle) skills become more refined, thus enabling children to perform such self-help skills as buckling, snapping, buttoning, and zipping. Mastering these skills involves a great deal of work and practice, but children enjoy the challenge. Older preschoolers and kindergarten children become even more agile; they show interest in sports, noncompetitive games, and physical fitness (Berk, 1996; Black & Puckett, 1996).

Social/Emotional Development. Preschool and kindergarten children begin to spend more time with people outside their own families. They have a strong need to be with and accepted by other children of similar ages, and often, they become very attached to their playmates. They are generally happy, curious, compliant, imaginative, and pleased with their own abilities to plan and complete projects, which are primarily carried out in imaginative play activities. New experiences interest them, and they want to know more about other people, what other people do, and what they themselves are capable of doing. They spend much time experimenting with adult roles that they have observed. Preschoolers show increased autonomy, although they still move back and forth between their need to be independent and their need for dependence. Although the ability to delay gratification of their needs and wants has increased, they still become easily frustrated, cannot tolerate waiting, and frequently cry when things do not go their way. Many children also experience an expanding range of emotions and learn how to express these emotions in socially acceptable ways. Fear and anxiety are common emotions during these years. Many preschoolers are fearful, especially 3- and 4-year-olds, who typically fear the dark, unfamiliar animals, and potentially dangerous situations such as fire and deep water. By the end of this period of development, most children outgrow these fears.

Cognitive Development. From the ages of 3 to 6, children's thinking is a combination of fantasy and reality, and their understanding is based upon their own limited experiences. Young preschoolers focus primarily on what they see in their immediate surroundings and upon present events. They have difficulty with concepts related to the past and the future, and they are able to think aloud about only one idea at a time. As they become more mature and have more experiences, preschoolers' thinking becomes more objective and realistic. Older preschoolers and kindergartners, for example, can put together objects based on more than one attribute (e.g., color, size, shape), but their thinking is not systematic and they often stop in the middle of what they are doing and go on to something else. Children between the ages of 3 and 6 ask many "why" questions. Although they sometimes do this to get attention, generally their questions stem from their strong need to find out about their world. This process of asking questions and finding out about things helps them learn.

Language Development. Children's vocabularies increase rapidly during this period. Usually, 3-year-olds have vocabularies of 200–250 words, 5-year-olds have vocabularies of about 2,500 words, and the vocabularies of 6-year-olds consist of about 20,000 words. Preschoolers usually understand more words than they actually speak. Most preschoolers love to talk and are curious about words. Sometimes, however, they use words that they do not understand merely for the practice and pleasure that new words bring. In doing this, they give the impression that they understand what they are saying. Adults, therefore, must be careful not to assume that young children understand all of the words they use. Table 3.3 describes the major age-related characteristics of preschool and kindergarten children.

Table 3.3

Age-related Characteristics of Preschoolers and Kindergarteners

Age	Physical/Motor	Social/Emotional	Cognitive	Language
3 years	**Gross Motor** • stands on one foot briefly • kicks and throws ball • rides tricycle • uses swings, slides, and climbers • walks on tiptoes • does forward somersault **Fine Motor** • makes simple drawings • dresses and undresses self but will still ask for help • copies figures (e.g., +) • cuts paper • uses paste with forefinger • builds eight block towers	• likes to please adults • has occasional, short temper tantrums • can be jealous of younger siblings • looks to adults for security, recognition, and encouragement • takes turns, shares, and uses language to settle disputes • tries to follow directions • shows an interest in family activities • may act like a baby • accepts suggestions • tests limits	• stacks objects by size • understands simple questions, statements, and directions • asks many questions and understands more words than he or she uses • counts by rote and recognizes some letter names • likes rhythm, repetition, and humor • puts simple geometric shapes into correct slots	• uses familiar words and longer sentences with plurals and past tense • talks to self • plays with language for fun and practice • names objects, people, and events in a picture • recites nursery rhymes and poems
4 years	**Gross Motor** • balances • runs, jumps, climbs, and hops in place skillfully • bounces and catches ball • builds bridges with blocks • walks backward **Fine Motor** • copies O and X • uses fork and safe knife • follows lines cutting paper • dresses self using zippers and buttons • prints letters • draws simple, recognizable figures	• is proud of what he or she can do • prefers own age mates • seeks attention by showing off, making up stories, and being silly • expresses displeasure loudly and through aggression • can tolerate some frustration • is developing a sense of humor • likes nonsense words • shows a balance between dependence and independence	• knows own sex, age, and last name • points to six basic colors when asked • gives long answers to questions • draws what he or she knows • has limitless imagination • sees differences among some shapes and colors • shows interest in books and printed words • counts objects when touching them	• answers out loud to "Hi" and "How are you?" • speaks clearly in sentences • makes up words • asks many "how" and "why" questions • speaks of imaginary conditions • tells tall tales • uses adverbs and five-word sentences • likes repetition of sounds and words

Table 3.3
(Continued)

Age	Physical/Motor	Social/Emotional	Cognitive	Language
5 years	**Gross Motor** • runs on tiptoe • skips, jumps rope, and walks a straight line • rolls ball to hit objects • rides two-wheeled bicycle with training wheels • dribbles and bounces ball **Fine Motor** • copies designs, letters, and numbers • can cut, paste, and fold paper • grips pencil correctly • shows handedness • copies the numerals 1–10 and a triangle	• plays together with others • enjoys friends and wants to visit with them alone • cooperates with adults and peers • recognizes the rights of others • tries to conform to rules • generally feels good about self and his or her world	• understands yesterday, today, and tomorrow • knows difference between reality and fantasy • can remember more than two ideas for a short time • is keenly interested in numbers and counting • remembers own address • identifies pennies, nickels, and dimes • asks for information and facts • hears differences and similarities in letter sounds • remembers number, letter, and counting sequences	• uses sentences with correct grammar • talks to others with poise and maturity • asks direct questions and wants real answers • uses longer sentences with connectors (e.g., *but, because*) • is interested in word meanings • tries out new words and can define some simple words • likes stories • understands nouns and verbs

What Are School-Age Children Like?

School-age children, ages 6–8, also show dramatic changes in development. They are losing temporary teeth and gaining permanent teeth, their motor coordination continues to be refined, and they work hard at mastering the fundamental skills of reading, writing, and mathematics. School-age children's thinking also changes during this period as it becomes more orderly and logical. Friends assume an important role in their lives, and they become increasingly aware of how they look to others (Berk, 1996; Dodge, Jablon, & Bickart, 1994; Wood, 1994). Older school-age children prefer to work with peers of the same sex. Most school-age children delight in group projects and activities, have a delightful sense of humor, and respond to adults with beaming smiles when they are praised and sad looks when they are criticized.

Physical/Motor Development. The average height of school-age children ranges from 45 to 51 inches, while the average weight ranges from 45.5 pounds at age 6 to 60 pounds at age 8 for boys and somewhat less for girls. As children grow taller, their body proportions again shift. During this period, their vision becomes sharper, they still have frequent illnesses, and they tire easily. Gross motor skills include such fundamental movements as running, kicking, and reaching, which prepare children for the more-complex coordination needed to play organized sports. Playground games such as tag and hopscotch are very popular with and important for school-age children. Fine motor development is evident in greater dexterity and control over drawing and writing, which

Table 3.4
Age-related Characteristics of School-Age Children

Age	Physical/Motor	Social/Emotional	Cognitive	Language
6 years	**Gross Motor** • enjoy challenging acrobatics and outdoor activities • ride two-wheel bike • can do standing long jumps • begin to use a bat **Fine Motor** • have good visual tracking • make simple figures with clay • sew simple stitches • use table knife for spreading food	• are competitive and enthusiastic • test boundaries • can be bossy, teasing, and critical of others • get upset easily when hurt • believe in rules for others but not self • have pride in work • like surprises • enjoy routines and have difficulty with transitions	• use symbols • work in spurts • begin to use logic • can put stories and events in sequence • sort and classify information, groups, and objects	• explain things in detail • use enthusiastic language • have some speech irregularities
7 years	**Gross Motor** • balance on one foot • walk balance beam • hop and jump in small spaces • can do jumping-jacks **Fine Motor** • brush and comb hair • use table knife for cutting	• are sometimes moody and shy • rely on adults for help • are afraid to make mistakes • are sensitive to others' feelings • have strong likes and dislikes • draw and write about same theme repeatedly • are eager for adult acceptance	• engage in abstract thinking • like maps and detailed information	• talk with precision • converse easily with others • are curious about word meanings • send notes and use secret codes
8 years	**Gross Motor** • are highly energetic and agile • alternate hopping to a beat • engage in rough and tumble play • have coordinated skills for sports **Fine Motor** • use common household tools (i.e., hammer, screwdriver)	• have keen awareness of adult and child worlds • show disappointment when things do not go their way • crave acceptance from peers and adults	• classify and sort spontaneously • discover, invent, and take things apart to investigate how they work • want perfection and erase constantly • work slowly	• explain things in detail • use enthusiastic language • have some speech irregularities

makes copying from the chalkboard easier (Puckett & Black, 1996; Wood, 1994). Older school-age children produce smaller and more detailed pieces of art.

Social/Emotional Development. School-age children are now more responsible and independent, are more prosocial in their peer interactions, work harder at making friends, and are more self-critical. Younger school-age children still seek adult approval and tend to tattle, whereas older school-age children are more interested in forming clubs and selected groups. Older children also have fears and worries that they carefully mask; these take the form of nail biting, inattention, or changed eating and sleeping patterns.

Cognitive Development. School-age children are eager, curious, and delightful learners who thrive on opportunities to discover and invent. They rely on learning through such forms of play as puppet shows, story retellings, games, and secret codes. Younger school-age children's thinking is intuitive and based on concrete, active experiences. Older school-age children's thinking changes from an intuitive, concrete understanding to a more logical understanding. They can now think, plan, and reflect on what they are learning, but their thinking, while growing more abstract, still needs to be related to familiar experiences. Older school-age children have a more focused attention span that enables them to think, plan, and reflect on their accomplishments; they also have an increased understanding of memory that facilitates cognitive processing. These abilities enable them to begin to understand differences, cause and effect, and different perspectives.

Language Development. School-age children have a good understanding of both oral and written language. Their oral language is quite adultlike, and they tend to dominate conversations. Their talk gleefully includes metaphors, jokes, puns, and riddles, for they now understand multiple meanings. They also use language to communicate their feelings and understand and use more appropriate grammatical structures such as plurals, possessives, and past tense in their oral and written language. Their vocabularies continue to expand, and they show a new interest in the meanings of words. The written language of school-age children typically includes invented spellings, which are evidence of their understanding of the connection between letters and sounds. Table 3.4 describes the major age-related characteristics of school-age children.

The miniportraits provided in Tables 3.1–3.4 of widely held characteristics of children from birth through age 8 can be a powerful tool for you. They can help you know what to expect and what challenges children may face at different periods of development. They also can give you a framework for understanding how to meet the needs of all children.

EXPLORING YOUR ROLE AS A CHILD DEVELOPMENT SPECIALIST

A NOTE TO FAMILIES ABOUT CHILD DEVELOPMENT

Many parents recount situations about their children and end with the question, "Is this typical?" which is followed by "What should I do?"

The following is part guessing game, part information. First are listed a few developmental characteristics and then some brief scenarios for you to mark *T* for typical and *D* for different.

Some Developmental Characteristics

- Each child develops at his or her own pace.
- Children between 3 and 7 years are learning to separate the real from the pretend.
- Most children can correctly make all the sounds of the English language by 7 years.
- Children begin losing their baby teeth between 5 and 8 years.
- Young children make sense of the world based on their own experiences.
- Curiosity and competence are powerful motivators in young children.

Common Scenarios (Mark T or D)

_____ 1. Emily, who is 20 months old, is scribbling on the walls with a crayon.

_____ 2. Sam, a 7-year-old, is commenting to a teacher, "I told my dad you were really old, maybe 20 or 21 years old."

_____ 3. Marty is a 6-year-old who has difficulty saying certain letters, mainly *r* words such as *frog* and *rabbit* and the beginning sounds. He talks with a slight lisp and just lost his two front teeth.

_____ 4. David, a first grader, wrote a story about his favorite dog, Spot, that looked like this:

Spt 12 n'is. He liks me dd liks mi fas.

_____ 5. Amy had a bad case of chicken pox and missed 8 days of school. Now she says she never wants to go back.

Even typical development can create problems. Early childhood teachers and parents can help children learn to overcome difficulties. If a behavior persists for a few months after active intervention, the family doctor may be a good person to call for further help.

Answers: All are typical most of the time.

1. Writing starts when a child learns how to make a mark. Scribbling is the first step. Children should be provided with paper and a place to write.

2. Children often view age based on their own ages, so "really old" may be 20 years, instead of a more realistic mature age.

3. If a child is understandable to his or her teacher and other children, speech problems are minor. The difficulties most often occur before age 7 and with the loss of teeth.

4. This is an example of invented spelling. David is using his understanding of letter sounds to write his story: "Spot is nice. He likes me and licks my face."

5. Preferring the security of home is not hard to understand. As on the first day of school, Amy does not know what to expect after missing so much school. Her teacher and family can help her re-enter the classroom in a variety of ways.

PAUSE AND REFLECT ABOUT ATTRIBUTES OF YOUNG CHILDREN

Think about a child you know very well. Make a list of the three most important age-related characteristics of the child that you think a teacher ought to know about to optimize the child's development. Use at least two of the developmental domains just discussed (i.e., physical/motor, social/emotional, cognitive, and language). Now that you have this information, what do you think this child needs to develop optimally?

Your Role as a Child Development Specialist

Child development is the study of the changes that occur in children from conception through middle childhood. As a teacher of young children, you will be making hundreds of daily decisions about children that are based, in part, on their growth and development. A good example of decision making based on child development comes from Ms. Cochran, a first-grade teacher.

One of Ms. Cochran's first graders, Vu, is a 6-year-old bilingual child who reads fluently. During free-choice time, children select from a variety of materials to play with and usually interact in small groups or pairs. Vu always chooses to play alone and seldom speaks with his classmates. During these times, Ms. Cochran interacts with Vu and talks with him about what he is doing. While he does answer her, the conversation is very one-sided—initiated by Ms. Cochran and finished when she no longer asks questions or makes comments. Ms. Cochran has observed that Vu also needs help taking turns, sharing, cleaning up, using words to ask for something or to respond to a question or request, and during transitions. Based on her observations and what she knows about 6-year-olds, Ms. Cochran spoke with other specialists and Vu's parents to see how the school could better meet Vu's developmental needs.

Ms. Cochran is demonstrating her role as a child development specialist. While child development knowledge is essential for all early childhood professionals, it alone is not sufficient. Your role as a child development specialist can be guided by the following attributes.

1. *Possess a thorough knowledge of child development.* Early childhood practitioners rank knowledge of child development the number-one competency for practitioners in all early childhood settings (Goffin & Day, 1994; Early Childhood Education Research Project, 1994). For example, Ms. Cochran knows that 6-year-olds typically talk to other children and to the teacher in one-to-one, small-group, and large-group interactions. Vu was not using oral language in these ways. Based on this knowledge, Ms. Cochran developed strategies to help Vu acquire the social skills that will enable him to become a more integral part of the group. She spoke with Vu's parents and encouraged them to establish a playtime for Vu each week, to have him play with children his own age, and to spend time talking with him at home.

2. *Be a keen observer of children.* Observation is essential for understanding and responding to children. It is your basic tool—your eyes and ears—and gives you important information about children's needs, interests, and strengths. Knowing what typical behavior is at certain ages enables you to observe actual behavior and compare it with expected behavior. When children's growth and development are not typical, your documented observations will help you identify a child who may require additional services from other professionals such as a pediatrician, counselor, speech and language specialist, or social worker. In the preceding scenario, Ms. Cochran was aware that Vu's social and oral language development were not typical of 6-year-olds and sought support for him early.

3. *Create a safe and caring environment for all children.* All children need a safe and healthy environment for their optimal development. In Ms. Cochran's first grade, she provided daily opportunities for children to choose their own activities and to choose their playmates for a long block of time every morning. Through her care, competence, and commitment to providing a supportive environment, she enlisted lots of support for Vu.

4. *Modify your environment to meet the needs of all children.* If you view each child as unique, you will want to know as much as you can about each child in your setting and you will adjust your goals based on each child's strengths, culture, interests, and abilities. Some children may require more individual instruction and may need to learn a skill at a slower pace, and some may need to have more sensory or concrete experiences for learning. Some may exhibit behaviors that are culturally appropriate. In Vu's case, Ms. Cochran knew that Vu needed to develop social skills, so she began asking him questions that could not be answered with a simple "yes" or "no." She also knew that children from Vu's culture often speak only when spoken to. Thus, Ms. Cochran enlisted other student helpers that Vu could contact if he needed something, and she chose children to be helpers who already had a trusting relationship established with Vu. These adaptations illustrate that children need predictable environments "so that they can develop the language skills, social competence, self-confidence, and ways of thinking that. . . help them discover how the world works" (Schorr, 1988, p. 182).

5. *Develop children's social and emotional competence.* We know that "educators who establish firm boundaries, foster warm personal relationships in the classroom, and enable students to have a say about their learning strengthen students' attachments to school, their interest in learning, their ability to refrain from self-destructive behaviors, and their positive behaviors" (Association for Supervision and Curriculum Development, 1997, p. 44). Ms. Cochran's concern for Vu's well-being, feelings, and social competence clearly will enable Vu to become part of the classroom community so that he can learn to become more socially competent.

Why Child Development Knowledge is Important

During the critical early years, children are not only establishing the basic foundations for physical, cognitive, and social/emotional development, but they also are forming beliefs, attitudes, and behavior patterns that influence how they view themselves and the world in which they live. Making good decisions about children's healthy growth and development considers their special needs and interests, as well as their cultural and social backgrounds (Bredekamp & Copple, 1997). We will discuss these important aspects of child development separately.

Children with Special Needs

By now, you are probably aware that there will be all kinds of children in the settings in which you will be working. Some may have physical or learning disabilities; others may have special gifts or talents. A *disability* is defined as "an inability to do something or a diminished capacity to perform in a specific way" (Hallahan & Kauffman, 1994, p. 6). *Special needs* are those areas in which a child needs individualized supports and services to help develop, learn, be happy, and be included with children of the same age (Hallahan & Kauffman, 1994). The term *special needs* refers either to children with disabilities or children with gifts and talents.

While you are not expected to have in-depth knowledge of every disability or talent, you do need to learn about specific needs of the children in your setting. As an early childhood educator, you will nurture and interact with these children in the same positive manner as you will with every other child, for children with special needs are more alike than they are different from other children. They have the same basic needs to be cared for adequately, to be treated fairly, and to be successful. It is beyond the scope of this book to discuss in depth each category of special needs. However, we do want to introduce you to important legislation and services, categories of disabilities, and the notion of inclusion for children with disabilities, as well as some characteristics of children with gifts and talents that are important aspects of their development.

Children with Disabilities

Legislation. Since the mid-1970s, there have been a variety of federal laws enacted to ensure that the educational needs are met for children with exceptionalities and that the abilities of children with disabilities are recognized. These laws provide funding and guidelines for federal, state, and local schools and agencies to educate eligible children with disabilities from birth through age 21 in the most appropriate settings. In addition, the laws require that classroom aides or resources, specialized training for classroom teachers, therapy services, family training and counseling, and home visits be made available when needed. Table 3.5 lists these major federal laws and describes the eligibility guidelines for service.

Categories of Disabilities. The *Individuals with Disabilities Education Act (IDEA)* (1990) lists 13 different disabilities that qualify children for special education services. Identifying these disabilities, their basic characteristics, and the services available for children who have them is essential to fulfilling your role as a child development specialist in a regular education setting. These 13 categories are as follows.

1. *Autism:* a developmental disability that affects verbal and nonverbal communication and social interactions. It generally appears in the first 3 years of life. Children who are autistic either do not speak or have immature speech patterns and limited understanding of ideas.

Table 3.5
Legislation for Children with Special Needs

Law	Year	Major Highlights
Public Law 94–142, *Education for All Handicapped Children* (EHA)	1975	• Identifies and provides all children between the ages of 3 and 5 with developmental disabilities with a free, appropriate public education • describes processes and procedures for determining eligibility for free intervention services • mandates provision of other services including transportation, testing, diagnosis, and parental rights to due-process hearings if parents disagree with an eligibility decision
Public Law 99–457, *Education of the Handicapped Act Amendments*	1986	• mandates intervention services for children with developmental delays or who are at-risk for developmental delays from birth through age 2 • requires that intervention services for very young children be provided in settings in which other infants and toddlers are being educated, such as child-care settings, preschools, and family-care settings • requires family involvement in decision making and in plans for the transition to preschool special education programs • mandates an individualized family service plan (IFSP) for infants and toddlers that includes goals, needed services, and plans for implementation
Public Law 101–476, *Individuals with Disabilities Education Act* (IDEA)	1990	• reauthorizes and extends PL 94–142 • changes language from "handicapped children" to "children with disabilities" and adds autism and traumatic brain injury to eligible categories for services • mandates that each state and local government must pay most of the costs of special education programs and must determine its own criteria and evaluation process for determining eligibility for services • critical mandates include the following: —free and appropriate public education —least restrictive environment (i.e., where possible, children are placed in regular education settings) —due process (i.e., schools and parents may protest an eligibility decision) —parental or guardian participation (i.e., they are to be included in all decision making)
Americans with Disabilities Act (ADA)	1990	• civil rights legislation that ensures that individuals with disabilities are protected from discrimination in the workplace and in all public facilities

2. *Deafness:* a hearing impairment that ranges from mild to severe. Children classified as deaf cannot process language without an amplification device.

3. *Deaf-blindness:* a combined hearing and visual impairment that causes severe communication and related educational problems. These children must be educated in programs that attend to both disabilities.

4. *Hearing impairment:* a sensory, physical disability that can be temporary or permanent and adversely affects children's speaking abilities.

5. *Mental retardation:* a cognitive delay in which children consistently function below the level of the average population.

6. *Multiple disabilities:* two or more disabilities that result in motor and sensory deficiencies, delay development, and affect learning.

7. *Orthopedic impairment:* a motor skill impairment that affects motor skill development and impedes self-help and other areas of development. It includes such impairments as clubfoot and impairments caused by other diseases such as cerebral palsy.

8. *Other health impairments:* ongoing medical attention for such health problems as heart conditions, tuberculosis, asthma, epilepsy, and diabetes. While these health problems do not directly affect children's ability to learn, they often affect development in a negative way because these children have limited physical and mental energy.

9. *Serious emotional disorders:* social/emotional disabilities include abnormal social relations, bizarre mannerisms, inappropriate social behavior, and unusual language that interfere with a child's daily adaptation.

10. *Specific learning disability:* a disability that causes difficulty with processing auditory and visual stimuli in children with normal intelligence. Learning disabilities may occur in the areas of memory, visual and auditory discrimination and association, perceptual motor skills, attending, or verbal expression, all of which lead to an inability to remember, express ideas, focus on tasks, or discriminate between likeness and difference.

11. *Speech or language impairment:* a communication disorder that includes stuttering, impaired articulation, or an inability to gain meaning from language that is basic to many of the other disabilities listed here, especially hearing impairment, mental retardation, and specific learning disability.

12. *Traumatic brain injury:* a neurological impairment caused by an outside influence that results in brain injury, either temporary or permanent, that may affect one or more areas of developmental functioning. This is a new category of disability under *IDEA* (1990) that provides services for children with brain injury.

13. *Visual impairment:* a disability that affects normal development, even with correction, including those with low vision, partial sightedness, or legal blindness.

Being knowledgeable about the different categories of needs that qualify for services is an important first step for all adults in regular early childhood settings. It will help your interactions with children who exhibit any of these special needs and perhaps help you to provide resources to them early, which will affect their development.

Inclusion. *Inclusion* is a way of educating all children with exceptionalities in the most natural settings within their community, particularly in the early years (Division for Early Childhood of the Council for Special Education, 1993; Sailor, Gerry, & Wilson, 1991). As a teacher of young children, it is important that you create an environment that maximizes the learning potential for *all* children, including those with special needs. Advocates of *full inclusion* believe that "all children, no matter what their disability . . . [should be educated] . . . in the regular education classroom, with both special and regular educators sharing joint responsibility in a team teaching . . . model that adapts the curriculum to meet the needs of all learners" (Bergen, 1997, p. 153). These educators do

ASK the Expert: Richard M. Gargiulo on Young Children with Special Needs

Common Questions Students Ask about Young Children with Special Needs

Richard M. Gargiulo

1. Why are so many early childhood teachers, especially those with limited exposure to young children with special needs, reluctant to teach them or have unwarranted fears because of the youngsters' disabilities or delays?

This perception is unfounded. Young children with disabilities are more like their typically developing classmates than they are different. I strongly encourage teachers to remember that a child with exceptionalities is first and foremost a child. Just because a youngster is labeled exceptional should never prohibit professionals from realizing just how typical he or she is in many other ways. Good teachers look for similarities between children with special needs and their peers, not differences. It is vitally important that early childhood teachers focus on the child, not the impairment; separate the abilities from the disability; and see the youngsters' strengths, not their weaknesses.

2. In what kind of environment should young children with disabilities be taught?

Contemporary thinking suggests that **all** young children with special needs should receive intervention and educational services in settings designed for youngsters without disabilities, that is, in normalized environments such as day-care centers, Head Start programs, or regular kindergartens. Known as **full inclusion**, this concept has the potential to polarize our profession. It has evolved into one of the most controversial and complex practices in the field of early childhood education. Some early childhood educators mistakenly believe that we are required by various federal laws to educate young children with special needs only in regular education classrooms. This simply is not true. To the extent that it is appropriate, we need to educate young children with disabilities in the least restrictive environment, that is, with their typically developing peers. This, of course, implies the need for a continuum of placement options, not solely a regular classroom. As an illustration, for some children with disabilities, a more restrictive setting, such as a preschool program for children with disabilities or for children with multiple impairments, is the more appropriate environment rather than serving these youngsters in a church-affiliated preschool or a public school kindergarten.

3. If children with disabilities are so much like their typical counterparts and there is a push for full inclusion, why are early childhood teachers in the field of special education prepared differently from their classmates?

This is a perfectly valid question. I wonder the same thing. In fact, I believe the time is right for a collaborative or integrative personnel preparation program. Support for this proposal is growing both in early childhood circles and in the field of special education. Many of my colleagues question the wisdom of training early childhood professionals via distinct preparation programs. I believe we need to develop a seamless or inclusive model for preparing teachers of young children so that all are prepared to teach all children regardless of the type of setting they work in. To me, good teaching is good teaching—we teach children, not disability labels. A unified model of preparation makes good sense. Preservice teachers would be able to draw upon effective and pedagogically sound practices from both parent fields and thus provide services that are age and developmentally appropriate while also being responsive to the individual needs of each learner. I am convinced that the time has arrived to put an end to segregated, categorical preparation programs. Young children need teachers with multiple competencies capable of providing effective instruction in a variety of settings. Such professionals will be well suited to meet the challenges of the workplace in the 21st century.

Richard M. Gargiulo is a professor of education at the University of Alabama, Birmingham.

not believe that separating children with disabilities into isolated classrooms allows them to develop in the best possible learning environment. On the other hand, there are others who support *partial inclusion,* a model that provides assistance when and where it is needed, as well as the full-inclusion option (Bergen, 1997). They argue that full inclusion may not meet the unique, special needs of all children either academically or socially because these children need more intensive, individualized instruction and separate, specialized settings that ensure an appropriate education.

Children Who Are Gifted and Talented

Gifted children are characterized by high academic ability; talented children show excellence in such areas as art, music, drama, or sports. A gift or talent can occur in one or more areas of development. In a regular early childhood setting, children with gifts and talents need to be challenged and stimulated just as every other child in your setting does. Intellectually gifted children progress faster than their peers academically and often have a deep interest in books and reading, large vocabularies, a wide range of interests, and a desire to learn. They need challenges to their creative thinking and many opportunities for participation in groups designed to challenge their abilities.

Children with special needs often experience greater academic and social challenges as they move forward with their education. Having knowledge of these needs will increase your awareness and sensitivity to all children. It will also enable you to explore new ways of viewing and educating children with disabilities and children with gifts and talents. All early childhood professionals must accommodate individual differences and develop the skills necessary to work with the entire professional support team to maximize the potential of every child. This process necessitates a more inclusive interpretation of developmentally appropriate practices (Puckett & Black, 1996).

PAUSE AND REFLECT ABOUT CHILDREN WITH SPECIAL NEEDS

Think about a child you know or may have seen who has a special need. Describe the characteristics of the child and what you think the child's teacher did or did not do to support his or her development. What concerns do you have about teaching children with exceptionalities at this stage of your professional development?

Children from Diverse Backgrounds

The social settings and cultural contexts in which children live significantly influence their development. Knowledge about these is critical "to ensure that learning experiences are meaningful, relevant, and respectful for the participating children and their families" (Bredekamp & Copple, 1997, p. 9). By *social setting,* we mean the significant people in children's lives who influence their development; by *cultural context,* we mean the values, behaviors, languages, dialects, and feelings about being part of a particular group that all children possess. These cultural influences are passed from generation to generation and significantly shape children's development (Banks, 1997; Bredekamp & Copple, 1997). As Barbara Bowman so eloquently states, "Rules of development are the same for all children, but social [and cultural] contexts shape children's development into different configurations" (Bowman, in Bredekamp & Copple, 1997, p. 12). The blend of diverse characteristics contributes to each child's uniqueness.

Since the civil rights movement of the 1960s, educators have become increasingly aware of, knowledgeable about, and sensitized to how deeply children's development is influenced by their social and cultural contexts. Just as you and I want to be accepted for who we are, so too do children from diverse backgrounds want the same, full acceptance. Being aware of different cultures will help you be more open and accepting of children from cultures with which you may not be familiar.

America has always been characterized by the blending of many cultures, which has shaped this country into what it is today. Yet its basic values still reflect a western European tradition (Stewart & Bennett, 1991). European-American characteristics, such as individual responsibility for one's own actions, a strong work ethic, and a focus on the individual rather than the group, dominate American culture (Berns, 1997).

The following generalizations suggest a few key values and behaviors that children from different cultural groups bring with them to early childhood settings. Use them to increase your sensitivity, but remember that while these characteristics serve as a starting point to understand other cultures, they do not necessarily apply to all children of a particular cultural group. Thus, they should not be used rigidly (Berns, 1997).

African-American Children

- tend to be oriented toward feelings and personal interactions
- are more proficient at nonverbal communication than Anglo children are
- respond best to teaching strategies that emphasize cooperation over competition, such as cooperative learning groups
- have a rich aural tradition and learn best through listening and oral activities, such as read-alouds (Bennett, 1995)

Asian-American Children

- emphasize conformity, respect for authority, and submergence of individuality
- value family loyalty and responsibility for relatives
- respect education, achievement, authority, and self-control
- view teachers as having high status
- respect elders, deferred gratification (Feng, 1994)

Hispanic-American Children

- have a strong tradition of family, community, and ethnic loyalty (Garcia, 1992)
- value interpersonal relationships and a commitment to help others
- have close and personal relationships with parents and teachers
- are highly valued in their culture

Native American Children

- value self-determination, cultural preservation, and cultural pluralism (Banks, 1997)
- have a holistic and shared view of the world (Banks, 1997)
- approach elders with respect and high esteem
- are highly valued in the family group
- value sharing and cooperation
- are expected to learn by observation and to be patient (Berns, 1997)

The values, behaviors, languages, and traditions of individual cultures shape the children you will be caring for and teaching. You will be learning ways to make each child feel accepted and valued by other children and adults so that children can each develop the necessary feelings of self-worth so vital to their healthy development (Chipman, 1997). Knowing that children's development is shaped within their social and cultural worlds makes it imperative that you become sensitive to children's rich, diverse backgrounds as you attempt to make the best educational decisions for them. As you grow in becoming a teacher of young children, you will learn to enjoy and appreciate the richness of the diversity of the children you teach.

Major Theoretical Models

The best early childhood professionals use their knowledge of young children to guide and change their practices by connecting their practices to theories. The theories that follow are regularly used to explain what children are like. We discuss four theories from the fields of psychology and anthropology to help you think about different influences on development. We describe the key ideas of each theorist and then apply them to early childhood practice.

Psychosocial Theory of Erik Erikson (1902–1994)

Erikson's (1963) psychosocial theory emphasizes that development occurs throughout the life span in a series of stages, with each stage contributing to and being influenced by the one preceding and following it. He proposed eight psychosocial stages that are each characterized by a conflict or crisis that influences our social development and reflects the particular culture unique to each individual (Berk, 1996). According to Erikson, healthy, life-long, social interactions come from the successful resolution of the unique developmental tasks that an individual faces. How individuals resolve the social conflicts at each stage influences their attitudes and skills. Erikson re-interpreted Freud's psychosexual stages and placed more emphasis on the interactive nature of development and less emphasis on biological factors. Consequently, Erikson believed that children play an active role in shaping their experiences by the way they interact with their environments. He emphasized the role of developmental needs as a way to understand what age-appropriate social and emotional behavior should be. Erikson's theory is the most widely read and influential of the psychoanalytic theorists. Erikson was a German psychoanalyst who was strongly influenced by his studies with Sigmund Freud, the father of psychoanalysis. Table 3.6 describes each of Erikson's eight psychosocial stages and suggests applications for you to use as a child development specialist.

Table 3.6
Erikson's Eight Psychosocial Stages

Psychosocial Conflict	Developmental Ages	Key Characteristics	Major Outcomes	Significant Persons
Trust Versus Mistrust	Infancy (0–12 months)	• Infants' conflict centers on care and nurturance. • Their needs must be satisfied.	• If needs are met consistently, infants develop trust in others and a hopeful, confident outlook. • If needs are met inconsistently, infants do not develop the hope that they will receive the care they need.	• Responsive, sensitive, and consistent caregiver
Autonomy Versus Shame and Doubt	Toddlerhood (1–3 years)	• Toddlers' conflict centers on their ability to exert ownership over their bodies and actions after they develop trust and good feelings about themselves and their environment	• If toddlers have the opportunity to manage themselves and their environments appropriately, they develop autonomy, a sense of an emerging separate self, and will. • If the environment is so rigid that children feel overcontrolled by others, they resist such control and may become filled with doubt about their ability to control themselves successfully.	• Significant, consistent adult
Initiative Versus Guilt	Preschool Years (3–5 years)	• Preschoolers struggle between their ability to undertake and complete tasks and their fear of failing at those tasks and feeling guilty. They go back and forth between the wish to be big and independent and also to be helpless like a baby. • They generally will take responsibility for self-care, want to belong to a group, and begin to play together cooperatively.	• Preschoolers who show initiative have a sense of direction and purpose to their work and play. • Preschoolers who cannot test their independence and are punished too quickly may feel unnecessarily guilty.	• Basic family

Table 3.6
(Continued)

Psychosocial Conflict	Developmental Ages	Key Characteristics	Major Outcomes	Significant Persons
Industry Versus Inferiority	School-age Years (6–12 years)	• School-age children become increasingly focused on doing and making things; they want to do things well and to be competent. • They want to master intellectual and social tasks.	• School-age children who show a sense of industry demonstrate feelings of competence by a can-do attitude toward school tasks. • School-age children who do not feel industrious feel incompetent and often demonstrate a can't-do attitude toward school tasks.	• Neighbors, peers, and those at school
Intimacy Versus Isolation	Early Adulthood (20s and 30s)	• Adults at this stage are ready to form deep relations.	• If young adults have resolved their sense of identity, they develop a sense of love and loyalty. • A weak sense of self hinders forming intimate relationships and leads to a sense of isolation.	• Partners in sex, friendship, and cooperative ventures
Generativity Versus Stagnation	Middle Adulthood (40s and 50s)	• The focus is on the future and preparing the next generation of citizens through productivity and care.	• Those who have resolved previous crises in a healthy manner nurture their own children or other younger generations for the future and have the virtue of caring. • An unhealthy resolution leads to questions about usefulness and a sense of purpose in life.	• Shared lives and mentoring relationships
Ego Integrity Versus Despair	Late Adulthood	• The focus is on reviewing life's accomplishments.	• Resolution in a healthy way leads to feelings of integrity, full growth, and wisdom about contributing to society. • Resolution in a negative way leads to feelings of despair and hopelessness in being able to contribute to society.	• Society at large and personal sphere of significant others

Children need warm, loving, caring adults who understand their social needs during each period of development. Adults are the social and emotional models for children and have an extremely important role in helping them learn appropriate social interaction feelings and competencies. For example, infants need adults who consistently meet their needs, talk with them calmly, and nurture their feelings of trust. It is through such interactions that infants develop "a sense of a safe, interesting, and orderly world where they are understood and their actions bring pleasure to themselves and others" (Bredekamp & Copple, 1997, p. 58).

From Erikson, we gain support for the important role of play, which provides children with opportunities to practice appropriate social skills and develop feelings of competence. Children use pretend play as a way to make choices and decisions that increase their sense of autonomy and competence, and to master the social and cultural world in which they live (Erikson, 1963).

Adults can use Erikson's developmental stages to select appropriate children's literature to help children more easily cope with the critical problems they face at certain ages. For example, the theme of autonomy is clearly evident in *Where the Wild Things Are* (Sendak, 1964); initiative and adventure can be found in such books as *Moss Gown* (Hooks, 1987) and *Min Yo and the Moon Dragon* (Hillman, 1992); and a sense of industry or task orientation can be understood through *Island of the Blue Dolphins* (O'Dell, 1960) for older children and *Daniel's Story* (Matas, 1993) for younger children.

Cognitive Development Theory of Jean Piaget (1896–1980)

Piaget's theory of the stages of children's intellectual development focuses on how children's thinking, reasoning, and perception differ from those of adults. Piaget's cognitive development theory is based upon his in-depth, observational studies of his own children. These studies were used as a means of figuring out how children think about their worlds. Piaget's background as a biologist, with its emphasis on adaptation, strongly influenced his theory of cognitive development. The following four assumptions about cognitive development underlie Piaget's theory (Glassman, 1994).

1. Biological and environmental influences interact continuously to develop an individual's thinking, reasoning, and perceptual ability.
2. Cognitive development is initially the result of direct experience in an environment; eventually, children become capable of transforming their experiences mentally through internal reflection.
3. The pace of an individual's development is influenced by the social milieu.
4. Cognitive development involves major qualitative changes in one's thinking.

Piaget hypothesized that the thinking ability of all children, including those with special needs and from diverse backgrounds, moves through a series of four cognitive stages. The rate of progress through these stages varies from individual to individual, but each stage has unique characteristics. The first three stages occur during the childhood years; these include (a) the sensorimotor stage (0–2 years), during which infants and toddlers use their senses and reflexes to respond to their immediate world but do not think conceptually; (b) the preoperational thinking stage (2–7 years), during which children have an increased ability to think symbolically and conceptually about objects and people outside of their immediate environment, which is evident through children's increasing use of language and imaginative play; and (c) the concrete operational stage (7–12 years), which is characterized by the ability to use logical thought to solve concrete problems related to concepts of space, time, causality, and number. The fourth stage, formal operations (ages 12 and on), marks the beginning of logical and scientific thinking and is characterized by the ability to make predictions, think hypothetically, and think about thinking. Table 3.7 summarizes Piaget's first three stages of cognitive development and lists the major characteristics of each. (Piaget's cognitive development theory is discussed in greater detail in Chapter 4.)

Applying Piaget's Theory in Early Childhood Practice

Although Piaget never claimed to be an educator, his theory has greatly influenced our thinking about what early childhood teachers should do to promote children's intellectual development. First, early childhood settings should include a wide variety of interesting materials and experiences for all children. Because young children's thinking is

Opportunities for children to practice new skills helps them gain confidence.

EXPLORING YOUR ROLE AS A CHILD DEVELOPMENT SPECIALIST

Table 3.7
Piaget's Stages of Cognitive Development

Cognitive Stage	Approximate Age Range	Key Behavioral Characteristics	Practical Applications
Sensorimotor	birth–2 years	• react to stimuli with simple reflexes, such as rooting and sucking • develop first habits, such as sucking when shown a bottle • accidentally reproduce interesting events, such as kicking a mobile and hearing music (primary circular reaction) • focus on the world outside of self, such as imitating sounds of others (secondary circular reaction) • are interested in and curious about novel objects, what objects can do, and what they can do with objects, such as rolling a ball and knocking an object with it (tertiary circular reactions) • develop the concept of object permanence: the understanding that objects exist even when they cannot be seen	• provide stimulating, colorful, safe objects for infants and toddlers to reach for, grasp, and explore • encourage sounds and responses to stimuli such as clapping, singing, and cooing
Preoperational Thinking	2–7 years	• have the ability to mentally represent an object that is not present, as in pretending to drive a care while playing (symbolic function) • are egocentric, able to focus only on own perspective, not on those of others • project animism, giving life to inanimate objects, as in thinking that clouds cry • show centration in thinking, focusing attention on one characteristic of an object or event, such as color, shape, or size to the exclusion of others • display a rapid increase in language • use fantasy and imaginative play as natural modes of thinking	• provide props to represent images in children's environment • talk about how certain behaviors (e.g., pushing, grabbing) make others feel to reduce egocentrism • encourage classification of objects by shape, size, weight, or color • provide rhymes, songs, and poems that play with the English language and note similar sounds • provide opportunities to work in groups of two or three • encourage new gross motor activities that stretch children's comfort zones • provide open-ended activities (e.g., blocks, art, writing, pretend play) • provide sensory experiences
Concrete Operations	7–11 years	• can coordinate attributes at one time (reversibility) • classify and divide sets and subsets and consider their relationships (e.g., understanding that one's mother can also be somebody else's sister or daughter at the same time) • become more analytical and logical in their approach to words and grammar	• use concrete, manipulative objects and materials to help children draw conclusions • provide concrete materials as a bridge to representational thought • provide opportunities to make decisions and exchange points of view

SOURCE: Adapted from Children by J. W. Santrock, 1995, Madison, WI: Brown & Benchmark.

based on motor experiences, the optimum learning environment has interesting materials available to children at different levels of development. Such materials might include colorful stacking toys for infants, ample puzzles and construction materials for preschoolers and kindergartners, and board games and manipulative materials for school-age children. These materials must be worthy of children's attention to enhance the development of their thinking through exploration, experimentation, hypothesis testing, and reflection (Bredekamp & Copple, 1997).

Opportunities for play enhance children's practice with symbols. During play, you will notice that children practice what they know and use important thinking abilities, such as problem solving, negotiation, and decision making. The opportunity to practice new skills in a safe context is inherently satisfying to children. Such repetition may be as simple as grasping and dropping an object in infancy or repeatedly working the same puzzle, in and out of the frame, until all variations have been mastered. From Piaget we learn that as children develop, they practice different and more varied skills, and thus become more effective in their interactions with their environments.

Several different early childhood programs and practices have been designed explicitly using Piagetian principles, particularly the interaction patterns between adult and child. One such program is Educating the Young Thinker, an inquiry approach aimed at promoting the development of representational competence using language to provoke cognitive disequilibrium (Copple, Sigel, & Saunders, 1979). A second approach uses group games to promote the development of children's logic and social and moral values (Kamii & DeVries, 1980).

Cultural Context Theory of Urie Bronfenbrenner (1917–)

Bronfenbrenner (1979), an American developmental psychologist, emphasizes social and cultural influences on development (Santrock, 1995). These contexts—the family, educational setting, community, and broader society—are interrelated, and all have an impact on the developing child. For example, even though a child with a disability may live in a nurturing, accepting family and have support from peers and neighbors, the child may be affected by stereotypes and biases held by the community at large that could affect his or her development. Bronfenbrenner's model includes the following four different societal systems, each of which influences the others as well as the child's development.

1. *The microsystem* is where the child lives and experiences most of his or her interactions, such as the home, school, and neighborhood.

2. *The mesosystem* involves the relations between the microsystem and the larger environment, such as the connections between the family and school and the relations between the family and the neighborhood.

3. *The exosystem* includes the social settings that affect, but do not include the child, for example, the parents' work environment and government services such as parks and libraries. If, for example, a parent is highly stressed in the work environment, that parent's stress will often influence how the parent interacts with the child after work.

4. *The macrosystem* includes cultural influences—the values, beliefs, laws, and customs of a child's culture that are transmitted from generation to generation and affect the interactions among the family, school, and community in the child's immediate world, the microsystem.

Applying Bronfenbrenner's Model to Early Childhood Practice

Bronfenbrenner's model has a significant impact on how early childhood educators interact with children and their families. The most important applications occur at the microsystem level, where early childhood teachers can provide consistent support for children and their families. A significant application of Bronfenbrenner's theory involves knowing children in more than one context. Observing children in different social settings (e.g., the school and the home) and inviting families to provide their perspective and knowledge is essential for obtaining the most complete picture of individual development.

Hierarchy of Needs Theory of Abraham Maslow (1908–1970)

Humanistic psychologist Abraham Maslow (1954) formulated a theory of personality development based upon a hierarchy of universal basic and growth needs. Maslow suggested that these needs motivate individual behavior and lead to healthy growth and development when they are satisfied. Basic needs include physiological needs (e.g., food and drink) and safety and survival needs (e.g., physical and psychological security). Growth needs emerge as children's basic needs are met. Growth needs include the need for love and belonging (e.g., being accepted and belonging to a group both in the family and in the school). They also include the need for esteem that comes from recognition, approval, and achievement from both peers and adults that leads to a sense of competence and can-do feelings. Such feelings of self-worth are derived from authentic, not trivialized, accomplishments. As needs are met, individuals naturally tend to seek higher needs, the highest of which is self-actualization, the desire to use one's abilities and talents to the fullest. Motivation to satisfy growth needs increases when they are being met and decreases when they are not being met. In Maslow's scheme, children whose basic safety needs are clearly being met will naturally seek stronger needs for love, belonging, and so forth, up the pyramid of needs.

Applying Maslow's Theory to Early Childhood Practice

Adults who care for children must know which of their basic and growth needs are or are not being met if they are to help children grow and develop in healthy ways. If children's needs for food, shelter, and safety are not being met, they will require additional support to be successful in school. Providing predictable routines offers children a sense of security in the daily schedule that makes them feel secure in their setting. On the other hand, some children may be well fed and housed but feel threatened or unloved and may protect themselves by withdrawing from group involvement. Because children's physical, health, and safety needs often are threatened today, all early childhood educators not only must be prepared to provide adequate health, safety, and nutrition, but also must know how to access other services, such as physical, dental, and social services. Additionally, parents and teachers must help children feel like a part of the family or school group to satisfy the needs for belonging and love.

From these four theorists, we learn that there are many approaches to learning about children's growth and development. We also learn that no one theoretical perspective tells us all we would like to know. Knowing about multiple approaches to child development enables us to select and use whatever is best for each child at a given time.

Conclusion

Understanding what children are like is a critical first step in facilitating their healthy growth and development. Thorough observations of children in all contexts, supplemented with a growing knowledge of typical patterns of growth and development through all periods of development, as well as a firm grounding in psychological theories, are necessary to meet the needs of all children and to detect special needs as early as possible. These understandings will help you make better decisions about your own educational practices in whatever early childhood setting you might be in.

One Child, Three Perspectives: *Angelica's Baby Pictures*

Angelica is a 4-year-old child who was adopted from Bolivia, South America, at age 2. Angelica lives with her mother, a single parent, in a diverse community near a major city.

Angelica's preschool class was studying about how living things grow and change. On this particular day, Angelica came home from school crying because she couldn't do her homework. Angelica's teacher, Ms. Kane, had sent home a piece of adding-machine tape with the following directions: "Cut the paper to the length you were when you were born, and please bring a photo of you when you were a baby, so we can see how much bigger you are now and how different you look now that you are older."

Angelica had spent her first 22 months of life living with a foster family in South America and came to this country with only the clothes on her body. There were no photos and only a little medical history. Angelica's mother will never know what Angelica looked like when she was a baby, when she said her first word, or when she took her first step.

Because Angelica was so sad, her mother made an appointment to speak with Ms. Kane. Ms. Kane explained that she was having her class make books about themselves, including special information about when they were babies. Ms. Kane seemed to think this was a perfectly appropriate activity for preschoolers and could not understand why Angelica was so upset.

During the course of the conversation between Angelica's mother and Ms. Kane, Angelica's mother shared how this seemingly harmless activity created a series of painful questions between Angelica and her mother about Angelica's past. She could not be told who her birth parents were, why they didn't want to keep her, whether there were pictures of her when she was a baby, what she looked like, or who friends were. Angelica's mother reminded Ms. Kane that she had filled out the family questionnaire at the start of the school year and reported that Angelica was adopted; she was surprised that Ms. Kane had selected an adoption-insensitive assignment for Angelica and her classmates.

Ms. Kane decided to seek more information about adoption sensitive assignments, so she talked with the community social worker who served the preschool. During their conversation, Ms. Kane learned that certain typical school projects, such as finding baby pictures, making family trees, learning about family heritage, and making Mother's Day presents, may cause emotional turmoil for children who are adopted. The social worker told Ms. Kane how important it was for her to be sensitive to the needs of adopted children, because even though they don't appear to be different, their needs are somewhat unique, and to never dismiss adoption-insensitive issues as insignificant, because, to adopted children, they are not. She also reminded Ms. Kane that children do not like to feel different and that anything teachers of young children can do to affirm who they are contributes to their sense of self. The social worker invited Ms. Kane to talk with the other preschool staff members and determine their interest in a staff development seminar entitled "Adoption Awareness in the Schools," which she would be happy to conduct.

REACT:	Think about how the perspectives of Angelica's mother, Ms. Kane, and the social worker are alike and different. What might be some reasons? With whom do you identify most in this case? Why?
RESEARCH:	Call several adoption agencies and look on the World Wide Web to locate information and materials that will help you learn more about what adopted children are like and what they need. A good source is the Center for Adoptive Families, 10230 New Hampshire Avenue, Suite 200, Silver Spring, MD 20903 (Telephone: 301 439-2900). What key characteristics of adopted children did you find that apply to child development?
REFLECT:	What assumptions about adopted children do Ms. Kane, the social worker, and Angelica's mother hold? Generate some ways you can be adoption-sensitive in your setting, such as having children make gifts for other family members on Mother's Day or Father's Day if children have only one or no parents.

IN-CLASS WORKSHOP

Understanding Inclusion

In the Ask the Expert feature earlier in this chapter, Richard Gargiulo talks about inclusion—the belief "that all young children with special needs should receive intervention and educational services in settings designed for youngsters without disabilities, that is, in normalized environments such as child-care centers, Head Start programs, or regular kindergartens." He urges all teachers of young children to focus on children's abilities, not on their disabilities, because a child is first and foremost a child. If you visit an inclusive early childhood setting, you will notice children with disabilities who are part of a community of learners in a regular classroom setting, a team of professionals (special and regular education teachers, paraprofessionals, and other support personnel) collaborating to modify and adapt the learning environment for individual children, and teachers who take responsibility for helping all children learn and succeed in the regular classroom.

FIGURE 3.1

The division for early
childhood of the
council for
exceptional children
position on inclusion*

Inclusion, as a value, supports the right of all children, regardless of their diverse abilities, to participate actively in natural settings within their communities. A natural setting is one in which the child would spend time had he or she not had a disability. Such settings include but are not limited to home and family, play groups, child care, nursery schools, Head Start programs, kindergartens, and neighborhood school classrooms.

DEC believes in and supports full and successful access to health, social service, education, and other supports and services for young children and their families that promote full participation in community life. DEC values the diversity of families and supports a family guided process for determining services that are based on the needs and preferences of individual families and children.

To implement inclusive practices DEC supports: (a) the continued development, evaluation, and dissemination of full inclusion supports, services, and systems so that options for inclusion are of high quality; (b) the development of preservice and inservice training programs that prepare families, administrators, and service providers to develop and work within inclusive settings; (c) collaboration among all key stakeholders to implement flexible fiscal and administrative procedures in support of inclusion; (d) research that contributes to our knowledge of state of the art services; and (e) the restructuring and unification of social, education, health, and intervention supports and services to make them more responsive to the needs of all children and families.

*Endorsed by NAEYC, April 1994

SOURCE: From *Position on Inclusion* by the Division for Early Childhood of the Council of Exceptional Children, 1993, Reston, VA.

Early childhood teachers are increasingly being expected to teach in inclusive settings. This movement has been supported by several national associations and is reflected in the position statement, shown in Figure 3.1, that was developed by the Council for Exceptional Children, Division for Early Childhood in 1993 and endorsed by the NAEYC in 1994. Read this position statement to help you (a) explore the ideas behind inclusion, (b) examine your own attitudes towards children with special needs, and (c) think about your beliefs about the capacity of children with special needs to learn in a regular early childhood setting. Then respond to the following questions.

1. What do think about these ideas? Do any of them cause you concern? If so, name them and try to describe what concerns you.

2. What questions does this position paper raise for you?

3. How do the ideas in this paper relate to those that Richard Gargiulo expressed in the Ask the Expert feature earlier in this chapter? Be prepared to share one of your ideas with the whole group.

What Is Inclusion?

There are many reasons to include young children with disabilities in the regular early childhood setting. Inclusion can benefit children with and without disabilities, teachers, and families of all of the children. Based upon your answers to the preceding questions, brainstorm statements that describe what inclusion is and what inclusion is not. Use the following example as a starting point then complete your own comparison chart.

INCLUSION IS	INCLUSION IS NOT
Children who have disabilities attending regular early childhood programs.	Placing children with disabilities in regular classrooms without the support and services they need to be successful.
Regular education teachers using innovative strategies for the varied learning needs of children in the class.	Separate pull-out programs for children according to their disabilities.

SOURCE: Adapted from "Discover the Possibilities, PEAK Parent Center," Winter, 1990, *Proceedings of the School Leaders' Institute on Inclusive Education, Syracuse University Inclusive Education Project*, 3(1).

Once you have completed your chart, think about why inclusion is or is not needed for children with special needs.

Exploring Your Role in Fostering Children's Learning

The overwhelmingly majority of teachers . . . are unable to name or describe a theory of learning that underlies what they do in the classroom, but what they do—what any of us does—is no less informed by theoretical assumptions just because these assumptions are invisible. Behind [teaching practice] is a theory that embodies distinct assumptions about the nature of knowledge, the possibility of choice, and what it means to be a human being.

—Alfie Kohn, 1993, p. 10

Learning Outcomes

✔ Understand the learning processes in early childhood education

✔ Examine the features of authentic learning

✔ Explore learner-centered teaching and learning and explain the cycle of learning

✔ Describe the major learning theories and their implications for the very young

✔ Examine the influence of teachers' beliefs on their teaching practices

✔ Consider the central role of play in children's learning

Meet the Teachers

Mrs. Suarez teaches toddlers in a local child-care setting. If you visit her class, you will see Mrs. Suarez sitting on an oversized pillow on the floor while reading books to a small group of children, one of whom is sitting on her lap. She is talking to them about the imaginary characters they have seen in their books. Mrs. Suarez believes that it is important to talk with and read to children regularly, and she helps the children's parents do the same in their homes. She suggests that parents use short, simple sentences to talk with their children and helps them find good books to read to their infants and toddlers, because, as she says, "Children's brains are being wired for learning from birth."

Ms. Burke coteaches in an inclusive preschool setting. She and her coteacher recently began to teach with themes that are planned in response to children's interests and questions. This different way of teaching raised several questions for Ms. Burke, such as, "Where will I find ideas for next week?" "How can I really plan for children's learning based on their interests and still meet the long-range goals that my school system requires?" Ms. Burke was asking herself these questions at the same time that her school was being renovated and the children expressed interest about the renovation—the trucks, the heavy equipment, and the demolition that was taking place daily in and around the school. She decided to take her children on a tour of the construction site. During the resulting theme study, she and the children photographed the workers and the machinery, created a pictorial time line that documented the transformation of the building, gathered a variety of picture books about construction, collected tools and toys for the children to use, and read *The Three Little Pigs* to help children extend their concept of building. Ms. Burke noticed that the children talked with each other more about the school construction, were less dependent on her for ideas in their play, and needed less adult direction in their learning experiences. Ms. Burke now considers children's needs and interests in her planning, writing an individualized education program, and initiating staff referrals for a child because, she says, "I am more in tune with how children's thinking and abilities influence their learning."

Ms. Dombrowski, the math lead teacher for the primary grades in her elementary school, uses math journals in her first grade as one way to integrate the 13 national mathematics standards in her curriculum. Ms. Dombrowski has read many articles about writing in mathematics to assess children's mathematical understandings. She uses the knowledge she has gained from them to introduce math journals to her first graders because, she says, "Communication in mathematics helps the children clarify their ideas and enables me to understand how they are thinking, what mathematical knowledge they possess, and how they express that knowledge." Ms. Dombrowski's first graders write word problems, counting sequences, and particular patterns that have to do with the mathematical concepts of missing addends, counting money, telling time, and place value. Sometimes the children write alone, but sometimes they write with a partner, because Ms. Dombrowski believes "that true understanding of mathematics comes from interacting and talking about ideas and strategies." She shared her students' mathematical progress with other teachers for the primary grades, and they now include journal writing as part of the mathematics curriculum.

Each of these teachers understands the different ways children learn. Using the following questions, consider these teachers' understandings about how children learn, and compare, contrast, and connect them with your thinking.

COMPARE:	What are some similarities in the ways that these three teachers help children learn?
CONTRAST:	What do these teachers think about how young children learn? What differences do you notice in the ways they have used to foster children's learning?
CONNECT:	What impressed you most about these teachers' views of learning? How do you think you will incorporate these ideas with children? Why?

A Definition of Learning

Picture the difference in yourself when you are learning something new and when you are doing something that you have already learned. In which situation do you feel more confident about demonstrating what you know? While there are many different theories about what learning is, most agree that learning is the natural process of making sense of information and experiences that is fostered through interactions with others. Learning "occurs when [there is] a relatively permanent change in an individual's knowledge or behavior that is dependent upon prior experience and can be determined through performance" (Woolfolk, 1995, p. 196). To illustrate, recall what it was like when you first learned to drive a car. You knew it was a natural activity for most teenagers and adults, but you first needed to figure out how to shift to drive forward, reverse, parallel park, brake, and so forth. The more practice you had behind the wheel with a more experienced driver, the deeper your prior knowledge of driving helped your driving become better each time. Now, some years later, you can see a permanent change in your driving behavior since the first day you took the wheel.

Recent research in multiple intelligences (Gardner 1991, 1993), multicultural education (Banks & Banks, 1997), and cognitive and neurosciences (Caine & Caine, 1997) has contributed to our deeper understanding of how all people think and learn. This research has clear implications for learning in early childhood settings, because it provides evidence that all children can and do learn regardless of their diverse backgrounds and innate learning abilities.

PAUSE AND REFLECT ABOUT LEARNING

Think about one of your most successful learning experiences. What made it meaningful, memorable, and enjoyable? Now think about one of your least successful learning experiences. What made it uninteresting, irrelevant, and discouraging? Make a list of the characteristics of each and compare and contrast them. What observations do you notice?

Features of Authentic Learning Experiences

People learn best when they believe in themselves and are confident that they can learn (Bandura, 1997). Authentic learning experiences resemble situations that people naturally encounter outside the classroom and that make sense to them (Kauchak & Eggen, 1998). The following scenario involving Danielle and Maria, two preschool children, illustrates what early childhood educators need to consider an authentic learning experience.

Danielle and Maria were building with large, hollow blocks during center time. Together, they decided to build a maze for their animal figures so they could have an animal relay race. They collected blocks, built large enclosed spaces with side openings and lanes to connect each space, wrote signs that said Start, Stop, and Tickets, and gathered a variety of animal figures from the box of accessories nearby. While the girls were concentrating intently on their building and deciding which animals were going to participate in the relay race, their teacher passed by the block building area. Here is what she noticed: Danielle and Maria were (a) measuring space, (b) writing their signs, (c) selecting the correct number of blocks to build each side of their enclosures, (d) using two small blocks to equal one long block (which demonstrated an understanding of equivalency), and (e) classifying when putting away their blocks according to like shapes at the end of their project.

The scenario involving Danielle and Maria shows these children naturally making sense out of their block play. Together, they are engaged in a project that enables them to demonstrate what they know about measurement, spatial relations, and early literacy through real, or authentic, learning. Authentic learning develops learners who see possibilities and want to know about things; nonauthentic learning develops learners who want to give correct answers and do exactly what their teachers want them to do (Elkind, 1989). The following features characterize authentic learning experiences for all children.

1. *Authentic learning experiences use children's prior knowledge to actively engage them in personally meaningful, purposeful activities.* All children learn by both doing and thinking about what they are doing. Merely manipulating objects does not assure that mental engagement will occur. For example, when young children are taught to use quality children's literature, such as *Chicken Soup with Rice* (Sendak, 1962), they are not only being exposed to a wide array of concepts and language, but they are also more likely to be interested in reading. Such an experience differs greatly from one that teaches children to read isolated words printed on flash cards. Older children enjoy mathematical experiences, such as using supermarket advertisements of familiar products to do price-comparison shopping for certain foods. Each of these examples actively connects children to their real world of experience.

2. *Authentic learning experiences promote strategic thinking.* Teaching children to be strategic thinkers is the heart of good teaching and learning, because we then teach specific skills in contexts that the learners need to use. In learning to become better readers, for example, all children need command of how and when to use a variety of strategies. Using picture cues, making predictions, and asking questions for advance organizers all help children apply the skills they need as readers. Strategic thinking allows children to discover new meanings and understandings and to develop the reflective skills that will make them independent learners (Gardner, 1991).

3. *Authentic learning experiences foster learning through social interactions.* Vygotsky (1978) argued that learning is a social process and that children first learn new knowledge through social relations with others, which they later internalize. Starting from birth, children's communication with others is essentially social. They use language for different purposes: to ask for something they need, to get things done, to find out information, and to maintain relations with others (Halliday, 1975; Santrock, 1995). Communicating and sharing ideas with others promotes improved collective understanding and provokes appropriate higher-level thinking skills.

4. *Authentic learning experiences are based on each child's different ways of learning and displaying their knowledge.* Because learning is individual and developmental, not all children learn in the same way or at the same rate, or have the same interests in how to learn. Howard Gardner (1993) suggests that we all construct knowledge through at least eight different intelligences, which provide multiple ways of learning skills, concepts, and strategies. (See Table 4.4 and the In-class Workshop at the end of this chapter for a description of Gardner's eight intelligences.) Similarly, we demonstrate what we know in different ways. A good example of this is a study of the rain forest by a second-grade class. The children read books about the rain forest, such as *Save My Rain Forest* (Zak, 1992), learned specific vocabulary words related to the rain forest, and wrote stories about tropical evergreens and endangered species. Some children counted and graphed a vast array of evergreens and endangered species, and some made a class mural depicting the different species of plant and animal life. Throughout their study, the second graders

transformed their classroom into a rain forest and invited their families to come and experience all that they had learned. Some children read and told stories about specific life forms in the rain forest; others tape-recorded information sessions and provided their parents with headphones to listen to their recordings about life and life cycles. What did the children learn? Aside from vocabulary words, they practiced the reading, writing, oral language, mathematical, and science skills that were expected at the second-grade level in their school district. When early childhood teachers consider children's multiple ways of learning, it means that children at any age can approach almost any topic from a variety of meaningful learning perspectives.

5. *Authentic learning experiences enable children to make sense of their learning by applying it to other situations.* Research from the cognitive and neurosciences suggests that most learners have difficulty appropriately applying knowledge learned in one setting to a different setting (Gardner, 1991). Being able to transfer knowledge, skills concepts, and strategies from one situation to another is an essential aspect of learning. When younger children learn to use picture cues to "read" a story from one book, they use that strategy over and over again in "reading" other books. When older children learn to read to the end of a sentence to get its meaning before sounding out an unfamiliar word, they are using the context of the sentence to increase their reading comprehension and then use that strategy in other reading situations.

What makes this an authentic learning experience?

These features of authentic learning highlight how central learners are to the learning process. Because teachers are expected to reach all learners, all early childhood educators need to consider these features in planning individual and group experiences for young children.

FEATURING FAMILIES

WHAT IS A GOOD LEARNING EXPERIENCE?

Children's interests are important sources of good learning experiences; these interests provide opportunities for developing and expanding knowledge and skills. The following example shows how teachers can help parents understand how to capitalize on children's interests as an important part of their learning.

Ms. Davis sent the following "homework" assignment to parents.

Dear _____:

Please take a few minutes to watch or remember your child at play. Then answer the following questions and return this paper to school **tomorrow**.

1. What activity does your child **spend the most time** doing?

2. How long does your child spend doing the above activity?

3. What activity does your child **spend the least time doing or does not do at all?**

4. List three or four of your child's favorite playthings.

This information will help me know your child better, so I can plan activities that will interest him or her. I'll share our activity calendar for next month in a few weeks and will send home an activity that is special for you and your child.

Thank you for your time.

Beth Davis

Child's Name _____

Adult's Signature _____

As a follow-up, Ms. Davis sent home the following activity to one family.

Dear _____:

Thank you for answering my questions the other day. You say that Antonio likes to play with cars and watch TV. For his homework tonight, I asked him to complete the activity on this paper and to ask you to help him with it.

Activity: Select a 10–15 minute segment of a TV show to watch with Antonio. About 10 minutes before the show, tell him you want him to keep track of the number and kind of cars in the show. Ask him what he will need to do this. Get his supplies together, then watch the show. After the show, ask him to show you how he kept track of the cars. Ask him how many of each kind of car he saw. Then ask him to draw a picture of the one he liked the best.

Did he have a method for keeping track of the cars?   Yes   No

Could he tell you how many cars were in the show?   Yes   No

Did he tell you about his favorite car?   Yes   No

Please have Antonio bring this sheet, plus his car record and picture, to school tomorrow. I hope you enjoyed this activity and discovered some of what Antonio is learning about numbers and solving problems.

Thank you for your help.

Beth Davis

Your Role as a Facilitator of Learning

Being a facilitator of learning—one who is a partner with children in the learning process—is one way to maximize your significant influence on the children in your care. As a facilitator, you view "learners as active participants in the learning process" (Caine & Caine, 1997, p. 18) and you view your role as engaging children in learning and promoting their understanding rather than simply transmitting knowledge. With this disposition to learn along with others, you become a life-long learner who has the capacity to explore, satisfy curiosity, meet new challenges, and love learning. Your commitment to learning enables children to value its importance—a message that is as critical as the content you teach. It also honors the reciprocity between you and the learner, and it exemplifies the simple but powerful words of Robert Fulghum, "All I ever needed to know I learned from my kindergarten students." Your role as a facilitator can be guided by the following principles about learning.

1. *Teachers' beliefs about learning affect children's learning.* What you believe about how children learn guides your interactions with individuals and groups of children, your daily schedule, and your room arrangement. In early childhood settings, teachers and

caregivers interact with children in different ways. Some use open-ended questions to probe children's thinking; others use closed questions that focus on factual information. These interactions reflect not only certain theoretical perspectives, but also your beliefs about how children learn. This personal belief system greatly influences what you do, constitutes a large part of your teaching, and has a powerful impact on your ability to promote learning (Good & Brophy, 1997).

2. Teachers create opportunities for colearning. As a partner in learning, you must be skilled at selecting the appropriate learning materials and play props that will help children move from learning with assistance to learning independently. For example, when young children can consistently solve a particular kind of math problem using manipulatives, they next need to try to solve it using pictures, and then finally solve it only in their minds. These different levels of learning indicate the types of support children require to internalize the concepts that lead them toward independence. As a colearner, planning how and when to use materials to support children's learning at different levels is one of the most challenging tasks you will encounter, because supporting children's learning helps them gain confidence in their own capacity to learn (Bodrova & Leong, 1996).

3. Teachers encourage social interactions and shared experiences to increase learning. Because social interaction is central to learning, learners need many opportunities to share and compare their thinking with that of others. The others can be peers or adults who provide opportunities to refine and develop thinking. As a facilitator, you can increase learning in your setting with some of the following strategies that rely on social interactions: cooperative learning, peer tutoring, cross-age tutoring, group investigations, sociodramatic play, and sociodramatic play centers. Each of these strategies respects students as resources in constructing their own learning.

4. Teachers model and teach life-long learning skills. Life-long learning skills enable you to engage in continuous learning. The following skills are needed to be a life-long learner: "confidence ("I can do it"), motivation ("I want to do it"), effort ("I'm willing to try hard"), responsibility ("I follow through on commitments"), initiative ("I am a self-starter"), perseverance ("I finish what I start"), caring ("I show concern for others"), teamwork ("I work cooperatively with others"), common sense ("I use good judgment"), and problem solving ("I use my knowledge and experience effectively")" (Rich, 1992, in Berns, 1997, p. 324).

The Importance of Learner-Centered Experiences

Think back to the way you learned in school. Were you mostly concerned with memorizing facts and reciting correct answers to your teachers' questions? Or do you remember having opportunities to ask questions about different subjects and processes, becoming involved in answering many of your own questions, and pursuing some of your own ideas? Both of these ways of learning are common in schools. While you probably remember what you learned in school, do you also remember how you felt while learning and what your teachers did to keep you interested in learning? Educators are changing their understanding of learning from a passive view of learners who accumulate information through a series of reinforcement techniques to an active view of learners who utilize learning strategies to discover and process information (American Psychological Association, 1993; Goleman, 1995; Gardner, 1991; Piaget, 1970; Vygotsky, 1978).

A learner-centered focus means that you know how each learner "understands his or her world and approaches the process of learning" (McCombs & Whisler, 1997, p. xii). This focus addresses (a) children's basic learning needs, (b) brain-based learning research principles, (c) life-long learning, (d) social and emotional learning as well as intellectual learning, and (e) child-initiated and child-directed learning. These five principles are described in the following paragraphs.

Learner-centered Experiences Meet Children's Basic Learning Needs. All children have three basic learning needs: the need to belong and feel supported, the need to have personal control and responsibility, and the need to demonstrate competence through meaningful educational experiences (Karsenti & Thibert, 1995; McCombs & Whisler, 1997; Thorkildsen, Nolen, & Fournier, 1994). A learner-centered approach to teaching addresses all of these needs by making learning relevant to children's lives, developing positive feelings, and maintaining children's motivation, involvement, and success in learning (McCombs, 1993).

Learner-centered Experiences are Based on Brain Research. New research in medical and cognitive sciences is increasing our knowledge of the brain's role in learning. This research suggests 12 brain-based learning principles that enable educators to help children become better learners (Caine & Caine, 1997) and confirm what early childhood educators have always known: that the early years are critical years for building a strong foundation for learning. Figure 4.1 lists four major principles of brain-based learning.

Brain research also illustrates the importance of the first 3 years of life for "wiring" pathways in the brain for a lifetime of learning. These pathways develop from children's positive stimulation with adults, events, and objects. They also affect how children learn, their interactions with others, and their beliefs about themselves, all of which they carry throughout life (Caine & Caine, 1997; Newberger, 1997). Understanding brain research is essential for preparing learners who can "learn spontaneously, independently, and collaboratively, without coercion" (Abbott, 1997, p. 10) in order to be successful citizens of the 21st century.

Learner-centered Experiences Focus on Life-Long Learning. Educational experiences involve all learners across the life span from birth through old age. In conceptualizing

FIGURE 4.1

Four major principles of brain-based learning

1. **Functioning.** The brain operates on different levels (for example, conscious and subconscious) and in different ways simultaneously. These functions include physiology, thoughts, emotions, imaginations, and predispositions.

2. **Feelings.** The brain is fundamentally social. Human relationships and emotions profoundly influence the ways in which the brain processes information.

3. **Patterning.** The brain searches for meaning through patterns. It identifies the familiar and responds to novel stimuli. It perceives parts and wholes.

4. **Learning.** The brain's tendency to seek greater complexity is enhanced and inhibited by threat.

SOURCE: Adapted from *Education on the Edge of Possibility*, by R. N. Caine and G. Caine, 1997, Alexandria, VA: Association for Supervision and Curriculum Development.

The brain is impacted by human relationships and emotions.

how we learn new knowledge, skills, attitudes, and dispositions, Bredekamp and Rosegrant (1992) propose a cycle of learning that all learners experience. They describe a four-step recursive learning cycle that begins with awareness, moves to exploration, then to inquiry, and finally to utilization. Think about yourself now as you begin to learn to teach young children. You are at the beginning of a new learning cycle about learning to teach. Suppose, for example, that you have observed a smoothly operating early childhood setting where children work at centers, and now you are trying to learn how to manage several small groups of children engaged in different learning tasks at the same time. Your *awareness* might consist of paying closer attention to how experienced teachers orchestrate several groups; your *exploration* might consist of trying it yourself and noticing what happens when you work with several small groups simultaneously; and your *inquiry* might involve further application of what you are learning as well as a comparison with what others are doing with the same skill. At this stage, you adapt your practice based upon what you know about the process and what you have experienced. Lastly, you *utilize* this skill in a way that enhances children's learning and enables you to monitor children's learning at multiple levels and of multiple tasks simultaneously. This cycle repeats itself many times over, because once you uti-

Table 4.1
The Cycle of Learning

	What Children Do	*What Teachers Do*
Awareness	Experience	Create the environment
	Acquire an interest	Provide opportunities by introducing new objects, events, people
	Recognize broad parameters	
	Attend	Invite interest by posing problem or question
	Perceive	Respond to child's interest or shared experience
		Show interest, enthusiasm
Exploration	Observe	Facilitate
	Explore materials	Support and enhance exploration
	Collect information	Provide opportunities for active exploration
	Discover	Extend play
	Create	Describe child's activity
	Figure out components	Ask open-ended questions—"What else could you do?"
	Construct own understanding	Respect child's thinking and rule systems
	Apply own rules	Allow for constructive error
	Create personal meaning	
	Represent own meaning	
Inquiry	Examine	Help children refine understanding
	Investigate	Guide children, focus attention
	Propose explanations	Ask more focused questions—"What else works like this?" "What happens if. . .?"
	Focus	
	Compare own thinking with that of others	Provide information when requested—"How do you spell. . .?"
	Generalize	Help children make connections
	Relate to prior learning	
	Adjust to conventional rule systems	
Utilization	Use the learning in many ways; learning becomes functional	Create vehicles for application in real world
	Represent learning in various ways	Help children apply learning to new situations
	Apply learning to new situations	Provide meaningful situations in which to use learning
	Formulate new hypotheses and repeat cycle	

SOURCE: From *Reaching Potentials: Appropriate Curriculum and Assessment for Young Children, Vol. 1* (p. 33), by S. Bredekamp & T. Rosegrant (Eds.), 1992, Washington, DC: National Association for the Education of Young Children. Reprinted with permission.

lize your knowledge of managing small groups, you develop new awareness about some of the gaps in what you know or do not know about managing small learning groups. The more you revisit the learning cycle, the deeper your knowledge or skill becomes. Table 4.1 illustrates the cycle of learning and the teacher's role in supporting children at each of its recursive stages.

Learner-centered Experiences Enhance Social and Emotional Competence as Well as Intellectual Learning. An essential outcome of school for all children is to become "knowledgeable, responsible and caring adults" (Association for Supervision and Curriculum Development, 1997). Learner-centered experiences help children become *knowledgeable* because they naturally motivate children to learn and help them use new information in their lives. They help children become *responsible* by offering them opportunities to make decisions that affect others as well as themselves; and they encourage *caring* behavior by providing opportunities to learn that caring is an essential component of a community in which individuals are concerned about others as well as themselves. The ability to manage the social and emotional aspects of one's life in a complex world is an important yet "different way of being smart" and is a basic responsibility of all educators (Goleman, 1995). Attending systematically to children's social and emotional competence increases children's academic achievement, decreases problem behaviors, and improves children's interpersonal relationships (ASCD, 1997).

Learner-centered Experiences are Child Initiated and Child Directed. Learning experiences that enable children to assume some responsibility for their own learning are referred to as child initiated or child directed. Recall your positive memories about learning. You probably remember being able to pursue ideas that interested you, being given reasons for why you were being asked to learn something, or being trusted to make other meaningful learning choices. These attributes help learners take control of and responsibility for their own learning and instill intrinsic motivation in the learner (McCombs & Whisler, 1997). Early childhood teachers who use child-directed learning experiences are reflecting Dewey's (1916) theory of progressive education, in which the overarching purpose of schooling is to prepare students for the realities of today's and tomorrow's world. Educators assume that children are capable of making good learning choices, that the process of learning is just as important as the product children produce, and that learning to make decisions is an important skill and a fundamental right in a democratic society. While child-initiated and child-directed learning is an important part of learner-centered experiences, it is important to realize that a balance between learner-centered and teacher-centered experiences must be found for children to have the learning opportunities they need to succeed in this complex world.

These five generalizations remind us as teachers of the centrality of our students in learning. This applies to both content and process ways of learning. In the next section, we focus on the role of play as one of the primary ways young children learn.

How Play Contributes to Children's Learning

Understanding how play helps children learn is an important part of becoming a teacher of young children. You might have overheard conversations with parents of young children who say, "But all my child does is play." or ask, "When is he or she going to learn something?" How will you respond when you are the child's teacher? Knowing why play is the catalyst for children's learning will help you answer these questions. It will also help you understand that the absence of play in young children is often an obstacle to their capacity for healthy growth, development, and learning.

A Definition of Play

Think about the following scenario in a Head Start classroom where two children are preparing a pretend birthday celebration for the child who plays the role of the mother. When they realize they need a present, one of the children says, "We can ask Mr. Bear." This is a reference to the book *Ask Mr. Bear* by Marjorie Flack (1932) in which Danny tries to find the perfect birthday present for his mother by asking many different animals for suggestions. After the children locate the book in their library center, they take on the roles of the different animals in the book—the goat, the cow, the hen, the goose, and the bear— as they search for a birthday present for their "mother." When they finish the celebration for their "mother," they plan another celebration for their pretend sister. The book becomes the content for role-playing, trying out different intonations that might sound like these animals, and talking with each other about how to enact their pretend birthday celebration. This particular scenario illustrates the definition of play as any activity that is freely chosen, meaningful, active, enjoyable, and open-ended (Fromberg, 1995). Play is an important condition for learning that demonstrates the following unique characteristics.

Play is symbolic and enables children to demonstrate what they know about certain concepts. Symbolic play enables children to represent reality as they mentally think through solutions to problems (a "what if" attitude) and deepen their thinking (an "as if" attitude). For the two Head Start children, the "what if" thinking

Adults need to value the importance of children's play.

occurred when they imagined the roles of the animals; the "as if" behavior occurred when they actually pretended to talk like the animals.

Play is meaningful and helps children make sense out of their experiences. In the preceding scenario, the children were relating what they knew about birthdays to the content of the book they had heard, *Ask Mr. Bear.*

Play is active and is a natural process of doing something both mentally and physically. The children's re-enactment of the familiar story demonstrates how they "learned by doing" by exploring the roles of the animals and inventing their own version of a birthday celebration.

Play is pleasurable and supports children's different ways of learning even when the activity is serious. The idea that children's enjoyment can actually enhance their learning is often difficult to understand and accept, yet we know that the two Head Start children are enjoying their re-enactment and at the same time seriously preparing a birthday celebration for the child who plays the role of the mother.

Play is voluntary and intrinsically motivating, and it capitalizes on children's curiosity through personally meaningful and purposeful experiences. The children's initiative in locating the book and establishing the scenario to enact is a good illustration of this characteristic.

Play is rule-governed, whether the rules are implied or expressed, and allows children to apply rules to different settings. In play, children establish and sometimes change the rules; nevertheless, there are rules for appropriate role behavior and the responsibilities of the players. These rules organize children's play, as is evident in the roles taken on in the preceding scenario.

Play is episodic in that there are emerging and shifting goals throughout the experience that foster children's strategic thinking. In the play scenario described earlier, the children completed their enactment of the birthday party for the child who plays the role of the mother and then immediately began to plan another birthday party for their sister, shifting the focus of the play.

In play, children construct understandings of their world, become empowered to do things for themselves, and experience social competence. These are essential learning processes. In addition, the play context contributes to children's learning across all of the domains (Isenberg & Jalongo, 1997; Wassermann, 1990).

The Importance of Play

Most educators do not understand how play or playful ways of knowing help children learn. If you ask teachers of young children what play is, they might say, "It is when children are dressing up and pretending, or using games, or going outside during recess." These views of play are limited mostly to physical activity and do not represent how play contributes to all aspects of children's development, how it helps children construct knowledge, or how it helps children learn.

In the field of early education, play has long been respected as the primary way young children learn. According to Bredekamp and Copple (1997), research and theories across disciplines support the notion that "play gives children opportunities to understand their world, interact with others in social ways, express and control emotions, and develop their symbolic capabilities" (p. 14). The work of Vygotsky and Piaget illustrates the important role of play. According to Vygotsky (1978), play is a "leading factor in development [because] in play a child behaves beyond his average, above his daily behavior; in play it is as though he were a head taller than himself" (p. 102). According to Piaget (1980), "play is a powerful form of activity that fosters the social life and constructive activity of the child" (p. viii). Moreover, through play, children also discover what they can do, test their physical and mental abilities, and compare these with those of their peers. While play is important for all children, it is particularly important for children with special needs (e.g., delays in motor, speech and language, or social development) and for children whose native language is not English (Dunlap, 1997; Gibbons, 1993).

Adults gain important insights into children's learning by understanding what to look for when children play. Young children's play provides adults with important information about children's cultural experiences. You can learn about special traditions, celebrations, and family values by watching and listening to children at play. In play, children "practice newly acquired skills and also function on the edge of their developing capabilities to take on new social roles, attempt novel or challenging tasks, and solve complex problems that they would not (or could not) otherwise do" (Bredekamp & Copple, 1997, p. 14).

Recall that earlier in this section, we defined play as a condition for learning that has unique characteristics. Children learn best when play is linked with other conditions (e.g., social interaction, concrete experiences, a sense of competence). The characteristics of play (e.g., that it is active, voluntary, and symbolic) are the same characteristics that are essential to developmentally appropriate practice (Bredekamp & Copple, 1997) because they support children's learning of specific academic skills across the content areas and growth in each developmental domain. (See Chapter 6 for a full discussion of content areas.) Table 4.2 illustrates the connections between play and learning.

Stages and Types of Play

Children's play develops in a typical sequence that parallels their cognitive and social development. Cognitive play reflects children's ages, understandings, and experiences. It includes sensorimotor play, symbolic play, constructive play, and games with rules (Piaget, 1970; Smilansky & Shefatya, 1990). Social play describes children's interactions with their peers. It includes onlooker, solitary, parallel, associative, and cooperative play (Parten, 1932). While both cognitive and social play develop sequentially over time, some types of play are more typical of particular periods of children's development. Nonetheless, all types of play occur in different forms throughout one's life. Table 4.3 lists the types of cognitive and social play, provides a definition of each, and supplies an age-appropriate example.

PAUSE AND REFLECT ABOUT PLAY

Think back to some of the pleasant moments when you were invited to "come and play." What characteristics of play were evident in these experiences? How do you think these experiences helped you learn? Having thought about these questions, what do you now think about how play contributes to children's development? Why?

ASK the Expert   Doris Pronin Fromberg on the Value of Play

Doris Pronin Fromberg

Common Questions Students Ask About the Value of Play in Helping Children Learn

1. If children play, how will teachers have time to cover the curriculum?

Consider analyzing what you mean by "covering" the curriculum in ways that can "cover" the children. Consider the image of world-to-child as contrasted with child-to-world. Analyze what concepts and tasks you think the world-to-child curriculum intends. It will invariably be less significant that what children can organize if you provide the settings, props, and opportunities. Children's thinking develops in both ways, but their awareness of their own ideas as compared with those of others takes place particularly during sociodramatic play. They learn an enormous amount about how to create oral playwriting as they negotiate sociodramatic play episodes with other children. The feedback that they receive from one another helps them to understand how effectively they communicate their child-to-world thoughts, a precursor to writing and comprehending stories.

2. When children play, how could teachers lose control of the class?

When children play, they are engrossed in what they are doing. In any case, children who seem out of control when they have true choice and autonomy to set the rules of the play may very well be stressed by too much teacher direction and too much sedentary activity. This suggests the need to re-evaluate the schedule of a class in order to reduce whole-class times, reduce the number of transitions, and lengthen blocks of time (not less than 45–60 minutes) in which children may select learning centers that include opportunities for all types of play.

3. If children play, will parents complain that they are not learning in school?

Some parents need to learn that the appearance of children actively engaged in play may mask the reality of their learning. Extensive research indicates that children who engage in pretend and sociodramatic play increase their literacy skills; cognitive development, particularly problem solving; social competence; and capacity to generate new connections in a creative way. Some ways to let parents know what children are learning in a class are the following: (a) save children's drawing and writing samples to show progress over time, (b) with photographic slides, document learning experiences that are active and show the uses of different materials and thematic props at parent meetings, (c) save language experience charts for display, (d) four-for-the-day: send four one- or two-line notes each day to four different parents informing them of something that their children learned that day and how their children participated, and (e) consider creating a collaborative newsletter with other teachers that records children's comments about their school activities.

4. What are the differences among work, exploration, and play?

Children usually define a particular activity as play if they autonomously chose to do it; they might define the same activity as work if the teacher asks them to do it. Philosopher John Dewey suggested a continuum of drudgery: . . . work . . . play . . . fooling, and proposed that a balance between work and play is appropriate for schools. Exploration is when we find out what something or someone can do, and play is when we see what we can do with it or another. Work, exploration, and play can be satisfying or challenging, but exploration and play are typically self-motivated and pleasurable, even when serious.

Doris Pronin Fromberg is a professor of education and Director of Early Childhood Teacher Education, Hofstra University, New York

Table 4.2
Play and Learning

Learning Domain	Play Experiences	Skills and Concepts Learned
Cognitive	• sorting objects • playing school at the chalkboard	• problem solving, hypothesis testing • problem solving, mental planning, self-evaluation
Language and Literacy	• repeating rhymes using nonsense words, telling jokes, asking riddles, and chanting jump-rope songs • role-playing a trip to the hospital and maintaining a complex play theme	• using language to organize and maintain play; understanding multiple meanings; understanding words, sounds, and grammatical structure; exploring the phonological, syntactic, and semantic rules of language • using purposeful verbal interactions with explanations, discussions, negotiations, and commands; exploring the forms and functions of language
Literacy	• pretending to read a book, write a shopping list, read environmental print, and re-enact stories	• developing interest in stories and books; comprehending stories and story structure; understanding fantasy in books; and symbolically representing the world
Social and Emotional Development	• engaging in dramatic and sociodramatic play, re-enacting stories, working through conflicts, learning how to enter an ongoing play event, and creating a puppet show	• seeing other perspectives; taking turns; sharing roles, materials, and responsibilities; communicating both verbally and nonverbally for needs and wants; waiting for a turn • developing empathy for others' feelings; expressing one's own feelings and coping with them (helps children think out loud about their experiences so they can cope with them more easily)
Physical	• using various writing and drawing tools (e.g., markers, paintbrushes, pencils) • engaging in running and climbing activities and games	• fine motor skills • gross motor skills • body awareness and fitness
Creative	• pretending to have a birthday party; using scraps of material and paper for creating art products; and interpreting familiar roles in new ways	• problem solving, internal imagery, flexible thinking, and alternative responses to situations

SOURCE: Adapted from *Creative Expression and Play in Early Childhood*, 2nd ed., by J. P. Isenberg and M. R. Jalongo, 1997, Upper Saddle River, NJ: Merrill/Prentice-Hall.

Table 4.3

Types of Children's Play

Type of Play	Definition	Age-appropriate Example
Cognitive Play		
Sensorimotor	Repeated movements with or without materials. Sensorimotor play is the primary type of play of infants and toddlers.	Infants and toddlers: stacking and unstacking rings on a pole Preschoolers and kindergartners: repeating a pattern while stringing beads School-age children: practicing jump-rope skills and rhymes
Symbolic	Early symbolic play involves transforming one object for another and later transforming self and object to satisfy needs in dramatic play. Symbolic play emerges around age 2 and dominates in ages 2–7.	Infants and toddlers: pretending to drink from a toy cup Preschoolers and kindergartners: pretending to rescue people from a burning building School-age children: using secret codes or made-up languages to communicate
Constructive	Making things from a preconceived plan. Constructive play combines sensorimotor and symbolic play, during which children make something according to a preconceived plan.	Preschoolers and kindergartners: constructing a plane from a building set School-age children: creating sets for a story re-enactment
Games with Rules	Predetermined rules that guide acceptable behavior and depend upon reciprocal behavior. Games with rules emerge in simple form in infancy but predominate in the school-age years and beyond.	Infants and toddlers: playing peek-a-boo Preschoolers and kindergartners: playing simple singing and circle games School-age children: playing card games, board games, and group games such as Squirrel and the Tree and Where's the Kitty?
Social Play		
Onlooker	Observing what others are doing, not joining in the play but involved as a spectator. Toddlers engage in a great deal of onlooker play.	Infants and toddlers: watching another paint at an easel Preschoolers and kindergartners: watching an ongoing play group before deciding to enter School-age children: watching a group game before participating
Solitary	Playing alone and independently while concentrating on the activity rather than on other children. Solitary play is typical of infants, toddlers, and young preschool children but may be seen in older children as well.	Infants and toddlers: playing alone and showing no interest in others Preschoolers and kindergartners: playing with own toys School-age children: choosing to play alone for privacy or to think about how to elaborate on a play theme

Table 4.3
(Continued)

Type of Play	Definition	Age-appropriate Example
Social Play		
Parallel	Playing side-by-side but not with others and using toys similar to those of others, sometimes imitating the behavior of other playing children. Parallel play is typical of toddlers and young preschool children.	Infants and toddlers: playing nearby others with little or no interaction Preschoolers and kindergartners: using shared toys but not sharing toys School-age children: using own materials but aware of others using the same materials
Associative	Playing with others in a loosely organized activity with a major interest in being with each other rather than in the play itself. Associative play first appears in young preschool children and is often the first attempt at group play.	Preschoolers, kindergartners, and school-age children: playing in the same area with the same materials but for different purposes and different ends
Cooperative	A complex form of play with shared goals focusing on social interaction. Children typically use negotiation, differentiated roles, and division of labor to create, coordinate, and enact a play theme. Cooperative play is most typical of older preschoolers and school-age children.	Older preschoolers and school-age children: building an airport and deciding how to get there; what to see; and how to build a lounge, air-traffic control tower, hangar, and parking lot

Major Learning Theories

As an early childhood teacher, how you think children learn strongly influences what and how you teach them. There are many scientifically tested theories of learning that have endured and are used in a wide variety of circumstances. But because learning is so complex, we cannot use one single theory to explain it. Thus, early childhood educators use multiple theoretical perspectives to understand how children learn.

What Is a Theory?

A theory is an organized system of knowledge that describes, explains, and predicts behavior. Theories "guide and give meaning to what we see. . . . theories that are verified by research often serve as a sound basis for practical action" (Berk, 1996, p. 5). The fields of psychology, anthropology, and sociology provide early childhood educators with most of the theories of how children learn. From these theories, you will begin to make decisions in your own classrooms about good learning environments, motivation, and appropriate expectations for young children's learning.

Some theories suggest that nature, or heredity, exerts the greatest influence on learning; others suggest that nurture, or the physical and social environment, exerts the most influence on children's learning. Most modern views of learning explore how nature and nurture work together to influence learning (Berk, 1996). In the sections that follow, we examine the major learning theories that influence how teachers approach learning. We describe the key ideas of each theory, identify the primary theorists associated with each theory, and apply each theoretical perspective to early childhood settings.

Nativistic Theory of Learning

Nativistic theory, sometimes called maturation theory, suggests that growth is hereditary and naturally unfolds through a predetermined sequence under the proper conditions. Nativist theory focuses on predictable patterns of development that are the result of maturation and assumes that efforts to teach behaviors before their natural occurrence are not necessary and may indeed be harmful to children's development. To illustrate, most children begin to sit, walk, talk, play, and read at about the same ages. These early developmental milestones set the stage for learning more complex skills throughout one's life. While all children progress through certain sequences of development, they do so at different rates. Consequently, nativist theorists assume that children who are not ready to learn a skill do not benefit from intervention.

Nativist Theorists

Arnold Gesell (1890–1961). Arnold Gesell was a physician who studied the process of maturation at the Yale University Clinic for Child Development. Gesell was the first theorist to provide systematic, normative descriptions of children's development in all domains—physical, language, intellectual, and social—through detailed observations of children from birth through age 10. His research, commonly referred to as "ages and stages," provides typical characteristics of children by ages that represent a predictable sequence of development for all children regardless of race or culture.

Other nativist theorists who have influenced our thinking about learning include Jean-Jacques Rousseau and Noam Chomsky. Rousseau (1712–1778), a French philosopher and author of *L'Emile*, believed that children are inherently good and should be left to develop naturally so their inherent goodness can develop. Rousseau was the first to identify "childhood" as a stage of life. Chomsky (1928–   ), a noted linguist, emphasizes the important role of maturation in learning language. He and other nativist linguists suggest that children are "prewired" for language development, thus explaining the differences in language development among children.

Applying Nativist Theory in Early Childhood Practice. Gesell's theory and research, completed in conjunction with Dr. Louise Bates Ames and Dr. Frances Ilg, have helped parents, pediatricians, and teachers clarify expected behaviors for children at particular ages. Among the applications of Gesell's theory to early childhood education are the following.

1. Early childhood teachers often use developmental milestones as the basis for their teaching. They assess children's progress and plan experiences based on what children can do today and what is anticipated that children will next be able to accomplish. However, some of these "ages and stages" data have been misused by educators who often label children as delayed rather than identifying children's strengths as individual learners as the starting point on the learning continuum.

2. Children develop at different rates in one or more areas. Because there are no fixed criteria for what constitutes delayed development, early childhood teachers must rely on their own ability to monitor the knowledge and skill acquisition of all children.

3. The notion of readiness has its roots in nativist theory and focuses on providing learning experiences at children's present level of ability. This assumption can be counterproductive by maintaining children's current level of learning rather than providing them with appropriate levels of challenging learning opportunities. Decisions about the appropriate time to enter kindergarten based solely on age and

Children need appropriate levels of challenging activities.

waiting to teach children to read until they are mentally ready are still evident in many early childhood settings today.

4. First-time parents often find that Gesell's emphasis on heredity is somewhat limiting to what their children can learn. They view the environment as the key element of learning.

Behavioral Theory of Learning

Behavioral theory identifies all learning in terms of behavior that can be observed, measured, and recorded. While behaviorists acknowledge that heredity somewhat limits what people can learn, they view the environment as the most influential element on learning. They suggest that learning is the accumulation of knowledge and responses through selective reinforcement, and that learning occurs when one reacts to aspects of the environment that are pleasurable or painful. From the behaviorist perspective, learning occurs in three ways: through association (classical conditioning), through reinforcement (operant conditioning), and through observation and imitation (observational learning). Learning through association means generalizing between events. When a young child says "bird" for all things that fly, adults provide reinforcing responses, such as, "We call that an airplane." Eventually, the child distinguishes birds from other flying things. Learning through reinforcement occurs when adults try to extinguish an inappropriate behavior by ignoring it or praise a behavior to ensure its continuance. Learning through observation happens when children watch the behaviors of peers and adults, form mental pictures of them, and later try to imitate those behaviors. How behaviors are reinforced determines how ingrained they become. Because behaviorists consider learners to be passive recipients of stimuli from the environment, they believe that learning results from adults' shaping and changing children's behavior through the use of cues and reinforcement techniques in a carefully designed external environment.

Behavioral Theorists

B. F. Skinner (1904–1990). Probably the best-known behavioral theorist is B. F. Skinner, who theorized that the behavior of all learners can be modified and that the basic principles of learning apply to all learners, regardless of age. He assumed that children's behavior can be increased through a range of reinforcers such as smiles and praise, and decreased through punishment, such as withdrawal of special privileges.

Other behavioral theorists who have influenced our view of learning are John Locke, Edward Thorndike, and John Watson. John Locke (1632–1704), a prominent English philosopher, theorized that environment and experience are the determinants of learning. He proposed that the environment is the primary factor in shaping individual development and learning. Locke's ideas paved the way for future behaviorists.

Edward Thorndike (1874–1949) studied learning through association and suggested the stimulus-response method. From his research on animals, Thorndike concluded that learning depends on associations, which in turn form learned habits. Complex learning is the result of combined associations.

John Watson (1878–1958), an American psychologist influenced by Russian psychologist Ivan Pavlov, is known for his ideas about classical conditioning. In his view, learning depends only on observable behaviors. Watson claimed that he could shape the entirety of a person's learning by taking full control of all events of a child's first year of life and by discouraging emotional and social connections between the parents and their child.

Applying Behavioral Theory in Early Childhood Practice. Behavioral learning theory is among the most influential views of learning today. It has given rise to the following practices.

1. Behavior modification, a behavior management tool, is widely used to change children's behavior. Many early childhood teachers use external rewards (e.g., stickers, smiley faces, and marbles) to motivate and control behavior. While reward systems do work for some children, early childhood teachers need to examine how and when they should be used, if at all.

2. Time-out, removing a child from a situation and ignoring the undesirable behavior, is another application of behavioral principles. While this technique promotes automatic responses to specific requests, it does not promote inner or self-control. Using time-out must be handled very carefully and sensitively.

3. Drill-and-practice exercises, such as memorizing word lists and multiplication tables, are typical examples of a behavioral approach to learning. Many teachers rely almost exclusively on this approach to learning. Whereas drill-and-practice exercises promote the learning of discrete facts and skills, they do not provide children with the opportunity to think about "big ideas" or to think conceptually about problems.

Social Learning Theory of Learning

Social learning theory suggests that children learn social behaviors by observing and imitating models, especially those of their parents. It accepts the key behavioral learning principles of conditioning and reinforcement but has expanded them to include how children learn social skills. Social learning theorists view learners as being active in shaping their own learning and believe that observational learning, a cognitive influence on learning, is central to how children learn. They also acknowledge the central role of children's identification with key family members in influencing their learning of language, dealing with aggression, developing a moral sense, and learning socially acceptable behaviors (Papalia & Olds, 1995). Today, social learning theory is more influential than behaviorism in viewing how children learn.

Albert Bandura (1925–   ). Albert Bandura, a contemporary behaviorist, expanded the principles of behaviorism and conceived the theory of social learning. He recognized that children learn much of their social behavior from imitating or watching others. As a result, modeling became a major principle of learning that has prompted parents and teachers to explicitly demonstrate expected forms of behavior. Bandura's current work underscores how children's thinking affects their learning. How children think about themselves and create and judge their own expectations about learning strongly influences their development of "personal standards for behavior and a sense of self-efficacy—beliefs about their own abilities and characteristics—that guide responses in particular situations" (Berk, 1996, p. 20).

Applying Social Learning Theory in Early Childhood Practice. The use of social learning techniques in early childhood education is widely used to help children learn appropriate behaviors, skills, and techniques. It bridges behavioral theories with cognitive theories because it acknowledges the active role that children play in their own learning and the cognitive influences on learning (Papalia & Olds, 1995). The following are applications of social learning theory to early childhood education.

1. Children play an active role in their own learning, particularly in choosing whose behavior to imitate. These models may be significant adults such as parents or teachers, or they may be television heroes. When children spend many hours watching cartoons or adult television programs, for example, they often adopt the behaviors of those characters as their own.

2. The learning environment of young children can be configured to promote or thwart positive modeling of expected learning behaviors. How you arrange furniture and materials, how you create daily routines and procedures that make sense to learners, and how you provide learning experiences that challenge children's thinking provide the environmental conditions that enable children to learn naturally and positively.

3. Modeling, or observational learning, is the basis for learning both appropriate and inappropriate skills and behavior. When young children have difficulty in getting along with other children, for example, adults can model appropriate ways of getting along to help children change undesirable interactions and understand the reasons for doing so. If a preschooler wants a toy from another child and grabs rather than asks for it, the teacher can model appropriate behavior by telling the child to use words to ask for what he or she needs. Secondly, observational learning is also used in sociodramatic play when young children are asked to imitate the behavior of important adults in their lives (e.g., parents, siblings, teachers) to demonstrate what these adults would like the children to accomplish; with guided practice, children often can complete the task.

4. Hearing adults' comments about their efforts (e.g., "I'm pleased that you didn't give up on that task even though it was hard and frustrating." or "I know you can

Children imitate behavior that they observe.

figure that problem out.") helps children view themselves as can-do rather than can't-do learners. Such comments also promote interest in learning through self-efficacy and the development of personal standards.

Constructivist Theory of Learning

Constructivist theory focuses on the mental processes children use in thinking and remembering. It views learning as the self-regulated changes in thinking that occur from the acquisition of knowledge through which learners seek solutions to cognitive challenges. Influenced by research in the cognitive, computer, and social sciences, constructivism emphasizes the active roles of the learner, prior knowledge, social interactions, and authentic tasks in constructing understanding rather than imposing knowledge (Woolfolk, 1995). Constructivist theory is rooted in the works of Jean Piaget, Jerome Bruner, and Lev Vygotsky and can be viewed from the interrelated perspectives of cognitive-developmental theory and sociocultural theory.

Cognitive-Developmental Constructivist Theory

Jean Piaget (1896–1980). Piaget, a Swiss biologist and theorist, studied how children acquire knowledge and how thinking and learning develop in children. Piaget assisted in standardizing the first intelligence test at the Binet Laboratory in Paris. While assessing the intelligence of French schoolchildren with this test, he became intrigued with children's incorrect answers to questions. Simultaneously, he noted that children's responses appeared to be age related.

Central to Piaget's cognitive theory is the concept of adaptation, which begins in infancy and continues over a lifetime. Adaptation is the process through which the mind develops cognitive structures to make sense of the outside world. According to Piaget, learning is the active construction of knowledge through interactions with people and the environment that takes place in stages. It is evident in behavior that reflects changes in thinking occurring in distinct stages with unique features that correlate with specific ages of development.

In Piaget's theory, children's minds develop in a series of four stages, each of which is characterized by distinct ways of thinking. Each stage builds upon the preceding one, which becomes the foundation for new ways of thinking about and responding to the world. From birth through age 2, children are in the *sensorimotor stage*. Infants learn about their world by using their senses to solve sensorimotor problems, such as shaking a rattle to hear noise or finding hidden objects. This sensorimotor thinking evolves into the *preoperational stage,* which lasts from ages 2–7. During this stage, children use symbolic thinking to show what they know, especially through pretend play and language. Preoperational thinking lacks the logical qualities that are characteristic of the thinking of older children and adults. In the next stage, the *concrete operational stage,* children ages 7–11 build upon preoperational thinking and think in more logical ways, but their thinking and learning are tied to concrete objects. While children organize objects into various categories and hierarchies at this stage, they are not yet ready to think abstractly. From about age 11 on, children in the *formal operational stage* are able to think and reason abstractly in ways that are similar to those of mature adolescents and adults (Berk, 1996).

Learning during each of these four stages results from the interactions among the reciprocal processes of assimilation, accommodation, and equilibration. From children's interactions with their environment, they organize mental structures that become the foundation for more complex thinking and learning. They do this by taking in new information into existing structures (assimilation) or by changing existing structures to accommodate the new information (accommodation), therefore creating a balance between the new and the old information that makes sense to them (equilibration). Imagine yourself arriving for your first class at your college or university. You first had to figure out certain features of the building, such as where your classroom was, how you got from the door of the building to your classroom, how you got from the classroom to the restroom, and perhaps how you could get a snack during a break (assimilation). Familiarizing yourself with the building enabled you to routinely enter the building and find essential places in the future so that you did not have to think each time about how to find your classroom. You changed your mental structures and used accommodation to learn your way around the building. Your need to learn your way around the building is an example of equilibration, the mental need to find ways to maneuver in a new environment.

Jerome Bruner (1915–). Influenced by the work of Piaget, Jerome Bruner studied the thought processes of perception, memory, strategic thinking, and classification. Unlike Piaget, Bruner does not propose stages of these thinking capacities; rather, he theorizes that they are simply less well developed in children. Bruner likens learning to a computer, because learning occurs as much from the outside in as from the inside out. Thus, the mind actively codes, transforms, and organizes information as it takes it in. Bruner views children as active learners who organize information into higher and more complex categories and modify their own thinking as it makes sense to them in their environments.

Applying Cognitive Developmental Theory in Early Childhood Practice. Cognitive developmental theory has fundamentally changed the way we view teaching and learning. It has been applied in the following ways.

1. Learning experiences are planned to stimulate children's curiosity through the use of concrete inquiries, experiments, and discovery learning that mentally involves hands-on use of open-ended materials. In a science study of shadows, for example, younger children might investigate how to make long and short shadows using flashlights and paper; older children might use shadows to determine the size of objects. Both of these experiences enable children to construct knowledge about sources of light.

2. The teacher's role in early childhood settings is to ask questions that encourage problem solving. It is also to provide meaningful activities that promote decision making and the exchange of viewpoints among children.

3. Early childhood settings must provide a variety of equipment and materials for children to use each day. Having time to explore and think about materials enables children to build conceptual understanding. To understand the concept that new colors are produced by mixing different proportions of colors, for example, children need time to experiment with mixing colors, observe the changes that occur, and infer how to match someone else's color mixture rather than having an adult tell them what will happen during this process.

Sociocultural Constructivist Theory

Lev Semenovich Vygotsky (1896–1934). Vygotsky, a Russian psychologist, asserted that social and cultural context strongly influences how children learn. Sociocultural theory is an outgrowth of Vygotsky's studies of educational practices for Russian children with disabilities. Many of these disabilities were caused by the years of war, famine, and poverty that beset Russia early in this century, suggesting that cultural influences strongly impact children's learning.

According to Vygotsky (1978), children learn primarily through their relationships with other people, particularly in dialogue between each child and a more knowledgeable person. These social relationships form the basis for later communication and thinking. Vygotsky emphasized the importance of family, social interaction, adults and more capable peers, and play as primary influences on learning and believed that as a result, learning occurs first on the social level and then on an individual level.

Three major concepts permeate Vygotsky's sociocultural theory: the zone of proximal development (ZPD), scaffolding, and the role of the adult. First, Vygotsky theorized that a child has an actual and a potential level of learning. The distance between what a child can do independently (actual level) and what that child can do with assistance (potential level) is called the zone of proximal development and substantially influences children's learning when they encounter a problem to solve (Vygotsky, 1978). When children work at their potential level, they experience what is possible to do independently before they can actually do it.

Vygotsky's second major concept is scaffolding, a support system that enables children to move along the learning continuum by building new competencies. For scaffolding to take place between an adult and a child, the child must be engaged in meaningful, problem-solving situations with mutual give and take between the child and the adult.

Lastly, Vygotsky ascribed major importance to the role of the adult in children's learning. Through the use of the zone of proximal development, supportive adults can guide

Children need time to think and experiment.

children's learning in many areas. Vygotsky viewed learning as a socially mediated process—as dependent upon the support that adults and more mature peers provide as children try new tasks.

Applying Sociocultural Constructivist Theory in Early Childhood Practice. Vygotsky's emphasis on the relationship between culture and learning has given rise to the following implications for early childhood practice.

1. Teachers must create a community of learners. Adults who take responsibility for children's learning must provide learning experiences that are slightly above the children's level of functioning and assist children's inquiry and investigations.

EXPLORING YOUR ROLE IN FOSTERING CHILDREN'S LEARNING

2. Cooperative learning activities provide important opportunities for children to learn. Classroom routines, such as multistudent projects and center-based learning, offer students opportunities to solve problems together through verbal exchanges and negotiation. The presence of imaginative play, small-group activities, mixed-age grouping, and children interacting with each other offer additional valuable learning experiences that capitalize on the social aspects of learning.

3. Early childhood settings need to include discovery and guided learning experiences with many opportunities for dialogue between children and adults. The richer the context for language usage in learning tasks, the more children will develop the knowledge and skills needed for a particular culture (Berk, 1996).

Multiple Intelligences Theory of Learning

Howard Gardner (1943–). Howard Gardner is a psychologist at Harvard University and codirector of Project Zero, a cognitive research project that measures intelligence. He is best known for identifying eight different intelligences: linguistic, logical/mathematical, musical, visual/spatial, bodily/kinesthetic, interpersonal, intrapersonal, and naturalist. Gardner (1993) views intelligence as the "ability to solve problems or fashion products that are of consequence in a particular cultural setting" (Lazear, 1991, p. xi). Problem solving enables a learner to figure out how to reach a stated goal; creating projects enables learners to display their knowledge, feelings, and understandings of their world. Grounded in brain research (see Figure 4.1), Gardner suggests that intelligence is more than a single ability that can be enhanced, taught, and changed. While each of us has certain intelligences that dominate, all of the intelligences work together to help individuals solve problems and accomplish tasks. This more inclusive view of intelligence differs from the narrower, traditional view that intelligence can be measured as a single entity that is demonstrated outside of one's natural learning environment through standardized testing. Table 4.4 describes each of Gardner's intelligences and suggests possible learning experiences for teaching to and through them.

Applying Multiple Intelligences Theory in Early Childhood Practice. If you consider for a moment the strengths in learning that your friends or family members have, you might notice that some are especially good at getting along with others. According to Gardner's theory, these individuals would have high interpersonal intelligence. Others you know may be especially capable of using language to express their knowledge and understand their world. In this case, they would have high verbal/linguistic intelligence. Knowing these different capacities enables you to teach for understanding, ensuring that you reach all types of learners when you are teaching skills and concepts and that children have an opportunity to show what they know and understand. While Gardner's research is still new, it provides insights into maximizing children's potential by connecting classroom learning to real-life experiences. Multiple intelligences theory asks the question, "In which ways is this child smart?" The following practices represent multiple intelligences theory.

1. Early childhood practices need curriculum approaches and assessment strategies that help students display their understandings in a variety of ways. Incorporating authentic assessment strategies (e.g., portfolios, projects) and giving children choices of how to display their learning (e.g., a play, a graph, a song) are consistent with this view of learning.

CHAPTER 4

Table 4.4

Ideas for Teaching To and Through Gardner's Eight Intelligences

Intelligence	Description	Applications
Verbal/Linguistic	using language to express ideas and to understand others	writing in a journal, reading a book, listening to a story, telling about an experience
Logical/Mathematical	using reasoning to discern numbers, quantities, and abstract patterns (sometimes called scientific thinking)	making projects following a plan, comparing and contrasting objects, making graphic organizers, performing calculations
Visual/Spatial	forming images of one's world in the mind	expressing ideas and feelings with no words (e.g., drawing, making posters, inventing an imaginary character), engaging in pretend play
Bodily/Kinesthetic	using all or part of one's body to make something or solve a problem	dancing, using movement, enacting a play; dramatic play, pantomime, noncompetitive games
Musical	thinking in music by hearing, recognizing, and remembering tonal patterns; sensitivity to rhythm and beat	creating raps and songs, playing musical instruments, appreciating different kinds of music (classical, folk); humming
Interpersonal	understanding, getting along, and working well with others; relies on all other intelligences	teams, projects, cooperative group learning, verbal and nonverbal communication
Intrapersonal	knowing who you are and what you can and cannot do	reflecting on own actions, metacognitive activities (e.g., thinking strategies used in reading), writing about self
Naturalist	discriminating among living things (e.g., plants, and animals) and sensitivity to the rest of the natural world	environmental units, caring for pets and plants observing and touching real plants and animals outside, asking questions about similarities and differences in plants and animals, categorizing natural materials

SOURCE: Adapted from "The First Seven . . . and the Eighth: A Conversation with Howard Gardner" by K. Checkly, 1997, *Educational Leadership 55*(1), pp. 8–13, and *Seven Ways of Knowing* by D. Lazear, 1991, Palantine, IL: Skylight Publishing.

2. Planning must acknowledge the different talents that children in your setting possess. How you perceive the objectives of projects, the nature of extension activities, and the arrangement of your room will influence how you help children tap into each of their intelligences over the course of their learning.

3. Approaches to education are personalized to meet the cultural and learning needs of the students. Linking learning to children's real-life experiences and their cultural backgrounds capitalizes on students' strengths and maximizes learning potential. Knowing, for example, that many African-American children often learn best through interpersonal relations, a teacher might tap into this intelligence through the use of cooperative projects that include experimentation and improvisation. Knowing that many Hispanic children prefer holistic, concrete, and social approaches to learning, a teacher might provide them with opportunities to express their knowledge through art, music, drama, and dance in addition to verbal and linguistic forms to affirm their dominant intelligences (Berns, 1997). Table 4.5 compares the key theoretical perspectives on how children learn.

EXPLORING YOUR ROLE IN FOSTERING CHILDREN'S LEARNING

Table 4.5
A Comparison of Theoretical Perspectives on How Children Learn

Theory	Theorist	View of Learning	View of Learner	Role of Adult	Practical Applications
Nativist	Gesell (1890–1961) Rousseau (1712–1778) Chomsky (1928–)	• develops naturally by age-related stages • maturation is the key factor in learning; learning occurs when children are ready	• passive • emphasis on nature	• nonintervening; allows child's learning to unfold	• reading readiness—waiting for readiness skills to appear before beginning formal reading instruction
Behavioral	Skinner (1904–1990) John Locke (1632–1704) Edward Thorndike (1874–1949) John Watson (1878–1958)	• behavior that can be observed, measured, and recorded • quantitative increase in learned behavior as children grow older • modeling and conditioning are primary principles of learning	• passive recipient of stimuli in environment	• shapes and changes behavior through cues and reinforcement techniques by direct intervention	• behavior modification • time-out • stickers and other rewards • behavioral charts • direct instruction
Social Learning	Bandura (1925–)	• learning is the result of observation and imitation of significant role models, especially parents • cognition is a strong influence on learning	• active in shaping own learning • how one thinks about one's own experiences influences beliefs about self-efficacy	• models expected behaviors and skills	• modeling • direct instruction
Constructivism: Cognitive Developmental	Piaget (1896–1980)	• mental structures determine how children understand their world • learning occurs in stages that are distinctly different from one another • new learning depends on prior understanding	• active, not reactive • independent effort to make sense of world by actively constructing knowledge	• Presents useful problems to solve that challenge and support children's innate drive to seek solutions to problems • prepares an environment with hands-on learning materials that challenge students' thinking while doing	• discovery and inquiry learning • using concrete experiences to teach concepts (e.g., manipulatives in mathematics)

Bruner (1915–)	• active processing of experiences • quantitative increase in perception, attention, memory, and problem-solving skills with age • learning occurs from the interaction of nature and nurture • cultural context impacts learning • imaginative play helps • children separate thought from action influences learning	• actively processes experiences • active		
Constructivist: Sociocultural	Vygotsky (1896–1934)	• learning occurs first on a social level and then on an individual level • dialogue and language are critical to learning; self-talk provides guidance and direction to learning	• focus on the social context mediated by dialogue with others • more capable peers and adults influence learning • children internalize the essential social and cultural values, beliefs, and attitudes that guide their behavior	• does not assume a direct teaching role • provides variety of materials to be used in different ways • asks questions that require investigative thinking and abilities • scaffolds learning to continue to build new competencies when learner is working at the edge of ability • teacher as a partner • cooperative learning • forms of play are leading learning activities • assisted learning and performance • shared activities • think-alouds and talk-alouds • discovery learning • children's interests

(continued)

Table 4.5
(Continued)

Theory	Theorist	View of Learning	View of Learner	Role of Adult	Practical Applications
Multiple Intelligences	Gardner (1943–)	• intelligence has more than one dimension	• active in seeking more than one way of knowing	• provides learning opportunities that use different intelligences in the teaching-learning process	• teaching concepts through different intelligences • learners choose ways to learn • learners choose how to demonstrate knowledge • interdisciplinary curriculum • projects • authentic assessment

ASK the Expert Janet Boies Taylor on Developmental Continuity

Common Questions and Misconceptions Students Have About the Continuity of Young Children's Development

Janet Boies Taylor

1. Do Piaget's explanations of the stages of children's intellectual development mean that you have to wait until the child is ready to learn something?

Children are active learners who continuously ask questions and seek answers to those questions, which in turn raise new questions. While their questions and answers differ from adult ways of thinking about the same experience, children's thinking follows predictable sequences that arise out of spontaneous convictions. Their convictions about what is true or right are not learned from adults and are quite uniform across all children at a certain level of reasoning. For example, when children of 4 or 5 years of age are asked who is older, their father or their grandmother, they will generally respond that their father is older. They based this spontaneous conviction on the idea that their father is taller than their grandmother, so he must be older. We can observe these early spontaneous convictions in children's ideas about written and spoken language, and in their ideas about what is real, what is alive, and the origins of things that exist in the physical world. This helps us understand that young children are always ready to learn and to think about things that interest them. However, they will build their ideas on what they already know and will not come to know something in the same way that an adult knows. Piaget's book **The Child's Conception of the World** provides more information about this topic.

2. Are all children of the same age at the same developmental level, and is the knowledge they bring to school the same?

This is not the case. There will be a wide range of development across domains of knowledge in any child. Thus, a child may exhibit a sophisticated understanding of how to solve a math problem but have a great deal of difficulty with reading. Or, at an earlier age, a child may have a sophisticated understanding of walking but have difficulty with talking. According to Piaget, the differences in the rates of development are attributed to four factors: maturation—the factor most closely linked to age, disequilibration—the conflict created in the child's mind when new information does not fit into the child's existing knowledge, and social interaction and experience—the kinds of interactions the child has with people and things in the world. Differences in development are the result of the different kinds of experiences each child has.

3. How can teachers provide for the continuity of development for all the children in their classrooms when their children exhibit such a wide range of developmental differences?

This is a very difficult, yet very important, question. Rather than trying to teach to the average level of the class, hoping that those at the lower levels will catch up and ignoring the needs of those at the other end of the developmental continuum, early childhood teachers should adopt a developmentally appropriate curriculum. In this kind of curriculum, teachers and children work together to make decisions about the kinds of activities in which they want to engage. Children are thought of as active constructors of their knowledge, and teachers build on the spontaneous interests of children by providing the materials and questions appropriate to each child's developmental level. Additionally, the teacher provides for considerable peer-peer interaction so that the children learn from each other. Developmentally appropriate practice differs from traditional approaches to the curriculum in that it puts the focus on the child's development rather than on the subject matter being taught.

Janet Boies Taylor is a professor of early childhood education at Auburn University, Auburn, Alabama

Given the vast array of theories on how children learn, it is important that you understand your own perspective on learning as well as that of the learner. The Pause and Reflect About Teaching and Learning feature provides a good opportunity for you to get a better sense of what it means to learn.

PAUSE AND REFLECT ABOUT TEACHING AND LEARNING

Think of a time when you taught something to a younger person. Describe the learner, the time and place, and what and how you taught that person. What theoretical perspectives were you using? Now that you have read this section, would you try other approaches? Why or why not? Compare and share your responses with a peer.

Conclusion

A review of how children learn best reveals clear relationships between the way teachers approach learning and its lasting impact. Understanding the diverse ways in which young children learn is a critical link to maximizing their learning potential. Teachers who have the greatest impact on children's learning relate to children's experiences, connect learning opportunities to real-life situations, facilitate the acquisition of knowledge by allowing children to be participants in their own learning, provide scaffolding, and love learning themselves. Developing a healthy respect for different ways of learning, knowing, and representing knowledge and skills is necessary in all early childhood settings.

One Child, Three Perspectives: *Alexander's Reading Difficulties*

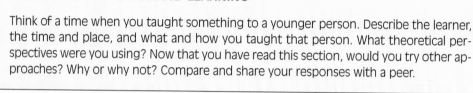

Alexander is in the third grade in a local public school. This is his first year in school in this country. In Russia, where he came from, Alexander was reading at grade level in Russian, his first language.

In Alexander's school, there are many children whose first language is not English. On the school support staff, there is an English-as-a-second-language (ESL) teacher and an English-as-a-second-language specialist who assesses children's literacy levels and provides support for both second-language learners and their teachers. Alexander's teacher, Ms. Myers, referred Alexander to the ESL assessment specialist with the following note: "Alexander is not doing well in reading and lacks comprehension in content-area reading. He does not pay attention in reading group, nor does he understand grammar or spelling, show word recognition, or answer questions at the end of a reading assignment. Alexander cannot sit still during reading time and is often excluded from the group. He has difficulty writing in English in his journal and completing long-term projects, and he has of late become frustrated and decreasingly confident in his ability to read and write even in his first language."

Each day Alexander goes to his ESL class, where the ESL teacher approaches reading and writing in English in a different way. Before beginning to read the text, his teacher formulates questions about the topic, finds out what Alexander knows about it, and helps Alexander through the text by using picture clues and other supports each step of the way. For content reading, the ESL teacher works with Alexander on strategies for gathering and recalling information. According to his ESL teacher, Alexander is making steady progress in English as a second language and is very attentive to the task of learning to read under her tutelage.

Soon after Alexander began having difficulty with reading and was becoming a behavior problem in her class, Ms. Myers called Alexander's parents, who are fluent in English, for a meeting with the ESL team and herself. Alexander's parents expressed surprise when Ms. Myers reported Alexander's lack of progress in learning to read and his lack of interest in school. In Russia and at home, Alexander has not been a problem. He reads a variety of things in Russian, his first language, and shows none of the behaviors Ms. Myers reports. Ms. Myers suggests that Alexander's parents stop using Russian at home and speak only English to Alexander. The ESL specialist suggests that he spend more time in her class using her ESL strategies. Alexander's parents do not want him to stop speaking Russian. They end the meeting without arriving at an agreement about what to do for Alexander.

REACT:	Think about how the perspectives of Ms. Myers, the ESL teacher, and Alexander's parents are alike and different. What might be some reasons? With whom do you identify most strongly in this case, and why?
RESEARCH:	Search the ERIC Web site and read several articles about second-language learning of young children. What are the key learning principles that apply to this topic?
REFLECT:	What assumptions about learning to read in a second language do Ms. Myers, the ESL teacher, and Alexander's parent make? Generate some key strategies for teaching reading to second-language learners.

EXPLORING YOUR ROLE IN FOSTERING CHILDREN'S LEARNING

Learning Environments for Multiple Intelligences

When you think about creating the best learning environments for children, you surely want to consider Howard Gardner's theory of multiple intelligences (MI). MI theory suggests that people have many forms of intelligence that are unevenly distributed and developed and can be improved through practice. As a teacher of young children, you will want to be aware of which intelligence(s) each individual child uses best to learn, understand, and construct knowledge. One way to facilitate this is to create a balance of learning opportunities that tap all of children's intelligences. This approach to teaching enables children to form and express their conceptual understandings through the intelligence(s) of their choice and make personal connections to their learning in all areas of the curriculum. It also provides opportunities to develop their untapped talents.

Using Gardner's theory of multiple intelligences, two first-grade teachers designed and implemented a mental health unit. They used three basic concepts to structure their unit: (a) physical affection can be an expression of friendship, celebration, or a loving family; (b) there is a difference between stressful and relaxing situations; and (c) individuals and the community need to be sensitive to persons with disabling conditions. Here is how they designed center-based learning experiences to deepen children's understandings (Liess & Ritchie, 1995).

INTELLIGENCE	LEARNING EXPERIENCES
Bodily/Kinesthetic	write in Braille by hole punching or gluing peas on a card; assist blindfolded friends around the school
Visual/Spatial	draw pictures of sounds you would miss if you could not hear or sights you would miss if you could not see
Musical/Rhythmic	write songs and raps about disabilities
Verbal/Linguistic	read stories about disabilities; decode sign language and Braille riddles
Interpersonal	select pictures from magazines of people assisting each other
Intrapersonal	reflect on learning in journals on the computer or by drawing
Logical/Mathematical	measure areas of the school for wheelchair use; examine the building to identify what needs to be done for people with disabilities

Procedure for Developing a Multiple Intelligences Learning Environment

1. **Select a topic or unit of study.** Select a topic or unit of study that your children show interest in or that you are required to teach. This topic can be from any area of the curriculum. Be sure you identify the major concepts or ideas you wish to teach.

2. **Brainstorm possible ideas, including room arrangement and the schedule.** Think about all the possibilities for teaching. Make a list or a chart of all of them.

3. **Select activities and learning experiences.** From your list of ideas, select at least two different learning experiences for each intelligence that are most appropriate for children in your own setting. Decide which activities are most appropriate for each intelligence and tell why.

4. **Plan for arranging the learning centers.** Think about how to arrange the room so children can choose different centers. Consider the space, the traffic flow, and the type of materials you will need.

5. **Evaluate the children's learning.** Decide how you will evaluate what the children learned. You might consider observation, anecdotal records, photography, interviewing the children, or looking at their journal entries.

6. **Think about the implications by considering these questions:**

   - How does using this approach to teaching help children learn?

   - How does it set the stage for further learning?

   - What kinds of planning do teachers need to use this approach?

SOURCE: Adapted from "Using Multiple Intelligence Theory to Transform a First-Grade Health Curriculum." by E. Liess and G. Ritchie, 1995, *Early Childhood Education Journal 23*(2), pp. 71–79.

5

Exploring Your Role in Designing a Safe, Healthy, and Appropriate Early Childhood Environment

The environment supports children's desire to find out about things, facilitates the process of discovery, and, in general, meets children's needs.

—Alfie Kohn, 1996, p. 54

Learning Outcomes

✔ Appreciate the influence of the environment on children's behavior and learning

✔ Use criteria to select and evaluate materials for play and learning

✔ Explore the early childhood educator's role in providing safe, healthy, and appropriate settings for children's learning

✔ Apply principles of design to planning and evaluating indoor and outdoor settings

✔ Adapt environments to meet the needs of all children

Meet the Teachers

Ms. Koen is a lead teacher of twelve 2-year-olds. During a recent graduate course, she learned that the "environment is the third teacher." The idea that the environment could be an important teaching and learning tool intrigued Ms. Koen, who was frustrated by the behavior of her toddlers. As she told her colleagues, "My classroom is small and everything seems to wind up all over the floor. The children argue endlessly over materials and often wander aimlessly from activity center to activity center." After reading about good environments for toddlers, sharing her concerns with her colleagues, and engaging in some personal reflection, Ms. Koen began to realize that toddlers' behavior is often affected by the classroom and materials provided for play. Ms. Koen then redesigned her classroom space on paper, starting with the housekeeping area. She created a corner by placing the sink, stove, and refrigerator catty-corner to each other, and she placed the dolls and dress-up materials in separate containers so the children could more easily locate and put away the items. Next, she enlarged the block center to facilitate building, added figures and other materials to extend the toddlers' play, and moved the sand table to a location where it could be easily wheeled onto a drop cloth and four children could use it at the same time. Almost immediately, Ms. Koen noticed a change in the toddlers' behavior from aimless wandering to longer, more sustained play.

Ms. Endo has been teaching in a Head Start setting for over 10 years and knows that her room must be safe, welcoming, and appropriate to meet the needs of all of the children. This year, her class includes a child who is confined to a wheelchair as a result of injuries suffered in an automobile accident and a child with a visual impairment who requires teaching modifications using other sensory skills. After consulting with other members of the Head Start team (the nurse, social worker, speech-language therapist, and psychologist) as well as the children's families, Ms. Endo modified some parts of the physical environment. She put adhesive-backed Velcro on the bottom of some fine-motor materials to help the child in the wheelchair attach items to the lap tray. She also cleared the pathways to accommodate the wheelchair and increase mobility for the child with low vision. Next, she adapted her instructional environment by altering the amount of light, distance, contrast, and colors, each of which affects how children process visual information. For example, she painted brightly colored letters on some wooden blocks to make them easier for the child with the visual impairment to see. She decided to use storytelling and flannel-board characters, and she located lots of big books with enlarged type and pictures, a molded plastic globe, an abacus, and a clock with a raised face. She even found a book in the library on how to make touch toys and games (Gallagher, 1978). Ms. Endo also uses tactile cues, such as marking the child's name on his cubby with a textured sign that can be felt and taping small objects or toys on the outside of bins so the child can identify where each piece of equipment belongs.

Ms. Mitsoff teaches first grade in an urban school. Early in the school year, she and the children establish simple rules for sharing materials and respecting each other in their first-grade community because she believes that "The relationships children have with one another deeply affect the amount of control they have in their environment. Children need to be able to clearly express their feelings and ask for what they need to live harmoniously in their world and the world in which they will be growing up." Yet even though she follows through on this belief by taking time to create classroom behavioral expectations with the children, some children have disagreements over materials, space, or taking turns. When this occurs, Ms. Mitsoff expects the children to talk through their problems by themselves and find a solution before she intervenes. One example of this occurred on a day when two first-grade boys were making puppets to dramatize stories they had created about a farm. The boys became increasingly silly, boisterous, and disruptive with their puppet making, so Ms. Mitsoff called them aside in a quiet corner to talk about the effect their interactions were having on the other first-grade children. Each of the boys blamed the other for the noisy behavior. After listening to each child, Ms. Mitsoff said, "Talk to each other until you can figure out how to act appropriately in the puppet-making center so all the children can learn without being disturbed. Then come and tell me how you plan to solve the problem." Ms. Mitsoff uses this strategy to create a learning environment that is influenced by the children and the teacher and helps children become self-sufficient, collaborative problem solvers who can live comfortably in the group.

These three teachers know how fundamental the environment is for children's learning, behavior, and identity. Use the following questions to compare, contrast, and connect these teachers' views on appropriate environments to your own ideas about establishing environments for young children.

COMPARE:	What are some similarities in the ways these three teachers design their environments?
CONTRAST:	What differences do you notice in the ways these teachers encourage children's exploration and curiosity?
CONNECT:	What impressed you most about how these teachers set up their classrooms and arrange materials to meet the special needs of their children? How could you incorporate some of these ideas in your own teaching?

A Definition of Environment

Imagine entering someone's home and immediately sensing that you are in a special place. There is music playing in the background; the smell of warm apple pie is in the air; there are comfortable places to sit, beautiful wall decorations and plants to admire, and light permeating through the house. Your host and hostess are interested in who you are and engage you easily in conversation. You feel welcome and valued. The attributes that convey this comfortable, homey feeling are the same ones that characterize good early childhood environments. Good environments invite children to discover, invent, create, and learn together in a community that is caring, respectful, and supportive.

By *environment*, we mean the combination of a planned arrangement of physical space, the relationships between and among the people, and the values and goals of a particular program, center, or school system. Environment is the sum total of these influences that affect particular individuals and groups of people. Yet each environment is unique because of how these influences interact. One useful way to think about environment is to consider its different parts: physical, human, and curricular. The physical environment includes such features as the space, room arrangement, equipment, and materials; the human environment comprises the social atmosphere and interactions between and among children and adults; and the curricular environment includes the curriculum content, experiences, routines, schedule, values, goals, and daily organization. Each part must be considered when you design the whole learning environment for young children.

Principles of Environmental Design and Materials Selection

Designing environments for young children is based on what we know about children's growth, development, and learning. These principles of environmental design apply to all early childhood settings. The differences in early childhood environments can be found in the types and uses of age-appropriate materials as well as how the different team members and families participate to make that environment unique. The following five research-based principles of environmental design will guide your development of a positive environment for all children.

Good Early Childhood Environments are Organized, Stimulating, and Aesthetically Pleasing. For children to respond favorably to an environment, it must be predictable and comprehensible to them (Bredekamp & Copple, 1997). Predictable environments have simple routines and rituals that enable children to feel secure and safe and to understand what behaviors are expected of them; predictable environments also have flexible structures that make it easy for everyone to work and be productive (Dodge, Jablon, & Bickart, 1994). Think back to Ms. Koen, the teacher of toddlers whom you met in the opening scenario. Initially, her environment was not orderly or predictable—indeed, it was quite chaotic! Nor was there a place to keep materials so the children could use them easily to engage in meaningful play. After Ms. Koen reorganized her space, the children knew where to find what they needed and how to maintain a sense of order. She had provided predictability for her toddlers. Moreover, Ms. Koen made clear her behavioral expectations about the use of materials. How you organize your environment reflects the needs and developmental levels of the children you teach, your beliefs about teaching and learning, and the goals and values of the community in which you teach (Edwards, Gandini, & Forman, 1993). Good environments are also pleasant places to be. They often have living green plants, attractive colors, comfortable furniture, soft lighting and colors, open spaces, and a clean fragrance. A pleasant environment for living and learning invites both adults and children into the learning process.

Good Early Childhood Environments Create a Caring Community of Learners. Early childhood settings must support positive relationships between and among adults and children, children and children, and teachers and families. Children need consistent, positive relationships with a limited number of adults and other children in a respectful setting to develop healthy relationships with others and to learn about themselves and their world (Bredekamp & Copple, 1997). These conditions enable children to feel like a part of their community, which connects them to others. Being part of a caring community of learners means including all children in all aspects of classroom life. It also enables children to appreciate individual differences and value the concept that each of them is unique and has something to offer. Cultivating a sense of belonging wherever possible is an essential principle of environmental design (Dodge et al., 1994).

Good Early Childhood Environments Reflect Clear Program Goals. The goals of every program are expressed directly in the arrangement and relationships of the environment. How you relate to children and families in your care, how you arrange physical space and select materials, and how you use space and time reflect the goals of the program. While the goals of early childhood programs and individual classrooms vary

(a)   (b)

Adults' ideas about effective learning environments have changed through the years.

widely because of age, community, culture, and experience, goals are essential to creating environments. If, for example, a goal of your program is to nurture children's curiosity and disposition to learn, your environment will likely include regular opportunities for children to engage in individual, small-group, and large-group problem solving and social interactions that offer multiple ways of learning and showing what they know. In contrast, consider the American classrooms earlier in this century that had students' desks bolted to wooden floors: Clearly the goal was to have all the children learn the same knowledge and set of skills at the same time and at the same rate. The focus in these classrooms was on whole-group activities during which children were doing the same tasks.

Good Early Childhood Environments Protect Children's Health and Safety. Early childhood environments must be designed to support children's physical and psychological safety and health and to meet both local and national standards for licensing. At a minimum, physical health and safety needs include adequate space and appropriate entrances and exits. It also includes food, clothing, shelter, rest, medical care, and a balance between active, sensory stimulation and quiet opportunities for reflection. Psychological health and safety needs include a consistent, predictable relationship with an attentive, caring adult who has high, positive expectations for children and enables strong peer acceptance and "freedom from exploitation and discrimination in their communities" (Weissbourd, 1996, p. 8). Children know they are in a safe place when they feel welcome and relaxed. This happens when their needs are cared for and met and when adults listen to and talk with them in a respectful way. Children who grow up having their basic physical and psychological needs met are likely to trust themselves and others and to rely on inner resources for coping with difficulties. On the other hand, children who grow up without having their basic physical and psychological needs met are at a clear disadvantage for becoming successful learners (Carnegie Task Force on Meeting the Needs of Young Children, 1994; Squibb & Yardley , 1999).

Good Early Childhood Environments Provide Appropriate Materials and Equipment.
The materials and equipment in the early childhood environment are learning tools that
suggest what children can do. They also support children's physical, intellectual, social,
and emotional development. Materials are classroom items, such as crayons, paints, and
paper, that are regularly replaced or replenished; equipment refers to large, more costly
items such as furniture and outdoor structures. The best materials for all children are attractive, have strong sensory appeal, invite children to imagine and create their own
ideas and interpretations, and allow for active exploration. These materials have the following characteristics:

- They are developmentally appropriate and match children's abilities and interests.
- They are open-ended and offer flexibility, variety, and multiple uses for children of
  different ages and abilities.
- They are culturally appropriate and nonsexist. They reflect the culture of the children's families and community and promote equality and tolerance rather than per-
  petuating stereotypical roles.
- They are safe, durable, nontoxic, well-designed, and of good workmanship (Essa,
  1996; Feeney & Magarick, 1984).

Infant and toddler environments have unique criteria—the six *S*'s (Lowman & Ruhmann, 1998):

1. Simplicity—areas are divided into large motor, messy, or quiet zones
2. Softness—there are comfortable, homelike qualities and textures
3. Seclusion—there are small spaces where infants and toddlers can be by themselves
4. Senses—there are appeals to all senses without sensory overload
5. Stimulation—there is a balance that allows children to feel successful yet still provides challenges
6. Stability—there is a slow and careful rotation of centers to provide a sense of security

The Compendium of Early Childhood Resources and Materials at the end of this book
suggests basic materials and equipment for infants and toddlers, preschoolers and
kindergartners, and school-age children.

A well-designed early childhood environment holds numerous possibilities for optimizing children's learning and development. If you follow the principles of a well-designed
environment, you will become a teacher who shows genuine interest in children's activities
and supports their efforts. You will also see children who are absorbed in learning and make
good learning choices (Isenberg & Jalongo, 1997). Table 5.1 describes the key features of a
good environment and gives practical applications of each.

PAUSE AND REFLECT ABOUT PRINCIPLES OF ENVIRONMENTAL DESIGN

Think about a college classroom where you are now studying to become a teacher. What
principles of design are evident or not evident, and how do they affect your learning?
What changes could you realistically suggest to make this classroom setting more powerful for learning?

Table 5.1
Key Features of a Good Learning Environment

Feature	Characteristics	Practical Applications
Ideas	• reflects concrete evidence of the teacher's beliefs about teaching and learning	• Children use materials independently or with support from an adult or more capable peer. • Children are given opportunities to choose activities and materials and take initiative about how plans will be completed. • Children are encouraged to identify and solve problems.
People	• promotes quality interactions between and among adults and children, adults and adults, and children and children • focuses on how adults behave toward children	• Adults show delight with children by smiling, listening, and attending. • Adults respect children and empathize with their feelings. • Adults support children's learning through probing questions, comments, coaching, and extensions. • Families and community resources are regular and integral to the program.
Time	• the schedule allows children to work at their own pace to complete projects	• Long-term investigations, representations, and interdisciplinary experiences are present. • There is a balance of large-group, small-group, and individual learning time. • Outdoor play is a priority. • Opportunities exist to work one-on-one with an adult, with another child, in groups, or alone.
Space	• attention is given to the arrangement of the physical environment (and the accessibility of materials	• Children and teachers arrange space as they explore and as interests change. • Centers are clearly defined by low shelving, carpets, or labels. • Areas are large enough to accommodate children's real and changing interests. • Areas contain adequate table and floor space for children to work together comfortably. • Areas exist where children can spend time alone if desired.
Resources	• concrete materials, objects, people, and ideas are available for children to explore and solve real problems	• Original children's artwork is displayed throughout the room. • Child- and adult-made materials reflect the children's families, cultures, and interests. • Materials include real items as well as replicas. • Transitions occur naturally for children.

SOURCE: Adapted from "Creating the Learning Environment: Context for Living and Learning" by S. V. McLean, 1995, in J. Moyer, Ed., *Selecting Educational Equipment and Materials for School and Home,* Wheaton, MD: Association for Childhood Education International.

Your Role in Designing a Safe, Healthy, and Appropriate Learning Environment

Designing an appropriate learning environment is an important skill for early childhood educators. Consider the following example of a first-grade teacher, Ms. Schutta, as you think about your role in providing good learning environments for all children.

The physical environment in Ms. Schutta's first-grade classroom is divided into areas designed for specific activities. There are clear entrances and exits to these areas, pathways within the classroom for the children to move about safely, and tables clustered together where children do their work. Ms. Schutta's classroom is full of plants, has displays of children's work, comfortable and cozy areas, and a few aesthetically pleasing prints and posters on clean, painted walls. The daily schedule begins first thing in the morning with a large block of time (45 minutes) called "breathing out" time, during which children transition from home to school and have time to settle into the school routines. (Wassermann, 1990). During "breathing out" time, Ms. Schutta observes from the sidelines and then works one-on-one with children who need specific instructional skill or concept development. There is also a 2-hour language arts block, during which children pursue individual projects, including a variety of hands-on, small-group learning experiences, followed by a sharing and debriefing time. During this workshop, the children choose from among three or four centers. Each center is clearly labeled; materials are accessible and inviting. Some of the centers in this class are a class library that contains collections of books of many different sizes and genres; an art center that has an easel stand with tempera paints and watercolors, a wikki center with a board for wikki sticks (e.g., wax-covered, bendable sticks the size of pipe cleaners that are used for construction and can stick to different surfaces); a game-and-puzzle center where children together or independently work with wooden puzzles, Lego blocks, pattern blocks, or unifix cubes or play checkers, dominoes, or board games; and a magnet center filled with a variety of magnetic letters that children put together to make sounds and words that they know. The content taught through Ms. Schutta's centers is based upon county and state standards of learning. One of the first things Ms. Schutta's first graders do upon arrival at school is to select an area for work by hanging a tag on a choice board, allowing them to occupy a space at a particular center. The morning block ends with a sharing time, during which children share important aspects of projects that are meaningful to them.

One of Ms. Schutta's first-graders, Jon, a child with learning disabilities, has difficulty with writing. When the class was studying the life cycle of the pumpkin, Jon drew pictures to tell the story of the pumpkin's stages of growth. He explained each stage of his drawing to Ms. Schutta, who wrote down his words so he could share them with his classmates. Chad, on the other hand, is receiving services because he is gifted and talented in math and reading, but he does not like to write. Ms. Schutta noticed how he loves baseball and provided him with trade books and research formats so he could learn more about the sport. Chad used the long blocks of time to draw and write about a baseball book he was reading. He created a baseball diamond, listed baseball facts, and used his love for baseball to develop his writing skills.

Ms. Schutta is demonstrating several key aspects of her role as designer of a safe, healthy, and appropriate environment. While there is no single set of criteria for such settings, educational researchers have identified the following guidelines for all early childhood environments.

Arrange Space to Meet the Needs of All Learners. One of the very first decisions you will make when you have your own setting is to determine how to utilize the space you have. How and where you place furniture, arrange materials, and organize space will influence the behavior and learning of your children (Kritchevsky, Prescott, & Walling, 1977; Loughlin & Suina, 1982; McLean, 1995). Space must be arranged to accommodate a variety of learning activities occurring in different-sized groupings. Finding the right use of space is a challenge for all teachers, both experienced and new; somehow, classrooms never seem to have enough of it. Notice that Ms. Schutta arranged her space into centers, or areas, where children work together on projects in small groups, in pairs, or individually. She labeled each area clearly and organized and displayed the learning materials so that the children can access them easily and independently. Figure 5.1 shows Ms. Schutta's room arrangement for school-age children. A sample room arrangement for infants and toddlers is provided in Figure 5.2, and a sample for kindergartners is provided in Figure 5.3.

Use Time Flexibly. Time affects student learning and reveals your priorities. Long blocks of time provide children with uninterrupted periods for active exploration, deeper understanding, and higher-level application of subject matter. At the same time, they enable you, the teacher, to help children understand complex concepts and ideas by providing them with more opportunities to apply those concepts to authentic problems (Association for Supervision and Curriculum Development, 1997; Edwards, Gandini, & Forman, 1993; Garreau & Kennedy, 1991). With longer blocks of time, you are more likely to use a variety of teaching strategies to keep children engaged in learning. In the preceding scenario, we witnessed how Ms. Schutta used two long blocks of time—"breathing out" first thing in the morning to help children transition from home to school and a language arts workshop with options for children to apply their developing language arts skills and knowledge. What is important to observe about Ms. Schutta's use of time is how she uses it to make learning interesting and engaging for her first-graders.

Select Appropriate Learning Materials. An environment that supports children's learning contains materials that capture and sustain children's interests and imagination, that are stored attractively on shelves, and that are organized to extend children's learning (Isenberg & Jalongo, 1997). Infants need materials that stimulate their senses, such as soft, textured toys, while toddlers need toys that challenge their emerging motor skills, such as climbing and push-and-pull toys. Older children, on the other hand, need materials that will strengthen their minds and muscles, such as group games. Notice that Ms. Schutta selected a wide variety of interesting learning materials for each of her centers.

Create a Positive Climate for Learning. Climate is the feeling children get from the environment that dictates to what extent they will be productive and engaged learners. A positive classroom climate is essential for a good learning environment. Perhaps the most important teaching decision Ms. Schutta made was to establish a setting that encourages children to exchange their ideas and progress, respect each other and each other's work, and feel a sense of community. Recall that Chad had the freedom to pursue his interests while practicing important writing skills. The 1997 Iowa Teacher of the Year and a National Teacher of the Year finalist, Jan Mitchell, uses five key attributes as a framework for creating a positive climate for learning. Figure 5.4 lists and defines the essential attributes of every learning setting.

Show Students That You Care about Them and What They are Learning. At this point in your preparation to become an early childhood educator, you might feel overwhelmed and uncertain about your ability to provide appropriate learning environments. As you

FIGURE 5.1

Room arrangement for school-age children

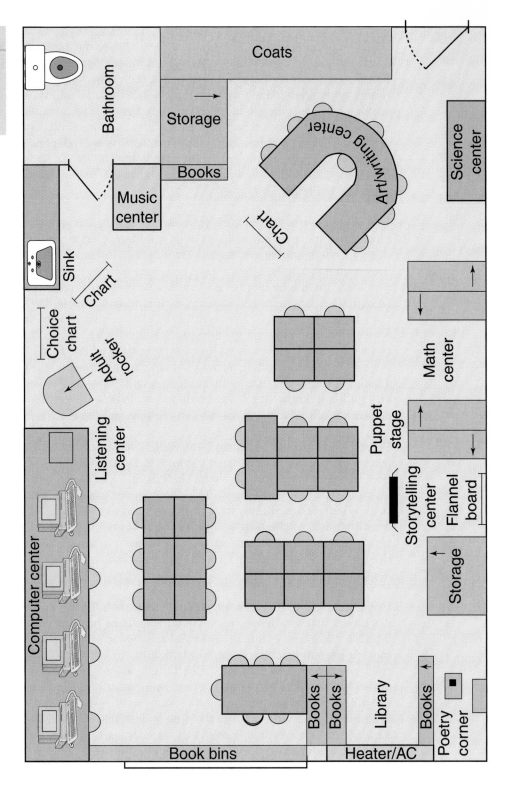

Courtesy of Mary Schutta and Robyn Cochran, Deer Park Elementary School, Fairfax, Virginia.

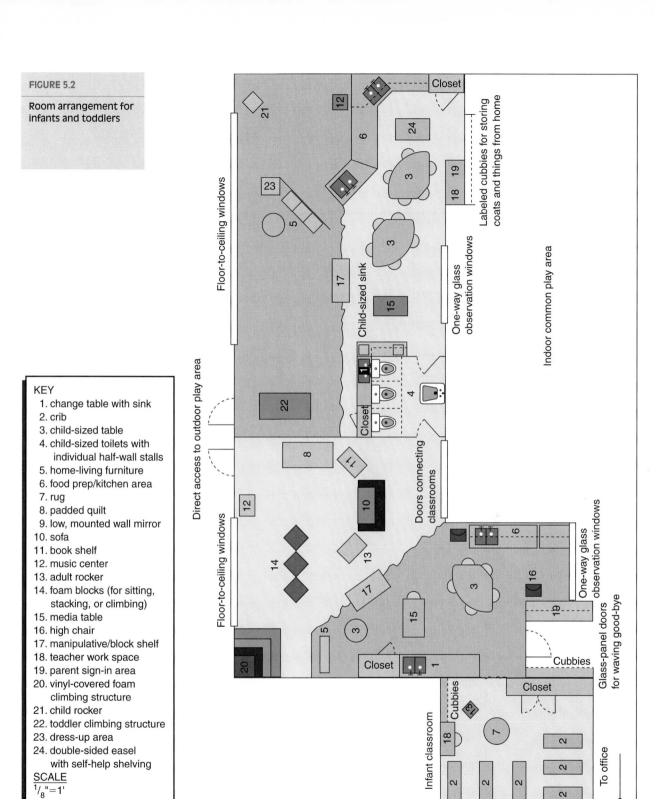

FIGURE 5.2

Room arrangement for infants and toddlers

KEY
1. change table with sink
2. crib
3. child-sized table
4. child-sized toilets with
   individual half-wall stalls
5. home-living furniture
6. food prep/kitchen area
7. rug
8. padded quilt
9. low, mounted wall mirror
10. sofa
11. book shelf
12. music center
13. adult rocker
14. foam blocks (for sitting,
    stacking, or climbing)
15. media table
16. high chair
17. manipulative/block shelf
18. teacher work space
19. parent sign-in area
20. vinyl-covered foam
    climbing structure
21. child rocker
22. toddler climbing structure
23. dress-up area
24. double-sided easel
    with self-help shelving

SCALE
$\frac{1}{8}" = 1'$

Courtesy of Nellie Bagley, Fairfax County Employees Child Care Center, Fairfax, Virginia.

157

FIGURE 5.3

Room arrangement for kindergartners

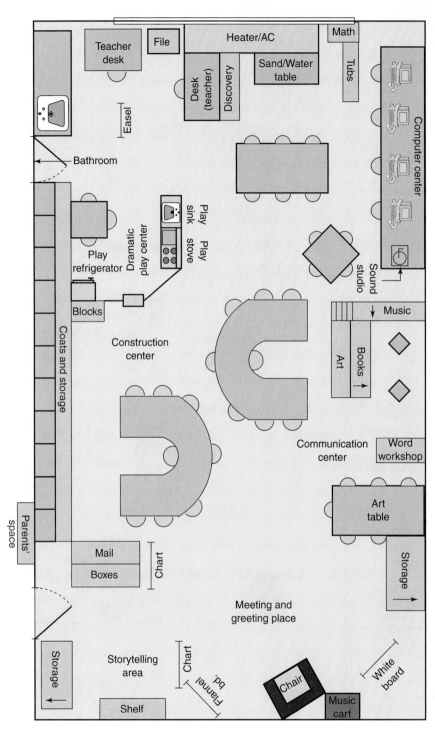

Courtesy of Gail Ritchie, Kings Park Elementary School, Fairfax, Virginia.

FIGURE 5.4		
Essential attributes of a positive learning climate	**Security**	Children must feel safe enough to take risks as they learn.
	Identity	Every child must be valued and appreciated as an individual with unique needs and abilities.
	Responsibility	A sense of belonging to a community is felt by the children.
	Dignity	Every child should have self-respect and respect for the thoughts and actions of others.
	Community	A sense of trust and responsibility is created and supported by the children, families, and teachers.

SOURCE: Adapted from "Making a Good Start," *Education Update 39*(6), p. 6, Association for Supervision and Curriculum Development, 1997.

gain experience and confidence in doing so, be certain to show children that you care about them and their learning. A true spirit of caring is at the heart of safe, healthy, and appropriate learning environments. You show caring when you find out about children's interests and offer them just enough support, structure, and expectations to be self-directed, responsible learners. The ethic of care is aptly discussed by Nel Noddings (1995): "Caring for students is fundamental in teaching and . . . developing people with a strong capacity for care is a major objective of responsible education" (p. 678). Ms. Schutta exhibited an ethic of care with both Jon and Chad. She took time to uncover their interests (e.g., Chad's love of baseball) and teach them skills in a supportive way through what is important to them (e.g., taking dictation from Jon about a pumpkin's life cycle so he could share his ideas). She provided different kinds of support to each child to increase their participation, achieve a sense of belonging, and become better connected with their learning.

Connect with the Children's Families. It is a well-known fact that strong families make strong schools. As a teacher of young children, you will want to find ways to connect with the children's families, because they are an indelible part of your classroom environment. Send home positive notes—you can always find something positive to say about each and every one of your students. Such notes let parents know that you have a vested interest in their children's learning and that you care about their children's progress. (See Chapter 10 for more specific suggestions about the family-school connection.) The following Featuring Families provides ideas about helping parents understand centers in the learning environment.

FEATURING *FAMILIES*

COMMUNICATING WITH FAMILIES ABOUT LEARNING CENTERS

Ms. Davis uses a center-based approach to learning. Because parents are sometimes unfamiliar with this approach to teaching and learning, they often question its purpose and value. Therefore, at the first open house for families, Ms. Davis plans a minicenter time so parents can get a flavor of what and how their children learn at school. Ms. Davis prepares the following note for each parent.

A planned classroom helps your child grow, develop, and learn. It is often organized around centers. This approach helps your child learn by doing and thinking about what he or she is doing. As your child changes activities, he or she will work with many different groups of children. In this way, your child will learn to talk with others about ideas and to meet and solve problems. Notice that I have prepared activities for you to do tonight in the different centers. Please choose a center and see what your child does there. Below is a list of centers. You will have 30 minutes to try one or more centers. I hope you enjoy yourself and will write down what you have learned as well as any questions you might have.

Construction	Computer	Listening	Mathematics	Science
Library	Art	Dramatic play	Writing	

Following is the parent activity that Ms. Davis posted in the Science center.

Materials

Living Things Area: hermit crabs in aquarium, 5-gallon aquarium with fish, food for the animals, a feeding log/journal, 3 magnifying glasses, a balance scale

Electricity Box: an open box with batteries, wires, switches, small lightbulbs, magnets, and tools

Other Materials: a small basket with a variety of familiar objects, an old radio and tools to take it apart, a collection of shells, books on fish and hermit crabs, paper, crayons, and pencils

Purpose: The more young children know about and understand their world, the more they become independent, confident learners. The science center encourages children to ask questions, to look for answers, to experiment, and to engage in a scientific method of learning. It conveys a message to children that their interests are important and gives them new ideas to think about. When children finish their investigations in the center, they show what they are learning in pictures, words, writing, or constructions with others.

Task 1: Using the materials in the electricity box, figure out more than one way to make the lightbulb shine.

Task 2: Observe the hermit crabs. Then feed them and look at them using the magnifying glass. Record your findings in the journal. What questions do you have? Look in some of the books to find your answers.

Conclusion: What did you notice about your learning experience?

Why the Environment Is Important

The classroom environment is as important as the role of the teacher because it directly affects how children behave, develop, and learn (Cooper, Hegarty, Hegarty, & Simco,

1996; Wortham, 1996). Many organizational or behavioral problems within early childhood settings can be reduced or eliminated by creating healthy conditions for learning. These conditions make learning safe and supportive, and they encourage all children to develop confidence, take risks, work independently, and strengthen their social skills. High-quality environments provide a wide range of authentic learning opportunities whenever and wherever possible. They also contain appropriate materials for individuals and groups of children to use independently; enable adults to observe, support, and meet the learning needs of each child; and support program goals and outcomes. Figure 5.5 describes seven conditions for learning and their implications for classroom environments (Cambourne, 1988).

There is a large body of research that documents the effect of the classroom environment on children's behavior, learning, and development and identifies key features that reflect high-quality environments (Cryer & Phillipsen, 1997; Trawick-Smith, 1992). These features—ambiance, privacy, size, density, arrangement of space, the meeting of individual needs, and cultural awareness—are discussed in the following paragraphs.

Ambiance: Light, Color, Texture, and Noise

Ambiance refers to sensory information that increases comfort, understanding, and learning. The sights, sounds, smells, and touches in every setting bring it to life for the present but also become part of long-term memory, to be recalled long after one has left that environment (Crumpacker, 1995). Light is one important aspect of early childhood environments. They should have as much natural light as possible through windows and doors. Hanging things in windows and mirrors on walls creates a spacious feeling. Where this is not possible, a variety of soft lighting, such as desk and floor lamps instead of glaring fluorescent lighting, should be used for a softer effect. Color also contributes to the feeling of an environment. Environments for children should have enough color to stimulate but not overwhelm the senses. Texture stimulates tactile learning, which is important for all children, especially those with special needs. Good early childhood environments have many materials with soft textures, such as finger-paints, modeling dough, and stuffed toys, and cozy furnishings, such as beanbag chairs, carpeting, and pillows (Jones & Prescott, 1978); soft and cozy items make children feel safe and secure. Noise that comes from children's natural interactions in active learning environments is

a.

b.

Which conditions for learning are apparent in these classroom environments?

FIGURE 5.5

Eight conditions
for learning

Condition	Implications for Environment
Immersion	Environments are organized to immerse children with materials and ideas in a variety of ways. For example, children learning to read should be immersed in print throughout the day.
Demonstration	Environments support children's learning with many models or examples of the concepts and processes they are learning. For example, children need examples of how to solve problems in mathematics.
Expectation	Environments contain adults who expect all children to learn and provide children with many opportunities to be successful with appropriate and interesting materials and experiences.
Responsibility	Environments enable children to actively participate in making good learning choices about when, how, and what to learn. When environments support children's independence, children learn self-management and self-control.
Approximation	Environments allow children plenty of time to work on a task and gradually achieve the desired goal. Children cannot do this if they become overly concerned about making mistakes and always having "right answers."
Employment/Use	Environments offer a variety of authentic learning experiences in all curriculum areas that apply to children's real-life experiences. For example, children build good habits about nutrition by eating and cooking healthy snacks.
Response/Engagement	Environments help children construct their own knowledge by being actively involved in authentic learning situations. Engaged learners think, "I can participate successfully in this activity," or "This learning is important to me in my life," or "If I try something new, I will not be ridiculed."

SOURCE: Adapted from "Toward a Relevant Theory of Literacy Learning: Twenty Years of Inquiry by B. Cambourne, 1995, *The Reading Teacher, 49*(3), pp. 182–190.

healthy. On the other hand, environments where children yell and scream or teachers raise their voices upset children and impede their ability to learn. In many early childhood classrooms, you will find special spaces designed for children to seek privacy and feel secure by being able to escape from the bustling activity of a classroom environment filled with engaged learners (Sanoff, 1995).

Privacy

Children have different needs for levels of interaction. Some children need time alone and enjoy silent periods; others do not. For children who easily become overstimulated, tired, or upset, places to be alone are important, because they respect such children's need to have a quiet moment. You can create private spaces in safe alcoves that contain soft features such as carpeting and pillows or as part of a loft where children can be quiet but still see the rest of the classroom. Quiet spaces set off by themselves and housed with some books and perhaps a few floor cushions send the message, "Here is a place where I can think, watch, and collect myself in a safe way." Private spaces nurture children's emotional health and also send a message about how to use the area or the materials. There should be space for children to play alone or with a friend, protected in some way from other children, in every classroom (Cryer & Phillipsen, 1997).

Size

Size refers both to the number of children in a learning group and to areas of the classroom. The best early childhood environments enable children to interact regularly and often in small groups within a small space. Research shows that small-group interactions improve children's attitudes, achievement, social skills, and voluntary participation (Moore, 1983; Moore & Lackney, 1995). In contrast, extensive large-group interactions have been associated with "decreased attention, lower task performance, behavioral problems, and social withdrawal" (Moore & Lackney, 1995, p. 18). Daily opportunities for learning in small groups enable teachers to use a wider array of interaction patterns with children, learning centers, student learning teams, peer tutorials, and other instructional strategies.

In regard to the size of areas of the classroom, again, smaller is better. Areas provided for small groups mean low numbers of children interacting together or with an adult. Small groups foster familylike feelings of sharing, connection, trust, and support. These feelings are what bind groups of people together (Crumpacker, 1995). How you create spaces for small-group interaction with the materials and equipment you have will send messages to children, such as "This is not a space for a lot of people. We will not be pasting or cutting with scissors here, or doing gymnastics." There are active places as well, which are wide open in the classroom. For example, there is enough room in the block area for children to work together, so that social development and shared thinking are encouraged. The block area has the blocks neatly organized so children can think through what they are doing and what they are planning to do.

Density

Density, the number of children who occupy the square footage of a space, or use available materials, is closely connected to classroom size. Because research shows the positive effects of small, intimate groupings, having environments with very high concentrations of children, adults, or materials would be counterproductive. There are two types of classroom density: social density, which refers to how many people are in a space, and spatial density, how many square feet are available per child (Trawick-Smith, 1992).

Social Density. From the literature on size, we know that children in large groups interact in less positive ways, regardless of how much space is available to them (Moore, 1983; Moore & Lackney, 1995). Having lots of children and adults in one area increases social density. Some studies have shown that social density can restrict peer interactions, verbalization, cooperative behaviors, and fantasy play (Clarke-Stewart, 1987). Smaller groups are more likely to create feelings of comfort and safety and to enable children to acquire independence and social competence when sharing classroom space with a moderate number of other children and adults (Trawick-Smith, 1992).

Spatial Density. Generally, the smaller the space available for each child, the more likely it is that children will have difficulty with their interactions. The National Association for

What impact can social density have on children?

the Education of Young Children (1991) requires a minimum of 35 square feet per child indoors and 75 square feet per child outdoors. Not enough square feet per child can lead to uninvolved, aggressive, and solitary behaviors. Similarly, not enough toys and materials can lead to such undesirable behaviors as teasing, hitting, fighting, and playing alone too much. Teachers might increase the amount of play materials, then, as one solution to problems of negative behaviors. When the environment is small and intimate, but with enough square footage and materials to allow active learning, it can foster the positive behaviors and learning we seek for all children.

Arrangement of Space

How materials, equipment, and furniture are arranged in a classroom can critically affect children's self-esteem, security and comfort, autonomy, self-control, and peer interactions (Sanoff, 1995). When teachers divide space into defined interest and learning areas, they protect children from visual and auditory distraction and promote a more intimate setting for learning. Separating the active from the quiet and the messy from the nonmessy areas also provides an organizational structure that can enhance children's persistence at tasks and improve the quality of their social interactions (Moore, 1983; McLean, 1995).

Learning Centers. Learning centers are well-defined, organized areas of the classroom that are set aside for specific learning purposes without the teacher's constant presence and direction. They enable teachers to integrate the curriculum, develop cultural awareness, enhance multiple intelligences, and nurture children's spontaneity and originality (Isbell, 1995; Isenberg & Jalongo, 1997). A center arrangement enables children to interact more frequently than they can in large groups. In centers, children are more likely to get immediate responses to their ideas, communication, and work. Centers allow for self-directed activities with opportunities to work individually or with a partner, thereby helping children to become more independent or to learn to work cooperatively.

The versatility of centers makes them an essential part of early childhood settings. Some possible learning outcomes for children in center-based learning environments include the following:

- problem-solving ability, by making good learning choices that determine the direction of their play and their work
- responsibility, by selecting, using, and caring for their materials
- persistence, by carrying out plans to completion (Isbell, 1995; Isenberg & Jalongo, 1997; Sanoff, 1995)

The Meeting of Individual Needs

High-quality environments meet the unique needs of individual children. For example, children from some family backgrounds and cultures have many privacy needs. Girls may show a greater need for personal space and may react more negatively than boys to wide-open spaces and classrooms with more teachers per child (Sanoff, 1995). Children with special needs may have specific space requirements. Teachers must ensure that children with physical disabilities have access to all play areas in the classroom; thus, for example, lofts may not be appropriate for them. Cultural, family, gender, and ability differences must be considered, then, in planning early childhood environments.

Cultural Awareness

Children begin to notice differences early; therefore, the physical and visual environment should reflect the lives of the children and families that it serves. Just as your lifestyle and home suit your needs, culture, and community, so, too should the setting in which children learn. Such an environment is called multicultural or antibias, because it helps children understand and appreciate their own backgrounds as well as the backgrounds of others. What does a multicultural setting look like? It might include posters on the walls that represent the cultures of the children in the room; a dramatic play center with dolls, toys, and books from a variety of cultures, and a classroom library containing a rich selection of books and music from many cultures (Jalongo, 2000).

You must take into account each of these environmental features when planning your own early childhood setting. We will consider them further in the next section.

You have learned about the key characteristics and essential attributes for creating a positive learning environment. Selecting appropriate materials; connecting with families; considering space, light, and noise factors—these details are only a few of the many critical aspects of providing an overall healthy environment in your classroom. In addition, one personal attribute for the early childhood practitioner which cannot be overemphasized is continued vigilance for each child's health and safety. Learning to anticipate problems before they occur is key. To do this, you need to experience the classroom from the child's perspective—actually getting down on hands and knees and seeing things from a child's vantage point is one practical way to prevent health and safety problems.

Viewing this video clip will increase your awareness of the differences between child-resistent products and making something child-proof. As you'll see, being vigilant is necessary and important when it comes to the health and safety of the children in your classroom. Even though most of the video centers around the home, the insights given here may prove useful when you meet resistance to health and safety rules like handwashing, locking purses and other personal items in drawers, and posting emergency numbers.

1. List six safety and health rules that you would post in a classroom. How can you incorporate these rules into your classroom daily?

2. What can you do to take precautions against any unnecessary accidents involving health and safety in your classroom?

3. You've decided to have a family activity at preschool. What special health and safety precautions might be worth consideration?

Planning and Evaluating the Indoor and Outdoor Environments

Think back to the teachers you met in the Meet the Teachers opening section of this chapter. Recall how Ms. Endo modified her environment so all children could participate and how Ms. Mitsoff believed in the importance of positive relationships between children. Reread that section and think about those teachers as you explore how to plan the indoor environment.

Planning the classroom environment is one of the most visible outcomes of your efforts. A well-planned environment provides a safe, supportive place for children to live, learn, and grow; provides a balance of teacher-directed and child-initiated activities; and invites children to use materials in purposeful and meaningful ways (Bredekamp & Copple, 1997; Kontos & Wilcox-Herzog, 1997). How well the teacher plans and organizes the environment determines how children grow, develop, and learn. It also determines the quality of the environment. Planning is necessary to encourage children to learn at their own pace, to provide appropriate experiences, and to offer options for pursuing special interests. We will examine the nature of both indoor and outdoor environments.

Preparing the Indoor Environment

The indoor environment is the place in which children acquire skills, concepts, and attitudes about the world. It is, in fact, children's home for learning that occurs each day. There should be planned opportunities for children to develop self-help skills, make good learning choices, become self-directed, and feel competent and confident. In this way, schools facilitate children's learning from the home environment to the school environment. Think about the essential elements of high-quality indoor environments for young children as you read the next section.

Room Arrangement and Space

Space can be arranged in two different ways: It can be arranged according to children's play and developmental needs, such as physical, social, or cognitive development, or by curriculum areas, such as writing, reading, science, and art. Regardless of how you arrange it, space should facilitate, not hinder, learning. Planning for room arrangement should include the following:

- a large group area to hold demonstrations, meetings, and discussions
- small-group areas for work in small groups, in pairs, and alone
- individual areas to facilitate independent work on projects
- display areas that invite children to "stop, look, touch, talk, question, and think" (Cooper et al., 1996, p. 2) about instructional materials, reference materials, or their own work
- clearly labeled work areas and easy access to materials to facilitate autonomy and independence

Large-group Area. Some teachers locate the large-group area in the center of the room and have smaller work and play areas around the room, others arrange a quiet corner of the classroom for it, and still others use a large classroom library for this purpose. In the large-group area, you will need an easel for group work such as class news and charts. Within easy reach, you will also want an organized supply of materials, such as markers of various colors, chart paper, scissors, a magnetic board or a cookie sheet with an assortment of magnetic letters and shapes, sentence strips, and masking tape or other tape.

Small-group Area. Teachers often use low bookshelves, tables, and other furniture to create centers or areas where groups of children can work together. Using these as dividers gives the room an open, uncluttered look and gives you an unobstructed view. Dividers can double as a display for instructions, examples of children's work, or storage for reference materials. Small-group work areas should have enough space, materials, and chairs for the number of children who will typically be working there. Crowded areas frustrate children and make it difficult for them to work together productively. If you have desks in your classroom, you might want to cluster some together to form a worktable.

Independent Area. Every classroom needs to have space for individual projects. Even though children can work independently at a common table, they need enough space for their own materials. Moreover, some individual areas should be quiet places where individuals can work without distraction, thereby providing more psychological than actual separation.

Displays. Classroom displays are resources that should encourage children to observe, question, and investigate, so you need to be especially mindful of how you use them. Crowded walls that are overstimulating and unplanned discourage rather than encourage learning (Cooper et al., 1996; Sanoff, 1995). Displays should be at the children's eye level so they can revisit their work and use reference materials easily. A large display space is best used for a piece of well-loved writing that becomes shared reading the children go back to again and again or for a classroom mural that many children had a hand in creating. Teachers use displays to allow children to reflect on and discuss their own work and the work of their classmates, and they point out the positive qualities of all pieces. Displays are changed after they have been appreciated. When walls and dividers are covered with children's work, appropriate posters, and aesthetically appealing art that reflects the culture of the children, they send the message that the children and families in the group are valued and valuable. On the other hand, when walls and dividers are covered with cartoonlike materials or oversized management tools, such as classroom rules, they can be visually noisy and stressful for children.

Clearly Labeled Centers and Easy Access to Materials. Most classrooms include a number of work areas. Some may be permanent centers, such as those for art and writing; others may be changed according to children's interests, needs, and the particular topic under study. These areas, or centers, have clear pathways so children can safely move in and out, are labeled clearly so children know what to do at each center and how many children can be there at one time, and contain materials that enable children's thinking and exploration. Following are some suggestions for making centers work.

- Identify the center with print or an appropriate picture.
- Arrange commonly used materials in clearly labeled baskets or other containers that are accessible from where the children are working independently. Children should know how the materials are used and stored.

FIGURE 5.6

Example of work board for self-help skills

Arrival

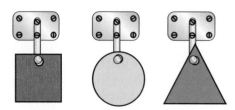

hang-up

check-in

choose a center

Courtesy of Mary Kleinpaste.

- Introduce centers one at a time, explicitly demonstrating and practicing the routines for using each one with the children.
- Have an adequate supply of materials.
- Use a work board to establish routines for participating in centers. The work board can be on an eye-level easel or can lean against a wall. Children can choose and monitor center use through this tool. Figures 5.6 and 5.7 show work boards

FIGURE 5.7

Example of work board for choosing centers

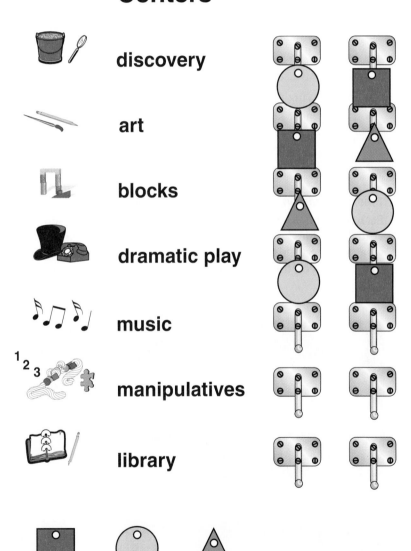

Centers

discovery

art

blocks

dramatic play

music

manipulatives

library

Name cards

Courtesy of Mary Kleinpaste.

used by Mary Kleinpaste in her classroom of preschool children with disabilities. Notice how she uses her boards to provide children with responsibility for developing independent self-help skills and choosing centers with the aid of pictorial representations.

Storage. You will need storage for materials and for children's daily work. Children need space in which to keep work-in-progress, finished work that will be used to assess their progress, and personal belongings. Materials, supplies, and work can be stored in a variety of ways but should be orderly and aesthetically pleasing. Here are some suggestions:

- Use easy-to-find storage containers that have different and interesting textures, such as berry baskets or decorated boxes.
- Consider balance and design when arranging materials, displays, and furniture.
- Store daily work in a labeled, clear plastic tub or box.
- Use a plastic crate with hanging files for finished writing.
- Try a drying rack for drying paintings.
- Use a plastic shoe rack for storing puppets.
- Cut cereal boxes in half, cover them with contact paper, and have students store their materials in them. These boxes can easily be placed in the center of worktables to designate particular children who should work there.

Time, Schedule, and Routines

Each day, you need to provide time for a balance of large-group, small-group, and individual activities. Your schedule should provide consistency for learners so they know what to expect; this gives children control over their day and conveys a clear message about what you think is important. For example, we know that long blocks of time en-

Labels help keep active classrooms organized and aid classroom volunteers.

able children to be more productive, self-directed, and self-expressive, and they send the message that children's work is important (Garreau & Kennedy, 1991; Isenberg & Jalongo, 1997). A good place to keep your daily schedule is in your meeting area, where you and the children can review it each morning.

Routines are the regular and predictable activities that form the basis of the daily schedule and ensure effective use of time and space. They help children sense the passage of time (e.g., snack follows cleanup) and enable them to anticipate events (e.g., a musical selection marks the end of the day). A consistent but flexible schedule and regular routines are foundational to appropriate indoor environments. They set the stage for learning and can thwart or create an atmosphere for learning that makes your classroom special for every child.

Figure 5.8 provides sample schedules for half-day preschool, full-day kindergarten, and second grade that can guide your planning. One note of caution: Adhering to a rigid schedule can impede children's thinking just as much as not having any schedule at all.

PAUSE AND REFLECT ABOUT WHY THE ENVIRONMENT IS SO IMPORTANT

Consider the floor plan shown in Figure 5.1, 5.2, or 5.3. Describe at least three features of good indoor environments that you notice in it. Now use the evaluation criteria listed in Figure 5.9 to determine its quality. What message does the room convey about the teacher's values? What changes could you suggest to make it more inviting and appropriate for young children?

FIGURE 5.8

Sample schedules

Half-day Preschool

8:45–9:00	Arrival and Greeting
9:00–9:15	Class Meeting
9:15–10:15	Choice and Centers
10:15–10:30	Cleanup
10:30–10:50	Sharing and Snack
10:50–11:20	Outdoor Play
11:20–11:45	Story and Preparation for Home

Full-day Kindergarten

8:50	Arrival, Greeting, Group Time
9:25	Centers and Work Time
10:45	Whole-group Sharing and Debriefing
11:00	Gross Motor Activity (indoors or out)
11:30	Lunch
12:00	Whole-group Story and Discussion
12:30	Integrated Language Arts, Science, Math
2:30	Group Share, Story, Music
3:00	Preparation for Home

Second Grade

8:15	Free Choice
8:30	Investigative Centers
10:00	Cleanup
10:15	Class Meeting
10:30	Outdoors
10:45	Integrated Science and Math
12:15	Lunch and Story
12:45	Integrated Language Arts/Social Studies/Arts
2:45	Music and Preparation for Home

Materials and Equipment

Materials are the tools children use to learn. Developmentally appropriate materials are concrete, real, and meaningful to children (Bredekamp & Copple, 1997). They enable children to investigate, explore, and experiment. Teachers choose materials that can be used by children with a wide range of abilities, are easily manipulated and safe, and meet the needs of the children in the group. All children are responsible for the care and cleanup of the materials. Following are some things to think about when providing good learning tools for children.

- Have plenty of materials available.
- Include adequate props and materials for play.
- Model the appropriate use of materials when necessary.
- Be creative in finding resources for your classroom. Use recycled materials, ask parents to provide and construct items, and begin your own collection of scraps and inexpensive resources.

Nutrition, Health, and Safety

Goal 1 of the *Goals 2000: Educate America Act* (U.S. Department of Education, 1994) states that "By the year 2000, all children in America will start school ready to learn." A major objective of this goal is to ensure that children receive the nutrition and health care they need to build healthy bodies and healthy minds. The relation between nutrition and development (i.e., how nutrition contributes to children's development and learning) is clear; thus, in early care and education settings, building healthy nutrition habits is essential to children's learning (Cesarone, 1993). There are a number of opportunities to promote such habits in your environment. Guidance for health and safety performance standards in early childhood is available in the document *Caring for Our Children* (American Academy of Pediatrics, 1992). The National Resource Center for Health and Safety in Child Care, located at the University of Colorado, provides information about these standards at its Web site, http://nrc.uchsc.edu, and offers a helpful guide, *Stepping Stones to the National Child Care Health and Safety Performance Standards* (1997). The NAEYC (1998) recommends the following hands-on health and nutrition activities for children to learn about healthy eating:

- Integrate learning activities about health and nutrition. Use seed catalogues and real vegetables to explore, taste, and talk about the nutritional value of different vegetables. The class might also want to make vegetable soup.
- Learn about diverse cultures. Use the cultural backgrounds of children in your classroom as a theme for the day's snacks, meals, or cooking experiences. Explore the different cultural influences on food.
- Visit local markets. Help children become aware of how food is grown and sold in places other than a market.
- Use replicas of healthy foods, such as fruits, vegetables, cheeses, and bread in the dramatic play area to serve as good models for play related to foods.
- Serve nutritious snacks in an atmosphere that encourages social or self-help skills.
- Engage in pleasant interactions during snack and mealtimes that will encourage children to accept new foods and develop healthy eating habits. Snacks and meals are more pleasurable when food is served on a predictable but flexible schedule, when there are small portions of food and drink so children can ask for more, and when the conversation focuses on the children, not the food. Table 5.2 lists some nutritious foods appropriate for children at different ages.

ASK the Expert
S. Vianne McLean on Good Learning Environments

S. Vianne McLean

Common Issues and Concerns about Arranging the Environment

1. How should teachers set the stage for learning?

In early childhood education, the design of the learning environment has long been seen as a hugely important part of teaching, and the child's actions in that environment a critical dimension of learning. Good learning environments for young children are multimeaning, multipossibility sorts of places that offer rich resources to explore and act on. Good learning environments for young children tell stories; they offer rich resources to explore and act on. Good learning environments for young children also document the individual and collective histories of this group of people and speak volumes about the shared experiences that have gone before, or are in progress, or that are foreshadowed for the future.

2. Are you saying that because the physical environment is so important, teachers should just let the children explore on their own?

The physical environment—the arrangement of space and provision of materials—is very important, but there really is no way to separate out the human environment from the physical. They are part of the same whole. The most enticing, wonderful resources, and the largest, most spacious classroom, will count for nothing unless children are given the opportunity to explore the environment, with the support, encouragement, and extension that adult facilitators can provide. This combination of a *physical environment* that is rich with materials and a supportive *human environment* really creates powerful learning opportunities for young children.

3. Can't having all those materials available to children and allowing them to decide how to use them lead to chaos?

They *can* lead to chaos, if the teacher is not well organized. To be able to support children's immediate learning needs effectively, the teacher needs materials that are carefully organized and readily accessible. The teacher also will be needed in many places at the same time, and to help ensure that she is able to attend to those who need her involvement the most, both the physical and human environment have to be structured in such a way that children are able to do a lot of routine things for themselves and for each other. For example, it needs to be made physically possible for them to locate the tools or materials they need, to clip paper on easels, and to hang paintings to dry. But from the human environment children also need encouragement for both self-sufficiency and collaborative problem solving, as well as assistance in developing the necessary practical skills.

4. Doesn't it often happen that when a teacher sets up a new center or activity, it doesn't go the way it was planned?

Teachers may sometimes feel like they have wasted time preparing a plan that then has to be abandoned when the children "don't cooperate." But that "in-advance" thinking is really time very well spent. Child-responsive teachers know that what they are planning is not a guaranteed route. It is a set of contingency plans. They are able to say in advance: "Okay, I know the general direction in which we are going. So if this happens, then I can respond this way, and that will still get us there," or "I've got the resources to support any of these three options the children might decide on. Any one of them will move us in the right direction."

S. Vianne McLean is Associate Vice-Provost for Academic Programs and Graduate Studies, Arizona State University—West Phoenix, Arizona.

Table 5.2
Nutritious Foods for Children at Different Ages

Age	Nutritious Foods	Foods to Avoid
Infants		
0–4 months	breast milk or formula	
4–6 months	iron-fortified cereals of barley or rice	eggwhites, seafood, chocolate, citrus fruits, tomatoes (allergies)
6–7 months	strained fruits and vegetables, fruit juices, teething foods, such as crackers, toast	honey, raisins, nuts, peanut butter, pieces of hot dog, and raw carrots (choking)
8–9 months	pureed meats, potatoes, rice, pasta	
10–12 months	finger foods such as cheese cubes, toast strips	
Toddlers/ Preschoolers	sandwiches cut into shapes; finger foods such as pretzels; cut-up vegetables; fresh fruit, such as apple slices, strawberries, orange and grapefruit sections; dried fruit, such as apples, pears, apricots; milk-group items such as cheese sticks, frozen yogurt, sherbet; bread-group items such as bagels, cookies, dry cereals, pretzels, rice cakes; vegetable-group items such as celery, cucumber slices, green beans; meat-group items such as hard-boiled eggs, peanut butter	big pieces of hot dog, jelly beans, nuts, popcorn, raisins, raw carrots, seeds, small hard candies, tough meat, whole grapes

High-quality early care and education settings provide a safe, secure environment for all children. Safe environments include adults who provide plenty of attention to children and who understand them and can meet their needs. Safe environments also are characterized by consistent, responsive caregiving for long periods of time, and by children who feel assured that they will be secure and protected (Jackson, 1997). Safe settings are especially healing for children who have been exposed to violence. "Without such access, no amount of intervention, whether in the form of nurturing first aid or clinical intervention, may be very helpful" (Jackson, 1997, p. 69).

It goes without saying that an important aspect of safe environments has to do with the materials available for children's use. This needs to be taken into account as you assess your indoor environment. Table 5.3 provides guidelines for safe and developmentally appropriate materials for children of all ages. These elements need to be planned for and also evaluated. In the following sections, we explore how to ensure that indoor and outdoor environments for all children are safe, healthy, and appropriate.

Table 5.3

Guidelines for Selecting Safe and Appropriate Materials for Children of All Ages

Age	Guidelines	Appropriate Materials
Infants (0–3 years)	• equipment should be sized appropriately • too large to swallow • washable • brightly colored • free of small or removable parts • free of sharp edges and toxic material • nonelectric • durable • soft and varied textures • rounded and smooth edges on furnishings	• soft cloth and thick cardboard books, musical toys • push-pull toys, infant bouncers • simple rattles, teethers, sturdy cloth toys, squeeze-and-squeak toys, colorful mobiles, activity boxes for the crib • soft rubber blocks, dolls, animals • soft hand puppets • tactile toys
Toddlers (1–3 years)	• nonelectric • painted with lead-free paint • easily cleaned • cannot pinch or catch hair • too large to swallow • no glass or brittle plastic • suited to child's skills, and the right size and weight • helps child learn new skills and practice learned skills	• simple picture books and poems about familiar places and people • toys to push and pull such as wagons, doll buggies • ride-on toys • low slides and climbers, tunnels for crawling, variety of balls • color paddles, dressing dolls, activity boxes, simple puzzles • stacking toys, sandbox toys, finger paints
Preschoolers and Kindergartners (3–5 years)	• durable, nontoxic, flame retardant • designed to promote children's large and small muscle development • designed to foster children's interest and skills in literacy • nonelectric • designed to enhance children's interest in adult roles, growing imaginations, and increasing motor skills	• props for imaginative play (e.g., old clothes, hats, cookware) • puzzles • art materials and media • simple board games • wheeled vehicles • woodworking sets (hammer, preschool nails) • sewing materials • bead-stringing materials • picture books, simple repetitive stories and rhymes • climbers, rope ladders, balls of all sizes, old tires • dressing frames, toys to put together and take apart • globe, flashlight, magnets, lock boxes
School-age Children (6–8 years)	• require involvement and concentration • some electric current but not enough to overheat • expand children's school experiences (e.g., computers, planting) • suited to individual children's skill level to promote interest	• simple card games • simple board and table games (e.g., Bingo) • collector's items (e.g., shells, rocks) • sports equipment (e.g., for baseball, hockey) • puppets, sand art kits, woodworking and sewing kits

SOURCE: Adapted from "Toy Safety and Selection" by S. Taylor, V. Morris, and C. Rogers, 1997, *Early Childhood Education Journal 24*(4), pp. 235–238; and *Creative Expression and Play in Early Childhood*, 2nd edition, by J. P. Isenberg and M. R. Jalongo, 1997, Upper Saddle River, NJ: Merrill/Prentice-Hall.

Evaluating the Indoor Environment

Periodic evaluation of your indoor environment will help you meet your learning objectives as well as the needs of each child. When assessing your overall environment, consider the physical characteristics, such as room arrangement, light, time, and relationships; the social characteristics, such as the cultural backgrounds and needs of the children; and the unique qualities of the local community, such as neighborhood safety, that affect the children. Figure 5.9 provides a list of questions that you should ask yourself to evaluate early childhood indoor settings.

FIGURE 5.9

Evaluating an indoor environment

Questions to Consider

- ✔ Are there large spaces for the whole group to meet comfortably?
- ✔ Are there medium spaces for small-group instruction? If there is team teaching, are these far enough apart to prevent interference?
- ✔ Are there small spaces for two to three children to work in together?
- ✔ Are there quiet spaces for individual tasks?
- ✔ Do table space and the room arrangement support cooperation?
- ✔ Are there moveable walls, furniture, or bookcases dividing interest centers?
- ✔ Are the interest areas clearly labeled and defined (e.g., dramatic play centers, writing centers)?
- ✔ Are there clear pathways and traffic lanes?
- ✔ Is there a quiet space for children to work or be alone?
- ✔ Are the furnishings and materials appropriate for learning tasks that are accessible to children?
- ✔ Is the children's work attractively displayed at eye level throughout the classroom?
- ✔ Are there attractive, up-to-date bulletin boards and pictures?
- ✔ Are there visual images that portray a range of roles and cultural backgrounds?
- ✔ Are there soft spaces with rugs, pillows, or cushions that make the room warm and inviting?
- ✔ Is safety considered in available supplies and equipment?
- ✔ Are there fresh, pleasant smells and living plants?
- ✔ Are there positively worded signs and messages?
- ✔ Are the materials easily accessible, aesthetically organized, and attractive to children?
- ✔ Are there diverse textures and shapes and natural materials that invite children to explore and discover?
- ✔ Is the space flexible and does it allow for expansion?
- ✔ Is there an ample supply of open-ended materials to challenge thinking and prevent frustration?
- ✔ Are the children's lives and interests represented throughout the room with work samples, photographs, sketches, and cultural artifacts?

ASK the Expert Joe Frost on Outdoor Play Environments

Common Issues and Concerns about Outdoor Play Environments

Joe Frost

1. Do children need adult-designed playgrounds?

Today's children do need planned playgrounds to compensate for crowded conditions in urban areas, to provide reasonably safe play areas, and to help ensure that children play. Children reared in rural areas have ample places and opportunities to play in rich natural environments filled with hills, streams, vegetation, and animals. In these environments, there is less threat from the hazards of cities—crime, traffic, and drugs. In urban areas, however, natural play spaces are limited or nonexistent. We must create spaces for urban children, including well-designed environments at schools, in public parks, and in children's museums. *Well-designed* means incorporating many of the advantages of the countryside into these built environments.

2. Must national playground safety standards result in uninspired, insipid, boring playgrounds?

The growing emphasis on national safety guidelines and standards for playground equipment *can* contribute to "cookie-cutter," boring playgrounds, which were the norm throughout the last half of the 20th century. The mentality that focused on limited conceptions of play in earlier periods unfortunately is alive and well today, but a growing number of contemporary playgrounds are lightyears ahead of those of even a decade ago. The most authoritative national play equipment guidelines and standards apply to standard equipment, for example, climbers, slides, and swings. The elements that most influence creative play—nature areas, gardens, storage facilities, building materials, pets, and water and sand areas—are virtually untouched by playground standards. Those who call most loudly for what has become an undue emphasis on safety are those who fail to understand that manufactured play equipment is a limited component of developmentally appropriate playgrounds.

3. What is the appropriate role of adults in children's play?

Several European countries, notably England, Sweden, and Denmark, surpass the United States in understanding how adults can best contribute to children's play. Over the past decade, they moved from the concept of "play leader" (one who leads children in play) to the present conception of "play worker" (one who interacts with children in a play atmosphere of cooperation and respect). The basic premise for play work is that children's play is free—freely chosen by the child, yet supported by adults who ensure that children have many opportunities for play in rich, reasonably safe environments. Adults provide the materials and places for play, allow ample time for play, and interact cooperatively about play, leaving the lead in play roles to children. Perhaps the most fundamental requirement for adults in enhancing children's play is that they value and understand play and allow children freedom to shape their own play worlds.

Joe Frost is Parker Centennial Professor, University of Texas

The Outdoor Environment

Although planning the outdoor environment is as essential as planning the indoor environment, it often is neglected. To maximize children's learning outdoors as well as indoors, the outdoor environment should be as enriching as the indoor environment. It should provide children with the following:

- a wide range of diverse activities, such as gross motor activities, pretend play, and group games
- plenty of well-organized space, such as sand and water areas, natural gardens, and pathways for wheeled vehicles
- easy access from the indoor environment
- adult supervision from many vantage points
- unstructured, moveable equipment and materials for use in different play areas
- aesthetic surroundings, including plants and well-cared-for equipment
- defined zones or areas for different activities and easy movement between play areas, such as digging and constructing, role-playing and enactment, mixing and pouring, and painting and splashing (Sanoff, 1995).

All children need outdoor time every day, weather permitting. For young children, long blocks of carefully planned and supervised outdoor periods each day are important for their total development. Older children usually have scheduled recess for an entire grade or grade level, and many primary-grade teachers use the outdoors to teach specific lessons in social studies and science. The rules of a classroom community should apply outdoors as well.

According to Joe Frost, a recognized international authority on children's play and playgrounds, "We are seeing physical differences in brain development for children who are stimulated through play and those suffering play deprivation" (personal communication, November, 1996). Read the "Ask the Expert" feature on page 177, which recounts our conversation with Joe Frost about why children need a well-planned outdoor play environment. Notice his mention of playground design, safety, and the appropriate role of the adult in the outdoor environment.

PAUSE AND REFLECT ABOUT OUTDOOR ENVIRONMENTS

In the "Ask the Expert" feature on Joe Frost, what surprised you about the importance of outdoor environments? Why? How will you use this new information in your design and use of the outdoors?

Adapting the Environment for All Children

Today, children with special needs have the same access to public education as all other children do. It is likely that you will have children with moderate, temporary, or permanent disabilities in your care. These children need the same type of classroom environments as other children, even though they may have different developmental needs.

In planning for these needs, you will want to make some adaptations by either adding something to the environment that is not there already or using something that is already there in a different way. Before making any modifications, be sure to contact these children's families about the child, the special need, or special equipment (Youcha & Wood, 1997). Following are some suggestions for adapting the environment for children with particular needs.

Adapting the Environment for Children with Limited Motor Abilities

Limited motor ability applies to children whose ability to move negatively affects that child's participation in an activity (Bigge, 1991). This could be the result of cerebral palsy, spina bifida, or other conditions that confine a child to a wheelchair either temporarily or permanently. These children need access in the classroom. The following are suggestions for adapting the environment for children with limited motor abilities (Sheldon, 1996):

- *Access.* Be sure children can enter the building and classroom through wide paths, doorways, and walkways. Have low sinks, water fountains, and table surfaces for a child in a wheelchair. Put lever-style handles on faucets and doors for simpler operating movements than those required by traditional knobs and faucets.
- *Circle Time.* Children with limited motor abilities often have difficulty finding a place to sit and see. You can have all children sit on chairs at circle time keeping everybody's eye level the same and making the child in a wheelchair feel less different.
- *Art.* Coloring, drawing, and illustrating are difficult skills for these children because of poor fine-motor skills or inability to reach the materials and equipment. You might provide a variety of more-accessible areas and surfaces for children to paint on, such as a window, a wall, or the back of a divider.
- *Books.* Many children have difficulty turning the pages or cannot reach the books from the bookshelves. You can arrange shelves at different levels so the books are accessible to everybody; provide headphones and tapes so children can listen to the stories; or provide books in several areas of the classroom, especially if your regular classroom library is in a loft or other inaccessible place.
- *Computers and Technology.* Technology for children with limited motor abilities is often an easy way to adapt your environment. Try touch-sensitive computer screens, hand-held devices, and voice-input computers (Breet, 1995); place stickers on keyboard keys for a particular program to help children locate keys more easily, or set a template over the keyboard so only certain keys show.
- *Space.* Entrances to centers need to be wide and free from materials for children who are in wheelchairs or who need a walker. Table height can be adjusted so a wheelchair can fit underneath. Adjusting legs on large pieces of equipment, such as an easel, will make activities accessible to more children.

Adapting the Environment for Children with Sensory Impairments

Children with visual or hearing impairments need multisensory experiences to feel like a part of the learning environment. Wald, Morris, and Abraham (1996) suggest the following circle-time adaptations that provide a more inclusive environment.

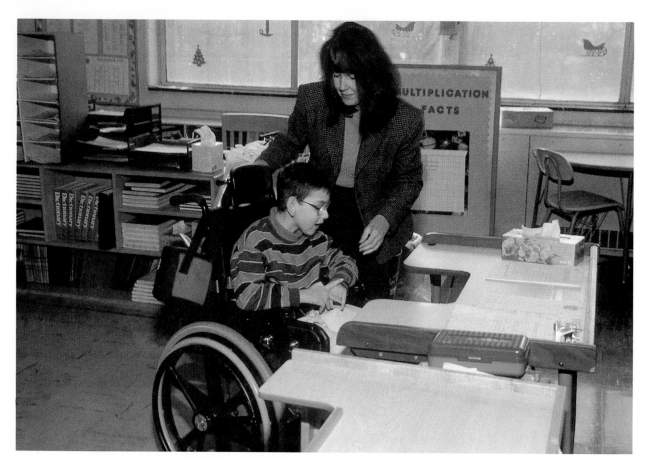

This teacher knows how to adapt the classroom environment to accommodate children with special needs.

- *Vision.* Use brightly colored boxes to hold objects for discussion. Illustrate main events of the day on your daily schedule. Use tactile and auditory cues for children to find their way around the room.
- *Hearing.* Vary the tone of your voice and the pace of your talk. Make sure you have audiotapes of sounds in children's natural environments such as the cafeteria or the school bus. Make sure there is a blinking light on the fire alarm in case of emergency.
- *Touch.* Use a "talking wand," a small tube held by the child who is speaking and then passed on to others so that the speaker is clearly identifiable. Make sure you introduce all new materials before adding them to the centers for children's exploration and use.
- *Smell.* Add scented items to containers with perforated tops and have a "smell and tell" instead of "show and tell" on some days.

Adapting the Environment for Children with Diverse Academic Needs

Every early childhood setting has children with a range of academic abilities. Following are some suggestions for meeting the diverse academic needs of each child.

- *Space.* Have a quiet place for children who are easily distracted or need to calm themselves down.

180

- *Time.* Allow sufficient time for all children to process and complete their play and work.
- *Transitions.* Moving from one activity to another or from one space to another creates difficulty for some children. Some may need more time to clean up, finish a project, or move from one activity to another.

McCormick and Feeney (1995) provide the following suggestions for facilitating transitions for children with special needs:

- Provide specific instructions and practice with transition behaviors, such as where to put away materials and how to move quietly from one area to the next.
- Reiterate what the next activity will be.
- Allow children who finish early to move independently to another activity.
- Give several notices that an activity will soon end before using an abrupt transition warning such as a light or bell.
- Allocate sufficient time to end an activity and clean up before beginning preparation for the next activity.

Adapting the environment to include all children is essential. The efforts you make to modify your environment can result in a new level of learning for all children and adults in the environment.

Conclusion

Early childhood environments are spaces where all children learn to live, grow, and learn together. Within these spaces, children need to become increasingly independent, feel safe and comfortable, and become confident and competent learners. Creating a good environment for all children "invites young children to action" (Jones & Nimmo, 1994, p. 17). This requires not only a substantial collection of concrete resources and equipment, but also, a great deal of skill and knowledge on the part of the teacher. A teacher who plans and evaluates developmentally appropriate indoor and outdoor environments has a "set of dispositions that enable the teacher to be a creative problem solver, a negotiator and a reflective practitioner" (McLean, 1995, p. 12).

One Child, Three Perspectives: Rashid at Circle Time

Rashid is a kindergartner who challenged his teacher, Mr. Thomas, every day during circle time. This was Mr. Thomas's first year as a kindergarten teacher, although he had taught preschool for the previous 5 years. Mr. Thomas came to his new kindergarten position enthused, proud, and ready to be the best kindergarten teacher ever. Now Rashid was challenging the way he conducted his circle time!

In Mr. Thomas's class, there is a daily morning circle time during which the children and teacher come together to review the day's events, complete the calendar and weather chart, and sing songs. Even though Mr. Thomas invited certain children to speak and allowed them to converse among themselves, he expected all the children to sit, listen, and respond when invited. Rashid, however, wouldn't sit down at circle time and do what Mr. Thomas asked. Rashid wasn't really angry or deliberately defiant; he just seemed to want to move and use his body. Mr. Thomas used all the techniques he knew at the time to get Rashid to sit down and listen: time-out, moving Rashid to the front of the circle within easy reach of him, and using a reward system for positive behavior.

When none of Mr. Thomas's techniques worked, he talked to Ms. Williams, the other kindergarten teacher, and to the school counselor about Rashid's inability to sit and listen during circle time. Mr. Thomas told his colleagues that Rashid played well with his peers and used wonderful language during activities in which he could move. Mr. Thomas said, "Rashid uses language, not necessarily when I want him to, but he chooses to use it in particular situations. I am at a loss for what to do during circle time."

Both of his colleagues suggested that he find an appropriate way for Rashid to move and still participate with the group. As a result of these conversations, Mr. Thomas realized that he needed to create an environment for Rashid that resembled his preschool classroom. That meant finding more appropriate materials and activities for Rashid. He went to the basement of the school and found an old slide, old wooden blocks, and several other beautiful old toys. He thought, "This is what Rashid needs!" Mr. Thomas brought the newfound materials into the room and placed the slide right in the middle of his classroom. At first, Mr. Thomas told his colleagues that he was really concerned about what the parents and other teachers would think and say about him when they noticed the old slide in the room. But the school counselor and Ms. Williams assured him that he was doing what was best for Rashid.

When Rashid arrived at school the next day, he saw the slide, stopped, looked up at it, and said, "Who is that for? Is that for all of us? Can I climb on it?" After the children all had an opportunity to climb on the slide, it was morning circle time. All the children except Rashid were in the circle. They liked circle time: It was fun and gave them a chance to communicate about what was important to them. Guess where Rashid was? Perched on top of the slide, looking over the children in the circle and smiling, as if to say, "I'm happy up here." Of course, the children kept reminding Mr. Thomas that Rashid was on the slide. Mr. Thomas replied, "Isn't it wonderful to see Rashid sitting during circle time!"

Mr. Thomas's determination to find out what kind of learning environment and materials Rashid needed to be successful during circle time also allowed him to more effectively meet the needs of all the other children. Following a "Let's find out what's best for you" approach to meeting Rashid's needs, Mr. Thomas expanded his own understandings about how the environment influences children's behavior. He took the challenge Rashid presented and grew with it.

All was not rosy, however, because the principal did not approve of Mr. Thomas's decision and many of the parents wanted to know why their kindergartners needed a slide in their classroom when they were supposed to be learning letters and numbers to get them ready for first grade. The parents believed that slides were for preschoolers. During his formal observation, the principal criticized Mr. Thomas for "not following the plan to have all children participate in circle time."

REACT:	Think about how the perspectives of Mr. Thomas, the principal, and Ms. Williams are alike and different. What might be some reasons? With whom do you identify, and why?
RESEARCH:	Interview at least two different kindergarten teachers about how they plan and conduct their circle times. Find out how long their circle times are, what kinds of activities they do, and how they respond to children who cannot sit and listen during that time. Compare the responses of the teachers you interviewed with the key features of a good learning environment described in Table 5.1. Chart your findings and draw one major conclusion from your research.
REFLECT:	What assumptions about children who need to move during circle time do Mr. Thomas, the principal, parents, and Ms. Williams make? Using the data gathered from your interviews, generate some ways you can more appropriately respond to children like Rashid during circle time.

Arranging the Learning Environment

Reread "Ask the Expert: S. Vianne McLean on "Good Learning Environments," presented earlier in this chapter. Respond to the following points that McLean makes about good learning environments by answering the two questions that follow. Then, share your response with a partner.

- Good learning environments for young children are multimeaning, multipossibility sorts of places that offer rich resources to explore and act on.
- To be able to support children's immediate learning needs effectively, the teacher needs materials that are carefully organized and readily accessible.
- Teachers who are responsive to children's interests sometimes feel like they have wasted time preparing a plan that then has to be abandoned when the children don't cooperate.

1. What do you think of these ideas?
2. How do you think you could implement them? Discuss why or why not.

6

Exploring Your Role as a Curriculum Developer

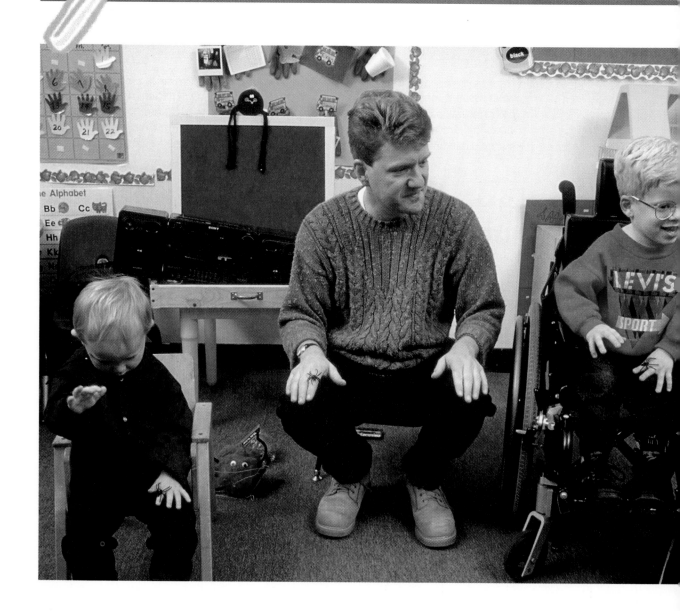

Teachers at all levels of their professional development must expect to learn along with the children in their class. I'm convinced that curriculum evolves from the teacher and learner in interaction with content and with each other. To accomplish this kind of exchange, beginning teachers must . . . know how to listen to children's cues when making their curriculum decisions . . . help children relate to classroom phenomena in such a way that the children can invent their own solutions to problems. . . . Throughout this process, teachers can provide children with opportunities to explore, investigate, and use symbolic representation to communicate their ideas to others.

Georgann Olson, 1994, p. 40

Learning Outcomes

✔ Define and describe high-quality early childhood curricula for children

✔ Explore the early childhood educator's role as a designer and collaborator of curricula

✔ Identify major issues and trends in early childhood curricula

✔ Understand curriculum theory and the process of curriculum evaluation

✔ Define, describe, and create developmentally appropriate practices for children

✔ Understand areas of the curriculum and ways to integrate subject matter

Meet the Teachers

Yvette Eagle has been a child-care provider for 7 years and is now the new owner and director of a child-care center in a rural area of her state. One of Yvette's first tasks as director was to develop the curriculum. At a recent conference, Yvette was sharing her new role with her colleagues: "At this point, I must implement a curriculum with an existing staff that is not used to planning for children's learning experiences. How will I get my teachers to view curriculum not as a series of unrelated, cute activities, but rather as a plan to guide children's learning?" Yvette believes that young children's learning should be organized to reflect their physical, social, emotional, language, and cognitive needs. She sees her biggest challenge as convincing her teachers that curriculum development is an important responsibility for early childhood teachers. At this point, Yvette is overwhelmed, but not discouraged, by the idea of developing an appropriate curriculum for her center.

Ms. Ornstein teaches a full-day kindergarten class. If you visit her classroom, you will notice children working on different projects. When Ms. Ornstein's kindergartners arrive at school, they choose two learning activities to work on for the day and immediately begin completing unfinished work from the previous day. Ms. Ornstein believes that "Children can be trusted to select learning activities that interest them and to develop the habit of completing work they started." An important part of Ms. Ornstein's curriculum is having her kindergartners record and chart their completed work to share with the group each day. On one particular day, Lukas was constructing a plane from his woodworking plan, Peter was recording his favorite part of *Peter Rabbit* after listening to the story on audiotape, and Elli had drawn a picture of the solar system that looked like a puzzle she had recently completed and was recording the names of the people who had helped her. Ms. Ornstein encourages children to record and chart their work each day because it "offers children an important way to communicate their ideas to others and to make sense of their experiences to themselves and to others."

Ms. Buscovich is a third-grade teacher who describes her class as "quiet, organized, and well planned, with lots of whole-group teaching for basic-skills instruction." While taking a graduate class on mathematics curricula in early childhood, she learned that teaching mathematical skills in isolation can be confusing to many children and that children need to apply mathematical operations to real-life situations. Thus, Ms. Buscovich decided to provide opportunities for children to learn math by doing math. She began by developing small-group learning activities with pattern blocks. Children observed, experimented, and discovered answers to questions about particular characteristics of the pattern blocks. They shared their findings with their peers and reused the pattern blocks in different ways after listening to classmates' ideas. The more Ms. Buscovich used authentic strategies for teaching math concepts, the clearer it became to her that all students were better able to connect what they were doing to larger mathematical concepts. For Ms. Buscovich, learning new ways of teaching mathematics helped her feel more confident and less overwhelmed.

All of these teachers are using three important curriculum principles to guide their decisions about teaching and learning. First, the teachers are considering what their children are like and then developing experiences to match those characteristics. Next, the teachers are considering which particular experiences influence children's classroom learning and behavior. Finally, the teachers respect the different ways children learn (Kostelnik, Soderman, & Whirren, 1999).

COMPARE:	What do these three teachers know about children that guides their teaching and learning decisions?
CONTRAST:	How do these teachers think about the curriculum, or what happens in the classroom? What are some commonalities and differences among them?
CONNECT:	What aspects of the curriculum do you think you will look for when you begin observing teachers of young children? Why do you think so?

A Definition of Curriculum

The curriculum is the pathway of education; it is what children actually experience in schools. According to Bredekamp and Rosegrant (1992), a curriculum is "an organized framework that delineates the *content* that children are to learn, the *processes* through which children achieve the identified curricular goals, what teachers do to achieve these goals, and the *contexts* in which teaching and learning occur" (p. 10). In other words, a curriculum is a broad-based plan for achieving the goals of education. It provides an overview of what children can be expected to learn and suggests ways to teach it.

Curriculum decisions include what children are expected to learn (content), how children will learn it (instruction), and when the material is best learned (timing) (Katz & Chard, 1989). Simply stated, what we teach differs from how and when we teach it. Early childhood professionals incorporate research and theory, various methodologies, and different program models in their definition of *curriculum.* Ultimately, however, the curriculum should help children develop the knowledge, skills, values, and dispositions they will need to become productive members of society.

Why the Curriculum Is so Important

It is common to think of a curriculum only as standards and academic content, but there are other important dimensions. Although there are some local, state, and national curriculum standards that teachers are expected to follow, differences in teaching practices lead to great variations in the quality of learning experiences for young children. A visitor could observe several early childhood classrooms in which the same lesson is being taught to young children and notice considerable variations in ways of teaching as well as clear differences in what and how children are learning. What makes the difference is not the required content, but the way in which each teacher interprets and enacts the curriculum. To fully understand the curriculum, a teacher would need to consider not only the curriculum standards and content, but also the intents of schooling and all of the experiences children have while they are in school. In other words, there is a written curriculum (documents and standards), a taught curriculum (the teacher's interpretation and methodology), and a tested curriculum (the instruments used to evaluate children's progress or overall program effectiveness). Some experts have even argued that there is a "hidden curriculum" (Jackson, 1968), meaning all of the lessons that children learn about school itself as an organization and as a mirror of the society's values.

Suppose, for example, that an early childhood teacher is presenting a lesson on shapes. The teacher decides to focus on the basic shapes of a circle, triangle, square, and rectangle. She begins the lesson by saying to the kindergartners, "What is a shape?" and "Name some shapes that you know." One child responds that a star is a shape. But the teacher is not expecting that answer and, without considering the child's point of view, replies, "No, that is not one of the shapes we are studying." It could be argued that the lesson the child learns from this interaction has very little to do with the curriculum standards or the subject matter. Instead, the child may have learned that being a "good" student means guessing what is on the teacher's mind or that conformity is the goal of education. The child actually may be learning to dislike school rather than learning to identify basic shapes, which was the intended goal; that is, children not only learn content, they also learn rules, both explicit and implicit, about what school is and what it means to become an educated adult. When the concept of curriculum is broadened in this way, it becomes virtually everything that occurs under the auspices of the school (Jalongo, 2000). Even though there is a local curriculum that all teachers are expected to

What curricular objectives are apparent in this classroom?

follow, the curriculum is interpreted according to each teacher's beliefs about teaching and learning. Thus, the curriculum is everything that happens in a school.

Influences on the Curriculum

When teachers create and interpret the curriculum broadly, it is affected by five key influences (Ball & Cohen, 1996).

1. *The curriculum is affected by teachers' perceptions about children.* Teachers build on children's prior knowledge, consider the children's interest in the topic under study, and draw upon their observations of the children's learning processes. For example, when a teacher believes that a particular child is very intelligent, the teacher is likely to give that child more time to think before expecting a response. Conversely, if the teacher believes that the child is not progressing well, the teacher tends to give the child less time to respond before calling upon another child to answer. Thus, even though curriculum standards exist to regulate quality, the quality of classroom interactions is influenced by teachers' beliefs about children in general, about groups of students, and about particular students.

2. *The curriculum is affected by teachers' interpretations of the content of material.* No matter how clearly specified the content may be, teachers have their own understandings of what the central ideas are, the types of questions that should be formulated, and the sort of teacher responses that are appropriate to each child's answers, com-

ments, or actions. For example, teachers who interpret the material in terms of young children's development will delight in the fact that the very young are frequently playful, spontaneous, unpredictable, and imaginative as they work to master the material they are learning. Conversely, teachers who interpret material as simply a body of facts to be delivered may be annoyed by young children's surprising responses and treat their active style of learning as behavior that is distracting, problematic, or deliberately difficult.

3. *The curriculum is influenced by how teachers shape the content for children to learn.* A teacher puts his or her own imprint on the curriculum by selecting illustrative examples, explaining how to accomplish tasks, monitoring the children's activities, and revisiting topics to make the material more readily understood by the children. Teachers who define learning as memorizing verbal material, for instance, will meet with limited success when working with diverse groups of young children. A heavy reliance on words and recall inhibits positive teacher-child communication, particularly when a child's ethnic background or first language differ from the teacher's or when a child has a language delay or disorder. If, on the other hand, a teacher decides to shape the content for the children through direct involvement with real materials, he or she has a much better chance of communicating effectively with a diverse group of students because the task is shaped by direct participation rather than through abstract ideas.

4. *The curriculum is influenced by classroom management issues.* Teachers pay attention to children's ways of knowing, interacting, and working and decide what is acceptable and unacceptable behavior in the classroom. When teachers become overly concerned with control, the effectiveness of instruction is diminished. A good example is the way that early childhood teachers manage a group of young children who are working on a project. Some overly controlling teachers might insist that children work in silence, but this requirement only deprives children of the opportunity to practice language and social skills at the same time that they are involved in creative expression. Effective instructional practice would suggest that the best way to handle this situation is to actively teach children how to talk quietly with peers by showing them how the volume of their voices needs to be adjusted for indoor and outdoor settings.

5. *The curriculum is influenced by the perspectives of the larger community.* Teachers comply with their local, state, and national curriculum, consider the program's goals, conform to the school administrator's policies, respond to input from families, rely upon their professional training, and refer to the recommendations of various professional organizations. At times, these influences send conflicting messages about appropriate courses of action in the classroom, and it is up to the teacher to reconcile such contradictions. In early childhood education, it is important to put the needs of children and families first and use them as a guiding principle in responding to the community at large. Maintaining this focus enables teachers to function as child advocates who not only teach but also support and defend all of the young children in their care.

Developmentally Appropriate Practice and the Curriculum

Developmentally appropriate practice is not a curriculum. It is a way of interpreting the curriculum that centers on what children know and can do by taking into account their needs and characteristics to make thoughtful and appropriate decisions about the early childhood curriculum. Everything that has been learned through research

These teachers are modifying the state's curriculum guidelines to meet the needs of their community.

and formulated into theory about how children develop and learn at various ages and stages is used to create a curriculum that matches children's abilities and needs. Developmentally appropriate practice is based on the following three elements.

1. Developmentally appropriate practice is based only on what is presently known and understood about children. It is not based on what adults wish children were like, or hope they will be like, or even expect they might be like.

2. Developmentally appropriate practice is characterized by planned learning experiences for each child that take into account his or her strengths, interests, and needs. This means that adults must recognize that children learn in different ways and at different rates.

3. Developmentally appropriate practice incorporates family needs, values, and cultural backgrounds in children's learning experiences. Treating children and families with respect is essential to making learning relevant to all learners, especially those children with diverse needs and from linguistically and culturally different backgrounds (Bredekamp & Copple, 1997). Figure 6.1 compares developmentally appropriate practice with less developmentally appropriate practice.

FIGURE 6.1

Comparison of
developmentally
appropriate practice
to less
developmentally
appropriate practice

Less Appropriate	Appropriate
• high adult-child ratios	• low adult-child ratios
• inadequate staff training	• staff are trained in the curriculum
• chronological age or test scores determine placement	• authentic assessment measures are used
• all children do the same activity	• individualization is occurring
• children are generally assigned to tasks	• children have some choice of their learning experiences
• teachers rely heavily on direct instruction	• teachers use different methods
• learners are passive and are expected to sit still and listen most of the time	• learners are actively engaged in interesting learning experiences
• paper-and-pencil tasks predominate	• active learning experiences dominate
• emphasis is on correct products	• emphasis is on balance of process and product
• subjects are taught separately	• subjects are integrated
• skills and memorization are emphasized	• concept development is emphasized
• children have no input into the curriculum	• children's ideas are recognized
• teachers rely heavily on extrinsic rewards and/or punishments to control behavior	• teachers value and reward self-discipline
• special learning projects are either absent or used as rewards	• varied learning experiences are central for all children
• communication with families is minimal and perfunctory	• family participation is valued

SOURCE: Adapted from *Developmentally Appropriate Practice: Curriculum and Development in Early Education.* (2nd ed.) by C. Gestwicki, 1999, Albany, NY: Delmar.

A curriculum based on these three elements of developmentally appropriate practice enables early childhood teachers and caregivers to provide a realistic range of experiences, learning materials, and activities. Such variety is needed to meet the special needs and interests that each child brings to the group learning experience. Note what Sue Bredekamp says about developmentally appropriate practice in the following "Ask the Expert" feature.

What Does Research Say About Appropriate Early Childhood Curricula?

Studies of programs and practices that produce successful results for all children suggest the following agreed-upon principles for appropriate curricula for children (Bredekamp & Copple, 1997; Carnegie Corporation of New York, 1996). These principles of practice

ASK the Expert
Sue Bredekamp on Developmentally Appropriate Practice

Common Issues and Concerns about Developmentally Appropriate Practice

Sue Bredekamp

1. Developmentally appropriate practice means watering down or oversimplifying what is taught to young children.

The NAEYC's 1987 publication on developmentally appropriate practice may have inadvertently contributed to this misconception because it was written in the context of a "push-down curriculum," in which next-grade expectations are routinely pushed down to younger children. Because the NAEYC opposed rote drill and practice on isolated academic skills and the overuse of whole-group, teacher-directed instruction with very young children, some people interpreted the statement to mean that in developmentally appropriate classrooms, children are not expected to learn anything. Nothing could be farther from the truth. To be developmentally appropriate, a curriculum must be intellectually challenging and engaging, because young children are naturally curious and eager to learn just about everything there is to know about their worlds. It is somewhat ironic, in fact, that one of the most developmentally appropriate programs in the world—the early childhood program in Reggio Emilia, Italy—is also among the world's most intellectually challenging and enriching.

2. Developmentally appropriate practice means that teachers are overly passive and do not teach.

Again, this misconception is counterintuitive; if we base our practices on what children need to develop their full potential, adults have to be highly involved and even directive. Young children do need opportunities to explore and make discoveries on their own, but they can do this best in contexts in which adults provide care, guidance, information, and a host of other things that adults, but not young children, know and are able to do.

3. Developmentally appropriate practice principles do not apply to children with disabilities or special learning and developmental needs.

This confusion is again puzzling, because one of the most well-known principles of human development is that there is a wide range of individual variation on every dimension; therefore, it is impossible to be developmentally appropriate without also being individually appropriate. These are not mutually exclusive terms. Because each child in a developmentally appropriate program must be viewed as an individual for whom teachers assess, plan, and adapt the curriculum and teaching, developmentally appropriate programs are ideal environments in which to include children with disabilities or special learning needs.

4. Developmentally appropriate practice is insufficiently sensitive to and responsive to cultural and linguistic diversity of children and families.

The very idea that any set of practices could be called developmentally appropriate for all children is criticized because it assumes that there are universals of development irrespective of cultures. This particular concern led to the most important modification in the NAEYC's 1997 revised edition of developmentally appropriate practice—a fundamental clarification of the definition takes into consideration at least three important pieces of information: age-related human characteristics (predictions about what is age-appropriate), knowledge of the individual children in the group, and knowledge of the social and cultural context. Because all development occurs in and is influenced by social and cultural contexts, early childhood programs cannot be developmentally appropriate unless they are also culturally appropriate.

Sue Bredekamp is Director of Research, The Council for Early Childhood Professional Recognition, Washington, DC.

apply not only to school and child-care settings, but also to adults who interact with young children in other educational settings such as scouting or recreational programs.

An appropriate curriculum provides for all areas of a child's development: physical, emotional, social, cognitive, linguistic, and aesthetic. An early childhood curriculum centers on the whole child (Bredekamp & Rosegrant, 1995). For example, the curriculum supports children's physical development through movement, climbing, or cutting experiences; social and emotional development through learning how to solve conflicts over materials, working cooperatively in groups, and caring for each other and for materials; and cognitive development through acquiring the skills of reading and writing, solving mathematical problems, and posing and answering questions about their world. Children's early learning experiences affect their performance in schools and beyond. Research on brain development, for example, indicates that during the first 10 years of life, a child's brain has already formed most of its lifetime connections (Caine & Caine, 1997).

An appropriate curriculum, which includes a broad range of content areas, is worth knowing, meaningful, and easily accessible to children. All young children need to learn content that does not trivialize learning and is worth knowing. Content that is worth knowing builds on big ideas and fosters deep understanding. While some early childhood teachers would shudder at the thought of teaching physics to young children, in fact, the content of physics, which includes the study of motion, can be made appropriate. To illustrate, at the simplest level, children can explore how objects move and what makes them move. For example, when preschool children experiment with the effect that changing the incline has on a ball, they are doing physics on a level that they understand. The same is true of children in the primary grades who place drops of colored water and oil in a pan and carefully tip the pan at different angles, speeds, and directions, then observe differences in the moving circles. Both of these activities are designed to help children discover information about their physical world by conceptualizing how objects move (Chaille & Britain, 1997).

An appropriate curriculum supports children's home culture and language while also developing all children's abilities to participate in the shared culture of the school. Children's first languages and their cultural values are essential to good early childhood practice. For example, when teachers and caregivers use stories written in a child's home language and then retell them in English, they are conveying an important message about the value of another language. Moreover, early childhood settings should display signs and labels in other languages, display children's writing, and incorporate culturally appropriate songs, dances, and drama to affirm children's culture and language.

An appropriate curriculum sets high expectations for children. An extensive body of research supports the conclusion that it is important for teachers to believe that all children can learn. Rosenthal and Jacobson conducted the classic study that reinforced this idea in 1968. This study, as well as many that followed it, demonstrated that children will rise

A successful curriculum provides a balance of support between home cultures and languages and the shared culture of the school.

or fall to the level of the teachers' expectations for them (ASCD Advisory Panel on Improving Student Achievement, 1995; Carnegie Corporation of New York, 1996). If, for example, teachers expected you to read well, you probably did. If, on the other hand, teachers thought that you would not learn to read well, you probably did not.

An appropriate curriculum helps children build stable, predictable, and trusting relationships with adults. Teachers and caregivers must create settings in which every child is known well by at least one adult. Such relationships are important for all aspects of children's development, including language, cognitive, social, emotional, and physical development. These relationships have lasting, life-long implications (Bowlby, 1969; Stern, 1985; Dyson & Genishi, 1993). In today's early childhood settings, it is common for children to spend the first 2 or 3 years together with one teacher rather than having different teachers who have to get to know them each year. Having the same teacher for more than 1 year builds trust by enabling children to bond with the teacher and with their peers. Such a curricular organization is referred to as "looping," or multi-age classrooms (Chase & Doan, 1994).

An appropriate curriculum is results oriented. Children who experience a developmentally appropriate curriculum have improved short-term and long-term cognitive and social gains. Studies show that children from low-income families who participated in such programs were less likely to drop out of school, be placed in special needs classrooms, or engage in criminal activity (Lazar & Darlington, 1982; Barnett, 1995; Schweinhart & Weikart, 1996).

An appropriate curriculum is enacted by teachers who believe in themselves and are confident that they can exert a positive influence on children's lives despite the complex challenges that characterize teaching today. Over and over again, research has indicated that the best teachers believe in their power to influence children's lives for the better (Ayers, 1996; Bandura, 1997). They do not blame the school, the family, or the child when learning is difficult. Instead, they do everything in their power to improve the situation so that all children can reach their full potential.

These seven research-based principles form the foundation of the early childhood curriculum. They make clear why it is important for teachers to believe that all children can learn.

PAUSE AND REFLECT ABOUT A DEVELOPMENTALLY APPROPRIATE CURRICULUM

In your own words, how would you define a developmentally appropriate curriculum? Include what characteristics you would look for in an early childhood setting, what kinds of activities you might see, and what kinds of activities would be of concern to you. Now, compare your responses to the seven principles of practice just described. Share one of your responses with a partner and tell which principle of practice it met and why.

Your Role as a Curriculum Developer

Your role as a curriculum developer for young children is an exciting one. You shape what children should learn and how they should learn it. Simply stated, you are the link between the child and the content to be learned. In John Dewey's (1933) words, "Teachers are the agents through which knowledge and skills are communicated and rules of conduct enforced" (p. 18).

Teachers connect students to learning experiences that help them develop knowledge, skills, cultural values, and appropriate behaviors. They do this by asking themselves the following questions:

- "What will I teach?"
- "To whom will I teach it?"
- "How will I teach it?"
- "When and for how long will I teach it?"

In designing a curriculum, you will rely as much on your own personal experiences and beliefs as you will on subject-matter knowledge and methodology. To create a developmentally appropriate curriculum for young children, you need to have understanding and skill in the following seven areas.

1. *Understand and use knowledge of children's growth and development to plan and enhance learning.* A primary principle of curriculum development is teaching the whole child. This means using your knowledge of children's typical developmental patterns, their needs and interests at different ages, and their different ways of learning best as you develop your curriculum. We know, for instance, that preschool children have high energy levels, so teachers plan short group times that offer these children many opportunities to talk and move. Likewise, we know that peer relationships are very important to children in second and third grade, so teachers provide many opportunities for these children to learn with and from each other (Barbour & Seefeldt, 1993).

2. *Be knowledgeable about each of the subject areas you teach to create a curriculum worth teaching.* Every early childhood teacher must have specialized knowledge in the content he or she teaches in order for it to have integrity. Thus, you must know the key concepts, facts, principles, and processes for each discipline, because they provide a coherent means of organization. To illustrate, suppose you were teaching key concepts about measurement to young children. You might have preschool children pour and measure sand and water, but second graders might weigh the containers to see which weighs the most (Barbour & Seefeldt, 1993). In this way, you would tailor a key concept from mathematics to the age and experience level of your students while teaching children accurate and interesting ideas.

3. *Understand which teaching methods work best with particular children and in particular disciplines.* Knowing content is different from knowing how to teach the content (methodology). Sometimes called "pedagogical content knowledge," teaching methods simply refer to how teachers present content to children so they can use it. Knowledge of methodology is not a recipe book but rather a repertoire of ways to help teachers pace instruction to maximize all children's learning. Some appropriate methods you might encounter are hands-on learning, investigations, choice of learning experiences, coaching or guiding children with skill acquisition, demonstrations, modeling, role-playing, and problem solving. Your knowledge of how and when to use different methodologies also includes what misunderstandings, challenges, and prior knowledge children bring to their learning (Bredekamp & Copple, 1997).

4. *Help children make connections within and across the curriculum.* Creating a meaning-centered curriculum (Bredekamp & Rosegrant, 1992) can be accomplished through thematic units and projects that include many content areas. You will want to include children in the planning. As you and the children experience learning in all the content areas, you will come to see, discover, and think in ways that open new possibilities. A study of space by one kindergarten class is a good example of helping children make connections across subject areas. The children and teachers explored space from a variety of perspectives—spatial relations, inside spaces, outside spaces, crowded spaces, outer space, and underneath spaces—which developed concepts, skills, and abilities in all of the subject areas (Pappas, Kiefer, & Levstik, 1995), thus opening up possibilities for learning within and across the content areas.

5. *Build on children's interests, cultural backgrounds, and prior knowledge.* When teachers consider children's prior knowledge, cultural backgrounds, and interests in planning a curriculum, it is referred to as an "emergent curriculum" (Jones & Nimmo, 1994). All children learn best when what they are learning interests them and means something in their personal lives. But what happens if children show no interest in what the class is studying? A child may not be interested in learning about magnetism, for example, unless she or he has experienced magnets, read books such as *Amazing Magnets* (Rowe & Perham, 1994) or *The Science Book of Magnets* (Ardley, 1991), and experimented with different objects to see which ones are attracted to magnetic force. When children have such experiences, they are more likely to show an interest in the content to be studied.

6. *Realize that your curriculum reflects your own personal experiences, values, and beliefs as much as your knowledge of content and pedagogy.* Your experiences with schools, teachers, and learning up to this point affect how you view the curriculum. These experiences are what will make you a unique teacher of your curriculum and at the same time will influence how you interpret and enact the how, why, and what of the curriculum you are developing. It is important for you to be in touch with your own, personal life experiences, which will influence your role as a curriculum developer.

Young children need concrete experiences, not just paper-and-pencil activities.

7. *Have realistic goals and expectations.* Today's teachers often feel pressured to add more rigorous content from later grades into early childhood settings; this is sometimes referred to as the "push down" curriculum. The expectations for such a curriculum are often unattainable because they include excessive amounts of paper-and-pencil, abstract experiences for children. We know, for example, that preschool and kindergarten children need concrete experiences with real people and objects to make sense of their learning. Engaging young children in meaningless experiences, such as memorizing tables of mathematical facts or copying words from the chalkboard for the sake of copying, only adds to frustration and a negative disposition toward learning (Bredekamp & Copple, 1997).

Understanding the Written Curriculum

The written curriculum contains the curriculum standards that guide educators' teaching and learning decisions. These standards can be local, state, or national. Most people believe that high academic standards lead to higher achievement.

Curriculum Standards

How do we know what children are supposed to learn at different grade levels? Most states have mandatory local and state curriculum standards that help early childhood teachers in public school settings decide what and how to teach. There are also voluntary national curriculum standards for each subject area for both public and private settings. Standards enable teachers to know what content to teach and how to assess children's understanding of that content. Consequently, when we talk about curriculum standards, we mean both content standards and performance standards (Bredekamp & Rosegrant, 1995).

Content Standards

Content standards clearly state what learners should know and be able to do in certain subject areas and at specific grade levels. Content standards include the knowledge, skills, and dispositions toward learning that children need to develop. For example, in a science study of plants, children at different levels might know the following: names of plants, different parts of plants (e.g., leaves, stems, blossoms, roots), how plants grow, and the particular botanical techniques that keep plants healthy and alive. Children would also need to know and use some of the scientific thinking processes, such as inquiry, observation, systematic description, and hypothesis testing, to gather and evaluate information and to communicate that information to others. The depth of this knowledge would differ for children according to their age, experience, and interest level.

As a result of the standards movement, the early childhood profession has developed its own curriculum guidelines, which address the most important curriculum content questions that affect children's learning. All teachers need to be able to answer the following curricular questions in a positive way: "Is the content worth knowing, meaningful, and relevant to the children I am teaching?" "Is the content I am teaching accurate according to the standards of the subject area?" and "Is it reasonable to teach specific skills and knowledge at this time, or would children benefit from learning it at a later time?" These questions are typical of those raised in the 20 guidelines for curriculum content that are published by the NAEYC (Bredekamp & Rosegrant, 1995). Figure 6.2 lists these Guidelines for Curriculum Content, which have been adopted by the profession.

Performance Standards

Performance standards differ from content standards by defining the degree to which learners have mastered particular subject matter. For example, in evaluating the writing of kindergarten children, teachers need to know what constitutes mastery along the literacy learning continuum. One child might be using drawings for writing; another might be stringing letters together; yet another might be writing conventionally. These indicators are essential in determining what children can do in particular content areas (Goals 3 and 4 Technical Planning Group, National Education Goals Panel, 1993, p. iii).

Early childhood educators are very much a part of the standards movement. While high content and performance standards are necessary, they are not sufficient by themselves. Standards are primarily used to set the direction for the teacher. Fundamentally, it is the way the teacher delivers (i.e., interprets and enacts) the curriculum—the quality of teaching—that in the end actually makes the difference in children's learning (Bredekamp & Rosegrant, 1995).

Content Areas of the Early Childhood Curriculum

What is appropriate content for young children? By *curriculum content,* we mean those key concepts, ideas, skills, and processes that are unique to the specific academic disciplines of science, math, technology, social studies, language arts, the creative arts, health, and physical education. For example, some key concepts in mathematics include number sense, estimation, and geometry. Having a deep understanding of this content as well as knowledge of what discipline concepts are appropriate for children at different ages to learn is essential to a good curriculum, because content makes up a large part of the early childhood curriculum. Table 6.1 lists the content areas of the early childhood

FIGURE 6.2

NAEYC guidelines for
curriculum content

Curriculum . . .

1. describes a theoretical and research base that supports how children learn.
2. achieves learning for children in all domains and enables them to participate in democratic living.
3. teaches knowledge and understanding, skills and processes, and attitudes and dispositions.
4. includes varied subject matter that is interesting and relevant to children.
5. specifies age-appropriate learning goals.
6. reflects the needs and interests of particular groups of children and incorporates varied teaching strategies and learning experiences to accommodate individual differences.
7. respects and supports children's home culture and language and builds positive relationships with families.
8. builds on and extends what children already know and can do.
9. uses broad concepts to organize learning experiences to meet individual learning needs, abilities, and interests.
10. integrates subject matter knowledge through themes and topics of study that allow for rich conceptual development.
11. uses the standards of the subject-matter areas to provide content that has intellectual integrity.
12. provides content that is meaningful and worth knowing.
13. engages children actively in learning through meaningful choices.
14. values children's errors as a necessary part of the learning process.
15. emphasizes development of children's thinking, reasoning, decision-making, and problem-solving abilities.
16. values social interaction as integral to the learning process.
17. supports children's basic physical needs.
18. protects children's physical and emotional safety needs.
19. strengthens children's sense of competence by ensuring successful learning experiences.
20. adapts to individual or group needs where appropriate.

SOURCE: *Reaching Potentials: Appropriate Curriculum and Assessment,* Vol. 2, S. Bredekamp and T. Rosegrant, Eds., 1995, Washington, DC: National Association for the Education of Young Children.

curriculum, defines them, and identifies key national standards for each content area that have been developed by each specialty association.

Teachers and caregivers must have a deep understanding of the various academic disciplines they teach, as well as an appreciation of the unique concepts, processes, inquiry tools, and applications to real-world settings of the knowledge in the different subject areas to develop appropriate curricula for children (Bredekamp & Rosegrant, 1995; The National Board for Professional Teaching Standards, 1995). Table 6.2 describes the goal for each content area and suggests an appropriate content area learning experience for toddlers, preschoolers and kindergartners, and school-age children.

Organizing the Written Curriculum

Once you understand the content of the curriculum, you can use it to organize what you teach. There are two primary ways to organize your curriculum: by developmental domains or by subject matter. A description of each follows.

Table 6.1
Overview of Content Areas in the Early Childhood Curriculum

Subject Area	Definition	National Content Standards	Specialty Association(s)
Mathematics	The search for sense and meaning, patterns and relationships, order and predictability Goal: Mathematical literacy	1. Mathematics as problem solving 2. Mathematics as communication 3. Mathematics as reasoning 4. Mathematical connections 5. Estimation 6. Number sense and numeration 7. Concept of whole-number operations 8. Whole-number computation 9. Geometry and spatial sense 10. Measurement 11. Statistics and probability 12. Fractions and decimals 13. Patterns and relationships	National Council of Teachers of Mathematics (NCTM)
Science	Knowledge about specific phenomena (characteristics, classifications, and principles that explain the universe) and the processes used to evaluate information Goal: Science literacy	1. The nature of science 2. The nature of mathematics 3. The nature of technology 4. The physical setting 5. The living environment 6. The human organism 7. Human society 8. The designed world 9. The mathematical world 10. Common themes 11. Habits of mind	National Center for Improving Science Education (NCISE)
Technology	The application of science to problems of human adaptation to the environment		
Health	The capacity of individuals to obtain, interpret, and understand basic health information and services and the competence to use such information and services in ways that enhance health Goal: Health literacy	1. Comprehends concepts related to health promotion and disease prevention 2. Health information and health-promoting products and services 3. Health-enhancing behaviors that reduce health risks* 4. Influence of culture, media, technology, and other factors on health 5. Interpersonal communication skills to enhance health 6. Set goals and make decisions to enhance health 7. Personal, family, and community health	National Health Education Standards of Association for the Advancement of Health Education (AAHE) and American Public Health Association (APHA)
Visual Arts	The ability to create visual images and interpret images that others have made	1. Understanding and applying media, techniques, and processes 2. Using knowledge of structures and functions	Consortium of National Arts Education Associations (NAEA)

*Most applicable for preschool health education

Subject Area	Definition	National Content Standards	Specialty Association(s)
		3. Choosing and evaluating a range of subject matter, symbols, and ideas	
		4. Understanding the visual arts in relation to history and cultures	
		5. Reflecting upon and assessing the characteristics and merits of their work and the works of others	
		6. Making connections between visual arts and other disciplines	
Music	Acquisition of song and melodic understanding	**For Preschool Children:** 1. Singing and playing instruments 2. Creating music 3. Responding to music 4. Understanding music **For Kindergarten and School-age Children:** 1. Singing, alone and with others, a varied repertoire of music 2. Listening to, analyzing, and describing music 3. Performing on instruments, alone and with others, a varied repertoire of music 4. Reading and notating music	Music Educators National Conference (MENC)
Social Studies	Fosters knowledge, attitudes, values, and skills believed necessary for citizens to participate, continually improve, and perfect society	**Geography Standards:** 1. The world in spatial terms 2. Places and regions 3. Physical systems 4. Human systems 5. Environment and society 6. Uses of geography	Geography Education Standards Project (GESP)
		History Standards 1. Family life now and past 2. History of local communities in North America now and past 3. People, events, problems, and ideas that created the history of the states in which children live 4. Origin of democratic values and how they are exemplified by people, events, and symbols 5. Causes of immigration to and nature of large groups of people within the U.S. now and past 6. Regional folklore and cultural contributions that helped form our national heritage 7. Selected attributes and historical development of various societies in Africa, the Americas, and Europe	National Council for History in the School (NCHS)

Table 6.1
(continued)

Subject Area	Definition	National Content Standards	Specialty Association(s)
		Civics Standards 1. Role of government and what it does 2. Basic values and principles of American democracy 3. How the U.S. government embodies purposes, values, and principles of American democracy 4. Relationship of U.S. to other nations and to world affairs 5. Role of the American citizen	The Center for Civic Education (CCE)
Physical Education	The acquisition of sequential movement skills and increased competency based on the unique developmental level of the individual	1. Competency in many movement forms and competency in a few other movement forms 2. Exhibits a physically active lifestyle 3. Maintains a health-enhancing physical fitness 4. Demonstrates responsible personal and social behavior in physical activity settings 5. Demonstrates understanding of and respect for differences among people in physical activity settings 6. Understands that physical activity provides the opportunity for enjoyment, challenge, self-expression, and social interaction	National Association for Sport and Physical Education (NASPE)
Language and Literacy	Acquisition and application of reading, writing, listening, speaking, viewing, and visually representing	1. Reads a wide range of print and nonprint texts to serve multiple purposes 2. Reads from a wide range of genres and periods of literature 3. Applies a variety of strategies to comprehend, interpret, evaluate, and appreciate texts 4. Communicates effectively with various audiences for different purposes 5. Uses a wide range of writing strategies appropriately 6. Applies knowledge of language to create, critique, and discuss various texts 7. Conducts research and communicate results 8. Uses a variety of technological and informational resources for research 9. Develops an understanding of and respect for diversity in language 10. Makes use of first language to develop competency in English and to develop understanding of curriculum content 11. Participates as a knowledgeable, reflective, creative, and critical member of literacy communities 12. Uses spoken, written, and visual language to accomplish own purposes	International Reading Association (IRA) and National Council of Teachers of English (NCTE)

Table 6.2
Goals of Content Areas and Age Appropriate Experiences

Content Area	Goal	Age-appropriate Activity
Mathematics	To develop a conceptual understanding of quantitative, logical, and spatial reasoning to understand the relationships between and among pieces of information To represent mathematical ideas with symbols and utilize appropriate mathematical procedures and processes to compute and solve problems	**Topic: Classification** Toddlers: Sort blocks by shape in a sorting box Preschoolers and kindergartners: Simple classifications by sorting objects that are alike (e.g., in shape, color, size) in one place School-age Children: Multiple classifications by sorting objects into two or more groups (e.g., by color and size)
Science	To explore the content of the physical sciences (e.g., physics and chemistry), Earth sciences (e.g., astronomy, geology), and life sciences (e.g., biology and ecology) To utilize science processes (e.g., observing, classifying, experimenting, relating, and communicating) and scientific methods (e.g., forming hypotheses, interpreting data) to form concepts and solve problems	**Topic: The Body** Toddlers: Name body parts, listen to heartbeat with stethoscope Preschoolers and kindergartners: Draw heart and arteries; build a person with construction toys and play doctor with a doll or stuffed animal School-age Children: Trace body and label key parts and muscles
Health	To understand basic health concepts and develop life-long healthful skills and attitudes related to nutrition, safety, personal hygiene, and exercise	**Topic: Nutrition** Toddlers: Provide healthful food snacks such as fruits and vegetables; taste and name foods Preschoolers and kindergartners: Provide healthful cooking activities such as making stuffed celery or fruit salads, or spreading cheese on crackers School-age Children: Categorize food into food groups using class and individual books, displays, or food charts; identify sources of food products
Visual Arts	To develop the ability to express ideas and feelings using the senses	**Skill: Making Art** Toddlers: Make marks on large paper using large, sturdy markers, crayons, or paint; use soft play dough for rolling and modeling Preschoolers and kindergartners: Draw and paint using brushes of various widths and markers of different styles (e.g., chisel, fine point) Experiment with making different kinds of lines (e.g., wavy, curly, zigzag) School-age Children: Draw or paint on different textures and surfaces (e.g., transparencies, fabric, wall paper) using different tools (e.g., yarn, tubes, marbles) to create different results

Table 6.2
(continued)

Content Area	Goal	Age-appropriate Activity
Music	To help children use their emotions to become more discriminatory and perceptive about their world	**Skill: Singing** Toddlers: Sing simple songs and chants, such as "Rain, Rain, Go Away," and "Twinkle, Twinkle, Little Star," that have a lot of repetition, rhyme, and action Preschoolers and kindergartners: Use longer songs with predictable structures (e.g., those based on colors or numbers) that have repetition and rhyme; use a variety of songs throughout the day for arrival, calendar, and weather; incorporate singing games School-age Children: Use vocal rounds and chants with parts, such as "Row, Row, Row Your Boat"
Language and Literacy	To help children communicate using both oral and written language	**Topic: Writing** Toddlers: Opportunities to make random marks on paper, chalkboard, and other surfaces Preschoolers and kindergartners: Let children set the purpose for communicating by choosing to communicate through pictures and letters; provide an environment rich with print including class lists, murals, group stories, song charts, and children's labeling of their own work using sound spelling School-age Children: Utilize different forms of writing such as diaries, editorials, journals, and stories
Physical Education	To develop life-long, positive habits of fitness	**Skill: Body Awareness** Toddlers: Use different body parts (e.g., feet, hands, legs) with movement activities to respond to music with different tempos Preschoolers and kindergartners: Switch body parts in movement activities such as changing "Skip, skip, skip to my Lou" to "Hop" "Jump" or "Crawl to my Lou" School-age Children: Improvise and match movements to the beat of music (e.g., clap in time, march to a different beat) and engage in simple folk dances

Developmental Domains

Kostelnik, Soderman, and Whiren (1999) suggest using areas of children's development, called developmental domains, to design and develop curricula for young children. Such an approach is truly learner centered, teaches the whole child, and enables children to integrate their developing knowledge, skills, abilities, and dispositions as the teacher decides what, how, and when to teach certain concepts and skills. Developmental domains provide a balanced view of the child as a total being and enable teachers to select content that matches each child's capabilities. When content is beyond a child's abilities, the result is often failure. Table 6.3 lists each of the eight domains and provides the purpose of each.

Table 6.3
Developmental Domains as Content Areas for Young Children

Domain	Purpose
Cognitive	To acquire information, develop basic skills, build understanding of complex concepts, and develop information-processing and problem-solving skills
Social	To develop social attitudes, learn social-interaction skills, appreciate and respect cultural and individual differences, and respect and accept responsibility for the environment
Affective	To develop self-awareness and self-esteem and to learn to handle powerful emotions
Aesthetic	To build awareness, appreciation, participation, and responses to the expressive arts: art, music, dance, drama, and puppetry
Physical	To build gross and fine motor skills, foster care and respect for the body, and encourage positive attitudes toward physical activity
Imaginative	To develop creative expression and play through the use of imitation, make-believe, role-playing, and drama
Language	To build upon listening and speaking abilities, develop emergent reading and writing abilities, and foster enjoyment and response to high-quality children's literature
Construction	To provide a wide range of opportunities for building and making objects that are symbolic representations of the child's experiences and ideas through blocks and other construction toys, woodworking, simple weaving and sculpting, collage, movable outdoor play equipment

SOURCE: Adapted from *Developmentally Appropriate Programs in Early Childhood Education* (2nd ed.) by M. Kostelnik, A. Soderman, and A. Whiren, 1999, Upper Saddle River, NJ: Merrill Prentice Hall.

Subject-matter Areas

A curriculum designed by the different subject areas provides a different focus. Because a large portion of the curriculum comes from the academic disciplines (i.e., the specialized knowledge of each subject area), a subject-matter approach to the curriculum makes sense to many teachers, school boards, and curriculum developers. Knowledge from the academic disciplines enables children to "learn about the world; describe what is learned; structure the knowledge; test assumptions and challenge understandings; and define and solve problems" (Bredekamp & Rosegrant, 1992, p. 69). For example, when studying science, children learn important scientific concepts, such as "Change is all around us" and "Things move in different ways." They also learn to use the scientific method to test hypotheses.

Using a subject-matter approach to the curriculum, however, causes some concerns for early childhood educators. Because a subject-matter approach to the curriculum is expert based, much of the content is difficult for children to understand. Making specialized knowledge accessible to children at their varying levels of understanding often leads to a watered-down, inaccurate, or confusing curriculum and places primary responsibility on the learner to make connections within and across the subject areas (Bredekamp & Rosegrant, 1992). Moreover, a subject-matter curriculum by itself is not adequate, because it often leads to "fragmented, isolated skill development or the exclusion of other kinds of knowledge and skills essential to children's ultimate success in society" (Kostelnik et al., 1999, p. 71).

An Integrated Curriculum

The word *integrated* means "joining all parts of something together to make a whole." Sometimes called interdisciplinary teaching, an integrated curriculum teaches skills and concepts from the different subject areas based on the study of a broad concept or theme and on the developmental needs of the learners. An integrated curriculum helps children connect their past experiences to what they are currently learning by focusing on processes and concepts within each subject area and connecting them to the other subject areas. It emphasizes children's actual experiences or interests; their interactions with each other, with materials, and with ideas; and ample time for children to experiment and explore ideas (Krogh, 1995; Morrow, 1997; Wortham, 1996). An example of integrated teaching is a second-grade class studying the topic of food. The children might be answering questions they asked, such as "Where does food come from?" They might also be measuring ingredients for recipes, illustrating stories or poems about food, reading literature about food, and perhaps creating advertisements for their favorite foods. Through a variety of activities related to the topic of food that combine different subject areas, children deepen their knowledge and skills in several content areas.

The idea of an integrated curriculum is not new; it has its origins in the ideas of John Dewey (1938), William Kilpatrick (1936), and Jean Piaget (1965). These respected thinkers suggested that curricula for children should be holistic; that knowledge should be integrated and include some child-directed activity; that children and teachers should decide together what to learn; and that content should be learned through the study of themes and larger ideas. Learning becomes more meaningful for children when they make connections among concepts, experiences, school, and life to what they know.

Whether you organize your curriculum by domains, subject matter, or a combination of both, your curriculum for children must reflect what we know about how children learn. If your school system typically organizes the curriculum by subject areas, you might try to match some of its goals and activities to the domain areas. If children need opportunities in one or two domains, it would be beneficial to supplement activities for them by developmental domains.

Understanding the Taught Curriculum

The taught curriculum is how a teacher makes the content meaningful to a particular group of children. A meaningful curriculum considers children's developmental needs and interests, the environment and culture in which they live, their subject-area knowledge, and the methodology that is appropriate for a particular group of children (Barbour & Seefeldt, 1993; Bredekamp & Rosegrant, 1995).

Characteristics of a Meaningful Curriculum

Wortham (1996) suggests the following four distinguishing characteristics of a meaningful curriculum.

1. *A meaningful curriculum is relevant to children.* Learning needs to be connected to children's real-life experiences, interests, and knowledge in order for it to make sense to them. Consider, for example, a first-grade class studying homes. A meaningful curriculum might have children reading books about homes such as *A House Is a House for Me* (Hoberman, 1978), *Noah's Ark* (Spier, 1978), or *The Village of Round and Square Houses* (Grifalconi, 1986), writing stories and drawing pictures about their own homes, or taking inventories of what is in each room of their own homes. Children might also take a field trip to look for different types of houses and notice the materials used to build those houses. In social studies, children might investigate houses that people lived in long ago, and in math, they might make blueprints of houses and then construct them from blocks using different shapes. In

Common Issues and Concerns about an Integrated Curriculum

1. What does curriculum mean in early childhood education?

Today, we have an impressive body of knowledge about child development, learning theory, and principles of pedagogy. Decades of research confirm the value and long-term, positive effects of early childhood programs that emphasize active learning and social competence. I believe that an early childhood curriculum should offer educators a vision of what an age-appropriate program looks like and a framework for making decisions about how to achieve that vision.

Diane Trister Dodge

2. Why would people who work with infants and toddlers need a curriculum?

Caring for babies should occur in a safe and healthy environment. It should also take advantage of the unique learning opportunities that occur during this period. The brain development that takes place in the first 3 years of life is astounding. These are critical years for emotional, social, and language development. According to Erik Erikson, infants and toddlers are discovering whether the world is a place they can trust and whether they can assert their independence and feel capable. They develop trust and autonomy in the context of relationships. A curriculum framework for programs serving infants and toddlers must reinforce relationships as the focus of decision making.

3. Is a preschool curriculum also appropriate for kindergarten?

Definitely. Children from age 3 to 5 are at the stage of initiative: they like to have choices, to come up with ideas for using materials and for play. In many ways, 5-year-olds are closer to preschoolers developmentally than they are to 6-year-olds. Most have not yet made the cognitive leap in reasoning and logical thinking that occurs around age 6 or 7. A curriculum that focuses narrowly on academic skills not only is potentially damaging to children's social and emotional development, but also fails to challenge children's intellectual curiosity. A curriculum for preschool and kindergarten should focus on the physical environment as the setting for learning. It should engage children in exploring, trying out their ideas, creating representations of what they have learned, and sharing ideas with others.

4. Why talk about constructing curriculum in the primary grades when teachers are required to follow subject-matter curriculum guides adopted by their schools?

Curriculum guides and textbooks offer teachers direction about what to teach in each subject, but classroom teachers must find a way to make the curriculum effective and meaningful for their children. Because every group is different and every child is unique, teachers create the curriculum each year. It is the individual teacher, with the input and involvement of parents, who knows the children well enough to make informed decisions about what each child needs to become a competent learner. The teacher has to plan how to teach.

Diane Trister Dodge is President, Teaching Strategies, Inc., Washington, DC science, they might explore homes for different animals such as turtles and hermit crabs. These learning activities are meaningful because they build on and extend what children already know. Contrast this type of curriculum with one in which a first grade class is studying the same topic of homes but the children primarily complete teacher-created worksheets about homes and listen to the teacher's facts about homes, about which they may or may not have prior knowledge. When teachers consider children's experiences and interest level in the curriculum, children utilize higher-order thinking skills to wrestle with real issues and problems (Bredekamp & Rosegrant, 1992; Drake, 1993; Wortham, 1996).

2. *A meaningful curriculum promotes active learning.* Active learning occurs when children are mentally involved in direct experiences that help them connect the information and skills they are learning to their own lives. For example, if a second-grade class is studying living things, children may choose to read books on the topic that interest them or to take a walking field trip through the neighborhood to identify living things unique to their school building, and practice literacy skills as they read, write, and draw about what they are learning. Active learning experiences encourage children to demonstrate true understanding by explaining, finding evidence, generalizing, applying, and representing the topic in a new way (Piaget, 1965; Vygotsky, 1978). Teachers create active learning environments by respecting children's ideas, modeling strategies such as thinking aloud, problem solving, problem posing, and helping them see familiar ideas in new ways (Ryan & Cooper, 1995).

3. *A meaningful curriculum is designed by and with children.* When children plan some of their learning, it is more likely that their needs, interests, backgrounds, and abilities will be taken into account. Joint planning bridges what is personally meaningful and relevant for children to what content needs to be taught. It allows for varied learning activities at different levels to occur simultaneously in the classroom (Katz & Chard, 1989; Wortham, 1996).

4. *Meaningful curriculum links child development and content knowledge.* Educators have discussed the importance of teaching the whole child for many decades. To teach the

FIGURE 6.3

Continuum of curriculum integration

	Separate Subjects	Subject Integration	Literature Units	Theme Integration	Concept/ Inquiry
	Least Integrated				Most Integrated
Emphasis	topics separate	topics combined	literature focus used as curriculum organizer	common theme focus	concepts, skills, affective goals emphasized
Example	schedule in which each subject has a designated time block	combines two or more content areas	begins with a children's book	teacher-selected topic and activities centered on that topic	children's interests are the basis for questions about the topic

SOURCE: Adapted from *Interdisciplinary Curriculum: Design and Implementation* by H. Jacobs, 1989, Alexandria, VA: Association for Supervision and Curriculum Development.

whole child, you need to consider all areas of development in the learning process. This approach is in sharp contrast to formal, academic instructional methods whose focus is almost exclusively on intellectual development. While intellectual development is clearly a priority for a meaningful curriculum, teachers must also consider other developmental domains in the learning experiences (Kostelnik et al., 1993; Wortham, 1996). Figure 6.3 portrays a continuum of curriculum integration from least meaningful to most meaningful.

FEATURING FAMILIES

COMMUNICATING WITH FAMILIES ABOUT THE CURRICULUM

Ms. Davis's children have been studying fairy tales. Each week, she invites a child to select a take-home pack (PAK), which contains a related activity to be completed by the child and an adult in the home. Families with limited English literacy skills may complete the activity and the feedback form verbally on a cassette tape. Following is an example of a PAK for *The Gingerbread Man.*

Materials Needed

One-gallon plastic bag, canvas bag, or small knapsack

A copy of *The Gingerbread Man* with cassette tape

A recipe for gingerbread cookies and cookie-cutter

An Activity Card

A Feedback Form

Gingerbread cookie mix (optional)

Format of Activity Card

Name of Activity
Cooking Activity

What the Child Will Learn
Measuring skills (math, science)

Use the senses of smell, taste, touch, seeing, and hearing (sensory/physical skills)

How substances (dough) change when baked (science)

Use small-motor skills (physical skills)

Count ingredients as added (math)

Describe steps taken to make the cookies (language)

What to Do

- Ahead of time, gather the ingredients, directions, and utensils necessary to make the cookies.
- Read *The Gingerbread Man* with your child (or listen to the cassette tape and follow along with the book). Ask your child, "Why was the fox so interested in the gingerbread man? Can cookies become real?"
- Then, suggest that together, you make some gingerbread cookies, and talk more about the story. Follow the directions by allowing your child to "read" the pictures on the recipe, make the cookies, and then enjoy!
- Clean up supplies and answer the questions on the Feedback Form.
- Send the PAK back to school.

Feedback Form

1. Did you complete the activity with your child?   Yes   No
2. Did your child "read" the recipe?   Yes   No
3. Did your child talk about measuring ingredients?   Yes   No
4. Did your child think cookies can come alive?   Yes   No
5. Did you have any problems with this activity?   Yes   No

   If yes, please tell me more: _____

   _____

6. What did your child like best about the activity? _____

   _____

7. What did you like best? _____

   _____

Signature _____ Date _____

PAUSE AND REFLECT ABOUT CURRICULUM ON WHEELS

Since it is good practice to offer children a wide variety of hands-on experiences in all of the developmental domains listed in Figure 6.5, how do caregivers obtain the resources to provide these experiences? Some caregivers utilize neighborhood story hours or play groups. Others take advantage of the latest "hands-on" museum or take "let's explore our neighborhood" walks or trips to the library. Some of the larger libraries even have a "toy library" with developmentally appropriate toys that can be borrowed in addition to books. All of these examples demonstrate how caregivers can plan meaningful learning experiences for children, and that is what curriculum is all about.

As this video segment shows, one community in Massachusetts has decided to model good teaching to caregivers and bring the "curriculum" to the children. On this segment, you'll see the "Discovery Van" in action. Each hour-long visit allows the driver, who is a trained instructor, to involve children in thematic units. As if this isn't enough, the caregivers benefit, too. While the children are learning, the caregivers are learning as well. Each visit counts as an hour of continuing education that goes toward certification and licensing requirements.

1. Brainstorm a quick plan for a Discovery Van thematic unit. Choose a theme and list ideas for integrating traditional "subject" areas, such as mathematics, reading, or science. How could you integrate other areas such as dramatic play, music, art?
2. List three places in your community that provide curriculum assistance for caregivers. How could they be better utilized?

Creating a Meaningful Curriculum

There are many different approaches to creating a meaningful curriculum. The two primary approaches typically used by early childhood professionals are thematic units and projects. However you organize your curriculum, the best curriculum for young children is created around broad concepts that reflect the content you need to teach and the processes unique to the subject-matter areas, as well as thoughtful consideration of the children's development, homes, neighborhood, and community.

Thematic Units

Theme teaching means that children study a particular topic using a variety of learning experiences in more than one content area. Thematic units are one way to organize learning around a key concept or idea about a topic that is relevant and interesting to children. Thematic units enable children to link their learning from many different subject areas, generalize knowledge and skills from one experience to another, and connect what they are learning to real life (Caine & Caine, 1997; Kostelnik et al., 1993).

Thematic units can take different forms. Some may center on a certain type of literature, such as fairy tales. In this theme, the children may read and listen to different fairy tales, talk about their characteristics, (e.g., royalty, magic, a setting in a faraway time and place, commoners finding great riches and power), and perhaps write or enact fairy tales using those characteristics. Other thematic units focus on a topic that links several content areas, including music, art, play, mathematics, social studies, and science. For example, the topic of farms in a thematic unit may drive the curriculum decisions. In this case, children would ask questions about what they wanted to find out about farms, and then read, write, and illustrate their findings. Skills would be taught where appropriate. Suppose, for example, in the study of farms, that children decided to plant individual and classroom vegetable gardens. They may make a classroom bar graph on the growth of the seedlings (mathematics), write or draw about the progress of the seedlings in journals (literacy), and illustrate and categorize the different plants in a class mural (art). Still other themes may be organized around multiple intelligences. (See the Chapter 4 In-class Workshop for an illustrative example.) Whatever form you use, theme teaching includes children's ideas and interests as a part of the entire study.

The teacher, the children and teacher together, or the children themselves may select topics for thematic units. When making decisions about topics for units and themes, teachers should consider the children's previous experiences and decide what knowledge is worth knowing (Katz & Chard, 1989). Thematic units can be based on topics that we know interest most children, or they can be based on something interesting happening in the school, in a child's family, in the community, or in the world. Figure 6.4 provides a list of commonly used early childhood theme topics. Chapter 7 provides detailed information on planning for thematic teaching.

A thematic approach to the curriculum also helps teachers make decisions that support the 10th NAEYC curriculum content guideline (Bredekamp & Rosegrant, 1995). This guideline states that "curriculum allows for focus on a particular topic or content while allowing for integration across traditional subject-matter divisions by planning around themes and/or learning experiences that provide opportunities for rich con-

FIGURE 6.4

Commonly used
early childhood
thematic units

Organizing a curriculum around broad themes encourages "meaning making" for children. The following commonly used themes can provide the foundation for meaning making. While they are categorized by content area, notice that many topics fit into multiple categories, making it ever so important to integrate your curriculum.

Social Studies

My Family and Me; My Neighborhood; My School; Jobs and Work; Friends; Transportation and Vehicles; Homes; The Food We Eat; Explorations; Familiar Things in Our World; Feelings; Values; Celebrations; My World, Working and Learning Now and Long Ago; Children Now and Long Ago; People Who Make a Difference; Beginnings: People, Places, and Events

Science

Environmental Studies (recycling, pollution); Caring for Pets; Endangered Species; The Rain Forest; Living Things; Light and Shadows; Night and Day; Water; Animals; Seasons; Weather; Things That Grow; Exploring Space; The Physical World (magnetism, light, color, sound, weather, seasons); Ways to Communicate; The Natural World; How Things Work (faxes, copy machines, computers), Sea Life; Mysteries and Secrets; Natural Science; Change and Continuity

Mathematics

Patterns; Opposites; Colors and Shapes; Numbers; Time; Measurement; Stores; Space

Literature

Fairy Tales; Fables; Folktales; Poetry; Author Study; Chants and Rhymes; Chapter Books

Interdisciplinary Themes

Transformations; Old and New; Near and Far; Above and Below; Patterns, Containers; Fasteners; Ways of Communicating; Diversity; Intergenerational Relationships; Cycles and Systems (light, heat, life, food); Clothing; Health and Wellness; Interdependence; Natural Science; Community Institutions (museums, aquariums, bowling alleys, zoos). Stores (department stores, farm stands, groceries, ice-cream parlors,

FIGURE 6.4

(continued)

shoes, banks, bakeries, gardens); Public Services (police, fire, libraries, dumps, town hall, hospitals, highways); Offices and Factories (banks, schools, construction sites, veterinarians, clothing); Similarities and Differences

Themes for Toddlers

Self-awareness; My Family and Me; Music and Movement; The Five Senses; Vehicles; Home Living

Resources for Thematic Teaching

Allen, D., & Piersma, M. (1995). *Developing thematic units: Process and product.* New York: Delmar.

Altheim, J., Gamberg, R., Hutchings, M., & Kwak, W. (1988). *Learning and loving it: Theme studies in the classroom.* Portsmouth, NH: Heinemann.

Kostelnik, M. (Ed.). (1991). *Teaching young children using themes.*, Glenview, IL: Good Year.

Raines, S., & Canady, R. (1989). *Story stretchers.* Mt. Rainier, MD: Gryphon House.

ceptual development" (p. 16). According to Katz and Chard (1989) and Kostelnik et al. (1993, 1999), to meet this guideline, effective thematic teaching should enable children to do the following:

1. build on what they already know, stimulate questions they want to answer, and relate information to their lives
2. understand basic concepts and processes from the subject areas rather than focusing on isolated facts
3. learn accurate facts and information related to the theme
4. integrate content and processes from all the subject areas
5. engage in hands-on activities as they inquire about the theme
6. grow in each of their developmental domains
7. use the same content in more than one way and at more than one time
8. capitalize on interests, because that is what motivates learning

To illustrate these principles, consider an example of a second-grade study of outer space during which children learn concepts and facts about the planets, sun, moon, and space exploration. In math, the children compare temperatures of the planets or measure distances between the sun and other planets; in social studies, they relate life on other planets to their own lives or illustrate life in a spacecraft; in science, they study different moon and cloud formations, or explore what life might be on other planets; and in language arts, they write about their knowledge of space or learn phonics skills from the books they are reading on space; this enables children to integrate content and processes from all subject areas, participate in hands-on activities to inquire about the theme, and use the same content in more than one way and at more than one time.

Themes and projects help integrate the curriculum.

Projects

Projects are focused, in-depth studies of something that children, in collaboration with teachers, initiate, direct, organize, and develop (Edwards, Gandini, & Forman, 1993; Katz & Chard, 1989). These deep investigations support children's natural ways of learning, provoke their thinking by making learning meaningful, and spark their curiosity by challenging their abilities. Teachers who use the project approach to the curriculum believe in children's capacity to pursue their own ideas and represent them through different media. Thus, teachers facilitate and document children's progress while ensuring their learning of "skills, content, and processes across various subject areas" (Dodge, Jablon, & Bickart, 1994, p. 163). Projects have their roots in Dewey's (1938) and Kilpatrick's (1936) ideas that experienced-based learning forms the foundation of education (Hartman & Eckerty, 1995). More recently, the schools in Reggio Emilia, Italy, have used the project approach successfully with the entire preschool community.

Projects can last for a day, a week, a month, or even a year and are characterized by five features: individual and group discussions, field trips, representations of children's knowledge, investigations, and displays of learning. The following example of a pet store project created by a class of kindergartners illustrates some of the key principles of the project approach.

Ms. Ornstein's kindergartners began the year studying about themselves and their interests. Their activities and conversations prompted extensive group and individual discussion about the children's pets, what they knew about them, and questions they had about caring for pets. The children regularly brought pictures of their pets to school, and many pets visited the classroom. From this expressed interest, Ms. Ornstein took the children's lead and added books and pictures about pets to her classroom library. The children's ques-

The children's interest in pets prompted a field trip to a pet store.

tions sparked an interest in planning a field trip to the local pet store to see what it included. Ms. Ornstein created a large word-and-picture chart for children that asked the question "What do you think we will see?"

Ms. Ornstein's kindergartners used a checklist to record which animals and pet toys they expected to see and then compared those data with what they actually saw after the trip. Planning the field trip sparked children's investigations of their pet study. They generated lists of what they already knew about pets and what they needed to know, read several more books about all kinds of pets, and planned specific questions to ask during the field trip to the pet store. The children represented what they already knew and what they were learning about pets by creating fact folders, drawing what they saw during their field trip, illustrating stories they read and stories they wrote, and making diagrams and sketches of the block and dramatic play area where they had created their own pet store, and they learned the basic economics of buying and selling through enactment of pet store scenarios. Small groups, called committees, planned and developed other experiences, such as a final sale for the other kindergarten and first-grade classes in the school and an open house for the parents and families to celebrate the children's accomplishments. Some children displayed their learning by explaining with confidence and assurance the key aspects of their pet store, while others shared their writings, labeling, and artwork. In this project, the kindergartners used math skills by classifying pets; science processes by using charts, graphs, and written reports to record scientific data; art skills by sketching, drawing, and painting pictures of real and imaginary pets; and writing skills by labeling, copying, and making

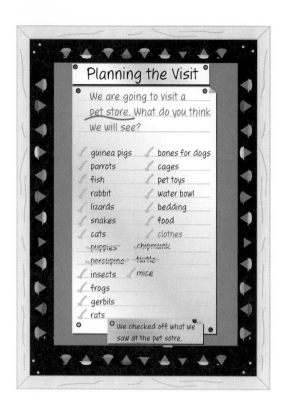

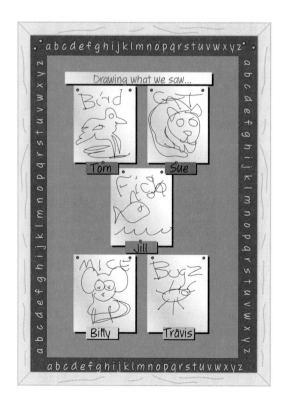

signs for the displays. This example clearly illustrates how projects help children acquire new knowledge and skills while developing dispositions toward learning and creating feelings of competence (Katz & Chard, 1989).

Curriculum Theory

Have you ever wondered about the behavior of certain animals, the nature of rainstorms, or why some things are easy for you to learn and others are not? These speculations are based on certain assumptions you make about those things and are called theories. A theory is knowledge that is systematically organized, applies to a wide variety of circumstances, and can explain or predict a set of phenomena. Consequently, you can prove or disprove a theory as you deepen your knowledge about it.

Curriculum theory focuses on one major question: What knowledge is worth knowing? (Bredekamp & Rosegrant, 1995; Kessler, 1991). This question has spawned many theories about what and how children should learn. While each theory offers different ideas about what to teach, to whom, when, why, and how, together they serve us well in designing and developing a curriculum for young children.

Eisner and Vallance (1974) suggest five theoretical orientations that shape the curriculum. These orientations to the curriculum are cognitive processes, academic rationalist, personal relevance, social reconstructionist, and technology.

The curriculum as *cognitive processes* centers on the development of cognitive skills and emphasizes thinking processes over content in all learning activities. This orientation has led to the development of materials and curricula for higher-order thinking skills, such as Bloom's taxonomy of thinking.

Academic rationalists view the curriculum as the traditional study of great ideas. They advocate teaching the same information and content to all children and view a core body of knowledge as essential for all learners. Teachers with this view consider knowledge to be unchanging and see their primary role as passing on that essential knowledge to all children.

A third orientation, *personal relevance*, emphasizes experienced-based learning matched with students' needs and interests as the source of the curriculum. This perspective views knowledge as constantly changing and seeks to develop a curriculum that is relevant to each learner at his or her level of understanding. Teachers with this orientation facilitate learning rather than transmit knowledge and view their classrooms as learning communities for solving problems.

Social reconstructionists stress the curriculum as an agent to change and improve society. This orientation to the curriculum emphasizes social values and critical thinking through peace education, awareness of social problems (e.g., war, poverty, violence), and community action projects at the individual, school, and community levels. Teachers with this orientation must be politically active and aware citizens, in addition to helping children learn subject-matter content.

The curriculum as *technology* is an efficient view of the curriculum quite common in American schools. In a technology orientation, the curriculum is predetermined to reach the same measurable outcomes for all students. It utilizes behavioral objectives to measure changes or test students' achievement in particular skill areas and assumes that curriculum standards must be explicitly stated, taught, and tested. The curriculum as technology leads to standardization.

How you view curriculum theory greatly influences your role as a curriculum developer. Table 6.4 lists the key dimensions of these theoretical orientations to the curriculum.

Table 6.4
Key Dimensions of Theoretical Orientations to the Curriculum

Category	Goal	Source of Knowledge	Teacher's Role	Methods
Academic Rationalist	intelligent citizens acquisition of knowledge	academic disciplines learners' needs and interests tied to acceptable standards	disseminate factual information through direct instruction	worksheets, workbooks, seatwork, drill and practice, isolated subject-area teaching
Cognitive Processes	development of thinking skills	manipulation of objects, ideas, and information using higher-order thinking skills	develop children's critical and creative thinking; teach children to learn how to learn through solving problems	learning experiences using the following taxonomy of thinking skills: knowledge, comprehension, application, analysis, synthesis, evaluation
Personal Relevance	growth of each student at his or her level of understanding	children's needs and interests; child development; cultural values of individuals and groups; whole child	interaction with learner to determine mutually agreed-upon learning goals; assess children's needs; connect students with materials and experience to best meet their needs and interests	self-directed learning; learning contracts; problem-solving experiences; experienced-based, child-centered practice
Social Reconstructionist	citizens who will transform society for the better	social problems and concerns; student interest in societal problems	political advocates for children and schools; problem-solving opportunities related to social issues; community building	group experiences and projects using real, active, and purposeful learning experiences related to social problems
Technology	maximized student achievement for clearly specified objectives; mastery learning	predetermined standards and goals; precise objectives; and carefully sequenced objectives in the content areas	efficient and effective means to achieve specific ends	scope and sequence of learning tasks; reinforce correct responses; modeling; guided practice; independent practice

Conclusion

Developing a good curriculum for young children takes into account three primary issues facing early childhood educators today: time to present the curriculum, the academic nature of a curriculum for young children, and depth versus breadth in curricular decisions (Raines, 1997). These issues provide the greatest curricular challenge to the profession. If you talk to many experienced teachers today, you might hear them say, "There is so much to teach and so little time to teach it." Teachers will tell you that the combination of daily distractions, a fragmented schedule, local and state curriculum mandates, and parental pressure allow little time for exploration of topics in depth. Whatever the reason for teachers' concerns over not having enough time to teach what they must in the way they wish, "the results are the same. When less time is spent on a topic, there are fewer opportunities to explore a topic in depth" (Raines, 1997, p. 83). Second, the trend toward teaching traditional curriculum content for the primary grades at earlier ages is also of concern to the entire early childhood community. Curriculum expectations that are too high are frustrating to children and lead to false labeling as immature, disruptive, and unready for school (Shephard & Smith, 1988). On the other hand, a curriculum that is not challenging enough leaves many children bored and disinterested while leading to wasted learning opportunities. Lastly, the issue of depth versus breadth is also a long-debated one. Given the recent emphasis on "meaning making," more educators are developing longer units to enable children to study topics in more depth through principles of integration and application by solving real problems common to all groups. The specialty organizations for each subject area support integration as long as children have ample opportunities to explore the discipline subjects in more depth.

One Child, Three Perspectives: *Benjamin's School Play*

Benjamin is in kindergarten at a school where the teachers plan an annual, elaborate kindergarten play. In this year's performance, *About the Presidents,* each child was assigned the part of a U.S. president. Benjamin was the 31st president, Herbert Hoover.

The teachers asked parents to go to the library with their children and help them find three or four interesting facts about the presidents their children were studying and to try to dress their children for the performance in clothing that represented their presidents' time periods. In school, the children practiced their parts, which consisted of facts they researched and memorized with the help of their parents, and sang songs about George Washington and Abraham Lincoln. Benjamin's teachers believed that having parents help their children research interesting facts, practice their parts, and prepare special clothing was a wonderful way to involve them in their children's learning.

Benjamin's mother, a single, working parent, first heard of her son's kindergarten play through a written notice from the teachers. When she learned that she had to go to the library with her son to help him research facts, Benjamin's mother was excited. But she soon discovered that Benjamin could not relate to learning about Herbert Hoover. He had little or no understanding of what a president is or does, of wars, or of what it means to be a humanitarian. Furthermore, the library books about Herbert Hoover were not written so a 5-year-old could understand them. The more Benjamin's mother explained to Benjamin about Herbert Hoover, the more frustrated she became, because Benjamin was not interested in this president. He wanted to be only George Washington, a name that had some familiarity to him. Thus, preparing Benjamin for his part in the school play became his mother's project.

On the day of the performance, the kindergartners were seated in a semicircle on the stage, the microphone was in the center, and the teachers were at each end coordinating the children's spoken parts. Some of the children spoke so softly that they could hardly be heard; others looked frightened and stiff but said their parts. One boy, who spoke too close to the microphone, received an electrical shock to his mouth and burst into tears. He never did get to say his part. Three months later, Benjamin cannot recall any facts about Herbert Hoover, but he can tell you which of his friends played certain presidents. He does enjoy watching the videotape his mother made of the performance and singing the class songs.

This profile of Benjamin, his mother, and the kindergarten teachers raises a number of issues about a developmentally appropriate curriculum. What is appropriate content for children? How can teachers make that content accessible to young children? How should children represent that content to each other and to their families?

REACT:	Think about how the perspectives of Benjamin, Benjamin's teachers, and Benjamin's mother are alike and different. What might be the underlying reasons? Which perspective do you identify most strongly with, and why?
RESEARCH:	Read about the appropriate roles of drama in early childhood settings. You might want to read *Creative Drama in the Classroom* by N. McCaslin (1990); *Literacy and the Arts for the Integrated Classroom* by N. Cecil and P. Lauritzen (1994), or *Radical Reflections* by M. Fox (1993).
REFLECT:	What values do all children gain from drama in the classroom? Generate a portrait of what appropriate drama for kindergarten children should look like.

IN-CLASS WORKSHOP

Brainstorming with Curriculum Webs

Curriculum webs are tools for planning an integrated curriculum. Webs can be used to brainstorm with other teachers and with children to develop a curriculum that is most relevant to the children whom you are teaching. Brainstorming, a method of problem solving in which all members of the group spontaneously contribute ideas, is a useful tool because it allows for many ways to plan the curriculum.

Using the ideas discussed in "Ask the Expert: Sue Bredekamp on Developmentally Appropriate Practice," which was presented early in this chapter, brainstorm a developmentally appropriate theme for a particular age group. Here are the steps to follow while brainstorming:

1. Choose a theme to explore by examining your school's or school district's curriculum.

2. Brainstorm with the children what they already know about the topic and what they want to know about the topic.

3. Brainstorm with your colleagues about the concepts or big ideas to be learned, the topics to be covered, and the activities and experiences to be integrated into each curriculum area or domain.

4. Organize your ideas into the form of a web. Figure 6.5 provides an example of a brainstorming web for a kindergarten theme on animals, and Figure 6.6 illustrates a third-grade theme on Greece.

5. Select resources and a means of assessment.

Then, construct a curriculum web by doing the following:

1. Brainstorm the possibilities related to a developmentally appropriate theme for the age level you are teaching (see Figure 6.4 for a list of suggestions).

2. Think of key words or terms and appropriate activities associated with your theme.

3. Group some of the ideas together by a common category to form a few broad categories.

4. Search for information, resources, and a broad range of reference materials to support the categories.

5. Finalize the web by selecting the major concepts to be learned and identifying the possible connections among the web strands created.

Finally, ask yourself, "How does this web compare to the characteristics of a developmentally appropriate curriculum?"

FIGURE 6.5

Brainstorming web for kindergarten about the theme animals

LANGUAGE ARTS

Listening
- Retell or act out
- Literature experiences → read *Q Is for Duck* (early finishers)
- Animal guessing game → clues
- Following directions for class book:
  - cut out shape of animal's head
  - cut clothes from magazine and paste
  (Animals Should Definitely Not Wear Clothing)

Reading
- *Make Way for Ducklings*, R. McCloskey
- *Find Demi's Sea Creatures*, Demi
- *Louis the Fish*, A. Yorinks
- *Big Red Barn*, M. W. Brown
- *Animal, Animal Where Is Your Home?*, J. B. Moncure
- *Visit to the Aquarium*, Aliki
- *Q Is for Duck*, M. Elting and M. Folsom
- *Animals Should Definitely Not Wear Clothing*, J. Barrett
- *Whose Baby?*, M. Yabunchi
- Big Books: *Sea Life* and *Wild Animals*, Educational Insights

Writing
- Journals → animals in unexpected places
- rewrite *Q Is for Duck*
- Make animal counting book (1 bear, 2 birds, etc.)
- Zoo books → writing animal names
- language experience chart to summarize unit

Social Studies
- Where do animals live? → house, farm, desert, mountain, etc.
  (Animal, Animal, Where Do You Live?)
- Animal habitats: aquarium, zoo, farm; What is the difference in animals?

THEME: ANIMALS
1. water   2. land/air

Science
- Different animals in different homes → land, air, water
- Fish aquariums → different sea life
- Water/land/air murals
- Discuss similarities and differences between animals and humans (Venn diagram)
- Compare animal and human coverings (skin, fur, feathers, etc.)

Math
- How many fish in your aquarium?
- Count how many different underwater animals we can think of
- Compare sizes of land animals
- Estimate weights of animals
- Animal counting books
- Animal crackers: sorting, counting, graphing
- Count number of animals on farm mural and write numbers
- Graph animals according to special homes (zoo, farm, and aquarium)

Art/Music
- "Old MacDonald Had a Farm"
- Torn-paper animals to make into book
- Fish aquariums
- Water/land/air mural
- Farm mural
- Make class books:
  1. *Animals Should Definitely Not Wear Clothing*
  2. *On the Farm* (Big book)

Special Activities
- Pet day
- Second-graders share zoo books
- Animal videos → National Geographic Society
- Movement → follow the leader (*Make Way for Ducklings*) or acting out animals
- Guess Zoo?, an animal-matching memory game

Courtesy of George Mason University interns.

FIGURE 6.6

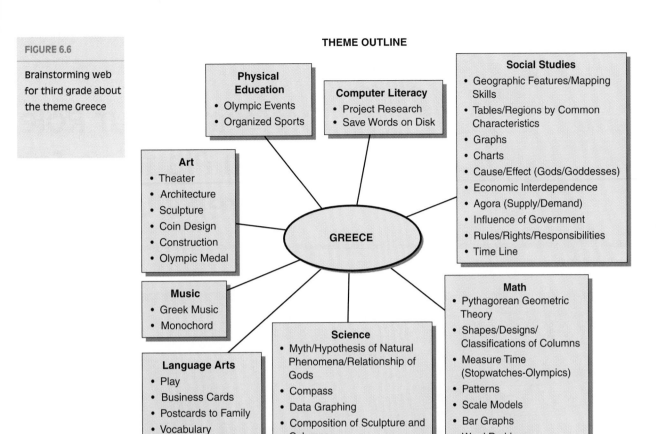

THEME OUTLINE

Brainstorming web for third grade about the theme Greece

Physical Education
- Olympic Events
- Organized Sports

Computer Literacy
- Project Research
- Save Words on Disk

Social Studies
- Geographic Features/Mapping Skills
- Tables/Regions by Common Characteristics
- Graphs
- Charts
- Cause/Effect (Gods/Goddesses)
- Economic Interdependence
- Agora (Supply/Demand)
- Influence of Government
- Rules/Rights/Responsibilities
- Time Line

Art
- Theater
- Architecture
- Sculpture
- Coin Design
- Construction
- Olympic Medal

GREECE

Music
- Greek Music
- Monochord

Math
- Pythagorean Geometric Theory
- Shapes/Designs/Classifications of Columns
- Measure Time (Stopwatches-Olympics)
- Patterns
- Scale Models
- Bar Graphs
- Word Problems
- Economic Transactions

Science
- Myth/Hypothesis of Natural Phenomena/Relationship of Gods
- Compass
- Data Graphing
- Composition of Sculpture and Columns
- Food Chain (by Region)
- Venn Diagrams

Language Arts
- Play
- Business Cards
- Postcards to Family
- Vocabulary
- Research/Report on Famous Person

Courtesy of George Mason University PDS8 interns.

Exploring Your Role in Planning for Children's Learning

Time spent in planning is essential to a well-run program. When goals and objectives are formulated, the purposes of activities chosen are made clear. When potential problems are anticipated in planning, barriers to learning and costly delays are prevented. When a schedule is planned, the best use of time and effort is assured. Planning significantly reduces teacher stress, as teachers are better prepared and more secure in what they do.

—Schikedanz, York, Stewart, and White, 1990, p. 19

Learning Outcomes

✔ Define and describe types and levels of planning

✔ Investigate the purpose of planning and its role in effective instruction

✔ Apply principles of planning to lessons, thematic units, and projects

✔ Develop daily, weekly, and monthly schedules to meet your goals and objectives

✔ Plan for individual needs and abilities of diverse learners

Meet the Teachers

Ms. Burke is a special education teacher of preschoolers who is intrigued by the beliefs and principles of the schools of Reggio Emilia. She has learned the importance of responding to children's interests as part of planning her curriculum. She says, "Teachers need to know that finding out about children's interests is a key tool for planning. I know children stay engaged in small- and large-group activities when they are of interest to them. In many ways, using children's interests in planning my curriculum allows children to operate on many different developmental levels and at their own pace. Many teachers I know think that brainstorming ideas around a seasonal theme or a subject that they choose is the best way to inspire learning. I say, " 'The theme is just the big umbrella under which different types of learning occur.' "

Ms. Kims is teaching in an inclusive, first-grade classroom for the first time. Although she includes a read-aloud time at some point each day, the children do not appear interested in the books she is reading. She concluded that "Children with special needs have short attention spans." Yet after talking with a colleague in the lunchroom about this concern, Ms. Kims realized that she never really planned for read-aloud time. She just read whatever picture books were available whenever there was a gap in the day. Ms. Kims began to plan for a regular and predictable read-aloud time each day, and she carefully selected short picture books that would be of interest to first graders. She began a schedule of regular read-alouds immediately after lunch to replace her random read-aloud times and experiences. Ms. Kims says, "By replacing a random read-aloud with a planned read-aloud using a variety of carefully selected books, I am providing my children with an exciting, meaningful learning experience that increases their appreciation of literature. Planning has also boosted my confidence as an educator in an inclusive classroom."

Mr. Pearlman has just completed his student teaching in a third-grade classroom. In his final journal, he wrote, "I learned that I can plan in advance, although what I plan may not be what I do. I love to research—to look for activities—to create my own lessons because I think I can better meet specific needs of the children. This takes so much time, and requires so many modifications, that I learned I cannot do it constantly. I was surprised by how much time planning consumed, and I was afraid of failing, of presenting poor lessons, or of losing the children." Mr. Pearlman simplified his plans well in advance of actually teaching them, tried them on in his imagination as he watched his cooperating teacher teach, and then talked through his ideas with his cooperating teacher. That strategy led directly to better planning, better teaching, and better learning outcomes for children.

These three teachers know how important planning is for children's learning. Use the following questions to think about the key elements of planning. Compare, contrast, and connect these teachers' views about planning to what you know about planning for all children's success in school.

COMPARE:	What are some similarities in the ways these teachers plan for children's learning?
CONTRAST:	What differences do you notice in how these teachers plan?
CONNECT:	What surprised you about how these teachers plan for all children? What idea do you think will be most useful to your planning? Why?

A Definition of Planning

Think about some of the best parties you have ever attended. Before those parties, your hosts or hostesses needed to think about whom to invite, what kind of party to have (e.g., barbecue, cake-and-ice-cream, dinner), when to have it, how long it should be, and any special items that were needed (e.g., paper plates, hats, gifts, games). During those parties, the hosts or hostesses made sure the food was ready, the guests were comfortable, and the gifts were opened at the appropriate time and place. And after the parties were over, the hosts or hostesses probably thought about what they might or might not do again for another party. To have a successful party, then, there has to be planning.

Planning is the ability to think ahead and anticipate what is likely to make an event run smoothly. Just as there needs to be planning for social events, so too does there need to be planning for teaching and learning. Planning for teaching involves creating and arranging events in your mind and continually thinking and rethinking about teaching and learning. Planning helps you manage time and events and make decisions that will benefit each child. It also includes troubleshooting, the ability to predict what parts are likely to be confusing or to require additional time or practice.

To maximize children's learning, teachers need to answer questions about planning before, during, and after each lesson or activity. Before teaching, ask yourself, "What do I want children to know and be able to do? Why and who should learn what I am planning? When and how can I meet the needs of both individual children and the group? How will I evaluate and assess children's learning?" During teaching, ask yourself, "Is what I planned really engaging the children? Do I need to make any adaptations or adjustments to my plan?" And after teaching, ask yourself, "What parts of this plan worked and what parts need to change? Why do I think so?" To answer the questions about what, why, and for whom planned learning occurs, you must be able to assess what children already know and what is worthwhile and appropriate for an individual child or a group of children to learn. To answer the questions about when and how requires careful planning to achieve your intended outcomes (Schickedanz, York, Stewart, & White, 1990).

When teachers talk about planning, they include planning for instruction as well as planning for a supportive environment, planning for the routines and procedures that provide the predictability of the day, planning for transitions between activities and lessons, and planning for children's interests and needs (see Chapter 5 for more specific details). Because children are learning throughout the school day, each part of the learning day must have a plan. Without planning, learning is left to chance. Good planning at every level is the road map that connects meaningful curriculum experiences to the overall goals of the program or school district. It helps ensure that legitimate learning activities are available that enable all children to achieve appropriate educational goals (Spodek & Saracho, 1994). Decisions made during planning have a profound influence on what children can and do learn.

Types and Levels of Planning

Most prospective teachers cannot wait to start planning lessons and activities for children. What they sometimes fail to realize is that they will be teaching in a program or school district that has predetermined goals and objectives for the children to meet. Even though there may be mandated goals, objectives, and content to teach in particular programs and school districts, teachers are continually shaping and reshaping lessons and activities, because teaching is a dynamic, interactive process. In many ways, you are like an architect of your own classroom world (Hansen, 1995), a professional decision maker who plans for children's learning based on both child development and curriculum knowledge.

Teachers engage in two basic types of planning: long-term and short-term. Long-term planning is very general and includes yearly planning, semester or quarterly planning, and unit or project planning. Each has its own purpose, yet each is connected to the other. Yearly plans provide an annual guide and direction for the school or program. They contain the broad goals, objectives, concepts, and skills that children should develop over the course of the year. Semester, quarterly, unit, and project plans contain more-specific goals, objectives, concepts, and skills that you hope children will achieve during a particular period of time. When you are engaged in long-term planning, you will decide the content and topics to cover (the what and why of planning), the sequence in which those topics will be covered (the how and where of planning), and the amount of time to be spent on each topic (the when of planning). In many cases, the school district, state, or program in which you are working will already have made some of these decisions. Even so, your long-term planning will focus on reviewing and fine-tuning such decisions (Reiser & Dick, 1996.)

Long-term planning guides your development of learning experiences that are based on children's prior experiences, and it helps you think through the topics that you might want to introduce during a semester or year. Once you have a general idea of what you are going to teach, you can begin to gather materials and plan field trips that will enhance children's learning. You will also be able to share your long-term plans with families so that they have advance notice of events that call for participation and a better understanding of what their children will be learning. Long-term plans should be flexible to meet the changing needs, interests, and abilities of your children. When your planning is flexible, you can capitalize on unanticipated learning opportunities, align your planning with stated goals, develop reasonable goals for each child, and determine the extent to which each child will be expected to achieve those goals (Spodek & Saracho, 1994). Figure 7.1 provides a sample yearly plan for kindergarten, and Figure 7.2 provides one for first grade. Notice how the teachers have developed their own methods for long-term planning.

Short-term planning is more specific and detailed than long-term planning because it addresses the day-to-day decisions that teachers make. It includes weekly and daily plans that identify the activities, experiences, and lessons to be used in the classroom. These plans contain specific objectives or anticipated outcomes of lessons and activities that are related to long-term goals. Short-term plans contain the schedule and sequence of lessons and activities. As you prepare your daily plans, consider which skills, concepts, and thinking processes children need to develop throughout the days and weeks ahead. Your planning will also include ways to organize your learning environment, how best to integrate the subject areas (e.g., math, literacy) across your units of study, and how to sequence and assess children's learning. Short-term planning also includes detailed lesson plans for particular parts of each day. These plans include a sequence of activities to meet children's basic needs and support their development of skills and concepts. Figure 7.3 provides a sample daily plan for infants and toddlers, primary children and a daily schedule for kindergarten. Again, notice the different formats that teachers use to plan. Figure 7.4 provides a sample daily schedule for full-day child care for 4- and 5-year-olds, and Figure 7.5 provides a sample daily plan for first grade. A sample weekly schedule for half-day preschool is shown in Figure 7.6.

A word of caution is needed about planning. While planning is essential to children's learning, becoming too rigid about continuing on with a plan regardless of children's engagement in it limits learning. Good planning in early childhood settings provides for a variety of self-selected learning activities within carefully prepared alternatives that are related to the needs and interests of particular children. Planning begins before the school year and continues until the children leave at the end of it.

Your Role as a Planner

Planning for children's learning is one of the most important skills possessed by successful early childhood teachers. You are responsible for what happens when children are with you, for selecting and establishing appropriate goals and methods, for setting the pace for learning, and for evaluating and assessing children's progress. How you plan can diminish or enhance children's learning and well-being. Consider the following example of five student teachers planning a kindergarten social studies unit on families. It included the mandated state and local social studies goals and the specific content that is required of kindergartners. As you read about these student teachers' planning process, think about your role as a planner.

The student teachers began their collaborative planning process for a social studies unit on families by first reviewing the information about their schools and students, which reminded them of the diverse nature of the student population. After looking at the statewide and districtwide objectives and standards, they created a general statement about how to make the topic of families relevant to the lives of kindergartners.

A unit on families needs to show sensitivity to nontraditional family groups.

EXPLORING YOUR ROLE IN PLANNING FOR CHILDREN'S LEARNING

FIGURE 7.1

Yearly plan for kindergarten

FT–Fairy Tale Unit
FLE–Family Life Education Optional Lessons
G/T–Gifted and Talented Required Lessons
POS–Program of Study
⬭–Teacher's Key Questions

"My World and Welcome to It"　　　　　　　　"Windows to the World"

Months/Themes	September Start School I Am Special Shapes/Colors	October We Are Special Change Seasons Properties	November Community Food/Nutrition Animals Changes	December Nursery Rhymes Fairy Tales* Number Concepts	January Senses Winter Patterns
Language Arts/ Verbal/ Linguistic	Intro. Roberts & ABC books Intro. Journals Apple book 1st qtr. interviews	Intro. —work folders —take-home books Pumpkin book Intro. blending activities (cont.)	Fall and animal poetry Intro. syllables— use names	Reading conferences See POS K4 Pocket chart poetry Minibooks ⬭ What are letters and words?	Winter poetry Begin alphabet dictation Writing conference Story retelling
Math/Logical-Mathematical	Shapes Colors Physical properties Intro Tool box	Begin Days of Kindergarten graph Sort Classify Map symbols and directions	Play money and HM math money Inventory #4	Number concepts ⬭ What are numbers?	Intro. Venn diagram (*The Mitten*) Patterning Inv. # 3 & 5
Science/ Naturalist	Explore Science table Rainbows, sun, shadows	Pumpkins and Apples ⬭ What's happening outside?	Animals Adaptations (Squirrels)	*Three Little Pigs* House Experiments ⬭ Which house will not blow down?	⬭ What are the senses?
Social Studies/ Interpersonal	Citizenship Making friends Classroom community	Friends and family project ⬭ What is a neighborhood?	Careers, Jobs, Helpers Thanksgiving Veteran's Day	Geography connection to fairy tales ⬭ Where do fairy tales come from?	Martin Luther King ⬭ Who was MLK? Chinese New Year
Health G/T	Safety Telephone numbers Business numbers G/T - 5 & 6 Faces and vehicles FLE - K.9(911)	FLE K.5 Working and playing with others K1.2.3 Families G/T 8 & 9 Sorting	Food and Nutrition project Helpers Changes Animal homes Substance abuse	⬭ How does food keep me healthy and help me to grow?	G/T Patterns Smell

February Magnets Germs/Health Comparing	**March** Weather/Water Geography Measuring	**April** Ecology Spring Sequencing	**May** Ants No. Experiments Rhyming	**June** Summer We Are Special (Revisit)
Weather poetry Five Senses books Intro R & W charts	Journal and Reading conferences *Read Aloud* *Rhymes for the Very Young* by Jack Prelutsky	3rd qtr. interviews Assessments Science experiment Write all letters and numbers you can	Paul Revere poem Rhyming poetry Journal and Reading conferences	(How many words can I write?)
Comparing (Rice table, mitten matching) HMV–c Inv. #2	Measuring: –length –height –weight –temp	Sequencing Inv. #6	Number experiments (What is . . . 5, 7, 9?) Consult POS	Revisit Days of Kindergarten graph
Magnets (How do magnets work?) Project - Five senses	Weather Water –erosion –sink/float –bubbles Peanuts	Growing plants Water table Butterflies –life cycles Recycling project	Ants/Insects (project) (How do plants and animals grow and change?)	Summer
Valentine's Day Love I like . . . Presidents' Day Chinese New Year	G.W. Carver Harriet Tubman Geography	Earth Day Conservation (Who cares about the world?)	Memorial Day	Booker T. Washington We Are Special (revisit) Flag Day—Betsy Ross
FLE K.4 Keeping healthy	G/T #1 Weather hazards (What causes weather?)	G/T #2 Planting machines	FLE Keep Safe G/T Pets	

EXPLORING YOUR ROLE IN PLANNING FOR CHILDREN'S LEARNING

FIGURE 7.1

FT–Fairy Tale Unit
FLE–Family Life Education Optional Lessons
G/T–Gifted and Talented Required Lessons
POS–Program of Study
⬭–Teacher's Key Questions

"My World and Welcome to It"　　　　　　　　　　　　　"Windows to the World"

Months/Themes	September Start School* I Am Special Shapes/Colors	October We Are Special Change Seasons Properties	November Community Food/Nutrition Animals Changes	December Nursery Rhymes Fairy Tales* Number Concepts	January Senses Winter Patterns
Computer	Explain programs Children, children who do you see? Kid Pix	Alphabet book Dr. Seuss	Sammy's Science House Thankful book	Math I Bugs in a Box	Patterning
Music/ Musical	I Am Special We All Live Together Rainbows	Mary Wore a Red Dress If You Are Happy and You Know It	Piggy Bank Squirrel song	FT chants and songs Where has the gingerbread man gone?	Five Senses songs and poems Rhythm –patterns (What patterns can I copy or create?)
P.E./Bodily- Kinesthetic	Play dough Imagination station and puppets Body parts	Magnetic letters Five Little Pumpkins	Grocery store (What will I be when I grow up?) Connect with our people	Play dough numerals FT props & puppets (Who can I pretend to be?)	Pass the Mitten game Texture patterns Senses –experiments
Visual/Spatial	Buildings, pod, neighborhood Blocks Monthly poster	Apple prints Fall people from natural materials	Wreath of thankfulness	FT Neighborhood in pod Candyland	Snowflake patterns Texture painting
Intrapersonal	I Am Special Intro. Kinds of Smart	Feelings (How do I fit in?)	Needs/wants (What am I thankful for?)	Favorite character Voting	(What if I were . . . blind, etc.?)

| | | "Discovering the Natural World" | | "Look How We've Grown" | |

February Magnets Germs/Health Comparing	**March** Weather/Water Geography Measuring	**April** Ecology Spring Sequencing	**May** Ants No. Experiments Rhyming	**June** Summer We Are Special (Revisit)
Computer valentines	(Individual Books) *Green Eggs and Ham*	Wind stories	*Down by the Bay* (Songbook) Old Lady (sequencing)	
New Year Bells Health songs	Irish music Follow the drinking sound	Taping selves singing (Can I sing?) Ecology songs	I Know an Old Lay Down by the Bay No More Pie Jamberry Star Spangled Banner	
Magnet –experiments	Experiments –leprechauns –water	Ecology experiments	Outdoor sports Hopscotch	Physical fitness test (What did we learn this year?)
Multimedia valentines	Construction Weather Maps Artwork	Block map of classroom	Ant pathways Sand art	End of Year poster Revisit "What We Did" posters
Personal habits of cleanliness	(Are leprechauns real?)	Environmental stewardship "Giving Tree"	(What have I learned this year?)	Portfolio conferences MI goal setting

Courtesy of Gail Ritchie, Fairfax County Public Schools, Virginia.

FIGURE 7.2

Long-range plans
for first grade

Subject	September	October	November	December	January
Social Studies	Families I Am Special All About Me rules Citizenship	Families I Am Part of a Family Christopher Columbus	Families Thanksgiving Veteran's Day Children of long ago	Families Traditions and celebrations Needs and wants	Families People of the World Martin Luther King
Reading	Reading Assessment Text levels Letter identification	Shared language: pumpkins, fall, trees	Shared language: families, homes	Shared language: *Gingerbread Man* Celebrations	Shared language: winter, snow
Writing	Writing assessment	Ongoing assessment is used to determine the needs of individual students and plan instruction accordingly. Scope of instructional emphasis includes •Using multiple strategies to attach meaning to print •Sentence structure •Word usage •Capitalization •Punctuation			
Math*	Investigating numbers: patterns, comparing number relationships	Addition sentences Counting on measurement: nonstandard units	Numbers 11–15 Shapes Subtraction	Numbers 16–19 Measurement: weights (nonstandard), money	Equal groups problem Solving with + Combinations Facts: zeroes, doubles
Science	Five senses	Leaves Adopt a tree Fall	Parts of a Tree Leaves	Evergreens	Seeds Recording plant growth Winter
Health	School safety Bus safety	Fire safety Police officer	Poison Pharmacist Mr. Yuck	Medicines Controlled substances	Nutrition
Handwriting	Formation of letters Fine motor skills	Formation of letters Fine motor skills	Formation of letters Fine motor skills	Formation of letters Fine motor skills	Formation of letters

*Graphing Calendar Activities integrated throughout the year

February	March	April	May	June

Families
The World:
  different types
  of families
Chinese New Year
	Families
	How the
	  environment
	  affects how we live
	Maps/Geography
		Families
		Local community
			Families
			Community
			Economics
				Families
				Review

Shared language:
  national
  celebrations
Plants
	Shared language:
	  plants, weather
		Shared language:
		  weather, flowers
			Shared language:
			  seasons
				Shared language:
				  summer

•Spelling •Structural analysis •Letters and sounds •Building vocabulary •Story structure •Author's craft •Writing in different forms •Using informational sources in the classroom •Planing before writing •Self-monitoring strategies •Initiating writing •Revising to help clarify or expand meaning •Developing oral language •Collaborating with others for the purpose of writing				

10's and 1's
Place value
Time duration
On the hour
	Measurement:
	  length
	Solid shapes
	Subtraction
	  sentences
		Relating addition
		  and subtraction
		Counting on/
		  counting back
		Money
			Measurement:
			  capacity, weight
			2-digit numbers
				Area
				Fractions
				Multiplication
				Division

Propagation:
  growth without
  seeds
	Clouds
	Tree growth
		Flowers	Grass
			Plants
			Flowers
				Flowers

Nutrition Dental health Personal Hygiene	Nutrition	Emergencies	Strangers Safety procedures	
Formation of letters	Formation of letters	Formation of letters	Formation of letters	Formation of letters

Courtesy of Diana Sparrgrove, Parklawn Elementary School, Fairfax, Virginia.

| Teacher | Brenda | | Day/Date | Tues./9–22 |

Theme _____ Families _____   Age group: _Walkers (10-15 mos.)_

	Child: Corey	Child: Mandy	Child: Mateo	Child: Lori
A.M. Language—books, pictures, conversation	Family picture collage Who Is That? game "Gamma"	Ma Ma, Daddy, baby	Point To game (family members from pictures)	Bubba (brother) Telephone dialogue
Large and small muscle activity	Play pat-a-cake Cruise activity area	→→→→ Arrange and climb, soft blocks	→→→→ Play stand up and sit down by ballet bar	→→→→ Arrange and climb, soft blocks
Creative—art, blocks, music, dramatic play				
Learning—size, nature, colors, numbers, five senses, shape				
P.M. Language—books, pictures, conversation				
Large and small muscle activity				
Creative—art, blocks, music, dramatic play				
Learning—size, nature, colors, numbers, five senses, shapes				

Notes: Mateo's mom reports he often cries standing at the rail of his crib. He needs help to get down. Corey's grandmother is visiting for a week.

FIGURE 7.4

Daily schedule for
full-day child care for
4- and 5-year-olds

Time	Activity
7:00–7:15	Prepare the room for the children. Put out selection of manipulatives, puzzles, and art materials on tables. Fill water table with either water or rice.
7:15–8:00	Children arrive. Classroom jobs. Choice of activities.
8:00–8:30	Breakfast. Brush teeth.
8:30–8:50	Continuation of morning activities.
8:50–9:00	Cleanup.
9:00–9:15	Circle time. Good morning song and story, poetry, game, felt-board activity, or movement.
9:15–10:00	Snack. Bathroom. Large motor activity.
10:00–10:30	Outdoor play.
10:30–11:15	Choice time. All centers are open.
11:15–11:30	Cleanup.
11:30–11:45	Story.
11:45–12:15	Lunch.
12:15–2:15	Rest.
2:15–3:00	Bathroom. Brush teeth. Snack.
3:00–3:30	Afternoon activities.
4:00–5:30	Songs, stories, or movement. Choice of centers. Multipurpose room.
5:30	Small snack, if needed.
6:00	Last time for children to be picked up. Housekeeping.

Courtesy of Nellie Bagley, Fairfax County Employee Child Care Center, Fairfax, VA.

They stated that studying the family was important because kindergartners are beginning to build a strong sense of self and to understand their relationships with others. Through discussion with one another, the student teachers agreed on three major goals of the social studies unit on families: students would be able to (a) identify historic events that happened while a family member was living, (b) experience a family member's work, and (c) understand where they live in relation to the school and their classmates. The student teachers identified the school district goals in each of the content areas (e.g., language arts, math, science, social studies, and the arts) that applied to their unit on families and that would guide their selection of activities. They also used the key concepts of self, others, needs, family, and responsibility that were described in their school district's curriculum guide to make decisions about the lessons and activities to prepare.

Guided by the content goals and standards, the student teachers located books, poetry, and media appropriate for their student population. They chose nonfiction books such as *I Love My Family* (Beal, 1991); picture books such as *Tell Me Again About the Night I Was Born* (Curtis, 1996); technology such as *Just Grandma and Me* (Living Books, 1994); and professional resources such as *Teaching Young Children Using Themes* (Kostelnik, 1991). They also discovered that many of the books and resources they located naturally formed categories such as What Is a Family?, Family Traditions, Family Changes, Where

FIGURE 7.5

Daily plan for
first grade

Tuesday

Date: _____

Special Information for today: _____

9:00–9:30   **Morning Choice Time/Announcements/Attendance**
- hang up backpacks and check job chart
- each child chooses an activity (read books; play games on rug; computer; explore manipulatives from math center; use writing center, art center, or listening center)
- morning announcements and pledge—about 9:15 A.M.
- take attendance after announcements; messengers take it to office

9:30–10:00   **Morning Meeting**
- children are on the rug, calendar helper fills in and reads calendar, schedule; does weather chart, number of days in school, ABC chart
- read poem: _____ *October* _____;
  Choose two children to share news; write news on white board
- Focus Lesson: *Interactive writing—What we will learn later about October*

10:00–10:45   **Writing Workshop**   Program of Study Link: _____
- Fill out individual calendars and weather graphs
- Writing activity: _____ or journals
- Group 1: _____ *Emari's: Kitty & the Birds/Tom Is Brave* _____

- Group 2: _____ *Jeremy's: Uncle Bunde/Our Granny* _____

- Group 3: *Ali's Little Brother/Me Magnetic letters: practice their names*

10:45–11:30   **Reading Workshop**
- Shared Reading: _____ *Health-Fire Safety—Jennifer* _____
- Reading Response: _____ *Stop-Drop-Roll* _____
- Small Group _____
- Quiet Reading from Book Boxes
- Sharing Circle

11:30–11:40   **Outdoor break, then bathroom break before lunch**

11:50–12:20   **Lunch (pick up children at door by main stairs)**

12:20–12:30   **Bathroom Break**

12:30–12:50   **Storytime and Discussion**   Book: *Finish Picking Apples and Pumpkins*

          Sharing

12:50–1:40	**Math**
	Program of Study Link: _____
	Developing Number Sense:_____*Math Happening**_____
	Concept Lesson: _____*Addition/Problem solving*_____
	Activity:_ *Ways to make 5—use cut-paper squares to record, in groups of three*_____
	Small Groups: _____
	_____
	_____
1:40–2:00	**Free Choice or Outdoor Break and Snack**
2:00–2:30	**Library**
2:30–3:00	Mrs. Prince every other week/Science (2:30–3:15 or 3:00–3:30)
	Concept Lesson: _____
	Activity: _____
	_____
	_____
3:15–3:30	**DEAR Time** (Drop Everything and Read) (independent reading or buddy reading) only when science ends at 3:15
3:35–3:45	**Prepare for Dismissal**
	• stack chairs, pick up things off floor, tidy centers
	• check cubbies and pack bags
3:45	**Dismissal** (children gather by door and sit on the floor)

*A Math Happening is an authentic math problem that occurs in children's natural daily activities (e.g., How many snacks are needed for the children after counting those who are absent and subtracting that number from the number of children in the class).

Courtesy of Diana Sparrgrove, Parklawn Elementary School, Fairfax, Virginia.

Families Live, and Family Roles and Responsibilities. These categories helped them brainstorm the topics, which led to a conceptual web they hoped to use during the unit. Figure 7.7 shows the concept web they used for this unit on families.

With their web created, the student teachers planned to find out what the children already knew about families as a starting point for their unit. They decided to assess children's prior knowledge during a class meeting on the first day of the unit by asking children, "What do you already know about families?" and "What would you like to know about families?" This inquiry technique allowed the children to have input into the learning and provided the student teachers with a starting place for the individuals in their classes (Wills, 1995). The student teachers planned a variety of teacher- and child-selected activities that would meet their goals, enhance the children's self-esteem, and build respect for others and their families. For example, in language arts, the children

FIGURE 7.6

Weekly schedule for
half-day preschool

Teacher's Name _____

Week of _____

	Monday	Tuesday	Wednesday	Thursday	Friday
Morning Meeting —Greetings —Calendar —Weather	Talk about water and its uses.	Discuss field trip to pond and ask children to take paper and crayons. Have clipboards to share.	Have children write in their News Books today. What might they write?	Remind children about store. Give out play money.	
Art	Add new collage materials.	Only in afternoon. Add new paint.	Sponge art.	Make sculptures for store.	
Literacy	Have books and posters on water (e.g., rivers, oceans).	Have books and posters on water (ponds, creeks, waterfalls).	New books. Miss P. will help.	Begin pricing for store.	Have blank books available (use colored paper) with markers.
Blocks	Add blue colored paper so children can make rivers.	Add pencils and paper so children can make plans for bridges.	Teacher supports bridge building.	Add boats and people.	
Dramatic Play	Include doctor and sailor props.	→→→→	Books about water and bridges.	Put rocker/boat in areas with sailor hats.	→→→→
Sand/Water	Use plastic tubing, funnels, measuring cups, spice containers.	→→→→	Put boats in water table.	Add cars, plants, and boats.	→→→→

Manipulatives	Introduce new lotto game. Teacher will join group.	In afternoon, play lotto again.	Remove stones from sorting tray.	Begin pricing new items for store.	Have buttons for sorting.
Outdoors	Take water table outside. For building bridges, use stones.	Water table outside in afternoon.	Free play. Nature walk.	Set up balance beam.	Balance beam.
Group Time	Music—Mrs. Z. will play guitar and teach songs. Story: *Cloudy with Chance of Meatballs.*	Flannel-board story: *Swimmy*	Group story on visit to the pond.	Read *Riptide.*	Read *Swimmy.* Play Who is Hiding?
Other Activities	Snack—make carrot sticks at square table in afternoon.	Visit local pond	Collect wood on nature walk.	Mary's birthday— cupcakes for snack.	Cooking—make fruit salad for afternoon snack.

Theme/Unit: Water

TO DO: Remember to send home note about trip to bridge. Invite parents to come.

Ask Jo's aunt to help with News Books time on Wednesday.

Send note to Mrs. Z.—Thank her for guitar playing.

Mary has birthday on Thursday.

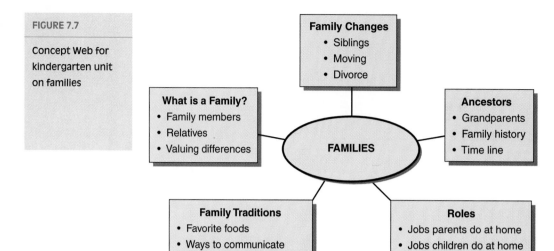

FIGURE 7.7

Concept Web for
kindergarten unit
on families

Family Changes
- Siblings
- Moving
- Divorce

What is a Family?
- Family members
- Relatives
- Valuing differences

Ancestors
- Grandparents
- Family history
- Time line

FAMILIES

Family Traditions
- Favorite foods
- Ways to communicate
- Family stories
- Celebrations and activities
- Hobbies and interests

Roles
- Jobs parents do at home
- Jobs children do at home
- Family work roles

would read and write stories about their own families and homes; in math, they might create a class graph about their family members and class pets; and in science, they might identify special sounds in their homes. The student teachers also developed integrated learning centers focusing on family-centered activities such as cooking and carpentry; a library center with special books on the topic, including books children would make; and career roles. To do this, they needed to ensure that the rooms were arranged to accommodate different centers.

After the student teachers organized the topics to be covered, they turned their attention to the development of learning activities. They identified special vocabulary terms (e.g., *adoption, divorce, nanny*) that were characteristic of some of the families of the children in their classes. They talked about these terms' meanings to develop sensitivity for children who were members of families that differed from the traditional nuclear family. This helped them get ready for the questions they anticipated children would ask about family unit terms.

Look at Figure 7.8 and notice how the student teachers planned assessment techniques, resource persons, field trips, and classroom displays that met the Guidelines for Developmentally Appropriate Curriculum and Assessment (Bredekamp & Rosegrant, 1995) as a benchmark of the choices they were making. Figure 7.9 illustrates week 1 of their kindergarten family unit. These student teachers have demonstrated the essential components of good planning (Feeney, Christensen, & Moravcik, 1996; Gordon & Williams-Browne, 1995; Reiser & Dick, 1996; Taylor, 1995) that are described in the following paragraphs.

Know the Children for Whom You are Planning. Successful curriculum planning begins with the children themselves. Developmentally appropriate practice (DAP) is an important principle of practice in early childhood education. It requires that teachers make decisions based on three important kinds of knowledge: (a) child development and learning, (b) individual needs, abilities, and interests, and (c) social and cultural contexts in which children live (Bredekamp & Copple, 1997). Understanding typical growth

FIGURE 7.8

Selected activities and teaching considerations for kindergarten unit on families

Literacy

Books: *All Kinds of Families*
  Adoption Is for Always
  The Boy Who Wanted a Family
  At Daddy's on Saturday
  Grandma Gets Grumpy
  I Dance in My Red Pajamas
  Peter's Chair

Talk About: What is family?
Interview families about jobs
Letters to family members

Art and Music

Silhouette collages of families
Build imaginary houses at carpentry table
Represent children's families using different media
Family-helper song
Sounds in the home
Things We Need booklet—Illustrate
Create Changes in My Family posters

Assessment Techniques

• KWL*
• Observations in all domains
• Individual conferences
• Anecdotal records
• Work samples

Social Studies

People and the *Past*
Similarities/Differences:
  • What is a family?
  • Me Museums
  • Family interests
  • Dream houses
  • Gingerbread people
Interdependence:
  • The class as a family
  • Things We Need booklet
  • Family members' jobs

Math and Science

Graphs: • Family members
  • Family pets
  • Family jobs
Make gingerbread people
Classify and sort family pictures
Create patterns with family pictures

FAMILIES

Dramatic Play Center

Housekeeping and family props
Books about families
Telephone books and telephones
Variety of dolls and animal figures

Resources

Field trips: Walking tour of neighborhood to observe different sizes and types of homes, vehicles, and other characteristics
People: Family members (Librarian to locate developmentally appropriate books, videos, software)
Displays: Classroom map, school and community graphs of family characteristics, family pictures at home and at work

Family-School Connection

Letters to parents explaining unit and inviting the families to call and contribute materials (e.g., family recipes)
Family Fair

*What I Know, What I Want to Know, What I Learned

FIGURE 7.9

Weekly plan for kindergarten unit on families

244

Week of _____

Week 1 of Kindergarten Social Studies Unit, "The Family"

Time	Monday	Tuesday	Wednesday	Thursday	Friday
8:30–9:30 12:15–12:45	Center Choice Family books, puppets, block people, carpentry	Center Choice	Center Choice	Center Choice	Center Choice
9:30–9:55 12:45–1:10	Morning Meeting Calendar, pledge, attendance, Morning Message, Share Time Intro. topic: "What Is a Family?" with KWL*	Morning Meeting Venn diagram: Family Pets	Morning Meeting Family recipes	Morning Meeting Read *Bread, Bread, Bread*	Morning Meeting Prepare for classroom visitor
9:55–10:10 1:10–1:25	Movement Family in the Dell	Movement Pantomime Pets	Movement Simon Says	Movement Heads, Shoulders, Knees, and Toes	Movement Carnival of the Animals
10:10–10:40 1:25–1:55	Snack/Recess	Snack/Recess	Snack/Recess	Snack/Recess	Snack/Recess
10:40–12:00 1:55–3:15	Read-aloud All Kinds of Families Centers Family Center: Class book: *My Family*	Read-aloud *Your Family, My Family* Centers Family Center: Graphing Family members	Read-aloud *The Relatives Came* Centers Family Center: Cover for recipe book	Visitor: Mr. Ramos will cook tortillas Centers Family Center: Making tortillas	Visitor: Grandmother Centers Family Center: Family crests
12:00–12:15 3:15–3:30	Class meeting	Class meeting	Class meeting	Class meeting	Class meeting

*What I Know, What I Want to Know, What I Learned
Courtesy of George Mason University PDS8 Interns

and development is the foundation for planning an age-appropriate curriculum and is necessary to understand individual needs, abilities, and interests. Considering children's ages, developmental levels, uniqueness, and social and cultural backgrounds will greatly enhance your planning. Younger children need large blocks of time for play and spontaneous exploration; older children need large blocks of time to engage in more project-oriented and structured planning to more accurately represent their learning (Feeney et al., 1995). Notice how the unit on families planned by the student teachers took into account the characteristics of 4- to 6-year-old children by providing many activities for them to work in small groups and expand their academic skills across the subject areas.

Be Knowledgeable about the Content and Concepts You Plan to Teach. Each academic discipline has identified key content and concepts considered essential to learn at different ages (Bredekamp & Rosegrant, 1995). (Many of these concepts are listed in Table 6.1 in Chapter 6.) One of the first sets of questions you will ask yourself in order to

Teachers need to be life-long learners, too.

EXPLORING YOUR ROLE IN PLANNING FOR CHILDREN'S LEARNING

make content accessible to children you are teaching is, "What content and concepts will I be teaching? What do the children already know and how can I build on that? What are the most effective age-appropriate ways to teach this content?" This kind of planning focuses on results. Children want to know many things about their world. They are particularly interested in knowing about themselves, about their families and communities, about how things work, and about the natural and physical aspects of their environment. You will want to plan experiences that are meaningful, challenging, and will extend children's thinking, but that also enable them to be successful learners. Whatever content and concepts you present to children must have integrity and be worth knowing, or they will be of little value to them (Katz & Chard, 1989). For the unit on families, we saw how the student teachers selected books on topics directly relevant to 5-year-olds and planned graphing activities using children's family members and pets to teach graphing concepts. Note, too, that most of the activities they planned were worth knowing and doing.

Plan a Variety of Experiences to Meet Individual Needs, Abilities, and Interests. Good planning consists of varied experiences that maximize learning. Planning for a broad range of developmental skills and interests is important, because not all children learn in the same manner. The abilities of children even of the same age vary, so activities must be open-ended and flexible enough to be used by a number of children with varieties of skills. Instead of working with one set plan for all children, stretch yourself to incorporate the different types of intelligences into your planning (Gardner, 1993). This effort recognizes that students learn differently and allows them to express themselves in their own ways. You can see that the student teachers who developed the unit on families planned a variety of activities, which met different learning styles. For example, they included graphing for those who prefer patterns, writing stories for those who prefer words, cooking and carpentry for those who like spatial activities, and individual activities for children to do alone, as well as activities to be done in a group. In this way, the plan was to work from children's strengths and choose teaching strategies that use multiple modes of representation and multiple modes of performance (Barba, 1998).

Planning a variety of experiences also takes into account children's interests. Most children have particular interests. The enjoyment that a person experiences in pursuing an interest usually leads him or her to find out more about it and to gain skill and expertise in it—sometimes lasting a lifetime. This can also lead to the person being exposed to other interests, which in turn leads to other competencies. For example, exposing kindergarten children to different family occupations may spark an interest in a particular career option in one or more children in the class.

Plan Appropriate Methods of Assessing and Evaluating Children's Learning. How will you know what children have learned? An important responsibility of all early childhood teachers is planned, ongoing assessment and evaluation of children's learning. Serious evaluation leads to better understanding of children and better planning (Taylor, 1995). The methods of assessment planned by the student teachers who developed the unit on families showed evidence of good planning. They planned to assess children's prior knowledge through the KWL strategy (What I Know, What I Want to Know, What I Learned), which will enable them to start the unit building on children's prior knowledge and increasing their understanding from that point. Teaching for understanding means children can do "a variety of thought demanding activities with a topic—like explaining, finding evidence and examples, generalizing, applying, and representing the topic in a new way" (Perkins & Blythe, 1994, pp. 5–6). The student teachers also planned to conduct ongoing observations in all domains, use work samples for portfolios, and conduct individual conferences. Each of these assessment strategies is tied to the unit goals and reflects the importance of unifying goals and assessment from the outset.

Plan Time to Reflect Upon your Teaching and Learning Activities. Reflection is part of every teacher's planning process. Thoughtful teachers reflect on questions about student learning and their own teaching methods. Ask yourself, "What have my students learned?" "What evidence do I have that shows they are learning?" Think about the outcome of your planning. Identify the aspects of your teaching that worked and those that did not, why your teaching was successful or not. Look at the part of the lesson or activity that did not work as well as you would have liked. What can you change about it to improve it? Thinking about your teaching and children's learning should be done every day to improve your teaching and better meet the learning needs of all children (Gordon & Williams-Browne, 1995).

Allow Plenty of Time to Plan Ahead. Your best teaching will occur when plans are made well in advance of the teaching day so you have enough time to gather materials, make contacts, and think through how to implement your ideas. You will want to find a regular planning time for yourself, and with your teaching team to ensure the best planning. Writing down your daily, weekly, and unit plans gives you the flexibility you need to implement your ideas. You might also consider planning extra or optional activities, even though you may not use them. Some of these extra activities can be planned to include families, as described in the following "Featuring Families." Additional planning "increases teacher confidence, allows for flexibility, and prevents teacher distress when planned activities take less time than expected, are not well received, or are clearly inappropriate for the children that day, based on such variables as mood, weather, or absenteeism" (Taylor, 1995, pp. 94–95).

FEATURING FAMILIES

COMMUNICATING WITH FAMILIES ABOUT MEANINGFUL LEARNING ACTIVITIES IN THE HOME

Each month, Ms. Davis sends home a calendar of things for children and families to do that are related to themes at school. Following is a portion of one of her February calendars. What other activities can you think of that would be appropriate for parents to use with their children?

February Home Activities				
Monday	*Tuesday*	*Wednesday*	*Thursday*	*Friday*
2 Ask me what *communicate* means.	**3** Read with your child the picture message or rebus chart brought home today.	**4** Write a rebus message about what you did after supper tonight.	**5** Sing *Little Cabin in the Woods* with and without words—just hand signs!	**6** Select and make a recipe from the *Home-to-School Cook Book*.
9 Collect 20 old envelopes with stamps on them—15 for home and 5 to take to school.	**10** Have your child sort the 15 envelopes. How many ways did your child sort your child sort the envelopes?	**11** Make a valentine to send to someone special. Address and stamp the envelope.	**12** Take the valentine to the mailbox or post office.	**13** Read *A Letter for Amy* by Ezra Jack Keats.
16 Finish the picture phone book with your child. Call a friend in the new phone book.	**17** Take turns acting out activities you do during the day. Guess what each other is doing.	**18** Select four or five pictures of your child at various ages. Play a sequencing game to see if your child can order the pictures from early ages to the present.	**19** Give your child a hug and say "I love you." How many ways can you tell each other "I love you?"	**20** On a piece of paper, write the word *Communicate*, then find pictures in magazines that show ways to communicate. Make a collage.

PAUSE AND REFLECT ABOUT YOUR ROLE AS A PLANNER

Think about your role as a planner in relation to the unit on families described in this section. What did you realize about planning when you read about these student teachers' plans? What questions do you have from reading this description? What do you agree and disagree with? What other thoughts do you have about planning a unit on families for kindergarten children?

Why Is Planning So Crucial to Success as a Teacher?

There is considerable evidence that planning is an essential aspect of successful teaching. Throughout your career as an early childhood teacher, you will be engaged almost continually in some kind of planning. It will occur in each phase of the teaching process: before teaching (e.g., making decisions about the purpose for learning and writing down the specific steps of the teaching-learning activity), during teaching, (e.g., making necessary changes with your procedures, materials, and the content as you are teaching), and after teaching (e.g., evaluating your lesson, thinking about what will affect your teaching for the next day or week, and noting changes you want to make). In each of these planning phases, teachers "utilize cognitive monitoring strategies such as visualizing, guiding, managing, decision making, and self-probing" (Freiberg & Driscoll, 1996, p. 77). Teachers plan to make decisions about individual and group learning; accountability to local, state, and national standards, and each learner's success (Reiser & Dick, 1996). These three fundamental principles of planning are discussed in the following paragraphs.

Planning Individual and Group Learning

When you understand and appreciate students' unique learning and developmental needs, you take into account what each child brings to the teaching and learning situation. You also recognize that no two children and no two groups of children come into the classroom in quite the same way. Children bring their own experiences, attitudes, skills, interests, questions, and problems with them to school. Only the teacher—knowing the children, their families, and the school environment—makes a deliberate effort to select and adapt teaching methods and structure learning experiences to meet current individual needs (Spodek & Saracho, 1994). When you are responsive to the wide range of abilities and learning styles of the children in your classroom, you demonstrate to children that accepting and responding to differences are important democratic values. The opposite approach assumes that all children respond equally to one particular teaching method and is often less effective for meeting individual needs.

One good way to facilitate individual learning is through a variety of grouping practices. Basically, there are four types of grouping patterns that you will regularly use: large groups, small groups, one-on-one interactions, and individuals. Generally, children learn more readily if they experience a variety of instructional groups. Grouping should be flexible and vary in size consistent with the learning activity, allow for child-initiated activities, foster self-esteem and social and emotional learning, and have appropriate pacing of learning activities to enhance learning. Table 7.1 lists and describes the different types of grouping patterns for children.

Planning Accountability to Local, State, and National Standards

Why do you need to be so clear about your goals for students? Unfortunately, if you do not have a clear idea of what goals you have for your students, you will not be able to do a good job of planning instruction for them. In many schools and programs today, you probably will be asked to teach specific units of study and will most likely be given goals, objectives, and a prepared curriculum guide to follow. It is likely that you will be given one or more of the following: a list of competencies that students are expected to achieve, specific textbooks to use to teach certain subjects, and perhaps some curriculum kits. You can incorporate these standards and materials into your own curriculum provided you can state your own goals and objectives for the children's learning and articulate them to others. When you are clear about your own goals and objectives, you have the means to incorporate any mandate into your program (Barbour & Seefeldt, 1993).

Quality early childhood programs and practices readily accept the principle of accountability. Accountability means that you evaluate student progress frequently and make plans for each child's future learning. Additionally, the staff, teachers, and program must also be regularly assessed. Results of these assessments are then used for planning individualized education programs when they are necessary (National Association of Elementary School Principals, 1998).

Table 7.1
Grouping Patterns for Children

Type	Description	Appropriate Uses
Large Groups/ Whole Class	• includes 10 or more children • economical with time but does not address individual needs and responses • children are generally passive participants	• share common experiences and hear the same thing • singing • story time and read-alouds • demonstrations • classroom visitors • group games • class meetings and discussions • group conferences
Small Groups	• provides opportunity for social interaction and leadership skills • involves 2–10 children to develop skills, concepts, and ideas with others • involves negotiation, interaction, and support	• peer teaching and tutoring • multiage groups • flexible skill groups (short-term) • activities that require teacher assistance (e.g., literacy and math skills) • cooperative groups learning • interest groups • social or random groups • centers, stations, choices
One-on-one Interactions	• involves focused adult-child interaction, generally to help a child acquire a skill or concept or pursue a need or interest • capitalizes on spontaneous learning and teachable moments encouraging dialogue and questioning	• observation and assessment of skill level and adaptive teaching based on observational data • concentrates on children's learning
Individuals	• enables a child to explore an idea on his or her own (e.g., insects, water, printing, building) • maintains control within the child • pursues interests and continues learning after instructional activities have ended	• hands-on, interactive learning opportunities (e.g., books, interactive bulletin boards, replicas to explore, activity centers) • contracts, centers, stations • peer tutoring • choices and projects • volunteers

Planning for Each Learner's Success

Teachers have a responsibility to address each student's individual and exceptional learning needs. Planning for each child's learning at every level depends to a large extent on the goals that you select, the strategies that you use to reach the goals, and the ways that you interact with each child and groups of children as learners (Eggen & Kauchak, 1996). Consider the way in which the three teachers you met in the chapter

FIGURE 7.10

Strategies for meeting individual needs of diverse learners

Strategies for Culturally and Ethnically Diverse Learners

1. Incorporate the home culture.
2. Encourage active participation from families.
3. Capitalize on students' backgrounds.
4. Use culturally relevant curriculum materials.
5. Identify and dispel stereotypes.
6. Create culturally appropriate learning environments.
7. Use various grouping patterns.

Strategies for Linguistically Diverse Learners

1. Integrate teaching approaches.
2. Use multiage and peer tutoring.
3. Incorporate thematic units and projects.
4. Have two or more children at a computer at a time to enhance communication.
5. Use language that invites children's participation and that they understand.

Strategies for Children with Exceptionalities

1. Use audiotape materials for children who cannot read successfully.
2. Provide visual reminders (pictures, graphs, maps, charts) for children who have difficulty attending.
3. Give directions in small steps.
4. Discover the special interests and strengths of each child and capitalize on them in the classroom.
5. Arrange seating so that every child can be seen and heard comfortably.
6. Be sensitive to the obstacles that prevent children from learning.

SOURCE: Adapted from *Educating Everybody's Children: Diverse Teaching Strategies for Diverse Learners* by R. W. Cole, Ed., 1995, Alexandria, VA: Association for Supervision and Curriculum Development.

opener try to ensure success for each learner: Ms. Burke said, "Teachers need to know that finding out about children's interests is a key tool for planning"; Ms. Kims now plans for a regular read-aloud time each day and uses a variety of books in her inclusive classroom; and Mr. Pearlman talked through his mental and written plans with his classroom teacher to better meet the needs of his students.

Building a planning repertoire that includes multiple instructional strategies is an important goal for beginning teachers and others who want to improve their teaching and enable children's learning. While it is beyond the scope of this book to present in-depth instructional strategies to address students' diverse learning needs, the general guidelines presented in Figure 7.10 are appropriate for teaching all learners with the goal of success.

Good planning also has other benefits, ranging from providing the total picture for a day, week, month, or quarter, to using time wisely and productively, to asking higher-level questions. Each of these functions empowers your teaching in the most positive way (Freiberg & Driscoll, 1996). Figure 7.11 lists the various functions of planning.

FIGURE 7.11

Various functions
of planning

1. Planning gives you the "big picture" of teaching and enables you to coordinate the many parts of the teaching day.
2. Planning facilitates good management and instruction by providing a sense of order to your day.
3. Planning enhances learning by ensuring a purpose.
4. Planning facilitates sequencing and pacing learning by determining appropriate "next steps" for individual children.
5. Planning connects classroom learning to the children's community through good use of resources and children's culture.
6. Planning alleviates disruptions and the need to waste time.
7. Planning increases student learning through identifying student outcomes.
8. Planning increases your repertoire of instructional strategies.
9. Planning enables you to ask higher-level questions.
10. Planning assists in having the necessary supplies and materials.
11. Planning serves as a guide for substitute teachers to ensure continuity of instruction.
12. Planning documents learning and increases accountability to program goals and objectives.

SOURCE: Adapted from *Universal Teaching Strategies*, 2nd ed., by H. J. Freiberg and A. Driscoll, 1996, Needham Heights, MA: Allyn & Bacon.

PAUSE AND REFLECT ABOUT WHY PLANNING IS CRUCIAL TO YOUR SUCCESS AS A TEACHER

Reread the opening section, "Meet the Teachers." How might these teachers have planned differently? What would be the advantages and disadvantages of alternative approaches?

Research on Teachers' Planning Efforts

Research on teachers' planning efforts supports what most experienced teachers have concluded: that instructional planning plays a critical role in teaching and school learning (Clark & Dunn, 1991). When do teachers engage in planning? Contrary to the notion that teachers don't start planning their instruction until the night before they must present it, researchers have found that teachers are constantly engaged in planning. In reality, teachers plan their instruction all the time—while driving home from school, grocery shopping, standing in the shower, and sitting on the beach (Reiser & Dick, 1996).

We know from research (Berliner, 1986; Borko, Bellamy, & Sanders,1992; Clark & Peterson, 1986; Lawler-Prince & Jones, 1997; Reiser & Dick, 1996) that there are qualitative differences in the planning process between novice (preservice) teachers and their more experienced counterparts. For example, novices and experts use different

Teachers plan all the time, not just the night before a lesson.

strategies for solving problems. Expert teachers have more pedagogical and subject matter knowledge than novices; they also have more highly developed mental systems for organizing and storing this knowledge. Consequently, expert teachers process information more efficiently than novices do during each of the phases of teaching.

Expert teachers are better able than novices to use their knowledge of children, content, and pedagogy to plan in their heads, making mental maps to guide their teaching and support children's learning. Their plans are more detailed and more richly connected to learning than those of novices. Expert teachers include a greater number of student actions, teacher instructional moves, and routines for common classroom activities (Borko et al., 1992). Figure 7.12 compares and contrasts the differences between expert and novice teachers' planning.

FIGURE 7.12

Planning
characteristics of
expert and novice
teachers

Expert Teacher	Novice Teacher
Before Teaching	**Before Teaching**
1. Has system for teaching successful lessons matched to unit and lesson topics previously used and modified (e.g., folders, files). 2. Uses extensive planning based on more pedagogical and content knowledge and better-developed conceptual systems. 3. Has experience with keeping lessons flowing through detailed mental planning to guide the direction of the learning.	1. Focuses on detailed, written lesson plans and gathering resources. 2. Has limited mental plans and experiences to draw upon.
During Teaching	**During Teaching**
1. Uses an extensive variety of teaching strategies to teach activities and lessons. 2. Has well-defined beliefs about student learning and content. 3. Has greater use of instructional and management routines and procedures leading to more efficient responses.	1. Uses a limited repertoire of teaching strategies. 2. Has untested and undefined pedagogical beliefs about student learning and content. 3. Uses a limited number of routines and procedures causing extensive thinking and a focus on surface features or events.
After Teaching	**After Teaching**
1. Uses an extensive variety of teaching strategies to make content accessible to learners of varying abilities. 2. Attends to children's performance and interests.	1. Has a limited number of ways to make content accessible to learners of varying abilities. 2. Attends primarily to children's interests.

Making Useful and Appropriate Plans

A beginning teacher recently said to us, "Planning is the hardest thing I do. Be sure your preservice teachers learn how to plan well so they can have more control over their teaching in their own classrooms and with their planning teams." This teacher has a good insight into one of the most important aspects of teaching appropriately: the various planning tools a teacher needs to implement good learning experiences for children. In this section, we provide you with practical information on how to make long-range plans (e.g., thematic units and projects) and short-range plans (e.g., activities and lessons). We begin with the basic elements of both types of planning.

Elements of Effective Planning

There are basically four elements that will guide both your long-term and short-term planning: goals and objectives, processes, activities and lessons, and assessments to help each child learn (Eddowes & Ralph, 1998; Feeney et al., 1996; Reiser & Dick, 1996).

1. *Goals and Objectives.* Goals are broad purposes for learning (e.g., in science and math, a goal is to build on children's natural interests in the world), whereas objectives define the specific behavior, skill, or concept you wish the children to attain. Goals take into account learners' needs, the content to be learned, and community values and interests. Whatever your goal, clearly identifying the purpose of a lesson or activity is necessary so you think about what children will learn. Goals and objectives can be based on children's needs, abilities, or interests or can result from your observations and assessment.

2. *Processes.* Processes are ways of thinking about and making sense of information. For example, children use the scientific processes of observing and classifying and the mathematical processes of measuring and counting to understand information; they use the reading processes of predicting and inferring to gain meaning from text. These basic process skills are necessary for conceptual understandings.

3. *Activities and Lessons.* These are specific learning experiences, designed by the teacher or together with a child or children, to meet intended goals and objectives. For example, writing responses to literature in language arts, graphing family members in mathematics, and formulating hypotheses about plants in science are typical lessons and activities in early childhood. Planning good activities and lessons requires that they be age appropriate and match the abilities and skills of individual children in a group (Bredekamp & Copple, 1997). It also requires identifying resources and materials needed and deciding how to present these learning experiences to children (e.g., procedures and methods to be used).

4. *Assessment and Evaluation.* These are methods selected to determine how well children are learning. The methods used should provide a way to determine what children know and can do following the lesson or activity. The results of your assessment will help you to determine the next steps you will take and to revise your instruction based on children's performance and responses.

Webbing as a Planning Tool

Webbing is a way for teachers to brainstorm possible key concepts, ideas, and learning experiences and then connect them through a pictorial or graphic representation (Katz & Chard, 1989; Jones & Nimmo, 1994). You can create a web around a theme (e.g., plants), a subject area (e.g., language arts, science), or a program or school district goal (e.g., multicultural education, critical thinking). Figure 7.13 illustrates curriculum webs organized around "The Self" for preschool children, and Figure 7.14 illustrates concept webs organized around "Famous Americans" for first-grade children. Note that one web for each age level is developed for concepts; the other is organized around subject areas.

Making Long-range Plans

There are primarily two kinds of long-range planning: planning for thematic units and planning for projects. We discuss each in the following paragraphs.

CONCEPT WEB

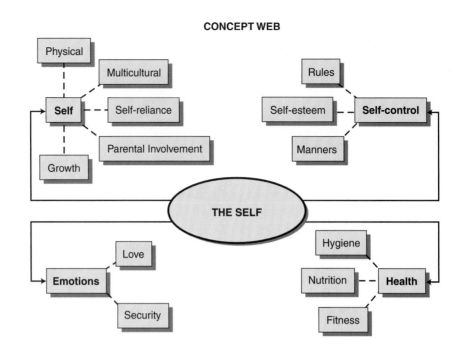

FIGURE 7.13

Concept and subject-area webs for preschool children

INTEGRATED SUBJECT-AREA WEB

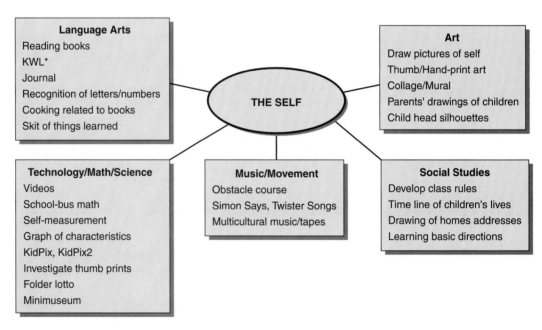

*What I Know, What I Want to Know, What I Learned
Courtesy of George Mason University PDS interns.

FIGURE 7.14

Concept and subject-area webs for first-grade children

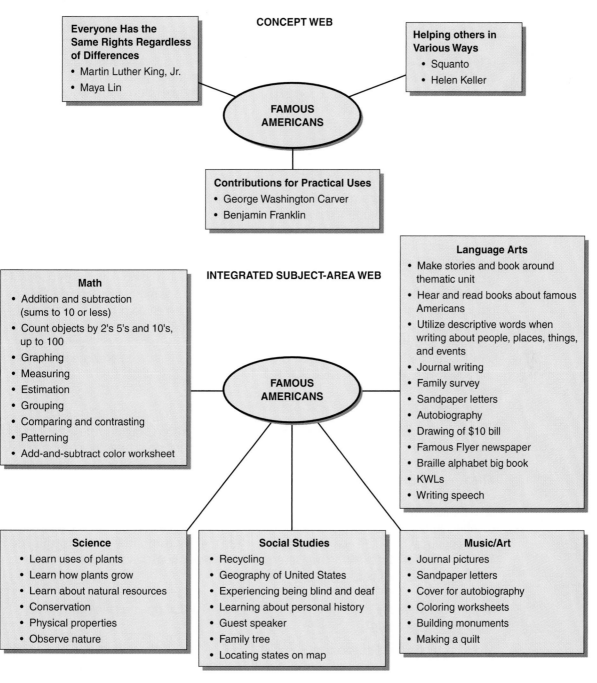

CONCEPT WEB

Everyone Has the Same Rights Regardless of Differences
• Martin Luther King, Jr.
• Maya Lin

Helping others in Various Ways
• Squanto
• Helen Keller

FAMOUS AMERICANS

Contributions for Practical Uses
• George Washington Carver
• Benjamin Franklin

INTEGRATED SUBJECT-AREA WEB

Math
• Addition and subtraction (sums to 10 or less)
• Count objects by 2's 5's and 10's, up to 100
• Graphing
• Measuring
• Estimation
• Grouping
• Comparing and contrasting
• Patterning
• Add-and-subtract color worksheet

Language Arts
• Make stories and book around thematic unit
• Hear and read books about famous Americans
• Utilize descriptive words when writing about people, places, things, and events
• Journal writing
• Family survey
• Sandpaper letters
• Autobiography
• Drawing of $10 bill
• Famous Flyer newspaper
• Braille alphabet big book
• KWLs
• Writing speech

FAMOUS AMERICANS

Science
• Learn uses of plants
• Learn how plants grow
• Learn about natural resources
• Conservation
• Physical properties
• Observe nature

Social Studies
• Recycling
• Geography of United States
• Experiencing being blind and deaf
• Learning about personal history
• Guest speaker
• Family tree
• Locating states on map

Music/Art
• Journal pictures
• Sandpaper letters
• Cover for autobiography
• Coloring worksheets
• Building monuments
• Making a quilt

Courtesy of George Mason University PDS interns.

Common Issues and Concerns About Teaching Children Using Themes

1. How do teachers choose topics that will make good themes?

Themes represent concepts. Concepts are big ideas supported by smaller bits of information such as terms, facts, and principles. Topics that do not meet these conceptual criteria lack substance and depth. This is exemplified by weekly plans centered around a letter of the alphabet, such as *B*. Since *B* is not a concept, it is a poor choice for a theme.

In addition to being *conceptual*, themes must be *relevant*. Relevant themes are directly tied to children's real-life experiences. Themes such as foods, night and day, homes, and backyard birds are relevant because they help children make sense of their lives and expand their understanding of life around them. Conversely, Ancient Rome, the rain forest, and penguins are less relevant because these topics fall beyond young children's first-hand experiences.

2. Do teachers have to make every activity relate to the theme?

Some teachers have the mistaken impression that every activity must relate to the theme. This can be problematic for several reasons. First, not everything worth learning is necessarily theme related. Children need a wide array of learning opportunities; some of these easily fit the theme of the moment, others stand apart. Both kinds of experiences benefit children. Second, when the classroom is overly saturated by a given topic, the theme loses its appeal for children and adults alike. Youngsters, initially excited by the theme, grow weary of dealing with it at every turn and children less interested in the topic have a hard time finding activities that genuinely excite their curiosity. To avoid these drawbacks, several nontheme-related activities should be interspersed throughout a unit plan. The most effective unit plans are ones in which children have several theme-related activities from which to choose each day as well as some other experiences that cover content or processes not addressed by the overall topic under study.

3. Can teachers plan a whole year of themes in advance?

Planning themes too far ahead overlooks an important criterion for effective theme planning: timeliness. Themes are timely when they build on children's current interests. Thus, themes should take advantage of teachable moments. Children who discover an anthill on the playground and become curious about it are ripe for a unit on insects. Likewise, discovering that several children in a class will become older brothers and sisters during the year could prompt a unit on babies. The chance to tap children's interests as they become evident is lost if all the topics are mapped out for the year. It is reasonable to have a few standard themes to cover annually. However, it is also important for teachers to leave time for themes particularly suited to the children with whom they are currently working.

4. Many teachers use holidays to plan their themes. What do you think about this approach to planning?

Several potential problems accompany holiday themes. First, holiday themes run the risk of being little more than a convenient backdrop for classroom decorations and craft projects. Young children usually come away from such experiences without having expanded their concepts or increased their skills across the curriculum. This is not effective theme teaching. Second, there are many opportunities for children to learn holiday lore at home and through the community. The same cannot be said for other concepts such as spiders, homes, friends, or storytelling. Limiting holiday themes allows more attention to be paid to those concepts for which early childhood programs can add richness, variety, and experiences not so easily obtained elsewhere. Third, the religious or cultural significance of certain holidays may be lost. For instance, the true importance of Easter may be overlooked in a flurry of bunny images and Easter baskets.

Such simplistic approaches promote stereotypes and assume that every family celebrates particular holidays and that their celebrations are similar. None of these assumptions is in keeping with the cultural and religious sensitivity that early childhood professionals strive to achieve. Holiday activities may appropriately comprise some of the non-theme-related concepts in a given unit, such as family traditions or 'people living together.' These concepts are inclusive, not exclusive. They support children's growing awareness of the similarities as well as differences among people.

Marjorie J. Kostelnik is a professor in the Department of Family and Child Ecology, Michigan State University, East Lansing, Michigan.

Planning Thematic Units

Thematic units involve a variety of planned learning experiences around a core concept in a manageable way. A core concept is a broad idea, question, or problem that helps children make connections and further their understanding of the world around them. It has intellectual integrity, is relevant and meaningful, and represents in-depth thinking and problem solving that can be studied at different age or grade levels. Examples of core concepts include human relationships, patterns, processes of change, traditions and celebrations, and communities. How a theme is studied and focused changes with the age, interests, and grade level of the children.

The Ask the Expert feature with Marjorie Kostelnik answers questions about thematic teaching, such as selecting topics, planning themes in advance, and using holidays as themes. (Recall, too, that Chapter 6 provided an extensive discussion of organizing a curriculum around themes.) Figure 7.15 provides an outline of the questions teachers should ask themselves to help them plan meaningful thematic units; the questions are answered in the context of the theme, Famous Americans, for which concept webs were provided in Figure 7.14.

Planning for Projects

Projects are planned, in-depth investigations of a topic worth learning about. The investigations are usually undertaken by a small group of children within a class, sometimes by a whole class, and occasionally by an individual child, about a topic posed either by the children, the teacher, or the teacher working with the children (Katz, 1994). The goal of a project is to learn more about the topic by applying higher-level thinking skills rather than to seek right answers to questions posed by the teacher (Katz, 1994). It epitomizes the collaborative nature of teaching, during which "teachers and children think, plan and critique together" (Gordon & Williams-Browne, 1995, p. 336).

FIGURE 7.15

Steps to planning
thematic units

1. *What is the core concept?*

   Many people have contributed to the way we think and live today.

2. *What is the theme and its origin?*

   The theme is famous Americans. This is a required unit of study to meet state standards. The social studies goals are to increase student awareness of historically significant deeds from past generations. Children will learn about Martin Luther King, Jr., Helen Keller, George Washington Carver, Benjamin Franklin, Maya Lin, and Squanto.

3. *What are the content areas that will be integrated? What are the corresponding concepts to be explored?*

   The content areas are language arts, mathematics, science, social studies, art, and music.

   Other concepts are helping others and rights and responsibilities. Skills in each content area will be taught.

4. *What are the materials, resources, and field trips needed?*

   Materials: peanuts and plants, Braille alphabet, books on these famous Americans, magazines, pencils, crayons, markers, scissors, glue, journal books, bandana, ear muffs, tag board and sandpaper, clay and play dough

   Resources: children and their families, guest speaker (person who uses Braille), school specialists, and community members; child- and teacher-made displays (e.g., class monument, sand letters, Earth friends made from recycled materials, and quilt replica)

   Multimedia: videos (Black Americans of Achievement series, *Squanto and the First Thanksgiving,* and *Franklin, What's the Big Idea?*)

Software:	Kid Pix, Make a Map
Web sites:	Ben Franklin
www.s/n.fi.edu/franklin/rotten.html
	Squanto and the Pilgrims' First Year in America:
www.ericir.syr.edu/plweb-cgi
	Martin Luther King, Jr.
www.splcenter.org/centerinfo/lci-2.html
	Maya Lin
www.splcenter.org/centerinfo/maya.html

   Field Trips: National Museum of American History, neighborhood nature walk

5. *What is the culminating activity?*

   Minimuseum containing exhibits of Braille alphabet letters and words, materials made from peanuts and sweet potatoes, kites with a key, map of places where Martin Luther King, Jr. lived and visited

6. *How will the unit be introduced?*

   KWL: Ask, "What makes a person famous?" "Who do you know that is famous?"

7. *How will children's learning be assessed? How will the teacher's teaching be evaluated? How will the unit be improved or extended?*

   Assessment Techniques: observation, recording, and documentation; anecdotal records; work samples and work folders; participation in project; skills tailored to individual needs

   Teacher Self-evaluation: reflective notes in journal, daily review of lessons and activities that are adapted for the next day

   Extensions: Children who exhibit particular interests may pursue those interests

In the following Ask the Expert feature on page 262, Jeanette Allison addresses the misconception that projects are unstructured and chaotic and answers questions about the difference between thematic units and projects, selecting topics, and getting started on projects. For even more information on the project approach, visit the Web site *www.ualberta.ca/~schard/projects.html*.

The following are steps to use when planning projects.

PHASE 1: GETTING STARTED

- Have several discussions to select and refine the topic. Topics must be (a) closely related to the children's experience, (b) integrated across subject areas, and (c) have enough depth to be explored for an extended time period.
- Brainstorm ideas with the children and make a web of the possible topics and subtopics for study. Invite children to ask questions they want to find answers to through investigation.

PHASE 2: FIELD WORK

- Provide many opportunities for direct investigations of the topic through field trips to places and for investigations of objects and people. In these investigations, children are learning from observation, constructing models, recording findings, predicting, discussing, and dramatizing their new understandings (Katz & Chard, 1989).

PHASE 3: CULMINATING AND DEBRIEFING EVENTS

- Children and their teacher(s) prepare and present the results of their investigations in the form of displays of findings and artifacts, talks, dramatic presentations, and/or guided tours of their constructions.

Planning for project work is not a one-time event. As children's needs and interests change and deepen, you can rebalance your curriculum by including project work periodically so that it reflects the children's current needs and interests. Additionally, be prepared to learn along with your children. Figure 7.16 provides an outline and Figure 7.17 provides a project planning web for a first-grade project on gardening.

Making Short-term Plans

Planning for daily or weekly learning experiences is what we refer to as short-term planning. Activity or lesson plans focus on a single teaching episode. In most preschool programs, the term *activity* is used for planning; in most primary and elementary schools, the term *lesson* is used. Both, however, have similar components. The term *activity* is preferred for younger children because it implies a less formal and rigid approach to learning. In this text, we make the distinction by age only.

Planning for Activities and Lessons

Activity and lesson plans provide the working documents of a program or classroom. These plans are part of the classroom structure and are determined, in part, by the schedule (see Chapter 5 for a discussion of varying schedules). At a minimum, the activity and lesson plans describe what is planned for that day, including the goals and objectives for the activities, the time frame within which they are to be carried out, and

ASK the Expert   Jeanette Allison on The Project Approach

Common Questions and Concerns About the Project Approach

Jeanette Allison

1. What is the difference between projects and thematic units?

This is the most frequently asked question, because projects and units appear to be similar. However, understanding the uniqueness of both approaches provides for more effective project work. Units have overlapping characteristics with projects and therefore can be natural stepping stones to project work. Still, units are not substitutes for projects. Projects and units differ in how much the following elements are emphasized, that is, more or less: investigation, inquiry, conceptual understanding, children's questions and input, problem solving, real-life artifacts, internal motivation, self-control, choice, creativity, time, and flexibility in the destination. For example, projects allow for more inquiry, understanding, curiosity, choice, and time investigating phenomena. Units have more predetermined outcomes and timeliness that the teacher monitors closely. Units are commonly implemented similarly each year, and usually on a predictable schedule each month, while projects change yearly. Another distinction between projects and units is that units tend to emphasize activities more than the children and entertainment more than engagement. Also, for units, fun and excitement are primary criteria in topic and activity choice; the learning cycle is terminal more than ongoing; pace and foci usually are predetermined by teachers. Projects are meant to cause children to question deeply and examine thoroughly real-world, "right-here" phenomena.

2. How do you suggest that a teacher start a project?

The first step in starting a project is choosing a topic. Find out what children want to investigate. Notice their interactions, activity preferences, and conversations. During group time, consult with children about things they would like most to explore. Together, decide on major milestones and events and initial plans. For example, I implemented a project with children that originated from a construction site next to the school. Daily, children scampered over to the windows and monitored the site. When I observed them closely, I began to appreciate their curiosity, and I asked, "Would you like to find out what is happening at the construction site?" From there, our project began. Within 5 weeks, the project's focus changed from construction site to house to post office to Laundromat to hospital. The overall focus, then, was on a community. Our major theme was structures.

3. How are topics chosen?

It is crucial to base topics on what children want to investigate. I cannot emphasize this enough. When the project approach is new to teachers, it may be helpful to begin with starter topics with which the teachers feel comfortable. But it is imperative that teachers quickly move away from teacher-determined topics. True benefits of project work cannot be realized until children are integral to the process from the outset. Their topic preferences are linked directly to the long-term motivation needed to sustain project work. Teachers must choose topics that focus on *concepts*, such as underlying meaning and ideas, rather than solely on facts and trivia. Instead of studying pets in a random fashion, for example, children should begin with a more focused idea, such as "people who take care of pets," guided by the overall theme of interdependence, or "what pets need to survive," centered on the theme of survival. And finally, topics must relate to children's lives. Learning must be determined largely by what they know and want to know.

4. Is the project approach unstructured?

At first glance, projects appear chaotic and goal-less. Admittedly, projects are less structured than traditional teaching, but they are not meant to be unstructured. The chaotic feeling can come from the natural and necessary shifts in children's interests and learning. A teacher not used to this can be caught off guard and interpret these shifts as straying off target. If the teacher does not begin with a concept-based theme, such as systems or communication, and consider major goals ahead of time, the project can be rather rocky. The goals and purposes of the project approach are supposed to help children develop useful knowledge, skills, and social conventions pertaining to their world.

Project activities help children understand their roles in the world and what the world has to offer them. Children develop research skills throughout a project's three main phases: getting started, main part, and culmination. Each phase's length depends on what is being investigated, children's wonderments, and teachers' resources and responsibilities. I encourage teachers to include projects as part of, if not central to, the program. Doing so honors a child-proven approach to early learning.

Jeanette Allison is an associate professor, College of Education, Arizona State University, West Phoenix, Arizona.

Jeanette Allison is an associate professor, College of Education, Arizona State University, West Phoenix, Arizona.

FIGURE 7.16

Outline for first-grade project on gardening

I. **Project Title:** Gardening (with a focus on the arts)

II. **Objectives:** Children will
- use the visual and constructive arts to express and communicate ideas about gardens and gardening
- develop their constructive, analytical, problem-solving, literacy, and oral-language skills through participation
- explore and use a variety of materials and discuss their potential for making art associated with gardens
- develop interpersonal intelligence through collaborative and cooperative experiences

III. **Planning Web**

IV. **Phase 1: Getting Started**

   Goal: To discover and develop children's knowledge about and experiences with gardening and gardens
   - Teacher-initiated KWL on gardens and gardening
   - Books, poetry, and songs about gardens
   - Artworks of gardens by other children and artists
   - Paint own gardens
   - Children interview families about types of gardens they have seen or had

FIGURE 7.16

(continued)

- Journal writing about starting a garden, what it needs to grow, and the kinds of gardens children would like
- Authentic props in dramatic play center relating to gardens
- Visit gardens with class and families

Questions to assess prior knowledge:
- What does a garden need to grow?
- What animals would you expect to see in a garden?
- Who has a garden? Why?
- What else would you see in or near a garden?

Phase 2: Finding out about gardens through investigative activities

Field Visits: Field visits to community gardens (involve families); look for evidence of animals, identify types and purposes of gardens, observe and confirm predictions of gardens and surroundings, generate own questions and find out the answers

Classroom Activities:
Visual Arts:
- Use watercolors to imitate impressionists' paintings of gardens
- Use a variety of materials (e.g., Popsicle sticks, pebbles, bark) to construct a three-dimensional representation of each group's garden
- Observe and note details in paintings of gardens by several different artists
- Explore works of art featuring gardens from around the world via books, videos, photos, posters, and the Internet

Dramatic Play:
- Enact a garden shop through use of authentic materials (e.g., gloves, plastic tools, hats) to enact various roles
- Provide authentic props (e.g., soil, water, pots, seeds, watering can) to create own minigardens

Constructive Play:
- Decide where and how to construct a minigarden in the most suitable place
- Design and build birdbath for the garden
- Plan for obstacles (e.g., rain, lack of wind, unwanted pests)

Creative Dramatics:
- Sing garden songs and create appropriate movements
- Retell stories through puppetry, miming, and readers theater
- Listen to garden sounds and enact them

Math:
- Graph numbers of each type of plant the class is growing

- Count how many pennies, nickels, dimes, and quarters children need for purchasing seed packets of their choice
- Sort seeds by color, size, and type

Science:
- Conduct experiments to see what happens when plants go without water
- Observe garden growth
- Examine plants to learn about their parts: leaves, stems, roots
- Observe an earthworm making its way through soil
- Reroot plant clippings in water and in soil to observe changes

Classroom Visitors and Resources:
- Local artists, museum curator, and resources on impressionist paintings
- Garden-shop employees, nursery employees, produce employees
- Architects and gardeners in the community to discuss upkeep
- Musicians from local community to explore musical movement through gardens
- Families and other resources on personal gardens that are different, have different needs and purposes
- Local community member who enjoys gardening
- Representative from local hardware store or home building supplier who can speak about garden materials and preparation
- Local farmers

Phase 3. Culminating Event (Choose from these possibilities)
- Field trip to a nearby farm to observe how gardens are constructed and maintained
- Family luncheon to view projects developed (e.g., minigardens), to enjoy a tasting of fruits and vegetables planted, and to exchange recipes of tasty dishes
- Family picnic during which families can view student art displays, seed-sorting graphs, slide show of children at work in their garden, displays of student-conducted experiments, and hear a retelling of *Stone Soup* by Ann McGovern

Assessment Strategies: (Choose from these possibilities)
- Share constructions
- Question individuals about projects
- Anecdotal records of children's participation during investigations
- Videotape and display children's work from projects
- Observe participation during culminating event with families
- Children's descriptions of what they liked and did not like about planning and growing a garden
- Have children complete a participation chart (e.g., I Turned the Soil, I Picked Weeds, I Watered Plants) and graph responses

FIGURE 7.16

(continued)

Children's Books:

Anderson, L., & Bjork, C. (1988). *Linnea's windowsill garden.* New York: R & S Books.

Carle, E. (1987). *The tiny seed.* Saxonville, MA: Picture Book Studio.

Chevalier, C. (1991). *Little green pumpkin.* New York: Bradbury.

Cole, H. (1995). *Jack's garden.* New York: Greenwillow.

Cooney, B. (1982). *Miss Rumphius.* New York: Viking.

Ehlert, L. (1988). *Planting a rainbow.* New York: Harcourt, Brace, Jovanovich.

Ehlert, L. (1994). *Red leaf, yellow leaf.* New York: Harcourt, Brace, Jovanovich.

Ernst, L. (1991). *Miss Penny and Mr. Grubbs.* New York: Bradbury.

Florian, D. (1991). *Vegetable garden.* New York: Harcourt, Brace, Jovanovich.

Ford, M., & Noll, S. (1995). *Sunflower.* New York: Greenwillow Books.

Krause, R. (1989). *The carrot seed.* New York: Harper Trophy Books.

Lionni, L. (1960). *Inch by inch.* New York: Astor-Honor.

McGovern, A. (1987). *Stone soup.*

Ryder, J. (1989). *Where butterflies grow.* New York: Dutton.

Zion, G. (1959). *The plant sitter.* New York: Harper & Row.

Teachers' References:

Bauer, K., & Drew, R. (1992). *Alternatives to worksheets K–4.* California: Creative Teaching Press.

Hart, A., & Mantell, P. (1996). *Kids garden! The anytime, anyplace guide to sowing and growing fun.* Charlotte, VT: Williamson.

Kite, P. (1995). *Garden wizardry for kids.* New York: Barron's Educational Series.

Muhlberger, R. (1993). *What makes a Monet a Monet?* New York: Viking.

Munro, E. (1961). *The encyclopedia of art.* New York: Golden Press.

Raboff, E. (1987). *Art for children: Renoir.* New York: Harper & Row.

Roalf, P. (1993). *Looking at paintings: Flowers.* New York: Harper & Row.

Steele, M. (1989). *Anna's garden songs.* New York: Greenwillow.

Venezia, M. (1988). *Getting to know the world's greatest artist: Van Gogh.* Chicago: Children's Press.

Optical Data School Media. (1994). *Kinder ventures user guide for laser disc multimedia program.* One of five modules. "Out and about: Exploring plants, animals, and the environment." Warren, NJ: Author.

Note: This project was developed by a group of early childhood Professional Development School interns. They were asked to develop a project with a focus on the arts.

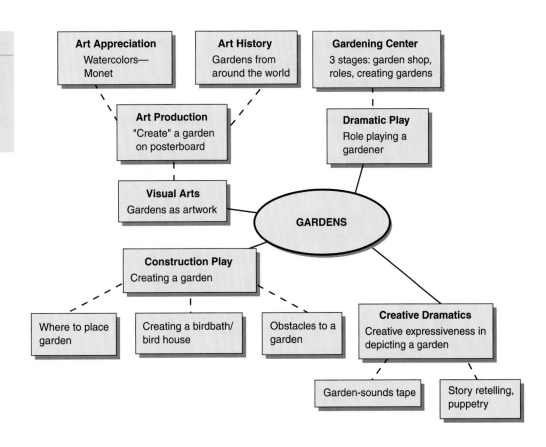

FIGURE 7.17

Planning web for
first-grade project
on gardening

Art Appreciation
Watercolors—
Monet

Art History
Gardens from
around the world

Gardening Center
3 stages: garden shop,
roles, creating gardens

Art Production
"Create" a garden
on posterboard

Dramatic Play
Role playing a
gardener

Visual Arts
Gardens as artwork

GARDENS

Construction Play
Creating a garden

Where to place
garden

Creating a birdbath/
bird house

Obstacles to a
garden

Creative Dramatics
Creative expressiveness in
depicting a garden

Garden-sounds tape

Story retelling,
puppetry

a means of assessment and evaluation. In addition, activity and lesson plans provide information about which teacher will be in charge of the activity, in what part of the classroom each activity is to be carried out, and what materials are needed. Although activity and lesson plans can take many forms, they should be complete enough so that any teacher can pick one up and know for any given day what is planned and why it is planned. Figure 7.18 shows two lesson planning forms. The first is a very short form providing the basic information; the second is a longer, more thoughtfully completed form that takes into account all aspects of a conceptual curriculum and speaks to the total development of the children and families within the classroom. Both forms can be used for different purposes.

PAUSE AND REFLECT ABOUT MAKING AND USING APPROPRIATE PLANS

Reread both Ask the Expert features in this chapter and then search the Internet for suggestions for projects and units. What did you find that would be useful to you in planning? What criteria will you use for judging the worthiness of units and projects located on the Internet? What questions do you still have?

FIGURE 7.18

Short and long forms
of activity or lesson
plans

Short Form for a Lesson or Activity Plan

I.   Activity or Lesson Topic: (What is the name of what you will teach?)

II. Lesson Overview: (What are the goals, concepts, or skills you will teach?)

III. Teaching Procedures: (What will you do before, during, and after teaching?)

IV. Materials: (What materials, resources, and space do you need?)

V.   Assessment: (How will you know what the children learned? How will you evaluate your own teaching?)

VI. Other Comments: (Is there anything specific you need to do for this lesson or activity?)

Long Form for a Completed Lesson or Activity Plan

I.   Lesson Topic and Subject: Layers of the Rain Forest, Science and Art

II. Time: 1.5 hours

III. Lesson Overview

   A. Concept: Each of the four layers of the rain forest has distinctive characteristics and plant life.

   B. Objectives: Students will
   - develop a perspective of each of the four layers of the rain forest
   - develop understandings of plant characteristics in each of these layers
   - construct pictorial representations of each layer

   C. Grouping Patterns:
   - Heterogeneous whole group for the introductory part of the lesson
   - Paired learning to discuss and construct pictorial representations

IV. Teaching/Learning Procedures

   A. Objectives for Each Group:
   - Each pair will discuss the different types of plant life for each layer of the rain forest
   - Each pair will construct the four layers of the rain forest

   B. Introductory Activities:
   - Sing the Rain Forest Song as children transition to the rug
   - Access prior knowledge through questioning
   - Read parts of *Nature's Green Umbrella*
   - Talk about characteristics (e.g., shapes and colors of leaves) that we see in the rain forest

   C. Developmental Activities:
   - Pair children to discuss characteristics of the rain forest
   - Pairs will plan a pictorial representation of the four layers of the rain forest using four different pieces of white paper

   D. Summary Activity:
   - Have each paired group meet with another paired group to share their representations and talk about the reasons they included particular details

E. Extensions:
- Add animals to the rain forest pictures in the appropriate layers
- Discuss animal habitats and why specific layers are more appropriate than others

V. Materials

A. Each Student:

Pencil, four pieces of large white paper, crayons, glue, tissue paper, construction paper, and markers

B. Teacher:

Book, 32 pieces of large white paper, and Rain Forest Song

VI. Family-School Connection
- Children will take home their pictures and share them with their families
- Teacher will send home paper to families asking them for comments about the rain forest creations

VII. Adaptations for Individual Learners
- Pair children with strong literacy skills with children who are still developing literacy skills
- Provide many visual resources that illustrate the different levels of the rain forest
- Discuss special vocabulary terms

VIII. Orchestration and Monitoring
- Use the marked spaces on the rug for whole-group instruction
- Use open-ended questions to engage children's participation
- Observe and monitor engagement of working pairs
- Use a familiar song to begin the lesson and to invite children to the rug; clap patterns if needed to get children's attention

IX. Assessment
- Observe children's planning abilities and record using anecdotal notes
- Listen for children's responses to questions for ability to describe the four layers of the rain forest
- Observe children's completed work

X. Lesson Effectiveness

A. Objectives:

How do you know you met the objectives?

What are the next steps you will take, and why?

B. Self/Teaching

What parts of this plan worked? Why?

What parts could use improvement? Why?

What are some possible changes for my future teaching?

What did I learn about myself as a teacher?

Courtesy of Lynelle Kerns, George Mason University PDS7 Intern, Fairfax, Virginia.

Conclusion

Planning provides the framework for teaching and learning and will probably require many adaptations along the way. Planning for the education of young children should be based on a blend of theory and practice that reflect how children grow and learn. It should always acknowledge young children as active and creative learners (National Association of Elementary School Principals, in press). Planning well makes the uncertainties of teaching easier to handle. To achieve the best outcomes for children's learning and development, you must become knowledgeable about and skilled in the various techniques of planning. When planning, always ask yourself, "Why am I asking children to do this activity or lesson?" "How will what I am doing help my children become better learners?" and "Will this lesson or activity help my students learn a concept, skill, or strategy, or will they simply be completing a task?" Having high yet realistic expectations for each child is the hallmark of effective planning, which leads to positive outcomes for young children.

One Child, Three Perspectives: *Shayna Goes to Kindergarten*

Shayna was a kindergartner who was curious and quick to learn but had difficulty adjusting to large groups of children and large-group activities. Shayna's teacher had been teaching for 25 years in a rigorous, skills-based kindergarten program with lots of group work. Each day, the children completed many papers. According to Shayna's teacher, the more papers they completed, the more it meant that everything was running smoothly. Shayna, who was already reading, was spending her days coloring pictures, cutting them apart, and gluing them in sequence. She also spent large amounts of time circling pictured objects beginning with the same letter, and then coloring all the pictures.

One day, as usual, Shayna's kindergarten teacher gave the children ditto sheets and workbook pages to complete, and she insisted that the children remain quiet while they worked on them. Suddenly, Shayna started to chant softly, "*Boring, boring, boring,*" and one of her classmates began to tap in rhythm to the words with a fat crayon. Soon, every child took up the chant, and, like the chant of penitentiary prisoners, "BORING, BORING, BORING" grew louder and louder. The teacher was incensed! Shayna was marched down to the principal's office and her parents were called, because Shayna had "started a kindergarten revolt"!

In a conference between Shayna's teacher and parents, Shayna's parents questioned why Shayna had to complete activities that seemed meaningless to her. Shayna's teacher reminded them that Shayna needed to conform to the kindergarten program and that these activities were expected of all kindergarten children; Shayna's behavior in the group was simply unacceptable, she said. Her parents were concerned that Shayna, already labeled the class clown, would lose interest and enthusiasm for kindergarten and learn that school was boring.

If Shayna's teacher had planned her curriculum with Shayna's needs, interests, and abilities in mind, she might have planned some meaningful activities for Shayna to do: Her planning decisions should have been different. Shayna's teacher should have planned for Shayna in three different ways. Before each activity, she should have considered what Shayna brought with her to school—her culture, her family background, the influences of her community, and her prior experiences—and what kind of grouping pattern would work best for Shayna. During each activity, Shayna's teacher should have noticed Shayna's reactions and interactions with the work and with her peers. After the lessons, Shayna's teacher should have evaluated Shayna's intellectual, behavioral, and attitudinal outcomes, as well as unintended effects. Taken together, that would constitute the whole of what we mean by planning.

But Shayna's teacher assumed that it was her job to get Shayna ready for first grade by teaching her with small, digestible pieces of information. Shayna's teacher felt obligated and pressured to cover the material and get every child on track by making them all conform to the demands of the written material. She believed that if her students were quiet and diligent, they would fit in with the school culture in which she worked.

REACT:	Think about how the perspectives of Shayna, her parents, and Shayna's teacher are alike and different. What might be some reasons? With whom do you most closely identify, and why?
RESEARCH:	Shayna's teacher is using the direct instruction model of teaching. Compare this way of teaching with thematic units and projects, as described by Marjorie Kostelnik and Jeanette Allison in the Ask the Expert features of this chapter. Consider again the kindergarten unit on families developed by the five student teachers. How did they plan to promote concepts and skills while using theme teaching?
REFLECT:	What alternatives does Shayna's teacher have in planning to meet Shayna's needs and keep her interested in kindergarten?

Planning for Different Age and Ability Levels

Planning for different ages and ability levels requires a learning plan, which is a systematic way to identify children's areas of strengths, areas that need strengthening, and appropriate activities to help them move along the learning continuum. To use a learning plan effectively, you must be knowledgeable about the widely held expectations for the physical, cognitive, language, social, and emotional development of the age range of the children you are teaching, as well as about age-appropriate learning experiences.

Using the developmental milestones for children of different ages described in Tables 3.1 through 3.4 in Chapter 3, examine the learning plan shown in Figure 7.19 and, in a small group of colleagues, discuss each of the three categories. Next, think about a child you know very well; it may be your own child, a niece or nephew, or someone from your field experience class. Fill out the learning plan for that child. Discuss with your group any information you have that does not fit on the chart. Finally, discuss the strategies you might use to compile your individual learning plan information into a classroom chart that allows for easy access to implementation. For example, the classroom chart shown in Figure 7.20 may be used as an overview of which children need help in particular areas; a check mark is made in areas that need to be strengthened. How do you think learning plans can improve children's learning?

FIGURE 7.19

Learning plan

Name _____

Date _____

Areas of Strength and Confidence

1. _____

2. _____

3. _____

Areas Needing Strengthening

1. _____

2. _____

3. _____

Activities to Help

1. _____

2. _____

3. _____

FIGURE 7.20

Classroom learning-plan chart

Name of Child	Physical Development	Cognitive Development	Language Development	Social Development	Emotional Development

EXPLORING YOUR ROLE IN PLANNING FOR CHILDREN'S LEARNING

8

Exploring Your Role in Documenting Children's Learning

Student assessment is a critical aspect of the educational encounter. At its best, it provides teachers with important knowledge of students and their growth as learners, informs ongoing curricular and pedagogical practice, is a basis for helping students reflect on their own learning, and serves as a window for parents into the power of the teaching-learning exchange that involves their sons and daughters.

—Vito Perrone, 1997, p. 305

Learning Outcomes

✔ Examine assessment issues and practices affecting young children

✔ Understand the purposes of assessment and delineate ways of sharing assessment information with families

✔ Develop skills for observing, recording, and analyzing information about children's learning and development

✔ Identify and describe the principles of performance assessment

✔ Understand the components of a balanced assessment program

Meet the Teachers

Laurie Stamp is a nursery school teacher who works with 3-year-olds. When Nam Sun, a newly immigrated child, enrolled in her class, she sought to welcome him into the group and to communicate with him despite the fact that he did not speak English. At the end of the day, when children were leaving, Laurie would often kneel down, give them a hug, and say, "See you tomorrow!" But Laurie was sensitive to the fact that hugging the teacher was not a part of Nam Sun's school departure ritual. One day when Nam Sun's mother came to pick him up after school, he paused in the doorway and bowed to Laurie. Laurie bowed back. The 3-year-old's face registered great surprise and delight, and he dashed to his mother's side, smiling and speaking in a very animated way. Then he paused, turned around, came slowly back to his teacher, raised his open arms, and looked at her. Laurie bent down and hugged Nam Sun, to his obvious delight. About this incident, Laurie remarked, "I will remember forever the day we learned to say good-bye in two languages" (Jalongo & Isenberg, 1995).

Maggie Pompa is completing the second half of her student teaching internship in first grade. One of her insights was that she needed a better system of assessment than what she observed in others. In speaking with her university faculty supervisor, Maggie said, "Most teachers seem to depend on their recollections, paper-and-pencil tests, and children's products to determine how a child is doing. I need a more systematic approach to collecting such information. What happens if records are not kept on a consistent basis and there is a parental question or a legal issue? I need the sort of documentation that will give me confidence in whatever I am reporting." Fortunately, she

275

was able to visit with several teachers who had such systems and were willing to share. The system that appealed to her most is multifaceted and includes observational notes, checklists, interviews, formal assessment, and carefully selected samples of students' work.

Mr. DeMarines, the principal of an elementary school, called a staff meeting last year to discuss a schoolwide assessment plan. Although many of the teachers were maintaining purposeful, well-organized collections of children's portfolios, Mr. DeMarines thought it would be useful to have reading and writing portfolios that would accompany children as they progressed from one year to the next. The goals of a schoolwide literacy portfolio system would be to inform others about what each child can do and to build students' skills in self-assessment. After a year of hard work, the principal speaks with pride about the system now in place: "It gives teachers a clearer idea of what children can do with language than a test score ever could. It also prepares teachers to conduct informative and well-planned conferences with parents and families."

COMPARE:	What are some commonalities among the assessment practices of these three educators, even though the first is focused on a single child, the second on her overall assessment practices, and the third on a schoolwide program?
CONTRAST:	How do these educators think about assessment? How would you characterize the outlook of each one?
CONNECT:	What made the greatest impression on you and how will you incorporate this into your teaching?

Assessment Defined

Suppose that you were going to apply for a $5000 scholarship and the application procedure required a 1000-word essay about your reasons for pursuing a career in early childhood education. Think about what you would want to know before beginning to write your essay. You would probably be wondering about the following things:

Competition: How many people usually apply?

Standards: What criteria will be used to evaluate the essays?

Format: How is the final copy of the essay to be prepared?

Support: Is there a previous recipient of the scholarship I can talk with to get some pointers?

Outcomes: When and in what way will the applicants be notified of the results?

Similar questions about competition, standards, format, support, and outcomes are raised when young children enter school. Parents wonder, "How is my child doing in comparison to other children? Will the teacher evaluate my child fairly? What types of information and work samples will be used to assess my child's performance? If my child is experiencing difficulty, what assistance is available? How will I be kept informed about my child's progress?" These concerns of parents and families not only have educational implications, but they also have social and ethical consequences for the child. That is why assessment is such an important issue for you as an early childhood educator.

What is assessment in early childhood? The National Association for the Education of Young Children defines assessment in early childhood as "the process of observing, recording, and otherwise documenting the work children do and how they do it, as a basis for a variety of educational decisions that affect the child" (Bredekamp & Rosegrant, 1992, p. 22). Assessment should not be used to label children, categorize them, define them as failures, or deprive them of intellectually stimulating opportunities. At its most basic level, "assessment is the ability to see children, to perceive what they can do in the hope of understanding how they learn" (Brainard, 1997, p. 163). At its best, assessment should help to inform instructional decisions, result in benefits to the child and family, and relate to what the child is learning in school. Four main purposes for assessment in early childhood are to *plan instruction for individuals and groups of children*, to *communicate with parents and families* about the progress of individual children, *to identify children and families* who need specialized programs and support services, and to *evaluate the effectiveness and quality* of early childhood programs and services. Figure 8.1 describes the purposes of assessment in greater detail.

PAUSE AND REFLECT ABOUT MISCONCEPTIONS ABOUT EARLY CHILDHOOD ASSESSMENT

What ideas do you have about assessment? Is it possible that your ideas reflect those of the general public rather than those of a professional educator? Read the following Ask the Expert feature, then make a list of the misconceptions that you now hold. After reading the chapter, revisit this list and consider how the newly acquired information has affected your thinking.

ASK the Expert Sue C. Wortham on Performance Assessment

Common Issues and Concerns About Performance Assessment

Sue C. Wortham

1. What are the limitations of standardized tests?

Preservice teachers frequently have misconceptions about the value of using standardized tests with school children. They remember well their own experiences with standardized tests and how uncomfortable and fearful they were (and still are) of how they would perform. They are surprised to find out that standardized tests have weaknesses and cannot necessarily be relied upon to accurately measure individual student achievement. It has not occurred to some prospective teachers that standardized tests vary in quality. When applying this information to the testing of young children, students become concerned about inappropriate administration of tests to preschool children, a concern shared at the national level.

2. What is informal assessment?

Students who have spent little or no time in early childhood classrooms are surprised to learn that there are many alternatives to formal assessment. Their experiences in elementary school with standardized tests and teacher-designed assessments have led them to believe that these are the only options available. It is a pleasant surprise for them to learn that they can use observation, work samples, and project products, among other possibilities, for assessment.

3. How is informal assessment used?

Students generally are in favor of alternative assessment once they understand when and how it is used. They have concerns about parental acceptance of this type of assessment, particularly the use of portfolios for reporting rather than traditional report cards. They question whether parents are in favor of assessment of performance in terms of learning outcomes rather than letter grades. They want to be able to use this type of assessment, but they are uneasy about parents who may demand letter grades and rank ordering of children in the class.

4. What is the connection between informal assessment and instruction?

The most difficult aspect of authentic assessment for preservice and in-service teachers to comprehend and use is the link between assessment and planning for instruction. It is easily understood that assessment is conducted to determine achievement or developmental progress. It is less-well understood that assessment should guide the teacher's planning for further instruction. The notion that assessment reveals strengths and weaknesses in instruction as well as student progress is difficult and unclear. This misunderstanding extends to the use of portfolio assessment. It is apparently a complex leap from portfolio contents to the learning objectives that have been used for instruction. Teachers and future teachers understand that portfolio entries reflect student progress and growth over time. They do not as readily accept that the contents of the portfolio also reflect curriculum objectives for the early childhood program and how well children have responded and expressed understanding of those objectives.

Sue C. Wortham is a professor of early childhood education, University of Texas at San Antonio, Texas.

FIGURE 8.1

Purposes for assessment

For Children and Families

to assess the value or worth of the program

to determine whether program goals are being met

to make planning decisions

to report to parents on the progress of individual children or the school

to make decisions about support services for children

to help children build skills in self evaluation

For Early Childhood Practitioners

to obtain feedback on ways to improve teaching

to gather, organize, and interpret information about children's abilities and interests

to identify steps to meet individual needs

Your Role as an Evaluator

One of the worst things that anyone could say about you as a teacher is that you identify favorite children in the group who receive preferential treatment. At first, this might seem out of the question, because you imagine a blatant instance of favoritism, such as a teacher's pet. But unfair assessment practices can creep into your practice in unanticipated ways. It might consist of expecting more from children who live in a wealthy neighborhood and less from children who live in housing projects. It might be allowing a few more seconds for one child to respond to a question and jumping in sooner for another child. Or, inequity might be expressed by giving a second chance to a child whose family is very vocal and involved in the school program while immediately reprimanding a child whose family is uninvolved in school events. Effective early childhood educators have a strong commitment to equity and fairness. It is this conviction that forms the foundation for assessment practices.

As a teacher, your assessment practices should be "a means to find out what children know, can do, and care about" (Smith & Goodwin, 1997, p. 117). Remember that "children depend on adults to help them discover all the capability and potential they possess. The unjust use of testing and assessment denies many children full knowledge of their own power to learn and grow. Children, especially those who are thus cheated, are not in a position to advocate for themselves; only adults committed to justice can press their needs forward in school and society." (Fennimore, 1997, p. 241).

Effective teachers try not to let a child's appearance influence expectations for achievement.

a.

b.

Early childhood teachers are expected to be competent in a number of areas related to assessment practices (McAfee & Leong, 1997); these are discussed in the following paragraphs.

Recognizing Unethical, Illegal, and Otherwise Inappropriate Assessment Methods and Uses of Assessment Information. Confidentiality is an important aspect of assessment. Clearly, it is entirely inappropriate for a teacher to sit in the lunchroom with colleagues and remark about a child, "What can you expect? He got the lowest score on the reading readiness test in the entire class . . . and everyone knows what his family is like." Such public pronouncements are likely to taint everyone's opinion of that child's abilities and do irreversible reputational damage to the family. When the child moves on to the next grade level, his teacher probably will recall some of these negative remarks and expect to experience difficulty with the child. If such negative remarks were overheard in conversation outside the school, it would be even worse, and it would reflect unfavorably on the teacher and on the entire school. Part of becoming a professional is knowing when to keep quiet and protect confidentiality. A useful guideline in making these decisions is to ask yourself how you would feel about a member of your family being treated in this way. If your sibling or child had scored low on a test, would you want it known by anyone who happened to pass by in the grocery store or broadcasted to every teacher in the school? Without a doubt, professional information can be shared in unprofessional ways with colleagues and with other members of the community; you must guard against such unprofessional behavior in yourself.

Choosing and Developing Appropriate Assessment Methods. Early childhood educators must carefully consider children's rights, the purposes for assessment, and the corresponding methods. Take, for example, the assessment of children's visual acuity. It is important to be well informed about different types of visual impairments, corrective measures, and, for impairments that cannot be corrected, ways of adapting materials and the curriculum to accommodate children's needs. Yet it is not cost-effective to subject every child to an exhaustive vision evaluation. Under these circumstances, most schools conduct a vision screening. The purpose of a screening is to detect the presence or absence of a problem and, if a problem exists, to make recommendations for more in-depth evaluation. Thus, children are given several different vision evaluation tasks administered by trained volunteers and are then referred to eye-care specialists if the quick screening instrument suggests that there might be a problem. This is an example of choosing an appropriate assessment method. It has the children's best interests at heart, it serves the purpose of making appropriate referrals to eye-care specialists, and it uses an efficient and cost-effective method of providing the needed level of service to all children.

Administering, Scoring, and Interpreting the Results of Various Assessment Methods. Teachers are notorious for carrying tote bags full of students' work back and forth between home and school. If you could look inside student teacher Tina Hidalgo's bag, you would see illustrated math problems that her first graders invented by working with a partner. They used the folktales and nursery rhymes with which they were already familiar to develop math sentences, then they represented them pictorially. One pair of children drew three bears, three bowls of porridge, three chairs, and three beds along with the equation $3 + 3 + 3 + 3 = ?$ The partners were also responsible for figuring out the correct answer, writing it on the back of the page, signing their names, and indicating how well they worked with their partners using a simple ☺ or ☹. As Tina evaluates these papers, she does much more than mark the answers right or wrong and hand out stickers or stars. Rather, she analyzes children's errors, makes notes about what to teach next, and plans for minilessons with small groups of children who share the same misunderstandings. Analyzing children's writing, artwork, and responses to various tasks is an assessment method commonly used by early childhood teachers. Just think of how much more Tina knows about her students' abilities than the teacher who gives a timed test on math facts! Not only can she see their mathematical reasoning from concrete drawings to abstract equations, but she also can tell if they are learning to use mathematical symbols and even find out something about their literacy skills, because the problems are based on the class's prior knowledge of stories. Varied assessment methods developed and evaluated by teachers make significant contributions to knowledge about what children know, can do, and still need to learn.

Using Comprehensive Assessment Data to Make Decisions about Individual Students, Instructional Planning, Curriculum Development, and Programmatic Improvement. In the case of principal Mr. DeMarines's schoolwide reading and writing portfolios, described at the beginning of this chapter, these data were used to communicate important information about what each child could do with written language. Knowing this helped teachers in subsequent years to plan for instruction. It pointed out areas of the curriculum that could be strengthened and ways to improve the portfolio system already in place. One of your roles as an early childhood practitioner is to make certain that assessment is ongoing, comprehensive, and put to good use.

Communicating Assessment Results to Students, Parents, Educators, and Other Audiences as Appropriate. As Mr. DeMarines concluded, the very fact that these portfolios were maintained by all of the staff members in his school helped every teacher to feel much better prepared for meetings with parents and other family members. The information gathered over time enabled each teacher to do more than report a test score or

Consider using student-led conferences as part of your overall assessment plan.

grade. It enabled the teachers to show children's effort and progress, and it did so in a way that is more understandable to laypersons than are technical, statistical terms, such as stanines, percentile ranks, and normal curve equivalents.

As the portfolio project in Mr. DeMarine's elementary school continued, *student-led conferences* became part of the assessment process. Instead of hearing about the results of their parents' conferences with the teachers after the fact, students actually participated in these home-school meetings. First, the children were encouraged to reflect on goals they had set for themselves in reading and writing. Some examples of kindergartners' self-selected goals included, "I want to make a big book and read it to the whole class," "I want to make a picture book about collecting beanie babies," and "I want to learn to spell all my friends' names." Next, the teachers sent home brief surveys to parents and families asking them what their goals were for their children during the first few weeks of school. Some examples were, "I hope that he learns to like reading," "If she can learn her alphabet, we will be very pleased," and "We want him to learn how to make the letters better when he writes." When student-led conferences are conducted, the child, the family, and the teacher all meet to discuss such goals, review the child's progress thus far, and make plans for achieving new goals in the future.

Involving Children and Families in the Assessment Processes. Think about your experiences with assessment as a child. Perhaps your parents or guardian met for 5 or 10 minutes with the teacher once or twice a year. They probably had to sign your report card and return it to the school. But assessment practices in some schools have changed in several significant ways. First of all, many schools and centers provide parents and families with more detailed, written reports, such as the sample progress report shown in Figure 8.2.

Contemporary parents and families are likely to be directly involved in setting goals for children, particularly those with special needs. A good example of this is the individualized

FIGURE 8.2

Sample progress
report

CONCEPTUAL SKILLS

Number Concepts

- Exhibits use of one-to-one correspondence
- Writes numerals 1–10 from memory
- Counts large numbers of items with ease
- Explores and understands combining numbers, explains how answer was achieved
- Records results of projects involving counting, measuring, and so on and can do these operations with help

Classifying and Graphing

- Sorts items into categories
- Records items on graphs to show one-to-one correspondence
- Notices similarities and differences

Geometry, Patterns, Reasoning

- Recognizes basic shapes
- Draws shapes from memory
- Recognizes more difficult shapes (e.g., oval, diamond, semicircle)
- Copies simple patterns
- Copies complex pattern designs with individual attention and help
- Helps use calendar to mark passage of time
- Learning to use days of the week and terms such as *yesterday, today,* and *to-morrow* to mark passage of time
- Developing an awareness of time using kitchen timer and sand timer

EMERGENT LITERACY SKILLS

Reading and Language

- Uses initial consonants
- Uses some final consonants
- Uses some medial consonants
- Experiments with vowels
- Uses the *-s* word ending
- Shows beginning sight vocabulary and spells common words (*I, me, yes, is*)
- Learning to space words appropriately while writing

Visual Discrimination and Memory

- Assembles a simple puzzle with help
- Writes all the letters in own name correctly

FIGURE 8.2

Sample progress
report *(continued)*

- Recognizes all capital and most small letters of the alphabet
- Writes letters from memory
- Recognizes written names of classmates

Associating Print with Written Words

- Understands the connection between oral language and written words
- Demonstrates the left-to-right progression of printed material
- Has difficulty rereading dictated stories from memory
- Recognizes frequently used words in dictated stories and in environmental print

Understands the Concepts of Letter, Word, and Sentence

- Locates first and last letters in a word
- Responds correctly to the question, "How many words are in that sentence?" after some initial confusion
- Copies words from left to right
- Associates letters with corresponding sounds

Learning the Use of Reading Clues

- Exhibits a small sight vocabulary of common words
- Uses picture clues at centers to read recipes and charts
- Uses picture clues to interpret words in books
- Has some knowledge that an initial consonant can unlock a word, but doesn't apply it without help

educational plan (IEP). Developing an IEP for a child typically includes a goal-setting meeting in which the parents/family, teachers, and various specialists all participate. For younger children, ages birth through 3 years, the plan is called the individualized family service plan (IFSP). If this team agrees upon a goal, such as supporting the ability of a child who is physically handicapped to feed himself or herself, each adult at the meeting would bear responsibility for carrying out this plan. The teacher would be responsible for helping the child to become more independent during meals served at school, the physical therapist would suggest some adaptive strategies to facilitate self-help skills (e.g., a special spoon, a bowl with a suction cup on the bottom, a stainless steel wheelchair tray with high edges), and the family members would agree to reinforce this learning during meals served at home by cosigning an IEP document with school and support services personnel. Figure 8.3 summarizes your multiple roles in early childhood assessment.

In fulfilling these roles, your first and most important responsibility is to be fair. When asked to explain fairness, most people say something like, "Everyone being treated the same." But equity is far too complex a concept to be explained by identical treatment at all times. To illustrate, imagine that a teacher is leading children in a rhythm band and has in her class a child with an attentional disorder who begins to wander around the room, a child who is hitting another child with the tambourine, and a child who keeps striking the triangle without trying to coordinate his efforts with the group. If you were

FIGURE 8.3

Your multiple
assessment roles

Evaluating the Learning Environment

- analyzing a good environment for learning
- noting what children can learn from different areas of the classroom
- observing what children learn through outdoor activities

Evaluating Children's Work

- evaluating the progress of individual children
- communicating assessment information to families, educators, and professionals in other fields
- protecting children's confidentiality
- planning individualized learning

Evaluating Program Effectiveness

- determining the success of the lesson
- evaluating the curriculum in various areas
- participating in large-scale evaluation of the total program

Evaluating Professional Performance

- documenting your own professional growth
- assessing the performance of colleagues
- learning to observe one's self and to become a better observer of children

interacting with these children, it would not be fair to treat them exactly the same way and would be even worse to assess them without considering their individual differences; rather, you would need to observe thoughtfully and think about what would enable each child to experience success at some level. You might, for example, invite the child who is playing the triangle to come forward and strike it only when the group claps, remind the child who has the tambourine of its proper use, and invite the child who is wandering around the room to rejoin the group by speaking softly in her ear and leading her back to the circle. This classroom example helps to illustrate why there is a trend toward assessing children's performance in real-world activities rather than using artificial samples of behavior, such as tests.

Approaches to Assessment

The appropriate outcome of assessment is to optimize children's learning and to improve classroom practice. The fundamental questions that early childhood educators ask as they assess include the following:

- What are these children able to do?
- What evidence can I collect to document every child's effort, progress, and achievement?

- When new learning takes place, how does each child go about putting it to use?
- What situations and contexts enable every child to demonstrate learning and attain success at some level?

Answers to such questions are difficult to measure for a variety of reasons. The next section examines major approaches to assessment and the advantages and limitations of each approach.

Norm-referenced, or Standardized, Tests

Of all the assessment tools used in America, group-administered tests are the most familiar. Tests are samples of behavior in a particular area or domain (e.g., reading readiness, mathematics achievement).

Norm-referenced, or *standardized*, tests are rooted in a comparative concept of assessment. The procedure is to administer the test to a large group of children who become the normative group to which later test takers are compared. Thus, if you were developing a standardized test for kindergartners, you would write the items, try them out, revise them, write standard instructions for administering the test, identify a group of kindergartners, give the test, and calculate the scores. Children who later would take the test would have their scores compared, or referenced back, to those of the normative group. This is where the terminology *norm-referenced* comes from. Usually, this comparison will tell you where a child ranks. For example, if a child has a percentile rank of 93%, this does not mean that the child got a score of 93 out of 100. Rather, it means that 93% of the normative group, that first reference group, scored lower than this child.

The advantages of published, formal, norm-referenced tests is that they are efficient, inexpensive, convenient, and considered by the general public to be objective (Madaus & Tan, 1993). Standardized tests are often used to

- *compare and categorize* people, educational institutions, and problems according to abstract, impersonal, and generalizable rules
- *measure the performance* of students and educators using a consistent "yardstick" to provide information to policy makers and bureaucrats
- *determine opportunities* on the basis of objectives, qualifications, or merit (Madaus & Tan, 1993).

The disadvantages of norm-referenced testing are numerous, however. Perhaps the most obvious failing of these tests is that they provide virtually no guidance in planning instruction (Popham, 1998). After the test scores arrive in the mail, the teacher has a number on a piece of paper for each child rather than information about what the child *can* do and specific information about what to teach next or how to present it.

Too often, a single test score becomes the basis for deciding such things as who will be admitted to a program (e.g., qualifying for a gifted and talented program), which programs will survive (e.g., determining how much money to allocate to Head Start), or which children will gain access to support services (e.g., deciding which infants are at-risk and qualify for intervention services). Where young children are concerned, the dangers of overreliance on testing are even more acute. First of all, young children are at the very beginning of their lives as learners, and errors in assessing their abilities can have profound consequences. If significant adults are told that the child is lagging far behind peers or has a learning disability, for instance, they may lower their expectations for the child and offer fewer intellectually challenging activities. Research on the human brain suggests that challenges are essential for optimal neural development (Caine & Caine, 1997), so children who are labeled as deficient in some way are further deprived of the very things they need to learn.

What is worse, the probability of making huge errors in assessing young children's performance and potential is very high. As Meisels (1995) points out, "Group-administered tests focus on the acquisition of simple facts, low-level skills, superficial memorization, and isolated evidence of achievement. The tests hold great power, and that power can be abused. Of greatest concern is that they rob teachers of their sense of judgment about how to help children develop to their optimal potential" (p. 1).

Because very young children cannot perform paper-and-pencil tests or, if they can, cannot attend to such a boring task for long, many of the assessment tools for young children rely on motor skill tasks to make predictions about success in school. An infant might be asked to drink from a cup, a toddler to construct a tower out of three wooden blocks, and a preschooler to copy a triangle shape. Yet when these children are older, virtually all of the standardized tests will emphasize verbal and, to a lesser extent, mathematical skills. None of the skills measured by the tests are directly related to the criteria used to measure school success later on. This situation makes tests given during the early childhood years poor predictors of later school achievement; if these long-term predictions are accurate no more than about half the time, the tests are not much more useful (and far more expensive) than the toss of a coin.

Additionally, young children do not understand testing procedures and the importance of tests. Common errors of naive test takers include not responding at all even when they know the answer, losing their place in a test booklet and getting most of the subsequent answers wrong, getting completely distracted from the task by something

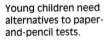

Young children need alternatives to paper-and-pencil tests.

EXPLORING YOUR ROLE IN DOCUMENTING CHILDREN'S LEARNING

else, talking to one another, and copying from someone else's test paper. For all of these reasons, young children are notoriously poor test takers, and their test scores are not necessarily a reflection of their true abilities.

A basic principle of assessment is content validity, meaning that there is a clear connection between what is taught and what is assessed. A major part of early childhood education is teaching children self-help skills such as feeding and dressing themselves and learning social skills such as taking turns and sharing materials. Young children also have experiences in play, art, music, and drama, and they do not lend themselves to evaluation through tests (Jalongo & Stamp, 1997). The range of abilities that is (or can be) evaluated through traditional tests is also a major limitation in testing. It would be difficult to imagine a group-administered, easy-to-score, paper-and-pencil test that could measure all the important outcomes of a high-quality early childhood program. For all of these reasons, assessment in early childhood must be fair, focus on what children can do, examine a range of behaviors, and optimize every child's learning potential.

Criterion-referenced Tests

Many professional organizations have issued position statements on assessment. A synthesis of several of these general standards challenges the long-standing purpose of testing: to sort, measure, and determine opportunities for people. Contemporary views of assessment argue for a very different set of goals (International Reading Association/National Council of Teachers of English, 1995; Penning, 1995; Perrone, 1991). Critics of norm-referenced tests for young children argue that assessment should do the following:

- Improve student learning, be fair to all students, and have beneficial consequences for children
- Promote processes that involve multiple perspectives on the child's learning that are supported by various data sources collected in different contexts
- Be systematic, regularly reviewed, and continuously improved
- Communicate regularly and clearly to and with all stakeholders: students, parents, teachers, administrators, policy makers, and the public
- Enable teachers to critically analyze the curriculum and instruction
- Recognize that teachers play a crucial role in comprehensive assessment
- Invite family and community participation
- Support collaboration between and among educators and other professionals dedicated to working with young children

Criterion-referenced tests have been proposed as a better way of addressing these issues. Unlike norm-referenced tests, which compare one child's performance with that of a reference group of peers, criterion-referenced tests analyze in considerable detail each child's attainment of objectives that are deemed reasonable and appropriate for young children, as does the sample progress report shown in Figure 8.2. With toddlers, a criterion might be naming a pictured object; with preschoolers, an objective might be identifying and naming the basic colors; with children in the primary grades, a criterion might be writing a paragraph that would be scored using a very detailed rating scale called a *rubric*. It is easy to see how the results of criterion-referenced assessment would provide more helpful information about what to teach next. In fact, most of these tests result in individual profiles of student performance that are designed to keep track of children's attainment of generally agreed-upon objectives, just like the progress report items listed in Figure 8.2.

Some disadvantages of criterion-referenced assessment are that these instruments are very detailed, have to be administered individually, and are therefore more time consuming. Additionally, educators need to be trained in how to use criterion-referenced assessment to monitor and facilitate children's progress, and, because the general public is oriented toward competition, single test scores, and comparisons, many adults are reluctant to accept criterion-referenced assessment.

Even though tests are the type of assessment tool that is most familiar to students, parents, and educators, tests—whether norm- or criterion-referenced—are not the only approach to comprehensive assessment. Increasingly, early childhood educators are using a variety of alternatives to tests.

Principles of Performance Assessment

In everyday use, the word *perform* refers to executing a task or process and bringing it to completion. Given this definition, learners' abilities are assessed as they produce work of their own by drawing upon their knowledge and skills, considering the context, and responding to a task (Wiggins, 1998). The difference between a traditional, paper-and-pencil test and performance assessment is like the difference between taking a test on math facts and running a cash register at a busy grocery store. Although it is important to master basic math in order to be a cashier, that knowledge is not adequate when one is called upon to make change, deduct coupon amounts, and figure out a grocery order purchased with food stamps. In other words, there is a difference between *knowing about* something and *knowing how* to do something. In performance assessment, children are called upon to produce something rather than merely select the correct answer from several choices and invited to complete tasks that they are likely to encounter outside the classroom (Hamayan, 1995). Because of this emphasis on practical application of skills, performance assessment is sometimes referred to as *authentic assessment,* and, because it is a departure from traditional testing methods, performance assessment is sometimes called *alternative assessment.* Many educators believe that performance/authentic/alternative assessment is a better means of developing and documenting higher-level thinking skills in students. Figure 8.4 summarizes different levels of assessment.

McTighe (1997) offers the following seven principles of performance assessment:

1. Establish clear performance targets that state what you expect children to have learned.
2. Strive for products and performance that relate to the real world.
3. Publicize criteria and performance standards.
4. Provide models of excellence.
5. Teach strategies explicitly.
6. Provide feedback to learners and enable them to make adjustments.
7. Document and celebrate progress.

Good teachers are constantly assessing how their students are doing, gathering evidence of progress, identifying problems, and adjusting instructional plans accordingly (Herman, Aschbacher, & Winters, 1992; Marzano, Pickering, & McTighe, 1993). Advocates

FIGURE 8.4

Levels of assessment
in early childhood

Large-scale Assessment

Federal and state mandated assessments

Examples:

- National Head Start evaluation
- Accreditation of early childhood programs by the National Association for the Education of Young Children
- On-site evaluation for state licensure in child care

District-, school-, and programwide assessments

Examples:

- Assessing the development of toddlers prior to their entry into a program
- Evaluation of all early childhood classrooms in a school using a rating scale
- Requiring all kindergarten children to take a reading-readiness test

Individual Assessment

Child

Examples:

- Teacher's anecdotal records of behavior and events
- Parent/family questionnaire data
- Notes taken on home visits

Teacher

Examples:

- Portfolio produced by the individual teacher to document attainment of competence
- Self-assessment of attainment of lesson plan objectives
- Observations of preservice teachers by an experienced teacher and college supervisor

of performance assessment argue that when students are called upon to apply what they have learned to meet significant challenges, they are better prepared, not only for the next grade in school, but also for later life. If educators can agree that learning and understanding are the primary goals of teaching, then children will need numerous opportunities to apply facts, concepts, and skills appropriately in new situations (Gardner & Mansilla, 1994). Rather than being a one-time, scheduled event that is separate from life in classrooms (as a standardized test is), performance assessment can be closely connected with instruction and generally is perceived as more relevant by the learners.

Controversies about whether to rely on traditional tests or to incorporate a wider variety of assessment strategies persist. Parents and families are familiar with test scores, letter grades, and comparisons of one child's abilities with another's (Culbertson & Jalongo, in press). As a result, they often express a preference for these methods of explaining how a child is doing at school. Administrators are understandably concerned with how a program, grade level, or school system is doing in comparison with others. As a result, they are often insistent on large-scale measures and are uninformed about or nonsupportive of teachers' efforts to amass detailed profiles on each child. Likewise, teachers themselves may regard alternative forms of assessment as too much work that is given too little consideration by other colleagues, supervisors, families, and the community at large. One workable solution to this controversy is to stop thinking of assessment as *either* standardized tests *or* teacher-developed methods. It should be both. Just as a medical doctor is interested in community health as well as the health of the individual patient, educators at all levels need to consider the overall learning successes of a program as well as the learning of each child.

Remember that "assessment is more than just the collection of information, it is collection with a purpose" (Salvia & Yesseldyke, 1995, p. 3). In essence, assessment is research about children's abilities. Tests, both those that are professionally published and those that are teacher-constructed, are plentiful in schools. The challenge, then, is to balance traditional means of assessment with performance-based methods of evaluation. Performance assessment rounds out the assessment picture by examining student performance in many contexts over a long period of time; reducing the gap between assessment, diagnosis, and teaching methods; and obtaining the most valuable data on individual effort, progress, and achievement (Chard, Katz, & Genishi, 1996). The sections that follow address the two major categories of performance assessment: evaluation of individual children's progress and overall program evaluation.

Evaluating Individual Children's Progress

The basic question answered by observation of individual children is, "How is this child doing?" For early childhood educators, observation consists of watching learners in action, recording significant details, interpreting the results, and using the observational data to guide and inform decisions. Figure 8.5 provides an overview of the observation process. To facilitate the observation process, Chard, Katz, and Genishi (1996) suggest that early childhood educators

- write just enough to jog their memories later, when they have time to elaborate
- try to keep objective descriptions of behavior separate from subjective interpretations or inferences
- keep materials handy for writing down anecdotes

Observations are sometimes written as anecdotes, or short, written descriptions of behavior and events (Power, 1996). When you think about your role as a thoughtful observer, think about the many purposes that the observations you produce will serve. Included among these purposes are to understand the learner, to plan the curriculum, to discover children's interests, to offer guidance and assistance, to measure children's progress, to intervene or make referrals, to communicate with parents and professionals, and to obtain feedback on the success of your teaching methods (Nilsen, 1999).

FIGURE 8.5

Observation
processes and
methods

THE PROCESS

Perception →

What you notice, based upon sensory input, prior experience, individual ways of reacting to experience, the cultural context, teacher education, beliefs about children, educational values, personal ethics, and society.

Description →

What you capture, in words, on tape, or on video and use to characterize the settings, events, and verbal and nonverbal behaviors based on direct observation or inferences from the data collected.

Interpretation

How you make sense of the behaviors and events you perceived. This process typically includes noting patterns, generating hypotheses, and making recommendations.

METHODS FOR OBSERVING AND RECORDING

- **Anecdotal records:** a narrative (storylike), factual account recorded after behavior occurs. Often used to obtain details on a child's behavior (e.g., early reading efforts) and plan appropriate learning experiences.

- **Specimen records or running records:** anecdotal information gathered during a specified time (e.g., during outdoor play) or over a period of time (e.g., a record of the verbal interactions with other children of a newly immigrated child who is learning English). Often used to discover causes and effects of behavior by studying what precedes and follows an event.

- **Time sampling:** tallies or other coding system used to show the presence or absence of a behavior during specified time periods (e.g., observing children's patterns of interaction at lunchtime).

- **Event sampling:** used during a particular event (e.g., charting children's questions in response to a read-aloud). Often used to get baseline data, information on how frequently a particular behavior occurs prior to an intervention strategy (e.g., a toddler crying when brought to child care).

- **Checklists:** charts of information that record yes/no, presence or absence of a behavior (e.g, a list of developmental tasks completed by the child's family with items such as "knows basic colors and color words").

- **Rating scales:** charts of information that add a dimension of kind or amount (e.g., an item such as "Prints name without adult assistance: Usually/Sometimes/Not Yet).

- **Observation using mechanical means:** audiotapes, videotapes, and photographs used to record observations (e.g., audiotaping circle time to make decisions about music instruction, videotaping a puppet play so that the children and teacher can critique it, or taking photographs of children working in groups to document a class project).

- **Interviews:** questions used to gather children's perceptions, ideas, and feelings about a topic or situation (e.g., interviewing children to determine their reading interests or asking them to provide explanations of friendship prior to beginning a unit on friends).

- **Children's drawings:** analyzing children's artwork and inviting them to talk about their work as a way of better understanding their concerns, interests, and lives (e.g., asking children to draw happy and sad things prior to a discussion).

Learning to say "good bye" in two languages is an example of an appropriate anecdotal assessment.

Shirley Tertemiz, a student who was observing a teacher at work in a kindergarten classroom, wrote this anecdote:

> Tchr. presented a lesson on colors. Ch. mixed food coloring and water to produce diff. colors. Ch. were instructed to use all eight colors in their crayon boxes to produce colorful pictures. Tchr. questions/comments: "How many diff. colors did you use?" "I see words in your picture, could you read them to me?" "Did anyone experiment with mixing colors?" "I noticed that you made shapes." "Could you tell me more about your picture?" To J., tchr says, "I like those railroad tracks" and walks away. J. says to E., "The tchr. didn't even know that it's a sidewalk!"

Note how she wrote just enough to jog her memory and described objectively what the children were doing in art, just as the experts suggest. Figure 8.6 identifies major errors that are commonly made when teachers are first beginning to conduct observations of young children. Be certain to study this information carefully before you begin gathering observational data.

After you have gathered many pieces of information about a child or your program for evaluation purposes, the next step is to compile that information.

Figure 8.7, on page 296 suggests some materials for collecting observations and organizing them in useful ways.

Student work portfolios are purposeful collections of children's work that document achievements and provide data on the processes involved in products. If traditional testing is like a snapshot, then portfolio assessment is more like a photo album—a collection of pictures showing growth and change over time (McTighe, 1997). A portfolio is an "organized,

EXPLORING YOUR ROLE IN DOCUMENTING CHILDREN'S LEARNING

FIGURE 8.6

Major errors in
observation

- **Error:** Being overly judgmental

  Example: "She's probably just lazy."

  Why Not? Judging children does not solve anything. If you judge them, you merely absolve yourself of responsibility for facilitating changes in behavior that will serve them better, both now and in the future.

  Alternative: Be careful about describing behavior, saying, for instance, "Janine sometimes moves from center to center without engaging in the activities there. We have found that it is important to invite her into the ongoing activities and get her started."

- **Error:** Overgeneralizing

  Example: "He never finishes any of his work."

  Why Not? It is not accurate to say that someone *never* finishes *anything*. This is clearly an overstatement.

  Alternative: Be precise, saying, for instance, "At the end of the day, Xi frequently has several activities that he has begun but not finished."

- **Error:** Labeling

  Example: "He is sloppy."

  Why Not? It is not fair to characterize someone's entire personality with a word.

  Alternative: Describe an actual behavior, saying, for instance, "Krish has a tendency to rush through his work, particularly when it involves handwriting."

- **Error:** Stereotyping

  Example: "These children from the housing projects aren't like other children."

  Why Not? It is prejudicial to categorize a group of children in this way based on family income.

  Alternative: Say what needs to be addressed and be a child and family advocate, saying, for instance, "It is often the case that these toddlers arrive at school without much prior experience with lap reading of picture books. We have been collaborating with the public library to use the bookmobile as a way to offer toddler story times and to provide greater access to high-quality literature."

- **Error:** Blaming

  Example: "The way she keeps acting out, it's clear that she doesn't get any discipline at home."

  Why Not? You have no basis in fact for making such an assumption. It could even be the case that the child is disciplined severely at home and that she is acting out at school as a cry for help.

  Alternative: Work to find out what might be causing the behavior, for instance, conferring with a parent or other family member and saying, "I am concerned that Sean has been giving other children karate chops and pushing them down on the playground. Can you think of any reason why he might be behaving in this way?"

- **Error:** Making long-term predictions

Example: "He's never going to amount to anything. I wouldn't be surprised to find out he's in trouble with the law while he is still in junior high school."

Why Not? Teachers cannot see into the future, and making dire predictions only results in lowered expectations that are communicated to children and may have a self-fulfilling prophecy effect.

Alternative: Note what the child is doing right, saying, for instance, "I noticed that Lucien really helped out when Adrianna fell at the bottom of the slide by comforting her and going to get help."

- **Error:** Comparing children to peers and adults

Example: "He's the best artist in the class. He draws even better than most adults."

Why Not? Teachers need to focus on what children can do, and it is better to encourage them than to praise them. The difference is that praise tends to say, in effect, "Just keep doing what you are doing to please me and stay ahead of the others." Encouragement, on the other hand, lets children know that their efforts are recognized and that they bear responsibility for self-evaluation.

Alternative: "Monroe frequently chooses to go to the art table first. I have noticed that he is interested in trying different media to produce pictures, including not only crayons, but also paints, chalk, colored pencils, and a variety of materials and tools."

purposeful compilation of evidence documenting a child's development and learning over time. It is not a 'method' of appraisal or assessment, but a way of keeping together and compiling information from many methods. It exhibits to the child and others the experiences, efforts, progress, and accomplishments of that child" (McAfee & Leong, 1997, p. 100).

FEATURING FAMILIES

A QUESTION-AND-ANSWER SESSION WITH PARENTS ON PORTFOLIOS

Read the following script of an actual conversation that took place between a teacher and a group of parents on Back-to-School Night, where parents had an opportunity to raise questions concerning the new school year.

PARENT A: I noticed you said that you will be using portfolios to grade the children. What's wrong with tests and regular grades?

TEACHER: I have used both approaches—portfolios, and tests and grades—in recent years and we have found that the children learn more about the subject matter and themselves with the use of portfolios. The problem that I see

FIGURE 8.7

Materials for
recording
observations

small notebook on
string around neck

smock with pockets or special garb

blank adhesive
address labels

self-adhesive notes

pens, pencils, highlighters, and clipboard

label dots

folio with pockets

file folders

small tape recorder (for interviews)

laptop computer

specially designed evaluation sheets

with relying exclusively on tests and grades is that children are placed in a competitive situation with their classmates.

PARENT B: But competition is what the *real* world is about. You should be preparing our children to compete, not make school a warm, fuzzy place!

TEACHER: Actually, I have wrestled with that point about helping children to develop skills that they will use throughout life. Business and industry tell us that teamwork is important. How do I reconcile teamwork and competition? I tell the children that they must compete with *themselves* to try to do better than they have done before. I also help them to realize that sometimes the best way to do a better job is to work with others and share ideas.

PARENT A: Can't you grade them on tests and homework assignments? My child has been working on a project for 2 weeks and I don't see any workbook pages or practice sheets. How do I or you know if she is learning anything?

TEACHER: Children can show us what they know in so many ways—by telling us, by writing a story, by drawing a picture, by performing a play they have written, by building with blocks, and so many others. Portfolios give me a means to document what a child has learned in a way that is meaningful to him or her. The children and I have many opportunities to discuss their work, and they select with me what they want to include in their portfolios. Think about your jobs. If the only information that was given about your work performance was a letter grade, you would probably feel that a grade alone would not adequately describe your capabilities. The same holds true for children in school. I want your children to control their own learning and to take responsibility for self-evaluation. When they reflect on their accomplishments, evaluate their work, plan revisions, and set goals, they are also developing their competence.

PARENT C: But how do you evaluate their work?

TEACHER: I use their work to assess their progress in achieving the standards of learning and the skills and knowledge within the school system's curriculum. I look for problem-solving skills and evidence that the child is really thinking. Portfolios may contain a variety of information, including such things as writing samples, a reading list, a spelling file, a video of a play, a recording of an original song, and so much more.

PARENT B: What can I do to help my child?

TEACHER: When you talk with your child about what he or she is learning at school, ask challenging questions, such as "Why do you think that happened?" or "What might have happened if you had . . .?" Help your child to understand that real learning is a thinking process, not just memorization of some facts.

PAUSE AND REFLECT ABOUT SYSTEMS OF ASSESSMENT

In most classrooms today, teachers continue to use folders, files, and paperwork to gather assessment information. Read the following Ask the Expert feature, then search the Internet for information about computer systems for storing student work portfolios. What systems do you expect to have in place by the time you are finished with your teacher preparation program? (For a detailed plan, see Power, 1996, and Nilsen, 1999.)

EXPLORING YOUR ROLE IN DOCUMENTING CHILDREN'S LEARNING

ASK the Expert Deborah Leong on Assessment, Development, and Technology

Common Issues and Concerns About Assessment, Development, and Technology

Deborah Leong

1. Is assessment the same thing as testing?

Assessment is more broadly defined than testing and encompasses many different ways of measuring the behavior of young children. Assessment may include testing, observations of children, samples of their work, interviews, and the performance of a skill or the solving of a problem. Sometimes the term *assessment* is used to avoid the negative connotations of the word *testing*. Testing usually refers to standardized tests or paper-and-pencil tests through which teachers elicit specific responses from children and the children's responses are scored in a numerical fashion.

2. Why do I need to assess more than once?

The primary purpose of assessment is to help children in their efforts to learn. If assessment is to be used to help teachers make decisions about learning in the classroom, than assessing a child only once a year or even twice a year is not enough. The purpose of beginning and end-of-year assessment is to sum up the child's performance. However, the real strength of good assessment information is that it helps the teacher really decide what will be the optimum steps in the teaching-learning exchange.

3. How can assessment help me teach?

Assessment can help the teacher identify a child's zone of proximal development (ZPD). The ZPD is the area that encompasses the skills that are just on the edge of emergence. Thus, scaffolding or supporting learning within the ZPD is most beneficial for later development. Through assessment, the teacher can discover the boundaries of a child's ZPD, what the child can do without help and what the child can do with assistance.

4. How will technology help me assess children in the future?

One of the most exciting developments today is the way that computers will support assessment in the future. Scanners and optical recognition programs make direct input of data into the computer possible so that teachers can easily process their own notes, which they ordinarily take while observing students. Voice recognition and graphic tablets, while they have limited application today, will someday enable even young children to assess themselves while interacting with a computer. The computer can keep records straight and track progress on skills as diverse as math facts and literacy. Computers can make the saving of images of children's work easy and can help teachers weave these together with coherent parent reports of child progress. With the advent of artificial intelligence, computers can spot error patterns, provide profiles of individuals, and provide alternative means of analysis of information. Computers will never be able to replace the experience and knowledge of an expert teacher, but they can make the management of assessment information easier.

Deborah Leong is a professor of psychology, Metropolitan State College of Denver, Denver, Colorado.

Ideally, a student work portfolio should represent the child's social, cognitive, emotional, creative, and physical performance and development pertinent to the educational environment (Gelfer & Perkins, 1996). In addition, student work portfolios can offer greater insight into complex, interactive learning experiences; provide a framework for teachers to organize and record children's progress; show the advantages of relevant learning experiences; enable the teacher to really understand children's abilities; and aid in planning for instruction. The In-Class Workshop at the end of this chapter will guide you in developing student work portfolios.

Evaluating Program Effectiveness

Program evaluation answers the question, "Am I providing a quality program?" Figure 8.8 provides a series of questions to guide the early childhood professional in rendering judgments about a program's overall effectiveness. Of course, program evaluation depends on who is responsible for deciding about program quality. A child enrolled in a program may view it differently from how a parent views it, and a trained external evaluator might regard a program differently from how the director of the program views it. Thus, it is important to look at quality from multiple perspectives, as described in Figure 8.9.

Documentation is the process of displaying children's work on a class project. The methods used for documentation are selected with these goals in mind: enhance children's learning, respect children's ideas and work, involve children in planning and evaluation, foster parent participation, and make the learning process visible (Chard, 1996).

The schools in Reggio Emilia, Italy, are known worldwide for their documentation practices. In these schools and in the traveling exhibits of children's work that have come out

---

FIGURE 8.8

Assessing the overall curriculum

Does the curriculum

- Promote interactive learning and encourage the child's construction of knowledge?
- Encourage active learning and allow children to make meaningful choices?
- Foster children's exploration and inquiry, rather than focusing on "right" answers or "right" ways to complete a task?
- Lead to conceptual understanding by helping children construct their own understanding in meaningful contexts?
- Embody expectations that are realistic and attainable at this time, or could the children more easily and efficiently acquire the knowledge and skills later on?
- Encourage the development of positive feelings and dispositions toward learning while leading to acquisition of knowledge and skills?
- Help achieve social, emotional, physical, and cognitive goals and promote democratic values?
- Promote and encourage social interaction among children and adults?

SOURCE: Adapted from *Reaching Potentials: Appropriate Curriculum and Assessment for Young Children* by S. Bredekamp and T. Rosegrant, Eds., 1992, Washington, DC: National Association for the Education of Young Children; "Teaching Young Children: Educators Seek 'Developmental Appropriateness' " by S. Willis, 1993, November, *ASCD Curriculum Update*, pp. 1–8.

FIGURE 8.9

Perspectives on
program evaluation

Katz (1993) suggests that there are five different perspectives on program quality. In order to provide a high-quality program, each of these perspectives must be considered simultaneously.

↘ The **top-down perspective** examines easily observed and measured characteristics. Top-down program characteristics set the stage for effective instruction to occur. Is the classroom space adequate? Are there sufficient toys and equipment in the room? Are there enough adults to work with the number of children in the class? These top-down considerations influence effective instruction by providing educators with the basic resources to establish a learning environment.

↗ The **bottom-up perspective** focuses on the quality of the daily experience of the child in the program. Does the child feel valued, accepted, and successful? Are there interesting activities for children to pursue? Are children's special needs and circumstances addressed appropriately? Is school a place that children want to be?

→ The **inside perspective** deals with the working conditions experienced by teachers. Are their basic needs being met through adequate salary and health care benefits? Are they treated with respect by colleagues and supervisory personnel? Is there support for their ongoing professional development?

↔ The **outside-inside perspective** emphasizes the relationship between early childhood educators and families. Do parents and other family members feel welcome at the school? Is there regular communication between teachers and families? Can families rely upon the educational system for support?

← The **outside perspective** deals with the relationships among the educational program, the community, and the larger social context in which it operates. How is the kindergarten program viewed in our community? How is the program regarded in our country? Is there a general belief among community members that the program is supporting children's development and preparing them for more productive lives?

of Reggio Emilia, you can see beautiful displays of children's work at various stages, photographs that chronicle the progress of projects, written comments on the children's work from teachers and parents, and transcripts of discussions with children about their work.

Large tables, display cases, and three-dimensional bulletin boards are all ways in which the life cycle of a class project can be communicated to others. Documentation is often used to capture the essence of a class or schoolwide project (Carter & Curtis, 1996; Helm, Beneke, & Steinheimer, 1998).

General Indicators of a Balanced Assessment Program

How will you know if your assessment plan is balanced and working well? One indicator is *student motivation to learn*. When learners understand why learning is important, know what is expected, and are confident that they will be treated fairly, they are much more likely to produce work that is of high quality. In a balanced early childhood assessment program, teachers realize that learning is far more complex than memorizing information. The connections between and among a child's knowledge, skills, attitudes, and values are recognized and respected. Think about yourself as a

Schoolwide projects create exciting assessment and program evaluation opportunities.

student trying to produce a lesson plan. If you understand that careful planning will enable you to become a much more effective teacher, if you see examples of outstanding lesson plans, and if you know that your instructor will work with you to improve instead of merely grading what you have turned in, you are going to adopt a more positive attitude and work harder than you would if these conditions were not met. The same holds true for children. They learn better when adults believe in their abilities, show them how something is done, provide guided practice, and set clear performance standards.

Another indicator that an assessment program is well balanced is *child and family participation in assessment.* A teacher we know of who sought to build her second graders' self-assessment skills in writing invited them to complete questions such as, "I already know how to . . ." "Right now I am learning how to . . ." and "Next, I want to learn how to. . . " Similarly, when this teacher sent home a questionnaire to parents, she asked them to set literacy goals for their children with questions such as, "This year, I hope that my child learns . . ." In both instances, the teacher was setting goals and encouraging families and children to develop a vocabulary of assessment.

A third indicator of a balanced assessment program is *recognition that errors are part of the learning process.* If evaluation takes the form of accurately guessing what is on the teacher's mind, young children will experience frustration and failure. A young child's thinking isn't merely less sophisticated or in-depth than an experienced adult's, it is qualitatively different. Children have naive perceptions about the world. They attribute human qualities to inanimate objects, as when they converse with a toy and believe it can eat or sleep as they do. They hear words and interpret them literally, as in thinking that "warm mittens" somehow give off heat like tiny furnaces. If they try to explain a complex phenomenon, such as the images on a television, they will probably resort to the idea that miniature people are inside the box. For all of these reasons, errors are an inevitable part of childhood. They are not easily eradicated, because the child's naive theories have to be replaced by more accurate ones, and this takes time, experience, and the ability to truly understand. Telling children the "right" answer—even getting them to memorize an answer and recite it back—is not sufficient to displace their naive theories about the world.

Balanced assessment programs also *provide varied opportunities for children to demonstrate what they have learned.* The concept of one-to-one correspondence is a good example. It is possible for a child to demonstrate understanding of this correspondence on a worksheet by drawing lines from a set of five dogs to a set of five food dishes. It is also possible for a child to demonstrate that understanding by putting one napkin, cracker, and cup of juice at each child's place at snack time; by enacting examples with toys and pieces of string; or by creating flannel-board shapes for one-to-one correspondence examples. In other words, mastery of a concept can be determined via daily routines and playlike activities rather than relying exclusively on worksheets.

A balanced assessment program also *recognizes the limitations of measurement.* Clearly, all forms of measurement are flawed in some way. A published, standardized test that arrives in neat little plastic-wrapped stacks along with a booklet that specifies all of the administration and scoring procedures certainly seems more official and objective than one teacher's anecdotal records, but it may not be truly reflective of what children can do under normal circumstances. The same child who has difficulty matching a clock face to the time written in numerals on a test can have a clear idea of his daily schedule at home and at school, including lunchtime, bedtime, and so forth. On the other hand, one teacher's anecdotal notes on the children in a class will not say much about how that child is functioning in comparison with peers. The underlying issue here is how educators pose problems to the learners. When problems are highly structured for the learner, the trade-off is that the learning being tested might not have much use in everyday experience. Even though a child can circle the letter that a pictured word begins with, that skill does not necessarily translate into reading words. When the problems are less well defined (as they more often are in real life), comparing one person's response to another's is far more difficult. If several toddlers are figuring out how to push and pull toys, a teacher can observe them as they struggle to solve this less-structured problem, but a standardized testing of their abilities would be virtually impossible.

Finally, a balanced assessment program *does not confuse measurement with a curriculum and instruction.* The mere fact that data on a child or program are collected is no substitute for really teaching. Just as taking a patient's temperature and recording it on a chart doesn't improve that person's medical condition unless it is coupled with appropriate treatment, evaluating children's work doesn't enhance learning unless these data are used to provide an appropriate curriculum and instruction. When the total curriculum (written), daily learning experiences (taught), and methods of evaluation are carefully orchestrated, children are far more likely to increase their understanding and improve their skills. As you consider the quality of the learning experiences that your program provides for students, use Figure 8.10.

FIGURE 8.10

Balancing
assessment in
early childhood

Purposes for Assessment

- to determine children's status and progress
- to provide information useful for classroom planning and decision making
- to identify children who might benefit from special help
- to collect and document information for reporting and communication

Targets of Assessment

- children's development: major child growth and development domains (e.g., motor skills, social/emotional development, growth in literacy)
- each child's progress: expected outcomes of the program for individual children
- children's uniquenesses: interests, attitudes, knowledge, and patterns of growth
- problem areas: issues or concerns about an individual child or a group
- programs: large-scale assessments of program quality at the local, state, regional, national, or international level

Processes in Assessment

- collect
- record
- compile
- summarize
- interpret
- use

MAJOR METHODS OF ASSESSMENT

Formal, Paper-and-Pencil Assessment Methods

teacher-constructed tasks and tests

standardized tests

norm-referenced: child's performance is compared with that of other peers, such as *intelligence tests* that attempt to characterize the child's potential as a learner by determining how it compares with the scores of other children on the test; *achievement tests* that attempt to evaluate what a child already has learned in a subject area (e.g., mathematics achievement); and *readiness tests* that attempt to predict how a child will fare in later literacy activities.

criterion-referenced: child's performance is assessed in terms of goals or criteria, such as "Identifies capital and lowercase letters of the alphabet."

Informal, Performance-based Assessment Methods

teacher observation

checklists

projects and exhibitions

portfolios

developmental screening: designed to detect the presence or absence of a problem and make recommendations for referral, such as a quick vision assessment that results in a yes/no decision about whether the child needs to consult an eye-care specialist.

SOURCE: Adapted from *Assessing and guiding young children's development and learning* 2nd ed., by O. McAfee and D. Leong, 1997, Boston: Allyn & Bacon.

Conclusion

As a teacher, you will find that you are expected to exert a powerful, positive influence on children's learning as well as on their motivation to continue to learn. This expectation is often referred to as teacher accountability, meaning that your performance is judged, not merely by your words and actions, but also by the effects of your teaching on learners. If you say, "We offer high-quality care for infants at this center," "These children are learning to read," or "This is a good program," you should expect that the standard response from parents, families, colleagues, community members, school administrators, and professionals in other fields will be, "How do you know?" "Show us that these children really are learning," or "Convince us that this is true." In your assessment role with the very young, your goal is to document that significant contributions were made to children's learning. This means that what they achieved with your guidance and support was appreciably better than what one would expect from normal maturation. The most fundamental question in early childhood assessment is one of "value added." How did the learning activities that you designed and the educational programs for which you are responsible improve the child's learning and life? When you can document that value has been added, you have fulfilled an essential dimension of your role as an early childhood educator.

One Child, Three Perspectives: *Damien, a Drug-exposed Child*

On a tour of a program for preschoolers at-risk, the program director said to a visiting early childhood professor, "I guess we should warn you. There is a crack-exposed child in the preschool classroom we will be visiting next. I know this is terrible, but he has kicked and bitten and thrown things so often that we call him 'the attack child.' He needs a full-time aide. Fortunately, he's a lot better now than he was at the beginning of the year. Our new principal, who was just transferred here from the high school, expelled the boy for 3 days. A lot of good that did! Everyone knows that this kid lives in a crack house. How is spending more time there supposed to solve his problems?"

They entered a classroom to see and hear a first-year teacher reading Eric Carle's picture book *The Very Hungry Caterpillar* aloud. A biracial boy with light brown ringlets and hazel eyes was seated on a young woman's lap. This was Damien, the child the visitor had been forewarned about.

When the children were actively involved in listening to the story and playing a game, Damien participated enthusiastically. But when they were assigned to color, he began to race around the room and scream. Then he swept a shelf of toys and a puzzle rack onto the floor with his arm while the other children watched him uneasily. His aide, a frail-looking young African-American woman who appeared to be fresh out of high school, managed to catch Damien and attempted to restrain him by speaking softly, leading him to another area of the classroom, and encircling him with her arms. Damien struggled at first, then he relaxed.

It was time for free play. Damien sat down, opened up a miniature barn, and took out the toy animals, people, and farm equipment stored inside. The other children kept their distance. It was as if a magnetic field had been created with Damien repelling every other person. All of the adults, including his aide, were positioned on the other side of the room.

The visitor approached Damien cautiously and knelt down on the carpet. He was making the plastic tractor and the wagon attached to it go around in a circle, over and over again. The visitor picked up a plastic spotted cow, waddled it over toward the roly-poly farmer who was positioned in the driver's seat, and said in a goofy voice, "Hi, Damien. I want to go for a ride. Can I, please? Huh? Huh? Can I please?" Damien peered at the cow intently, then at the visitor, his jaw dropping in amazement. He nodded affirmatively. The play continued in this way with different toys sometimes leaping over fences, screeching into the barn, losing a passenger, or giving Damien a noisy kiss on the cheek. Some of the other children stopped by to watch and ask what Damien was doing and why he was laughing. What they were really wondering, the visitor concluded, was whether it was safe to play with Damien.

Later that day when all of the adults had an opportunity to talk, the teacher, aide, and program supervisors wanted to know what the visitor thought about Damien. "I would capitalize on the fact that Damien has the services of a full-time aide. Her time might be better spent in one-to-one playful interaction rather than in attempting to control Damien during group time. As long as everyone is wary of Damien and tends to keep away, his social development will be arrested. I think the most pressing issue is Damien's acceptance into the group. You need to give yourselves permission to treat him differently, to focus on furthering his social and emotional development, rather than being overly concerned about making sure that he covers the content." The aide shared her frustration with the situation and reported that they had been working with social services to try to have Damien removed from his mother's custody. So far, all of their efforts had been futile (Jalongo, 1996).

REACT:	In what ways are the perspectives of the program director, the visiting professor, and the aide in the class alike?
RESEARCH:	Investigate the subject of prenatal drug exposure and identify the major issues and recommendations. What beliefs did the adults in this situation seem to be acting upon? How did their responses to Damien compare with the recommendations you found?
REFLECT:	Which perspective do you identify most strongly with, and why?

Designing Portfolios of Children's Work

Now that you have seen what might go into a child's portfolio, work in a group to invent a different type of portfolio. You could, for example, design a portfolio for all areas of the curriculum (MacDonald, 1997; Nilsen, 1999) or for one curricular area, such as the arts (Jalongo & Stamp, 1997). You might prepare a portfolio that documents the life cycle of a project (Borgia, 1996). There are also three general types of portfolios, one of which you may want to develop. A permanent portfolio is a very selective sampling of work from each year that is advanced to the next grade to communicate with the child's new teacher (Gullo, 1994). The other two types of portfolios are a work-in-progress portfolio of what a child is currently working on in school and a current-year showcase portfolio that documents accomplishments chosen by teacher and child (Gullo, 1994).

Goals of Student Work Portfolios

Keep in mind the main goals of student work portfolios as you work in your groups:

- **Portfolios should incorporate actual classroom work.** The systematic collection of student work throughout the year helps to document student progress and achievement. The student work serves as a lens through which the faculty can reflect on their successes and adjust their instructional strategies.

- **Portfolios should enhance students', teachers', and families' participation in the assessment process.** Students accept more responsibility for their own learning and take pride in their achievements when they share their accomplishments and evidence of growth with others. School-family-community communication is enhanced when laypersons can really see evidence of effort, progress, and achievement.

- **Portfolios should meet the accountability concerns of school districts and funding agencies.** Portfolios are unlikely to replace large-scale assessment efforts in schools, districts, and programs, but they can do much to complete the assessment picture in ways that provide in-depth information. Large-scale assessment is like a telescope; portfolios are like a microscope on the same programs (Gullo, 1994).

How to Develop Portfolios

Use the following steps and resources to develop your portfolio plan (Genishi, 1996).

1. **Why?** What do you want to assess? Why create a portfolio for each child? What is it that you are trying to learn or reveal via this portfolio? Refer to Figure 8.1 for a list of reasons for assessment.

2. **What?** Which documents best demonstrate development? Which work samples are typical of the child's play or work? Which samples show what is unique about the child's work? What products document the attainment of curricular goals? See Figure 8.10 for an overview of the assessment process and a list of types of assessment data to collect.

3. **How and When?** How will you schedule the collection of samples of children's work? (For example, would you compare a sample taken the first and last months of school, or would you take the child's choice of three best examples?) How will you obtain child input? (For example, through individual interviews, small-group contacts, or coaching children how to select and discuss their choices of products for the portfolio?) (See Benson and Smith [1998] for an example of a first-grade portfolio.)

4. **Where?** Where will work samples be stored? (In a plastic crate, in a file drawer, or in magazine files?) In what formats? (Folders, videotapes, audiotapes, photographs, or binders?) How will they be organized? Who will need access to them?

5. **What Else?** Determine whether there are gaps in the profiles for each child or in the "developmental story" of your class or program. If so, what other work samples could you collect to make the information more comprehensive?

6. **Who?** Will what you have collected tell a clear story to the intended audience? Decide how to share the portfolio and with whom (e.g., parents and other family members, administrators, future teachers of the child, other children). Refer to Figure 8.5 for guidelines on effective documentation.

Presenting Your Plan

Make a list, chart, web, or sketch of your portfolio plan on the chalkboard, an overhead transparency, newsprint, or computer that can be shared with the total group. As each group presents its portfolio plan, evaluate it using the goals and questions in this workshop.

Exploring Your Role in Guiding Children's Behavior

My argument is that our first question should be "What do children need?"—followed immediately by "How can we meet those needs?"—and from that point of departure we will end up in a very different place than if we had begun by asking, "How do I get children to do what I want?"

My argument is that how students act in school is so bound up with what they are being asked to learn as to raise serious questions about whether classroom management can reasonably be treated as a separate field.

—Alfie Kohn, 1996, p. xv

Learning Outcomes

✔ Learn the components necessary in developing a classroom that is a community of learners

✔ Understand children's rights and needs and the ways in which those rights and needs shape a child guidance philosophy

✔ Become aware of the effects of a violent society on the development of young children

✔ Understand aggressive behavior in children and appropriate responses to it

✔ Define conflict, common types of conflict, and ways to resolve conflict in the classroom

✔ Develop greater confidence in your ability to function as a mediator and teach children self-control

✔ Acquire more skillful ways of communicating with children when difficult issues arise

Meet the Teachers

Charles works in a child-care program at the local hospital. His job is to work with medical personnel to determine each child's physical condition and limitations, then plan appropriate activities for the children in the playroom. He also works with families to help them get things back to normal as much as possible when the child is well and ready to return home. Over the years, he has found that after a hospital stay, young children often resist separation from their parents. As Charles sees it, "A big part of my role is to help the adults consider the child's point of view, give additional support when needed, and set reasonable limits for the child's behavior."

Mrs. Davis runs a child-care program for low-income families supported by the county. She cares for a mixed-age group of five preschool children in her home. The general rule in her classroom setting is that nobody owns any of the toys or materials; children are expected to share. But when a toddler brought his favorite teddy bear to school and didn't want to share, Mrs. Davis felt that he was entitled to cling to his toy and say, "It's mine!" because this situation was different. She decided to read several children's books during the week about "attachment objects" (blankets, soft toys, and other items that young children form a connection with) and then talk with the children about the treasured objects that most of them still sleep with or fondly remember.

Mrs. Davis was surprised by the children's idea to modify the rules about very special toys. They decided that when it comes to these very special items, "Other kids can look at them, but not take them away" and that, "Sometimes, you don't have to share."

Ms. Pettit has a child in her class this year who is well known throughout the school and community. Seven-year-old Tonya lives with her chronically ill mother and 3-year-old brother in a remote rural area. As a result, Tonya has responsibilities far beyond her years at home for cooking, cleaning, and babysitting. Although she is a bright and competent child, Tonya's school performance has been poor, because she frequently arrives at school tired, hungry, and neglected. Despite the research against retention at grade level, the professional staff members decide to keep Tonya in first grade for another year. Ms. Pettit describes what happened during the first few weeks of school: "Other children arrived with new school supplies, and Tonya, who can be quite persuasive, started to make deals with her classmates in which they ended up with the bad end of the bargain—such as Kim's new pencil box being traded for one marker that is going dry. Then I received an angry telephone call and a note from parents asking me what was going on. My first reaction was to punish her, but instead, I explained to her that it wasn't right for her to make unfair trades. Then I used my $100 allocation from the local parent group to equip several writing and drawing backpacks with various supplies so that children could use them at school or borrow one and take it home. That solved the problem, because now, Tonya has access to the materials that she needs."

COMPARE:	What are some commonalities among these three teachers, even though they are working with children of various ages?
CONTRAST:	How do these teachers think about teaching? How would you characterize the outlook of each one?
CONNECT:	What made the greatest impression on you, and how will you incorporate this into your teaching?

Children's Needs and Rights

Any discussion of child guidance or children's inappropriate behavior must begin by considering their basic needs as human beings. What is it that children have a right to expect? First and foremost, children have a right to caring relationships. They deserve adults who take time, listen to their concerns, support their efforts, treat them with dignity, and protect them from harm. Human beings remain helpless longer than any other species and therefore require a tremendous investment of love, care, and attention from families, educators, and other professionals, as well as from the communities in which they live. The following story about a child we know helps to illustrate why there is no effective substitute for nurturing.

> Unlike several of his kindergarten classmates, Jason adjusted readily to a full-day kindergarten program when school started in September. Later on in the school year, however, Jason started to cry, not at the start of the school day, but in the afternoons shortly before the buses arrived. His teacher was sympathetic at first but eventually lost patience with him and complained to anyone who would listen that Jason's crying was "driving her crazy." In desperation, she resorted to the behavioristic approach recommended by a more experienced teacher, convinced that if she ignored the crying it would eventually stop. Yet as the winter began, Jason's tears and protests became, if anything, even more intense.
>
> Clues to the puzzling pattern of Jason's behavior began to emerge after a concerned neighbor reported the child's situation to Children and Youth Services. Jason's mother had abandoned the family during the summer, and his father, who had a demanding job and a long commute, suddenly had sole responsibility for the boy. Monday through Friday, 5-year-old Jason was getting off the school bus, unlocking the front door, and staying home alone until his father arrived around 7:00 P.M. When the social worker spoke with Jason, the kindergartner confided that he had been frightened by some advertising for a horror movie that he saw on television and was terrified to stay by himself when it was dark outside. (Isenberg & Jalongo, 1997, p. 9)

We begin with this story because it reminds us that adults in crisis, such as Jason's father and teacher, sometimes make bad decisions in the absence of appropriate support. Such errors in judgment occur when adults disregard the child's needs or neglect their collective responsibility to care for the child. As Valora Washington (1996) reminds us, in an ideal world,

> *Every child should be*
> *cherished in families,*
> *supported by communities,*
> *considered holistically,*
> *nurtured with care. (p. 136)*

All human beings have fundamental needs for such things as food, shelter, clothing, adequate rest, and freedom from threat (Maslow, 1968). Yet with nearly half of America's children living in poverty, many children arrive at school without even these basic needs having been met (Children's Defense Fund, 1997). When a child is hungry, it is cruel to

How many of these children will be home alone until parents return from work?

Home life

berate the child for not paying attention in class. When a child's father is in jail, it is inconsiderate to sponsor a father-son event. When a child has witnessed a drive-by shooting, it is disrespectful to act as if nothing has happened. As an intervention specialist puts it, "Children carry their home lives to school as easily as the books and papers in their backpacks" (Krahl & Jalongo, 1998). Any teacher who overlooks this is failing to really *see* children.

In addition to the basic needs, all human beings have fundamental personal and social needs, including (a) *autonomy*, the need to exert an influence on decisions and events rather than feeling powerless and the victim of circumstance, (b) *relatedness*, the need for love, affirmation, and a sense of connectedness with others and belonging to a group, and (c) *competence*, the need to accomplish new things, acquire new skills, and successfully put these learnings to use (Deci & Ryan, 1985; Rodgers, 1998). In fact, some experts on guiding children's behavior believe that all children are striving to belong and that when they cannot feel like a valued part of the classroom community, they resort to antisocial behaviors such as seeking attention, exerting their power, trying to even the score through revenge, or resisting passively by withdrawing from adult demands (Dinkmeyer & McKay, 1989). Children also have the right to expect certain things from their educational experiences, as described in Figure 9.1.

312

FIGURE 9.1

Children's rights

Children have a right to . . .

be greeted warmly every day

be noticed in positive ways

exercise choices throughout the school day

enjoy their educational experiences

be heard and responded to by adults and peers

be allowed to converse with their peers

gain competencies, skills, and confidence

have their abilities recognized and regarded

know they can think and solve problems

learn about their world

expect daily and weekly routines

learn the skills of independence

give and receive compliments

establish warm and supportive relationships with adults

have adventures that involve new challenges or risks

expect fairness in class rules, policies, and procedures

be able to give and get help

learn to resolve conflicts

understand how to make, keep, and be a friend

be accepted into the classroom community and make contributions to it

be able to make mistakes, break a rule, or act wrongfully and then make amends, repair, and recover their place in the group

SOURCE: Adapted from R. S. Charney, 1992. *Teaching children to care: Management in the responsive classroom.* Greenfield, MA: Northeast Foundation for Children.

Additionally, every child has a right to hope—to have a sense of moving forward, making progress, and anticipating a brighter future. Hope is what enables us to believe that "we *can* get there from here" (Gannon & Mncayi, 1996, p. 55). Some ways that teachers build hope include communicating the following important messages to every child (Gannon & Mncayi, 1996).

> *People like me here; I can come back.*
> *I have my own space here; I can leave my stuff and it will be safe.*
> *Nice things happen here; I can depend on good things happening again.*
> *I might not get finished today, but I can work on it some more later.*
> *There are nice people here; I can become like them.*
> *I am getting better at this, and I can learn new things.*
> *What I want and think matters; I can make responsible choices.*
> *I don't have to depend on others all of the time; I can do some things well all by myself.*
> *My work matters to me and to the group; I can do outstanding work.*
> *What I am learning at school works in other places and at other times, too.*
> *There are so many choices, I can try and succeed at new things.*

When you see a child misbehave, ask yourself what might be motivating him or her. William Glasser (1992) argues that there are just four fundamental motivations for doing something: love, power, freedom, or fun—or some combination of these. Consider something as simple as brushing your teeth. You do it because you want to avoid dental fillings and pain (freedom) and enjoy good food (fun). You also do it because others will be more attracted to you than if your teeth were decayed (love), and because they may hold you in higher esteem if you have a dazzling smile (power). Likewise, children behave as they do, good or bad, in response to one or more of these motivating factors. The great majority of the time, young children strive to please adults and comply with their requests. The rest of the time, you will need to dig deeper to learn what might be causing a behavior. Figure 9.2 suggests some underlying causes of children's behavior.

FIGURE 9.2

Some underlying
causes of children's
behavior

Physical environment	• the child may be new to an environment and unfamiliar with procedures
	• there may not be enough materials to go around, and this leads to disputes
	• the classroom layout may be poor and fail to clearly demarcate quiet and noisy areas
	• the room may not be arranged in ways that encourage children to access materials and put them away independently
Child's basic needs are unmet	• the child may be neglected, abused, ill, tired, or hungry
	• the child may feel inadequate or incompetent
	• the child may feel unaccepted by peers and/or adults
Curriculum problems	• the academic demands may be unrealistic for the child's age or stage
	• an inflexible schedule might cause the child to act out
	• the child may be generally unchallenged and disinterested in the required activities
Cultural differences	• the child and family may feel overwhelmed by the adaptive demands of a new culture
	• the child may not have mastered the language well enough to make his or her needs known

	• the child may have suffered traumatic experiences in the process of immigrating
	• the family's values may conflict with certain school or class policies/procedures
Special needs	• the child may be abused or neglected, subjected to physical harm, sexual molestation, emotional maltreatment, or a disregard of the child's basic needs
	• the child may have attention deficit disorder, characterized by a child's inability to concentrate on a task long enough to process information or accomplish a goal
	• the child may be autistic, a severe impairment of two-way verbal or nonverbal social interaction in which the child's activity is dominated by repetitive behaviors and ritualistic behavior
	• the child may have a behavioral disorder, characterized by a difference from the norm in the *amount* and *intensity* of the child's reactions
	• the child may have a learning disability, a variety of problems manifested as difficulty with verbal or mathematical skills, with fine or gross motor skills, or with visual, auditory, and tactile perception

SOURCE: Adapted from *Children with Special Needs in Early Childhood Settings* by C. L. Paasche, L. Gorrill, and B. Strom, 1990, Menlo Park, CA: Addison-Wesley.

Your Role in Child Guidance

When a child misbehaves, it is difficult for most adults to avoid rushing to the question of how to stop the behavior and think instead about what might be causing it. Before you assume that the child is at fault, you will need to consider whether what we expect is necessary, productive, fair, and age appropriate (Kohn, 1996).

Is It Necessary? A day-care provider who works with 3-year-olds insists that every child lie down and take a nap in the afternoon. For the children who are in the habit of taking an afternoon nap, this procedure is fine. For those who are unaccustomed to naps, it is a constant struggle. She spends much of her time leading them back to their cots or saying "Shhhh!" loudly and frequently. The real question is not whether children are napping or

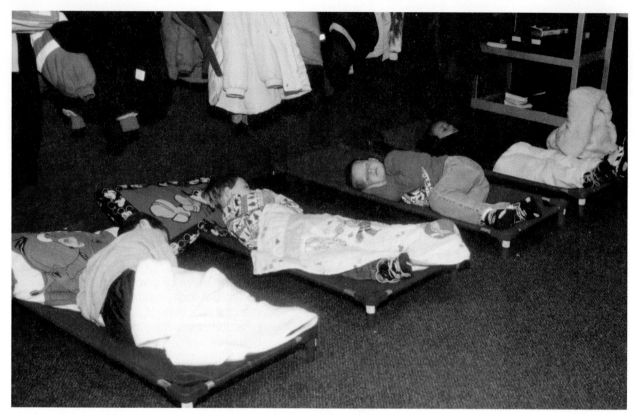

Does every child need a nap at the same time? What alternatives can you suggest?

not but whether a nap is necessary. If the nap is designed to keep children from getting overtired, and some children clearly are not tired, then who is the nap for? Wouldn't it be sufficient to have a quiet time instead of attempting to enforce a nap? Might the naptime be more for the teacher's benefit than the children's?

Is It Productive? In a Head Start classroom, all of the 4-year-olds are required to assemble in a circle and seat themselves on pieces of masking tape placed on the carpet. The circle time lasts for nearly 30 minutes, and every time a child moves from the tape, the teacher sends the child to a "growing-up chair." By the time the large group session is over, about a third of the children are or have been placed in chairs as punishment for failing to sit still. In fact, by the end of this excessively long and boring circle time, it almost looks like a game of musical chairs! The teacher persists at this unsuccessful practice and accepts it unquestioningly because it is what she remembers from her own experience in kindergarten. If you talk with her, she will tell you that the children come from poor families and "just don't know how to behave." What she really needs to do is to rethink group time. Ironically, what she considers to be a punishment (moving to chairs) is actually a momentary escape from the tedious work she repeats day after day.

Is It Fair? A second-grade teacher has attended a workshop on assertive discipline, and one of the recommended strategies is to list the names of children who misbehave and place a check mark next to the child's name with each new incident of violating classroom rules. She decides to do this on the chalkboard so that everyone can see who the offenders are. After a child accumulates three check marks, that child loses a privilege. When a regular visitor to the classroom asks about the names on the board and the teacher explains, the visitor says, "I just wondered. I see the same names up there all the time." Afterwards, the teacher thinks about what the visitor said and wonders to herself, "How can I say that this system is working if none of the children who need to learn self-control are learning it?"

Is It Age Appropriate? A private nursery school in a wealthy suburb has high tuition and a long waiting list. The director knows that parents and families send their children there in the hopes that their children's development will be accelerated, so she pressures the teachers to "get more out of" the children to build her program's reputation for developing precocity in children. Because the competition for the available slots in each class is keen, the director decides to institute more-stringent policies about entrance requirements and a more academic focus. The curriculum is deliberately "pushed down," so that toddlers are now expected to do what was once part of the program for 3-year-olds, the 3-year-olds do what was once part of the program for 4-year-olds, and so forth. When several of the toddlers do not sit quietly during stories, memorize songs and fingerplays, or paste shapes cut out by the teachers in the correct way, the director invites the parents in and asks them to remove their children from the program to make room "for those who can benefit." This child-care program director has lost sight of the developmental appropriateness of her curriculum. Situations such as these illustrate that guiding young children's behavior is a complex and challenging task, particularly when adults have different expectations and beliefs (Scarlett, 1997).

PAUSE AND REFLECT ABOUT DISCIPLINE

Which of the following did you experience as a child? How did you feel about such statements? What connections do you see between these statements and the children's rights listed in Figure 9.1?

- "All of you will sit here and miss recess until the person who broke the rules comes forward."
- "If everyone gets 100% on the spelling test on Friday, we will have a popcorn party."
- "You know the rules. Now you have to write 'I will not throw snowballs' 500 times."
- "I like the way that Heather is working. Look at Heather's picture, everyone."

Discipline and Child Guidance

What is "old-fashioned" discipline? Usually, it consists of some combination of rewards and punishments. Punishments are unpleasant or painful experiences that are imposed upon others to "teach a lesson" and enforce compliance, as in, "Go sit by yourself in time-out. I asked you twice to clean up the toys and you did not do it." Corporal punishment is physical pain inflicted to force compliance, as in spanking; in most states, corporal punishment is against the law. Threats are warnings about the punishments that will occur if compliance with the rules is not forthcoming, as in, "If you do not finish your work on time, you will sit there until you do." Rewards are pleasant experiences that are held out to recognize compliance, as in, "Those of you who did well on your papers got a sticker." Bribes are promises of future rewards, as in, "If you work quietly for the next 10 minutes, we will get to make play dough this afternoon." The trouble with these methods is that they require constant group surveillance (Kohn, 1996). Figure 9.3 compares and contrasts discipline with child guidance and praise with encouragement.

A student teacher who had been told that the best way to manage children's behavior was to "catch them being good" decided to put a chart on each of her first graders' desks. As she walked around the room, she would stamp stars on the charts of children who were working quietly. After accumulating five of these stamps, a child was permitted to get a piece of candy from a jar. Stamps could also be crossed off for inappropriate behavior. After experimenting with this system, the teacher recognized several drawbacks:

- Instead of talking with the children about what they were doing, she was preoccupied with scanning the room for good and bad behavior.
- Children started to tattle more, particularly after she had been out of the room or when they were under someone else's supervision at music, art, library, gym, or recess.
- A parent complained that her daughter's dentist found an unusually high number of cavities; the parent blamed the sugary treats that were given almost daily to her well-behaved daughter.
- The student teacher had little money, and it was becoming expensive to keep the candy jar filled with treats.
- The children who had been well behaved previously continued to be the "winners," while those who had difficulty complying with classroom rules continued to be "losers," except on rare occasions.
- The custodian complained that hard candy was being spit out and trampled into the carpet.

Notice that the student teacher did not question her own behavior at all. She operated on the assumption that children needed to do whatever she asked. This is one of the great fallacies of working with children—the assumption that whatever adults request is appropriate and that the only legitimate role for the child is to obey. A contemporary definition of discipline is quite different: Discipline is "helping children to learn personal responsibility for their behavior and to judge between right and wrong for themselves" (Fields & Boesser, 1998, p. 5).

The basic minimum requirement for any appropriate way of guiding young children's behavior begins by building a relationship with them and depends upon effective communication. Effective communication occurs when teachers do the following:

- Demonstrate understanding, respect the child's point of view, and identify with the child's situation
- Use a pleasant, calm, and normal tone of voice
- State clear, simple, polite, and firm expectations in a positive way
- Offer appropriate suggestions and alternatives for behavior
- Enjoy and verbally appreciate children's appropriate behavior
- Express feelings, especially anger, in an appropriate and constructive manner
- Use humor and see the funny side of situations to diffuse tension

FIGURE 9.3

Child guidance
versus discipline

Child Guidance

Child is encouraged to . . .

exercise self-control over emotions and override impulses

distinguish what is right, just, and good from what is wrong, unfair, and bad

internalize a code of conduct

recognize others' feelings and consider the consequences of behavior

cope with powerful emotions and act autonomously

engage in problem solving and consider underlying motives

Discipline

Child learns to . . .

yield to impulse in the absence of a threat of punishment

wait for an adult to pass judgment on behavior

fear punishment or expect rewards

dismiss others' feelings and focus instead on avoidance of punishment or attainment of rewards

repress emotions temporarily and retaliate later when authority figure is absent

keep score of who wins and loses

Encouragement

Teaches children to evaluate their own efforts
Examples: *"Was that fun?" "Are you glad you tried to . . ." "You seem pleased about . . ."*

Does not judge children or their work
Examples: *"I noticed that you were . . ." "Which of your paintings do you like best?"*

Focuses on the process rather than the outcome
Examples: *"How did you use the software to do this?" "It looks like you are working on your sign." "I see you are enjoying . . ."*

Is a **private** event that does not embarrass children in public or compare them with each other
Examples: *"Thanks for helping to clean up today." "I appreciate that you . . ." "Aren't you pleased that you were able to . . ."*

Praise

Teacher is the judge of what is good and bad
Example: *"You have been very good today, so here is a sticker for you."*

Judges children and their work
Examples: *"What a great story!" "You had the best idea."*

Focuses on the outcome
Examples: *"I am putting the best papers up on the bulletin board." "Who has their work finished?"*

Is a **public** announcement or event
Examples: *"Room 5, you have been very good today." "Look at Sheri's paper, everyone. She did it correctly." "The winners of the contest are . . ."*

SOURCE: Adapted from "Discipline in Early Childhood" by L. Porter, 1999, *Landscapes of Development: An Anthology of Readings* (pp. 295–308), L. E. Berk (Ed.), Belmont CA: Wadsworth.

- Be consistent and predictable in responses to children's behavior
- Use positive, affectionate nonverbal communication such as smiles, nods, hugs, or laughter (Lerman, 1984; Rodd, 1996)

PAUSE AND REFLECT ABOUT AGGRESSIVE TODDLERS—WHAT ARE THEY TELLING US?

Seeing the pattern and solving the puzzle of children's "out of control" or inappropriate behavior can be one of the most rewarding roles of the early childhood practitioner; however, it can be one of the most frustrating roles as well. When you encounter these feelings of frustration, consider the child; if you as an adult with your wide array of coping skills are experiencing frustration, how is the child feeling? Read over the Children's Rights outlined in Figure 9.1. Children should be able to count on these rights and expect to learn in an environment that fosters these rights. As an early childhood practitioner, you can make this happen.

In this video segment, you will see how one child development specialist has ensured that the rights outlined in Figure 9.1 are enacted in the learning environment of her nonprofit organization. Notice how this environment seems to be changing children's aggressive behavior.

1. Which of the children's rights as listed in Figure 9.1 are being addressed by the solutions presented in this video segment?

2. List three options for dealing with a child's aggressive behavior when the parent is present, but seems to be ignoring the behavior. How are these options different from the ways you would deal with a child's behavior when a parent is not present?

Guiding young children's behavior requires a strong commitment to communicating effectively.

Violence, Aggression, and Conflict

As American society moves into the 21st century, parents, educators, and professionals in related fields are expressing concern about the escalation of violence in children's lives. There are three broad categories of violence that exert a powerful influence on children's lives (Groves, 1996). *Media violence* refers to the aggressive acts that children see depicted in television programs, newscasts, videos, movies, newspapers, and magazines. On television alone, the average child sees 12,000 acts of violence each year (Dietz & Strasburger, 1991). Television violence is deceptive, because it "sanitizes" violence, seldom showing the pain, anguish, suffering, or even the blood that results from violence (Simmons, Stalsworth, & Wentzel, 1999). More often than not, the "bad guys" simply fall down and die instantly. One type of media violence that is frequently overlooked by adults, because it does not involve real people, includes the brutal acts of cartoon characters who magically spring to life after being cut up, run over, dropped from a cliff, and so forth. *Family violence* refers to the injuries, both physical and emotional, that children suffer as a result of abuse or neglect, as well as the acts of violence that children witness between and among adults and other family members. Increasing numbers of children watch the hostility that comes from a bitter divorce, for example. *Community violence* refers to the violence that children witness in their communities, such as fights, stabbings, and shootings. Children and families who live in high-crime areas often do not have the financial resources to leave the area. As a result, they live in fear for their lives.

Many Americans would like to think that violence is exclusively an urban problem or a racial problem that exists among certain ethnic groups, but the reality is that media violence is present in virtually every home, with 99% of American families owning at least one television set (Comstock & Strasburger, 1990). Likewise, domestic violence can erupt anywhere without regard to race, class, or ethnicity, although families who do not live in crowded areas may be better able to maintain secrecy than others. There is little question that some communities are more crime-ridden than others, but recent research suggests that poverty, not race, is the major risk factor for violence (American Psychological Association, 1993).

The effects of an increasingly violent society are evident in children's responses to conflict in early childhood settings (Carter, 1992; Eisenberg, 1992; Stone, 1993). Young children's aggressive behavior is on the rise, and incidents that used to involve an exchange of words now often result in an explosion of anger and a resort to hitting, kicking, and biting (Carlsson-Paige & Levin, 1992). As one teacher puts it, "It used to be that an angry child would storm off or a frightened child would cry. Now they are more apt to lash out, not by knocking over blocks or throwing down a toy, but by being aggressive toward one another."

Conflict refers to competing wishes, desires, or behaviors that evoke powerful emotions. It is, of course, possible for a person to have conflicting inner emotions (e.g., "Should I cheat on the test to get a good grade or should I be honest and suffer the consequences of not studying?"). Conflict also occurs when two or more people are on opposite sides of an issue (e.g., Child: "I was sitting there first, it's *my* chair." Sibling: "But you got up, so now *I'm* sitting here. If you get up, it's not your seat any more.").

One of the most important things that any adult responsible for the care and education of young children can do is to try to prevent behavior problems before they occur. Figure 9.4 provides an overview of prevention strategies.

Although conflicts do occur frequently in educational settings, students can be taught constructive ways to resolve conflicts (Johnson & Johnson, 1996). One type of conflict that teachers find most frightening in children is aggression. Aggression refers

FIGURE 9.4

Preventing behavior problems

As an initial step, consider the general goals of child guidance:

1. To create order so that the group can function effectively and so that all children can learn
2. To teach children to take responsibility for their own actions and to acquire self-discipline
3. To teach children to handle powerful emotions and express their feelings in socially appropriate ways
4. To foster cooperation between and among children and adults
5. To teach children the social responsibility and ethical principles necessary to enable them to function as citizens in a democratic society

Know children's abilities and limitations. For example, it is not fair to expect a child with attention deficit disorder to stay on-task for the same amount of time as peers without this problem, and you may find that adaptive equipment is needed to help a child who is physically disabled sit upright, feed himself or herself, or help himself or herself to paint at an easel. Try to foster independence so that children's frustrations are reduced. Avoid rushing children, as this usually results in stress and acting out. Avoid leaving children waiting with nothing to do, such as lining them up too early to go to the cafeteria. Time pressures (too little, too much) frequently erupt into problems.

Have a well-organized classroom and clearly established routines. If everyone decides that the blocks go on the shelf, for example, this makes it clear what is expected when the blocks are to be put away. Engage as many senses as possible when teaching routines. For instance, if a child is supposed to be responsible for watering the plants, announce this in the morning by placing a card with the helper's name next to a picture of a flowerpot, have a stick-person poster near the plants to show what the helper is expected to do, and establish an auditory signal for helper time. Demonstrate how to water the plants. Ask children to repeat the instructions before they actually perform the task. In this way, children with special needs can get the message in several different ways.

Discuss rules and consequences. Remind children of the rules that they have helped to set, and keep those rules simple and clear, such as "No water on the floor." Make consequences clear too, such as, "If you spill water on the floor, you have to mop it up." At times, there may be natural consequences of children's actions that it may be better for them to experience directly. For instance, a child in the primary grades might have a very messy desk and be unable to find things when needed. Rather than criticizing the child, this situation could be used to help him or her see the value of organizing materials.

Teach, practice, and review appropriate behaviors. Trust children and believe in them. They are not trying to make you look bad or being difficult deliberately. If they are behaving inappropriately, it is probably because they want power (to be noticed), fun (to enjoy themselves), freedom (to assert their independence), or love (to belong and be warmly regarded) (Glasser, 1992). Instead of *telling* children what they should not do, *show* them what they should do. Also, learn to be a troubleshooter and be alert to signs of difficulty and situations that will require special support.

Avoid inadvertently reinforcing the wrong sort of behavior. If a teacher sees a child pinching another child and says, "Come and sit by me," that action may be perceived as a reward by the child who is engaging in inappropriate behavior.

Think before you speak. Do not threaten children, saying, for instance, "You will have to stay after school if you don't get your work done" when the child rides the bus and there is no way this will happen. Learn to say what you mean and mean what you say.

Choose your battles. Don't feel that you have to respond to every inappropriate behavior, but don't be afraid to change something when things are falling apart, either. Beginning teachers who are striving to be liked by children will sometimes smile sweetly at virtually any behavior. It is better to project a serious, concerned facial expression when difficulties arise rather than be afraid of taking steps to stop a behavior.

Use children's literature. Children's books are a rich source of examples of children who engage in inappropriate behaviors, the consequences of those behaviors, and different ways of "trying on" solutions.

SOURCE: Adapted from *Positive Discipline for Preschoolers: For Their Early Years—Raising Children Who Are Responsible and Resourceful* by J. Nelsen, C. Erwin, and R. Duffy, 1995, Rocklin, CA: Prima Publishing; "Discipline in Early Childhood" by L. Porter, 1999, *Landscapes of Development: An Anthology of Readings* (pp. 295–308), L. E. Berk (Ed.), Belmont, CA: Wadsworth; and *How to Reach and Teach ADD/ADHD Children: Practical Techniques, Strategies, and Interventions for Helping Children with Attention Problems and Hyperactivity* by S. F. Rief, 1993, West Nyack, NJ: The Center for Applied Research in Education.

Established teaching routines can prevent behavior problems.

to a deliberate act that is designed to harm or diminish another person in some way. Aggression is a common response to conflict, a situation in which the needs or desires of one individual or group are at odds with the needs or desires of another individual or group. Research on children's aggressive behavior has revealed some interesting results, including the following:

Aggression Is in the Eye of the Beholder. A group of 3-year-old children is seeing how Silly Putty stretches as well as placing it on the Sunday newspaper comic strips to make imprints of the colored-ink pictures. One of the boys grabs all of the Silly Putty, stretches it out, and then presses it onto the face of another child while saying, "Put Caitlin's face on here." Is this an innocent experiment or an act of aggression? Does it depend, to some extent, on Caitlin's reaction? If Caitlin's feelings are hurt and she feels violated or humiliated, most teachers would say that it is an act of aggression. But what if she laughs and says, "I asked him to try it"? Clearly, what counts as an act of aggression is influenced by the social situation.

Some Children Evidence Behavior Patterns That Give Them Precisely What They Do Not Need. Visit Rashid's first-grade classroom on any given day, and you are likely to see him in time-out. Time-out is the classroom equivalent of being sent to one's room; it temporarily removes a child from the group when he or she becomes disruptive. Virtually anyone who recommends this practice is quick to point out that it is a last-resort measure and should be used infrequently and limited to 3 to 5 minutes. But Rashid's teacher continues to use time-out, even though it is obvious that it has done absolutely nothing to improve Rashid's behavior. Because Rashid is repeatedly isolated from the group, his peers treat him as untrustworthy and reject his overtures of friendship. Children like Rashid, who are less adaptable, more distractable, and more intense, really need to learn how to adjust to new circumstances, to concentrate, and to calm themselves. None of these things can be learned in isolation (Tobin, 1991). Child behavior that disrupts ongoing play and elicits negative responses usually leads to even stronger feelings of isolation, anxiety, and hostility. Knowing this, it is particularly important for teachers to guide children's behavior rather than merely judge it or police it.

Teachers Tend to Focus on Individual Children Who Are Aggressive, When It Would Be More Effective to Work with the Total Group. When invited to talk about "kids who are bad," 5-year-old David said, "Kalessha is *really* bad. She moved away and I'm glad. 'Cause one time, I was trying to write in my journal and she was holding my arm so I couldn't even write! And Oliver, he's really bad too. One time the teacher made him go to the principal's office because he was kicking other kids." Visit most classrooms for just half an hour and you will know who the "bad" children are, because you will hear their names all the time. Yet social conflict does not belong to a child; it is a consequence of relationships. Intervention efforts, such as those used with troubled youths at Boys' Town, are more effective when they concentrate on the group, demonstrate the desired behavior through role play, and discuss the role-play situation afterwards (National Educational Service, 1996). Instead of calling out the offender's name over and over again, a teacher should clearly demonstrate what the child needs to do in order to be accepted by the group.

Aggressive Behavior Frequently Occurs in Groups. "We're the Baywatch guys! Look out, we're coming through in our powerboats." With this announcement, a group of 4-year-olds comes running through the housekeeping area leaving dishes, plastic food, and babydolls in their wake. Research suggests that groups of aggressive children, clustered together, are frequently responsible for as much as a third of aggressive acts (Perry, Kussel, & Perry, 1988). Often, this aggression is related to media violence that is re-enacted in the classroom, as in superhero play. One intervention that a teacher can institute is to form flexible groups that will create new alliances and networks and restructure the social network of the group.

Aggressive Acts Occur Less Frequently Than Teachers Assume. In a study of preschoolers, aggressive acts accounted for approximately 3 to 6% of all the interactions between and among children (Cairns, Gariepy, & Kinderman, 1990). All things considered, this is not a high incidence of inappropriate behavior. The rate of openly aggressive acts depends to some extent on a child's ability to use words rather than actions to express emotions. For example, two toddlers are ambling about the child-care center when one stops, watches the actions of the other's pull toy, and grabs the toy away. The first toddler retaliates by biting the offending arm that took the toy away, then they both begin to cry. Although many adults would cite this as evidence that children are cruel, these toddlers are no more cruel than adults; they simply express their hostility in more concrete ways (Da Ros & Kovach, 1998). Whereas adults in a traffic jam have access to a repertoire of aggressive acts, such as cutting one another off, blowing the horn, shouting insults, and even making obscene gestures, the young child's repertoire of aggressive responses is often limited to inflicting physical harm on another. We know that most incidents of aggression in young children involve disputes over objects, territory, or access to privileges. Therefore, paying attention to the physical environment and establishing procedures for sharing are particularly important.

Teachers Sometimes Intervene Too Quickly When Aggression Occurs. Although it is important for every child to feel safe and protected from harm, children need to be taught to work out some of their problems. For example, two children in the dress-up corner reach for an old bridal veil at the same time, and a tussle ensues. This is a good example of an incident that can be negotiated. Rather than rushing in and quickly dispatching a solution, the teacher can "narrate" the argument with statements such as, "I see that Lisa and Shawneen both want to play brides," "How can you play brides if there is just one veil?" or "It wouldn't be much fun to play brides all by yourself." Whenever possible, skillful teachers encourage children to use their own problem-solving resources rather than always playing the role of referee. Your job is to help children develop the social skills they will need for a lifetime. In fact, your intervention in children's conflicts may be thought of as a continuum, ranging from most to least invasive or direct. Figure 9.5 illustrates the child guidance continuum (Gordon & Browne, 1996).

Positive Guidance Strategies

If children's needs and motives are disregarded, if "old-fashioned" discipline does not work, and if teachers' typical responses to children's aggressive acts are not particularly effective, what *should* teachers and caregivers of the very young be doing to guide children's behavior? Begin by learning something new rather than resorting to what you already know. Far too many teachers defend their practices on shaky grounds, saying, for example, "That's what my parents did to me and I turned out okay," "I always heard that you were supposed to make an example out of the ones who break the rules," or "All the teachers I know use stickers to get the children in their classes to cooperate." It is the rare educator who admits that, "In the face of inappropriate behavior my job is to create a change in order to effect a change. I may change the structure of the classroom,

FIGURE 9.5

The child guidance continuum

This continuum ranges from the least intrusive (1) to the most intrusive (10). Part of being a skillful teacher is deciding which approach is best suited to the situation. Child guidance is not a "one size fits all" strategy.

1. **Ignore.** Let the children work it out for themselves. After they do, you may want to comment: "I noticed that you were sharing the trucks today" or "It was great to see you playing together with the blocks."

2. **Listen and watch.** Let children see you watching and listening intently so that they are assured you are available. Again, you may want to comment afterwards: "I'm glad to see the sand staying inside the box" or "You were right to make room for Juanita."

3. **Act as a reporter or narrator.** Comment on what you hear, saying, for example, "I hear shouting," "There are seven people at this center and only four are allowed at one time," "I see clay all over the table," or "Remind me, Elise, of the rule about the woodworking center."

4. **Step in and restate the rules.** Set limits and protect the children: "Stop throwing the blocks right now," "You cannot leave the playground; there are cars going by," or "Everyone who played with the puzzles has to help put them away. Darien, you were playing here."

5. **Ask questions.** Rather than rushing in to size up the situation, hear the children out: "What happened here?" "Do you think that is fair?" or "Who can help me hang up these paintings?"

6. **Brainstorm.** Encourage children to say what to do: "Who has an idea about what to do when everyone wants to pet the rabbit?" "Is there a way that you could both play with the new wagon?" or "What could we do to keep your blocks from being knocked down?"

7. **Offer ideas.** Suggest possible solutions to the children: "The table is all sticky from snack. It needs to be washed with a sponge," "That's enough Power Rangers for today. Jenny and Rick, choose a center," or "Maybe Ms. G. (the aide) could help you glue your wood sculpture back together."

8. **Offer a choice.** Give children a limited number of options: "You can make your snack as soon as you come in in the morning, or you can wait until you are hungry" or "Everyone has to help clean up the room. You may work at the water table or in the block corner."

9. **Take action.** Plan a solution and let the children know you will monitor it. "Tomorrow when you come to preschool, we will put the shopping cart away. The cart is not for crashing into other people" or "You were late coming in from recess again today. Let's make a plan so that this won't happen tomorrow."

10. **Direct children in what they are to do.** Take command and tell children exactly what must be done. Often, this is reserved for situations that are hazardous or extremely inconsiderate of others: "Now someone has slipped and fallen on the floor. Tanya and Michelle, please go and get the mop and sweep up the sand that you spilled," "Everyone can play hide and seek. Give Weiwei a turn," or "Lisa is crying because you pushed her off the swing. Help her up and go get a wet paper towel for her elbow, Melissa."

SOURCE: Adapted from *Guiding Young Children in a Diverse Society* by A. Gordon and K. W. Browne, 1996, Boston: Allyn & Bacon.

the method of instruction, the peer interaction, my actions or thoughts or expectations, or I may simply command change in the actions of the child. Of these, the last is the least effective" (Tobin, 1991, p. 38).

Walk by any number of classrooms and you can hear teachers relying upon these least-effective methods with statements such as, "Eyes up here, please," "Shari, pay attention," "Brian, remember to raise your hand," "We always take turns in preschool," "I'm going to have to call your mother if you don't settle down," and "One more time, Carlos, and you are going to the principal's office." How do teachers begin to change this talk and replace it with something that will actually *teach* children how to get along with others? Six basic precepts follow.

First, Learn to Identify with the Child, Not with the Label. It is possible to see that a child *has* a problem without seeing that child *as* the problem. Approach a difficult child with the goal of understanding that child rather than with the goal of obtaining instant obedience, as difficult as that may be when disruptions occur. Maintain sufficient curiosity to find out why a child might act in a certain way and realize that in that quest, the child is your best teacher. In other words, you must see yourself in the child so that you can affiliate with him or her (Strachota, 1996). Suppose that a toddler is very high-spirited. He dashes to the carpet when you offer to read a story, pushes down another child, and handles the book roughly. Try thinking to yourself, "When do I get carried away? When was I reprimanded for this as a child? How did it feel?"

Second, As Educators, We Have to Focus on the Child's Needs Rather Than Our Own Fear of Failure. Put aside your worries about appearing inept and losing face. Think about the child and realize that the child's behavior may be invoking exactly the opposite of what that child truly needs from adults. Second-grader Marjorie is a good example. When the teacher directed everyone to draw pictures of their families, Marjorie grew sullen and refused to comply. The more the teacher pressed, the more adamant Marjorie became, and her teacher saw it as a power struggle. What her teacher did not realize is that Marjorie's father had abandoned the family to move in with his new girlfriend. Marjorie was mourning the loss of her father and had overheard her mother talking about being without money. The second grader was terrified that they would be poverty-stricken in the desperate ways she had seen portrayed in movies. Finally, Marjorie relented and drew the picture, but when she arrived at home, she cried bitterly about the fact that she "lied at school," because her picture depicted the entire family "even though I know Daddy doesn't live with us anymore."

Third, When Confronted with the Most Difficult Teaching or Learning Situations, Go Back to Basics—and We Don't Mean the Three R's. What is truly basic for young children is what they respond to naturally from the beginning: sensory experiences, play, and enactment. Newborns are soothed by sensory experiences such as being touched and listening to pleasant sounds; toddlers enjoy active play such as pushing, pulling, emptying, and filling; and 3-year-olds typically take delight in enacting familiar routines such as pretending to sleep, eat, or care for a baby. These are the things that mark a return to the basics for young children and are usually a good starting point for reaching a child who seems difficult to reach. Recall from Chapter 8 the case of Damien, the child who was exposed prenatally to crack cocaine. His kindergarten teacher discovered that instead of having his aide attempt to control his disruptive behavior as it arose, more could be accomplished when his aide sat alongside him and they played with various toys together, inviting other children to join in.

Fourth, Don't Expect That You Can Make It All Better. We are teachers, not miracle workers. Admitting that we cannot set everything right, however, is no excuse for ignoring what is right for the child. We are powerless to make it all better, yet we have tremendous power to make our corner of the world, our classrooms, better places for children to be. Stephanie, a private nursery-school teacher, was deeply frustrated and saddened by the painfully slow process of trying to remove a child who was being sexually abused by her adoptive father from his custody. This teacher punished herself because she could not be a rescuer, yet she had done everything within reason by discussing it with the program director, reporting it to Social Services, and discussing the evidence with a psychologist. Sometimes, the best we can do as teachers is to make our classrooms a safe haven while children are in our care.

Fifth, Follow the Child's Lead. Adults have their own agendas in mind, agendas that are quite different from the child's. It is well known that children who are successful at joining in other children's play have learned to merge with the activity that is taking place rather than disrupting it or simply asking, "Can I play?" A quiet moment when the child is at play is often the most opportune time to gain acceptance from that child. Particularly when children are aggressive, adults often treat these quiet moments as a "breather" and ignore the child at the very time he or she is most approachable. Coplaying, or merging with the child's spontaneous play, is a way to build trust between an adult and a child, because it is less intrusive, less threatening, and less controlling than other types of teacher-student interactions. Some of the themes in a self-control curricu-

A quiet moment when a child is at play is often a good time to approach the child and gain acceptance.

lum include learning to control impulses, follow school rules, manage stress, work in groups, and solve social problems (Henley, 1996).

Sixth, Learn How to Talk with Children About Inappropriate Behavior. Beginning teachers often do not know what to say when a child's behavior is inappropriate and surprising. The In-class Workshop at the end of this chapter will give you practice in speaking with young children in ways that promote appropriate behavior yet do not damage children's self-esteem.

Conflict Resolution and Classroom Communities

Beaty (1995) defines conflict as "interpersonal encounters needing a positive emotional resolution" (p. 5). Experts on conflict resolution have identified three main outcomes of conflict: (a) *domination,* in which one side is victorious over the other, (b) *compromise,* in which an agreement is reached through negotiation, and (c) *integration,* in which both sides get their way and neither side has to sacrifice anything (Graham, 1995). Thus, conflict does not have to be viewed as negative. Conflict can be looked upon as providing a creative opportunity for development, because children can learn to be more confident, independent, and competent when adults serve as facilitators (Dinwiddie, 1994). Ideally, conflict is resolved through a form of cooperative negotiation that leads to a mutually acceptable solution. This outcome, in which no one feels like the loser in the dispute and everyone wins, is referred to as conflict resolution. The current emphasis on conflict resolution is a response to concerns about violence and war in society (Slaby, Roedell, Arezzo, & Hendrix, 1995). As Lantieri (1995) puts it, "The world yearns for 'a new way of fighting,' one in which people can be strong without being mean" (p. 387). The goal of conflict resolution is to promote peace and equity as well as to build a sense of community in the classroom (Smith, 1993).

A classroom community is characterized by clearly understood goals, a sense of belonging to the group, effective communication, fair treatment, agreed-upon standards for behavior, opportunities to deal with ideas and values, care and concern for all members, and dynamic, interactive learning (Boyer, 1995; Jalongo, 1992). This attention to community is more than a pleasant approach to classroom dynamics. Recent research on the human brain and how it functions suggests that the social environments teachers build exert a powerful influence on learning for the following reasons (Sylwester, 1994):

1. Emotions simply exist, and they are resistant to change. Students *can* learn how and when to control emotions, but it is often useful to allow children some venting of their feelings before attempting to teach them to override their emotions using rational thought processes. A frequently overlooked part of learning to handle powerful emotions is acknowledging that they exist in the first place. Too often, teachers try to repress intense emotional responses in children to avoid unpleasantness. Often, the outcome is that these emotions erupt later with greater force, undermining the sense of community that is being built.

2. Activities that enable students to talk about their emotions, listen to their classmates' feelings, and think about the motivations of others teach children how to articulate emotions through words rather than lash out physically. One frequently recommended approach for talking about feelings is the class meeting (McClurg, 1998). Figure 9.6 offers some guidelines for making group decisions via a class meeting (Church, 1994).

FIGURE 9.6

Making group
decisions

Keys to Keeping Children Engaged in the Process

- **Respect and Tolerance.** Be tuned into children's interests and concerns. Teach them to be considerate of others.

    Example: If there is a new classroom pet, everyone is thinking, "Will I get a turn to feed the bunny? When can I expect a turn?"

- **Timing and Patience.** Adjust time devoted to discussion to children's developmental levels. Teach them to try to stick with a topic long enough to discuss it.

    Example: For preschoolers, just 5 minutes may be long enough. For third graders, it might be as much as 15 or 20 minutes.

- **Imagination and Leadership.** Use props to focus children's attention and harness their imaginations.

    Example: Allow a child to use play binoculars to scan the room for a problem area when children have failed to clean up. Give the group leader an object to wear (e.g., a special scarf) or to hold (e.g., a yarn pompom).

- **Cooperation and Communication.** Use activities that build a sense of cooperation and group unity.

    Example: Have children play a tossing, in which everyone grasps the edge of a round plastic tablecloth or a blanket and works together to bounce a ball in the center; hold hands and sway to the music while singing a spirited song together; invite children to demonstrate a new skill (such as skipping or whistling) and clap for them.

General Procedure

1. **Explain what a decision is.** Offer some concrete examples, such as choosing what to wear or eat for breakfast, then ask children to give some examples. Start with simple decisions, such as where to put a poster or what song to sing. Progress to more challenging decisions whereby children may need to give up something in order for things to work out, such as allocating computer time or taking a message to the office.

2. **Brainstorm and record ideas.** Keep a written record of what each child contributes to the discussion. It could be a list, a web of ideas, a prioritized list of activities, or a chart on an overhead transparency. Try breaking the group into smaller discussion groups that meet with an aide or parent volunteer so that everyone has a chance to speak.

3. **Decide what most children want to do.** Strive to arrive at agreement, but consider also that there usually are ways to keep some children from getting hurt feelings or being left out. For younger children, you may want to just look around to see if most children agree. For older children, you may want to take a vote. Teach children to respect one another's special talents, interests, and limitations.

4. **Follow through with the plan.** Let children implement their group decisions immediately so that they can see the positive outcomes of the group planning process.

SOURCE: Adapted from Making Decisions As a Group by E. B. Church, 1994, *Scholastic Early Childhood Today,* 8(8), pp. 40–41.

3. Emotional responses are affected by the context; thus, situations that draw out emotions and engage the entire body in life-like situations, such as simulations, role play, and cooperative projects, are most likely to help. When students practice the skills of community in real-world situations, they are actively constructing their knowledge about how to get along with others in a social situation.

4. Emotionally stressful school environments are counterproductive because they interfere with students' ability to learn. Learners must have a sense of control over their environment and develop self-esteem in order to maximize their learning power. Conversely, "a joyful classroom atmosphere makes students more apt to learn how to solve problems in potentially stressful situations" (Sylwester, 1994, p. 61).

Coping with Different Types of Conflict

Modern methods of early childhood conflict resolution are grounded in the belief that if teachers can guide the young child in learning to feel empowered, then the child will no longer have a need to do unkind things to others to bolster self-esteem. Stubbs (1992) contends, for example, that "Every unkind or harmful act committed on the planet has been done by someone who felt powerless in some way, and the stronger the feeling of powerlessness, the greater the unkindness or harm in the act" (p. 74). Additional support for implementing conflict resolution approaches comes from the humanistic psychology of Rollo May (1972). In his book *Power and Influence,* he contends that "Deeds of violence are performed largely by those who are trying to establish their self-esteem, to defend their self-image, and to demonstrate that they, too, are significant" (p. 23). Thus, a relationship exists among self-esteem, conflict, and conflict resolution. In thinking about the issue of conflict resolution, it is appropriate to ask yourself four questions:

1. When should I intervene in children's disputes?
2. When is it better to let children work it out for themselves?
3. Are the methods that I would use instinctively recommended by experts?
4. What new strategies can I incorporate into my conflict resolution repertoire?

In the following paragraphs, we list Beaty's (1995) eight basic types of conflict and provide recommendations for responding to each of these common situations.

Possession Disputes

Possession disputes occur when arguments arise over ownership. This is the number-one reason for conflict between children. Many teachers grow weary of intervening in these arguments and of the aggressive behaviors that sometimes accompany them. Here are some suggestions for avoiding possession disputes:

Analyze the Materials, Equipment, and Organization of Your Classroom. If a material is in short supply (e.g., one new wagon) you can *prevent* disputes from happening by establishing a policy in advance, such as having a sign-up sheet for turns, setting an egg timer for the length of the turns, and so forth.

Remember That Children Live and Play In Other Environments Where Materials Are Not Shared All That Much. They may be regularly prohibited from playing with an

When should an educator intervene in children's disputes?

older sibling's toys, for example, because they are "too little" to know how to use them. When children who are accustomed to such prohibitions arrive at school, they may welcome the opportunity to assert their possession over items in the classroom. Take the time to actively build children's understanding that the materials in the classroom are for everyone to use and enjoy.

Discourage the Practice of Bringing Items That Children Will Not Or Should Not Share to School. Parents sometimes send in an expensive toy or family heirloom, then they become upset if it is damaged. Likewise, children may bring in *transition objects*, items they are particularly fond of that usually offer some sort of tactile stimulation, such as a blanket, a teddy bear, or other stuffed toy. These items are called transition objects because they are a nonsocial substitute for the primary caregiver's physical closeness and are often used by children at bedtime or stressful times (Jalongo, 1987). Children should not be required to share these items; rather, they should learn to respect one another's right to have something that is not community property.

Attention Getting

Attention getting refers to using aggressive or inappropriate behavior to demand attention. At first, it might be difficult to imagine that *inappropriate behavior* would be used to gain attention, but negative responses may be preferable to no response at all to the child who is generally overlooked. Yet if children are told that they are bad or stupid or will never amount to anything, they may accept these pronouncements, internalize these low expectations, and act in ways consistent with the negative labels. Remember that children who want attention probably need it.

Greet Every Child Personally Every Day. Say hello and goodbye to every child every day. When you talk with children, let them hear their names in positive ways throughout the day, saying for example, "Kayla is making a very interesting dinosaur out of clay," "Tyler, you really like this book, don't you? Would you like to take it home and read it again?" or "Let's sing Carmy's verse for our song." Do not use children's names as a shorthand way of correcting inappropriate behavior by saying "Jenny!" to mean "no" or "stop" (Kostelnik, Stein, & Whiren, 1988).

Hear Children Out and Listen to What They Say As Well As How They Say It. Make it a habit to have at least one more extended interaction with every child every day, even if that means chatting with them at recess or at lunch. Because young children are fairly inexperienced users of language, it is essential to listen not only to children's words, but also, to the feelings that underlie those words (Jalongo, 1996). Be patient when the communication is not completely clear and give the child as much undivided attention as possible. Make comments that really let the child know you have understood and care about what he or she has to say.

Identify the Behavior That Is Unacceptable and Why It Is Occurring. Early childhood educators need to develop more skillful ways of talking to young children, such as, "Cherie, keep the blocks on the floor. We do not throw blocks in preschool because someone could get hurt," "Terri and Sheila, can you figure out a way that Min can join the hopscotch game?" and "Miguel, I can't let you push Crystal down. Look at her face. She doesn't like it when you pounce on her like a tiger." Try to be matter-of-fact about these things and state them plainly and concretely. The teasing sarcasm that peers may find humorous is entirely inappropriate for the young child. If you say, "Oh, *that* was a really great idea" when a child does something wrong, the child is apt to be confused by the inconsistency between your words and the situation.

Power Struggles

Power struggles refer to conflicts that result when children want to be first or to compel others to play "their way." Remember that children are inexperienced in negotiating and that part of your job is to teach them how to negotiate.

Try Making Suggestions That Will Lead to a Mutually Beneficial Conclusion. If two children are arguing because they both want to play the mother and neither wants to play the baby, you might suggest that they *both* be mothers and use dolls as babies.

Reassure Children That They Will Get a Turn and Make Sure That They Do. Often, children's insistence on being first comes from repeated experiences with the teacher discontinuing an activity before everyone has a turn. Even though it is necessary to stop an activity before children get bored with it, you can let them know that the activity will be available during free play or repeated throughout the week.

Keep Track of Who Gets a Turn At Something. Busy teachers often forget who had a turn at something and, if they call on the same person again, the children may protest, "But he already *had* a turn!" One way to avoid this situation is to make a set of magnetic cards with the children's names on them and use them to keep track of turns when it seems particularly important to do so. You will probably want to use a bulletin board to indicate whose turn it is to water plants, distribute snacks, and so forth. If you want to monitor the number of children at a learning center, a choice board that puts their names next to a drawing that represents each center can help to manage the flow of traffic to and from centers.

Personality Clashes

Personality clashes occur when children reject one another because of incompatible temperaments or jealousy. One typical personality clash that occurs often in early childhood settings is conflict between a group of children who want to play quietly and a group of children who want to be more boisterous. Often, the boisterous children will interrupt play, knock down a block structure, or leave the scene of quiet play in disarray. Personality clashes also occur when children differ markedly in their ways of interacting, as in when a child protests, "She always wants to be the boss."

Be Scrupulously Fair in Everything That You Do. Avoid competitions and prizes that leave some children feeling like winners and others like losers. Young children do not clearly understand games with rules and can be expected to react with tears or frustration to competitive situations (see the Featuring Families feature at the end of this section). When working with the very young, it is better to emphasize participation and effort rather than competition, which leads to jealousy.

Clearly Designate Quiet and Noisy Areas of Your Classroom. Use bookcases or other large objects to demarcate a quiet area and prohibit wild chasing throughout every corner of the room. Do not assume that children will understand the rules by words alone. Try role playing. For example, you can ask a child to get on a tricycle, then whisper in his ear to yell and ride through the housekeeping area; this is followed by a group discussion about why this behavior is not acceptable.

Set Up Situations In Which the Children's Differences In Personality Represent an Advantage. For example, a timid child might be paired with a more outgoing child on a field trip so that more questions are asked and ideas are discussed. Dramatizations that enable children to "try on" different personalities, such as play with puppets, can also help them to identify with classmates whose characteristic style of interaction is quite different from their own. A shy child may delight in assuming the persona of a sassy and mischievous puppet, for example.

Group-entry Disputes

Group-entry disputes occur when children try to join the ongoing play of another group. Well-known kindergarten teacher, author, and researcher Vivian Paley (1992) considered the following to be one of the most important rules in her classroom: "You can't say you can't play." In her book by the same title, Paley discusses how she instituted this rule to deal with the problem of insiders and outsiders and to counteract prejudice.

Make It Clear That Everyone Is Expected to Get Along with Everyone Else. Children can identify with being excluded because they are "too little" to do something. Children's books, such as *Bailey Goes Camping* (Henkes, 1985), *You'll Soon Grow Into Them, Titch* (Hutchins, 1983), and *Much Bigger Than Martin* (Kellogg, 1976), can be used to spark a conversation about the pain and anger that are caused by exclusion. Using this universal experience of young children can then serve as a basis for making it clear that it is not acceptable to treat anyone in the class as an outcast. Accompany a child who has been excluded, saying brightly, "Make room for Juanita! She wants to play house too," or "Don't forget, no closed games in second grade."

Model the Correct Way of Approaching a Group That Is Playing. Research suggests that the most successful strategy is to join in without disrupting the ongoing play or asking permission. With preschoolers or primary grades children, you may want to involve them in role-play situations that will give them practice in avoiding group-entry disputes.

Aggressive Play

Aggressive play is conflict that is caused by boisterous play, such as superhero play. Young children are attracted to superheroes because these figures are supremely powerful, and young children are not. Virtually all of the important decisions in a young child's life are made by others—what to do, where to go, when to do various things—so it is not surprising that superhuman characters who are even more powerful than adults are particularly appealing to children.

Set Reasonable Limits on Play. If children engage in a persecutor-victim theme such as wild animals chasing their prey, and the child identified as the prey is clearly unhappy about it, then it is time to intervene. If groups of children go crashing through a quiet area, disturbing those who are at play, then it is time to stop the theme.

If a Small Group Is Responsible for the Aggression, Temporarily Disband the Group. Three preschoolers who decided that they wanted to give karate chops and kicks to others started running through the Head Start classroom during free play, a time when children are free to choose centers and materials. Within moments, three children were crying or shouting. Their teacher knelt down next to the boys and said calmly, "I see that your friends do not want karate chops and kicks. I want each one of you to choose a different center . . . Okay, Rickie has chosen to observe our class rabbit and draw in the journal. That leaves . . . What will you choose, Kayla?" and so forth.

Teasing and Name Calling

Teasing and name calling are disputes that result when names that are hurtful or embarrassing to one child are used by another (National Association for the Education of Young Children, 1996). Although some insensitive teachers dismiss such behavior as an inescapable part of growing up, remember that you are a significant adult in children's lives and, as such, you can influence children for the better.

Model Respect, Caring, and Patience. As everyone knows, children are more influenced by the behaviors they observe in others than by their words. Simply saying, "That's not very nice" is not sufficient, because it does not specify what is objectionable.

Many children's books depict teasing and bullies and model coping strategies.

Be concrete: "Jason, calling people names like 'stupid' makes them sad. Please do not use that word when talking to our friends in this class."

Use Children's Literature That Depicts Teasing and Bullies. Many children's books model how children can cope with these difficult situations and resolve conflict (see Luke & Myers, 1994).

Shifting Blame

Shifting blame occurs when children deny responsibility for their actions and try to shift the blame to someone or something else.

Make It Clear That Telling the Truth and Admitting a Mistake Are Expected. Young children are at the stage of moral development where they want to avoid punishment. If your punishments consist of setting things right and making restitution rather than harsh discipline, this will tend to support the development of self-discipline. It also is helpful to admit to your own mistakes and say how you will correct them.

Give Children a Chance to Offer an Explanation for What Happened Before Rushing Into a Decision About How to Respond. Ask children to offer suggestions about what might solve the problem. For example, "I see that there are Cuisenaire rods all over the floor where Kahlesha and Nicole were working on their math problems. What could the two of you do to have the materials ready for the next math class?"

Now that you have examined Beaty's eight different types of conflict that typically occur in classrooms, try to explain how each one is a child's effort to say, in effect, "I am important."

FEATURING FAMILIES

COMMON CONFLICT SCENARIOS

The following is a column that appeared in a parent newsletter.

THE BIG D—DISCIPLINE

One definition of discipline is to guide or to teach self-control. To better explain how I guide children's behavior in my class, I will describe a common conflict scenario. Then I will look at two different responses and what the child might learn from each one.

Scenario: Bill, Robbie, and Samantha are playing a board game together. The game requires children to take turns. Whoever gets to the last space on the gameboard first is the winner. After several turns, Robbie finds that he is falling behind the other two players. At that point, he overturns the gameboard and sends the pieces flying. "That's a stupid game!" he yells out. Bill and Samantha are confused and upset. As the teacher, I approach the table. What would you do?

Response #1: Robbie is told that he is not using the materials correctly and is to blame for stopping the game. He is told that his behavior is wrong and that he has to pick up the pieces and apologize to his friends.

What would this action teach? (a) Adults are in charge of all the rules, so children always need to turn to adults to be the referees; (b) Feelings that caused the outburst are not discussed; (c) Saying that you are sorry settles conflict (even if you don't mean it); and (d) Robbie has lost by being declared the troublemaker, so he will probably try to find an opportunity to be the winner (for example, by tattling on someone else), or he will accept the idea that he is basically bad and make little effort to change that judgment.

Response #2: The adult approaches the children and asks what has happened while she gently touches each child's shoulder to bring them into a small circle. Each child is given a turn to say what he or she thinks happened and how he or she felt about it. The adult summarizes the comments and states the problem, "You were all playing the game and now the game is over with all the pieces on the floor. It seems that Robbie wanted to stop the game because he decided that he didn't like it and didn't know what to do." The adult then asks if there are other ways to solve this problem. The children suggest that you could leave the game just by saying you wanted to leave, removing your game piece, and going on to another activity. That way, the other children who liked the game could continue. The children also decided to pick up the pieces and restart the game. Bill and Samantha asked Robbie if he wanted to play this time.

What would this action teach? (a) Everyone has feelings, which should be respected; (b) There are many solutions to a problem, and some are better than others; (c) Adults are not the only ones who can solve problems; children can participate in and practice this process; and (d) Adults can be counted on to guide children's problem solving.

Young children need to learn that feelings are okay, but that how you express your feelings is not always okay. They need to develop skill and confidence in their ability to handle their own problems in socially acceptable ways rather than being branded as "bad." They need to learn how to live with others and work things out instead of constantly running to adults to serve as judge and jury. Think about how you might apply the second type of response to some of the behaviors that you like least. Imagine a long car trip during which two siblings are fighting about space in the back seat. How might the first response actually fuel the arguments? How might the second response build a truce?

Guiding Children to Appropriate Behavior

When you begin teaching, you will no doubt wonder what your colleagues who have such well-behaved classes do to make this happen. Yet even if you were afforded the opportunity to observe in these classrooms, your questions about discipline might remain unanswered. Here is what one educator who visited the classrooms of outstanding teachers to study behavior management observed: "I rarely got the chance to see these teachers work their magic with misbehaving children because it seemed as though the children in their classes almost never misbehaved. Evidently, I just happened to show up on unusually harmonious days—or else I wasn't staying long enough. After a while, however, it dawned on me that this pattern couldn't be explained just by my timing. These classrooms were characterized by a chronic absence of problems. . . . During my visits, I've been struck not only by what such teachers are doing, and how successful it is, but by what they are *not* doing. They are not concentrating on being effective disciplinarians. This is partly because they have better things to do, and those better things are preventing problems from developing in the first place" (Kohn, 1996, pp. xi–xii).

Most teachers are uncomfortable with emotional outbursts from children, angry disputes between or among children, and power struggles with children. Part of becoming a professional is responding to such situations differently from the way the average person might. Skillful teachers have learned to separate the behavior from the child, to be objective and not take it personally. Mainly, teachers fear such conflict situations for one of several reasons.

- *Teachers fear a loss of control over the classroom environment.* A chaotic classroom is the nightmare of teachers, both figuratively and literally. As one of our students expressed it, "I couldn't sleep the night before school started. I had a dream that I was teaching and the kids weren't listening to me at all. They were running around the room, throwing things and screaming. Did you ever have a nightmare like that?" The answer is "Yes!" Even experienced teachers have anxieties about children's behavior in school. Teachers are correct in assuming that an unruly group of children will reflect unfavorably on them in the culture of the school, where maintaining order and quiet frequently is prized. Moreover, a classroom that is chaotic is obvious to anyone who happens to pass by. The report that a classroom is out of control can quickly be communicated throughout a school or center.

- *Teachers fear that they will say the wrong thing.* When a tearful child says, "My grandmother doesn't have any hair. She gets chemo. She has cancer," what should a teacher say? Many teachers are so uncomfortable dealing with tragic situations that they change the subject, say nothing, or offer some formulaic response, such as, "Don't worry, she'll be all right." The first thing to remember with young children is that it may not be necessary to *say* anything. It might be better to gently touch the child's face, give a sympathetic look, be a little more understanding throughout the day, and talk over the situation with the family and a counselor rather than trying to give a speech.

- *Teachers fear a loss of face with the group.* Suppose that a child is directed to sit down and completely ignores the direction. Many teachers worry that such defiance will be contagious and infect the rest of the group with a spirit of rebellion when they see a classmate "getting away with" noncompliance. Many teachers find it helpful to get down to the child's eye level, make eye contact, and speak directly to the child. Until you are certain that the child has heard and understood, you should not assume defiance.

These common concerns help to explain why teachers view conflict so negatively. Actually, conflict is like stress in that it is inherently neither good nor bad. Stress results from anything that requires an extra effort of adaptation, including good things such as a job promotion and getting married. Likewise, conflict is "an interpersonal encounter requiring a positive emotional resolution" and can be viewed as an opportunity to learn about one's self in relationship to others (Beaty, 1995, p. 2). Learning to deal with conflict in a calm, confident manner is an important part of becoming an early childhood practitioner.

After reading this section on coping with conflict, you might have some reservations about or objections to the approach. Your first thoughts might be that it is too permissive, too time consuming, and too dependent upon verbalization skills. Why not just demand obedience and reprimand children to show them that you are a strict teacher? Why not just take the often-repeated advice to be somber at first in your interactions with children and "Don't smile until Christmas," as the old saying goes? The real reason for taking the time and investing the effort is because this method really teaches children how to get along with others, so it will become a way of life. You can no doubt remember situations in your own life as a child in school in which your teacher left the room for a few moments and the classroom instantly went out of control. When children rely on all of the control to come from outside (extrinsic) rather than from inside (intrinsic), they frequently grow up to be adults who have difficulty monitoring their own behavior and who need someone else to direct them in order to work.

One of the more controversial aspects of conflict resolution has to do with young children's capacity for responding to other children's suffering. Many educators who have some familiarity with Jean Piaget's cognitive-developmental theory would argue that young children are too embedded in their own perspective—too egocentric, to use Piaget's terminology—to take the perspective of another child. But Patricia Ramsey (1991),

ASK the Expert Edyth Wheeler on Conflict Resolution

Common Questions and Concerns About Conflict Resolution

Edyth Wheeler

1. Don't I have to prevent children from engaging in conflicts in order to create a peaceful classroom environment?

Most teachers will agree that conflicts occur naturally among young children. Some may be surprised to know that children actually learn important social and cognitive skills as they engage in conflicts with peers. During these interactions, they develop logical thinking, perspective taking, and problem solving, and they practice rich and often complex language. When teachers begin to think of conflict as a natural phenomenon and of children's ability to manage conflict as a developing capability, they will approach this area just as they do other areas of children's development, such as language and motor ability. The teacher's goal, then, is to support children's learning as they work through conflict situations.

2. Won't conflicts lead to aggressive behavior?

Conflict is an interaction in which children object to each other's actions; in other words, a mutual opposition or disagreement. Generally, children engaged in a conflict are trying to resolve the issue at hand. Most conflicts do not involve aggressive behaviors. However, aggression, which is defined as an unpro- voked attack, can precipitate retaliation. Conflicts, too, can develop in different ways. As teachers observe children's conflicts, they will decide whether the interaction is a constructive conflict, through which children learn, or a destructive conflict, which escalates in intensity as tempers flare and frustration rises.

3. How can teachers create a peaceful classroom and help children resolve conflicts?

It has been pointed out that "peace is not the absence of conflict" (Wichert, 1989, p. xi). A peaceful classroom depends on two conditions: first, that children want to resolve conflicts; and, second, that they have the ability to do so. The first condition can occur in a classroom that is a caring community where adults and children value and demonstrate cooperation, kindness, respect, and concern for others. Teachers can create the second condition by providing children with words to use in conflict situations and by adding curriculum experiences that encourage children's collaboration, perspective taking, and generation of alternative solutions to problems.

4. When should I step in to guide children, and when should I allow children to work things out on their own?

Children are often able to resolve conflicts without adult help. There are two things teachers can look for as they decide whether to intervene: If children have been playing together before the conflict begins, and if they are using reasoning and negotiation during their conflict, they are more likely to settle their dispute agreeably. Teachers who observe these conditions would be wise to give children the opportunity to manage the conflict themselves.

5. How can teachers create a caring classroom where conflicts are resolved agreeably?

I suggest an approach that I call "a three-layer cake." The bottom layer, the foundation, is the teacher's commitment to a peaceful classroom. The middle layer is made up of

340

curriculum ideas and activities that promote prosocial behavior and conflict resolution. The top layer contains strategies for children and teachers to use when conflicts occur. The icing on the cake is the family-school connection.

Here are a few suggestions for making your "three-layer cake." First, the bottom layer: Demonstrate your commitment to a caring classroom. Model prosocial behavior. Adults can be powerful models of both positive and negative words and actions. Be aware of the pervasive prosocial and empathetic behavior that happens naturally among children. I ask teachers and parents or caregivers to watch for acts of caring and kindness. Acknowledge these acts to children with words of encouragement.

The middle layer: Curriculum elements to build a caring classroom community include morning meetings, peer sharing and supportive routines in whole-language classrooms, cooperative activities and games, and discussions of good children's literature. We often see words such as *respect* and *consideration* on posters in classrooms, but without discussion of exactly what these words mean to children and how they are to act to show respect and consideration, the posters on display have little meaning.

The top layer: Begin by observing children in conflict and resist the temptation to step in right away. Allow for as much child control of the outcome as possible. Respect children's mutual decision making, even if it is not the solution you would have recommended. You may want to encourage children to use more complex reasoning and negotiation through scaffolding. If you observe a conflict that is escalating and may lead to violence, do intervene and allow children to calm down before guiding them to resolution.

The icing on the cake: Remember the importance of ongoing family-school communication to develop a mutual understanding of conflict issues and strategies and to provide continuity from home to school. Additional strategies include school visits from family and community members and joint workshops for families and teachers.

6. Are these expectations for conflict-resolution skills for all children?

Very young children are capable of empathy and understanding for others. As they learn to communicate effectively, they can resolve conflicts. Children as young as 3 years old have intervened as spontaneous peer mediators to help others. In inclusive and diverse classrooms, guiding children to resolve conflicts is a powerful tool. Experiences with those who are different in some way from themselves help children develop the perspective taking needed for conflict resolution. In turn, the perspective taking learned through conflict helps children understand others. In supporting children's learning about conflict resolution, teachers need to be aware of culture, language, and socioeconomic factors. Concepts of sharing and ownership, interaction and language styles, and social and cognitive development play a part in the issues, strategies, and outcomes of children's conflicts. As with any area of learning and development, teachers will provide appropriate guidance for individual children according to their particular needs. In some schools, a few children are selected to become peer mediators. It is important for teachers to communicate a belief that all children can, and should, be peacemakers.

7. Will what we do in classrooms carry over to the world outside the classroom?

Young children live in a world of widespread violence. They witness angry reactions to disagreements among family members, friends, strangers, and nations.

They are exposed to violence through first-hand experiences and through the pervasive presence of the media. Teachers, parents, and caregivers can play a vital role in helping children work toward peaceful resolution of their conflicts. In schools and classrooms, there is a growing movement to incorporate peace education and violence prevention. In your own school, share your caring classroom approach so that children may continue to practice peaceful conflict resolution from one year to the next. Strong family-school partnerships will help children bring their conflict-resolution skills from the classroom to the neighborhood. Communities can work to support prosocial children's television programming. As early childhood professionals, we face a critical, challenging, and yet promising undertaking, an opportunity to help children make a difference in their world, both now, as children, and later, as adults.

Edyth James Wheeler is an assistant professor of early childhood education, Towson University, Maryland.

a leading expert on young children's peer relationships, argues that "because even very young children resonate to others' emotions, children can empathize and communicate on an emotional plane before they are consciously aware of others' perspectives" (p. 18).

Beginning teachers often err on the opposite side and are too permissive. This sometimes occurs because the teacher draws upon his or her knowledge of being responsible for one child, such as a sibling or a child whom he or she babysat. But working with a group of children as their teacher is different from the casual style of interaction that characterizes these familiar situations. You are responsible for promoting every child's development and facilitating every child's learning. One child-care provider we know offers a good example of this. Kurt really enjoyed being in the company of children and had had many prior experiences supervising young children for his family and friends. When he decided to work as an aide in the summer to gain more experience, he interacted with the children in the same way that he had previously, cheerfully teasing them with remarks such as, "Hey, buddy! C'mon over here. Where'd you get that haircut? Are you having a bad hair day? I think so!" and then tousling the child's hair or roughhousing with the children, particularly the boys. Kurt was completely shocked when the other teachers asked to speak to him about his unsatisfactory work performance and the gender bias that was evident in his behavior. Clearly, Kurt had selected the wrong "script" for how to interact with young children in a child-care center. This does not mean that he was incapable of becoming an effective caregiver, only that he would have to make significant changes in his customary way of responding to the children in order to become their teacher. He would have to learn to resist acting like one of the children himself. Fortunately, Kurt was able to admit that his current style was "headed for disaster," because the children had begun to test the limits of how far they could go and some had insulted and even hit him. Kurt had to begin all over again and set new standards for behavior that were not so permissive. He was able to do so with time, training, and experience.

Conclusion

There is no question that violence is escalating and that some children live in places that adults would find frightening. Although this exposure to violence in the media, in families, and in the community is appalling, it is an unrealistic goal to eliminate violence altogether. Interestingly, "the word violence comes from the Latin word *vis*, meaning 'life force'. . . in violence, the thrust of life is making itself visible. It would be a mistake to approach violence with any simple idea of getting rid of it" (Moore, 1992, p. 126). As an early childhood educator, your role is to guide children in finding socially constructive outlets for that "life force." Far too often, children arrive at school with a long list of negative labels that are based on the situations of their families, their communities, or both. But children do not get to choose to whom they are born, and even the most dedicated educator cannot alter the desperate life circumstances in which increasing numbers of young children in America live. As Marian Wright Edelman (1992), the director of the Children's Defense Fund, reminds us, "We need to stop punishing children because we don't like their parents. The truth is we are punishing ourselves in escalating welfare, crime and lost workers and productivity by failing to value, invest in and protect all of our children" (pp. 45–46).

Early childhood practitioners *do* have the power to make centers and schools a haven, a safe community where children can feel accepted and learn valuable lessons. One of our most important roles is to help children understand who they are and how they can become admirable human beings.

One Child, Three Perspectives: *Earl's Disruptive Behavior*

Earl is a first grader who already has a police record. It seems that he was standing in his front yard pitching rocks as cars passed by, and one of the rocks hit a driver's windshield and broke it, causing an accident. At school, Earl is frequently in trouble despite the fact that he has the attention of the school psychologist, a foster grandparent, a social services caseworker, his teacher, and a student teacher. Within a one-hour period, the following observational notes were taken on Earl.

E. arrives at school in blue jeans, cowboy boots, and a house key chained to his belt. He is excited about a badge his father gave him that reads, "Kiss me if you love truckers." E. sits down at the desk, looks at the girl sitting next to him, and remarks, "Your eyes are really blue. Do you wear contacts?" The girl frowns and says, "No!" Then she turns away. E. says, "Well, I do. See?" and blinks his eyes rapidly. Then he says, "Look, I can stick this pin in my skin and not bleed—want to see me do it?" "No. That's disgusting," the girl responds. With that, E. slides the point of the pin under his skin and demonstrates that the pin is now attached to his finger. "Want to see me do it again?" E. asks. Again, a no. At this point, the teacher takes the pin away from E. and puts it in her desk drawer.

Time for partner reading. Children go to various corners of the room, arrange plastic tub chairs side-by-side, or stretch out on the floor. Most settle down and begin reading. E. stacks chairs on top of a table, and just as he is ready to climb on, the student teacher stops him, reminding him that chairs stay on the floor. E. walks by the restroom and sees two boys, absorbed in a book. "Hey, man! Get out of my chair," E. says to the boys. The boys look at him blankly and E. continues, "If you ain't outta my chair when I come back, you and me's gonna have words." E. takes a few steps away, then walks back, saying, "I mean it, man. That's my favorite chair." When E. emerges from the restroom, he challenges the boys to a fight. The student teacher directs E. to wash his hands and sit down. E. complies, then walks up to the teacher's desk, puts on some hand lotion, and pulls the desk drawer open to look at his badge. The teacher asks what he is doing and E. replies, "Nothing."

Time for the children to write in their journals. E. stares at the paper, then begins to wail loudly that he doesn't know how to write, puts his head down on the desk and moves his head and shoulders slightly as if sobbing. He glances around to see if anyone has taken notice. The student teacher kneels down next to E. and reminds him of some of the things that he might write, such as his name, letters of the alphabet, stop, no, *etc. With that, E. brightens. He says, "I want to copy the words off the badge that my dad gave me. My dad is a trucker. When he's on the road, I can take care of myself."*

Earl's teacher says, "Earl is a troublemaker. I have to watch him like a hawk. When he was absent for a couple of days, my classroom was peaceful. I have tried everything to get him to behave, but nothing seems to work," while Earl's student teacher says, "Based upon comments that Earl has made, he is left by himself much of the time since his mother abandoned him. I know that he is hurting and wants so much to be accepted, but he is often rejected by his peers."

The social worker says, "We are currently investigating Earl's case, and it is clear that Earl is neglected. If this situation continues, Earl's father may lose custody."

The foster grandparent says, "Earl is a very needy little boy. I hear all of these horror stories about him, but whenever I work with him one-to-one, he never gives me any real problems. I enjoy the time we spend together."

REACT:	In what ways are the perspectives of these adults alike? How do their approaches to meeting Earl's needs vary?
RESEARCH:	Read several articles at the library about children with difficult family circumstances. What recommendations were made?
REFLECT:	What might be the underlying reasons for the differences in the responses to Earl's situation? Which perspective do you identify most strongly with, and why?

Role-playing Ways of Talking with Children

Following are some examples of early childhood professionals speaking with young children in ways that can effectively guide their behavior. Try writing several of your own examples and role-playing them for the class.

- "Don't worry, everyone will get a turn. I will put the new baby carriage in the housekeeping area for everyone to use. Remember, only five people at a time in the center."

- "Look at Gita's face, Charley. I don't think she likes to get bear hugs, do you? Let's see if we can think of a better way to let Gita know that she is your friend."

- "Second graders, you all know that even though we have new gravel on the playground, it is not for throwing. Why?"

- "It bothers me when I hear you call your friends at school stupid, Mikey. When you are playing together, you need to talk things over so that it is more fun."

- "Yes, you can write your own name on your painting, Erica. But Kira is only 2 years old, and she needs help writing her name."

- "Tony, when the other third graders made their model of a zoo out of boxes and paper, they did not want anyone to ruin their work. How can you help them feel less angry with you for messing up their project?"

- "Trish, please don't yell across the room. Walk right up to your friends and speak softly."

- "On this walk, we will be looking for signs of fall. It will be very important for everyone to stay together and hold your partner's hand. That way, nobody will get lost."

- "Our custodian, Mr. Lowell, was very disappointed to see our classroom so messy yesterday when school was over. He had to work much harder cleaning our room and was very tired. How can we do better today? What could we do to let Mr. Lowell know that we are sorry?"

- "Please stay in our story circle until story time is over. Lamont, you are part of our group. Come back and join us."

- "I noticed that Jerry and Sandy were at the tape recorder listening to books. Now it is time to put the tapes away in the right place on the shelf until tomorrow."

- "Brad, I can't let you kick other people or give them karate chops, even if you are playing. Remember our rule? It's not okay to hit. How can you still play Power Rangers without hurting anyone?"

- "Wipe your brush on the side of the jar, like this. That way your paint won't run down your picture when you are at the easel."

- "I know that it is hard to wait for your turn, Bahar. Let's look at the list on the wall together. You just had a turn to go get the milk. We can mark on the calendar the day that it will be your turn again, but don't forget that there are lots of different jobs to do in first grade."

- "No putting chairs on the tables or standing on the tables, please. Every first grader has a chair to sit in and chairs have to stay on the floor."

- "Remember the rule about using the slide: one person at a time gets to stand on the top step."

- "I put the apple juice in this little plastic measuring cup so that you can pour your own. Pour it very slowly, like this, and watch to see how much will fill the cup. Who would like to try it?"

- "I see that your art project is starting to fall apart. Can I help you fix it?"
- "Some children were playing at the water fountain and got the floor all wet. Who has a good idea about how to solve this problem?"

Applying What You Have Learned

In *So This Is Normal Too?* Hewitt (1995) identifies several common developmental issues that early childhood educators typically encounter. For each of the following incidents, consider everything that you have learned from this chapter and try to formulate a response with your group. Refer to the guidance continuum in Figure 9.5 to identify a variety of strategies.

1. **Separating from Parents and Caregivers**
   A teenage father brings his 4-year-old son to class on the first day of nursery school. When the child begins to cry, the father says, "Stop being such a wimp! You're embarrassing me. Be a man."

2. **Seeking Attention and Tattling**
   A teacher is on playground duty and hears the following comments from children. "Teacher, look at me!" Gerri calls out while on climbing equipment. "Ms. B., look at what I can do. I can pump my legs and swing really high."
   "Ms. B., didn't you tell us not to climb the fence? Look at Jason and Miguel. They're climbing the fence."
   "It was my turn next on the seesaw and Charlene pushed in front of me."

3. **Telling Tales**
   Cheryl is talking to her kindergarten classmates about what she did over the summer. She says, "Me and my mama went to Disneyworld and we saw Mickey and Donald and then we ate french fries and ice cream and . . ." "Uh uh," says Denny, "I live on her street and she didn't go nowhere this summer. She was right here all the time."

4. **Taking Turns and Sharing**
   Two toddlers are playing on the carpeted floor of their day-care provider's home. They both want to use the plastic vacuum cleaner at the same time, and one child knocks the other to the floor.

5. **Having Tantrums and Swearing**
   A group of first graders is singing together, and the teacher asks if there are any special requests. Geoff wants to teach the group a song and begins to sing "Frosty the Snowman," but he forgets the lyrics. When the other children grow restless, he becomes increasingly frustrated. He scowls, turns bright red, and then screams loudly, "Just shut up, all of you. I can't think." Then he stomps away from the group and yells over his shoulder, "Assholes!"

6. **Behaving Aggressively**
   Within a first-grade classroom, children are busy working at learning centers. Suddenly, screams are heard from inside the restroom. As the teacher scans the room, she notices that Danny is nowhere in sight. She approaches the restroom door and asks, "Danny are you in there? Are you okay?" In response, she hears screeches of laughter and Danny's voice singing, "D-A-N-N-Y, Danny! Danny! Danny!" The teacher recalls the previous week, when Danny bit a fourth grader, and two days earlier, when he decided to "be a bowling ball" and roll down the hallway ramp. She knocks on the door again, saying, "Danny, please come out. Other children need to use the restroom. You are missing your play time." Silence. Soon the first-grade teacher hears scribbling, followed by a tearing sound. She unlocks the door to find Danny standing in the newly decorated restroom, surrounded by crayon drawings and strips of masking tape that he has put all over the new wallpaper (Conrad, 1997).

7. **Toileting or Eating Problems**

   A professional couple brings their son to preschool to meet his teacher. The boy is 3 1/2 years old but is not toilet trained. When they discuss this issue, the parents say that they do not want to toilet train him until he is ready. While they are talking, their son goes over into the corner, squats down, and has a bowel movement in his diaper. He then sticks his finger inside his diaper to show the parents that his diaper needs to be changed. Later, when the boy begins at the preschool, a group of children begin to ridicule him for still wearing diapers.

8. **Gaining Acceptance from Peers**

   Liddie has become the "little mother" of the child-care center, according to her teachers. Yet observations of Liddie suggest that her attentions are frequently rebuffed by peers. After a child falls and scrapes his knee, for example, Liddie follows him around with a wet tissue and persistently attempts to press the tissue against the scrape. "Get away from me, Liddie!" the boy finally shouts, "That hurts!"

A Problem-solving Strategy for Practitioners

Now try applying the following problem-solving strategy (Tobin, 1991) to each of the situations just described. Work in small groups, then be prepared to share your ideas with the total group.

1. What bothers you about the behavior?

2. Does it seem like typical behavior or something unusual?

3. What are your hypotheses about possible reasons underlying the behavior?

4. On your own, consider possible teacher responses, both good and bad. Then try to formulate a statement that reflects a skilled way of talking to the child and his or her family.

5. As a group, choose the most effective statement.

6. What might be the intended or unintended outcomes of your choice?

Exploring Your Role in Supporting Families

Early childhood educators need to identify with and respect families despite the fact that perspectives on childhood may differ drastically; we need to collaborate with families in ways that place children's needs uppermost and optimize growth and learning socially, physically, emotionally, cognitively, and artistically; and we need to build mutual trust and respect, particularly for those families who have had negative experiences with the educational system. To accomplish these goals, we must confront our own biases, embrace diversity, respect the knowledge that families have about children, and willingly share power. In every situation early childhood educators face, the overarching purpose is how to respond in ways that serve children's best interests.

—Nancy L. Briggs, Mary Renck Jalongo, and Lisbeth Brown, 1997, p. 56

Learning Outcomes

✔ Be introduced to the parent involvement traditions in the field of early childhood education

✔ Examine goals and models of home-school communication, collaboration, and support

✔ Recognize the early childhood professional's unique role in promoting home-school collaboration

✔ Learn general techniques and practical strategies for building mutual trust and respect with families

✔ Apply knowledge of school-community partnerships to various early childhood settings

✔ Identify exemplary practices in parent involvement and model programs for working with families

Meet the Teachers

Theo Spewock has been responsible for coordinating a program in her school district for many years, and she has become convinced that they need to establish communication with parents and families *before* children are struggling in school. She coordinates a national, federally funded program that provides learning support services to children who are experiencing difficulty with reading and mathematics. The program is called Title I. One of Spewock's many brainstorms was successful in connecting the family and school more closely: She decided to initiate contact with parents as soon as the babies were born, while the mothers were still in the hospital. After that, she communicated directly with the family every year on the child's birthday until the child entered school. Each year, all of the families in the school district received a birthday packet containing information about the child's development, appropriate learning activities, local services and agencies, and—with some financial support from the community—a picture book to begin building a home library for the child.

Ms. Cole is a teacher in a program for infants and toddlers with vision impairments. She works on a team consisting of the child's parent(s), the program director, an infant development specialist, and an eye-care professional to conduct a thorough assessment of each child. The team wrote learning outcomes for Kirsten, an 18-month-old who is blind. As Ms. Cole astutely observed, "Over the years, I have worked with dozens of parents who are grieving about their children's visual impairments and who feel helpless. I am confident that this program can offer needed support to Kirsten and her family." Some of the outcomes that have been identified include teaching Kirsten to feed herself, move around the classroom safely, and develop listening skills through recorded music. All of these goals for Kirsten are combined with a course of action, periodic review, and parent reports of progress into a document called an individual family service plan (IFSP). As part of this plan, Ms. Cole, her team members, and Kirsten's single-parent mother participate in "putting the services where the children are" by coordinating early intervention, developing an instructional plan, arranging services, and meeting periodically together.

Ms. Latall is the director of a private school for children from ages 3 to 8. Several years ago, the parents of children enrolled in a half-day public-school program for special needs preschoolers invited her to a parent meeting to inquire about having their students join hers for an afternoon of music or story time. Ms. Latall's immediate response was, "We can do better than having visitors who drop in for special occasions!" and, with the assistance of one of her parents and the school-based special education coordinator, a new program was begun. She called it Together in Play, or TIP. Two afternoons a week, Ms. Latall's preschoolers joined with a group of children with disabilities. Ms. Latall invited one of the student's mothers, who was blind, to be her aide in TIP. Together the children initiated the study of topics that interested them, including birds and snow. Meanwhile, the teachers and aide planned several experiences that were intended to help children understand disabilities, such as wearing bulky ski gloves and attempting to pick up small objects to simulate the grasping difficulties associated with cerebral palsy and wearing a pair of old plastic sunglasses scribbled with permanent marker to simulate a vision impairment. During the time that the children were together, the parents met to share ideas and focus on common concerns.

COMPARE:	What are some commonalities among these three teachers, even though they are working with different families and in different situations?
	Working with parents including parents in child's educational development
CONTRAST:	How do these teachers think about families? How would you characterize the outlook of each one?
	I think the parents think the families should be included in their educational development and it also helps because it involves both parties
CONNECT:	What made the greatest impression on you, and how will you incorporate this view of families into your teaching?
	That the parents and Teachers were able to effectively work together. They were all working toward the same goal the success of the children. I would incorporate these views by meeting with the parents on a regular basis and discuss goals for the child

Understanding Contemporary Families

What is a family? When most Americans hear the word *family*, they think of a mother, a father, and a child or children. The majority of families in America, however, do not fit this pattern. In fact, the most common family structure in the U.S. is a single-parent mother with one or more children. Many other children live in blended families formed by remarriage. Some children reside with family members from different generations, such as grandparents, aunts and uncles, or older siblings. Others live with certain family members at different times of the year and stages in their lives. Still others reside with no family member, such as those in foster care, those who are adopted, and those who are homeless (Swick, 1999). Artificial reproductive technology offers another definition of what constitutes a family member by making it possible for a child to be conceived outside the human body or for a biological child to be borne by someone else, with none, one, or both of the biological parents' heredity (Hanson & Gilkerson, 1996). Thus, it no

American families have changed dramatically over the last half-century.

Table 10.1
Sociohistorical Eras as They Relate to Families and Schools

	Premodern (prior to 1500s)	Modern (1500s –1950)	Postmodern (1950s –)
View of Child	miniature adult	innocent	competent
Social Orientation	obedience to authority; knowledge as a fixed body of thought	reason and thought as subjective; search for universals	ongoing adjustment to ideas that are too broad or narrow; emphasis on particulars and the influence of context variables
Family Characteristics	extended family—not just parents and siblings but also maternal and paternal grandparents, aunts and uncles, cousins, and in-laws	nuclear families consisting of parents and their children	permeable families consisting of single, divorced, remarried, and adoptive relationships
Family Functions	socialization, religious training, domestic training for girls, apprenticeships/employment for boys; emphasis on parental responsibility	contribute emotional resources and make financial sacrifices to child rearing; emphasis on parenting as instinctive and intuitive	balancing the demands of family and work in a complex, rapidly changing society; parents seen as needing support
Family Sentiments	survival	lifelong romantic and maternal love, mothers responsible for homemaking and child care; togetherness	changing partners and relationships; shared parenting, autonomy of individuals valued
School Characteristics	formal structure, survival skills taught	formal structure; greater emphasis on personal adjustment	child perceived as competent; introduced to complex ideas earlier

Courtesy of Nancy L. Briggs, adapted from *Ties That Stress: The New Family Imbalance* by D. Elkind, 1994, Cambridge, MA: Harvard University Press; and "School and Family in the Postmodern World" by D. Elkind, 1995, *Phi Delta Kappan, 77*(1), 8–14.

longer makes sense to think of families strictly in terms of shared genetic material, nor even in terms of a shared residence. For all of these reasons, the word *family* is difficult to define (Kagan, Powell, Weissbourd, & Zigler, 1987).

David Elkind's (1995) definition of family includes both biological and social influences. He defines the family as "a social system characterized by a kinship system and by certain sentiments, values, and perceptions" (p. 10). He further describes today's families as "postmodern" and their structures as "permeable." This means that, not only have families changed dramatically since the 1950s, but also, the divisions between parent and child, public and private lives, and work and home lives have "become blurred and difficult to discern" (Elkind, 1995, p. 1). Table 10.1 chronicles the major sociohistorical periods and society's view of the child, the family, and the school.

Of particular importance for early childhood professionals is the shift to the postmodern family. Elkind contends that the family is moving away from children's needs and toward the needs of adults, who are seeking fulfillment. Although new lifestyle options are associated with divorced, single-parent families, blended families, women working full-time out of the home, adults returning to higher education and training programs, out-of-home child care, and movement away from extended families, such changes have been unsettling and are sometimes detrimental to children (Elkind, 1994). Therefore, it is essential that we as early childhood educators understand the importance of families for children's growth and development.

FIGURE 10.1

Characteristics of
well-functioning
families

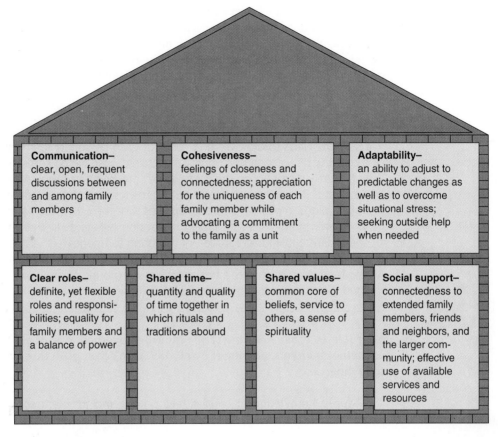

| Communication– clear, open, frequent discussions between and among family members | Cohesiveness– feelings of closeness and connectedness; appreciation for the uniqueness of each family member while advocating a commitment to the family as a unit | Adaptability– an ability to adjust to predictable changes as well as to overcome situational stress; seeking outside help when needed |
| Clear roles– definite, yet flexible roles and responsi-bilities; equality for family members and a balance of power | Shared time– quantity and quality of time together in which rituals and traditions abound | Shared values– common core of beliefs, service to others, a sense of spirituality | Social support– connectedness to extended family members, friends and neighbors, and the larger com-munity; effective use of available services and resources |

Source: Adapted from "Enough Analysis and Blame: Let's Strengthen All Families" by J. W. Sipe and D. S. Sipe, 1994, *Student Assistance Journal, 6*(5), pp. 16, 40.

Following an extensive review of the literature on families and discussions by a group of family experts, the U.S. Department of Health and Human Services (1990) concluded that in general, strong, successful families

- value togetherness
- encourage individual differences
- effectively adjust to change or stress

Clearly, early childhood education can play a major role in fostering each of these attributes. Figure 10.1 further describes the characteristics of families that are functioning well.

Your Role as a Family Resource Person

Seeking out the strengths of families is an important part of your role in working with children and families. Increasingly, early childhood educators in diverse settings are accepting responsibility for children in ways once thought to be the exclusive duty of parents and families. Rather than seeing your role solely as instructional, you need to view yourself as a *family resource person* who builds trust and respect between, among, and with families and the larger community. In this role, you will view parents as equal partners in education, support their efforts to help children learn at home, provide for children's basic needs such as supplying breakfast at school and assisting with proper dental care, and be able to refer parents to the many school and community resources that can provide support to the parents and families of the children in your setting.

PAUSE AND REFLECT ABOUT FAMILY CONFIGURATIONS

Use index cards to draw pictures, one for each person in your family. Pets can be included! Don't worry about your artistic talent, just sketch something that represents your family members on the cards. Write your first name and last initial on the back of each card. Then spread the cards out on the floor and take a look at the different family groupings. Try some different activities with the cards, such as making a class chart of different family sizes, grouping by relationships (e.g., all the grandparents), talking about different kinds of families, or inventing categories (e.g., family with the most sisters, family with the youngest children, family with the most generations). Then think about how you might use a similar activity with young children or a group of parents to send the message that there are all kinds of families (Berry & Mindes, 1993).

Your role as a *family resource person* must be governed, first of all, by a traditional interest in the children's learning (Powell, 1991). To accomplish this, you will need to do the following:

- Apply knowledge of child development and problem solving when interacting with families
- Acknowledge and respect parents' feelings
- Remain focused on both the individual child's and the group's needs
- Maintain a professional demeanor when working with families and community agencies (Bredekamp & Willer, 1993; Katz, 1993)
- Form dynamic, supportive interrelationships with programs, schools, and community agencies
- Begin as early as possible in the family's life and continue throughout the early childhood years (Gage & Workman, 1994; Swick, 1991)

Understanding the Family as a Social System

Early childhood educators who view families as part of a larger social system understand that all members of a family affect each others' lives (Kantor & Lehr, 1975). To best understand children, early childhood teachers must understand not only their relationships with their parents, but also, their relationships with their extended family members and with the community at large. Understanding the family as a social system is important for the following three reasons.

Children and Parents Influence Each Other as They Adapt Over the Years. When discussing family relationships, most adults first consider the many ways that parents and families influence children. What is sometimes overlooked is the fact that this influence is reciprocal. New parents who assume that their lives won't change that much with a new baby in the house are in for a big surprise. As any parent or guardian can attest, every imaginable aspect of life changes with the addition of that new human being. Children affect parents and families in other significant ways, too. A parent who has a child with a learning disability, for example, may become more patient over the years in the process of adapting to a child with special needs. The parent-child relationship also influences the many social contexts in which the parent operates: the role of spouse, relationships with extended family members, relationships with friends and coworkers, and connections to the larger community.

Family Problems and Issues Are Inextricably Related to Children's Development as Learners. If a parent loses a job, is chronically ill, or suffers injuries in an automobile accident, these changes affect children's lives. Young children cannot leave their problems at the door when they arrive at school, and the fact that they do not fully understand adults' problems can make these situations even more troubling for children. A father can say to his son, "I lost my job," but what does that mean to a child in preschool or the primary grades? Mostly, young children build their understandings of such ideas through concrete consequences. Some consequences might be, as some children we have known over the years have put it, "Now we have to go on vacation in the backyard instead of Disneyland," or "My dad watches TV all the time and my mom yells at him," or "I get my clothes at yard sales." Early childhood teachers must be keenly aware of such comments from children and strive to help families gain access to needed resources in the community that will support them in adjusting to their changed circumstances.

Connections to the Community—Including the School, Church, and Community Center—Are Significant for Children and Families' Well-Being. Goldberg (1997) characterizes children's and families' situations in the 20th century as follows:

> Society has changed, but children have not. Society has become more technologically advanced, faster paced, more competitive, and more materialistic; but children still need coddling, nurturing, and care. Society brought many children into the homes of two busy parents, working hard to make a living. It brought many children into homes where schedules were a thing of the past and expectations changed from time to time and from caregiver to caregiver. It brought still others into homes where there was one busy parent, working hard to do the jobs of two. Many children who still needed vast amounts of attention from parents found themselves with a multitude of caregivers giving shallow, unstructured, diverse care. (pp. 12–13)

In response to these trends, contemporary parents and families often turn to people outside their immediate or extended family for support. A child who attends summer camp sponsored by the local church or synagogue and held in the community center or school is bridging several social institutions. Participation in special activities within this community setting provides the bonds children and families need for healthy development because it involves the sharing of information, social and intellectual support, and strong role models for learning. When families are closely tied to the community, children's adjustment and development are enhanced.

When you take a systems approach to viewing families, you think about them holistically and respect them as human beings, regardless of their circumstances. A systems approach recognizes the need for parents and teachers who work with children to join together so that every child can learn.

Since parents are children's first teachers, it is important to invite them to continue their teaching role when their children enter school. Some parents may assume that because their children have entered this next stage of life, their job as parent-educator is lessening, but in reality it is growing. As an early childhood practitioner, you have the power to ensure that parents and families continue to stay involved in their children's lives.

On the surface, it can appear that including families is just "not worth it." It takes a lot of extra effort and there are disappointments and moments of frustration; however, when over 30 years of research has shown that parent involvement is the *single most important factor* in a child's educational achievement, how can we justify not including families in their child's educational life?

How do caregivers get *and keep* parents and other appropriate family members involved in their classrooms? Statistics show that there are between six and seven million parents enrolled in parent/teacher associations. This video segment will demonstrate just how successful parent/family involvement can be for everyone concerned—the child, the parents, and the teacher.

1. What can you do to nurture parent/family involvement in your classroom? Would you try to incorporate some of the ideas discussed in the video clip? What extra steps on your part might be necessary to foster family involvement?

2. What options are there for children whose parents don't speak English to be involved in their children's education?

Engaging Parents and Families in Educare

Parental involvement in children's education is not a new strategy. On the contrary, since the beginning of civilization, parents have been the first teachers and socializers of their children, passing on the skills, customs, and laws of their cultures, intentionally or otherwise, so that their children would be able not only to meet their own basic needs but also to be productive citizens and carry on their cultural traditions (Berger, 1995).

Parent involvement efforts over the past several decades have been widely criticized for being inflexible, superficial, and gender biased. Parents were invited to school at the school's convenience, for example, with conferences scheduled during the day or one evening per year. Often, when parents did volunteer time, they were given menial tasks to do such as cleaning up the classroom. Moreover, the focus was on homemaker mothers who could bake cookies, plan party games, accompany children on field trips, or assist at book sales (Henderson, Marburger, & Ooms, 1992). Frequently, there were few ways for fathers to participate without feeling like outsiders (McBride & Rane, 1997). As families made the shift from giving help to seeking it, the parent education movement began. Yet parent education also had some major limitations.

Previous efforts to educate parents were based on three erroneous assumptions: (a) learning flows only from school to parent to child; (b) learning occurs only in formal, school-like contexts; and (c) learning that reflects white, middle-class values is preferred (Briggs, Jalongo, & Brown, 1997). Although there is widespread agreement among early childhood educators about the importance of families' interest in and commitment to their children's education, there is far less agreement about the best ways to involve and support the postmodern family.

What is known, however, is that parent involvement is critical to children's success. In the agenda for school reform, for example, the national legislation *Goals 2000: Educate America Act* (U.S. Department of Education, 1994) acknowledges the need across this nation for parents' involvement in their children's education. Goal 8 is that every school will promote partnerships that will increase parental involvement and participation in enhancing the social, emotional, and academic growth of children. This last goal acknowledges that parents are indeed partners in their children's education, and that all teachers must assume a role that facilitates such partnerships. It also recognizes the need for all early childhood settings to create family-friendly policies that truly support today's families.

Working Effectively with Families

Research suggests that improved home-school relationships are characterized by support, collaboration, and open communication (Berger, 1995; Epstein, 1995; Williams, 1992). The following six basic types of involvement build partnerships between schools and families and communities (Epstein, 1995).

1. Parenting—helping all families establish home environments that support children as students
2. Communicating—designing and conducting effective forms of communication about school programs and children's progress
3. Volunteering—recruiting and organizing support for school functions and activities
4. Learning at home—providing information and ideas to families about how to help students with schoolwork and school-related activities
5. Decision making—including parents in school decisions.
6. Collaborating with the community—identifying and integrating resources and services from the community to strengthen and support schools, students, and their families.

More specifically, it is recommended that those entering the early childhood field recognize the following six guidelines for working effectively with families.

Be Aware That the Boundaries Separating Responsibilities for Children Are Blurring, with Schools Being Expected to Meet Far More Than Just the Academic Needs of Today's Students. The mission of America's education has been seriously broadened. Many Head Start programs provide children with breakfast, a place for each child to keep a toothbrush and comb, a snack, and transportation to and from school. Many of the responsibilities for basic needs once assumed by families have become part of the school program. Yet early childhood education cannot by itself respond to all of the elements of family functions (Chavkin, 1990; Coleman, 1991; Edwards & Young, 1992). Therefore, early childhood programs must align themselves with other social institutions that have complementary expertise and function as "multiple-service brokers for children" (Edwards & Young, 1992, p. 78) who put families in contact with agencies, services, and organizations that can lend support to families.

Confront Your Own Biases about Families. A recent Carnegie Foundation report found that a higher percentage of adults in the United States than in any other developed nation agreed with the statement that "parents are not taking responsibility for their children"

By providing families with information and ideas about how to help students with schoolwork, parents may become more active participants in their children's education.

(Boyer, 1995). It is not uncommon for those entering the teaching profession to use their own family experiences as a sort of yardstick for evaluating the families of others. When personal experience is used as the standard, a teacher can find other families lacking, use derogatory labels, or even use families' situations as the reason for failing to teach. Destructive comments such as, "Well, his parents are divorced, you know. What can you expect?" and "That's not her husband, that's her live-in boyfriend," and "Can you imagine? Seven people in that little house!" reflect a bias against diverse families. The attitudes that underlie these statements also can lead to adversarial relationships between families and educators, and when they do, the child is caught in the middle. Instead of rating families as "good," "average," "poor," or "dysfunctional," keep an unswerving focus on the child's needs. It is true that increasing numbers of children arrive at school without even their basic needs for food, shelter, and clothing having been met. This is a reason for early childhood educators to help. Even complimentary comments, such as "They're such a nice family," can cause children who never hear any positive comments about their families to feel ashamed of their family situations. It is far better to make specific, nonjudgmental comments that recognize the care and attention that families give to their children, such as, "It looks like somebody braided your hair for you." or "I see that you brought in some leaves for the collection." or "Mmmm. Somebody packed a good lunch for you." or "I see you are wearing your warm scarf and gloves today."

Recognize That Early Childhood Educators Are in a Unique Position to Identify Children's Needs and Inaugurate Families' Interactions with Schools. As soon as Lizzie arrived in second grade, it was clear to her teacher that she needed medical attention. The child's teeth were black with decay and the infection was upsetting her stomach. When the teacher called the home to speak with Lizzie's mother, the grandmother answered and said that her daughter was at the beauty shop having her hair done. Lizzie's teacher hung up the telephone, bristling with anger and ready to march down to the teachers' room to tell this story to her colleagues. On further thought, however, Lizzie's teacher realized that an indictment of the second grader's family would not do the family any good and could certainly do lasting damage to the child. Wouldn't it be better, she asked herself, if I deal with the problem instead of rushing to judge? Although the teacher confided in her husband and a good friend who taught in another state to let off steam, she resolved not to discuss the incident at all in the community out of respect for Lizzie.

Early childhood educators are in a key position to lead the way in restructuring efforts to work with families because they are in contact with families at a time when parents are most receptive to becoming involved in their children's educational experiences. Additionally, they are the community professionals who see children and their families on the most consistent basis throughout the year (Chavkin, 1990). The early childhood educator can also serve as an advocate for families, referring them to appropriate agencies to satisfy their family needs, or speaking out to get needed services in the neighborhood (Allen, Brown, & Finlay, 1992).

Appreciate the Importance of Effective Communication and Professionalism in Interactions with Families. Krista was a 6-year-old who had been in first grade for 2 weeks when her mother called the school and asked to see the teacher. The purpose of the meeting was to find out why Krista was not reading independently yet. When Krista's teacher heard this, her first reaction was to be defensive and say, "Give me a chance! School just started!" Instead, she arranged an appointment and listened carefully, not only to what Krista's mother said, but also "between the lines" to her underlying concerns. It seemed that Krista's father had a reading disability, and her parents were very worried that their daughter might be affected, too. Because the teacher really *heard* what Krista's mother had to say, an angry confrontation was defused and a positive plan of action was put into place. Krista's mother left with books and ideas instead of frustration, because the teacher had sought to communicate effectively and professionally instead of defending herself. Figure 10.2 is an overview of appropriate and inappropriate communication practices between early childhood educators and families.

Be Aware That Today's Early Childhood Educators Must Reach Out to Families and Communities. There is little place in contemporary society for the teacher who closes the door and has virtually no contact with families and the larger community. Instead of sitting behind the desk and waiting for parents to attend conferences, many early childhood educators are making home visits, traveling to homes to confer with parents or work with children as part of an early intervention program, like Ms. Cole, who was featured in this chapter's Meet the Teachers. Increasingly, early childhood educators are also functioning as part of a professional team assembled to help a child and family. A team assembled to support the learning of a drug-exposed child might include a social worker, medical professional, teacher, instructional aide,

Appropriate Practice	Inappropriate Practice
Frequent one-on-one, face-to-face, pleasant home-school contact	Families are left without attention for long periods
Teachers speak in pleasant, calm voices, with frequent eye contact	Teachers speak harshly or impatiently or use educational jargon
Teachers respond to all families' efforts at communication	Teachers ignore family attempts to communicate verbally or focus on some families to the exclusion of others
Teachers respond quickly to family distress signals (problems, emergencies, concerns) in a warm manner	Teachers ignore distress signals (problems, emergencies, concerns) or respond at their convenience
Interactions are carried out with sensitivity to the family's needs.	Teachers intimidate or criticize families
During interactions, teachers offer comments, suggest ideas, and encourage family's own exploration	Teachers interrupt, impose their own ideas, and seek to impose control over families
Varied communication, informal dialogue, newsletters, handbooks, phone calls, notes, conferences, and meetings	Little communication occurs; families are left to themselves in the hopes that the families will reciprocate and leave the school alone
Every family and every child is warmly greeted	Families and children are received indifferently or not greeted
Teachers accommodate individual differences in family circumstances and schedules when attempting to involve families	Families are expected to conform to schedules for meetings and conferences that suit teacher

SOURCE: Adapted from *Developmentally Appropriate Practice in Early Childhood Programs* rev. ed., S. Bredekamp and C. Copple, Eds., 1997, Washington, DC: National Association for the Education of Young Children.

school administrator, and the parent(s). The early childhood educator's response to the needs of today's families must be governed, first of all, by a genuine interest in every child's learning (Powell, 1991).

Explore the Many Dimensions of Your Role in Working with Families and Communities. The field of early childhood education has identified those behaviors that lead to supportive relationships with children and families. Figure 10.3 is an overview of the National Association for the Education of Young Children's standards for promoting positive family and community relationships.

Collaboration with other professionals is often necessary to find appropriate options for helping young children and their families.

PAUSE AND REFLECT ABOUT THE INFLUENCE OF YOUR FAMILY ON THOUGHTS ABOUT FAMILIES

Think about your own family's involvement in your education. List the ways your own family was involved in your early school experiences and with your teachers. How are these ways similar or different from those suggested in the preceding guidelines? Which of these ideas could you try? Talk about your experiences with a classmate. What would you like to know more about involving families in their children's education?

Allying with Parents and Families

In the field of early childhood education, it is common to speak of partnerships between families and schools. For a true partnership to exist, there must be mutual respect, shared decision making, and appreciation for the contributions made by each person. Hayes (1987) suggests that educators treat parents and guardians like professional child rearers who have extensive on-the-job experience. Family members know children in ways that the school can never know them. Usually, family members have been with children over extended periods of time and have witnessed many developmental milestones. The adults in a child's family typically have been involved with the child on a one-to-one basis in a wide variety of contexts, such as in the backyard, at the grocery store, at religious ceremonies, at the shopping mall, in the swimming pool, at family reunions, or at a family vacation spot.

On the other hand, educators know the child as one of many other children who are her or his age. They are trained to see evidence of the child's growth in all areas: physical,

These Behaviors from Teachers:

Establish and maintain positive, collaborative relationships with families.

- Respect parents' choices and goals for children and communicate effectively with parents about the curriculum and children's progress
- Involve families in assessing and planning for individual children, including children with disabilities, developmental delays, or special abilities
- Support parents in making decisions related to their children's development and parenting

Demonstrate sensitivity to differences in family structures and social and cultural backgrounds.

- Apply family systems theory, knowledge of the dynamics, roles, and relationships within families and communities
- Use intake interviews and home visits to get a sense of what families are like

Link families with a range of family-oriented services based on identified resources, priorities, and concerns.

- Document children's progress and families' concerns
- Seek in-house help from coworkers

Communicate effectively with other professionals concerned with children and with agencies in the larger community to support children's development, learning, and well-being.

- Ask, "What does this family need?" "What can I do to help them meet their needs?"
- Branch out into the community to establish interprofessional collaborations on behalf of children and families

Lead to These Benefits:

Benefits of families' communication with educators

- Insight into the school or center and the professional personnel and environment
- A sense of involvement and accomplishment
- Knowledge of the goals and objectives of the school or center
- Opportunities to reinforce educational goals and objectives at home through activities that help the child
- Children who are more successful students and happier individuals

Benefits of educators' communication with families

- Insight into families' concerns and aspirations
- Insight into the child's home environment
- A sense of involvement with and support for families

- Support from families
- Reinforcement of goals and objectives through home activities
- More successful, self-assured, and competent students
- Greater pride in their success as teachers or caregivers

SOURCE: Adapted from "Communication: The key to parent involvement" by E. H. Berger, 1996, *Early Childhood Education Journal, 23*(3), 179–183; and *What are the benefits . . . of high-quality early childhood programs?* by the National Association for the Education of Young Children, 1996, Washington, DC: Author.

cognitive, social, emotional, and creative. Teachers also have insights into the child's progress relative to the progress of a child's peers, because they work with children of the same age all of the time. When viewed in this way, it is easy to see why families' and educators' views of the same child are different yet complementary, with each contributing pieces to the puzzle of who a child is, how he or she is doing, and what might be causing a particular behavior.

Research consistently identifies positive home-school relationships as a characteristic of effective schools and associates a high level of parental involvement with increases in student achievement (Rosenthal & Sawyers, 1996). The many benefits of home-school collaboration are reciprocal—they accrue to both educators *and* families. Yet in order to reap these benefits, five barriers must be overcome (Berger, 1995; Isenberg & Jalongo, 1997):

1. *Cultural differences.* Sometimes parents and teachers have different expectations regarding discipline, timeliness, or celebrations. Some mannerisms, such as touching, can unintentionally offend culturally diverse families. A useful resource through which to learn about cultural variations in parenting is *Knowing and Serving Diverse Families* (Hildebrand, Phenice, Gray, & Hines, 1996).

2. *Seeming lack of interest in participation.* Sometimes parents do not feel welcome or comfortable in the school because of previous negative experiences or anxiety about discussing their children's progress. Some families do not know how to access resources; others fear that if they ask questions or complain, it will be "taken out on" their children later. You can overcome this barrier by building mutual trust and by offering a wide range of ways for families to participate both at home and at school (see the following Featuring Families).

3. *Time and transportation.* Many parents have difficulty finding the time and transportation to attend conferences and meetings during the workday. Schools and centers committed to families set up carpools, provide babysitting, and create a space where parents can meet informally.

4. *Difficult parents.* Some parents have difficulty dealing with other adults in authority. They may deny that a problem exists, become aggressive when challenged, or become overly protective about their children. In all cases, seeking joint solutions is essential.

5. *Teachers' and caregivers' lack of knowledge.* Although you may never reach all parents, all early childhood educators must develop skill in reaching families. You might practice speaking in ordinary language instead of educational jargon, use active listening to encourage participation, and avoid using judgmental words, such as *lazy,* or labels, such as *hyperactive.*

Conducting home visits is often a dimension of the early childhood practitioner's role. One way to break the ice with families is to conduct an initial interview that will provide helpful information about the child and family.

Parent/Family Questionnaire

Child's Name: _____

          (first)   (last)

Parent's or Guardian's
Name: _____

          (first)   (last)

Address: _____

_____

Telephone Numbers: _____

          (home)   (work)

Best Days/Times to Call: _____

Visits/Tours: Does your place of employment permit children of your child's age to visit or tour? _____ Yes _____ No

If yes, please provide contact information for the company or organization:

_____

_____

Lunch: Are you available to have lunch with your child at school between 11:15 and 11:45? _____ Yes _____ No

---

Participation: Are you willing to visit the classroom during this school year? _____ Yes _____ No

If yes, please indicate **all of the days/times** when you are available:

Monday _____   Tuesday _____   Wednesday _____   Thursday _____

8–9 A.M. _____   9–10 A.M. _____   10–11 A.M. _____   11–12 A.M. _____

12–1 P.M. _____   1–2 P.M. _____   2–3 P.M. _____

Activities:

Please check any activity that you would be willing to do:

_____ Read to a child

_____ Read to a group of children

_____ Tutor one to three children in reading

_____ Assist with routines (arrival, departure, lunch)

_____ Make a learning game for the class

_____ Supervise a classroom center (woodworking, cooking, art, etc.)

_____ Help to assemble toys

_____ Assist in typing children's stories

_____ Supervise on the playground

_____ Assist with a field trip

_____ Tutor one to three children in math

_____ Assist with a class celebration

_____ Organize a class event

_____ Serve on the phone committee

_____ Help children at the computer

_____ Help with sewing books and toys designed by children

Special Interests: *Please list any hobbies, abilities, or items that you are willing to share with the children, for example, playing a musical instrument, preparing a simple recipe, learning how to use basic woodworking tools, telling a story, or sharing items you have collected that children could pass around and observe, such as seashells or postcards.*

_____

_____

_____

Many strategies exist for overcoming obstacles and fulfilling your duty to help every child learn. *Philadelphia Teacher* (1997) offers the following general suggestions for working with urban families:

- Be positive—treat families with respect and share good news, not just problems.
- Extend a personal invitation—get on the telephone and ask each parent or family member to participate.
- Be persistent—keep trying until you find something that will meet the needs of families.
- Celebrate together—let families see what their children are learning.
- Be creative—try activities other than meetings in places other than classrooms.
- Make it convenient—consider parents' schedules and support their efforts to get involved.
- Be specific—give parents detailed suggestions about how they can help, for instance, a Saturday workshop on how to read aloud to your child.

It is clear that old ways of involving families are not adequate to face today's challenges. A partnership model emphasizes the contributions that both parents and teachers make to promote children's success in school and society. While there are many ways to share information and communicate with parents, you must remember that these require careful planning. Be sure to check the Compendium of Resources at the end of this book for Web sites and a host of other information to support your efforts.

The following are some "family friendly" ways to achieve successful partnerships.

- *Try to ease families' concerns about children's adjustment.* Orientation days are opportunities for children to become familiar with school and school routines before officially beginning school. Many schools use a buddy system, in which, for example, current kindergartners are paired with incoming kindergartners to help ease new students' transition to school.

- *Strive to communicate by keeping professional jargon to a minimum and speak in ways that the family understands.* One way to stimulate a family's interest in and a child's answer to the age-old question "What did you learn in school today?" is an Ask-Me-About badge. These are short sentences written on paper badges that invite parents to talk with their children about particular activities or experiences that they had in school or at the center. The badges supply information to parents and also provide children with opportunities to recall and describe particular learning activities, such as having a guest storyteller or going on a walking field trip.

- *Keep it easy for the family to stay informed.* Newsletters that feature children's work and are sent to the home let parents and families know about classroom experiences, open the door to two-way communication, and invite parents into their children's learning. Newsletters can cover a variety of topics, such as an upcoming family night, special projects under study, and good books to read. Computer software makes it increasingly easy to produce a professional-looking newsletter. This is a great way to have parents help out as well. No matter how confident you are about your writing skills, however, be certain to have others help you proofread the finished product. Other possibilities for contacting parents include a homework hot line, E-mail, and a home page on the Internet.

- *Offer opportunities for families to gather informally and network.* School-sponsored family gatherings, such as a summer picnic before school begins or a noncompetitive family game night, offer opportunities to make connections. A parent who has a child with Down syndrome may feel that contacts with other families who are raising children with special needs offer a particularly beneficial type of support. When families are closely tied to the community, children's adjustment and development are enhanced. Social events enable families and educators to get to know one another as people.

- *Schedule meetings at various times so that more families can participate.* Meetings scheduled at different times and locations meet the particular needs of families and invite more participation. For example, working parents could come to see a display of the children's work and be served a light breakfast by the children. Meetings could be scheduled on an evening or a Saturday morning with child-care provided.

- *Use a variety of strategies to enhance communication with families.* Be sensitive to the fact that not all parents have English as their first language or take time to read written messages from school. Some ways to let parents know how their children are doing at school that don't depend on the family's reading skills include messages in different languages recorded on the telephone about upcoming classroom events; videotapes of school events, such as the children singing, that can be circulated or viewed at home or at the library; and audiotapes of a child reading aloud.

- *Strive to identify with and meet the special concerns of families.* Each family has a unique set of circumstances that influences how parents and families respond to teachers' efforts to work with them. For example, when children have physical handicaps, families can be excessively protective, and when children are chronically ill, families sometimes fail to set reasonable limits on children's behavior. In such situations, families often appreciate an information sheet about appropriate learning games to play at home, a professional magazine article, or an informational brochure written especially for parents. Some excellent materials are those published by the Consumer Information Center in Pueblo, Colorado; professional association brochures (e.g., those published by the Association for Childhood Education International, the National Association for the Education of Young Children, and the International Reading Association); and a wide variety of literature from community and social service agencies and organizations.

- *Be sensitive to some family members' discomfort in the school setting.* Not all parents have had positive prior experience with schools or helpful interactions with teachers and administrators. Home visits or meetings held at a location other than the school, such as the public library or the neighborhood community center, are sometimes more appealing to families.

- *When difficulties arise, keep a problem-solving focus instead of blaming.* During a parent conference, it is sometimes tempting to blame the parent for a child's behavior at school. One way to bring up a difficult issue, such as a child who seldom completes activities at school, is to first ask the parent to share his or her views on the child's work habits at home. Often you will find that parents are already aware of the difficulty and are willing to collaborate on a mutually agreed-upon solution.

- *Focus on all families instead of being satisfied with the participation of a few with higher income levels or more leisure time.* Very often, you will hear teachers say that the parents whom they really want to see never come to school for conferences or school events. Making everyone feel welcome is the teacher's responsibility. For example, an evening when children share their accomplishments and every child has an equal opportunity to participate encourages all family members to participate (Liess, 1996).

- *Give parents the latitude to contribute in their own ways.* Some teachers develop a family questionnaire to find out about parents' jobs, hobbies, cultural specialties (e.g., songs, games, recipes), or travel pictures, or their interest in helping provide recycled materials, participating in special events such as birthdays, or volunteering in the classroom (see Featuring Families earlier in this section). Invite parents at various times throughout the year to demonstrate a skill, tell a story, or play a musical instrument.

- *Admit that you are sometimes in over your head and need to seek outside assistance.* Part of the skill of being a teacher is to know the limits of your professional preparation. If, for example, you are faced with a child whose mother was killed in an automobile accident or a child who is having difficulty adjusting to the birth of a new sibling, seek the advice of other professionals who work with young children. Figure 10.4 provides guidelines about how to make referrals.

Conferences with parents are an important way for significant adults in children's lives to exchange information about their learning and development. Conferences

367

FIGURE 10.4

Guidelines for making referrals

1. Recognize when you are in over your head and need to gain additional support.
2. Look upon this need for additional support as a professional response rather than a personal defeat.
3. Know the agencies, organizations, and services in your area.
4. Identify competent people in those groups with whom you can work.
5. Make referrals to these specific individuals, not just a general referral.
6. Secure family members' agreement that they will participate.
7. Ask family members to predict what might prevent them from participating and get them to identify ways to overcome obstacles to participation.
8. Check out the family's progress on proposed solutions and have alternative resources available in case difficulties arise.
9. Plan for a follow-up meeting to determine how the referral is benefitting the child.

Source: Adapted from "Building Successful Home/School Partnerships" by D. M. Rosenthal and J. Y. Sawyers, 1996, *Childhood Education, 72*(4), pp. 194–200.

provide an opportunity to support home-school partnerships through a free exchange of insights and observations about a particular child. They can be routinely scheduled (e.g., semi-annually) or can be spontaneous, as when you chat with families informally when you are waiting for the bus or out in the community. Sending home an information sheet before routine conferences helps many parents feel more comfortable, know what to expect, and share information more freely. The following checklist will help you prepare, conduct, and evaluate formal conferences.

PREPARING FOR A CONFERENCE

- Suggest several times for the conference, let the parent select, then confirm by making sure the parent knows the time, date, place, and length of the conference.
- Be prepared. Know what you are going to say and what evidence of the child's progress you are going to share. Have a written outline, if needed.
- Prepare the child. Ask the child what information he or she wants to share with parents.
- Arrange an inviting environment, and get all the children involved in preparing the classroom for visitors.
- Have student work samples ready in a folder and be ready to explain how and what that child is learning.
- Eliminate distractions. Give the parent you are speaking with your undivided attention.

CONDUCTING A CONFERENCE

- Establish rapport by welcoming the parent to the room and stating your pleasure in seeing him or her. Sit beside the parent, not at or behind your desk. Share a positive anecdote about the child.
- State the purpose of the conference and how you plan to conduct it.
- Begin sharing information about the child's strengths or what the child *can* do.

- Share the child's work samples, arranged to highlight progress and effort.
- Encourage parental information and questions. Remember that some parents are uncomfortable sharing information. Ask open-ended questions.
- Listen to what the parent has to say about his or her child. Listening enables you to gain new information and help solve problems.
- Be alert to nonverbal cues and the way that things are said rather than focusing on the words alone. Get in the habit of "listening between the lines."
- Suggest ways the home and school can collaborate and agree upon a plan of action. Set goals together.
- Always summarize the conference, and end on a positive note.

FOLLOWING UP ON A CONFERENCE

- Make a note of important points discussed during the conference or agreements that were reached so that you can refer to them later.
- Review conference notes and share them with other school personnel, if needed and appropriate.
- Summarize follow-up responsibilities, who is responsible for what, and how participants will know they have fulfilled their agreed-upon obligations. Make plans for monitoring progress toward goals.
- Tell the child about the conference so that he or she will know areas in which you have reached agreement.
- Send the parent a thank-you message for participating—a note, a telephone call, E-mail, or some other sign of appreciation.

Some teachers and schools like the children to participate in conferences; others do not. When children are included in conferences, teachers need to plan ahead with them, help them select appropriate work samples to discuss, and ensure adequate participation from them. Including children in conferences helps them take more responsibility for their own learning by enabling them to contribute insights about their progress in all developmental areas. Some teachers have students lead conferences and share their goals and accomplishments. It is equally important to prepare parents for conferences at which children are present. If you do not set their expectations, some parents may assume that the purpose of meeting with you is for them to demonstrate to you that they are strict disciplinarians who can demand obedience and get it by reprimanding their children in your presence. Even if children are not included in conferences, it is a good idea to share some things about the conferences with them after the conferences have taken place.

Collaborating with Families in Inclusive and Diverse Settings

Two primary concerns facing early childhood educators are working with families from diverse cultures and working with families who have children with disabilities. Maintaining a strong home-school connection with multiple cultures is a concern of many soon-to-be teachers. Usually, schools and centers with a high percentage of families who speak a language other than English (e.g., Spanish in the Southwest) already have forms, notices, and other written materials translated into the home language of these families. Be sure to ask for them if they are not automatically provided. If your school does not provide this service, or if the home language of a family is not commonly spoken in your community, enlist the help of another parent or an international student at a university who can translate for you. Sending home bilingual notices communicates a welcoming message to parents and families who speak languages other than English. Additionally, get into the habit of regarding these families as important resources who can share "cultural items like magazine pictures, family recipes, dramatic play props, family experiences, stories, and artifacts" (Swick, Boutte, & van Scoy, 1995, p. 2).

When a child has a disability, parents and families frequently look to teachers and schools for support. Often, parents of children with disabilities need additional services and resource materials to meet the special challenges. As a future teacher, you must be sensitive to the special needs and dynamics of parents of a child with a disability. Having enough information and background about families increases the likelihood of establishing good rapport and a good working relationship with the child and family.

Seeking out the *strengths* of families is an important part of your role in preparing a "family friendly" classroom or center. Contemporary society is faced with broadening its perspective of family structure and function, recognizing changes in family dynamics, realistically acknowledging the contemporary family's influence on children, and determining the impact these changes have on the school. Increasingly, early childhood programs in diverse settings will need to assume responsibility for children in ways once thought to be the exclusive domain of parents and families. Rather than seeing your role solely as instructional, you need to view yourself as a *family resource person* who builds trust and respect between, among, and with families and the larger community. In this role, you will view parents as equal partners in education, support parents' efforts to help children learn at home, provide for children's basic needs (e.g., supplying breakfast at school, assisting with proper dental care), and be able to refer families to the many school and community resources that can provide support.

Major Models of Home-School-Community Collaboration

Contemporary approaches to allying with families are moving toward a comprehensive services model. Suppose that you were the parent of a child with a hearing impairment. In the past, you would have traveled to and worked with a wide variety of individuals and organizations: an audiologist, a speech/language pathologist, a sign-language tutor, the school, and the National Speech, Hearing and Language Association. If you had relocated to another area of the country, you would have started all over again. Increasingly, today's families are seeing a sort of "one-stop shopping," whereby, for example, support services for a child with a hearing impairment are all coordinated at the school.

When parents, educators, and social service agencies form community collaborations, everyone benefits (Kagan & Rivera, 1991; Kirst, 1991; Stone, 1995). These alliances offer more equitable distribution of goods and services, improved access to and continuity of services for families, minimization of expenses, the elimination of the duplication of services, and the improvement of training opportunities for agency and school staff members (Epstein, 1995; Rutherford & Billig, 1995; Stone, 1995). The emphasis is on support, resources, empowerment, and meeting individual needs. Instead of large-group gatherings for which parents are expected to leave work, arrange for child care, come to school, and sit and listen to a lecture about effective parenting, new models of home-school collaboration are being implemented. These programs, called family resource or family support programs, recognize and respect the fact that while all families share many of the same needs, they do not all need the same type of information or service at the same time. The major goal of such programs is to provide services that will enhance family life, thereby improving the personal, social, and academic development of children and empowering families to help themselves (Davies, 1991; Kagan et al., 1987). Family support programs are a definite departure from the 1950s concept of parental involvement as being mothers working as volunteers or assistants to classroom teachers. In Table 10.2, traditional efforts to work with parents are contrasted with the new, family support services concept.

The issue of family support needs to be addressed as a national public policy issue so that a more coordinated effort can be put into action (Galinsky, Shubilla, Willer, Levine, & Daniel, 1994). Comprehensive family support programs require a great deal of political action. As Madeline Grumet (1988) asserts, there can be no community until educators begin to develop a sense of responsibility for everybody's children. It is not until families, educators, and other community members accept nothing less for every child in the program than they would for their own children that genuine progress can be made.

Beginning teachers often feel overwhelmed when working with families. First of all, the focus of new teachers understandably has been on teaching the children, and those who choose to spend their lives in the company of the very young may not be as confident or relaxed in the company of adults. Moreover, new teachers who are not parents themselves may feel that their knowledge about children is dismissed as "book learning" and lacks authority in the parents' eyes. The more candid among our undergraduate students have sometimes admitted that they don't know what to say to parents or that they feel awkward around them. The best approach is to focus on what you have in common: the child. A Carnegie Foundation for the Advancement of Teaching survey of parents found that the number-one thing parents expect from a teacher is the ability to motivate their children to learn (Boyer, 1995). Considering all this, a good way to begin with parents is to share the interesting activities you have planned that will support their children's learning. Instead of worrying about whether parents will judge you as less skillful because you are not a parent, simply acknowledge that they are the experts in this area and that your contributions will focus on the learning aspect. If you know

Table 10.2
A Comparison of Traditional Programs and Family Support Services

	Traditional Programs	Family Support Services
Emphasis	identifying family deficiencies	building upon family strengths
Timing	intervene after needs intensify or crises occur	help to prevent crises by providing resources and support early
Focus	the individual child's behavior	the family unit
Eligibility for Services	strict eligibility requirements; often have waiting lists	reach out to families; respond quickly and flexibly
Setting	services provided by appointment during specified hours	services offered in homes on an as-needed basis or in homelike centers with drop-in services
Collaboration	often provide services that overlap with those of other agencies, creating a competitive situation	avoid duplication of services and encourage interagency collaboration
Range of Services	offer only specific services or treatments	offer comprehensive services such as help in meeting basic needs, special services, and referrals

Source: Adapted from *Helping Children by Strengthening Families* by M. Allen, P. Brown, and B. Findlay, 1992, Washington, DC: Children's Defense Fund.

EXPLORING YOUR ROLE IN SUPPORTING FAMILIES

nothing about toilet training, do not fake it! A much better response is to locate expert advice at the library and to talk with experienced parents about this issue. When asking parents for help, try something like, "I know about early childhood education, but I don't know much about toilet training. You've toilet trained three children. Can you offer some advice?" The public library and your local bookstore will probably be better resources for you than an academic library, because they emphasize practical information for nonspecialists. Look for books by leading authorities, such as Penelope Leach's (1978) now-classic reference, *Your Baby and Child from Birth to Age Five,* John Rosemond's (1992) *Parent Power: A Common Sense Approach to Parenting,* Charles Schaeffer's (1984) *How to Talk to Your Child About Really Important Things,* or Dorothy Rich's (1997) *What Do We Say? What Do We Do? Vital Solutions for Children's Educational Success.*

Other valuable resources for early childhood educators are the many different comprehensive programs that can serve as shining examples of parent participation in children's education. In a joint statement of the National Parent-Teacher Association and the National Coalition for Parent Involvement in Education (1997), six research-based standards for parent/family involvement programs were identified:

Standard I: Communicating. Communication between home and school is regular, two-way, and meaningful.

Standard II: Parenting. Parenting skills are promoted and supported.

Standard III: Student Learning. Parents play an integral role in assisting student learning.

Standard IV: Volunteering. Parents are welcome in the school, and their support and assistance are sought.

Standard V: School Decision Making and Advocacy. Parents are full partners in the decisions that affect children and families.

Standard VI: Collaborating with Community. Community resources are used to strengthen schools, families, and student learning.

A variety of initiatives at the programmatic, state, national, and international levels have successfully met these standards. Table 10.3 highlights several of the most highly regarded parent involvement and support programs in the field of early childhood education.

Conclusion

Today, more than ever, families need help in ensuring that their children develop the values, attitudes, and behaviors that will help them succeed in school and beyond. Communities, schools, and programs must all recognize and accept that "yesterday's strategies will not be able to address tomorrow's realities or meet the needs of tomorrow's children" (Kagan, 1990, p. 272). As a result, one of the most persistent themes in the current school reform movement has been the strengthening of the connections among families, schools, programs, and communities—the issue of parental engagement in children's care and education. The steps that you will need to take to achieve this are summarized in Figure 10.5.

Three things are needed for social reform: a knowledge base, a public will, and a social strategy (Richmond & Kotelchuck, 1984). Where family support is concerned, American society certainly has a knowledge base and research support for greater home, school, and community collaboration (Roberts, Wasik, Casto, & Ramey, 1991). The thing that is lacking is a public will to act upon that knowledge (Lewis, 1991).

Table 10.3

Models of Successful Family Involvement and Education

Program and Focus	Brief Description of Activities with Families	Sources for Additional Information
Reggio Emilia: a municipality of Italy that is considered to have some of the finest preschool programs in the world and serves as a model of meaningful family and community involvement	Teachers meet with parents to discuss the child as part of the group Teachers meet with parents to discuss the individual needs of the child, and provide ongoing information Meetings are held to develop parenting skills Parents and teachers work together to improve the school environment by donating time to build furnishings or rearrange classroom space Parents and community members contribute time to the school	Edwards, Gandini, and Forman (1994), *The Hundred Languages of Children: The Reggio Emilia Approach to Early Childhood Education* Goldberg (1997), *Parent Involvement Begins at Birth*
Head Start and Home Start: federally funded national intervention programs for low-income children and families with a strong tradition of parent involvement and education	Provides a support system for families under stress that offers services in health, nutrition, and education Provides a career ladder for parents that enables them to begin as parent volunteers, become teachers' aides, and with subsidized training, eventually become teachers or administrators in the program Home visitors work with families in the home environment to model effective parenting and enhance children's learning	Zigler and Styfco (Eds.) (1993), *Head Start and Beyond: A National Plan for Extended Childhood Intervention* Zigler and Muenchow (1992), *Head Start: The Inside Story of America's Most Successful Educational Experiment*
Family Literacy and Even Start: federally funded intergenerational literacy programs that support literacy learning of both children and adults in the family	Administered by the states and operated by local school systems to support literacy growth at all levels Establishes lending libraries for books, toys, and games to be used by families enrolled in the program Home visits to support literacy activities Provides adult literacy instructors and materials for parents Adult literacy activities such as parents reading to children	Auerbach (1995), "Which Way for Family Literacy: Intervention or Empowerment?" Morrow (1995), "Family Literacy: New Perspectives, New Practices"
Family Math: links home and school by promoting gender and race equity in mathematics education and giving families access to high-quality mathematics instruction and materials education	Meetings are sponsored by the local schools and taught by a teacher-parent team for each grade level Problem-solving tasks such as measuring, estimating, and spatial relationships are designed so that a child and adult work on them together	Stenmark, Thompson, and Cossey (1986), *Family Math* Carnegie Corporation of New York (1996), *Years of Promise: A Comprehensive Learning Strategy for America's Children*
Home Instruction Program for Preschool Youngsters (HIPPY): an international home-instructional program for parents of 4- and 5-year-old-children	Designed to have a positive, sustained impact on the academic achievement and school adjustment of 4- and 5-year-old children Home visits conducted twice a month over a 2-year period to introduce a curriculum of activities that enhance learning Provides an extensive set of guidelines and instructional resources	Berger (1995), *Parents as Partners in Education: Families and Schools Working Together* Carnegie Corporation of New York (1996), *Years of Promise: A Comprehensive Learning Strategy for America's Children*

(continued)

Table 10.3
(continued)

Program and Focus	Brief Description of Activities with Families	Sources for Additional Information
Kentucky's Parent and Child Program (PACE): a statewide program designed to raise parents' educational levels while teaching them how to improve the learning skills of their young children	A strong parent-education component teaches parents how to teach their children	Carnegie Corporation of New York (1996), *Years of Promise: A Comprehensive Learning Strategy for America's Children*
Minnesota's Early Childhood and Family Education (ECFE): a statewide program offering information to parents of children from birth through kindergarten; services are available to all income levels and populations	Offers 2-hour classes once a week at times and settings convenient to parents Sessions begin with parents and children working together on thematic learning activities Parents then attend educational sessions determined by their needs while children participate in a preschool program Offers early screening for health and developmental problems as well as resource libraries for toys and books	Berger (1995), *Parents as Partners in Education: Families and Schools Working Together* Carnegie Corporation of New York (1996), *Years of Promise: A Comprehensive Learning Strategy for America's Children*
Missouri's New Parents as Teachers: a statewide intervention program that emphasizes establishing positive parenting styles beginning in the third trimester of pregnancy and continuing until the child reaches age 3	Provides information and guidance on child development and handbooks describing typical characteristics of children at each stage of development Hearing and vision screening for children Access to a school-based resource center, monthly individualized conferences, and monthly group meetings	Berger (1995), *Parents as Partners in Education: Families and Schools Working Together*

Recently, a neighborhood in Pennsylvania was selected by a national organization as one of the best places in America to raise a child, based on such variables as school achievement, crime rate, parent involvement in the schools, and so forth. Perhaps surprisingly, this was not one of the wealthiest neighborhoods. The houses are in an old section of Pittsburgh, but they are well maintained. When residents were interviewed by reporters and asked why the community had been so honored, one of them replied, "Maybe it's because everyone around here is nebby [western Pennsylvania slang for *nosey*]. We look out for one another and ask questions or pick up the phone if something doesn't look right. And, you pay attention to all of the kids here, not just your own."

Similarly, fulfilling your role as an early childhood educator requires you to care about all the children in your care and the families they come from, however different they are from your own. By working effectively with children, families, and the community at large, you are much better equipped to make a significant difference in the lives and the learning of the children entrusted to your care.

FIGURE 10.5

Steps toward
parent/family
engagement in
educare

**Strides Forward: Three-way and
Many-way Collaboration**

- Home visits
- Student-led conferences
- Establishing parent resource rooms
- Contacting parents/families on a regular basis to convey good news
- Functioning as a family advocate in the community
- Building a personal knowledge base of families' and community members' interests, occupations, and affiliations
- Providing opportunities for families to improve their situations
- Involving parents and families in decision making

Intermediate Steps: Two-way Communication

- IEP and IFSP meetings
- Language translators to facilitate communication
- Parent-teacher conferences
- Open houses
- Potluck dinners
- Sending children's work home and asking for comments back
- Workshops in which parents/families acquire new skills
- End-of-year celebrations

Initial Steps: One-way Communication

- Newsletters, school calendar
- Notes, tapes, and videos sent home
- Grades or progress reports sent home
- Announcements of events
- Contacting parents/families when problems arise
- Requesting parent volunteers
- Guest speakers

ASK the Expert Eugenia Hepworth Berger on Family Involvement

Common Questions and Concerns About Family Involvement

Eugenia Hepworth
Berger

1. Are parents truly interested in their children's education?

If schools are "family friendly," parents will feel welcome. When they feel welcome, they are able to express their interest. It is the school's attitude that enables parents to participate.

Most parents want their children to succeed, to achieve academically, and to be confident, positive, and able throughout their school experiences. Those who have marginal jobs hope that their children will be able to use academic success as a way to a better life. Some parents may have a negative or reluctant attitude toward participating in their children's schools as a result of their own life experiences. Perhaps they were unsuccessful in school, or for other reasons they may fear or want to avoid school contact. But when they come to view the school as wanting to help their children they feel more comfortable, and they are able to participate. Schools need to reach out to these parents.

Parents may work with schools at many levels. Most important is the family's basic belief in the school, support for the teacher, and encouragement of and positive interaction with their children. Parents may also become involved by tutoring, assisting in the classroom, being a paid or a volunteer aide, participating in the parent-teacher-student association, or participating in decisions and governance. This higher level of parent involvement is positive, but most important of all is the productive, caring connection between family and school. Schools want children to succeed; so do parents.

2. Does involvement of parents really help the child's education?

After **Goals 2000** had been approved, two goals were added. One of these, Goal 8, states, "By the year 2000, every school will promote partnerships that will increase parental involvement and participation in promoting the social, emotional, and academic growth of children." This goal was added because it was recognized that it takes more than the school to help all children become literate adults who are able to promote their own well-being and contribute to the overall good of the nation. Research and examination of successful schools support the value of parent involvement. It is particularly essential for at-risk children. If you look at schools with high success rates, you will find schools in which parents are involved, not always, but sometimes actively working in the schools.

3. How can teachers work with parents?

When I teach a course on parents as partners, I include quite a number of sessions on communication as well as sessions on activities that connect parents and teachers. Sometimes, students ask how they can work with parents, as if parents were a different species! The same communication skills that are positive with children and adults are appropriate when talking with parents. I tell students to remember that their mothers and fathers were parents, teachers are often parents, and they may be or may become parents. They should treat parents as they would like to be treated. When parents are culturally different from a teacher, the teacher should attempt to understand the differences and, most important of all, treat all parents with care and respect. Parents should also treat teachers with the same care and respect.

376

CHAPTER 10

Should teachers find that in spite of their positive overtures, parents are unhappy with them or their classrooms, it helps to let the parents explain what it is that makes them dissatisfied. Teachers must listen to parents' protests, let them express their concerns, and be considerate of their feelings and insights. Although it may be difficult, teachers should not be defensive. They should listen, let parents vent their concerns, and then try to come to an understanding and a plan of action together.

Teachers need to plan activities that encourage parents to connect with the school. These may include a note of introduction with the teacher's photo sent prior to the beginning of school, an early open house, or a breakfast for all parents, especially those who work outside the home. Other things to consider are family-friendly newsletters, weekly telephone calls (with something positive to relate), "up slips" and "happy grams," calendars with home activities that reinforce the curriculum, and home visits. If possible, parents should have telephone access to teachers or tutors and be provided with homework hot lines. Teachers need to set aside ample time for conferences, be aware that they can learn more about children when they listen to the parents, and make conferences a sharing, caring time. Monthly parties, planned by teachers for families, are a wonderful way to connect. Examples include pumpkin measuring and decorating in October, book making in November, winter-holiday celebrating in January, multicultural sharing in March, reading in April, and celebrating spring in May.

Teachers need to remember that parents are partners in the education of children. They were children's first educators, and they continue to be team members.

Eugenia Hepworth Berger is a professor emeritus, Metropolitan State College of Denver, Denver, Colorado.

One Child, Three Perspectives: *David, a Newly Immigrated Child*

While there are many kinds of families, people have strong opinions about the ability of single parents to provide the appropriate environments in which to raise children. Much of the concern centers around whether or not single parents can appropriately raise a well-socialized child who will become a productive and contributing citizen. Increasingly, however, women who have never married are choosing to become parents and adopting children to create a family. The case of David is a good example.

David was adopted from a Russian orphanage at 26 months of age. His never-married adoptive mother, Marsha, had invested 18 months of working intensely with a social worker through extensive interviews, a personal history, financial statements, fingerprinting, evaluations by a psychologist and a psychiatrist, and a series of parenting classes. Next, Marsha worked with adoption agencies until a child was identified as a good match. She spent 2 weeks in Russia getting to know David and preparing to bring him home. Although Marsha knew very little about David's birth history, she did learn that he had been in the orphanage since he was 2 weeks old.

The orphanage was well maintained and had a staff of women teachers and doctors. In David's group, there was a large, open room with areas designated for play and small tables and chairs for eating together. The children spent time each day going outside but never left the property. David's basic physical needs had been met and his daily routine was very structured, with meals and bathroom time strictly controlled. However, the food supply was limited, and David's treat for the day and primary means of getting milk was a yogurt shake. David was extremely shy, frightened, and withdrawn. One of

David's teachers described him as the runt of the litter and thought he might be retarded because he had not begun to talk at 26 months.

When David came to the United States, he still had no language. He exhibited fear of unfamiliar people and things (e.g., animals, males, bathtubs, strangers), could not walk steadily without support nor climb stairs, did not smile, and was very small for his age. In his first week in this country, he vomited in the car until he became used to the motion and sounds, clung to his new mother, or sat in one place with one toy until he was encouraged to move or to try another. He was also fascinated with looking at himself in the mirror, having never seen his own image. Still, no language or smiles.

At his new home, David experienced a stimulating, warm, and nurturing environment. He had his own room, a space for toys and books, friends to visit, and daily opportunities to explore toys and talk about what he was doing. Even though he did not speak, David's mother talked to him throughout the day as they were getting dressed, eating meals, or getting ready for bed. While in the car, she pointed out interesting objects, such as school buses and traffic lights, and remarked on them. As he grew older and more comfortable at home, David's mother had clear expectations for him in the home such as setting the table and recycling paper.

David's mother enrolled him in a local child-care setting upon a recommendation from her friend, an early childhood educator. With the director's encouragement and confidence, Marsha visited the center with David at different times of the day and stayed with him until he felt comfortable. Adapting to the life and culture of a new country was a challenge.

Each day, David cried and cried as his mother left him in the arms of Miss Gail, his caring and sensitive teacher, and his mother struggled with the question of what would help both David and her adjust to this new setting. David eventually became attached to Miss Gail, who welcomed him every day with open arms and soft, comforting words while he made the very difficult transition from home to school.

David's mother and teachers talked to him every day and read stories to him regularly. At school, David had a regular routine with teachers who cared about children's socialization, comfort level, and learning. David had opportunities to work alone, in small groups, and in whole-group experiences, and he engaged in many different kinds of learning activities. His teachers supported his efforts to adjust to his new school through conversations, pictures, and regular communication with David's mother. After a while, David began to say a few words, then a phrase, then a sentence, and eventually, he could connect thoughts together. When David was 4 years old, he still could not produce certain sounds or say certain words but was communicating easily about his needs and played with others in his child-care group and at home. Several people expressed concern about his language and suggested that David be referred to Child Find, a public program that identifies and serves children with exceptionalities at an early age. Others suggested that David be left alone and that his speech be allowed to develop naturally. His mother, always seeking what was in her child's best interests, struggled with the conflicting information and recommendations. She opted to wait and continue the supportive care and education. This obviously was a wise decision, because David is now a nonstop talker with clear speech and an enormous vocabulary that he uses to make his needs, ideas, and wishes known. Those who never knew David when he first arrived in this country would find it hard to believe that his first words were not uttered until he was almost 3 years old.

REACT:	In what ways are the perspectives of David's mother, David's teachers in Russia, and his teachers in America alike? How do their approaches to meeting David's needs vary? What might be the underlying reasons for these differences?
RESEARCH:	Locate several journal articles on second-language learners who are newly immigrated. What is recommended by the experts?
REFLECT:	Which perspective do you identify most strongly with, and why?

IN-CLASS
WORKSHOP

Creating an Informational Brochure on a Topic of General Interest to Parents

When you teach, you will find that it is important to communicate with parents and families in a variety of ways. One way of informing parents about important ideas is to create a tri-fold brochure on a topic. Examples of the titles for brochures that our students have developed for parents have included the following:

Books for Babies

What Does a Baby Know?

How Toddlers Learn

Guiding Children's Behavior

Understanding Developmentally Appropriate Practice

Why Children Need to Play

Ten Reasons to Read to Your Child

Summertime Activities for Preschoolers

How to Raise a Creative Child

Homework: How You Can Help

Questions Parents Ask About Starting School

There's Always Something New at the Library

Learning Mathematics Through Everyday Experiences

Where to Find Help: Services in Our Community

Procedure for Developing a Brochure

1. *Locate examples of brochures.* Collect and examine several brochures written for parents. Some good sources include professional organizations (e.g., the National Association for the Education of Young Children, the International Reading Association, the National PTA, Association for Childhood Education International). Places where you can usually find brochures include pediatricians' offices, shopping-mall displays, schools or child-care centers, mental health associations, and women's shelters. Also check the organizations in the Compendium of Resources at the end of this book. Bring at least one example of a high-quality brochure written for parents to class.

2. *Analyze the way that the material is written for parents.* Read publications such as *Parent's Magazine, Our Children* (published by the National PTA), *Working Mother Magazine,* and *Children Today* or the columns written for parents in popular magazines such as *Redbook* and *Family Circle.* Some of the leading authors who write for parents include T. Berry Brazelton, Penelope Leach, Eda LeShan, and John Rosemond.

3. *Research your topic.* Locate several authoritative sources on your topic using professional journals and books. Gather sufficient information to support the points that you will be making in your brochure, and identify other articles, books, software, or information about organizations (name, address, telephone number, Web site) that relate to your topic. Before you begin writing, formulate a rationale that states the reasons why you are bringing families and this information together. State specifically how the information will benefit children and those who care for them.

4. *Make a draft of your brochure.* Remember that your information will need to be clear, concise, and logically organized. Experiment with different arrangements, headings, formats, and illustrative materials until you discover the best way to get your message across. Advances in computer software and desktop publishing have made it possible to design high-quality brochures. If you or someone in your group has the skills and access to this type of software, consider using these resources in producing the final copy. If not, type the text of the brochure and sketch or cut-and-paste art or photographs that have been enlarged or reduced to the appropriate size. Use samples of children's work and comments, if appropriate. Include bulleted lists of important points or ideas from experts in the field. Intersperse short, thought-provoking direct quotations from authoritative sources in the text. Be certain to list the full names of all of the people who worked on the project directly on the brochure. When your draft is complete, seek the feedback of other parents and professionals before making your final copy.

5. *Complete the final, edited version.* Be sure to run a spell check on the text and proofread carefully. Ask someone with good editorial skills to read it one last time before the final copy is produced.

Evaluation Criteria

A high-quality brochure for parents

- focuses on ideas that are important for parents and families to understand

- provides a rationale and how this information will benefit children and families

- effectively synthesizes and translates material from a variety of professional sources into language that is understandable to general audiences
- offers a clear, concise explanation supported by concrete examples (e.g., children's comments, samples of children's work, common situations parents can identify with)
- makes appropriate use of the work of leaders in the field of education (e.g., brief quotations from experts, bulleted lists of recommendations compiled from various sources, all work cited appropriately)
- presents material in an original, engaging, and visually appealing way
- supplies a complete list of references in APA style as well as agencies, organizations, or companies that can serve as resources
- has been carefully proofread and edited to make certain the writing style is conversational and the text is error free
- uses the strategies that professional publishers use to invite readers to take the time to read it, such as an interesting title and a question-answer format, a self-test, or other ways to display the material (one of our students made the back of the brochure into a growth chart; another used a calendar format for summertime activities)

Scoring Sheet

5 = got it
4 = working on it
3 = trying
2 = not yet
1 = begin again

Significance of message	5	4	3	2	1
Clarity of rationale and benefits	5	4	3	2	1
Synthesis of numerous professional sources	5	4	3	2	1
Clear and concise explanation supported by concrete examples	5	4	3	2	1
Appropriate use and citation of reference materials	5	4	3	2	1
Originality and visual appeal of brochure	5	4	3	2	1
Quality of supplemental resources included	5	4	3	2	1
Evidence of careful proofreading and editing	5	4	3	2	1
Professional style of finished product	5	4	3	2	1

Comments: _____

_____

_____

11

Exploring Your Role as a Professional in the Field of Early Childhood Education

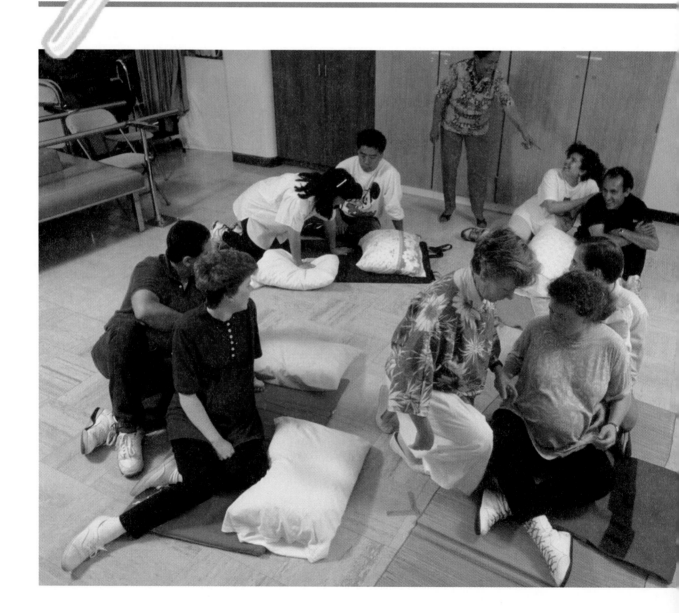

Every act of self-improvement is an act toward improved teaching. A very exciting aspect of teaching is knowing that development of oneself as a person goes hand in hand with development of oneself as a teacher. Skills of organization, communication, breadth of knowledge, sensitivity, all of which are helpful in one's daily life, become especially important in teaching. Every teacher who helps children helps them according to his or her own strengths. Teaching is far more than the application of techniques. A teacher's personal qualities make teaching either boring and abrasive or rich and meaningful for children. It is difficult to think of any area of personal development that would not somehow improve teaching.

—Lay-Dopyera and Dopyera, 1993, p. 20

Learning Outcomes

✔ Define professional development

✔ Reflect upon the stages in teachers' professional growth

✔ Develop strategies for managing personal and professional growth

✔ Understand the value of a research base to support teaching practice

✔ Document growth as an educator through a professional portfolio

Meet the Teachers

Ms. Huong has just begun working with toddlers at a private infant-and-toddler care facility in the program director's home. When she accepted the position, she "had no illusions that the center was top quality." Yet she decided to work there, partly to gain experience, partly because it was in her home town, and partly to make a difference in the educare for infants and toddlers in the program. She knew from talking to the director that the center wanted to earn a credential from the Academy of the National Association for the Education of Young Children (NAEYC) and this seemed like the perfect time to initiate improvements in the program. First, Ms. Huong consulted numerous resources on infant-and-toddler programs. She made a copy of a photo essay on the credentialing process from the journal *Young Children* (Cryer & Phillipsen, 1997), and she located expert advice on quality in infant-and-toddler programming in *Dimensions of Early Childhood, Early Childhood Education Journal, Child Care Information Exchange,* and the online Education Resources Information Index (ERIC). Ms. Huong also visited the NAEYC website at *http://www.naeyc.org/naeyc* and printed out the most up-to-date material on the credentialing process. Then she organized all of the information by topic, and when issues were discussed at staff meetings, she "just happened" to have some very useful resources on hand. Later, when the center was accredited by the NAEYC, Ms. Huong's colleagues kept saying, "We never could have done it without you!"

This year has been, by **Ms. Wilden's** own description, her "most challenging experience in 5 years of teaching third grade" in an urban setting. Ms. Wilden realized early in the year that two of the boys in her class were experiencing serious difficulty in learning to read and sought help from her fellow teachers, the reading specialist, and the school psychologist, as well as information from national organizations, to deepen her understanding of dyslexia.

383

She was surprised to discover that colored overlays—sheets of plastic that look like tinted transparencies—were very helpful to one student, while the other made the greatest progress with the recorded-book method (Carbo, 1997), in which he listened to an audiotape of the book as he looked at the words. Ms. Wilden remarked, "I was delighted to discover that there are some research-based strategies that enable dyslexic children to experience greater success in learning to read. I also wonder, though, what might have happened to the two boys if I hadn't taken the time to investigate dyslexia."

 Ms. Renzulli has been teaching kindergarten for 25 years. Although she was always regarded as a good teacher by her coworkers and in the community, over the last 5 years, she felt a growing dissatisfaction with the way she was teaching kindergarten. "I used to be the worksheet queen," Ms. Renzulli admitted. "When I first started teaching, everybody accepted lots of paperwork for kindergarten children as proof that they were learning. Now I have a poster outside my classroom door that reads, 'Real learning isn't measured by the weight of your child's backpack!' I couldn't really say that there was any outside pressure to change. It's just that I saw that my methods weren't working well with my students. Also, I was inspired by the many excellent student teachers who came into my classroom full of enthusiasm and bursting with ideas that they wanted to try. I would let them go, let them do things in their own way, and sometimes marvel at how successful they were. So, I revolutionized my teaching, had a great burning of the busy work from my files, and I love teaching again."

COMPARE:	What are some commonalities among these three teachers, even though they work in different settings and are at different stages in their careers?
CONTRAST:	How do these teachers think about teaching? About learning? How would you characterize the outlook of each one?
CONNECT:	Reflective teachers are *open minded*, willing to admit or consider that they are wrong; *responsible*, willing to look at the consequences of their actions; and *wholehearted*, willing to accept all students and to practice what they preach (Grant & Zeichner, 1984). What evidence did you see of these characteristics in the three teachers profiled? How will you go about becoming more wholehearted, responsible, and open-minded in your teaching?

A Definition of Professional Development

Professionalism refers to an intrinsic code of ethics, values, commitments, and responsibilities that guide thoughts and actions. Professionalism is what keeps a teacher striving for excellence and working hard to help every child learn, even when no one is observing or evaluating. Developing as a professional depends upon your commitment to continue to learn, even after you have completed your initial or advanced preparation program (Lieberman, 1995). (To review the National Association for the Education of Young Children's Code of Ethical Conduct, see the Compendium of Resources at the end of this book.)

Generally speaking, there are four dimensions that differentiate a professional role from other types of occupations (Darling-Hammond & Sykes, 1999; Darling-Hammond, Wise, & Klein, 1999; Saracho & Spodek, 1993).

1. *A defined **body of specialized knowledge** not possessed by the general public.* Figure 11.1 highlights the types of professional knowledge that teachers are expected to master.

2. ***Control over licensure**, certification, entrance requirements, and standards for responsible practice that are monitored by the professionals themselves.*

3. ***Autonomy of practitioners** to apply their professional knowledge in diverse situations, make decisions, and exercise judgment in their workplaces.*

4. ***High prestige and economic standing** in the larger community.* This means that professionals earn respect for their specialized skills and training and receive adequate compensation for their work.

Considered from these four dimensions, it is debatable whether or not teaching qualifies as a profession in the same way as law or medicine. Most people do not appreciate the special talents that are required to work effectively with the very young and assume that this type of work is fun and easy. Control over the standards of the profession is often external, emanating from federal, state, and local policies rather than from experts in the field of early childhood. Frequently, the early childhood educator's authority to make decisions is limited. Moreover, it is widely known that early childhood educators, particularly those in child care, are underpaid and held in low regard by the general public. Child caregivers, for example, have an annual turnover rate of between 35 and 50%, partially as a result of low salaries. In 1989, Ellen Galinsky reported that "seventy percent of child care workers earn less than poverty wages" (p. 108), and the situation has not changed much. If one also considers that caregivers rarely receive retirement or medical benefits, it is amazing that there are any child-care professionals at all (Gharavi, 1993). For all of these reasons, the professional status of teaching in general and the early childhood field in particular is a controversial topic.

Teaching has some unique characteristics that differ considerably from other professions (Farris, 1996; Swick & Hanes, 1987):

1. Unlike most other professionals, teachers seldom have any say about who their "clients" will be, and, under normal conditions, their work involves hundreds of hours in the company of those clients.

2. The test of a teacher's professional abilities is performance oriented and situation specific. Effectiveness is determined by the skills the teacher demonstrates in particular classrooms at particular times.

FIGURE 11.1

Types of professional knowledge

- **Case Knowledge:** acquired through direct experience with actual cases that become part of a teacher's "case files." Teachers return to these cases, sifting through them to find similarities to new cases they encounter.

Example: Making adaptations in the physical environment to meet the needs of a child. The teacher may be working with a young child with cerebral palsy for the first time and, in preparation, will refer to all prior personal experiences with making adaptations in the environment to offer guidance in this unfamiliar situation. The teacher may also borrow a case file from a more experienced colleague or professional in another field in order to respond appropriately to the child's needs.

- **Episodic Knowledge:** gained from personally meaningful, deeply affecting events.

Example: A teacher whose neighbor lost a child to Reyes' syndrome obtains literature on this life-threatening illness and writes an article for the school newsletter alerting parents to the symptoms of this devastating illness.

- **Procedural Knowledge:** the physical sequence of events associated with a particular task.

Example: A teacher who has learned the proper procedure for taking children on a field trip, including such things as permission forms, adequate adult supervision, safety procedures on the bus, and so forth.

- **Propositional Knowledge:** terminology, facts, concepts, and underlying principles learned through reading and study. Propositional knowledge is brought to bear on experience when teachers use it to more thoughtfully observe, analyze, and discuss real-world teaching.

Example: A beginning teacher who has experienced difficulty during large-group circle time experiments with some of the strategies that were presented in class, such as sitting close to a child who has difficulty with self-control, making group times more active and interactive, keeping large-group sessions short, providing a small carpet square to keep each child's space distinct, and restating the rules. The teacher institutes these changes, observes, adapts them to the situation, and shares the results with student-teaching seminar participants.

SOURCE: Adapted from "Developmental Stages in the Lives of Early Childhood Educators" by D. C. Berliner, 1994, in S. G. Goffin & D. E. Day, Eds., *New Perspectives in Early Childhood Education: Bringing Practitioners into the Debate* (pp. 120–128), New York: Teachers College Press.

3. Teacher education, while ostensibly focused on adults, is actually intended for children. Teachers have responsibility not only for their own learning but also for the effects of that learning on children's learning.

4. Unlike many other professions, in teaching, reciprocal emotional ties between the professionals and the clients are accepted rather than discouraged. It is a breach of professionalism when a psychologist becomes emotionally involved with a patient, while it is perfectly acceptable for young children to love their teachers and for their teachers to say that they love children.

5. Teaching is the only profession that virtually every person in America has had ample opportunity to observe, at least from the other side of the desk. The average

Most people don't realize the special talents required to work with young children.

high school graduate has spent more time in the company of teachers than on any activity other than sleeping and watching television (Ryan, 1986).

Thus, a career dedicated to the care and education of children, while commonplace, is unique among the professions.

Your Role as an Early Childhood Professional

An experienced third-grade teacher had saved for many years to travel to Australia. The study of Australia was part of her social studies curriculum, and the teacher was seeking both personal and professional development through travel. She described her reason for pursuing this goal by saying, "In this job you have to take care of yourself." The idea that a teacher should be in charge of his or her own professional development may be a rather startling concept. Educators are, as a group, very altruistic; most people would expect a great teacher's life to be a path of self-sacrifice rather than a plan for self-fulfillment. But becoming a masterful teacher is not a choice between attending to our professional growth and the needs of others; it is doing both (Sparks & Hirsh, 1997). The belief that dedicated teachers deny their needs and attend exclusively to the needs of students is a destructive myth. No matter how supportive the institutions in which early childhood educators work may be, it is up to teachers to identify their needs for professional growth and to monitor their own progress toward the goal of becoming better teachers.

Teachers who learn to take care of themselves professionally are smart rather than selfish. As architects of their professional growth, they recognize how their level of satisfaction with teaching influences relationships with colleagues and ultimately affects children's learning. The three timeless questions that guide professional development are

- Who am I?
- What do I need?
- How can I get help? (Clark, 1996, p. 125)

The first assumption of any effort at professional development is that it is "a complex, human task. It requires a climate conducive to learning and change . . . It is promoted by the effective use of diverse resources. It includes opportunities for field-testing, feedback, and adjustment. All of these things take time to achieve" (Wood, Thompson, & Russell, 1981, p. 88).

PAUSE AND REFLECT ABOUT YOUR OWN DEVELOPMENT AS A PROFESSIONAL

1. *What have you learned?* How would you explain the difference between teaching young children and teaching students at other developmental levels to someone who is unfamiliar with the field of early childhood?

2. *What will you do?* How do you plan to go about fulfilling the traditional mission of the early childhood educator: educating the whole-child and fostering total learning—cognitive, physical, social, and emotional? If you were asked to draw a path or diagram of your hoped-for career, what would it look like?

3. *Where will you find guidance?* What philosophical or theoretical orientations, powerful ideas, and effective strategies do you use to guide your professional practice? Who are your mentors and role models? What are your future goals?

What obstacles face men who want to work with young children?

Professionalism in the field of early childhood has been greatly affected by the belief that working with young children is a natural extension of maternal instincts. Historically, the care of young children has been relegated to women, and, because women and children were generally regarded as property in the eyes of society and the law, females and young children were powerless in a "man's world." Today, many people still assume "that preschool and kindergarten are just preparation for the serious learning of first grade—they are not 'real school.' This same attitude influences pay scales; generally, the younger the children, the lower the status and salary of the educator" (Feeney, Christensen, & Moravcik, 1996, p. 75).

Despite all of these obstacles, people all over the world dedicate their lives to the care and education of young children. The best in our profession think this is because we are captivated by the very young—their candor, their innocence, their active imaginations, and their delight in the world they experience afresh every day. One of the greatest rewards of working with the very young is observing their total involvement in learning. As you work with young children, those consummate novices, you too can keep learning, because each child is unique and every situation is individual. There will be daily challenges to your understanding of child development, teaching methods, and conflict resolution skills, because teaching is perpetually complex and engaging. In the process, you can become not only a better teacher, but also, a more caring person. Early childhood education and care are a paradox in that so much is demanded for relatively small financial compensation and such great emotional investment; but that investment is in that greatest of our nation's resources: children.

FEATURING FAMILIES

CONDUCTING HOME VISITS

An important part of professional development is learning how to interact with parents and families in ways that build mutual trust and respect. Keep in mind that any information shared with you during home visits is privileged and confidential. Here is one example of a form you might use or adapt when conducting home visits.

Interviewer: *CK*   Date: *Oct. 7*

Child's Name: *Jesus Martinez*   Grade: *2nd*

Parents' Names: *Miguel and Yolanda Guiterrez*

Siblings: *1 younger sister, 1 older sister*

Language(s) used: *English and Spanish*

Address: *1 Sonoma Lane, Phoenix, AZ*

Telephone: *602 357-2417*

E-mail: *Guiterrez@hotmail.com*

1. What are your child's interests? (art, sports, hobbies, activities)
   J. likes animals, computers, numbers—can do math in his head. Reads to younger sister. Likes stepfather to read to him. Watches Wheel of Fortune. Saving his money for a cat. Rides bike and swims. Loves Net surfing.

2. How does your child seem to feel about going to school?
   Moved in July and does not know many neighborhood kids. Wants to make friends and exchange phone numbers and E-mail addresses. Does not want to go to school because of "homework he doesn't know."

3. What do you expect your child to accomplish this year?
   Oral language in English needs improvement. He's more fluent in Spanish.

4. What signs of progress were you pleased to see over the summer?
   More confident with numbers, can figure out calorie and cholesterol counts in his head to help stepfather with a special diet! Started to play word games and use rhyming words.

5. Are there any concerns that you have about your child?
   May not be challenged in math at school. Expressed concern about husband's new job and the long hours worked—J. is very close to stepfather.

6. What have you discovered about your child's particular ways of learning?
   Looks for patterns in numbers and can do some of this with letters and words.

7. What is the most important thing your child could learn this year?
   To build his confidence in speaking English. (But he wants to learn to play soccer.)

8. What hopes do you have for your child in the future?
   Has a head for numbers and math—maybe an accountant or an engineer? Dream of him working at NASA—very good at problem solving.

9. Is there anything else that I should know as I work with your child?
   J. is very sensitive and feelings are hurt easily. Has a food allergy to seafood and is allergic to bee stings.

Thank you for your time and for inviting me to your home.

Ways of Supporting Professional Development

What conditions are most likely to foster professional development? Variables that affect teachers' overall job satisfaction and contribute to their professional development are depicted in Figure 11.2.

Preservice or in-service educators may be given information, but it is up to each individual to integrate and use that information. No one can simply tell you how to teach.

Consider the people you know who are majoring in education. Can you imagine who is most likely to become outstanding, average, or marginal? One way to predict is to consider how adult learners tend to behave. Teachers who are maturing as professionals

- pursue information today about what will help them to teach better tomorrow
- learn from tapping into their experiences and reflecting upon them
- work hard to fulfill the professional roles they have chosen for themselves
- move from dependence on others to greater self-direction and self-evaluation (Knowles, 1975)

FIGURE 11.2

Influences on teachers' professional development

People

The establishment of friendly, supportive, and trusting relationships with teachers, student teachers, aides, administrators, families, school support personnel (e.g., clerical workers, janitors, bus drivers), and other professionals (e.g., nurse, counselor, psychologist, consultant) that build a sense of community

Programs and Systems

An emphasis on personal and professional growth and a staff-development system that enables all educators to learn about the best that the field has to offer

Roles

Clearly defined roles and policies combined with leaders who have clear expectations, plan carefully, function efficiently, and encourage and support staff members

Fairness and equity regarding promotions, raises, and other rewards

Democracy

Meaningful staff involvement in decision making and agreement among staff members on goals and objectives.

Environments and Natural Resources

Physical environments that are well equipped, maintained, and organized

Innovation and Improvement

Professionals who have developed the ability to adapt flexibly to new demands and change in ways that continuously improve the curriculum, teaching, and learning

Relationships with Families and Communities

Effective ways of working with families and educating the public about the realities of teaching and learning so that continuous improvement becomes a reality

SOURCE: Adapted from *Achieving Center-based Change Through Staff Development* by P. J. Bloom, M. Sheerer, and J. Britz, 1991, Lake Forest, IL: New Horizons.

To illustrate, let's look at Jennifer and Kelly, two college students who are required to observe and participate in a second-grade classroom. Kelly can usually be found sitting at her desk, waiting for the teacher to stop and give her instructions. She is, in her own words, "totally clueless about what to do" during her field assignment, even though a detailed student handbook sits on her desk. When Kelly is confused about something, she complains to anyone who will listen. One requirement is to write in her journal every day, but this is Friday and she has not written anything all week. When Kelly encounters a challenge in the classroom, she panics and protests that she "wasn't prepared" for this particular situation by her teacher-preparation program.

In contrast, Jennifer pitches in and suggests a way she might help whenever an opportunity arises in the classroom. She has entered the due dates for each assignment on her calendar and refers to it frequently to pace herself. Jennifer reads the information carefully before formulating a specific question, then she decides who would be the best

FIGURE 11.3

Performance
standards for
beginning teachers

The teacher understands . . .

- the central concepts, tools of inquiry, and structures of the disciplines he or she teaches and can create learning experiences that make these aspects of subject matter meaningful for students.
- how children learn and develop and can provide learning opportunities that support their intellectual, social, and personal growth.
- how students differ in their approaches to learning and creates instructional opportunities that are adapted to diverse learners.
- and uses a variety of instructional strategies to encourage students' development of critical thinking, problem solving, and performance.
- individual and group motivation and behavior to create a learning environment that encourages positive social interaction, active engagement in learning, and self-motivation.
- and uses knowledge of effective verbal, nonverbal, and media communication techniques to foster active inquiry, collaboration, and supportive interaction in the classroom.
- and uses formal and informal assessment strategies to evaluate and ensure the continuous intellectual, social, and physical development of the learner.
- reflective practice and uses it to continually evaluate effects of his or her choices and actions on others (students, parents, and other professionals in the learning community) and actively seeks out opportunities to grow professionally.
- fosters relationships with school colleagues, parents, and agencies in the larger community to support students' learning and well-being.

SOURCE: Adapted from "Standards for Teachers: Potential for Improving Practice" by G. Ambach, 1996, *Phi Delta Kappan, 78*(3), pp. 207–210.

person to answer that question. When an autistic child joins the class, Jennifer reads several articles about autism, attends a presentation on the topic at the local Council for Exceptional Children meeting, stops by the local mental health association to get information, and speaks with teachers and professors who have training and experience in special education. Jennifer has learned to be self-directed, to use resources to solve problems, and to reflect upon her experiences.

Kelly is still entirely dependent upon others, while Jennifer is making steady progress toward her goal of becoming a caring, competent professional who has learned how to evaluate herself (see Black & Davern, 1998, for more on collaborative relationships with other adults). Figure 11.3 summarizes the performance standards for competent beginning teachers.

Stages in Teachers' Professional Development

Every teacher has the choice of seeking growth or resisting growth as a learner: "Professionalism is not an end in itself—a state of being—but an ongoing effort—a process of becoming" (Caulfield, 1997, p. 263). Just as there are stages in child development, there also are stages in teacher development. Knowing these stages may help you to better understand your own experiences on your journey to becoming a teacher of the very young.

Using symbolic language, or metaphors, is one way to talk about stages in teachers' professional development. A metaphor consists of an image or a phrase that symbolizes something else and captures the essence of something profound. For example, a college student who was miserable teaching junior high school and wished that she had pursued early childhood instead chose the metaphor of "a bird in a cage," because anyone could walk by her classroom and see her struggling. All the while she felt trapped, yet obligated to finish the semester. By way of contrast, an early childhood major who was working in a public school prekindergarten for at-risk children chose the metaphor of "a covered-dish dinner" to characterize her experience. She worked on an instructional support team consisting of the classroom teacher, a special education teacher, a social worker, and a medical professional to meet with families and make plans for each child. She selected the "covered dish" metaphor because her experience as a teacher thus far had taught her that "everyone brings something important to the experience, and when all of those contributions are combined, the result is wonderful."

In the section that follows, we have synthesized the work of several experts on teacher education to identify the following stages, themes, metaphors, descriptions, and recommended resources (Berliner, 1994b; Katz, 1977, 1995; Swick & Hanes, 1987).

Stage 1: Novice   **Theme:** Survival   **Question:** Am I cut out to be a teacher?

Metaphors: "Just learning the ropes." "Barely keeping my head above water." "Wondering if I have what it takes to be a teacher."

Description: Garrett Keizer (1988) poignantly characterizes the novice teacher's dilemma when he writes, "I never cared less whether I lived or died than I did my first year of teaching" (p. 1). Most student teachers and even first- or second-year teachers are considered to be novices who are striving to define themselves as professionals. Beginning teachers frequently feel overwhelmed by the daily demands of teaching and ill-prepared for the complexities of the teaching role.

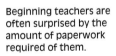

Beginning teachers are often surprised by the amount of paperwork required of them.

"The realization of the great responsibility they have for the group of children, as well as the discrepancy between the success they expect and the reality of the classroom, result in anxiety and feelings of inadequacy" (Essa, 1996, p. 95).

Many preservice teachers are still in the process of making their career decision about teaching. They usually have the idealism characteristic of their age, but they are also fearful of failure. As they move into their first "survival" year, new teachers are generally shocked by several things: the stamina required of the job, the amount of paperwork, the range and intensity of students' needs, the parents who lack confidence in them, and the lack of support for their efforts within the school and district (Ryan, 1986). Early childhood educators at this stage have training but limited experience. Usually, they are relatively immature as professionals and are still under direct supervision, such as a student teacher who works with a veteran teacher and a college faculty member as supervisors or a first-year teacher who is assigned to a master teacher or mentor. The persistent questions of the beginning teacher usually are "Who am I?" and "What can I do?" (Baptiste & Sheerer, 1997, p. 266).

Recommended Books: For more on first-year teachers, read autobiographical accounts such as Conroy's (1987) *The Water Is Wide,* Kohl's (1967) *36 Children,* Meier's (1997) *Life in Small Moments: Learning in an Urban Classroom,* Kane's (1991) *The First Year of Teaching: Real World Stories from America's Teachers,* and Dollas's (1992) *Voices of Beginning Teachers: Visions and Realities.* Also read studies of beginning teachers (Clandinin, Davies, Hogan, & Kennard, 1993; LaBoskey, 1994; Reynolds, 1992) or consult handbooks for beginning teachers (MacDonald, 1991; Wong & Wong, 1997).

Stage 2: Advanced Beginner   **Theme:** Consolidation   **Question:** How can I grow in competence and confidence?

Metaphors: "Putting it all together." "Finding my way." "Hitting my stride."

Description: During the consolidation phase, the teacher begins to focus on specific tasks, individual children, specific behavior problems, and challenging situations. Another hallmark of this stage is developing a more personalized approach to teaching, or a teaching style. The early childhood educator at this stage has completed professional training, worked directly with young children, and made a commitment to the profession. Practitioners at this stage are better equipped to identify possible courses of action, make rational decisions, and predict the consequences of their actions for children, families, colleagues, and professionals in other fields (VanderVen, 1991).

Recommended Books: *Notes from a Schoolteacher* (Herndon, 1985), *Among School Children* (Kidder, 1989), and *One Child* (Hayden, 1980). For research on teachers who are in the consolidation stage of their careers, see Connelly and Clandinin, 1988.

Stage 3: Proficient   **Theme:** Renewal   **Question:** What will I do to improve with experience rather than diminish my effectiveness?

Metaphors: "Avoiding falling into a rut." "Seeking new challenges"

Description: After working for 3 to 5 years, many teachers seek professional enrichment that will bolster their enthusiasm, offer a fresh perspective, enrich their storehouse of ideas, and inspire them to do their best. The teacher at the renewal phase is typically interested in exploring new ideas and resources that will enhance effectiveness. Activities such as collaboration with colleagues; perusal of the professional literature (books, journals, magazines); attendance at conferences, seminars, and workshops; visits to model programs; and the pursuit of an advanced degree are all ways that teachers seek renewal.

Recommended Books: *Joyful Learning: A Whole Language Kindergarten* (Fisher, 1991), *Finding Our Own Way* (Newman, 1990), *Stirring the Chalkdust: Case Studies of Teachers in the Midst of Change* (Wasley, 1994), and *Oops! What We Learn When Our Teaching Fails* (Power & Hubbard, 1996).

Stage 4: Expert   **Theme:** Maturity   **Question:** What impact has my life had on the lives of children and families?

Metaphors: "Really making a difference." "Taking on the mentoring role."

Description: Teachers who have attained maturity have arrived at a personal and professional teaching style and are most concerned with the long-term consequences of their teaching for learners. Profound and abstract questions characterize their quest to make an enduring contribution to children's learning: "What will their world be like?" "How important is it for children to know this?" and "Which experiences and activities will have the most enduring effect on learning?" It is also during this stage that teachers often assume leadership roles that emanate from expertise in the field, a secure sense of self, and the admiration of colleagues. Remember the veteran teacher, Ms. Renzulli, from the opening scenario? She completely changed her teaching because she regained her focus on the impact of her teaching.

Recommended Books: *The Languages of Learning: How Children Talk, Write, Dance, Draw, and Sing Their Understanding of the World* (Gallas, 1994), *The Transcendent Child: Tales of Triumph Over the Past* (Rubin, 1996), *Portraits in Courage: Teachers in Difficult Circumstances* (UNESCO, 1997), *Mentors, Master Teachers, and Mrs. MacGregor: Stories of Teachers Making a Difference* (Bluestein, 1995), and *On Their Side: Helping Children Take Charge of Learning* (Strachota, 1996). See issues of the journal *Teacher Researcher* for a wide array of articles about teaching. For some fine examples of early childhood educators who have reached maturity, read Carol Hillman's (1988) *Teaching Four-year-olds: A Personal Journey,* Mem Fox's (1993) *Radical Reflections: Passionate Opinions on Teaching, Learning, and Living,* or any of Vivian Paley's books, particularly *Wally's Stories* (1981) and *The Girl with the Brown Crayon* (1997). For more on teachers at all of these career stages, read *Teachers' Stories: From Personal Narrative to Professional Insight* (Jalongo & Isenberg, 1995).

PAUSE AND REFLECT ABOUT WHAT YOUR METAPHOR IS

An early childhood administrator had this to say about her role: "I see myself as a change agent, a coach, a mentor, and a facilitator whose job it is to remove obstacles so that people can teach." On her lapel was a button that read "Children First." Early childhood educators use a variety of metaphors or symbols to characterize our professional roles. One teacher from a neighborhood with a high crime rate referred to his classroom as "a safe sector of the city, a haven." A kindergarten teacher described her approach to the curriculum as "like building with blocks—first you make the base, then stack them, one at a time, on top of one another." We also use short statements or mottos that characterize our beliefs, values, and attitudes. Some current examples are "Leave no child behind," "Caring for other people's children," and "Celebrating diversity." What metaphors or mottos do you live by as a teacher of the very young? Give this some thought, then share your ideas with the class.

Beginning teachers sometimes assume that after they log more hours in early childhood settings, they will automatically become the teachers they aspire to be. Yet experience alone does not necessarily lead to more caring, competent teaching. It is possible to repeat the mistakes of that first "survival" year over and over again and learn little from experience, time after time. Nor will accumulating more formal education or collecting advanced degrees guarantee quality. Becoming an outstanding early childhood educator depends upon the personal investment you make in your learning and teaching, all the while keeping children at the center of your practice. There are many career paths in the early childhood field, as Figure 11.4 depicts.

Life-long Learning and the Early Childhood Practitioner

At this stage in your career, you might be dreaming about the day when you have completed your program. That hopeful dreaming might include abandoning your books, tests, presentations, trading them for exciting lessons, and spending your time in the company of young children. Perhaps you have thought to yourself, "When I get my certificate/degree/first job, I will finally be ready!" The bad news is, no matter how excellent your program is, it is only the beginning. There are several reasons why teacher-preparation programs cannot fully prepare teachers for what they will encounter in a classroom.

Change versus Status Quo. In every teacher-preparation program, your instructors have to deal with the conflict between preparing you for early childhood settings as they are and preparing you for early childhood settings as they should and could be. In other words, your instructors hope that you will go forward and improve education, not merely fit in, as important as that may be, particularly at first. Striving for change can sometimes cause you to feel frustrated with veteran teachers who are satisfied with the way things are. Although you need to respect their experience and acknowledge their strengths, you also have an obligation to improve the quality of care and education for young children.

General versus Specific. Early childhood teacher-preparation has to prepare teachers for a wide range of possibilities (see Figure 11.4). A student graduating from a 4-year program with a teaching certificate, for example, might be hired to teach third grade in a parochial school, teach prekindergarten in a public school, direct a child-care center, or provide instruction to young children who are ill in hospitals or in their homes. No program can be expected to provide you with guidance on the daily details of how to function in such diverse situations. That is why teachers must continue to be avid learners and develop professionally.

FIGURE 11.4

Career paths in early childhood

Path	Career
At least a high school diploma or equivalent	Nanny, licensed babysitter, child-care provider, family child-care provider
At least a child development associate credential	Classroom aide or assistant, child-care or family child-care provider
At least a 2-year associate's degree in child-care development and/or family relations	Child-care professional
At least a bachelor's degree in early childhood or child development	Early childhood teacher, public or private school teacher
A bachelor's degree plus experience working with young children, possibly a master's degree	Early childhood specialist, administrator, supervisor
At least a master's degree in early childhood or child development and significant prior experience working with young children	Early childhood teacher educators in community colleges, colleges, universities
A doctorate (Ph.D. or Ed.D.) in early childhood education or child development, prior experience with young children and college-level teaching experience	Early childhood professor, researcher, scholar

Real versus Ideal. Even though introductions to the real world of teaching occur more often and earlier through field experiences, no teacher-preparation program can eradicate the feelings of inadequacy during the first year. All professionals enter their profession with some fanciful notions of what their chosen careers will bring. It is surprisingly difficult to keep the right amount of that idealism intact throughout a career rather than deteriorating into a disillusioned or burned-out professional. Teaching well is an expression of who you are as a person and as an early childhood professional. There is no way to become completely prepared to teach, because even if you could be completely prepared for today, tomorrow will bring about changes that will demand new understandings and skills.

Promise versus Perfection. When you think about it, your instructors are in the business of making predictions about who will become effective early childhood practitioners. When you are a student teacher, they observe you in the context of the college or university classroom and try to imagine how you will perform in various early childhood settings. Then they observe you in someone else's early childhood setting with someone else's students and envision how you will function on your own. Although it may sometimes seem otherwise, your supervisors do not expect you to be perfect in either situation. Rather, they are looking for promise and progress at a level characteristic of other teacher candidates with your level of training and experience.

A good teacher-preparation program can inaugurate a teacher's journey as a learner but never fully prepare you for the realities and complexities of teaching. Each teacher must make the difficult adjustment from college to the real world of the center or classroom. Even when teachers are equipped with a repertoire of effective teaching behaviors, they still have to decide which to use, when and how to use them, and which students to use them with (Clark & Yinger, 1977). Much of what you will need to do and understand as a teacher is learned through on-the-job training.

When you become a teacher, you become your own project. Becoming a better teacher is never finished. There will never come a day when you say to yourself, "At last, I am a perfect teacher!" Rather, there are components of professional practice that every competent, caring teacher addresses throughout life. These components are outlined in Figure 11.5.

The Concerns of Beginning Teachers

Each teacher gradually builds a theory of the world of teaching and continually tests the theory in the classroom. Three experienced teachers were having dinner together when one of them said, "I can tell that I am lacking confidence about something when I have the teaching nightmares I used to have as an undergraduate. In this dream, the children are completely unruly and I can't get them to pay any attention to me at all." Another teacher agreed, saying, "My nightmare is a little different. In it, I find out that I forgot to attend a class and now I can't graduate." A third teacher laughed and said, "Me too! Only in my nightmare, they take back my teaching degree!" Beginning teachers often approach teaching with a mixture of excitement and anxiety. Some of the most common worries of student teachers and beginning teachers include the following:

- *Relationships with children and families.* What should I expect from children of this age? What if they misbehave? How will I respond? Will my response be appropriate? What if children, parents, or families don't like or respect me? What if a child has a problem that I know nothing about how to handle? How will I talk with parents and families during conferences? I've never done this before!

- *Relationships with adults.* What if my supervisors don't like or respect me? What if I make a terrible mistake? What if I am observed on my very worst day of teaching? If my supervisors think that my teaching is bad, what will I do? Will I be encouraged and helped, or simply branded as a bad teacher? What about my grade point average or other types of evaluation? What if my supervisors don't agree on what I should be doing? Will I be caught in the middle?

- *Learning activities.* What if the activity that I have planned turns out to be a disaster? What if children are disinterested or won't cooperate? What if I plan something for half an hour and the children are done in a few minutes? How will I

FIGURE 11.5

Components of
professional practice

Planning and Preparation

- Demonstrates knowledge of content and pedagogy
- Demonstrates knowledge of students
- Selects instructional goals
- Demonstrates knowledge of resources
- Designs coherent instruction

The Classroom Environment

- Creates an environment of respect and rapport
- Establishes a culture for learning
- Manages classroom procedures
- Manages student behavior
- Organizes physical space

Instruction

- Communicates clearly and accurately
- Uses questions and discussion techniques effectively
- Engages students in learning
- Provides feedback to learners
- Demonstrates flexibility and responsiveness

Professional Responsibilities

- Reflects on teaching
- Maintains accurate records
- Communicates with families
- Contributes to the school and district
- Grows and develops professionally
- Shows professionalism

SOURCE: Adapted from *Enhancing Professional Practice: A Framework for Teaching* by C. Danielson, 1996, Alexandria, VA: Association for Supervision and Curriculum Development.

ever find the time to plan adequately for everything I am expected to do? How am I going to assess children's learning? What can I do to make sure that I treat children fairly?

- *Future career.* Will I be able to find a good job? How will I conduct myself during interviews? How will I make sure that prospective employers know what I can do and give me a chance? (MacDonald, 1991).

Figure 11.6 suggests a variety of ways that teachers can contribute to their own personal and professional development.

FIGURE 11.6

Strategies for
professional
development

Observing to Learn: paying attention to nonverbal, verbal, and other behavioral responses from children and adults

- In college classes: conducting a case study of a particular child, noticing what classmates plan that is particularly effective, learning from instructors
- In schools and centers: noticing what good teachers do, looking at the work that children have accomplished, analyzing the classroom floor plan, visiting model programs
- In other settings: noticing what other professionals who work with young children and young children's parents do during story time at the library, in a hospital nursery, at a health fair at the mall, at a church fair, at a community playground, at a family reunion picnic, and so forth

Participating to Learn: gaining experience with young children whenever the opportunity arises

- In college classes: working in required student teaching and practicum experiences, volunteering to participate at special campus events for children (e.g., a face-painting booth on homecoming day, a field trip to campus, a "read-in" or a Saturday workshop for parents sponsored by a professional organization)
- In other settings: babysitting for friends and family, volunteering to work with young children in the community (e.g., provide short-term child care for parents attending a meeting), teach a religion class for young children at your church

Writing to Learn: using writing skills to become a reflective practitioner

- In college classes and during teaching: keeping a journal, writing plans, taking notes from teacher resource books, making curriculum webs, communicating with families, documenting what children are learning through bulletin boards, submitting news items to the newspaper, corresponding with a trusted teacher and friend, writing a philosophy statement, creating a portfolio, writing a paper on a topic of interest for a class

Raising Questions to Learn: formulating good questions for yourself and children

- In college classes and during teaching: questioning personal assumptions and biases, raising questions about cultural influences, asking political questions about policies, power, and control issues

Collaborating to Learn: combining your skills and abilities with those of other adults to become a more effective early childhood practitioner

- In college classes: forming a study group, working on projects with partners or groups, finding a faculty mentor, joining a professional organization, planning and teaching with another student teacher
- During teaching: coteaching with fellow teachers, working with administrators, parents, families, professionals in other fields, and community members to provide services or plan special events for children
- In other settings: attending workshops and professional meetings, joining organizations that work on behalf of children

Using Resources to Learn: gaining access to a wide variety of materials and people who will support and enhance learning

- In college classes: borrowing children's books, teacher resource books, and scholarly books from the library; using the Internet to locate current information on a topic; consulting experts from other areas of specialization (e.g., talking with a special education teacher about a child's physical handicap); subscribing to professional journals; beginning a collection of children's books; communicating with other professionals or professionals in training through E-mail and the Internet
- During teaching: knowing what support services are available in your community and how to access them to help families; borrowing materials from the public library, school library, or other agencies and organizations; identifying people you can trust in the community to help solve problems (e.g., the Lions Club to assist in getting children eyeglasses, the Shriners to assist with the cost of surgery for orthopedic problems); joining teachers' book clubs; traveling to learn about education in other lands; corresponding with other teachers using E-mail; joining professional discussion groups on the Internet

Learning as much as possible about classroom management can help beginning teachers "survive."

Conclusion

"Professional development today also means providing occasions for teachers to reflect critically on their practice and to fashion new knowledge and beliefs about content, pedagogy, and learners" (Darling-Hammond & McLaughlin, 1995, p. 597). Furthermore, teachers who continue to develop professionally have learned to accept responsibility for their own professional growth, to exercise sound professional judgment, and to use a wide array of human and material resources to foster life-long learning. Effective early childhood practitioners fully appreciate the paradox that self-development is intertwined with making significant contributions to the care and education of the very young.

ASK the Expert
Sharon Lynn Kagan on Public Policy and Teachers' Professional Growth

Some Common Misconceptions About Public Policy and Teachers' Professional Growth

Sharon Lynn Kagan

Misconception 1: Policy construction is expected to be rapid and predictable.

We all learn in many ways, but those of us who get to teach learn a great deal from our students and from the questions they ask and the ideas they bring to discussions. For the most part, my students are very, very bright. They have shown some interest in child development and policy because they have taken the prerequisites for the formal courses; those seeking individual guidance (via independent study or thesis advisement) are already quite advanced in their work. They ask good questions, have keen insights, and are in a policy hurry. They want to be policy makers—quickly.

I have been interested that they perceive policy construction as a linear, predictable, and fully knowable process. In their desire to "master" it—to have all the tools in hand before they plunge into the real world—they want it to be rational, to follow a formula. Often, students are mystified that policy is as much about chance, electability, and favors as it is about social justice and equity. They are stunned—and often intrigued—to hear the behind-the-scenes nuances of the policy process. Their surprise and freshness delights me and makes me realize that no work in policy can be complete without a policy practicum. Students constantly remind us, then, that the real work of teaching is to infuse reality without diminishing hope.

In their haste to make waves in the policy world, students often want to move fast. They usually feel that while it is desirable to be theoretically grounded in a discipline, it takes time—and a lot of it. Consequently, many launch into the policy world lacking any empirical understanding of young children and their development, lacking understanding of different theoretical approaches to pedagogy, and lacking any historical exposure to the complexities of the early care and education world. I lament this, because there is simply no substitute for rich empirical, theoretical, and historical understandings—they are the intellectual bedrock of policy work, providing both wisdom and credibility. Many students, therefore, need to learn that there is no substitute for academic training; simultaneously, we need to learn to help them understand the practical value of the empirical, theoretical, and historical perspectives that undergird our discipline.

Misconception 2: Real leadership is simple and effortless.

Beyond being well grounded in practice and theory, students need to realize that real leadership doesn't come easy. Leaders do tend to make leadership look simple: The President waltzes onto the podium and delivers the perfect speech effortlessly; we waltz into our classes and deliver the perfect lectures or seminars; master teachers waltz into their classrooms and seem to magically create the perfect learning environment for children. But behind all this apparent effortlessness are years of hours of work, and countless trials and errors, coupled with some dashed ideals and probably some embarrassing mistakes. We need to let our students know that it isn't all easy and without effort. They need to learn that leadership means having courage and using it; it means having integrity and using it; it means being willing to take risks; it means working hard and sticking to it; and sometimes it means lots of personal sacrifice. My biggest concern and students' most common misconceptions, then, is that many students perceive child-related policy work to be glamorous, effortless, and somewhat substanceless. My big job is conveying that it is precisely and fully the exact opposite.

Sharon Lynn Kagan is Senior Associate, The Bush Center in Child Development and Social Policy, Yale University, New Haven, CT.

One Child, Three Perspectives: *Rolando's Mother Gets Involved in Head Start*

When Twila, a Head Start teacher, knocked on her door, Mrs. Garcia suddenly realized that she had completely forgotten about the home visit she had scheduled several weeks ago. Mrs. Garcia's infant daughter had just spit up on her, and the house was a complete mess as a result of a family visit over the weekend. As she spoke with Twila, Mrs. Garcia held her front door half closed and tried to rush through the interaction. Sensing her discomfort, Twila said, "This doesn't seem like the best time to talk. Would you like to reschedule?" With a smile of gratitude, Mrs. Garcia agreed.

After she shut the door, Mrs. Garcia started to think about this opportunity for her son Rolando. Rolando was born with spina bifida: a place in his spine did not fuse together. He moved around by using the upper part of his body to drag his legs across the floor or by using a special wheelchair. What if the other children made fun of Rolando? If they did, then he surely would be better off at home. But the teacher had seemed very kind and had invited Mrs. Garcia and her husband to visit the classroom any time they wished. They even had a special orientation day when Rolando could attend a full day of school with a peer as his guide, and Mrs. Garcia would be permitted to be there throughout the day. She felt hopeful that Head Start would give Rolando a chance to learn and to make friends.

When Mrs. Garcia later discussed this with Rolando's father, he was opposed to the whole idea. "What if Rolando picks up all those childhood illnesses? Doesn't he have enough problems to deal with? Besides, you are home all day. It's your job to take care of him."

In the car after leaving the Garcia's home, the Head Start teacher wondered whether this family would agree to participate in the program. "Why would they refuse all of this help for their son?" she thought to herself. "He needs to form good peer relationships as much as strong family ties."

REACT:	In what ways are the perspectives of the three adults alike? Which perspective do you identify most strongly with, and why?
RESEARCH:	Locate information on spina bifida at the library. What are some ways of helping children with this condition to be accepted by their peers and have a successful learning experience?
REFLECT:	Rolando's mother, father, and the Head Start teacher have definite ideas about how to meet this young child's needs. What might be the underlying reasons for these differences? How do they compare with what you have read?

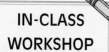

IN-CLASS WORKSHOP

Beginning Your Professional Portfolio

What Is a Professional Portfolio?

The concept of a portfolio in education is much like the portfolio of an artist: It is a carefully selected collection of your professional work. Actually, your portfolio will go through two stages: the process stage and the product stage. During the process stage, your portfolio will be a work-in-progress as you add, delete, and refine the contents. As you complete your training, your portfolio will become a finished product, something that is polished, professional, and ready to be shared with a prospective employer to document your competence as an early childhood practitioner.

Why Create a Portfolio?

A professional portfolio enables you to chronicle your own professional growth as a teacher and the effects of that growth upon student learning. There is extensive research to support the contention that the best teachers are those who reflect deeply about

404

- their personal and professional role as teachers
- their knowledge about children, subject matter, and teaching methods
- the impact of their teaching on student learning
- the quality of their interactions with students
- their goals for professional development
- the quality of their interactions with colleagues, supervisory personnel, and the families of students with whom they work

Teachers' professional portfolios contribute to their professional growth by (a) promoting self-analysis and critical reflection; (b) documenting learning, growth, and development over time; (c) meeting institutional, state, and national certification requirements; and (d) preparing them to work in schools where more balanced and comprehensive forms of assessment are valued (Potthoff, Carroll, Anderson, Attivo, & Kear, 1996).

How Is the Portfolio Developed?

Remember that the portfolio enables teachers to show how they make "decisions to create and use instruction and assessment to improve student performance over the long run" (Hibbard, cited in Sparks & Hirsch, 1997, p. 27). To do this, you will need to document that you have accomplished goals, met requirements, or shored up deficiencies. Perkins and Gelfer (1993) suggest areas of competence to be documented in a portfolio; these are outlined in Figure 11.7. Of course, there are other ways of organizing and developing your professional portfolio. The Childhood Development Association's national credentialing program suggests an autobiography, a class profile, and evidence that the candidate has met six goals (to establish and maintain a safe, healthy learning environment; to advance physical and intellectual competence; to support social and emotional development and provide positive guidance; to establish positive and productive relationships with families; to ensure a well-run, purposeful program responsive to participant needs; and to maintain a commitment to professionalism) and the related 13 functional areas (safe, healthy, learning environment, physical, cognitive, communication, creative, self, social, guidance, families, program management, and professionalism). The National Standards Board also has set guidelines for early childhood teachers' professional portfolios (see Figure 11.3) that can be used to structure portfolios. In addition, some teacher-preparation institutions have prepared their own goals, which also may be used to structure portfolios.

What Might Be Included?

Generally speaking, portfolios contain four different types of evidence:

1. *Artifacts* are documents produced in the normal course of work of the teacher developing the portfolio, such as lesson plans.
2. *Reproductions* are documents about typical events in the work of the portfolio developer that are not captured directly, such as a photograph of a bulletin board or a film clip from a class.
3. *Attestations* are documents about the portfolio developer's work prepared by someone else, such as an evaluation prepared by a teacher who worked with the student teacher.
4. *Productions* are documents prepared specifically for the portfolio (Collins, 1992).

Most portfolios include a philosophy statement that has been revised many times and developed over years of study in education. Some topics to consider include equity in education, reflectivity in teaching, empowerment of students, an appreciation for diversity and skill in meeting

FIGURE 11.7

Areas of competence
to document in a
portfolio

Communicates Effectively

- Is sensitive to the rights, needs, and concerns of children, families, colleagues, and community members
- Reflects good judgment and communicates accurately and appropriately with others in written and oral communication

Exhibits Professionalism

- Accepts constructive criticism and is willing to admit mistakes
- Is dedicated and enthusiastic, with a demonstrated commitment to the profession

Uses Appropriate Resources

- Consults professional resources and uses them to guide practice
- Matches instructional resources to learners' needs and developmental levels

Plans

- Identifies learning goals and develops key concepts carefully
- Selects materials and equipment and prepares them for use in the instructional setting

Uses Appropriate Content and Curriculum

- Designs learning activities that promote children's problem solving, decision making, and creativity
- Prepares lessons, experiences, activities, and projects that are relevant to young children's experiences

Demonstrates Methodology and Classroom Organization

- Uses flexible grouping strategies related to the needs and interests of different students
- Explores significant issues and concepts with children

Manages Classroom Instruction and Behavior

- Poses questions that are sufficiently open-ended to allow creative and divergent thinking to occur
- Guides young children's behavior and establishes rules and procedures with children's input

Evaluates Students' Performance

- Uses a variety of assessment and evaluation procedures to monitor children's progress
- Reports progress to parents in ways that foster communication

SOURCE: Adapted from Portfolio Assessment of Teachers by P. Perkins and J. Gelfer, 1993, *Clearing House*, 66(4), pp. 235–237.

individual needs of learners, knowledge of developmentally appropriate practice and an integrated approach to teaching, a holistic view of young children's learning (intellectual, social, emotional, physical, and aesthetic), and continuous commitment to scholarship and professional growth. Following is a sample philosophy statement of a student teacher, Bonnie Olinto, from George Mason University in Fairfax, VA.

Philosophy Statement of a Beginning Teacher

Good teachers believe the statement, "All children can learn." Teachers must make a pledge that they will go beyond first impressions to ensure that they will help all children to learn. I believe that an educator of young children must take the time to learn about child development and the cultures of the children, and consequently see each and every child as an individual.

The quality of a child's education depends directly upon the quality of his or her teachers. No other variable is as important as a child's education. A good teacher knows that children vary in their temperaments, maturity, abilities, and interests, and the teacher applies that knowledge to his or her style of teaching. I believe that a good teacher displays respect for children as individuals, shows enthusiasm for his or her work, shows fairness in dealing with individuals and the class, and has skill in communicating, as well as knowledge about and competence in what he or she does in the classroom.

Because each child is an individual, each child has a different style of learning. According to Howard Gardner's theory of multiple intelligences, there are at least eight different ways of knowing, perceiving, and understanding the world around us, and everyone possesses all of these intelligences to some degree. It is a teacher's responsibility to search out the intelligence of every one of the students.

Teachers who understand the complexity of the classroom environment realize the importance of finding ways to gain students' cooperation and involvement. The environmental factors in a classroom that foster learning include caring and support, high expectations for children, and opportunities for active participation. When organizing the physical setting, effective teachers consider ways to coordinate concrete materials to facilitate learning.

Schools must engage parents in the education of their children. There are several ways in which schools might involve parents and the community. Parents might become instructional aides or members of the school council, becoming visible participants in school life and symbolizing for students the community's commitment to education. Schools might sponsor programs in adult literacy or child rearing, or offer academic courses in continuing education. There are many avenues available for schools to use and to get parent and community involvement.

If the education of our children is to improve, then schools must be staffed by talented and committed teachers. Teachers who combine excitement about children's learning and enthusiasm for teaching, and who look at each and every child as an individual are good educators. All children are capable of learning.

In addition to a philosophy statement, you definitely will want to gather and carefully select materials such as the following.

- **A resumé:** Include a goals statement that identifies the type of position you are seeking as well as a chronological (most recent first) list of your professional experiences and other relevant work experiences; also include copies of certificates, awards, and honors. Use the format recommended by your teacher-preparation institution

- **Official documents:** such things as transcripts, PRAXIS test scores, criminal record clearance, certificates or licenses held, and evidence of specialized training (e.g., CPR)

- **Evidence of a suitable environment for learning:** classroom floor plans, daily schedule, class meeting notes, classroom rules, learning-center design plans, helper charts, and participation charts

- **Evidence of effective teaching:** samples of your best lesson, unit, theme, or curriculum web; your evaluation on each and samples of children's work; photographs of the best projects, centers, bulletin boards, and teaching materials you developed; and film clips of your teaching performance

- **Evidence of student assessment:** observational note-taking methods and assessment measures that you designed to evaluate student learning, photographs of displays of children's work, plans for student-work portfolios, student work samples, and a description of your IEP process

- **Evidence of working with parents and families:** family intake interview forms, home visits schedule, communication with parents/families (e.g., newsletters, conferencing schedule, IFSP procedures), a description of special events or projects that encourage family engagement in the program, and evidence of collaboration with the community

- **Evidence of ongoing professional growth:** a statement about other relevant work experiences and memberships in professional and community organizations, professional growth plans, and certificates of workshops or conferences attended

How Should the Final (Product) Portfolio Be Prepared?

As you go through the materials you have collected during your program, be selective. If there are materials in your portfolio that show your progress and were part of your process portfolio, save them in a separate file. The purpose of your final, or product, portfolio, is to highlight your achievements as you complete student teaching and secure a teaching position. Remember that a professional portfolio is assessed by quality, not by volume. Most of your portfolio should fit into a small three-ring binder. For bulky items such as a videotape or unit plan, you may want to add plastic pockets large enough to hold these materials or keep them in a separate envelope. Your portfolio should have a professional look. Type (and retype, if necessary) the material in your portfolio and make sure that it is error free. Visit a store that stocks office supplies to find the notebook, folders, dividers, and other materials that will make you proud to share your portfolio. Naturally, you will need to be thoroughly familiar with the items in the portfolio and practice using it so that you can skillfully weave it into your interview. You may want to explore the possibility of recording all of your material on a rewriteable CD or a Web page so that you can produce an electronic portfolio (Milone, 1995).

Additional Resources on Portfolios

Campbell, D. M., Cignetti, P. B., Melenyzer, B. J., Nettles, D. H., & Wyman, P. M. (1997). *How to develop a professional portfolio: A manual for teachers.* Boston, MA: Allyn & Bacon.

Guillame, A. M., & Yopp, H. K. (1995). Professional portfolios for student teachers. *Teacher Education Quarterly, 22*(1), 93–101.

McLaughlin, M., & Vogt, M. (1996). *Portfolios in teacher education.* Newark, DE: International Reading Association.

Milone, M. N. (1995). Electronic portfolios: Who's doing them and how? *Technology and Learning, 16*(2), 28–29, 32, 34, 36.

Compendium of Early Childhood Materials and Resources

Note to Students

As an *early childhood teacher*, you will always be looking for new ideas. You will need to gather, identify, evaluate, and use resources that will enhance your teaching and facilitate children's learning. When you begin to work with children, you will probably be concerned about the cost and availability of materials and resources to use. Thus, we have compiled this beginning collection of resources, many of which can be accessed with little or no cost. As you work with children, remember these resources and use them often. There is an abundance of information, ideas, and materials out there waiting for you.

This Compendium of Early Childhood Materials and Resources lists a wide range of resources that are available from diverse sources for your use. It is intended to provide a starting point for you to obtain information and assistance, add to regularly, and make it work for you; it is *not intended* to be a definitive list of every available resource that is available to you. Categorized as either material or human resources, the information is presented in alphabetical order for easy reference.

Material Resources

Young children need a large variety of materials. They are the powerful tools with which children explore, experiment, investigate, and understand their world. Gathering materials and creating a resource file will make your teaching more efficient. Again, we encourage you to add to this regularly to make it work for you.

Basic Materials and Equipment by Age Range

Infant and Toddlers (Birth–3 Years)

Infants learn by sensory exploration and social interaction. They need a variety of textured objects to view, hold, and reach for. They also need materials that make sounds, are soft and squeezable, and are simple, realistic, and safe. Toddlers are actively seeking independence and have a high energy level. They need action toys that they can take apart and put together and materials that are scaled to their size and require different kinds of manipulations such as nesting, stacking, and bouncing. Following are some beginning suggestions.

Basic Indoor Equipment
bulletin boards, cabinets, chairs (adult and child sized), clothes rack, cubbies, file cabinet, infant stroller, safety gates, shelves (high and low), storage bins on rollers, tables (changing table at adult height, other tables at child height), toilet facilities, wastebaskets (covered)

Housekeeping Equipment
brooms (adult and child sized), brushes (bottle, counter, hand), dishpan, dishtowels, disinfectants, hand-held portable vacuum, heating and serving dishes, sponges, towels, trays

Health and Safety Materials
first-aid and toilet supplies, food service supplies (bibs, bottles, flatware), resting facilities (cots, cribs), diapers, sanitation supplies (diaper changing pads), smocks, towlettes, washcloths

Gross Motor Equipment (Indoor/Outdoor)
apparatus (boxes, climbers), dramatic play (dishes, housekeeping), large-muscle toys (balls, blocks, push toys), sand play (cups, spoons), water play (dump-and-fill containers)

Manipulatives
Infants: clutch balls, infant gyms, squeeze toys, teething toys
Toddlers: beads, Duplos, giant pegboard, plastic vehicles

Sensory Materials
listening (bells, chimes), smelling (sealed spices), tasting (foods), touching and feeling (textured materials), visual (color paddles)

Cognitive Development
aquarium, blocks, books, floating and sinking pieces, gear-turning toys, nesting toys, number puzzles, plants, shells and rocks, stacking toys, sorting toys

Creative Arts
music (autoharp, tape recorders), art (brushes, paints easel, smocks), media (chalk, crayons, play dough, paper of assorted colors), movement and pretend play (props, hats, scarves)

Communication
books, pictures for discussion, feel box, flannel board, language games, puppets

Record Keeping
attendance sheets, booklets for observation notes, card file, parent forms, health sheets

Preschoolers and Kindergartners (Ages 3–5)
Preschoolers and kindergartners show increasing social ability, fascination with adult roles, growing mastery over their small and large muscles, and an interest in pretend

play. The materials and equipment for this age group should support their developing social skills and interests in these areas. The following materials and equipment will help you get started.

Basic Indoor Equipment
bookcase, bookshelves, bulletin board, cabinets (movable), chairs (adult and child sized), chalkboard, cubbies, drinking fountain (child height), filing cabinet, rugs, sink, smoke alarm

General Maintenance
broom, buckets, electrical extension cord and plug, plunger, toolbox

Housekeeping Supplies
brooms (push, regular), cleansers, cleaning cloths, dishpan, drying rack (folding), mops, soap, sponges, toilet paper, towels, vacuum cleaner

Health and Safety
first-aid supplies, flashlight, food preparation and service supplies (blender, bottle opener, can opener, flatware), measures, plates, storage containers, tablecloths, trays

Audiovisual Equipment
cassette recorder, CDs, film strips, record player, records, tapes, cassettes

Psychomotor Development
balls, bars for hanging, bean bags, bowling pin sets, crates, hoops, pails, pulleys, rakes

Perceptual Development
beads and laces, counting rods, dressing frames, games, linking toys, magnetic board

Building and Construction
blocks (assorted), boards, building sets, carpentry, sand and water play, vehicles, wheels

Creative Arts
aprons (plastic or cloth), brushes and holders, chalk, collage materials, containers, newspapers, paints (assorted), paper (assorted), play dough, printing materials, scissors

Dramatic Play
animals, camping, doctor/nurse, family living, cooking and eating equipment, doll equipment, dress-up, furniture for housekeeping, transportation, puppets, traffic signs

Music
autoharp, rhythm instruments (bells, maracas, triangles, tambourines, wooden blocks)

Language Arts
alphabet letters, books, camera, chart paper, computer, felt board, puzzles, typewriter

Mathematics
counters, food to cut and divide, geometric figures and shapes, matching sets, measuring equipment, money (play, homemade), number games, peg boards, shapes, sorting containers

Science
air experiments, animal foods and types, books about science concepts, food and gardening, seeds, light and heat, machines, magnets, picture collections

Office Supplies and Record Keeping
bulletin board, calendar, diskettes for computer, file cabinet, manila folders and envelopes, message pads, paper clips, pencils and pens, stationery, thumbtacks, yardstick

School-age Children (ages 5–8)
School-age children are refining skills and talents that they prize, are relying more and more on support from their peers, and are becoming more organized and logical thinkers. Materials and equipment for this age group should reflect their need for realistic, rule-oriented, and peer activities. Following are some suggestions.

Basic Indoor Equipment
air conditioner (where appropriate), boards, book racks, easels, cabinets, carpeting, chairs, chart holders, clock (wall), file cabinet, floor pillows, mirror, sink, towels, wastebaskets

Consumable Materials
chalk, chalkboard erasers, chart tablets, colored folders, fasteners, markers, metal rings, paper (assorted), paper clips, pencil erasers, tagboard (assorted), transparencies

Maintenance Materials
brooms, brushes, buckets, dishpan, mops, sponges, towels

Health and First Aid
items available in nurse's or director's office or first-aid cabinet fully stocked

Perceptual Motor
balance beam, balls, bean bags, climbing apparatus, cones for obstacle course, hoops, jump ropes, parachute, records and cassette tapes for movement, slide, tires

Media/Computing
audiovisual player, AV carts, books, book racks, camera, cassette recorder, cassettes, easel for book display, headphones, listening station, VCR

The Arts
aluminum foil, brushes, chalk, containers, crayons, drying rack, glue, laundry starch, markers, needles, paint, paper, paper cutter, pens, pipe cleaners or wikki sticks, stapler

Language Arts
alphabet wall cards and sets, bookends, book holder, books, chart tablets, flash cards, letters, pocket wall chart, puzzles, recordings, rubber stamps

Mathematics
blocks, calculators, cash register, clock, counting frames and sticks, dice, flannel board and cut-outs, floor graph, magnetic board, measures, number lines, chart to 100, pegs

Music
autoharp, bell sets, castanets, cymbals, drums, listening station equipment, music books, records, rhythm sticks, sand blocks, teaching aids, tone block, triangles

Science

ant farm, aquarium, bulbs (garden), cages, cooking equipment, flower containers, garden equipment, magnets, magnifying glasses, microscope, prisms, pulleys, timers

Social Studies

block accessories, blocks, community resource file, construction toys, dramatic play materials, games, globe, magazines, maps and atlas, newspapers, puppets, and puppet stage

Source: Adapted from *Selecting Educational Equipment and Materials for School and Home,* J. Moyer, Ed., 1995, Wheaton, MD: Association for Childhood Education International; and *Creative Expression and Play in Early Childhood,* 2nd ed., by J. P. Isenberg and M. R. Jalongo, Upper Saddle River, NJ: Merrill/Prentice-Hall.

Curriculum Resources

Selected Resources for Learning Centers

Carefully designed centers are a valuable resource for teachers and children. They enable teachers to integrate the curriculum, overlap subject areas, develop multicultural awareness, and teach to all of children's intelligences. Thus, carefully designed centers contain a variety of materials that are concrete, durable, and real. The following examples are listed by center.

ART CENTER MATERIALS

easel	water, tempera, and finger paint	paintbrushes
paste	newsprint, tissue, construction paper	tape
chalk	markers, crayons, colored pencils	hole punches
clay	books related to art topics	sponges

BLOCK CENTER MATERIALS

unit blocks	hardwood hollow blocks	brick blocks
traffic signs	play people and animals	Legos and Duplos
play vehicles	architectural drawings	street signs
books related to building and construction		

DRAMATIC PLAY MATERIALS

kitchen furniture	cooking utensils, cookbooks, recipes	play money
dress-up clothes	paper, pencils, food coupons	telephone
telephone books	various dolls	
books, magazines, and newspapers about families		

prop boxes containing other theme-related topics such as a restaurant, grocery store, transportation, post office

LIBRARY CENTER

A variety of teacher-made and child-made books, blank books, big books, books on tape, headphones, props to act out stories, pillows, soft chairs, magnetic board and letters

MANIPULATIVES AND PUZZLES

beads for stringing	pegboards and pegs	lacing cards
dressing frames	parquetry blocks	puzzles

teacher-made and commercial board and lotto games

constructions toys (bristle blocks, star builders, Lincoln Logs, Tinkertoys, Legos)

MATH CENTER MATERIALS

nesting cubes	geoboards and rubber bands	play money
abacus and rulers	counters and scales	cash register
playing cards	dice	yardstick

assortment of real objects (shells, rocks, buttons, leaves) for sorting and classifying

books about mathematics, counting, and math themes

MUSIC MATERIALS

drums and bells	rhythm sticks	record, tape, and CD players
toy instruments	graduated bottles	instrument-making materials
real instruments	child-made and teacher-made instruments	

books about music, musicians, and musical themes

SAND AND WATER MATERIALS

wet and dry sand	sand or water table	bulb syringes, squirt bottles
assorted cups and molds	assorted sticks, strainers	pots and pans, shovels, scoops
colanders, sifters, funnels	small vehicles	flower pots, flowers
small plastic animals	small garden tools	ice cubes, liquid soap
floating and sinking objects	straws	egg beater, ladle, sponges

SCIENCE MATERIALS

assorted bolts, nuts, washers, magnets, magnetic letters, buttons, fabric swatches, balls, paper, hand lenses, empty plastic containers, droppers

assorted dried legumes, stones, pebbles, yarn, thread, cord, wire, pipe cleaners

variety of real insects and bugs in covered containers

pets appropriate for a classroom (gerbils, guinea pigs, fish)

plants with and without flowers

things to take apart and put together, things to smell

paper, clipboard, and writing supplies

books, charts, posters, magazines, photo word cards about specific topics

instruction cards for completing experiments

WOODWORKING MATERIALS

wooden wheels, spools

7-oz. claw hammer and plane

hand drill

7-inch screwdrivers

woodworking bench

safety glasses

variety of rulers, protractors

Styrofoam for sawing, hammering, and drilling

instruction cards to sequence actions such as hammering a nail into the wood

tools labeled with written words

posters and charts for building furniture, a deck, or shelves

WRITING CENTER MATERIALS

variety of types of paper	alphabet letter stamps	props to enact stories
stapler, hole punch, ink pads	scissors, erasers, glue	books and magazines
book of wallpaper samples	stationery, magic slates	tape recorder, tapes

Source: Adapted with permission from Terri Cardi, Conneaut Lake, PA.

Free and Inexpensive Materials for Teachers

There are many resources and materials that enable all learners to participate in the learning process. Here are some places to start:

Teaching Tolerance

A free semi-annual publication of the Southern Poverty Law Center that provides teachers with suggestions for promoting more harmonious classrooms
400 Washington Ave.
Montgomery, AL 36104

Educators' Index of Free Materials

Educators Progress Services, Inc.
214 Center Street
Randolph, WI 53956
(414) 326-3126

Household and Found Materials

A large variety of household and found materials enable children to experiment with, imagine, and explore what materials can do and what they can do with materials. These materials help children make discoveries and find answers to their own questions. In this way, they learn naturally how to identify, classify, observe closely, make comparisons, ask questions, describe what they discover, and make predictions.

Household Materials

buttons, pots and pans, carpentry tools, plastic containers, bottle caps, cooking utensils, real objects that appeal to children's imaginations, simple camera, old typewriter, paper and pencils

Natural or Found Materials

sticks, shells, twigs, leaves, rocks, pinecones, sand, mud, water, buttons, candy boxes, cardboard tubing, catalogues, coffee cans, gift-wrapping paper, plastic items and containers, ribbon bits, scraps of carpeting and cloth, Styrofoam packing

Local Retailers

Try your local retailers for discarded items, samples, and other unwanted items (carpet stores for carpet samples for group meetings; ice-cream shops for discarded displays for dramatic play, wallpaper stores for discontinued wallpaper books for book covers, bulletin boards, and collage material).

Materials Request Form

Dear _____ :

We are studying about _____. To do our projects, our class needs _____. If you can help us with any of these materials, please send them to school this week.

Thank you.

Health, Nutrition, and Safety Resources

Health, nutrition, and safety are part of early childhood programs that traditionally get overlooked. Following are some resources to help you in this area.

Films

Some Children Need Special Care (Disabilities)
　　Modern Talking Pictures
　　5000 Park Street North
　　St. Petersburg, FL 33709-9989
　　(Free loan) (813) 541-6661

The Wellness Revolution (Preventive Health Care)
　　Modern Talking Pictures
　　5000 Park Street North
　　St. Petersburg, FL 33709-9989
　　(Free loan) (813) 541-6661

Organizations and Associations

American Alliance for Health, Physical Education, Recreation, and Dance (AAHPERD)
　　1900 Association Drive
　　Reston, VA 22091
　　www.aahperd.org
　　Journal: *Journal of Health Education*

American Academy of Pediatrics
   141 Northwest Point Blvd.
   Elk Grove Village, IL 60009-0927
   TIPP: The Injury Prevention Program (Parts are available on-line at *www.aap.org*
   and pamphlets are available)

American Academy of Ophthalmology
   P.O. Box 7424
   San Francisco, CA 94120-7424
   (Free eye chart and a variety of pamphlets on eye problems)

American Automobile Association
   Traffic Safety Department
   (Check with local branch office for address)
   Pamphlet: *Bicycling Is Great Fun*

National SAFE KIDS Campaign
   Children's Hospital National Medical Center
   111 Michigan Avenue, NW
   Washington, DC
   Pamphlet: *Safe Kids Are No Accident*

U.S. Department of Agriculture
   Food and Nutrition Service
   U.S. Govt. Printing Office
   Washington, DC 20402
   Two pamphlets: *Food Buying for Child Nutrition Programs* and *A Planning Guide for
   Food Service in Child Care Centers*

Web Resources

1. *www.healthychild.net*
   An on-line magazine with articles about child health and safety

2. *www.floridajuice.com*
   Recipes and nutritional information for children

3. *www.kidshealth.org/index2.html*
   Medical information from experts on such topics as immunizations, illnesses, and
   ADHD

4. *www.kidsource.com/kidsource/pages/health/prevention.html*
   Provides activities for children, answers to questions, and a changing spot with
   prevention hints

5. *http://cpsc.gov*
   The national consumer product safety site with information on toy and safety-seat
   recalls and links to other sites

Professional Resources for Teachers

Knowing where to access appropriate information and resources enhances your ethical
responsibility, your accountability to the profession, and your advocacy for children.

Common Questions about Learning Opportunities Beyond the School

Joan Moyer

1. If not in school, where do children acquire knowledge?

It is within the family that a child learns initial self-identity, his or her first language, ethnic heritage, values, and the culture of the family. This is meaningful knowledge that the child brings to his or her first formal schooling experience. If a child has access to a computer, he or she may be introduced to its possibilities and information in a comfortable, relaxed environment. Beyond the family, the neighborhood in which a child lives is an influential source of learning. As the child plays with other children in the backyard, on the sidewalk, on the playground, or at the park, he or she learns interaction techniques and observes different values, cultural practices, and interaction styles that other children use.

2. Where can teachers suggest that children and families find opportunities for learning beyond the family and neighborhood?

The extended neighborhood of the school abounds in rich learning opportunities. The fire station, police station, post office, supermarket, and bank all provide opportunities for children to learn about available resources and the world of work as well as the services that workers provide. Supermarkets, for example, provide learning opportunities as children research where products originate; learn about the processing, packaging, and delivery systems of the products; and study the job possibilities there. Children who live on farms, or who have the opportunity to visit farms for significant periods of time, gain valuable information about caring for animals, chores to be done, and the importance of farming as a source of food. Zoos are another avenue of learning about animals and their care. Trips to the zoo may be the only opportunity for some children to observe exotic animals as well as animals that are indigenous to their local area or state.

The beach also can provide information about oceans, the difference between salt water and fresh water, many types of marine life, and shell collecting, as well as offer unlimited opportunities for sand play.

The public library provides a myriad of sources for learning. For some children, the public library is their introduction to the world of books, storytelling, and puppetry. In public libraries, computers are available to children who may not have them in their homes; this opens up a fascinating introduction to the world for many children. The magazine and newspaper collections become first-hand sources for research projects, and library exhibits and visiting lecturers provide alternative learning options.

Interactive exhibits at museums also are sources of innovative, first-hand learning experiences, and clubs and organizations can provide vital role models in the lives of children who may not live in intact families.

3. How can teachers utilize this learning in the classroom?

They can begin by recognizing and honoring the learning that each child brings to school from his or her family. Teachers must build strong relationships with families, incorporating families' suggestions and sharing their own for determining the opportunities for learning in the home, the neighborhood, and the locale in which children live.

Joan Moyer is a professor in the College of Education, Arizona State University, Tempe, Arizona.

The National Association for the Education of Young Children Code of Ethical Conduct

Preamble

NAEYC recognizes that many daily decisions required of those who work with young children are of a moral and ethical nature. The NAEYC Code of Ethical Conduct offers guidelines for responsible behavior and sets forth a common basis for resolving the principal ethical dilemmas encountered in early childhood education. The primary focus is on daily practice with children and their families in programs for children from birth to 8 years of age, such as infant/toddler programs, preschools, child care centers, family day care homes, kindergartens, and primary classrooms. Many of the provisions also apply to specialists who do not work directly with children, including program administrators, parent and vocational educators, college professors, and child care licensing specialists.

Core Values

Standards of ethical behavior in early childhood education are based on commitment to core values that are deeply rooted in the history of our field. We have committed ourselves to

- Appreciating childhood as a unique and valuable stage of the human life cycle
- Basing our work with children on knowledge of child development
- Appreciating and supporting the close ties between the child and family
- Recognizing that children are best understood and supported in the context of family, culture, and society
- Respecting the dignity, worth, and uniqueness of each individual (child, family member, and colleague)
- Helping children and adults achieve their full potential in the context of relationships that are based on trust, respect, and positive regard

Conceptual Framework

The Code sets forth a conception of our professional responsibilities in four sections, each addressing an arena of professional relationships: (1) children, (2) families, (3) colleagues, and (4) community and society. Each section includes an introduction to the primary responsibilities of the early childhood practitioner in that arena, a set of ideals pointing in the direction of exemplary professional practice, and a set of principles defining practices that are required, prohibited, and permitted.

The ideals reflect the aspirations of practitioners. **The principles** are intended to guide conduct and assist practitioners in resolving ethical dilemmas encountered in the field. There is not necessarily a corresponding principle for each ideal. Both ideals and principles are intended to direct practitioners to those questions which, when responsibly answered, will provide the basis for conscientious decision making. While the Code provides specific direction for addressing some ethical dilemmas, many others will require the practitioner to combine the guidance of the Code with sound professional judgment.

The ideals and principles in this Code present a shared conception of professional responsibility that affirms our commitment to the core values of our field. The Code publicly acknowledges the responsibilities that we in the field have assumed and in so doing supports ethical behavior in our work. Practitioners who face ethical dilemmas are urged to seek guidance in the applicable parts of this Code and in the spirit that informs the whole.

Ethical Dilemmas Always Exist

Often, "the right answer"—the best ethical course of action to take—is not obvious. There may be no readily apparent, positive way to handle the situation. One important value may contradict another. When we are caught "on the horns of a dilemma," it is our professional responsibility to consult with all relevant parties in seeking the most ethical course of action to take.

Section I: Ethical Responsibilities to Children

Childhood is a unique and valuable stage in the life cycle. Our paramount responsibility is to provide safe, healthy, nurturing, and responsive settings for children. We are committed to supporting children's development, respecting individual differences, helping children learn to live and work cooperatively, and promoting health, self-awareness, competence, self-worth, and resiliency.

Ideals:

I-1.1 To be familiar with the knowledge base of early childhood education and to keep current through continuing education and in-service training.

I-1.2 To base program practices upon current knowledge in the field of child development and related disciplines and upon particular knowledge of each child.

I-1.3 To recognize and respect the uniqueness and the potential of each child.

I-1.4 To appreciate the special vulnerability of children.

I-1.5 To create and maintain safe and healthy settings that foster children's social, emotional, intellectual, and physical development and that respect their dignity and their contributions.

I-1.6 To support the right of each child to play and learn in inclusive early childhood programs to the fullest extent consistent with the best interests of all involved. As with adults who are disabled in the larger community, children with disabilities are ideally served in the same settings in which they would participate if they did not have a disability.

I-1.7 To ensure that children with disabilities have access to appropriate and convenient support services and to advocate for the resources necessary to provide the most appropriate settings for all children.

Principles:

P-1.1 Above all, we shall not harm children. We shall not participate in practices that are disrespectful, degrading, dangerous, exploitative, intimidating, emotionally damaging, or physically harmful to children. *This principle has precedence over all others in this Code.*

P-1.2 We shall not participate in practices that discriminate against children by denying benefits, giving special advantages, or excluding them from programs or activities on the basis of their race, ethnicity, religion, sex, national origin, language, ability, or the status, behavior, or beliefs of their parents. (This principle does not apply to programs that have a lawful mandate to provide services to a particular population of children.)

P-1.3 We shall involve all of those with relevant knowledge (including staff and parents) in decisions concerning a child.

P-1.4 For every child we shall implement adaptations in teaching strategies, learning environment, and curricula, consult with the family, and seek recommendations from appropriate specialists to maximize the potential of the child to benefit from the program. If, after these efforts have been made to work with a child and family, the child does not appear to be benefiting from a program, or the child is seriously jeopardizing the ability of other children to benefit from the program, we shall communicate with the family and appropriate specialists to determine the child's current needs, identify the setting and services most suited to meeting these needs, and assist the family in placing the child in a more appropriate setting.

P-1.5 We shall be familiar with the symptoms of child abuse, including physical, sexual, verbal, and emotional abuse, and neglect. We shall know and follow state laws and community procedures that protect children against abuse and neglect.

P-1.6 When we have reasonable cause to suspect child abuse or neglect, we shall report the evidence to the appropriate community agency and follow up to ensure that appropriate action has been taken. When appropriate, parents or guardians will be informed that the referral has been made.

P-1.7 When another person tells us of a suspicion that a child is being abused or neglected, we shall assist that person in taking appropriate action to protect the child.

P-1.8 When a child protective agency fails to provide adequate protection for abused or neglected children, we acknowledge a collective ethical responsibility to work toward improvement of these services.

P-1.9 When we become aware of a practice or situation that endangers the health or safety of children, but has not been previously known to do so, we have an ethical responsibility to inform those who can remedy the situation and who can protect children from similar dangers.

Section II: Ethical Responsibilities to Families

Families are of primary importance in children's development. (The term *family* may include others, besides parents, who are responsibly involved with the child.) Because the family and the early childhood practitioner have a common interest in the child's welfare, we acknowledge a primary responsibility to bring about collaboration between the home and school in ways that enhance the child's development.

Ideals:

I-2.1 To develop relationships of mutual trust with the families we serve.

I-2.2 To acknowledge and build upon strengths and competencies as we support families in their task of nurturing children.

I-2.3 To respect the dignity of each family and its culture, language, customs, and beliefs.

I-2.4 To respect families' child rearing values and their right to make decisions for their children.

I-2.5 To interpret each child's progress to parents within the framework of a developmental perspective and to help families understand and appreciate the value of developmentally appropriate early childhood programs.

I-2.6 To help family members improve their understanding of their children and to enhance their skills as parents.

I-2.7 To participate in building support networks for families by providing them with opportunities to interact with program staff, other families, community resources, and professional services.

Principles:

P-2.1 We shall not deny family members access to their child's classroom or program setting.

P-2.2 We shall inform families of program philosophy, policies, and personnel qualifications, and explain why we teach as we do—which should be in accordance with our ethical responsibilities to children (see Section I).

P-2.3 We shall inform families of and, when appropriate, involve them in policy decisions.

P-2.4 We shall involve families in significant decisions affecting their child.

P-2.5 We shall inform the family of accidents involving their child, of risks such as exposures to contagious disease that may result in infection, and of occurrences that might result in emotional stress.

P-2.6 To improve the quality of early childhood care and education, we shall cooperate with qualified child development researchers. Families shall be fully informed of any proposed research project involving children and shall have the opportunity to give or withhold consent without penalty. We shall not permit or participate in research that could in any way hinder the education or development of the children in our programs.

P-2.7 We shall not engage in or support exploitation of families. We shall not use our relationship with a family for private advantage or personal gain, or enter into relationships with family members that might impair our effectiveness in working with children.

P-2.8 We shall develop written policies for the protection of confidentiality and the disclosure of children's records. These policy documents shall be made available to all program personnel and families. Disclosure of children's records beyond family members, program personnel, and consultants having an obligation of confidentiality shall require familial consent (except in cases of abuse or neglect).

P-2.9 We shall maintain confidentiality and shall respect the family's right to privacy, refraining from disclosure of confidential information and intrusion into family life. However, when we have reason to believe that a child's welfare is at risk, it is permissible to share confidential information with agencies and individuals who may be able to intervene in the child's interest.

P-2.10 In cases where family members are in conflict we shall work openly, sharing our observations of the child, to help all parties involved make informed decisions. We shall refrain from becoming an advocate for one party.

P-2.11 We shall be familiar with and appropriately use community resources and professional services that support families. After a referral has been made, we shall follow up to ensure that services have been adequately provided.

Section III: Ethical Responsibilities to Colleagues

In a caring, cooperative workplace, human dignity is respected, professional satisfaction is promoted, and positive relationships are modeled. Based upon our core values, our primary responsibility in this arena is to establish and maintain settings and relationships that support productive work and meet professional needs. The same ideals that apply to children are inherent in our responsibilities to adults.

A—Responsibilities To Co-workers

Ideals:

I-3A.1 To establish and maintain relationships of respect, trust, and cooperation with co-workers.

I-3A.2 To share resources and information with co-workers.

I-3A.3 To support co-workers in meeting their professional needs and in their professional development.

I-3A.4 To accord co-workers due recognition of professional achievement.

Principles:

P-3A.1 When we have concern about the professional behavior of a co-worker, we shall first let that person know of our concern, in a way that shows respect for personal dignity and diversity to be found among staff members, and attempt to resolve the matter collegially.

P-3A.2 We shall exercise care in expressing views regarding the personal attributes or professional conduct of co-workers. Statements should be based on firsthand knowledge and relevant to the interests of children and programs.

B—Responsibilities to Employers

Ideals:

I-3B.1 To assist the program in providing the highest quality of service.

I-3B.2 To do nothing that diminishes the reputation of the program in which we work unless it is violating laws and regulations designed to protect children or the provisions of this Code.

Principles:

P-3B.1 When we do not agree with program policies, we shall first attempt to effect change through constructive action within the organization.

P-3B.2 We shall speak or act on behalf of an organization only when authorized. We shall take care to note when we are speaking for the organization and when we are expressing a personal judgment.

P-3B.3 We shall not violate laws or regulations designed to protect children and shall take appropriate action consistent with this Code when aware of such violations.

C—Responsibilities to Employees

Ideals:

I-3C.1 To promote policies and working conditions that foster mutual respect, competence, well-being, and positive self-esteem in staff members.

I-3C.2 To create a climate of trust and candor that will enable staff to speak and act in the best interests of children, families, and the field of early childhood care and education.

I-3C.3 To strive to secure an equitable compensation (salary and benefits) for those who work with or on behalf of young children.

Principles:

P-3C.1 In decisions concerning children and programs, we shall appropriately utilize the education, training, experience, and expertise of staff members.

P-3C.2 We shall provide staff members with safe and supportive working conditions that permit them to carry out their responsibilities, timely and nonthreatening evaluation procedures, written grievance procedures, constructive feedback, and opportunities for continuing professional development and advancement.

P-3C.3 We shall develop and maintain comprehensive written personnel policies that define program standards and, when applicable, that specify the extent to which employees are accountable for their conduct outside the workplace. These policies shall be given to new staff members and shall be available for review by all staff members.

P-3C.4 Employees who do not meet program standards shall be informed of areas of concern and, when possible, assisted in improving their performance.

P-3C.5 Employees who are dismissed shall be informed of the reasons for their termination. When a dismissal is for cause, justification must be based on evidence of inadequate or inappropriate behavior that is accurately documented, current, and available for the employee to review.

P-3C.6 In making evaluations and recommendations, judgments shall be based on fact and relevant to the interests of children and programs.

P-3C.7 Hiring and promotion shall be based solely on a person's record of accomplishment and ability to carry out the responsibilities of the position.

P-3C.8 In hiring, promotion, and provision of training, we shall not participate in any form of discrimination based on race, ethnicity, religion, gender, national origin, culture, disability, age, or sexual preference. We shall be familiar with laws and regulations that pertain to employment discrimination.

Section IV: Ethical Responsibilities to Community and Society

Early childhood programs operate within a context of an immediate community made up of families and other institutions concerned with children's welfare. Our responsibilities to the community are to provide programs that meet its needs, to cooperate with agencies and professions that share responsibility for children, and to develop needed programs that are not currently available. Because the larger society has a measure of responsibility for the welfare and protection of children, and because of our specialized expertise in child development, we acknowledge an obligation to serve as a voice for children everywhere.

Ideals:

I-4.1 To provide the community with high-quality (age and individually appropriate, and culturally and socially sensitive) education/care programs and services.

I-4.2 To promote cooperation among agencies and interdisciplinary collaboration among professions concerned with the welfare of young children, their families, and their teachers.

I-4.3 To work, through education, research, and advocacy, toward an environmentally safe world in which all children receive adequate health care, food, and shelter, are nurtured, and live free from violence.

I-4.4 To work, through education, research, and advocacy, toward a society in which all young children have access to high-quality education/care programs.

I-4.5 To promote knowledge and understanding of young children and their needs. To work toward greater social acknowledgment of children's rights and greater social acceptance of responsibility for their well-being.

I-4.6 To support policies and laws that promote the well-being of children and families, and to oppose those that impair their well-being. To participate in developing policies and laws that are needed, and to cooperate with other individuals and groups in these efforts.

I-4.7 To further the professional development of the field of early childhood care and education and to strengthen its commitment to realizing its core values as reflected in this Code.

Principles:

P-4.1 We shall communicate openly and truthfully about the nature and extent of services that we provide.

P-4.2 We shall not accept or continue to work in positions for which we are personally unsuited or professionally unqualified. We shall not offer services that we do not have the competence, qualifications, or resources to provide.

P-4.3 We shall be objective and accurate in reporting the knowledge upon which we base our program practices.

P-4.4 We shall cooperate with other professionals who work with children and their families.

P-4.5 We shall not hire or recommend for employment any person whose competence, qualifications, or character makes him or her unsuited for the position.

P-4.6 We shall report the unethical or incompetent behavior of a colleague to a supervisor when informal resolution is not effective.

P-4.7 We shall be familiar with laws and regulations that serve to protect the children in our programs.

P-4.8 We shall not participate in practices which are in violation of laws and regulations that protect the children in our programs.

P-4.9 When we have evidence that an early childhood program is violating laws or regulations protecting children, we shall report it to persons responsible for the program. If compliance is not accomplished within a reasonable time, we will report the violation to appropriate authorities who can be expected to remedy the situation.

P-4.10 When we have evidence that an agency or a professional charged with providing services to children, families, or teachers is failing to meet its obligations, we acknowledge a collective ethical responsibility to report the problem to appropriate authorities or to the public.

P-4.11 When a program violates or requires its employees to violate this Code, it is permissible, after fair assessment of the evidence, to disclose the identity of that program.

Copyright 1998 by the National Association for the Education of Young Children, Washington, D.C.

Interstate New Teacher Assessment and Support Consortium Standards (INTASC)

An agreed-upon set of 10 standards for preparing, licensing, and certifying educators as beginning teachers. The teacher

1. understands the central concepts, tools of inquiry, and structures of the discipline(s) he or she teaches and can create meaningful learning experiences from them.

2. understands how children learn and develop, and can provide learning opportunities to support each aspect of their development.

3. understands the ways students learn and adapts learning to meet each child's needs.

4. understands and uses a variety of instructional strategies.

5. creates positive learning environments.

6. uses effective communication techniques that foster active inquiry in the classroom.

7. plans instruction based on knowledge of subject matter, children, the community, and curriculum goals.

8. uses formal and informal assessment strategies to ensure continuous growth of the learner.

9. is a reflective practitioner who continually evaluates choices and who actively seeks out professional growth opportunities.

10. fosters professional relationships.

Source: Adapted from *Model Standards for Beginning Teacher Licensing and Development: A Resource for State Dialogue* by the Interstate New Teacher Assessment and Support Consortium, 1992, Washington, DC: Council of Chief State School Officers.

National Education Goals

The eight National Education Goals provide educational direction at the state and federal levels for what all children should have achieved by the year 2000. The eight goals are as follows:

Goal 1: All children in America will start school ready to learn.

Goal 2: The high school graduation rate will increase to at least 90 percent.

Goal 3: American students will leave grades 4, 8, and 12 having demonstrated competency in challenging subject matter . . . and every school in America will ensure that all students learn to use their minds well, so they may be prepared for responsible citizenship, further learning, and productive employment in our modern economy.

Goal 4: The nation's teaching force will have access to programs for the continued improvement of their professional skills . . . needed to instruct and prepare all American students for the next century.

Goal 5: Students will be first in the world in science and mathematics achievement.

Goal 6: Every adult American will possess the knowledge and skills necessary to compete in a global economy and exercise the rights and responsibilities of citizenship.

Goal 7: Every school in the United States will be free of drugs, violence, and the unauthorized presence of firearms and alcohol and will offer a disciplined environment conducive to learning.

Goal 8: Every school will promote partnerships that will increase parent involvement and participation in promoting the social, emotional, and academic growth of children (U.S. Department of Education, 1994).

ASK *the Expert*

Jerlean Daniel

Common Questions about the NAEYC

1. What makes the NAEYC unique as a large-membership organization?

Founded in 1926, the NAEYC has more than 100,000 members. The NAEYC is the nation's largest organization of early childhood professionals and others dedicated to improving the quality of early childhood education programs for children from birth through age 8 years. The NAEYC's primary goals are to improve professional practice and working conditions in early childhood education and to build public understanding and support for high-quality early childhood programs.

2. What kinds of issues does the NAEYC address?

The NAEYC, like other large-membership organizations, faces two major tensions. The *first* pertains to the dual roles of the governing board to serve and to lead the membership. If the governing board acts only in response to the concerns and directives of the membership, then it runs the risk of failing to lead. Leadership requires vision and the ability to anticipate, thus staying on the cutting edge of issues. But leadership without responsiveness to the membership is doomed. The *second* tension exists in part because of the low priority of children's issues on the national social agenda and the corresponding low valuation of direct service work with children. That tension revolves around the primacy of children's needs versus the needs of the profession. The majority of the NAEYC's membership affirms the primacy of children's needs. The balancing of the two major tensions, following versus leading and children versus profession, create a synergy, which represents the political realities of progress toward optimal services for children and families. I, for one, see no real competition, but rather an interdependent convergence toward mutually inclusive goals.

3. How does the NAEYC work to increase standards in the field of early childhood?

An example of the productive convergence of the two major tensions is NAEYC accreditation. Accreditation was a leadership vision brought to the membership by the staff and governing board. While the membership had not specifically requested accreditation, the commitment to better standards of early care and education, the NAEYC mission, was why people joined the NAEYC. The membership responded positively to the idea, and the organization put into place a process of consensus building, which created the accreditation criteria. Consensus building has long been one of the NAEYC's strengths. It is the link between responsiveness and leadership.

It is important to note here that the commitment of all parties was such that the accreditation criteria were not easy, self-serving benchmarks, but rather a set of professional standards that exceeded the licensing standards of most states. Because the NAEYC has no authority to require programs to become accredited, the process pivots around *voluntary* self-study and subsequent *validation* of the self-study results.

NAEYC accreditation also balances the second set of organizational tensions. The accreditation criteria set a higher standard for early care and education programming, establishing the primacy of children's needs. The self-study process enhances professional development, thereby setting a professional standard. Self-study is a valuable, classroom specific in-service training tool. It allows staff members to cooperatively evaluate their performance, expand their developmental knowledge, make appropriate adjustments, and achieve better-quality job performance.

The innovation of accreditation also generated further clarification of practice in the field in the form of developmentally appropriate practices (DAP). Again, consensus building was used to define exemplary practice and enhance professionalism.

4. Why should I belong to the NAEYC or any other professional organization?

The NAEYC, along with many other professional associations, offers a framework for our combined talents to make a difference, to efficiently focus our passion, and to effectively use our knowledge base to advocate for what ought to be. If any reader should think that he or she is not counted among the legions of committed, knowledgeable professionals charged with the responsibility to make early care and education services what they ought to be for young children and their families, I must ask, if not us, together, now, then who, and when?

Jerlean Daniel is a past president of the NAEYC and an assistant professor, University of Pittsburgh.

The following resources are available from the National Education Goals Panel:

Goal 1: All Children in America
Will Start School Ready to Learn
1-800-USA-LEARN
www.ed.gov/pubs/resdir.html.

National Education Goals Panel
1255 22nd Street, NW, Suite 502
Washington, DC 20037

Source: U.S. Department of Education. (1994). *Goals 2000: Educate America Act.* Washington, DC: Author.

Professional Associations, Organizations, Journals, and Materials
Professional Associations, Organizations, Journals, and Newsletters for Early Childhood Practitioners

The following organizations provide information, services, and materials to early childhood teachers.

American Montessori Society (AMS)
150 Fifth Avenue
New York, NY 10011
www.amshq.org

Association for Childhood Education International (ACEI)
(Infancy through adolescence)
11501 Georgia Ave., Suite 315
Wheaton, MD 20902
www.udel.edu/bateman/acei
Journal: *Childhood Education*

Canadian Association for Young Children
Regina CAYC
496 Dalgliesh Dr.
Regina, Saskatchewan, Canada S4R 6M8
www.gpfn.sk.ca/health/children/cayc

Canadian Child Care Federation
   30 Rosemount, Suite 100
   Ottowa, ON K1Y 1P4
   www.cfc.efc.ca/cccf/
   Newsletter: *Interaction*

Children's Foundation
   725 15th Street NW, Suite 505
   Washington, DC 20005
   www.childrensfoundation.net
   Provides a voice for caregivers, children, and their families
   Newsletters on projects undertaken

Council for Early Childhood Professional Recognition
   2460 16th Street NW
   Washington, DC 20009
   www.cdacouncil.org
   CDA headquarters and information on *Reggio America*

Day Care and Child Development Council of America
   805 Fifteenth Street NW
   Washington, DC 20005

International Montessori Society
   912 Thayer Ave. #207
   Silver Spring, MD 20910
   www.wdn.com/trust/ims
   Newsletters: *Montessori Observer* and *Montessori News*

National Association for the Education of Young Children (**NAEYC**)
   1509 16th Street NW
   Washington, DC 20036
   www.naeyc.org
   Journal: *Young Children*

OMEP (Organisation Mondiale pour l'Education Pre'scoliare)
   World Organization for Preschool Education
   2460 16th St NW
   Washington, DC 20009-3575
   http://omep-us.crc.uiuc.edu
   Journal: *International Journal of Early Childhood*

National Association of Family Child Care
   206 6th Avenue, Suite 900
   Des Moines, IA 50309-4518
   (515) 282-8192
   www.assoc-mgmt.com/users/nafcc
   Provides technical assistance to Family Child Care Association
   Newsletter: *National Perspectives*

Child Advocacy Groups

Action for Children's Television

Administration for Children, Youth, and Families

Canadian Day Care Advocacy Association

Child Care Action Campaign

Children's Defense Fund

Child Health Alert

Child Trends, Inc.

Child Welfare League of America

Families and Work Institute

National Black Child Development Institute

National Child Care Information Center

National Committee for the Prevention of Child Abuse

Reading is FUNdamental

Save the Children

Stand for Children

Society for Developmental Education

The Children's Foundation

UNICEF

Zero to Three: National Center for Infants, Toddlers, and Families

Other Professional Associations and Journals That Publish Some Materials About Early Childhood

Association for Supervision and Curriculum Development (ASCD)
1250 N. Pitt Street
Alexandria, VA 22314-1403
www.ascd.org
Journal: *Educational Leadership*

Council for Exceptional Children (CEC)
(Special Education)
920 Association Drive
Reston, VA 22091-1589
www.cwc.sped.org
Journal: *Exceptional Children*

International Reading Association (IRA)
800 Barksdale Road
PO Box 8139
Newark, DE 19714-8139
www.reading.org
Journal: *The Reading Teacher*

National Art Education Association (NAEA)
1916 Association Drive
Reston, VA 22091-1590
www.naea-reston.org
Journal: *Art Education*

National Association for Bilingual Education (NABE)
1220 L Street NW, Suite 605
Washington, DC 20005-4018
www.nabe.org
Journal: *Bilingual Research Journal*

National Association for Gifted Children (NAGC)
1707 L Street NW
Washington, DC 20036
www.nagc.org
Journal: *Gifted Child Quarterly*

National Council for the Social Studies (NCSS)
3501 Newark Street NW
Washington, DC 20016
www.ncss.org
Journal: *Social Studies and the Young Learner*

National Council of Teachers of Mathematics (NCTM)
1906 Association Drive
Reston, VA 22091-2970
www.nctm.org
Journal: *Teaching Children Mathematics (PK–6)*

National Science Teachers Association (NSTA)
1840 Wilson Blvd.
Arlington, VA 22201-3000
www.nsta.org
Journal: *Science and Children (Elementary)*

Other Journals and Professional Magazines Dedicated to Early Childhood Education

Beginnings

The Canadian Journal of Research in Early Childhood Education

Child Development
(Research journal of the Society for Research in Child Development)

Children Today
(Published by the U.S. Government Office of Human Development Services)

Child Care Information Exchange

Dimensions of Early Childhood
(Publication of the Southern Early Childhood Association)

Early Childhood Education Journal

Early Childhood Research Quarterly
(Research journal of the National Association for the Education of Young Children)

Early Childhood Today

Today's Child

Other Journals That Publish Some Articles About Early Childhood

American Journal of Orthopsychiatry

Canadian Children

Developmental Psychology

Merrill-Palmer Quarterly of Behavior and Development

Journal of Research in Childhood Education
(Published by the Association for Childhood Education International)

Peabody Journal of Education

Phi Delta Kappan
  (Journal of the National Honor Society, Phi Delta Kappa)

Review of Educational Research
  (Publication of the American Educational Research Association)

Language Arts
  (Publication of the National Council of Teachers of English)

Teacher Research: The Journal of Classroom Inquiry

Topics in Early Childhood Special Education

Book Publishers/Distributors That Feature Early Childhood Materials

Allyn & Bacon

Crystal Springs Books

Gryphon House

Merrill/Prentice Hall

Modern Learning Press

Redleaf Press

SkyLight

Teacher Ideas Press

Educational Resources Information Center (ERIC) Clearinghouses

ERIC is a national clearinghouse of information that can be accessed on-line.

U.S. Department of Education
  National Library of Education
  Office of Educational Research and Improvement (OERI)
  555 New Jersey Avenue, NW
  Washington, DC 20280-5720
  www.ed.gov

Disabilities and Gifted Education
  The Council for Exceptional Children
  1920 Association Drive
  Reston, VA 20191-1589
  www.cec.sped.org/ericec.html

Elementary and Early Childhood Education
  University of Illinois at Urbana–Champaign
  805 West Pennsylvania Avenue
  Urbana, IL 61801-4897
  http://ericeece.org

Child Care
  National Child Care Information Center
  301 Maple Avenue West, Suite 602
  Vienna, VA 22180
  http://nccic.org

National Parent Information Network
  www.npin.org

Storage and Organizational Resources

As you create your own personal system for locating, gathering, and using materials and resources, you will need to create a system for organizing them. We have provided suggestions for finding materials and resources and deciding what to include in your professional resource file.

Finding Materials for a Good Resource File

- Materials distributed from instructors, leaders, and consultants
- Bulletins and publications from your local, state, and federal government, professional organizations, and commercial organizations
- Magazines, pictures, professional journal articles
- Ideas shared by colleagues
- Books from the public library
- Notes taken during workshops, course work, and national, state, and local conferences
- Your own growing file of activities, catalogues, and professional publications

Materials to Include in a Resource File

- Art suggestions (e.g., recipes for play dough, fingerpaints, materials collection)
- Bulletin board and display ideas (e.g., pictures, themes)
- Dramatics (e.g., prop boxes, theme-related materials)
- Equipment sources, catalogues, and teacher-made materials
- Field trips and excursions
- Finger plays, songs, records, tapes
- Health and safety information and learning activities
- Literacy information and learning activities
- Math and science suggestions
- Social studies (e.g., ideas for community, understanding the self, rights and responsibilities)
- Themes appropriate for a particular age group
- Transition activities and ideas
    Children as Resources
    Families as Resources
    School Resources
    Community Resources
- Other

Technology Resources

The following Web sites provide information and ideas about all areas of early childhood. Use this list as a beginning for your own list of useful sites.

Children's Books

www.ghbooks.com
Free activities from resource books

www.eric-carle.com
Children's author and illustrator's Web site

Children with Special Needs

www.irsc.org/disability.htm
Information on disabilities

www.dftoys.com
Catalogue of toys for children with disabilities

Curriculum Resources

www.att.com/learning
Provides K–12 curriculum-based multimedia learning circles

www.naeyc.org
NAEYC's home page

perpetualpreschool.com
Preschool activities and resources

Lesson Plans

teachernet.com
Searchable database of classroom projects and bulletin board ideas for teachers

www.mcps.k12.md.us/curriculum/xocialstd/mbd/lessons-index.html
Offers preschool and multicultural lesson plans

Music

www.kididdkes.com
Variety of songs for children

Software Evaluation Criteria

Technology has become an integral and accessible part of children's learning. Here are criteria for selecting and using software with young children.

Technical Features

Are the basic function keys (e.g., delete, return) used appropriately?

Can children easily start, stop, and move about the program with little or no help?

Can children save or print their work?

Learning Features

Are there visual, auditory, and tactile features that make it easy for children to understand?

Can the learner control the pace and path of the program (i.e., make it faster or slower)?

Do children receive quick feedback so they stay involved in learning?

Content Features

Do the activities help the child learn new content, processes, or skills?

Can the learner explore concepts on several levels of difficulty?

Developmentally Appropriate Features

Are the content, skills, or processes used appropriate to the age range suggested?

Does the program enable children to be playful or construct elements on their own (e.g., draw pictures, move characters, create stories)?

Is there a range of activities that differ in complexity (e.g., does a mathematics program have activities that include one-to-one correspondence, estimation, and simple addition)?

Do children experience success when using this program?

Source: Adapted from "Thoughts on Technology and Education" by B. Bowman and E. Beyer, 1994, *Young Children: Active Learners in a Technological Age,* pp. 19–30, J. Wright and D. Shale, Eds., Washington, DC: National Association for the Education of Young Children; and "Children and Technology" by J. Isenberg and T. Rosegrant, 1995, *Selecting Educational Equipment and Materials for School and Home,* pp. 25–29, J. Moyer, Ed., Wheaton, MD: Association for Childhood Education International.

Human Resources

Human resources involve the services that *people* provide to children, families, teachers, and schools. As an early childhood teacher, it is important that you know what services are available to you to support children's growth and development, and also to help parents access and use them. Keeping track of the many available resources requires some kind of organizational system.

Community Resources

The following community resources are valuable sources of information and assistance in your teaching community. Following is a form to use to identify public and private agencies, consultants, and your own network. Some of the items listed are more useful to child-care workers; others are more useful to teachers of primary school-age children; some are useful to both. These resources provide a beginning list, which will grow with you as you identify other important human resources. You can also use this list to *organize* information, forms, and contact people in one easy location. We have listed community resources in alphabetical order. You might also want to organize these resources by public or private agencies, consultants, or your own personal contacts.

SERVICE	NAME	TELEPHONE NUMBER
Accounting		
Air Conditioning Service		
American Red Cross		
Ambulance		
Arts and Cultural Organizations		

Appliance Service _____

Attorney _____

Auditing _____

Carpenter _____

Center, Chair of the Board _____

Center, Director _____

Chambers of Commerce _____

Child Abuse: Hot Line _____

Child Abuse: Protective Services _____

Child Care Resource and Referral _____

Child Development Clinic _____

Cooperative Extension Office _____

Dance Studios _____

Electric Company _____

Family Services _____

Fire Department _____

Gas Company _____

Health Department _____

Heating Service _____

Hospital _____

Information and Referral _____

Insurance _____

Landlord _____

Legal Aid Society _____

Museums _____

Parks and Recreation _____

Physician _____

Plumber _____

Police Department, State _____

Police Department, Local _____

Public Library _____

Radio and TV Stations _____

Repair Service _____

Rescue Squad _____

Roofer _____

Service Organizations _____

Sheriff's Office _____

Taxi Service _____

Public School Specialists

Most public schools provide support services from specialists who are located throughout the building. Following is a list of some of the specialists who might provide support to you, the children, and families.

Art Teacher
Computer Teacher
English-as-a-second-language (ESL) Teacher
Foreign Language Teacher
Learning Disabilities Specialist
Librarian
Music Teacher
Physical Education Teacher
Reading Specialist
School Counselor
School Secretary
School Nurse
School Psychologist
Social Worker
Speech Teacher

Public Library-linked Services for Children and Families

Many public agencies and organizations provide various kinds of services to schools and families. As a teacher, you want to be creative in how you use these resources. Figure A.1 is a representation of some ways the public library serves to link the school and community to needed resources.

Community Building Strategies

Most communities provide various types of services to schools and community members. As a teacher, you need to know how to access the many resources your community offers. Table A.1 lists services provided, identifies referral agencies often associated with the services, notes typical services provided, and includes questions that you can ask to find out more information.

Linking libraries with community resources

Adult Education Programs

Directory of education; ESL; GED classes
Adult basic education, e.g., Federal Office of Refugee Resettlement;

Grant money, e.g.,
Literacy tutoring;
educational services;

Schools

Homework help center; Computers; Films;
Meeting place for homebound students
and teachers; Support for programs;
Children bring parents; Youth advisory councils
Volunteers; students, retired teachers

LIBRARY

Artists and Cultural Institutions

Display case; Artwork contests; Publicity; Visibility
to organization; Ethnic dance group meeting place

Lending of art and cultural collections; Entertainment,
music recitals; Classes and workshops

Community Agencies

Human services; Counselors

Referrals; Contacts in the
community; Meeting place
to counsel teens; Outreach;
Master instructional
technology on Internet

Business

Money, donations for prizes, sponsorship opportunities;
e.g., Storytellers for Children; Volunteers

Publicity, humanitarian focus in community;

Community Based Organizations; Civic Associations

Public meeting rooms; Blood drives; Real estate
classes; Home owner associations; Sport groups;
Boy/Girl scouts; Consumer credit counseling

Neighborhood information; Promotion of
library in community; Friends of the Library;
Computer equipment

Local Residents

Tax forms; Provide job experience and staff advisory;
forms; Provide job counseling; Job search resources; Immigrant
Volunteers; Serve on patron and Foundation gifts
groups; Friends of the Library;

Courtesy of Marshann Snyder.

439

Support Services for Children and Families

Type of Service	Referral Agencies	Typical Services	Information Gathering Questions
Health Services	Acquired Immune Deficiency Syndrome (AIDS) Hot Line	Braces, hearing aids, vision testing	What do you do?
	Alcohol and Drug Abuse Services	Clinic visits—prenatal/well baby	Whom do you serve?
	American Lung Association	Information and referral	What area do you serve?
	American Cancer Society	In-home services; home-delivered meals	How much does it cost?
	American Heart Association	Insurance and medical-form counseling	Is there help to pay for your service?
	American Red Cross	Labwork, medications	What happens after I call?
	Army Community Services	Limited hospitalization	Is there help for families who don't speak English?
	Community Health Centers	Medical, health, and dental care	What else should I know about your service?
	Dental Hygiene Clinics	Nutrition information and training	
	Health Department	Support groups	
	Home Health Care		
	Food Allergy Network		
	Juvenile Diabetes Foundation		
	Meals on Wheels		
	Poison Control Center		
	Shriners Hospital		
Economic Assistance	American Red Cross	Self-sufficiency: employment services, job counseling, job search, employability skills workshops and training	What do you do?
	Department of Housing and Human Services	Benefit programs for food stamps, temporary assistance/medical care for children or adults who are disabled or ill	Whom do you serve?
	Social Services		What area do you serve?
	Salvation Army		How much does it cost?
	Shelters	Medicaid to cover medical and health care to the elderly, those who are disabled, those who are blind, pregnant women, some needy children, and caretakers	Is there help to pay for your service?
	Social Security Administration		What happens after I call?
	Temporary Assistance to Needy Families (TANF)	Refugee assistance	Is there help for families who don't speak English?
	United Community Ministries	Assistance with hospital bills	What else should I know about your service?
	Other	Temporary cash assistance to families in need	

Intervention Services

Association for Retarded Citizens

Children and Adults with Attention Deficit Disorder (CHAD)

Department of Pediatrics

Early Intervention Services

Easter Seal Society

Family and Early Childhood Education Program

Preschool Child Find

Public Health Department

Public Schools Special Education Services

Speech and Hearing Clinics

Other

Americans with Disabilities Act

Information

Assistive Technology Services

Audiology Services

Developmental Evaluation

Equipment and Resources

Family Training, Counseling, and Home Visits

Health and Nursing Services

Information and Referral

Medical Services

Occupational Therapy

Physical Therapy

Psychological Services

Respite Care

Service Coordination

Social Work Services

Speech Therapy

Support Groups

Transportation

Vision Services

What do you do?

Whom do you serve?

What area do you serve?

How much does it cost?

Is there help to pay for your service?

What happens after I call?

Is there help for families who don't speak English?

What else should I know about your service?

Courtesy of Marshann Snyder.

Chapter by Chapter Cross Reference of Early Childhood Materials and Resources

The following grid provides a summary and cross reference for a beginning list of resources for emerging early childhood teachers. The topics covered in the Compendium are matched with the chapters which they support. For example, the National Education Goals are mentioned in Chapter 11 and a summary of the goals and additional web sites about the goals are included in this Compendium.

Chapter/Topic	1	2	3	4	5	6	7	8	9	10	11
MATERIAL RESOURCES											
Basic Materials by Age Range					•						
Learning Centers Materials						•	•				
Free, Inexpensive Materials					•	•					
Health, Nutrition, & Safety					•						
Professional resources for teachers	•	•					•	•			•
Code of Ethics	•										
INTASC Standards											•
National Education Goals											•
E.C. Professional Organizations		•						•			•
Child Advocacy Groups		•	•								•
Other Journals & Organizations											•
ERIC			•							•	•
Storage & Resource Organization Information					•	•	•				
Technology Resources						•	•				
Software Evaluation Criteria						•					
HUMAN RESOURCES											
Community Human Resources		•								•	
Public School Specialists			•	•							
School-linked Services										•	
Support Services for Families										•	

References

Preface

Ayers, W. (Ed.). (1995). *To become a teacher: Making a difference in children's lives.* New York: Teachers College Press.

National Association for the Education of Young Children. (1995). *Guidelines for preparation of early childhood professionals.* Washington, DC: Author.

Introduction

Carter, M., & Curtis, D. (1994). *Training teachers: A harvest of theory and practice.* St. Paul, MN: Redleaf Press.

Pressley, M. (1995). *Advanced educational psychology for educators, researchers, and policymakers.* New York: HarperCollins College Publishers.

Saracho, O. N. (1988). A study of the roles of early childhood teachers. *Early Child Development and Care, 38,* 43–56.

Chapter 1

Abbs, P. (1974). *Autobiography in education.* London: Heinemann.

Ayers, W. (1995). (Ed.). *To become a teacher: Making a difference in children's lives.* New York: Teachers College Press.

Ayers, W. (1989). *The good preschool teacher: Six teachers reflect on their lives.* New York: Teachers College Press.

Borko, H. (1989). Research on learning to teach: Implications for graduate teacher preparation. In A. Woolfolk (Ed.), *Research perspectives on the graduate preparation of teachers* (pp. 69–87). Upper Saddle River, NJ: Prentice Hall.

Boyer, E. L. (1995). *The basic school: A community for learning.* Princeton, NJ: The Carnegie Foundation.

Bredekamp, S. (1997). Preface. In J. P. Isenberg & M. R. Jalongo (Eds.). *Major trends and issues in early childhood: Challenges, controversies, and insights.* New York: Teachers College Press.

Bredekamp, S., & Copple, C. (Eds.). (1997). *Developmentally appropriate practice in early childhood pro-*

grams (rev. ed.). Washington, DC: National Association for the Education of Young Children.

Bruer, J. T. (1993). The mind's journey from novice to expert. *American Educator, 17*(2), 6–15, 38–46.

Burke, K. (1997). *Designing professional portfolios for change.* Arlington Heights, IL: SkyLight.

Carothers, S. A. (1995). Taking teaching seriously. In W. Ayers (Ed.), *To become a teacher: Making a difference in children's lives* (pp. 23–33). New York: Teachers College Press.

Carter, M., & Curtis, D. (1994). *Training teachers: A harvest of theory and practice.* St. Paul, MN: Redleaf Press.

Carter, M., & Doyle, W. (1989). Classroom research as a resource for graduate preparation of teachers. In A. E. Woolfolk (Ed.), *Research perspectives on the graduate preparation of teachers* (pp. 51–68). Upper Saddle River, NJ: Prentice Hall.

Clark, C. M. (1996). *Thoughtful teaching.* New York: Teachers College Press.

Cochran-Smith, M., & Lytle, S. (1990). Research on teachers and teacher research: The issues that divide. *Educational Researcher, 19*(2), 2–11.

Cruickshank, D. (1987). *Reflective teaching.* Reston, VA: Association of Teacher Educators.

Csikszentmihalyi, M. (1993). *The evolving self: A psychology for the third millennium.* New York: HarperPerennial.

Dewey, J. (1933). *How we think: A restatement of the relation of thinking to the educative process.* Boston, MA: D. C. Heath.

Eby, J. W., & Kujawa, E. (1998). *Reflective planning, teaching, and evaluation: K–12* (3rd ed.). Upper Saddle River, NJ: Merrill/Prentice Hall.

Eisner, E. (1994). *The educational imagination: On the design and evaluation of school programs* (3rd ed.). Upper Saddle River, NJ: Merrill/Prentice Hall.

Elkind, D. (1987). *Miseducation: Preschoolers at risk.* New York: Knopf.

Fennimore, B. S. (1989). *Child advocacy for early childhood educators.* New York: Teachers College Press.

Fuller, B., Holloway, S. D., & Bozzi, L. (1997). Evaluating child care and preschools: Advancing the interests of government, teachers, or parents? In B. Spodek & O. N. Saracho (Eds.), *Issues in early childhood educational assessment and evaluation* (pp. 7–27). New York: Teachers College Press.

Glasgow, K. (1994). A problem of theory for early childhood professionals. *Childhood Education, 70*(3), 131–132.

Glatthorn, A. (1996). *The teacher's portfolio: Fostering and documenting professional development.* Rockport, MA: Proactive Publications.

Goodman, Y. M. (1978). Kidwatching: An alternative to testing. *National Elementary School Principal, 57*(1), 41–45.

Gordon, A. M., & Williams-Browne, K. (1995). *Beginnings and beyond.* (4th ed.). Albany, NY: Delmar.

Hendrick, J. (1998). *Total learning* (5th ed.). Upper Saddle River, NJ: Merrill/Prentice Hall.

Hildebrand, V., & Hearron, P. (1998). *Guiding young children* (6th ed.). Upper Saddle River, NJ: Merrill/Prentice Hall.

Isenberg, J. P. (1995). Whole language and play in the expressive arts. In S. R. Raines (Ed.), *Whole language across the curriculum: Grades 1, 2, 3* (pp. 114–136). New York: Teachers College Press.

Jalongo, M. R., & Isenberg, J. P. (1995). *Teachers' stories: From personal narrative to professional insight.* San Francisco, CA: Jossey-Bass.

Katz, L. (1972). *Talks with teachers.* Washington, DC: National Association for the Education of Young Children.

Kochendorfer, L. (1994). *Becoming a reflective teacher.* West Haven, CT: NEA Professional Library.

Krall, C. M., & Jalongo, M. R. (1998). Creating caring communities in classrooms: Advice from an intervention specialist. *Childhood Education, 75*(2), 83–89.

Kramer, J. F. (1994). Defining competence as readiness to learn. In Goffin, S. G., & Day, D. E. (Eds.), *New perspectives in early childhood teacher education: Bringing practitioners into the debate* (pp. 29–36). New York: Teachers College Press.

Law, N., Moffit, M., Moore, E., Overfield, R., & Starks, E. (1966). *Basic propositions for early childhood education.* Washington, DC: Association for Childhood Education International.

McCarthy, J. (1988). *State certification of early childhood teachers: An analysis of the 50 states and the District of Columbia.* Washington, DC: National Association for the Education of Young Children.

McDevitt, T. M. (1990). Encouraging young children's listening. *Academic Therapy, 25*(5), 569–577.

McIntyre, D. J., & O'Hair, M. J. (1996). *The reflective roles of the classroom teacher.* Belmont, CA: Wadsworth.

Minuchin, P. (1987). Schools, families, and the development of young children. *Early Childhood Research Quarterly, 2,* 245–259.

National Association for the Education of Young Children (1998). *Code of ethical conduct and commitment.* Washington, DC: Author.

National Board for Teacher Certification (1995). *Early childhood/generalist: Standards for National Board Certification.* Washington, DC: Author.

Noddings, N. (1984). *Caring: A feminine approach to ethics and moral education.* Berkeley: University of California Press.

Raywid, M. A. (1995). In W. Ayers (Ed.), *To become a teacher: Making a difference in children's lives* (pp. 78–85). New York: Teachers College Press.

Ryan, K. (1986). *The induction of new teachers.* Bloomington, IN: Phi Delta Kappa (Fastback #237).

Sapon-Shevin, M. (1995). Building a safe community for learning. In W. Ayers (Ed.), *To become a teacher: Making a difference in children's lives* (pp. 99–112). New York: Teachers College Press.

Schon, D. A. (1983). *The reflective practitioner: How professionals think in action.* New York: Basic Books.

Schubert, W. H., & Ayers, W. C. (1992). *Teacher lore: Learning from our own experience.* White Plains, NY: Longman.

Shulman, L. (1986). Those who understand: Knowledge growth in teaching. *Educational Researcher, 19,* 4–14.

Sparks-Langer, G. M., & Colton, A. B. (1991). Synthesis of research on teachers' reflective thinking. *Educational Leadership, 48*(6), 37–44.

Tennyson, W. W., & Strom, S. M. (1988). Beyond professional standards: Developing responsibilities. *Journal of Counseling and Development, 64*(5), 298–302.

Chapter 2

Aries, P. (1962). *Centuries of childhood.* London: Jonathan Cape.

Athey, C. (1990). *Extending thought in young children.* London: Paul Chapman.

Bloch, M. N., & Price, G. G. (Eds.). (1994). *Essays on the history of early childhood education.* Norwood, NJ: Ablex.

Bronfenbrenner, U. (1974). *A report of longitudinal evaluation of preschool programs.* Washington, DC: U. S. Government Printing Office.

Carbo, M. (1995). Educating everybody's children. In R. W. Cole (Ed.), *Educating everybody's children: Diverse teaching strategies for diverse learners: What research and practice say about improving achievement* (pp. 1–8). Alexandria, VA: Association for Supervision and Curriculum Development.

Clark, C. M., & Peterson, P. L. (1986). Teachers' thought processes. In M. Wittrock (Ed.), *Handbook of Research on Teaching* (3rd ed.). (pp. 255–296). Upper Saddle River, NJ: Prentice Hall.

Clawson, D., & Chick, K. (in press). Inclusion: Celebrating contributions while meeting new challenges. In M. R. Jalongo (Ed.), *Resisting the pendulum swing: Informed perspectives on educational controversies.* Olney, MD: Association for Childhood Education International.

Cleverley, J., & Phillips, D. C. (1986). *Visions of childhood: Influential models from Locke to Spock.* New York: Teachers College Press.

Cryan, J. R. (1995). The banning of corporal punishment. *Dimensions of Early Childhood, 23*(3), 36–37.

Cryer, D., & Phillipsen, L. (1997). Quality details: A close-up look at child care program strengths and weaknesses. *Young Children, 52*(2), 51–61.

DeMause, L. (Ed.). (1974). *The history of childhood.* New York: The Psychohistory Press.

Driscoll, A. (1995). *Cases in early childhood education: Stories of programs and practices.* Boston, MA: Allyn & Bacon.

Education Week and Pew Charitable Trust (1998). Quality counts '98. *Education Week,* January 8, 1998, pp. 21, 67.

Epstein, A. S. (1993). Training for quality: Improving early childhood programs through systematic inservice training. *Monographs of the High/Scope Educational Research Foundation, 9* (PS 022 104).

Erwin, E. J. (1996). *Putting children first: Visions for a brighter future for young children and their families.* Baltimore, MD: Paul Brookes.

Feeney, S., Christensen, D., & Moravcik, E. (1996). *Who am I in the lives of children? An introduction to teaching young children.* Upper Saddle River, NJ: Prentice Hall.

Gallas, K. (1994). *The languages of learning: How children talk, write, dance, draw and sing their understanding of the world.* New York: Teachers College Press.

Glasgow, K. (1994). A problem of theory for early childhood professionals. *Childhood Education, 70*(3), 131–132.

Goffin, S. G., & Lombardi, J. (1988). *Speaking out: Early childhood advocacy.* Washington, DC: National Association for the Education of Young Children.

Greenspan, S., & Wieder, S. (1998). *The child with special needs: Encouraging intellectual and emotional growth.* Reading, MA: Addison Wesley.

Grunwald, L. (1996/97). The amazing minds of infants. In K. M. Paciorek & J. H. Munro (Eds.). *Early childhood education 96/96* (17th ed.). (pp. 45–50). Guilford, CT: Dushkin/McGraw-Hill.

Harms, T., & Clifford, R. M. (1997). Early childhood environment rating scale (2nd ed.). New York: Teachers College Press.

Hendrick, J. (Ed.). (1996). *First steps toward teaching the Reggio way.* Upper Saddle River, NJ: Merrill/Prentice Hall.

Isenberg, J. P., & Jalongo, M. R. (1997). *Major trends and issues in early childhood education.* New York: Teachers College Press.

Jalongo, M. R., Bauer, K., Conrad, N. K., & Cardy, T. (1998). National public school pre-kindergarten: Issues and future directions. *Dimensions of Early Childhood, 26*(3 & 4), 3–11.

Jensen, E. (1998). *Teaching with the brain in mind.* Alexandria, VA: Association for Supervision and Curriculum Development.

Kamerman, S. B., & Kahn, A. J. (1994). *A welcome for every child: Care, education and family support for infants and toddlers in Europe.* Arlington, VA: Zero to Three/National Center for Clinical Infant Programs.

Kozol, J. (1991). *Savage inequalities: Children in America's schools.* New York: Crown.

LeFrancois, G. (1998). *Of children.* Belmont, CA: Wadsworth.

Neugebauer, R. (1995, November/December). The movers and shapers of early childhood education. *Child Care Information Exchange,* 9–13.

Osborn, D. K. (1980). *Early childhood education in historical perspective.* Athens, GA: Education Associates.

Postman, N. (1982). *The disappearance of childhood.* New York: Dell.

Roberts, R. N., Rule, S., & Innocenti, M. S. (1998). *Strengthening the family-professional partnership in services for young children.* Baltimore, MD: Paul H. Brookes.

Rogoff, B. (1993). *Apprenticeship in thinking: Cognitive development in social context.* New York: Oxford University Press.

Sameroff, A., & McDonough, S. C. (1994). Educational implications of developmental transitions: Revisiting the 5- to 7-year shift. *Phi Delta Kappan,* 188–193.

Santrock, J. W. (1997). *Children* (5th ed.). Dubuque, IA: Times Mirror/Brown and Benchmark.

Schweinhart, L. J. (1994). *Lasting benefits of preschool programs.* (ERIC Digest No. EDO-PS-94-2).

Smith, A. B. (1996). Quality programs that care and educate. *Childhood Education, 72*(6), 330–336.

Snyder, A. (1972). *Dauntless women in childhood education.* Washington, DC: Association for Childhood Education International.

Sylwester, R. (1995). *A celebration of neurons: An educator's guide to the human brain.* Alexandria, VA: Association for Supervision and Curriculum Development.

Tanner, L. N. (1997). *Dewey's Laboratory School: Lessons for today.* New York: Teachers College Press.

Tuchman, B. (1978). *A distant mirror.* New York: Alfred A. Knopf.

Wortham, S. (1992). *Childhood: 1892–1992.* Olney, MD: Association for Childhood Education International.

Wyman, A. (1995). The earliest early childhood teachers: Women teachers of America's Dame Schools. *Young Children, 50*(2), 29–32.

Chapter 3

Association for Supervision and Curriculum Development. (1997). *Promoting social and emotional learning: Guidelines for educators.* Alexandria, VA: Author.

Banks, J. A. (1997). *Teaching strategies for ethnic studies* (6th ed.). Boston: Allyn & Bacon.

Bennett, C. I. (1995). *Comprehensive multicultural education: Theory and practice.* (3rd ed.). Boston: Allyn & Bacon.

Bergen, D. (1997). Perspectives on inclusion in early childhood education. In J. P. Isenberg & M. R. Jalongo (Eds.), *Major trends and issues in early childhood education: Challenges, controversies, and insights* (pp. 151–171), New York: Teachers College Press.

Berk, L. E. (1996). *Infants, children, and adolescents* (2nd ed.). Boston: Allyn & Bacon.

Berns, R. (1997). *Child, family, school, and community* (4th ed.). Fort Worth, TX: Harcourt Brace Jovanovich.

Bredekamp, S., & Copple, C. (1997). *Developmentally appropriate practice in early childhood programs* (rev. ed.). Washington, DC: National Association for the Education of Young Children.

Bronfenbrenner, U. (1979). *The ecology of human development.* Cambridge, MA: Harvard University Press.

Chipman, M. (1997). Valuing cultural diversity in the early years: Social imperatives and pedagogical insights. In J. P. Isenberg & M. R. Jalongo (Eds.), *Major trends and issues in early childhood education: Challenges, Controversies, and Insights* (pp. 43–55). New York: Teachers College Press.

Copple, C., Sigel, I., & Saunders, R. (1979). *Educating the young thinker.* New York: D. Van Nostrand.

Division for Early Childhood of the Council of Exceptional Children (1993). *Position on inclusion.* Reston, VA. Author.

Dodge, D., Jablon, J., & Bickart, T. (1994). *Constructing curriculum for the primary grades.* Washington, DC: Teaching Strategies.

Erikson, E. H. (1963). *Childhood and society.* New York: Norton.

Feng, J. (1994). *Asian-American children: What teachers should know.* Urbana, IL: Clearinghouse on Elementary and Early Childhood Education. (ERIC Digest No. EDO PS 94 4).

Garbarino, J. (1995). *Raising children in a socially toxic environment.* San Francisco: Jossey-Bass.

Garcia, E. E. (1992). Linguistically and culturally diverse children: Effective instructional practices and related policy issues. In H. C. Waxman, J. Walker de Fleix, J. E. Anderson, & H. P. Baptiste, Jr. (Eds.), *Students at risk in at-risk schools: Improving environments for learning* (pp. 65–86). Newbury Park, CA: Corwin Press.

Glassman, M. (1994). All things being equal: The two roads of Piaget and Vygotsky. *Developmental Review (14)*, 186–214.

Goffin, S., & Day, D. (Eds.). (1994). *New perspectives in early childhood teacher education: Bringing practitioners into the debate.* New York: Teachers College Press.

Hallahan, D. P., & Kauffman, J. M. (1994). *Exceptional children: Introduction to special education.* (6th ed.). Boston: Allyn & Bacon.

Hildebrand, V. (1997). *Introduction to early childhood education* (6th ed.). Upper Saddle River, NJ: Merrill/Prentice-Hall.

Hutchison, B. L. (1994). The value of developmentally appropriate practice for all children. In S. Goffin & D. Day (Eds.), *New perspectives in early childhood teacher education: Bringing practitioners into the debate,* (pp. 146–155). New York: Teachers College Press.

Individuals with Disabilities Education Act, Public Law 101–476, (30 October, 1990).

Isenberg, J. P. (1997). Development issues affecting children. In J. P. Isenberg & M. R. Jalongo (Eds.). *Major trends and issues in early childhood education: Challenges, controversies, and insights* (pp. 29–55). New York: Teachers College Press.

Kamii, C., & DeVries, R. (1980). *Group games in early education: Implications of Piaget's theory.* Washington, DC: National Association for the Education of Young Children.

Katz, L. (1996). Child development knowledge and teacher preparation: Confronting assumptions. *Early Childhood Research Quarterly, 11*(2), 135–146.

Maslow, A. H. (1954). *Motivation and personality.* New York: Harper & Row.

Nelsen, J. (1996). *Positive discipline* (rev. ed.). New York: Ballantine Books.

Piaget, J. (1952). *The origins of intelligence in children.* New York: New American Library.

Puckett, M., & Black, J. (1996). *The young child: Development from prebirth through age eight.* (2nd ed.). Upper Saddle River, NJ: Merrill/Prentice-Hall.

Sailor, W., Gerry, M., & Wilson, W. (1991). Policy implications of emergent full inclusion models for the education of students with severe disabilities. In M. Wang, H. Walberg, & M. Reynolds (Eds.), *Handbook of special education* (Vol. 4, pp. 175–193). New York: Pergamon Press.

Santrock, J. W. (1995). *Children.* Madison, WI: Brown & Benchmark.

Schorr, L. (1988). *Within our reach: Breaking the cycle of the disadvantaged.* New York: Anchor Books.

Stewart, E. C., & Bennett, M. J. (1991). *American cultural patterns: A cross-cultural perspective* (rev. ed.). Yarmouth, ME: Intercultural Press.

Vygotsky, L. (1978). *Mind in society: The development of higher psychological processes.* Cambridge, MA: Harvard University Press.

Weissbourd, R. (1996). *The myth of the vulnerable child.* Reading, MA: Addison-Wesley.

Wood, C. (1994). *Yardsticks.* Greenfield, MA: Northeast Foundation for Children.

Children's Books

Hillman, E. (1992). *Min Yo and the moon dragon.* Dallas, TX: Harcourt Brace.

Hooks, W. (1987). *Moss gown.* New York: Clarion.

Matas, C. (1993). *Daniel's story.* New York: Scholastic.

O'Dell, S. (1960). *Island of the blue dolphins.* Boston: Houghton Mifflin.

Sendak, M. (1964). *Where the wild things are.* New York: Harper.

Chapter 4

Abbott, J. (1997). To be intelligent. *Educational Leadership 54*(6), 6–10.

American Psychological Association, Presidential Task Force on Psychology in Education. (1993). *Learner-centered psychological principles: Guidelines for school redesign and reform.* Washington, DC: American Psychological Association/Mid-continent Regional Educational.

Association for Supervision and Curriculum Development. (1997). *Promoting social and emotional learning: Guidelines for educators.* Alexandria, VA: Author.

Bandura, A. (1997). *Self-efficacy: The exercise of control.* New York: Freeman.

Banks J. A., & Banks, C. A. (Eds.). (1997). *Multicultural education: Issues and perspectives* (3rd ed.). Boston: Allyn & Bacon.

Berk, L. (1996). *Infants, children, and adolescents.* (2nd ed). Boston: Allyn & Bacon.

Berns, R. M. (1997). *Child, family, school and community: Socialization and support* (4th ed.). Fort Worth, TX: Harcourt Brace College Publishers.

Bodrova, E., & Leong, D. (1996). *Tools of the mind: The Vygotskian approach to early childhood education.* Upper Saddle River, NJ: Merrill/Prentice-Hall.

Bredekamp, S., & Copple, C. (1997). *Developmentally appropriate practice in early childhood programs* (rev. ed.). Washington, DC: National Association for the Education of Young Children.

Bredekamp, S., & Rosegrant, T. (Eds.). (1992). *Reaching potentials: Appropriate curriculum and assessment for young children.* (Vol. 1). Washington, DC: National Association for the Education of Young Children.

Caine, R. N., & Caine, G. (1997). *Education on the edge of possibility.* Alexandria, VA: Association for Supervision and Curriculum Development.

Dewey, J. (1916). *Democracy and education.* New York: Macmillan.

Dunlap, L. L. (1997). *An introduction to early childhood special education.* Boston: Allyn & Bacon.

Elkind, D. (1989). Developmentally appropriate practice. *Phi Delta Kappan 71*(2), 113–117.

Fromberg, D. P. (1995). *The full-day kindergarten: Planning and practicing a dynamic curriculum* (2nd ed.). New York: Teachers College Press.

Gardner, H. (1993). *Frames of mind: The theory of multiple intelligences* (2nd ed.). New York: Basic Books.

Gardner, H. (1991). *The unschooled mind.* New York: Basic Books.

Gibbons, P. (1993). *Learning to learn in a second language.* Portsmouth, NH: Heinemann.

Goleman, D. (1995). *Emotional intelligence.* New York: Bantam.

Good, T., & Brophy, J. (1997). *Looking in classrooms* (7th ed.). New York: Harper Collins.

Halliday, M. A. K. (1975). *Explorations in the function of language.* London: Edward Arnold.

Isenberg, J. P., & Jalongo, M. R. (1997). *Creative expression and play in early childhood.* (2nd ed.). Upper Saddle River, NJ: Merrill/Prentice-Hall.

Karsenti, T. P., & Thibert, G. (1995, April). What type of motivation is truly related to school achievement? A look at 1,428 high school students. Paper presented at the annual meeting of the American Educational Research Association, San Francisco.

Kauchek, D. P., & Eggen, P. D. (1998). *Teaching and learning: Research-based methods.* (3rd ed.). Boston: Allyn & Bacon.

Kohn, A. (1993). *Punished by rewards: The trouble with gold stars, incentive plans, A's, and other bribes.* Boston: Houghton Mifflin.

Lazear, D. (1991). *Seven ways of knowing.* Palatine, IL: Skylight Publishing.

McCombs, B. L. (1993). Learner-centered psychological principles for enhancing education: Applications in school settings. In L. A. Penner, G. M. Batsche, H. M. Knoff, & D. L. Nelson (Eds.), *The challenges in mathematics and science education: Psychology's response* (pp. 287–313). Washington, DC: American Psychological Association.

McCombs, B. L., & Whisler, J. S. (1997). *The learner-centered classroom and school: Strategies for increasing student motivation and achievement,* San Francisco: Jossey-Bass.

Morrow, L. M. (1997). *Literacy development in the early years.* (3rd ed.). Boston: Allyn & Bacon.

Newberger, J. J. (1997). New brain development research—A wonderful window of opportunity to build public support for early childhood education. *Young Children (52)*4, 4–9.

Papalia, D., & Olds, S. (1995). *Human development.* (6th ed.). New York: McGraw-Hill.

Parten, M. (1932). Social participation among preschool children. *Journal of Abnormal and Social Psychology, 27*(2), 243–269.

Piaget, J. (1980). Foreword. In C. Kamii & R. DeVries, *Group games in early education* (p. vii). Washington, DC: National Association for the Education of Young Children.

Piaget, J. (1970). Piaget's theory. In P. Mussen (Ed.), *Carmichael's manual of child psychology* (3rd ed., Vol. 1, pp. 703–732). New York: Wiley.

Pool, C. R. (1997). Maximizing learning: A conversation with Renate Nummela Caine. *Educational Leadership 64*(6), 11–16.

Rich, D. (1992) cited in Berns, R. M. (1997). *Child, family, school, and community.* (4th ed.). Fort Worth, TX: Harcourt Brace.

Santrock, J. W. (1995). *Children.* Madison, WI: Brown & Benchmark.

Smilansky, S., & Shefatya, L. (1990). *Facilitating play: A medium for promoting cognitive, socio-emotional, and academic development in young children.* Gaithersburg, MD: Psychosocial and Educational Publications.

Thorkildsen, T. A., Nolen, S. B., & Fournier, J. (1994). What is fair? Children's critiques of practices that influence motivation. *Journal of Educational Psychology 86*(4), 475–486.

Vygotsky, L. (1978). *Mind in society.* Cambridge, MA: Harvard University Press.

Wassermann, S. (1990). *Serious players in the primary classroom.* New York: Teachers College Press.

Woolfolk, A. (1995). *Educational psychology* (6th ed.). Boston: Allyn & Bacon.

Children's Books

Flack, M. (1932). *Ask Mr. Bear.* New York: Macmillan.

Sendak, M. (1962). *Chicken Soup with Rice.* New York: Harper.

Zak, M. (1992). *Save My Rain Forest.* Volcano, CA: Volcano Press.

Chapter 5

American Academy of Pediatrics. (1992). *Caring for our children.* Elk Grove Village, IL: Author.

Association for Supervision and Curriculum Development. (1997). Making a good start. *Education Update 39*(6). Alexandria, VA: Author.

Bigge, J. (1991). *Teaching individuals with physical and multiple disabilities* (3rd ed.). Upper Saddle River, NJ: Merrill/Prentice Hall.

Bredekamp, S., & Copple, C. (Eds.). (1997). *Developmentally appropriate practice in early childhood programs* (rev. ed.). Washington, DC: National Association for the Education of Young Children.

Cambourne, B. (1995). Toward a relevant theory of literacy learning: Twenty years of inquiry. *The Reading Teacher, 49*(3), 182–90.

Cambourne, B. (1988). *The whole story: Natural learning and the acquisition of literacy.* Auckland, New Zealand: Ashton/Scholastic.

Carnegie Task Force on Meeting the Needs of Young Children. (1994). *Starting points: Meeting the needs of our youngest children.* New York: Carnegie Corporation of New York.

Cesarone, B. (1993). *Health Care, Nutrition, and Goal One.* ERIC Digest, Champaign, IL: Clearinghouse on Elementary and Early Childhood Education.

Children's Defense Fund. (1994). *Wasting America's future: The Children's Defense Fund report on the costs of child poverty.* Boston: Beacon Press.

Clarke-Stewart, A. (1987). Predicting child development from child care forms and features: The Chicago Study. In Phillips (Ed.), *Quality in child care: What does research tell us?* (pp. 57–59). Washington, DC: National Association for the Education of Young Children.

Cooper, H., Hegarty, P., Hegarty, P. & Simco, N. (1996). *Display in the classroom: Principles, practice, and learning theory.* London: David Fulton Publishers.

Crumpacker, S. (1995). Using cultural information to create schools that work. In A. Meek (Ed.), *Designing places for learning* (pp. 31–42). Alexandria, VA: Association for Supervision and Curriculum Development.

Cryer, D., & Phillipsen, L. (1997). Quality details: A close-up look at child care program strengths and weaknesses. *Young Children 52(5),* 51–61.

Dodge, D., Jablon, J., & Bickart, T. (1994). *Constructing curriculum for the primary grades.* Washington, DC: Teaching Strategies.

Edwards, C., Gandini, L., & Forman, G. (Eds.). (1993). *The hundred languages of children: The Reggio Emilia approach to early childhood education.* Norwood, NJ: Ablex.

Essa, E. (1996). *Introduction to early childhood education* (2nd ed.). Albany, NY: Delmar.

Feeney, S., & Magarick, M. (1984). Choosing good toys for young children. *Young Children, 40(1),* 21–25.

Garreau, M., & Kennedy, C. (1991). Structure time and space to promote pursuit of learning in the primary grades. *Young Children, 64(4),* 46–51.

Isbell, R. T. (1995). *The complete learning center book.* Beltsville, MD: Gryphon House.

Isenberg, J., & Jalongo, M. (1997). *Creative expression and play in early childhood.* Upper Saddle River, NJ: Merrill/Prentice-Hall.

Jackson, B. R. (1997). Creating a climate for healing in a violent society. *Young Children 52(7),* 68–70.

Jalongo, M. R. (2000). Early childhood language arts: Meeting diverse literacy needs through collaboration with families and professionals (2nd ed.). Boston: Allyn & Bacon.

Jones, E., & Nimmo, J. (1994). *Emergent curriculum.* Washington, DC: National Association for the Education of Young Children.

Jones, E., & Prescott, E. (1978). *Dimensions of teaching— Learning environments II: Focus on day care.* Pasadena, CA: Pacific Oaks College.

Kohn, A. (1996). What to look for in a classroom. *Educational Leadership 54(1),* 54–55.

Kontos, S., & Wilcox-Herzog, A. (1997). Influences on children's competence in early childhood classrooms. *Early Childhood Research Quarterly 12(3),* 247–262.

Kritchevsky, S., Prescott, E., & Walling, C. (1977). *Planning environments for young children: Physical space.* Washington, DC: National Association for the Education of Young Children.

Loughlin, C., & Suina, J. (1982). *The learning environment: An instructional strategy.* New York: Teachers College Press.

McCormick, L., & Feeney, S. (1995). Modifying and expanding activities for children with disabilities. *Young Children 50(4),* 10–17.

McLean, S. V. (1995). Creating the learning environment: Context for living and learning. In J. Moyer (Ed.), *Selecting educational equipment and materials for school and home.* Wheaton, MD: Association for Childhood Education International.

Moore, G. T. (1983). *Some effects of the organization of the socio-physical environment on cognitive behavior in child care settings.* Paper presented at the annual meeting of the Society for Research in Child Development, Detroit.

Moore, G. T., & Lackney, J. A. (1995). Design patterns for American schools: Responding to the reform movement. In A. Meek (Ed.), *Designing places for learning* (pp. 11–22). Alexandria, VA: Association for Supervision and Curriculum Development.

Moyer, J. (Ed.). (1995). *Selecting educational equipment and materials for school and home.* Wheaton, MD: Association for Childhood Education International.

National Association for the Education of Young Children. (1998). *Healthy eating from the start: Nutrition education for young children.* Washington, DC: Author.

National Association for the Education of Young Children. (1991). *Accreditation criteria and procedures of the National Academy of early childhood programs.* (rev. ed.). Washington, DC: Author.

National Resource Center for Health and Safety in Child Care. (1997). *Stepping stones to the national child* care health and safety performance standards: Guidelines for out-of-home child care programs. University of Colorado: Author.

Noddings, N. (1995, May). Teaching themes of care. *Phi Delta Kappan 76*(9), 675–679.

Sanoff, H. (1995). *Creating environments for young children*. Mansfield, OH: BookMasters.

Sheldon, K. (1996). "Can I play too?" Adapting common classroom activities for young children with limited motor abilities. *Early Childhood Education Journal 24*(2), 115–120.

Squibb, B., & Yardley, K. (1999). Playing healthy, staying healthy: A prevention program for contagious disease. *Early Childhood Education Journal, 26*(3), 143–148.

Trawick-Smith, J. (1992). The classroom environment affects children's play and development. *Dimensions 20*(2), 27–31.

U.S. Department of Education. (1994). *Goals 2000: Educate America Act*. Washington, DC: Author.

Wald, P., Morris, L., & Abraham, M. (1996). Three keys for successful circle time: Responding to children with diverse abilities. *Dimensions of Early Childhood 24*(4), 26–29.

Wassermann, S. (1990). *Serious players in the early childhood classroom: Empowering children through active learning experiences*. New York: Teachers College Press.

Weissbourd, R. (1996). *The myth of the vulnerable child*. Reading, MA: Addison-Wesley.

Wortham, S. (1996). *The integrated classroom: The assessment-curriculum link in early childhood education*. Upper Saddle River, NJ: Merrill/Prentice-Hall.

Youcha, V., & Wood, K. (1997). Enhancing the environment for all children. *Child Care Information Exchange, 114*, 45–47.

Chapter 6

ASCD Advisory Panel on Improving Student Achievement. (1995). Barriers to good instruction. In R. W. Cole (Ed.), *Educating everybody's children: Diverse teaching strategies for diverse learners* (pp. 9–20). Alexandria, VA: Association for Supervision and Curriculum Development.

Ayers, W. (1996). *To become a teacher: Making a difference in children's lives*. New York: Teachers College Press.

Ball, D., & Cohen, D. (1996). Reform by the book: What is—or might be—the role of curriculum materials in teacher learning and instructional reform? *Educational Researcher, 25*(9), 6–8.

Bandura, A. (1997). *Self-efficacy: The exercise of control*. New York: Freeman.

Barbour, N. H., & Seefeldt, C. (1993). *Developmental continuity across preschool and primary grades: Implications for teachers*. Wheaton, MD: Association for Childhood Education International.

Barnett, W. S. (1995). Long-term effects of early childhood programs on cognitive and school outcomes. *The Future of Children, 5*(3), 25–50.

Bowlby, J. (1969). *Attachment and loss; Vol: 1. Attachment*. New York: Basic Books.

Bredekamp, S., & Copple, C. (Eds.). (1997). *Developmentally appropriate practice in early childhood programs* (rev. ed.). Washington, DC: National Association for the Education of Young Children.

Bredekamp, S., & Rosegrant, T. (Eds.). (1995). *Reaching potentials: Transforming early childhood curriculum and assessment, Volume 2*. Washington, DC: National Association for the Education of Young Children.

Bredekamp, S., & Rosegrant, T. (Eds.). (1992). *Reaching potentials: Appropriate curriculum and assessment for young children, Volume 1*. Washington, DC: National Association for the Education of Young Children.

Caine, R. N., & Caine, G. (1997). *Education on the edge of possibility*. Alexandria, VA: Association for Supervision and Curriculum Development.

Carnegie Corporation of New York. (1996). *Years of promise: A comprehensive learning strategy for America's children*. New York: Author.

Cecil, N. L., & Lauritzen, P. (1994). *Literacy and the arts for the integrated classroom: Alternative ways of knowing*. White Plains, NY: Longman.

Chaille, C., & Britain, L. (1997). *The young child as scientist: A constructivist approach to early childhood science education*. New York: Longman.

Chase, P., & Doan, J. (1994). *Full circle: A new look at multi-age education*. Portsmouth, NH: Heinemann.

Dewey, J. (1938). *Experience and education*. New York: Collier Books.

Dewey, J. (1933). *How we think*. Boston: D. C. Heath.

Dodge, D.T., Jablon, J. R., & Bickart, T. S. (1994). *Constructing curriculum for the primary grades*. Washington, DC: Teaching Strategies.

Drake, S. M. (1993). *Planning integrated curriculum: The call to adventure*. Alexandria, VA: Association for Supervision and Curriculum Development.

Dyson, A. H., & Genishi, C. (1993). Visions of children as language users: Language and language education in early childhood. In B. Spodek (Ed.), *Handbook* of research on the education of young children, (pp. 122–136). New York: Macmillan.

Edwards, C., Gandini, L., & Forman, G. (Eds.). (1993). *The hundred languages of children: The Reggio Emilia approach to early childhood education.* Norwood, NJ: Ablex.

Eisner, E. W., & Vallance, E. (Eds.). (1974). *Conflicting conceptions of curriculum.* Berkeley, CA: McCutchen.

Fox, M. (1993). *Radical reflections: Passionate opinions on teaching, learning, and living.* San Diego, CA: Harcourt Brace.

Goals 3 and 4 Technical Planning Group. (1993). *Promises to keep: Creating high standards for American students.* Washington, DC: National Education Goals Panel.

Hartman, J., & Eckerty, C. (1995). Projects in the early years. *Childhood Education 71*(3), 141–148.

Jackson, P. (1968). *Life in classrooms.* New York: Holt, Rhinehart, & Winston.

Jacobs, H. (1989). *Interdisciplinary curriculum: Design and implementation.* Alexandria, VA: Association for Supervision and Curriculum Development.

Jalongo, M. R. (2000). *Early childhood language arts: Meeting diverse literacy needs through collaboration with families and professionals* (2nd ed.). Boston: Allyn & Bacon.

Jones, E., & Nimmo, J. (1994). *Emergent curriculum.* Washington, DC: National Association for the Education of Young Children.

Katz, L. G., & Chard, S. C. (1989). *Engaging children's minds: The project approach.* Norwood, NJ: Ablex.

Kessler, S. A. (1991). Alternative perspectives on early childhood education. *Early Childhood Research Quarterly, 6*(2), 183–197.

Kilpatrick, W. H. (1936). *Remaking the curriculum.* New York: Newson & Co.

Kostelnik, M., Soderman, A., & Whiren, A. (1999). *Developmentally appropriate programs in early childhood education.* (2nd ed.). Upper Saddle River, NJ: Merrill/Prentice-Hall.

Krogh, S. L. (1995). *The integrated early childhood curriculum.* (2nd ed.). New York: McGraw-Hill.

Lazar, L., & Darlington, R. (1982). Lasting effects of early childhood education: A report from the consortium for longitudinal studies. *Monographs of the Society for Research in Child Development, 47*(2–3, Serial No. 195). Chicago: University of Chicago Press.

McClaslin, N. (1990). *Creative drama in the classroom* (5th ed.). New York: Longman.

Morrow, L. M. (1997). *Literacy development in the early years: Helping children read and write* (3rd ed.). Boston: Allyn & Bacon.

National Board for Professional Teaching Standards. (1995). *Early childhood generic standards for National Board certification.* Detroit: Author.

Olson, G. (1994). Preparing early childhood educators for constructivist teaching. In S. G. Goffin & D. E. Day (Eds.), *New perspectives in early childhood education: Bringing practitioners into the debate* (pp. 37–47). New York: Teachers College Press.

Pappas, C. C., Kiefer, B. Z., & Levstik, L. S. (1995). *An integrated language arts perspective in the elementary school* (2nd ed.). White Plains, NY: Longman.

Piaget, J. (1965). *The moral judgment of the child.* New York: Free Press.

Raines, S. R. (1997). Developmental appropriateness: Curriculum revisited and challenged. In J. P. Isenberg & M. R. Jalongo (Eds.), *Major trends and issues in early childhood education: Challenges, controversies, and insights* (pp. 75–89). New York: Teachers College Press.

Ryan, K., & Cooper, J. M. (1995). *Those who can, teach* (7th ed.). Boston: Houghton Mifflin.

Schweinhart, L. J., & Weikart, D. P. (1996). Lasting differences: The High/Scope preschool curriculum comparison study through age 23. *Monographs of the High/Scope Educational Research Foundation, 12.* Ypsilanti, MI: High/Scope Press.

Shephard, L. A., & Smith, L. (1988). Escalating academic demands in kindergarten: Some nonsolutions. *Elementary School Journal, 89*(2), 135–146.

Stern, D. (1985). *The psychological world of the human infant.* New York: Basic Books.

Vygotsky, L. (1978). *Mind in society: The development of higher order psychological processes.* Cambridge, MA: Harvard University Press.

Wortham, S. C. (1996). *The integrated classroom: The assessment-curriculum link in early childhood education.* Upper Saddle River, NJ: Merrill/Prentice Hall.

Children's Books

Ardley, N. (1991). *The science book of magnets.* New York: Harcourt, Brace, Jovanovich.

Grifalconi, A. (1986). *The village of round and square houses.* Boston, MA: Little Brown.

Hoberman, M. A. (1978). *A house is a house for me.* New York: Scholastic.

Rowe, J., & Perham, M. (1994). *Amazing magnets.* London: Watts.

Spier, P. (1978). *Noah's ark.* New York: Doubleday.

Chapter 7

Barba, R. H. (1998). *Science in the multicultural classroom* (2nd ed.). Boston: Allyn & Bacon.

Barbour, N., & Seefeldt, C. (1993). *Developmental continuity across preschool and primary grades.* Wheaton, MD: Association for Childhood Education International.

Berliner, D. C. (1986). In pursuit of the expert pedagogue. *Educational Researcher, 15*(7), 5–13.

Borko, H., Bellamy, M. L., & Sanders, L. (1992). A cognitive analysis in science instruction by expert and novice teachers. In T. Russell & H. Mundby (Eds.), *Teachers and teaching: From classrooms to reflection* (pp. 49–70). London: Falmer Press.

Bredekamp, S., & Copple, C. (1997). (Eds.). *Developmentally appropriate practice in early childhood programs* (rev. ed.). Washington, DC: National Association for the Education of Young Children.

Bredekamp, S., & Rosegrant, T. (1995). *Reaching potentials II.* Washington, DC: National Association for the Education of Young Children.

Clark, C., & Dunn, S. (1991). Second generation research on teacher planning. In H. C. Waxman & H. J. Walberg (Eds.), *Effective teaching: Current research* (pp. 183–210). Berkeley, CA: McCuthan.

Clark, C. M., & Peterson, P. L. (1986). Teachers' thought processes. In M. C. Wittrock (Ed.), *Handbook of research on teaching* (3rd ed.), (pp. 198–243). Berkeley, CA: McCutchan.

Eddowes, E. A., & Ralph, K. S. (1998). *Interactions for development and learning.* Upper Saddle River, NJ: Merrill/Prentice Hall.

Eggen, P. D., & Kauchak, D. P. (1996). *Strategies for teachers: Teaching content and thinking skills* (3rd ed.). Boston: Allyn & Bacon.

Feeny, S., Christensen, D., & Moravcik, E. (1996). *Who am I in the lives of children?* Upper Saddle River, NJ: Merrill/Prentice Hall.

Freiberg, H. J., & Driscoll, A. (1996). *Universal teaching strategies* (2nd ed.). Needham Heights, MA: Allyn & Bacon.

Gardner, H. (1993). *Frames of mind: The theory of multiple intelligences* (2nd ed.). New York: Basic Books.

Gordon, A., & Williams-Browne, K. (1995). *Beginnings and beyond* (4th ed.). New York: Delmar.

Hansen, D. T. (1995). *The call to teach.* New York: Teachers College Press.

Jones, E., & Nimmo, J. (1994). *Emergent curriculum.* Washington, DC: National Association for the Education of Young Children.

Katz, L. (1994). *The project approach.* ERIC Digest, EDO–PS–94–6.

Katz, L., & Chard, S. (1989). *Engaging children's minds: The project approach.* Norwood, NJ: Ablex.

Kostelnik, M. (Ed.). (1991). *Teaching young children using themes.* Glenview, IL: Good Year Books.

Lawler-Prince, D., & Jones, C. (1997). Development of pre-service early childhood education teacher's instructional planning. *Journal of Early Childhood Teacher Educators, 18*(3), 77–85.

National Association of Elementary School Principals. (1998). *Early childhood education and the elementary school principal: Standards for quality programs.* Alexandria, VA: Author.

Perkins, D., & Blythe, T. (1994). Putting understanding up front. *Educational Leadership*(51), 4–7.

Reiser, R. A. (1994). Examining the planning practices of teachers: Reflections on three years of research. *Educational Technology 34*(3), 11–16.

Reiser, R. A., & Dick, W. (1996). *Instructional planning: A guide for teachers.* Needham Heights, MA: Simon & Schuster.

Schickedanz, J., York, M., Stewart, I., & White, D. (1990). *Strategies for teaching young children* (3rd ed.). Upper Saddle River, NJ: Prentice Hall.

Spodek, B., & Saracho, O. (1994). *Right from the start: Teaching children ages 3 to 8.* Needham Heights, MA: Allyn & Bacon.

Taylor, B. J. (1995). *A child goes forth: A curriculum guide for preschool children* (8th ed.). New York: Macmillan.

Wills, C. (1995). Voice of inquiry: Possibilities and perspectives. *Childhood Education* (Annual Theme Issue), 261–265.

Children's Books

Beal, K. (1991). *I love my family.* Reading, MA: Addison-Wesley.

Curtis, J. L. (1996). *Tell me again about the night I was born.* New York: HarperCollins.

Technology

Just Grandma and Me. (1994). Novato, CA: Living Books.

Chapter 8

Benson, T. R., & Smith, L. J. (1998). Portfolios in first grade: Four teachers learn to use alternative assessment. *Early Childhood Education Journal, 25*(3), 173–180.

Borgia, E. (1996). Learning through projects. *Scholastic Early Childhood, 10*(6), 22–28.

Brainard, M. B. (1997). Assessment as a way of seeing. In A. L. Goodwin (Ed.), *Assessment for equity and inclusion* (pp. 163–180). New York: Routledge.

Bredekamp, S., & Rosegrant, T. (Eds.). (1992). *Reaching potentials: Appropriate curriculum and assessment for young children.* Washington, DC: National Association for the Education of Young Children.

Caine, R. N., & Caine, G. (1997). *Education on the edge of possibility.* Alexandria, VA: Association for Supervision and Curriculum Development.

Carter, M., & Curtis, D. (1996). *Spreading the news: Sharing stories of early childhood education.* St. Paul, MN: Redleaf Press.

Chard, S. C. (1996). Documentation: Displaying children's learning. *Scholastic Early Childhood Today, 11*(1), 56–58.

Chard, S. C., Katz, L., & Genishi, C. (1996). A profile of every child. *Scholastic Early Childhood Today, 11*(1), 55–62.

Culbertson, L., & Jalongo, M. R. (1999). "But what's wrong with letter grades?" Explaining alternative assessment to parents. *Childhood Education, 75*(3), 130–135.

Fennimore, B. S. (1997). Moving the mountain: Assessment and advocacy for children. In A. L. Goodman (Ed.), *Assessment for equity and inclusion* (pp. 241–259). New York: Routledge.

Gardner, H., & Mansilla, V. (1994). Teaching for understanding: Within and across disciplines. *Educational Leadership, 51*(5), 4–8.

Gelfer, J. I., & Perkins, P. G. (1996). A model for portfolio assessment in early childhood education programs. *Early Childhood Education Journal, 24*(1), 5–10.

Genishi, C. (1996). Portfolios: Collecting children's work. *Scholastic Early Childhood Today, 11*(1), 60–61.

Gullo, D. F. (1994). *Understanding assessment and evaluation in early childhood education.* New York: Teachers College Press.

Hamayan, E. V. (1995). Approaches to alternative assessment. *Annual Review of Applied Linguistics, 15,* 212–226.

Helm, J. H., Beneke, S., & Steinheimer, K. (1998). *Windows on learning: Documenting young children's work.* New York: Teachers College Press.

Herman, J., Aschbacher, P., & Winters, L. (1992). *A practical guide to alternative assessment.* Alexandria, VA: Association for Supervision and Curriculum Development.

International Reading Association/National Council of Teachers of English. (1995). *Standards for the assessment of reading and writing.* Newark, DE: International Reading Association.

Jalongo, M. R. (1996). Editorial: Looking beyond the labels. *Early Childhood Education Journal, 23*(3), 187–188.

Jalongo, M. R., & Isenberg, J. P. (1995). *Teachers' stories: From personal narrative to professional insight.* San Francisco, CA: Jossey Bass.

Jalongo, M. R., & Stamp, L. N. (1997). *The arts in children's lives: Aesthetic experiences in early childhood.* Boston, MA: Allyn & Bacon.

Katz, L. (1993). *Five perspectives on quality in early childhood programs.* Urbana, IL: ERIC Clearinghouse on Elementary and Early Childhood Education (ERIC Document Reproduction Service No. ED–351–148).

MacDonald, S. (1997). *The portfolio and its use: A road map for assessment.* Little Rock, AR: Southern Early Childhood Association.

Madaus, G. F., & Tan, A. D. A. (1993). The growth of assessment. In G. Cawelti (Ed.), *Challenges and achievements of American education* (pp. 53–79). Alexandria, VA: Association for Supervision and Curriculum Development.

Marzano, R., Pickering, D., & McTighe, J. (1993). *Assessing student outcomes.* Alexandria, VA: Association for Supervision and Curriculum Development.

McAfee, O., & Leong, D. (1997). *Assessing and guiding young children's development and learning* (2nd ed.). Boston: Allyn & Bacon.

McTighe, J. (1997). What happens between assessment. *Educational Leadership, 54*(4), 6–12.

Meisels, S. J. (1995). Performance assessment in early childhood education: The work sampling system. (ERIC Digest No. EDO–PS–95–6).

Nelsen, J., Erwin, C., & Duffy, R. (1995). *Positive discipline for preschoolers: For their early years—raising children who are responsible and resourceful.* Rocklin, CA: Prima Publishing.

Nilsen, B. A. (1999). *Week by week: Plans for observing and recording young children.* Albany, NY: Delmar.

Penning, N. (1995). Guidance for politics-free student assessment. *The School Administrator, 11*(52), 31–32.

Perrone, V. (1997). Toward an education of consequence: Connecting assessment, teaching, and learning. In A. L. Goodman (Ed.), *Assessment for equity and inclusion* (pp. 305–315). New York: Routledge.

Perrone, V. (1991). On standardized testing. *Childhood Education, 67,* 131–142.

Popham, W. J. (1998). Farewell, curriculum: Confessions of an assessment convert. *Phi Delta Kappan, 79*(5), 380–384.

Power, B. M. (1996). *Taking note: Improving your observational notetaking.* York, ME: Stenhouse.

Salvia, J., & Yesseldyke, J. E. (1995). *Assessment* (6th ed.). Boston: Houghton Mifflin.

Smith, Y., & Goodwin, A. L. (1997). The democratic, child-centered classroom: Provisioning for a vision. In A. L. Goodwin (Ed.), *Assessment for equity and inclusion* (pp. 101–120). New York: Routledge.

Stiggins, R. J. (1994). *Student-centered classroom assessment.* Upper Saddle River, NJ: Merrill/Prentice Hall.

Wiggins, G. (1998). *Educative assessment: Designing assessments to inform and improve student performance.* San Francisco, CA: Jossey Bass.

Willis, S. (1993, November). Teaching young children: Educators seek "developmental appropriateness." *ASCD Curriculum Update,* 1–8.

Recommended Web Sites

Alternative Assessment
www.ncrel.org/sdrs/areas/issues/content/cntareas/science/sc5alter.htm

Authentic Assessment
mailer.fsu.edu/jflake/assess.html

Measurement and Evaluation: Criterion- Versus Norm-referenced Testing
www.valdosta.edu/~whuitt/psy702/measeval/crnmref.html

Modern Thinking on Assessment
www.ed.psu.edu/dept/~ae-insys-wfed/insys/esd/assessment/menu.html

Chapter 9

American Psychological Association. (1993). *Report of the American Psychological Association on violence and youth, Vol. I.* Washington, DC: Author.

Bauer, K. L., & Detorre, E. (1997). Super hero play: What's a teacher to do? *Early Childhood Education Journal, 25*(1), 17–21.

Beaty, J. (1995). *Converting conflicts in preschool.* Fort Worth, TX: Harcourt Brace.

Boyer, E. (1995). *The basic school: A community for learning.* Carnegie Foundation for the Advancement of Teaching.

Cairns, R., Gariepy, J., & Kinderman, T. (1990). *Identifying social clusters in natural settings.* Unpublished manuscript.

Carlsson-Paige, N., & Levin, D. E. (1992). When push comes to shove—reconsidering children's conflicts. *Child Care Information Exchange, 84,* 34–37.

Carter, M. (1992). Disciplinarians or transformers? Training teachers for conflict resolution. *Child Care Information Exchange, 84,* 46–51.

Children's Defense Fund. (1997). *The state of America's children: Yearbook 1997.* Washington, DC: Author.

Church, E. B. (1994). Making decisions as a group. *Scholastic Early Childhood Today, 8*(8), 40–41.

Comstock, G., & Strasburger, V. C. (1990). Deceptive appearances: Television violence and aggressive behavior. *Journal of Adolescent Health Care, 11,* 31–34.

Conrad, N. K. (1997). Unpublished manuscript.

Daros, D., & Kovach, B. A. (1998). Assisting toddlers and caregivers during conflict resolutions: Interactions that promote socialization. *Childhood Education, 75*(1), 25–30.

Deci, E. L., & Ryan, R. M. (1985). *Intrinsic motivation and self-determination in human behavior.* New York: Plenum.

Dietz, W. H., & Strasburger, V. C. (1991). Children, adolescents, and television. *Current Problems in Pediatrics, 21,* 8–31.

Dinkmeyer, D., & McKay, G. (1989). *Systematic training for effective parenting* (3rd ed.). Minneapolis, MN: American Guidance Service.

Dinwiddie, S. A. (1994). The saga of Sally, Sammy, and the red pen: Facilitating children's social problem solving. *Young Children, 49*(5), 13–14.

Edelman, M. W. (1992). *The measure of our success: A letter to my children and yours.* Boston, MA: Beacon Press.

Eisenberg, N. (1992). *The caring child.* Cambridge, MA: Harvard University Press.

Fields, M. V., & Boesser, C. (1998). *Constructive guidance and discipline* (2nd ed.). Upper Saddle River, NJ: Prentice Hall.

Gannon, B., & Mncayi, P. (1996). You *can* get there from here. *Reaching Today's Youth, 1*(1), 55–57.

Glasser, W. (1992). *The quality school: Managing students without coercion.* New York: Harper & Row.

Gordon, A., & Browne, K. W. (1996). *Guiding young children in a diverse society.* Boston, MA: Allyn & Bacon.

Graham, P. (1995). *Mary Parker Follett—Prophet of management: A celebration of writings from the 1920s.* Boston: Harvard Business School.

Groves, B. M. (1996). Growing up in a violent world: The impact of family and community violence on young children and their families. In E. J. Erwin

(Ed.), *Putting children first: Visions for a brighter future for young children and their families* (pp. 31–52). Baltimore, MD: Paul H. Brookes.

Henley, M. (1996). Teaching self-control to young children. *Reaching Today's Youth, 1*(1), 13–16.

Hewitt, D. (1995). *So this is normal too? Teachers and parents working out developmental issues in young children.* St. Paul, MN: Redleaf Press.

Isenberg, J. P., & Jalongo, M. R. (1997). *Creative expression and play in early childhood* (2nd ed.). Upper Saddle River, NJ: Merrill/Prentice Hall.

Jalongo, M. R. (1996). Looking beyond the labels. *Early Childhood Education Journal, 23*(3), 127–129.

Jalongo, M. R. (1992). *Creating communities: The role of the teacher in the 21st century.* Bloomington, IN: National Educational Service.

Jalongo, M. R. (1987). Do "security" blankets belong in preschool? *Young Children, 42,* 3–8.

Johnson, D. W., & Johnson, R. T. (1996). Conflict resolution and peer mediation programs in elementary and secondary schools: A review of the research. *Review of Educational Research, 66*(4), 459–506.

Kohn, A. (1996). *Beyond discipline: From compliance to community.* Alexandria, VA: Association for Supervision and Curriculum Development.

Kostelnik, M. J., Stein, L. C., & Whiren, A. P. (1988). Children's self-esteem: The verbal environment. *Childhood Education, 65*(1), 29–32.

Krahl, C., & Jalongo, M. R. (1998). Creating caring classroom communities: Advice from an intervention specialist. *Childhood Education, 75*(2), 83–89.

Lantieri, L. (1995). Waging peace in our schools: Beginning with the children. *Phi Delta Kappan, 76*(5), 386–387.

Lerman, S. (1984). *Responsive parenting.* Circle Pines, MN: American Guidance Service.

Luke, J. L., & Myers, C. M. (1994). Toward peace: Using literature to aid conflict resolution. *Childhood Education, 71*(2), 66–67.

Maslow, A. (1968). *Toward a psychology of being* (2nd ed.). Princeton, NJ: Van Nostrand.

May, R. (1972). *Power and influence.* New York: W. W. Norton.

McClurg, L. G. (1998). Building an ethical community in the classroom: Community meeting. *Young Children, 53*(2), 30–35.

Moore, T. (1992). *Care of the soul.* New York: Harper-Perennial.

National Association for the Education of Young Children. (1996). *Early years are learning years: Teaching children not to be—or be victims of—bullies.* Washington, DC: Author.

National Educational Service. (1996). Boys' Town. *Reaching Today's Youth, 1*(1), 50–51.

Nelsen, J., Erwin, C., & Duffy, R. (1995). *Positive discipline for preschoolers: For their early years—raising children who are responsible and resourceful.* Rocklin, CA: Prima Publishing.

Paasche, C. L., Gorrill, L., & Strom, B. (1990). *Children with special needs in early childhood settings.* Menlo Park, CA: Addison-Wesley.

Paley, V. (1992). *You can't say you can't play.* Cambridge, MA: Harvard University Press.

Perry, D. G., Kussel, S. J., & Perry, L. C. (1988). Victims of peer aggression. *Developmental Psychology, 24,* 807–814.

Porter, L. (1999). Discipline in early childhood. In L. E. Berk (Ed.), *Landscapes of development: An anthology of readings* (pp. 295–308). Belmont, CA: Wadsworth.

Ramsey, P. G. (1991). *Making friends in school: Promoting peer relationships in early childhood.* New York: Teachers College Press.

Rief, S. F. (1993). *How to reach and teach ADD/ADHD children: Practical techniques, strategies, and interventions for helping children with attention problems and hyperactivity.* West Nyack, NJ: The Center for Applied Research in Education.

Rodd, J. (1996). *Understanding young children's behavior.* New York: Teachers College Press.

Rodgers, D. B. (1998). Research in review: Supporting autonomy in young children. *Young Children, 53*(3), 75–80.

Scarlett, W. G. (Ed.). (1997). *Trouble in the classroom: managing the behavior problems of young children.* San Francisco, CA: Jossey-Bass.

Simmons, B. J., Stallsworth, K., & Wentzel, H. (1999). Television violence and its effects on young children. *Early Childhood Education Journal, 26*(3), 149–154.

Slaby, R. G., Roedell, W. C., Arezzo, D., & Hendrix, K. (1995). *Early violence prevention: Tools for teachers of young children.* Washington, DC: National Association for the Education of Young Children.

Smith, C. A. (1993). *The peaceful classroom: 162 easy activities to teach preschoolers compassion and cooperation.* Mt. Ranier, MD: Gryphon House.

Stone, J. (1993). Caregiver and teacher language—Responsive or restrictive? *Young Children, 48*(4), 12–18.

Strachota, B. (1996). *On their side: Helping children take charge of learning.* Greenfield, MA: Northeast Foundation for Children.

Stubbs, T. (1992). *An ascension handbook.* Livermore, CA: Oughten House Publications.

Sylwester, R. (1994). How emotions affect learning. *Educational Leadership, 52*(2), 60–65.

Tobin, L. (1991). *What do you do with a child like this?* Duluth, MN: Whole Person Associates.

Washington, V. (1996). Creating an ideal world for children. In E. J. Erwin (Ed.), *Putting children first: Visions for a brighter future for young children and their families* (pp. 135–136). Baltimore, MD: Paul H. Brookes.

Children's Books

Henkes, K. (1985). *Bailey goes camping.* New York: Greenwillow.

Hutchinson, P. (1983). *You'll soon grow into them, Titch.* New York: Penguin/Puffin.

Kellogg, S. (1976). *Much bigger than Martin.* New York: Dial.

Chapter 10

Allen, M., Brown, P., & Finlay, B. (1992). *Helping children by strengthening families.* Washington, DC: Children's Defense Fund.

Auerbach, R. (1995). Which way for family literacy: Intervention or empowerment? In L. Morrow (Ed.), *Family literacy: Connections in schools and communities* (pp. 11–27). New Brunswick, NJ: International Reading Association.

Berger, E. (1995). *Parents as partners in education: Families and schools working together* (4th ed.). New York: Prentice Hall.

Berger, E. H. (1996). Communication: The key to parent involvement. *Early Childhood Education Journal, 23* (3), 179–183.

Berry, C. F., & Mindes, G. (1993). *Theme-based curriculum: Goals, themes, activities and planning guides for 4's and 5's.* Glenview, IL: GoodYear.

Boyer, E. L. (1995). *The basic school: A community for learning.* Princeton, NJ: Carnegie Foundation for the Advancement of Teaching.

Bredekamp, S., & Copple, C. (Eds.). (1997). *Developmentally appropriate practice in early childhood programs.* (rev. ed.). Washington, DC: National Association for the Education of Young Children.

Bredekamp, S., & Willer, B. (1993). Professionalizing the field of early childhood education: Pros and cons. *Young Children, 48*(3), 82–84.

Briggs, N. L., Jalongo, M. R., & Brown, L. (1997). In J. P. Isenberg & M. R. Jalongo (Eds.), *Major trends and issues in early childhood: Challenges, controversies, and insights.* New York: Teachers College Press.

Carnegie Corporation of New York. (1996). *Years of promise: A comprehensive learning strategy for America's children.* New York: Author.

Chavkin, N. (1990). Joining forces: Education for a changing population. *Educational Horizons, 68*(4), 190–196.

Coleman, M. (1991). Planning for the changing nature of family life in schools for young children. *Young Children, 46*(4), 15–20.

Davies, D. (1991). Schools reaching out: Family, school, and community partnerships for student success. *Phi Delta Kappan, 72*(5), 376–382.

Edwards, C., Gandini, L., & Forman, G. (1994). *The hundred languages of children: The Reggio Emilia approach to early childhood education.* Norwood, NJ: Ablex.

Edwards, P., & Young, L. (1992). Beyond parents: Family, community and school involvement. *Phi Delta Kappan, 74*(1), 72–80.

Elkind, D. (1995). School and family in the postmodern world. *Phi Delta Kappan, 77*(1), 8–14.

Elkind, D. (1994). *Ties that stress: The new family imbalance.* Cambridge, MA: Harvard University Press.

Epstein, J. (1995). School/family/community partnerships: Caring for the children we share. *Phi Delta Kappan, 76*(9), 701–712.

Gage, J., & Workman, S. (1994). Creating family support systems: In Head Start and beyond. *Young Children, 50*(1), 74–80.

Galinsky, E., Shubilla, L., Willer, B., Levine, J., & Daniel, J. (1994). State and community planning for early childhood systems. *Young Children, 49*(2), 54–57.

Goldberg, S. (1997). *Parent involvement begins at birth.* Boston, MA: Allyn & Bacon.

Grumet, M. (1988). *Bitter milk: Women and teaching.* Amherst, MA: University of Massachusetts.

Hanson, M. F., & Gilkerson, D. (1996). Children born from artificial reproductive technology: Implications for children, parents, and caregivers. *Early Childhood Education Journal, 23*(3), 131–134.

Hayes, R. L. (1987). The reconstruction of educational experience: The parent conference. *Education, 107*(3), 305–309.

Henderson, A. T., Marburger, C. L., & Ooms, T. (1992). *Beyond the bake sale: An education guide to working with parents.* Washington, DC: National Committee for Citizens in Education.

Hildebrand, V., Phenice, L., Gray, M., & Hines, R. (1996). *Knowing and serving diverse families.* Upper Saddle River, NJ: Prentice Hall.

Isenberg, J., & Jalongo, M. (1997). *Creative expression and play in early childhood* (2nd ed.). Upper Saddle River, NJ: Prentice Hall.

Kagan, S. (1990). Readiness 2000: Rethinking rhetoric and responsibility. *Phi Delta Kappan, 72*(4), 272–279.

Kagan, S., & Rivera, A. (1991). Collaboration in early care and education: What can and should we expect? *Young Children, 47*(1), 51–56.

Kagan, S., Powell, D., Weissbourd, B., & Zigler, E. (1987). *America's family support programs: Perspectives and prospects.* New Haven, CT: Yale University Press.

Kantor, D., & Lehr, W. (1975). *Inside the family.* San Francisco: Jossey-Bass.

Katz, L. G. (1993, June). School-Parent relations: General principles. Paper presented in Brussels, Belgium.

Kirst, M. (1991). Improving children's services: Overcoming barriers, creating new opportunities. *Phi Delta Kappan, 72*(8), 615–618.

Leach, P. (1978). *Your baby and child from birth to age five.* New York: Knopf.

Lewis, A. (1991). Coordinating services: Do we have the will? *Phi Delta Kappan, 72*(5), 340–341.

Liess, E. (1995). Eat-in, share-in, read-in: An integrated, cooperative, end-of-year program for parents of first graders. *Day Care and Early Education, 22*(4).

McBride, B. A., & Rane, T. R. (1997). Father/male involvement in early childhood programs: Issues and challenges. *Early Childhood Education Journal 25*(1), 11–15.

Morrow, L. (1995). Family literacy: New perspectives, new practices. In L. Morrow (Ed.), *Family literacy: Connections in schools and communities* (pp. 5–10). New Brunswick, NJ: International Reading Association.

National Association for the Education of Young Children. (1996). *What are the benefits . . . of high-quality early childhood programs?* Washington, DC: Author.

The National Parent Teacher Association/National Coalition for Parent Involvement in Education. (1997). *Our Children, 22*(4), 4.

Philadelphia Teacher. (1997, May). *Philadelphia Teacher, 2*(1), pp. 4–5.

Powell, D. (1991). How schools support families: Critical policy tensions. *The Elementary School Journal, 91*(3), 307–319.

Rich, D. (1997). *What do we say? What do we do? Vital solutions for children's educational success.* New York: Forge/Tom Doherty Associates.

Richmond, J., & Kotelchuck, M. (1984). Commentary on changed lives. In J. Berrueta-Clement, L. Schweinhart, S. Barnett, A. Epstein, & D. Weikart (Eds.), *Changed lives: The effect of the Perry Preschool Program on youths through age 19.* Ypsilanti, MI: High Scope Press.

Roberts, R., Wasik, B., Casto, G., & Ramey, C. (1991). Family support in the home: Programs, policy, and social change. *American Psychologist, 46*(2), 131–137.

Rosemond, J. (1992). *Parent power: A common sense approach to parenting.* Kansas City, MO: Andrews/McMeel.

Rosenthal, D. M., & Sawyers, J. Y. (1996). Building successful home/school partnerships. *Childhood Education, 72*(4), 194–200.

Rutherford, B., & Billig, A. (1995). Eight lessons of parent, family, and community involvement. *Phi Delta Kappan, 77*(1), 64–68.

Schaeffer, C. (1984). *How to talk to your child about really important things.* New York: Harper & Row.

Sipe, J. W., & Sipe, D. S. (1994). Enough analysis and blame: Let's strengthen all families. *Student Assistance Journal, 6*(5), 16, 35, 40.

Stenmark, J. K., Thompson, V., & Cossey, R. (1986). *Family math.* Berkeley, CA: University of California.

Stone, C. (1995). School/community collaboration: Comparing three initiatives. *Phi Delta Kappan, 76*(10), 794–800.

Swick, K. J. (1999). Empowering homeless and transient children and families: An ecological framework for early childhood teachers. *Early Childhood Education Journal, 26*(3), 195–202.

Swick, K. J. (1991). *Teacher-parent partnerships to enhance school success in early childhood education.* Washington, DC: National Education Association.

Swick, K. J., Boutte, G., & van Scoy, I. (1995). *Family involvement in multicultural learning.* (ERIC Digest EDO–PS–95–2). Urbana, IL: ERIC Clearinghouse on Elementary and Early Childhood Education.

U.S. Department of Education (1994). *Goals 2000: Educate America.* Washington, DC: Author.

U.S. Department of Health and Human Services (1990). *Project Head Start.* Washington, DC: Department of Health and Human Services.

Waller, J. A. (1998, April). Promoting parent/community involvement in school. *Educational Digest,* 45–47.

Williams, D. (1992). Parental involvement and teacher education preparation: Challenge to teacher education. In L. Kaplan (Ed.), *Education and the family* (pp. 243–254). Boston: Allyn & Bacon.

457

Zigler, E., & Muenchow, S. (1992). *Head Start: The inside story of America's most successful educational experiment*. New York: Basic Books.

Zigler, E., & Styfco, S. J. (Eds.). (1993). *Head Start and beyond: A national plan for extended childhood intervention*. New Haven, CT: Yale University Press.

Chapter 11

Ambach, G. (1996). Standards for teachers: Potential for improving practice. *Phi Delta Kappan, 78*(3), 207–210.

Baptiste, N., & Sheerer, M. (1997). Negotiating the challenges of the "survival" stage of professional development. *Early Childhood Education Journal, 24*(4), 265–268.

Berliner, D. C. (1994a). Developmental stages in the lives of early childhood educators. In S. G. Goffin & D. E. Day (Eds.), *New perspectives in early childhood education: Bringing practitioners into the debate* (pp. 120–128). New York: Teachers College Press.

Berliner, D. C. (1994b). Expertise: The wonder of exemplary performances. In C. C. Block & J. Mangieri (Eds.), *Creating powerful thinking in teachers and students: Diverse perspectives*. Fort Worth, TX: Harcourt Brace.

Black, A., & Davern, L. (1998, February). When a preservice teacher meets the classroom team. *Educational Leadership*, 52–54.

Bluestein, J., (comp.). (1995). *Mentors, master teachers, and Mrs. MacGregor: Stories of teachers making a difference*. Deerfield Beach, FL: Health Communications.

Carbo, M. (1997). *What every principal should know about teaching reading*. Syosset, NY: National Reading Styles Institute.

Caulfield, R. (1997). Professionalism in early care and education. *Early Childhood Education Journal, 24*(4), 261–264.

Clandinin, J. D., Davies, A., Hogan, P., & Kennard, B. (1993). *Learning to teach, teaching to learn*. New York: Teachers College Press.

Clark, C. M. (1996). *Thoughtful teaching*. New York: Teachers College Press.

Clark, C. M., & Yinger, R. J. (1977). Research on teacher thinking. *Curriculum Inquiry, 7*(4), 270–304.

Collins, A. (1992). Portfolios in science education: Issues, purpose, structure, and authenticity. *Science Education, 76*(4), 451–463.

Connelly, M. F., & Clandinin, J. D. (1988). *Teachers as curriculum planners: Narratives of experience*. New York: Teachers College Press.

Conroy, P. (1987). *The water is wide*. New York: Bantam.

Cryer, D., & Phillipsen, L. (1997). Quality details: A close-up look at child care program strengths and weaknesses. *Young Children, 52*(2), 51–61.

Danielson, C. (1996). *Enhancing professional practice: A framework for teaching*. Alexandria, VA: Association for Supervision and Curriculum Development.

Darling-Hammond, L. (1993). Reframing the school reform agenda: Developing capacity for school transformation. *Phi Delta Kappan, 74*(10), 753–761.

Darling-Hammond, L., & McLaughlin, M. (1995). Policies that support professional development in an era of reform. *Phi Delta Kappan, 76*(8), 597–604.

Darling-Hammond, L., & Sykes, G. (Eds.). (1999). *Teaching as the learning profession: Handbook of policy and practice*. San Francisco, CA: Jossey-Bass.

Darling-Hammond, L., Wise, A. E., & Klein, S. P. (1999). *A license to teach: Raising standards for teaching*. San Francisco, CA: Jossey-Bass.

Dollas, R. H. (1992). *Voices of beginning teachers: Visions and realities*. New York: Teachers College Press.

Essa, E. (1996). *Introduction to early childhood*. (2nd ed.). Albany, NY: Delmar.

Farris, P. J. (1996) *Teaching: Bearing the torch*. Madison, WI: Brown & Benchmark.

Feeney, S., Christensen, D., & Moravcik, E. (1996). *Who am I in the lives of children?* (5th ed.). Upper Saddle River, NJ: Prentice Hall.

Fisher, B. (1991). *Joyful learning: A whole language kindergarten*. Portsmouth, NH: Heinemann.

Fox, M. (1993). *Radical reflections: Passionate opinions on teaching, learning, and living*. San Diego, CA: Harcourt Brace Jovanovich.

Galinsky, E. (1989). In U.S. Congress Joint Economic Committee, *The Economic and Social Benefits of Early Childhood Education*, Senate HRG 101–298, 101st Congress, 1st sess., 1989, 108.

Gallas, K. (1994). *The languages of learning: How children talk, write, dance, draw, and sing their understanding of the world*. New York: Teachers College Press.

Gharavi, G. J. (1993). Music skills for preschool teachers: Needs and solutions. *Arts Education Policy Review, 94*(3), 27–30.

Grant, C., & Zeichner, K. (1984). *Preparing for reflective teaching*. Boston, MA: Allyn & Bacon.

Hayden, T. L. (1980). *One child*. Boston: Little, Brown.

Herndon, J. (1985). *Notes from a schoolteacher*. New York: Simon & Schuster.

Hillman, C. B. (1988). *Teaching four-year-olds: A personal journey*. Bloomington, IN: Phi Delta Kappa.

Jalongo, M. R., & Isenberg, J. P. (1995). *Teachers' stories: From personal narrative to professional insight.* San Francisco, CA: Jossey-Bass.

Joyce, B., & Calhoun, E. F. (1996). Beyond the textbook: A matter of instructional repertoire. *Educational Horizons, 74*(4), 163–168.

Kane, P. R. (Ed.). (1991). *The first year of teaching: Real world stories from America's teachers.* New York: Teachers College Press.

Katz, L. (1995). *Talks with teachers of young children: A collection.* Norwood, NJ: Ablex.

Katz, L. (1977). *Talks with teachers.* Washington, DC: National Association for the Education of Young Children.

Keizer, G. (1988). *No place but here: A teacher's vocation in a rural community.* New York: Penguin.

Kidder, T. (1989). *Among schoolchildren.* Boston: Houghton Mifflin.

Knowles, M. (1975). *Self-directed learning: A guide for learners and teachers.* Boston: Cambridge.

Kohl, H. (1967). *36 children.* New York: American Library.

LaBoskey, V. K. (1994). *Development of reflective practice: A study of preservice teachers.* New York: Teachers College Press.

Lay Dopyera, M., & Dopyera, J. E. (1993). *Introduction to early childhood.*

Lieberman, A. (1995). Practices that support teacher development. *Phi Delta Kappan, 76*(8), 591–596.

MacDonald, R. E. (1991). *A handbook of basic skills and strategies for beginning teachers: Facing the challenge of teaching in today's schools.* White Plains, NY: Longman.

Meier, D. (1997). *Life in small moments: Learning in an urban classroom.* New York: Teachers College Press.

Milone, M. N. (1995). Electronic portfolios: Who's doing them and how? *Technology and Learning, 16*(2), 28–29, 32, 34, 36.

National Board for Teacher Certification. (1995). Early childhood generalist: Standards for National Board Certification. Washington, DC: Author.

Newman, J. (Ed.). (1990). *Finding our own way.* Portsmouth, NH: Heinemann.

Paley, V. G. (1997). *The girl with the brown crayon.* Cambridge, MA: Cambridge University Press.

Paley, V. G. (1981). *Wally's stories.* Cambridge, MA: Cambridge University Press.

Perkins, P., & Gelfer, J. (1993). Portfolio assessment of teachers. *Clearing House, 66*(4), 235–237.

Potthoff, D., Carroll, J., Anderson, P., Attivo, B., & Kear, D. (1996). Striving for portfolio integration: A portfolio content analysis. *Action in Teacher Education, 18*(1), 48–58.

Power, B. M., & Hubbard, R. S. (1996). *Oops! What we learn when our teaching fails.* York: ME: Stenhouse.

Reynolds, A. (1992). What is competent beginning teaching? A review of the literature. *Review of Educational Research, 62*(1), 1–35.

Rubin, L. (1996). *The transcendent child: Tales of triumph over the past.* New York: Basic Books.

Ryan, K. (1986). *The induction of new teachers.* Bloomington, IN: Phi Delta Kappa (Fastback #237).

Saracho, O. N., & Spodek, B. (1993). Professionalism and the preparation of early childhood education practitioners. *Early Child Development and Care, 89,* 1–17.

Sparks, D., & Hirsh, S. (1997). *A new vision for staff development.* Alexandria, VA: Association for Supervision and Curriculum Development.

Strachota, B. (1996). *On their side: Helping children take charge of learning.* Greenfield, MA: Northeast Foundation for Children.

Swick, K. J., & Hanes, M. L. (1987). *The developing teacher.* Champaign, IL: Stipes.

UNESCO. (1997). *Portraits in courage: Teachers in difficult circumstances.* Paris, France: Author.

VanderVen, K. (1991). The relationship between notions of caregiving held by early childhood practitioners and stages of career development. In B. Poking Chan (Ed.), *Early childhood towards the 21st century: A worldwide perspective.* Hong Kong: Yew Chung Publishing.

Wasley, P. (1994). *Stirring the chalkdust: Case studies of teachers in the midst of change.* New York: Teachers College Press.

Wong, H. K., & Wong, R. T. (1997). *The first days of school: How to be an effective teacher.* Alexandria, VA: Association for Supervision and Curriculum Development.

Wood, F. H., Thompson, S. R., & Russell, F. (1981). Designing effective staff development programs. In B. Dillon-Peterson (Ed.), *Effective staff development/organization development.* Alexandria, VA: Association for Supervision and Curriculum Development.

Name Index

Chaille, C., 193
Chard, S. C., 187, 208, 211, 213, 214–217, 246,
    255, 261, 291, 299
Chase, P., 194
Chavkin, N., 357, 359
Checkly, K., 137n
Chick, K., 54
Chipman, M., 94
Chomsky, N., 128, 138
Christensen, D., 42, 242, 389
Church, E. B., 329, 330n
Clandinin, D. J., 394
Clandinin, J. D., 394
Clark, C. M., 12, 65, 252, 388, 398
Clarke-Stewart, A., 163
Clawson, D., 54
Cleverley, J., 45, 49
Clifford, R. M., 60
Cochran, R., 156n
Cochran-Smith, M., 22
Cohen, D., 188
Cole, R. W., 251n
Coleman, M., 357
Collins, A., 405
Colton, A. B., 22
Comensius, J., 40, 43n, 49
Comstock, G., 321
Connelly, M. F., 394
Conrad, N. K., 53, 346
Conroy, P., 394
Cooper, H., 159, 167
Cooper, J. M., 208
Copple, C., 19, 72, 73, 74, 88, 93, 95, 100, 101,
    122, 123, 150, 166, 172, 190, 191, 196, 197,
    242, 255, 360n
Cossey, R., 373
Cruickshank, D., 6
Crumpacker, S., 162, 163
Cryan, J. R., 44
Cryer, D., 60, 160, 163, 383
Csikszentmihalyi, M., 6–7, 26
Culbertson, L., 291
Curtis, D., 12, 300
Curtis, J. L., 237

Daniel, J., 371
Danielson, C., 399n
Darling-Hammond, L., 385, 401
Darlington, R., 194
Da Ros, D., 325
Darwin, C., 49–50
Davern, L., 392
Davies, A., 394
Davies, D., 371

Day, D., 87
Deci, E. L., 312
DeMause, L., 44
DeVries, R., 101
Dewey, J., 5, 6, 42, 120, 195, 206, 214
Dick, W., 228, 242, 249, 252, 255
Dietz, W. H., 321
Dinkmeyer, D., 313
Dinwiddie, S. A., 329
Doan, J., 194
Dodge, D., 83, 150, 207, 214
Dollas, R. H., 394
Dopyera, J. E., 383
Doyle, W., 7
Drake, S. M., 208
Driscoll, A., 50, 52–53, 55, 249, 251, 252n
Duffy, R., 323n
Dunlap, L. L., 123
Dunn, S., 252
Dyson, A. H., 194

Eby, J. W., 9
Eckerty, C., 214
Eddowes, E. A., 255
Edelman, M. W., 48, 343
Edwards, C., 150, 155, 214, 373
Edwards, P., 357
Eggen, P. D., 111, 250
Eisenberg, N., 321
Eisner, E., 5, 217
Eliot, A. A., 49
Elkind, D., 28, 112, 352
Epstein, J., 357, 370
Erikson, E. H., 72, 74, 95–98
Erwin, C., 323n
Erwin, E. J., 58, 63
Essa, E., 152, 394

Farris, P. J., 385
Feeney, S., 42, 152, 181, 242, 245, 255, 389
Feng, J., 94
Fennimore, B. S., 18, 279
Fields, M. V., 318
Finlay, B., 359, 371n
Fisher, B., 395
Flack, M., 121
Forman, G., 150, 155, 214, 373
Fournier, J., 117
Fox, M., 395
Freiberg, H. J., 249, 251, 252n
Freud, S., 95
Froebel, F., 41, 43n, 57
Fromberg, D. P., 121, 124–125
Frost, J., 177

Fulghum, R., 115
Fuller, B., 15

Gage, J., 354
Galinsky, E., 371, 385
Gallagher, 148
Gallas, K., 35, 395
Gandini, L., 150, 155, 214, 373
Gannon, B., 313
Garbarino, J., 74
Garcia, E. E., 94
Gardner, H., 48, 111, 112, 113, 116, 117, 136, 139, 144, 246, 290
Gargiulo, R. M., 92–93
Gariepy, J., 325
Garreau, M., 155, 171
Gelfer, J. I., 299, 405, 406*n*
Genishi, C., 194, 291, 306
Gerry, M., 91
Gesell, A., 50, 128–129, 138
Gestwicki, C., 191*n*
Gharavi, G. J., 385
Gibbons, P., 123
Gilkerson, D., 351
Glasgow, K., 23, 51
Glasser, W., 314, 322
Glassman, M., 98–101
Glatthorn, A., 6
Goffin, S. G., 37, 39*n*, 87
Goldberg, S., 355, 373
Goleman, D., 48, 116, 120
Good, T., 116
Goodman, Y. M., 18
Goodwin, A. L., 279
Gordon, A., 27, 242, 247, 259, 325, 326*n*
Gorrill, L., 315*n*
Graham, P., 329
Grant, C., 384
Gray, M., 363
Greenspan, S., 48, 54
Grifalconi, A., 206
Groves, B. M., 321
Grumet, M., 371
Grunwald, L., 54
Gullo, D. F., 306

Hallahan, D. P., 89
Halliday, M. A. K., 112
Halongo, M. R., 395
Hamayan, E. V., 289
Han, E., 9
Hanes, M. L., 385, 393
Hansen, D. T., 227
Hanson, M. F., 351

Harms, T., 60
Hartman, J., 214
Hayden, T. L., 394
Hayes, R. L., 361
Hearron, P., 32
Hegarty, P., 159, 167
Helm, J. H., 300
Henderson, A. T., 356
Hendrick, J., 57
Hendrix, K., 329
Henkes, K., 335
Henley, M., 329
Henrick, J., 17
Herman, J., 289
Herndon, J., 394
Hewitt, D., 346
Hildebrand, V., 17, 71, 363
Hill, P. S., 43*n*, 49
Hillman, C. B., 395
Hillman, E., 98
Hines, R., 363
Hirsh, S., 387, 405
Hoberman, M. A., 206
Hogan, P., 394
Holloway, S. D., 15
Honig, A. S., 48
Hooks, W., 98
Hoot, J. L., 61–62
Howe, H., 56
Hubbard, R. S., 395
Hutchins, P., 335
Hutchison, B. L., 69
Hymes, J., 48

Ilg, F., 128
Innocenti, M. S., 54
Isbell, R. T., 165
Isenberg, J. P., 4, 32, 57, 74, 122, 125*n*, 152, 155, 275, 291, 305, 311, 363, 395

Jablon, J., 83, 150, 214
Jackson, B. R., 174
Jackson, P., 187
Jacobs, H., 208*n*
Jacobson, 193
Jalongo, M. R., 24, 32, 53, 57, 122, 125*n*, 152, 155, 165, 171, 187, 275, 288, 291, 305, 306, 311, 312, 329, 332, 333, 349, 356, 363
Jensen, E., 54
Johnson, D. W., 321
Johnson, R. T., 321
Jones, C., 252
Jones, E., 162, 181, 196, 255

Kagan, S., 352, 370, 371, 372, 402–403
Kahn, A. J., 57
Kamerman, S. B., 57
Kamii, C., 48, 101
Kane, P. R., 394
Kantor, D., 354
Karsenti, T. P., 117
Katz, L. G., 6, 28–29, 48, 71, 187, 208, 211, 213, 214–217, 246, 255, 259, 261, 291, 300, 354, 393
Kauchak, D. P., 111, 250
Kauffman, J. M., 89
Kear, D., 405
Keizer, G., 393
Kellogg, S., 335
Kennard, B., 394
Kennedy, C., 155, 171
Kessler, S. A., 217
Kidder, T., 394
Kiefer, B. Z., 196
Kilpatrick, W. H., 206, 214
Kinderman, T., 325
Kirst, M., 370
Klein, S. P., 385
Kleinpaste, M., 169n, 170
Knowles, M., 390
Kochendorfer, L., 30
Kohl, H., 394
Kohn, A., 109, 147, 309, 315, 318, 338
Kontos, S., 166
Kostelnik, M. J., 204, 205n, 209, 211, 238, 258–259, 333
Kotelchuck, M., 372
Kovach, B. A., 325
Kozol, J., 57
Krall, C. M., 24, 312
Kramer, J. F., 10n
Kritchevsky, S., 155
Krogh, S. L., 206
Kujawa, E., 9
Kussel, S. J., 325

LaBoskey, V. K., 394
Lackney, J. A., 163
Lantieri, L., 329
Law, N., 11
Lawler-Prince, D., 252
Lay Dopyera, M., 383
Lazar, L., 194
Lazear, D., 136
Leach, P., 372, 380
LeFrancois, G., 44n
Lehr, W., 354
Leong, D., 116, 280, 295, 298, 303n

Lerman, S., 320
Levin, D. E., 321
Levine, J., 371
Levstik, L. S., 196
Lewis, A., 372
Liess, E., 144–145, 367
Locke, J., 40, 130, 138
Lombardi, J., 37, 39n
Loughlin, C., 155
Lowman, 152
Luke, J. L., 336
Luther, M., 40, 49
Lytle, S., 22

MacDonald, R. E., 394, 399
MacDonald, S., 306
Madaus, G. F., 286
Magarick, M., 152
Malaguzzi, L., 48
Mann, H., 41
Mansilla, V., 290
Marburger, C. L., 356
Marzano, R., 289
Maslow, A. H., 74, 101–102, 311
Matas, C., 98
May, R., 331
McAfee, O., 280, 295, 303n
McAuliffe, C., 49
McBride, B. A., 356
McCarthy, J., 14n
McClurg, L. G., 329
McCombs, B. L., 117, 120
McCormick, L., 181
McDevitt, T. M., 28
McDonough, S. C., 46
McIntyre, D. J., 7
McKay, G., 313
McLaughlin, M., 401
McLean, S. V., 153n, 155, 165, 173–174, 181
McTighe, J., 289, 293
Meier, D., 394
Meisels, S. J., 287
Milone, M., 408
Mindes, G., 354
Minuchin, P., 19
Mitchell, J., 155
Mncayi, P., 313
Moffit, M., 11
Montessori, M., 42, 43n
Moore, E., 11
Moore, G. T., 163, 165
Moore, T., 343
Moravcik, E., 42, 242, 389
Morris, L., 179

Morris, V., 175*n*
Morrow, L., 206, 373
Moyer, J., 9, 153
Muenchow, S., 373
Myers, C. M., 336

Nelsen, J., 70, 323*n*
Neugebauer, R., 47, 48*n*
Newberger, J. J., 117
Newman, J., 395
Nilsen, B. A., 291, 297, 306
Nimmo, J., 181, 196, 255
Noddings, N., 25, 159
Nolen, S. B., 117

O'Dell, S., 98
O'Hair, M. J., 7
Olds, S., 131
Olinto, B., 407
Olson, G., 185
Ooms, T., 356
Osborn, D. K., 45, 48
Overfield, R., 11
Owen, R., 41

Paasche, C. L., 315*n*
Paley, V. G., 48, 334, 395
Papalia, D., 131
Pappas, C. C., 196
Parten, M., 123
Pavlov, I., 130
Peabody, E., 49
Penning, N., 288
Perham, M., 196
Perkins, D., 247
Perkins, P. G., 299, 405, 406*n*
Perrone, V., 275, 288
Perry, D. G., 325
Perry, L. C., 325
Pestalozzi, J. H., 41
Peterson, P. L., 65, 252
Phenice, L., 363
Phillips, D. C., 45, 49
Phillipsen, L., 60, 160, 163, 383
Piaget, J., 50, 72, 76, 98–101, 116, 122–123, 132–133, 138, 206, 208
Pickering, D., 289
Plato, 40
Popham, W. J., 286
Porter, L., 319*n*, 323*n*
Postman, N., 44, 63
Potthoff, D., 405
Powell, D., 352, 354, 360
Power, B. M., 291, 297, 395

Pratt, C., 43*n*, 49
Prescott, E., 155, 162
Preyer, W., 49
Price, G. G., 45
Puckett, M., 80, 83, 93

Raines, S. R., 218, 219
Ralph, K. S., 255
Ramey, C., 372
Ramsey, P. G., 339, 342
Rane, T. R., 356
Raywid, M. A., 19
Reiser, R. A., 228, 242, 249, 252, 255
Reynolds, A., 394
Rich, 116
Rich, D., 372
Richmond, J., 372
Rief, S. F., 323*n*
Ritchie, G., 144–145, 158*n*
Rivera, A., 370
Roberts, R., 54, 372
Rodd, J., 320
Rodgers, D. B., 312
Roedell, W. C., 329
Rogers, C., 175*n*
Rogoff, B., 46
Rosegrant, T., 118, 119*n*, 187, 193, 196, 197, 198, 199, 205, 206, 208, 212, 217, 242, 245, 277, 299*n*
Rosemond, J., 372, 380
Rosenthal, 193
Rosenthal, D. M., 363, 368*n*
Rousseau, J. J., 40–41, 128, 138
Rowe, J., 196
Rubin, L., 395
Ruhmann, 152
Rule, S., 54
Russell, F., 388
Rutherford, B., 370
Ryan, K., 27, 208, 387, 394
Ryan, R. M., 312

Sailor, W., 91
Salvia, J., 291
Sameroff, A., 46
Sanders, L., 252
Sanoff, H., 162, 164, 165, 167, 178
Santrock, J. W., 63, 72, 74, 78, 101, 112
Sapon-Shevin, M., 24
Saracho, O., 227, 228, 249, 385
Saunders, R., 101
Sawyers, J. Y., 363, 368*n*
Scarlett, W. G., 317
Schaeffer, C., 372

Schickedanz, J., 225, 227
Schon, D. A., 7
Schorr, L., 88
Schubert, W. H., 7
Schurz, C., 48
Schutta, M., 153–154, 155, 156n, 159
Schweinhart, L. J., 48, 62, 194
Seefeldt, C., 195, 196, 206, 249
Sendak, M., 98, 112
Sheerer, M., 391n, 394
Shefatya, L., 123
Sheldon, K., 179
Shephard, L. A., 219
Shubilla, L., 371
Shulman, L., 22
Sigel, I., 101
Simco, N., 159, 167
Simmons, B. J., 321
Sipe, D. S., 353n
Sipe, J. W., 353n
Skinner, B. F., 130, 138
Slaby, R. G., 329
Smilansky, S., 123
Smith, A. B., 48
Smith, C. A., 329
Smith, L., 219, 306
Smith, Y., 279
Snyder, A., 48
Socrates, 49
Soderman, A., 204, 205n
Sparks, D., 387, 405
Sparks-Langer, G. M., 22
Sparrgrove, D., 239n
Spier, P., 206
Spodek, B., 48, 227, 228, 249, 385
Squibb, B., 151
Stalsworth, K., 321
Stamp, L. N., 288, 306
Starks, E., 11
Stein, L. C., 333
Steinheimer, K., 300
Stenmark, J. K., 373
Stern, D., 194
Stewart, E. C., 94
Stewart, I., 225, 227
Stone, C., 370
Stone, J., 321
Strachota, B., 327, 395
Strasburger, V. C., 321
Strom, B., 315n
Strom, S. M., 25, 26
Stubbs, T., 331
Styfco, S. J., 373
Suina, J., 155

Surbeck, E., 6, 8–9
Swick, K. J., 351, 354, 370, 385, 393
Sykes, G., 385
Sylwester, R., 54, 329, 331

Tan, A. D. A., 286
Taylor, B. J., 242, 246, 247
Taylor, J. B., 141–142
Taylor, S., 175n
Tennyson, W. W., 25, 26
Tertemiz, S., 293
Thibert, G., 117
Thompson, S. R., 388
Thompson, V., 373
Thorkildsen, T. A., 117
Thorndike, E., 130, 138
Tobin, L., 324, 327, 347
Trawick-Smith, J., 160, 163
Tuchman, B., 44

Vallance, E., 217
VanderVen, K., 394
van Scoy, I., 370
Vygotsky, L., 72, 112, 116, 122–123, 134–135,
    139, 208

Wald, P., 179
Walling, C., 155
Washington, V., 311
Wasik, B., 372
Wasley, P., 395
Wassermann, S., 122, 154
Watson, J., 130, 138
Weikart, D. P., 48, 194
Weissbourd, B., 352
Weissbourd, R., 74, 151
Wentzel, H., 321
Wheeler, E., 340–342
Whiren, A., 204, 205n, 333
Whisler, J. S., 117, 120
White, D., 225, 227
Wieder, S., 54
Wiggins, G., 289
Wilcox-Herzog, A., 166
Willer, B., 354, 371
Williams, D., 357
Williams-Browne, K., 27, 242, 247, 259
Willis, S., 299n
Wills, C., 239
Wilson, W., 91
Winters, L., 289
Wise, A. E., 385
Wong, H. K., 394
Wong, R. T., 394

Wood, C., 83
Wood, F. H., 388
Wood, K., 179
Woolfolk, A., 111, 132
Workman, S., 354
Wortham, S. C., 48, 159, 206, 208, 209, 278
Wyman, A., 48, 56

Yardley, K., 151
Yesseldyke, J. E., 291

Yinger, R. J., 398
York, M., 225, 227
Youcha, V., 179
Young, L., 357

Zak, M., 112
Zavitkovsky, D., 48
Zeichner, K., 384
Zigler, E., 48, 352, 373
Zurbruegg, E., 19s

Subject Index

needs of, 309, 311–314. *See also* Needs
neglect of, 311, 315
nurturing of, 48–49
observing, 87–88
optimizing potential of, 50
rights of, 311–314
Children's Defense Fund, 311
Children's Foundation, 430
Choices, 326
Circle time, 179–180, 181–183
Classroom(s). *See* Environment(s)
Classroom arrangements, 167–170
  for infants and toddlers, 157
  for kindergartners, 158
  for school-age children, 156
Classroom management. *See* Behavior
        management; Child guidance
Classroom materials. *See* Materials
Climate, positive, 155, 159
Cognitive development
  as content area, 205
  of infants, 76–77
  Piaget's theory of, 98–101, 132–133, 138–139
  play and, 125
  of preschoolers and kindergartners, 81,
        82–83
  of school-age children, 84, 85
  of toddlers, 78, 79–80
Cognitive-developmental constructivist
        theory of learning, 132–134, 138–139
Cognitive play, 126–127
Cognitive processes, 217, 218
Colearning, 116
Collaboration
  with community, 357, 370–372
  with families, 369–372, 375
  home-school-community, 370–372
  with other professionals, 361, 362
  seeking, 12, 24–25
  as strategy for professional
        development, 400
Colleagues, ethical responsibilities to, 26
Color, 162
Commitment, as goal of early childhood
        practitioner, 12, 17–18
Communication
  of assessment results, 281–282
  behavior and, 318, 320, 329, 345–347
  benefits of, 362–363
  child guidance and, 318, 320, 329
  about curriculum, 209–210
  with families, 161–162, 209–210, 247–248,
        281–282, 359, 362–363,
        366–367, 375

about inappropriate behavior, 329
about learning activities in home, 247–248
about learning centers, 161–162
role-playing, 345–347
Community
  building sense of, 12, 24–25, 159
  collaborating with, 357, 370–372
  conflict resolution and, 329, 331
  curriculum and, 189, 190
  expectations of, 55–56
  family's connection to, 355
  in positive learning climate, 159
  positive relationship with, 360, 362–363
  violence in, 321
Community resources, 436–441
Comparisons, as observation error, 295
Competence
  documenting in professional
        portfolio, 406
  need for, 74, 312
Compromise, 329
Computers
  for children with special needs, 179
  planning for instruction with, 252–253
Concept development, 58–59
Conceptual skills, progress report on, 283
Concrete operations, 99, 133
Conferences, with families, 282, 367–369
Conflict, 321–325
  aggression and, 335, 340
  attention getting and, 332–333, 346
  blame shifting and, 336
  coping with, 331–336
  defined, 321
  discipline and, 337–338
  group-entry disputes, 334–335
  personality clashes, 334
  possession disputes, 331–332
  power struggles, 333–334
  teasing and name calling and, 335–336
  types of, 331–336
Conflict resolution, 329, 331, 340–342
Consortium of National Arts Education
        Associations, 200–201
Construction domain, 205
Constructive play, 126, 264
Constructivist theory of learning, 132–136,
        138–139
  cognitive-developmental, 132–134,
        138–139
  sociocultural, 134–136, 139
Content, curriculum, 198, 199, 200–205
Content knowledge, 22
Content standards, 198

Formal operational stage, 133
Full inclusion, 91

Games with rules, 126
Gardening project, 263–267
Gender, of early childhood practitioners, 388, 389
Generativity vs. stagnation, 97
Geography Education Standards Project (GESP), 201
Gifted and talented children, 91, 93
Goals
    of child guidance, 322
    curriculum and, 197
    of early childhood practitioners, 12, 17–27
    of early childhood programs, 58
    environment and, 150–151
    National Education, 198, 428–429
Goals 2000: Educate America Act, 172, 357
Greece, early childhood education in, 40, 45
Gross motor skills
    of preschoolers and kindergartners, 80, 82, 83
    of school-age children, 83, 84
    of toddlers, 79, 80
Group(s)
    aggression in, 324–325
    decision making and, 330
    planning for learning in, 249, 250, 251
Group-entry disputes, 334–335
Growth, 71
Guidance. *See* Child guidance

Handwriting instruction, planning for, 234–235
Head Start program, 121–122, 357, 373, 403
Health
    environment and, 151, 172, 174–175, 177
    resources for, 417–418
Health and Human Services, U.S. Department of, 353
Health impairments, 90–91
Health instruction
    as content area in curriculum, 200, 203
    planning for, 230–231, 234–235
Health services, 440
Hearing impairments, 89, 180
Hierarchy of needs, 101–102
Hispanic-American children, 94
Home-based programs, 10
Home Instruction Program for Preschool Youngsters (HIPPY), 373
Home-school-community collaboration, 370–372
Home Start program, 373

Home visits, 389–390, 403–404
House Is a House for Me, A (Hoberman), 206
Human resources, 56, 436–441
Hunchback of Notre Dame, The (Hugo), 45–46

IDEA (Individuals with Disabilities Education Act) (P.L. 101–476), 89, 90, 91
Identity, in positive learning climate, 159
IEP (individualized educational plan), 282, 284
I Love My Family (Beal), 237
Immigrant child, 377–379
Inclusion
    of children with disabilities, 91, 104–106
    defined, 91, 105–106
    of ethnic groups, 60
    full, 91
    partial, 91
Independence, need for, 74
Independent areas, 167
Individual, evaluating progress of, 291–295
Individual differences, respect for, 60
Individualized educational plan (IEP), 282, 284
Individual learning, planning for, 249, 250, 251
Individuals with Disabilities Education Act (IDEA) (P.L. 101–476), 89, 90, 91
Indoor environments, 166–176
Industry vs. inferiority, 97
Infants
    brain of, 71–72
    child care programs for, 10, 17
    classroom arrangement for, 157
    development of, 75–77
    environment for, 152
    materials for, 17, 152, 175, 410–411
    nutrition for, 174
    planning for, 236
Informal assessment, 278, 303
Initiative vs. guilt, 96
Inquiry, in cycle of learning, 118, 119
Instructional Support team (IST), design of educational plan by, 30–31
Integrated curriculum, 205–206, 207, 208
Intelligences, multiple, 136–137, 140, 144–145, 230–234
Intelligence tests, 303
Interdisciplinary approaches, 60
Interdisciplinary themes, 212–213
International early childhood programs, 61–62
International Montessori Society, 430
International Reading Association (IRA), 202, 288, 431
Internet, as source of information about early childhood programs, 63

Licensing, 14, 385
Light, 162
Literacy
    difficulties with, 142–143
    play and, 125
    progress report on, 283–284
    as subject area in curriculum, 202, 204
Literature, 212
    on dealing with bullies, 336
    in prevention of behavior problems, 323
Little Man Tate (film), 46
Logical/mathematical intelligence, 137, 144,
        230–231
Long-term planning, 228, 234–235, 255,
        259–261
Love, need for, 74

Macrosystem, 101
Management. *See* Behavior management;
        Child guidance
Materials, 410–414
    access to, 168
    early childhood programs and, 56–57
    environment and, 152, 153, 155, 172, 175
    free and inexpensive, 416–417
    historical view of, 43
    for infants, 17, 152, 175, 410–411
    for kindergartners, 175, 411–413
    in learning centers, 161–162
    learning to use, 12, 24
    possession disputes and, 331–332
    for preschoolers, 17, 175, 411–413
    for recording observations, 296
    for school-age children, 175, 413–414
    selecting, 150–153, 155, 172, 175
    for thematic units, 260
    for toddlers, 17, 175, 410–411
Mathematical intelligence, 137, 144,
        230–231
Mathematics
    in first-grade gardening project,
        264–265
    planning for, 230–231, 234–235, 239
    as subject area in curriculum, 200, 203, 212
Measurement, limitations of, 302
Media violence, 321
Meetings, scheduling, 366
Men, as early childhood practitioners, 388
Mental retardation, 89
Mesosystem, 101
Metaphors, 393–396
Methods, 196
Microsystem, 101
Mistakes. *See* Errors

Models and modeling
    of family involvement and education,
        373–374
    of group-entry strategy, 335
    of home-school-community collaboration,
        370–372
    of learning skills, 116
    of respect, 335–336
Motivation, as indicator of balanced
        assessment program, 300–301
Motor abilities, limited, 179
Motor development
    of infants, 75, 76
    planning for, 236
    of preschoolers and kindergartners, 80,
        82–83
    of school-age children, 83, 84
    of toddlers, 78, 79–80
Multiple intelligences theory of learning,
        136–137, 140, 144–145, 230–234
Music
    planning for instruction, 232–233
    as subject area in curriculum, 201, 204
Musical intelligence, 137, 144, 232–233
Music Educators National Conference
        (MENC), 201
My Left Foot (film), 45

Name calling, 335–336
Naps, 315–316
National Art Education Association
        (NAEA), 431
National Association for Bilingual Education
        (NABE), 431
National Association for Gifted Children
        (NAGC), 432
National Association for Sport and Physical
        Education (NASPE), 202
National Association for the Education of
        Young Children (NAEYC), 56,
        62, 163–164, 172, 192, 335, 360,
        427–428, 430
    Code of Ethical Conduct and Commitment of,
        18, 420–426
National Association of Early Childhood
        Teacher Educators, 56
National Association of Elementary School
        Principals, 249
National Association of Family Child
        Care, 430
National Board for Professional Teaching
        Standards, 199
National Center for Improving Science
        Education (NCISE), 200

elements of, 255
of environment, 166–175, 177–178
for first grade, 234–235, 238–239, 257, 263–267
functions of, 252
of individual and group learning, 249, 250, 251
for infants, 236
for instruction about families, 229, 237, 239, 242, 243, 244
for kindergartners, 229, 230–233, 237, 239, 242, 243, 244, 270–271
knowledge of children and, 242, 245
for lessons, 261, 267–269
long-term, 228, 234–235, 255, 259–261
of methods of assessing and evaluating children's learning, 246–247, 255
need for, 225, 248–252
for preschoolers, 237, 240–241, 256
for projects, 259, 261, 262–267
research on, 252–254
for school-age children, 234–235, 238–239, 257, 263–267
short-term, 228, 261, 267–269
thematic units, 259, 260
for toddlers, 236
types and levels of, 227–228
webbing and, 255, 256, 257, 267
Play
adult roles in, 133–134
aggressive, 335
associative, 127
characteristics of, 121–122
cognitive, 126–127
constructive, 126, 264
cooperative, 127
defined, 121–122
dramatic, 240, 264
importance of, 122–123
of kindergartners, 219–220
learning and, 111–112, 120–127
onlooker, 126
parallel, 127
solitary, 126
stages and types of, 123–127
symbolic, 126
Play environment, 177–178
Portfolios
in assessment, 295, 297, 299, 306–307
designing, 306–307
discussing with parents, 295, 297, 299
professional, 404–408
Positive outlook, importance of, 12, 19
Possession disputes, 331–332

Power struggles, 333–334
Praise, 319
Predictions, 295
Preoperational thinking, 99, 133
Preschoolers
child care programs for, 10, 17
curriculum for, 207
development of, 78, 80–81, 82–83, 103–104
materials for, 17, 175, 411–413
nutrition for, 174
planning for, 237, 240–241, 256
schedule for, 171
Privacy, 162–163
Private schools, child care programs for, 11
Problem-solving strategies, 12, 25–26
Procedural knowledge, 386
Professional associations and organizations, 429–432
Professional development, 383–408
defined, 385–387
dimensions of, 385
fostering, 390–392
home visits and, 389–390, 403–404
influences on, 391
public policy and, 402–403
specialized knowledge and, 385, 386
stages in, 392–396
strategies for, 400–401
Professional goals, 12, 17–27
Professional journals, 431–433
Professional portfolios, 404–408
Professional practice, components of, 399
Professional resources, 401, 418–433
Proficient teachers, 394–395
Programs. *See* Early childhood programs
Progress report, 282, 283–284
Projects
curriculum and, 214–217
first-grade gardening, 263–267
planning for, 259, 261, 262–267
thematic units vs., 262
topics of, 262–263
Propositional knowledge, 386
Psychosocial theory, 95–98
Public Law 94–142 (Education for All Handicapped Children), 54, 90
Public Law 99–457 (Education of the Handicapped Act Amendments), 90
Public Law 101–476 (Individuals with Disabilities Education Act), 89, 90, 91
Public policy, and professional development, 402–403. *See also specific laws*

Public schools
    child care programs for, 11
    specialists in, 438
Punishment, 317. *See also* Discipline
"Push down" curriculum, 197, 317

Rating scales, 60, 292
Reading difficulties, 142–143
Reading instruction, planning for, 234–235, 238
Records, 292, 296
Referrals, guidelines for making, 368
Reflective practice, importance of, 7
Reflective practitioners
    characteristics of, 9, 10
    journal keeping by, 8–9
    role of, 6–11
Reflective thinking, 6–7
Reggio Emilia, Italy, 299–300, 373
Regular class, placement in, 24
Relatedness, 312
Relevance, personal, 217, 218
Research
    on curricula, 191, 193–195
    on planning, 252–254
Residential facility, placement in, 24
Resource(s)
    community, 436–441
    curriculum, 414–418
    financial, 56–57
    health, nutrition, and safety, 417–418
    human, 56, 436–441
    Internet, 63
    for learning centers, 414–416
    library-linked, 438, 439
    material, 410–414. *See also* Materials
    professional, 401, 418–433
    storage and organizational, 434
    technology, 434–436
    Resource room, placement in, 24
    Respect
    for individual differences, 60
    modeling, 335–336
    need for, 74
Responsibility
    ethical, 26
    learning and, 120
    need for, 74
    in positive learning climate, 159, 160
    professional, 399
Resumé, 82, 407
Rewards, 317–318
Rights, of children, 311–314
Risk taking, 12, 21–22
Role-playing, 345–347

Rome, early childhood education in, 45
Roots (miniseries), 47
Routines, 171, 322, 323
Rules
    games with, 126
    in prevention of behavior problems, 322
    restating, 326
Running records, 292

Safety
    environment and, 151, 172, 174–175, 177
    resources for, 417–418
Scaffolding, 133
Schedule
    for children, 170–171
    for meetings, 366
School-age children
    child care for, 11
    classroom arrangement for, 156
    development of, 81, 83–85
    materials for, 175, 413–414
    planning for, 234–235, 238–239, 257, 263–267
    schedule for, 171
    themes for, 222–223, 234–235
Science
    in first-grade gardening project, 264–265
    planning for, 230–231, 234–235
    as subject area in curriculum, 200, 203, 212
Script, 7
Security
    need for, 74
    in positive learning climate, 159
Sensorimotor stage of cognitive development, 99, 126, 133
Sensory impairments, 89, 91, 179–180
Short-term planning, 228, 261, 267–269
Small-group areas, 167
"Smell and tell," 180
Social density, 163
Social development
    as content area, 205
    early childhood practitioner and, 88
    of infants, 76
    learning and, 120
    play and, 125
    of preschoolers and kindergartners, 81, 82–83
    of school-age children, 83, 84, 85
    of toddlers, 78, 79–80
Social interaction
    learning experiences and, 112, 116
    opportunity for, 59
Social-learning theory, 130–132, 138